European Intermediary Liability in Copyright

Information Law Series (INFO)

VOLUME 39

Editor

Prof. P. Bernt Hugenholtz, Institute for Information Law, University of Amsterdam.

Objective & Readership

Publications in the Information Law Series focus on current legal issues of information law and are aimed at scholars, practitioners, and policy makers who are active in the rapidly expanding area of information law and policy.

Introduction & Contents

The advent of the information society has put the field of information law squarely on the map. Information law is the law relating to the production, marketing, distribution, and use of information goods and services. The field of information law therefore cuts across traditional legal boundaries, and encompasses a wide set of legal issues at the crossroads of intellectual property, media law, telecommunications law, freedom of expression, and right to privacy. Recent volumes in the Information Law Series deal with copyright enforcement on the Internet, interoperability among computer programs, harmonization of copyright at the European level, intellectual property and human rights, public broadcasting in Europe, the future of the public domain, conditional access in digital broadcasting, and the 'three-step test' in copyright.

The titles published in this series are listed at the end of this volume.

European Intermediary Liability in Copyright

A Tort-Based Analysis

Christina Angelopoulos

Wolters Kluwer

Published by:
Kluwer Law International B.V.
PO Box 316
2400 AH Alphen aan den Rijn
The Netherlands
Website: www.wklawbusiness.com

Sold and distributed in North, Central and South America by:
Wolters Kluwer Legal & Regulatory U.S.
7201 McKinney Circle
Frederick, MD 21704
United States of America
Email: customer.service@wolterskluwer.com

Sold and distributed in all other countries by:
Turpin Distribution Services Ltd
Stratton Business Park
Pegasus Drive, Biggleswade
Bedfordshire SG18 8TQ
United Kingdom
Email: kluwerlaw@turpin-distribution.com

Printed on acid-free paper.

ISBN 978-90-411-6835-1

e-book: ISBN 978-90-411-6841-2
web-PDF: ISBN 978-90-411-8650-8

Printed in the United Kingdom.

Table of Contents

List of Abbreviations

Berne Convention	Berne Convention for the Protection of Literary and Artistic Works
BGB	*Bürgerliches Gesetzbuch* (the German Civil Code)
BGH	*Bundesgerichtshof* (the German Federal Court of Justice)
BVerfG	*Bundesverfassungsgericht* (the German Federal Constitutional Court)
C.civ.	*Code civil* (the French Civil Code)
CA	*Cour d'appel* (a French Court of Appeal)
CDPA	(The UK's) Copyright, Designs and Patents Act 1988
Charter	Charter of Fundamental Rights of the European Union
CJEU	Court of Justice of the European Union (former European Court of Justice)
COM	European Commission Document Number
CPI	*Code de la propriété intellectuelle* (the French copyright act)
DMCA	Digital Millennium Copyright Act 1998
DCFR	Draft Common Frame of Reference
ECHR	European Convention on Human Rights
ECJ	European Court of Justice
ECtHR	European Court of Human Rights
EGTL	European Group on Tort Law
EU	European Union

GEMA	*Gesellschaft für musikalische Aufführungs- und mechanische Vervielfältigungsrechte* (German society for musical performing and mechanical reproduction rights)
GDP	Gross Domestic Product
HADOPI	France's *Haute Autorité pour la Diffusion des Oeuvres et la Protection des Droits sur Internet.* Also refers to the law that set up this authority, the ***loi n° 2009-669 du 12 juin 2009 favorisant la diffusion et la protection de la création sur internet***
HADOPI 2	*Loi n° 2009-1311 du 28 octobre 2009 relative à la protection pénale de la propriété littéraire et artistique, Journal officiel du 29 octobre 2009*
J	Abbreviated title of a judge of the High Court of Justice of England and Wales
LCEN	***Loi n° 2004-575 du 21 juin 2004 pour la confiance dans l'économie numérique***
LG	*Landgericht* (a German regional court)
LJ	Lord Justice of Appeal, an ordinary judge of the Court of Appeal of England and Wales
OECD	Organisation for Economic Co-operation and Development
OJ	Official Journal of the European Union
OLG	*Oberlandesgericht* (a German higher regional court)
PETL	Principles of European Tort Law
SCPL	(in France) *service de communication au public en ligne,* i.e., an online service of communication to the public
TEU	Treaty on European Union
TGI	*Tribunal de grande instante* (a French regional court)
TMG	*Telemediengesetz* (the German Telecommunications Law)
TRIPS	Agreement on Trade-Related Aspects of Intellectual Property Rights
TPB	The Pirate Bay
UCC	Universal Copyright Convention
UK	United Kingdom of Great Britain and Northern Ireland

UrhG	*Gesetz über Urheberrecht und verwandte Schutzrechte* (the German copyright act)
US	United States (of America)
WCT	WIPO Copyright Treaty
WIPO	World Intellectual Property Organisation

Acknowledgements

First and foremost, I am immensely grateful to my supervisor Bernt Hugenholtz, as well as my daily advisor Stef van Gompel. Vast knowledge, faultless instincts and constructive commentary I knew they were going to bring to the job of thesis supervision, but their patience, encouragement and support was much more than what I could have expected. PhD candidates always delight in exchanging stories of their supervisors' indifference, peremptoriness and absence – I was awkwardly left with nothing to contribute to such discussions. I could not have been luckier.

I would also like to extend my thanks to the rest of the IViR staff. I was always conscious of the special environment IViR provided to researchers in information law and moving on to the world beyond its confines has only emphasised how true that is. I joined IViR in 2008 and worked there for a total of eight years. During that time, IViR embraced and encouraged me and I benefited enormously from being surrounded by the knowledge, enthusiasm and support it provided. I can say without doubt that I would never have contemplated attempting a PhD thesis had I not been lucky enough to find myself there. Over the years, I have worked alongside too many colleagues to mention, but a small number deserve special thanks: Tarlach McGonagle, who was so enormously supportive during my IRIS years, Lucie Guibault, a mentor if ever there was one, Anja Dobbelsteen, always efficient, helpful, competent and friendly, Nico van Eijk, my first IViR supervisor and Rosanne van der Waal, who somehow managed to dig up even the most obscure material I could request.

Thanks must also be extended to a number of people outside the institute who kindly offered me their comments and advice on the topic of intermediary liability from the point of view of their particular expertise. In particular, I am grateful to Valérie-Laure Benabou, who patiently answered all my questions on the French situation, Lionel Thoumyre and Ronan Hardouin, who let me pick their brains over a long lunch, Lionel Bently, who gave me helpful suggestions on English material, Matthias Leistner, whose careful emails cleared up my doubts on the German regime, Paul Davies, Claire McIvor and Jaani Riordan, whose enormously helpful books guided me through English accessory liability, Willy Duhen, who kindly let me read his thesis, Catherine Jasserand, a wonderful sounding board on the French system, Cedric Manara, who shared his insights and his book with me, Martijn Hesselink for his help on the European Legal Method and Stijn Smet, without whom the doctrine of fair balance would still be a mystery to me. I would also like to thank Francisco Cabrera, whose idea it was back in 2008, when I was out of inspiration for an IRIS plus topic, that I write about intermediary liability in copyright. Finally, my thanks are also due to Judith Townend and Jules Winterton, who have welcomed me so warmly at IALS. I look forward to three more productive years in information law research.

Naturally, no page of acknowledgements would be complete without mentioning my friends. They turned Amsterdam from the place where I happened to live into my home. Again the list of names is long, but extra special thanks go to Ana Ramalho and Kim de Beer, my intrepid paranymphs.

Last but not least, I would like to thank my fiancé Daniel, who rather bravely decided dating a PhD candidate was a good idea, and my parents, who warned me what I was getting into and did not mind when I did not listen.

Christina Angelopoulos
London, 11 January 2016

Chapter 1

Introduction*

The internet is by far the most efficient means of information exchange humanity has invented to date. As a result, it has rapidly progressed to the centre of modern social, political and economic life. With this development, internet intermediaries, the providers of all internet-related infrastructure and services, have been catapulted to prominence: they are the conduits of our communications, our gateways to knowledge, the guardians of our data and, increasingly, the backbone of our economy.

Because of its great efficiency, the internet has also proven a convenient vehicle for the commission of unprecedented levels of copyright infringement.[1] For the most part, these infringements are executed by numerous, anonymous and impecunious infringers, often hidden in inaccessible jurisdictions far from right-holders' reach. As such, they make unappealing defendants for copyright owners trying to enforce their rights: chasing individual infringers is, as has been said many times, 'a teaspoon solution to an ocean problem'.[2] In their search for deeper pockets, easier targets and long-term fixes, right-holders have instead turned against the internet's middlemen, attempting to hold these parties accountable for the wrongdoings of the small-scale offenders using their services to commit their infringements.[3]

---

* The research for this book was completed on 31 December 2015. Subsequent developments in the relevant law are therefore not reflected in this book.

1. I Iglezakis, 'The Legal Struggle in the EU against Online Piracy' in T-E Synodinou (ed.), *Codification of European Law* (Kluwer Law International 2012) 283.
2. The oft-quoted expression originates with R C Picker, 'Copyright as Entry Policy: the Case of Digital Distribution' (2002) 47 (2-3) Antitrust Bulletin 423.
3. OECD, 'The Role of Internet Intermediaries in Advancing Public Policy Objectives' (OECD Publishing 2011) 144; J Ginsburg, 'Separating the Sony Sheep from the Grokster

As a result, the issue of the liability of internet intermediaries for third party copyright infringements – that is to say, of intermediary accessory copyright liability – has entered into the political agenda across the globe, giving rise to one of the most complex, contentious and fascinating debates in modern copyright law.

Three main opposing sides emerge to the debate: while copyright holders maintain that internet intermediaries are at a minimum facilitating, if not soliciting infringement, and should therefore be forced to bear some of the costs they help to create, the intermediaries themselves counter that they are simply 'dumb pipe' that should not be used as a scapegoat for the misdeeds of others. Entangled in the discussion is the issue of end-users' fundamental rights,[4] as well as, more broadly, the interests of the public at large in the promotion of technological innovation, electronic commerce, net neutrality and a fair and equitable information society.[5]

Goats: Reckoning the Future Business Plans of Copyright-Dependent Technology Entrepreneurs' (2008) 50(2) Arizona Law Review 577; T Wu, 'When Code Isn't Law' (2003) 89 Virginia Law Review 679; M Bartholomew & P F McArdle, 'Causing Infringement' (2011) 64(3) Vanderbilt Law Review 675; J Riordan, The Liability of Internet Intermediaries (PhD thesis, University of Oxford 2013, forthcoming Oxford University Press 2016) N McBride & R Bagshaw 14-17; D Llewelyn, 'Intellectual Property Liability of Consumers, Facilitators and Intermediaries: Concepts under Common Law' in A Kamperman Sanders & C Heath (eds.), *Intellectual Property Liability of Consumers, Facilitators and Intermediaries* (Kluwer Law International 2012) 26; N Elkin-Koren, 'After Twenty Years: Copyright Liability of Online Intermediaries' in S Frankel & D J Gervais (eds.), *The Evolution and Equilibrium of Copyright in the Digital Age* (Cambridge University Press 2014) 29; S K Högberg, 'The Search for Intent-Based Doctrines of Secondary Liability in Copyright Law' (2006) 106(4) Columbia Law Review 909; M Bartholomew & J Tehranian, 'The Secret Life of Legal Doctrine: the Divergent Evolution of Secondary Liability in Trademark and Copyright Law' (2006) 21(4) Berkeley Technology Law Journal 1363.

4. Whether the term 'fundamental rights' or 'human rights' is used depends on the relevant source: rights derived from international law are termed human rights, while rights derived from domestic national constitutional law, as well as from European law are termed fundamental rights. The substantive differences between the two correspond only to any differences in the contents of the relevant provisions. See P Kinsch, 'Human Rights and Fundamental Rights (ChFR and ECHR)' in J Basedow, K J Hopt, R Zimmermann & A Stier, *The Max Planck Encyclopedia of European Private Law* (Oxford University Press 2012) 839.
5. See Commission Staff Working Paper, 'Online Services, Including E-Commerce, in the Single Market', SEC(2011) 1641 final, 11 January 2012, p. 24; T Wu, 'When Code Isn't Law' (2003) 89 Virginia Law Review 679; T Verbiest et al., 'Study on the Liability of Internet Intermediaries', EU Commission study (MARKT/2006/09/E), 12 November 2007; B Martinet Farano, 'Internet Intermediaries' Liability for Copyright and Trademark Infringement: Reconciling the EU and US Approaches' (2012) TTLF Working Paper No 14, 2; L Edwards, 'Role and Responsibility of Internet Intermediaries in the Field of Copyright and Related Rights', WIPO Study (2011); A Kamperman Sanders, 'Intellectual Property Liability of Consumers, Facilitators and Intermediaries: Comparative Concepts' in A Kamperman Sanders & C Heath (eds.), *Intellectual Property Liability of Consumers, Facilitators and Intermediaries* (Kluwer Law International 2012) 14.

While to date within Europe this issue has been largely handled on a country-by-country basis, this book aims at the formulation of harmonised European norms to govern this complicated topic. What are the substantive rules of European intermediary liability in copyright? The question is one that has vexed European legislators for almost two decades,[6] but continues to have no real answer. Moreover, the current polarised European debate on the topic does not leave much room for one to arise on a policy basis alone. Instead, the proper starting point for the European harmonisation of intermediary copyright liability should be searched for on more stable ground: the general rules of law. Only once the legal issues have been addressed should political or economic arguments for or against deviations from the otherwise applicable norms be considered.

The exploration of the law-based avenue towards the introduction of a substantive European intermediary liability is the topic of this book. This chapter introduces it. To this end, the sections below present the issue in greater detail. The chapter will begin with a description of the current European legal backdrop (section 1.1), before moving on to the two basic successive steps of defining the research question (section 1.2) and outlining its scope (section 1.3). After this introductory exposition, the more technical questions of terminology and methodology will be covered in sections 1.4 and 1.5. An outline of the chapters to follow is given in section 1.6. Finally, a brief note on the inevitable ideology underlying the choice of subject matter will be given (section 1.7).

1.1 SETTING THE SCENE

What is the current condition of EU intermediary liability harmonisation in copyright? For the time being, the relevant legal provisions remain largely superficial, eschewing the truly substantive.

Their history goes back to the early 1990s, when, in order to manage the building tensions and shield both copyright holders and the budding internet industry from the legal uncertainty caused by the roll-out of new technologies, a number of EU Member States turned to the introduction of special liability laws for internet intermediaries.[7] In an effort to forestall the parallel development of multiple disparate national European intermediary liability

6. The idea of the European harmonisation of intermediary liability in copyright was discussed in the EU as far back as 1996, when, in its Communication on Copyright and Related Rights in the Information Society, the Commission flagged the question of liability for the infringement of intellectual property rights as requiring potential EU-level clarification or harmonisation, see Commission Proposal for a European Parliament and Council Directive on certain legal aspects of electronic commerce in the internal market, 18 November 1998, COM (1998) 586 final.
7. For more information on this, see K Koelman, 'Liability for On-Line Intermediaries', Imprimatur/Institute for Information Law, Amsterdam, 1997.

regimes and the fragmentation of the EU's internal market that this threatened,[8] the European legislator pushed forward with the formulation of its own solution. This was two-pronged. At a first stage, in 2000, the E-Commerce Directive[9] was adopted. Following international trends in favour of internet self-regulation,[10] this established a set of conditional liability-free zones for internet intermediaries: the famous 'safe harbour' provisions. These grant immunity from claims for monetary compensation to intermediaries for any kind of liability incurred in the supply of three types of services: mere conduit, caching and hosting.[11] Specifically for the area of copyright, this generous regime was balanced out in the following year with the introduction of the Copyright Directive.[12] Article 8(3) of this requires that Member States ensure that injunctions be made available for the protection of right-holders against intermediaries whose services are used by a third party to infringe a copyright or related right. The resultant division between damages and injunctions allows the two directives to dovetail seamlessly into each other.[13] The Copyright Directive's injunction obligation was later confirmed by Article 11 of the 2004 Enforcement Directive,[14] which expands it to all intellectual property rights (IPRs) and provides further clarification.

Yet the resultant European framework is patchy.[15] Its limitations are particularly evident with regard to the safe harbours, which are: (a) conditional, (b) limited to the provision of only three types of services and (c) worded in an evasive, negative fashion, dictating only when Member States cannot impose liability for intermediary activities, not when they

8. Recital 40, E-Commerce Directive (see note 9 below). See also Commission Proposal for a European Parliament and Council Directive on certain legal aspects of electronic commerce in the internal market, 18 November 1998, COM (1998) 586 final.
9. Directive 2000/31/EC of the European Parliament and of the Council of 8 June 2000 on certain legal aspects of information society services, in particular electronic commerce, in the Internal Market (Directive on Electronic Commerce), [2000] OJ L 178/1 (hereinafter: 'E-Commerce Directive').
10. D Tambini et al., *Codifying Cyberspace* (Routledge 2008) 1-28.
11. See Arts 12-15 of the E-Commerce Directive.
12. Directive 2001/29/EC of the European Parliament and of the Council of 22 May 2001 on the harmonisation of certain aspects of copyright and related rights in the information society [2001] OJ L167/10 (hereinafter: 'Copyright Directive').
13. On this see Recital 16 of the Copyright Directive and Recital 50 of the E-Commerce Directive. See also P van Eecke, 'Online Service Providers and Liability: A Plea for a Balanced Approach' (2011) 48 Common Market Law Review 1455.
14. Directive 2004/48/EC of the European Parliament and of the Council of 29 April 2004 on the Enforcement of Intellectual Property Rights [2004] OJ L 157/45 and Corrigendum to Directive 2004/48/EC of the European Parliament and of the Council of 29 April 2004 on the enforcement of intellectual property rights [2004] OJ L 195/16 (hereinafter: 'Enforcement Directive').
15. M Leistner, 'Structural Aspects of Secondary (provider) Liability in Europe' (2014) 9(1) Journal of Intellectual Property Law & Practice 75.

ought.[16] This has created a two-tiered answer to the crucial question of whether and when damages can be demanded of intermediaries for the copyright infringements of others in Europe: at a first stage, whether a given intermediary attracts, in its pursuit of a certain activity, liability according to the standards ensconced in the individual Member State's legislation must be examined. Only if that is the case does, in the second instance, the question of immunity become relevant.

As a result of these shortcomings, the E-Commerce Directive provides only a buffer zone against intra-EU intermediary liability fragmentation: it merely forecloses liability under certain circumscribed conditions, while barring these, domestic courts are forced to fall back onto national liability standards. At the moment, these remain greatly divided. The substantive rules on intermediary liability for copyright infringement which determine whether the safe harbours will be necessary or redundant thus remain unharmonised.[17] This discrepancy has consequences not only for businesses engaging in activities not currently covered by the safe harbours, e.g., search engines, but also for intermediaries providing protected services that fail to abide by the requirements of the safe harbours and thereby forfeit immunity, such as hosting providers that refuse to expeditiously take down notified infringements or caching providers that do not appropriately update cached content.[18]

Admittedly, the Copyright and Enforcement Directives' provisions on injunctive relief do to a large extent avoid this problem: they are positively stated, daring to tell the Member States not only what they cannot do, but also what must be done. They have consequently been described as containing the real 'nucleus' of a truly European intermediary copyright liability.[19] At the same time however, the two provisions are remarkably thin on the details, consisting of only of two brief, essentially identical one-liners, which do nothing more than simply demand injunctions for right-holders. The scope of the obligation they impose is, as a result, entirely unclear: if injunctions must be ensured by the Member States for the benefit of copyright holders, what type of injunctions should those be and under which circumstances should they be made available?[20] No common European answer is currently provided. Indeed, Recital 59 of the Copyright Directive

16. C van der Net, 'Civil Liability of Internet Providers Following the Directive on Electronic Commerce' in H Snijders & S Weatherill, *E-Commerce Law: National and Transnational Topics and Perspectives* (Kluwer Law International 2003) 49.
17. C Angelopoulos, 'Beyond the Safe Harbours: Harmonising Substantive Intermediary Liability for Copyright Infringement in Europe' (2013) 3 Intellectual Property Quarterly 253.
18. See Arts 13 and 14 of the E-Commerce Directive.
19. M Leistner, 'Common Principles of Secondary Liability?' in A Ohly, *Common Principles of European Intellectual Property Law* (Mohr Siebeck 2012) 117.
20. M Leistner, 'Common Principles of Secondary Liability?' in A Ohly, *Common Principles of European Intellectual Property Law* (Mohr Siebeck 2012) 117.

explicitly leaves the relevant conditions and modalities up to the national law of the Member States.

A final insufficiency in the EU framework can be found in the lack of explicit guarantees for the parallel dimension of user rights and the public interest. Precisely as a result of its immense success, the internet has evolved into a significant source of danger in this regard. So, for example, given that the internet is 'one of the principal means by which individuals exercise their right to freedom of expression and information' in the modern world, any limitation to the access to or use of internet services by end-users represents a potential limitation of that right.[21] Likewise, in view of its origins, interferences with user-generated data will necessarily risk interference with those users' privacy and data protection rights as well.[22] These dangers could, *inter alia*, result from measures undertaken for the enforcement of copyright and applied through the medium of internet intermediaries. Despite the obviously high stakes involved however, and although these issues receive express recognition in the recitals to all three relevant EU directives,[23] no concrete legal devices aimed at ensuring the effective protection of these rights are, to date, elaborated in the operative parts of their texts.[24] Any guarantees that are included are, instead, entirely incidental to the protection of the intermediaries themselves, offering no comprehensive protection to users. As a result, it has been said that current EU information law 'construes the internet as a system of property rights whose exercise can be restricted', thereby essentially leaving user rights and the general interest empty-handed in the EU harmonisation process.[25]

---

21. This was made clear by the ECtHR in *Ahmed Yildirim v. Turkey*, application no. 3111/10, 18 December 2012. See also, European Parliament, MEMO/09/219, 6 May 2009.
22. CJEU, C-70/10, *Scarlet Extended SA v. Société belge des auteurs, compositeurs et éditeurs SCRL (SABAM)*, 24 November 2011; case C-360/10, *Belgische Vereniging van Auteurs, Componisten en Uitgevers CVBA (SABAM) v. Netlog NV*, 16 February 2012.
23. See Recitals 9, 14 and 46 of the E-Commerce Directive, Recitals 3 and 57 of the Copyright Directive and Recital 2 of the Enforcement Directive.
24. This is arguably the case for the prohibition of general monitoring obligations in Art. 15 of the E-Commerce Directive.
25. E Dommering, presentation at 'The European Harmonisation of Intermediary Accessory Liability for Online Copyright Infringement: at the Intersection of Tort Law and Fundamental Rights', Roundtable Discussion, Institute for Information Law (IViR), Amsterdam, 13 April 2015. See also M Horten, *The Copyright Enforcement Enigma – Internet Politics and the 'Telecoms Package'* (Palgrave Macmillan 2012) 212-215. In 2009, as part of the Telecoms Package, the EU legislator did introduce an obligation that any '[m]easures taken by Member States regarding end-users' access to, or use of, services and applications through electronic communications networks […] respect the fundamental rights and freedoms of natural persons.' But again, the protection granted here remains vague and little indication is given of what the necessary respect should look like. See Article 1(1)(b) of Directive 2009/140/EC of the European Parliament and of the Council of 25 November 2009 amending Directives 2002/21/EC on a common regulatory framework for electronic communications networks and services, 2002/19/EC on access to, and interconnection of, electronic communications networks and associated facilities,

The Court of Justice of the European Union (CJEU) has attempted to fill this gap through direct recourse to the Charter of Fundamental Rights of the European Union (hereinafter 'Charter').[26] Through this lens, the question of intermediary liability has been jurisprudentially reconfigured into a search for a 'fair balance' between competing fundamental rights. In this way, far from being exiled beyond EU reach, intermediary liability is provided with a high-level legal basis for its harmonised European regulation. Although this approach arguably does achieve a better representation of all implicated interests, it stumbles against the inevitable vagueness of the Charter's provisions, which offer very little in the way of interpretative material. The resultant rulings have consequently suffered from the same disadvantages as the ambiguous references incorporated into the directives, being supported by sparse and aphoristic normative underpinnings and offering limited instructive capabilities for the resolution of future cases.

1.2 PROBLEM DEFINITION

Despite the current stagnation, given the transnational nature of the question, the appeal of a true substantive harmonisation of intermediary accessory copyright liability remains consistent:[27] national divergences in legislation do not make sense in the online environment, which by its very nature mocks country borders.[28] This reality is particularly striking in the area of copyright, an area of law whose international dimension has been cultivated since the

---

and 2002/20/EC on the authorisation of electronic communications networks and services [2009] OJ L 337/37. The provision amended Article 3b of Directive 2002/21/EC, the so-called Framework Directive.

26. Charter of Fundamental Rights of the European Union [2000] OJ C 364/1 (hereinafter: 'the Charter').
27. Indeed, there are those that suggest not only the harmonisation of the liability of internet intermediary on the European level, but on a trans-Atlantic or even global level as well, see e.g., B Martinet Farano, 'Internet Intermediaries' Liability for Copyright and Trademark Infringement: Reconciling the EU and US Approaches' (2012) TTLF Working Paper No 14; C van der Net, 'Civil Liability of Internet Providers Following the Directive on Electronic Commerce' in H Snijders & S Weatherill, *E-Commerce Law: National and Transnational Topics and Perspectives* (Kluwer Law International 2003) 49 and J-F Thery & I Falque-Pierrotin, 'Internet et les réseaux numériques: étude adoptée par l'Assemblée générale du Conseil d'Etat le 2 juillet 1998' (La Documentation française 1998) 6-7. On that note, it should be mentioned that the current version of the leaked Transatlantic Trade and Investment Partnership (TTIP) treaty still being negotiated does include a section on intermediary liability in its chapter on intellectual property rights, see: Wikileaks, 'TPP Treaty: Intellectual Property Rights Chapter – 5 October 2015', available at: https://wikileaks.org/tpp-ip3/.
28. C van der Net, 'Civil Liability of Internet Providers Following the Directive on Electronic Commerce' in H Snijders & S Weatherill, *E-Commerce Law: National and Transnational Topics and Perspectives* (Kluwer Law International 2003) 49.

mid-nineteenth century.[29] Indeed, in Europe in particular, primary copyright liability already enjoys an exceptionally high level of harmonisation[30] through the adoption of no less than nine EU directives over the past twenty-five years,[31] while the push for further harmonisation continues.[32]

---

29. See P Goldstein & P B Hugenholtz, *International Copyright: Principles, Law, and Practice* (3rd ed. University Press 2012); L Bently et al. (eds.), *Global Copyright* (Edward Elgar 2010); S Ricketson & J Ginsburg, *International Copyright and Neighbouring Rights – The Berne Convention and Beyond* (2nd ed. University Press 2006).
30. See M Walter & S von Lewinski, *European Copyright Law: A Commentary* (Oxford University Press 2010); T Dreier & P B Hugenholtz (eds), Concise European Copyright Law (2nd ed., Kluwer Law International, forthcoming); M van Eechoud et al., *Harmonizing European Copyright Law* (Kluwer Law International 2009); J Pila & A Ohly (eds.), *The Europeanization of Intellectual Property Law: Towards a European Legal Methodology* (Oxford University Press 2013); C Geiger, *Constructing European Intellectual Property – Achievements and New Perspectives* (Edward Elgar 2013); T-E Synodinou (ed.), *Codification of European Law* (Kluwer Law International 2012).
31. Aside for the aforementioned Copyright Directive and Enforcement Directive, these are the following: Council Directive 91/250/EEC of 14 May 1991 on the legal protection of computer programs [1991] OJ L 122/42 and Council Directive 2009/24/EC of the European Parliament and of the Council of 23 April 2009 on the legal protection of computer programmes (codified version) [2009] OJ L 111/16 ('Computer Programmes Directive'); Council Directive 92/100/EEC of 19 November 1992 on rental right and lending right and on certain rights related to copyright in the field of intellectual property [1992] OJ L 346/61 and Directive 2006/115/EC of the European Parliament and of the Council of 12 December 2006 on rental right and lending right and on certain rights related to copyright in the field of intellectual property (codified version) [2006] OJ L376/28 ('Rental and Lending Rights Directive'); Council Directive 93/83/EEC of 27 September 1993 on the co-ordination of certain rules concerning copyright and rights related to copyright applicable to satellite broadcasting and cable retransmission [1993] OJ L 248/15 ('SatCab Directive'); Council Directive 93/98/EEC of 29 October 1993 harmonising the term of protection of copyright and certain related rights [1993] OJ L290/9 and Directive 2006/116/EC of the European Parliament and of the Council of 12 December 2006 on the term of protection of copyright and certain related rights [2006] OJ L372/12 (codified version) ('Term Directive'); Directive 2011/77/EU of the European Parliament and of the Council of 27 September 2011 amending Directive 2006/116/EC on the term of protection of copyright and certain related rights [2011] OJ L265/1 ('Term Extension Directive'); Directive 96/9/EC of the European Parliament and of the Council of 11 March 1996 on the legal protection of databases [1996] OJ L 77/20 ('Database Directive'); Directive 2001/84/EC of the European Parliament and of the Council of 27 September 2001 on the resale right for the benefit of the author of an original work of art [2001] OJ L272/32 ('Resale Rights Directive'); Directive 2012/28/EU of the European Parliament and of the Council of 25 October 2012 on certain permitted uses of orphan works [2012] OJ L299/5 ('Orphan Works Directive') and Directive 2014/26/EU on collective management of copyright and related rights and multi-territorial licensing of rights in musical works for online use in the internal market ('Collective Rights Management Directive').
32. For example, in 2010 a model European Copyright Code was drafted by the Wittem Group of European academics, see: Wittem Group, *European Copyright Code,* April 2010, available at: copyrightcode.eu. The adoption of an EU copyright law was also suggested by the so-called Monti Report, see M Monti, *A New Strategy for the Single*

These considerations are accentuated by the legal uncertainty that surrounds the issue of intermediary accessory copyright liability on the intra-EU national level. Unhelpfully, the issue remains one of the most badly understood areas of copyright law. Indeed, as shall be shown, if there is one similarity that stands out between the national rules in this area, it is the persistent confusion they all display: lacking well-reasoned set standards for the attribution of liability to one person for participation in the copyright infringements of another, domestic courts are forced to rely on open-ended, haphazard, improvisational tests, while conflicting decisions are rampant not only between Member States, but even within the same jurisdiction.[33] It is therefore apparent that a cogent solution to the problem of intermediary accessory copyright liability will require significant doctrinal reform across the board of EU Member States. Indeed, in a number of EU countries, the case law already relies heavily on the existing European system for legal certainty and structure, incomplete though that currently is. This indicates that an opportunity has emerged for the introduction of a single European solution: if twenty-eight accessory copyright liability birds must be killed anyway, European harmonisation would provide a much more efficient single stone solution. The Europeanisation of intermediary accessory copyright liability offers an opportunity for a re-conceptualisation and rationalisation of the applicable law, in a way which additionally better accounts for the cross-border nature of the internet.[34]

Right on cue, in May 2015, in its Communication on a Digital Single Market Strategy for Europe, the Commission committed to putting forth legislative proposals in 2015-2016 for 'a modern, more European copyright framework'.[35] This is intended to include legal reforms aimed at 'clarifying the rules on the activities of intermediaries in relation to copyright-protected content and, [...] modernising [the] enforcement of intellectual property rights, focusing on commercial-scale infringements (the "follow the money" approach) as well as its cross-border applicability'. The Communication's legislative roadmap also promised the creation of a 'fit for purpose'

Market – At the Service of Europe's Economy and Society, Report to the President of the European Commission, José Manuel Barroso, 9 May 2010.

33. C Angelopoulos, 'Beyond the Safe Harbours: Harmonising Substantive Intermediary Liability for Copyright Infringement in Europe' (2013) 3 Intellectual Property Quarterly 253; DLA Piper, 'EU Study on the Legal Analysis of a Single Market for the Information Society – New Rules for a New Age?', November 2009, available at: http://ec.europa.eu/information_society/newsroom/cf/itemdetail.cfm?item_id=7022. See also, C McIvor, *Third Party Liability in Tort* (Hart Publishing 2006) 1 and P S Davies, 'Accessory Liability: Protecting Intellectual Property Rights' (2011) 4 Intellectual Property Quarterly 390.
34. K Oliphant, 'European Tort Law: A Primer for the Common Lawyer' (2009) 62(1) Current Legal Problems 440.
35. Communication from the Commission to the European Parliament, the Council, the European Economic and Social Committee and the Committee of the Regions, 'A Digital Single Market Strategy for Europe', COM(2015)192 final.

regulatory environment for intermediaries, among other things through the adoption of new measures to tackle illegal content on the internet. According to the Communication, these could involve rigorous procedures for removing illegal content, while also avoiding the take-down of legal content, as well as the introduction of a duty of care requiring intermediaries to exercise greater responsibility and due diligence in the way they manage their networks and systems. This language indicates both an awareness of the deficiencies of the current framework and an emergent political will for its substantive improvement. This is appropriate: the EU legislator should take advantage of the attention currently focused on intermediary liability in copyright to pass, not just stop-gap measures addressing the most pressing problems, but a comprehensive solution that attacks the real issues.

How should the substantive harmonisation of intermediary accessory copyright liability be approached? While primary European copyright liability was pulled together primarily on the basis of the 'harmonising effect'[36] of the preceding international treaties in the area, accessory liability has been sidestepped by those texts.[37] In its default, the existing national rules must instead lead the way. These indicate unambiguously towards the area of tort law. And indeed, while a number of desultory attempts have been made to tackle the question of accessory liability directly in the national copyright laws of Europe, these are mostly ill-suited for the information era.[38] Absent satisfactory intra-copyright solutions in all EU Member States, the broader realms of national tort law are instead left as the most appropriate area in which to search for answers to the questions of intermediary accessory liability.[39] This should not be surprising: after all, copyright

36. M van Eechoud et al., *Harmonizing European Copyright Law* (Kluwer Law International 2009) 32.
37. See: Berne Convention for the Protection of Literary and Artistic Works (adopted 9 September 1886, entered into force 5 December 1887) 1161 UNTS 3, as amended (hereinafter: 'Berne Convention'); WIPO Copyright Treaty (adopted 20 December 1996, entered into force 6 March 2002) 2186 UNTS 121 (hereinafter: 'WCT'); Agreement on Trade-Related Aspects of Intellectual Property Rights, Annex 1C of the Marrakesh Agreement Establishing the World Trade Organization (adopted 15 April 1994, entered into force 1 January 1996) 1869 UNTS 299 ('TRIPS Agreement'); Universal Copyright Convention (adopted 6 September 1952, entered into force 10 July 1974) 943 UNTS 178, as amended ('UCC').
38. See below Ch. 3.
39. It is indicative that the famous US doctrine of secondary liability arose from the common law of tort: 'contributory liability' is derived from enterprise liability and 'vicarious liability' is an outgrowth of the principles of *respondeat superior*) see A Yen, 'Third-Party Copyright Liability after Grokster' (2007) 16(3) Information & Communications Technology Law 233; A Yen, 'Internet Service Provider Liability for Subscriber Copyright Infringement, Enterprise Liability, and the First Amendment' (2000) 88(6) Georgetown Law Journal 1833; R J Mann & S R Belzley, 'The Promise of Internet Intermediary Liability' (2005) 47 William and Mary Law Review 239; P S Menell & D Nimmer, 'Legal Realism in Action: Indirect Copyright Liability's Continuing Tort Framework and Sony's

infringement is a tort[40] and copyright law, although traditionally developing sui generis solutions with regard to primary liability,[41] remains a subcategory of that area of law. Where the dedicated European norms do not apply and national copyright law remains silent, domestic judges have thus turned to tort law to parse the issue.[42]

Arguably, the EU legislator should follow their lead: tort law, with its centuries-long specialisation in the elaboration of refined guiding formulae for the optimum regulation of every aspect of the extra-contractual interactions between private parties,[43] provides precisely the right tools for the governance of the complex question of intermediary accessory copyright liability. If that is so, perhaps now is the time to formulate a European tort law – if not more generally, then at least for this tiny corner of that field. Indeed, the CJEU's forays into the fundamental rights dimension of the issue can be interpreted precisely as an attempt to guide national tort law through the vehicle of higher legal norms. But such indirect input has clear limits. If the EU is to provide a truly substantive harmonised solution to intermediary accessory copyright liability, it must move past the simple imposition of outer limits to national pronouncements as provided by fundamental rights and grapple with the heart of the issue: the formulation of positively stated and much more detailed tort-based norms.

In the context of the above analysis, the research question addressed in this book takes concrete shape. This shall be the following:

> How can the substantive harmonisation of European intermediary accessory liability in copyright take shape, bearing in mind the existing national and EU rules on the topic, the principles of European tort law and the EU law of fundamental rights?

In other words, the objective of this book shall be the formulation of a model or reference tool for a future substantive harmonisation or unification

---

De Facto Demise' (2007) 55(1) UCLA Law Review 143. See also, *Metro Goldwyn Mayer Studios Inc. v. Grokster* (2005) 545 U.S. 913 and *Fonovisa v. Cherry Auction*, 76 F.3d 259 (9th Cir. 1996).

40. S Hetcher, 'The Kids are Alright: Applying a Fault Liability Standard to Amateur Digital Remix' (2010) 62(5) Florida Law Review 1275; S Hetcher, 'The Immorality of Strict Liability in Copyright' (2013) 17(1) Marquette Intellectual Property Law Review 1; A Jacob & A Dorfman, 'Copyright as Tort' (2011) 12(1) Theoretical Inquiries in Law 59; P R Goold, 'Is Copyright Infringement a Strict Liability Tort?' (2015) 30(1) Berkeley Technology Law Journal 305.
41. C van Dam, *European Tort Law* (2nd ed., Oxford University Press 2013) para. 701-1; N McBride & R Bagshaw, *Tort Law* (4th ed, Pearson 2012) 512.
42. This thought process is laid bare in a particularly clear manner by Justice Arnold in the English trademark case of *L'Oreal S.A v. eBay International AG* [2009] EWHC 1094 (Ch) at 344-346.
43. W van Gerven, J Lever & P Larouche, *Tort Law* (Hart Publishing 2000) 13.

of intermediary accessory copyright liability at the European level.[44] This shall be pursued on a basis of classic doctrinal legal research. The starting point shall be found in the current, limited EU harmonisation of the area, supplemented by the comparative consideration of relevant national law. Further guidance shall be searched for in the broader, overarching principles of fundamental rights and what can be discerned of a developing single European law of tort.

Some final consideration is necessary at this point on the meaning of the term 'harmonisation'. It should be noted that, strictly speaking, harmonisation refers to the 'approximation or co-ordination' of different legal solutions through the elimination of major differences and the creation of minimum requirements or standards.[45] By contrast, unification aspires to a vision of total uniformity, through the replacement of two or more legal systems with one single one. Harmonisation therefore sets a less demanding standard, although it can be seen as a step towards unification and does arguably strive towards that ultimate result.[46] From the onset it should be understood that whether harmonisation or unification should be pursued is not something addressed in this book. With this in mind, in the following the more moderate term 'harmonisation' shall be used as a shorthand reference to both objectives – essentially, to a general 'Europeanisation' of the law, whatever avenue that might follow.

1.3 SCOPE

The subject of this book has now been established: it examines the European accessory liability of internet intermediaries for online copyright infringement. What is the analytical scope of the analysis? From the previous sentence's description it immediately becomes apparent that this must be limited in three ways: the relevant liability must be accessory, it must be of an internet intermediary and it must be for a copyright infringement committed online. A fourth additional limitation arises from the definition of the notion of liability with regard to its consequences: the remedies in which

44. For similar projects in other areas of law see: Wittem Group, *European Copyright Code*, April 2010; European Group on Tort Law, *Principles of European Tort Law – Text and Commentary* (Springer 2005); C von Bar et al. (eds), *Principles, Definitions and Model Rules of European Private Law: Draft Common Frame of Reference (DCFR)*, prepared by the Study Group on a European Civil Code and the Research Group on EC private law (Acquis Group) (Sellier 2009).
45. W J Kamba, 'Comparative Law: A Theoretical Framework' (1974) 23 International and Comparative Law Quarterly 486.
46. K L Bhatia, *Textbook on Legal Language and Legal Writing* (Universal Law Publishing 2010) 243.

it results. In this section, a brief note on each of these scope-delineating elements shall be made.

1.3.1 Accessory Liability

What is accessory liability? Broadly speaking, a person may commit a tort in one of two ways: she can either commit the tort herself or she can contribute to the commission of that tort by somebody else.[47] The latter case is what here is called 'accessory liability'. This description indicates accessory liability's more prominent characteristic and limitation: it is not inchoate, but 'parasitic', i.e., contingent upon the commission of an initial tort by somebody else.[48] Accessory liability can therefore not arise unless accompanied by the primary liability of another party. Given that copyright infringement is a tort, accessory copyright liability is the liability of one person – the 'accessory' – for their participation in an infringement of copyright committed by another – the 'primary' or 'principal' wrongdoer.[49]

In most European legal systems, accessory liability is a relatively novel area of tort law.[50] Arguably, this is due to the limited need for an accessory liability rule in the traditional analogue world – the development of the internet has pushed for an expansion of tort beyond the track heretofore beaten. As a result, the contours of accessory liability align badly with the traditional structures of national tort systems – indeed, most European jurisdictions have not consciously conceived of a comprehensive principle of accessory liability for the tortious actions of others.[51] Instead, accessory liability tends to be handled in the tort laws of the Member States through constellations of miscellaneous isolated doctrines that fail to be understood as instances of a single overarching category of liability.[52] Importantly, more often than not, these doctrines fail to even identify cases of accessory liability as such, but instead formally classify them as instances of primary liability, with the accessory treated either as a 'joint tortfeasor', who stands alongside the person who committed the material act of infringement as an equal principal in a single tort, or as the perpetrator, not of a participation in the wrong of somebody else, but of an independent act of negligence consisting

47. N McBride & R Bagshaw, *Tort Law* (4th ed, Pearson 2012) 860; P S Davies, *Accessory Liability* (Hart Publishing 2015) 2.
48. P S Davies, *Accessory Liability* (Hart Publishing 2015) 1-2, 12. The term 'parasitic' first arose in the criminal law, see *R v. Gnango* [2011] UKSC 59.
49. T Hays, 'The Evolution and Decentralisation of Secondary Liability for Infringements of Copyright-Protected Works: Part 1' (2006) 28(12) European Intellectual Property Review 617.
50. Williams explains: 'The law relating to parties to a tort has not been so well worked out as that relating to parties to a crime', see G Williams, *Joints Torts and Contributory Negligence* (Stevens & Sons Ltd 1951) 11.
51. See e.g., R Stevens, *Wrongs and Rights* (Oxford University Press 2009) 276.
52. C McIvor, *Third Party Liability in Tort* (Hart Publishing 2006) 1.

of that participation.[53] As a result, the current law of accessory liability is, as had been said, 'unstructured, unprincipled and incoherent'.[54]

This under-theorised, crazy-quilt nature of accessory liability clearly contributes to the confusion regarding the accessory liability of internet intermediaries: as Bagshaw suggests, where there is doubt as to liability in the online world, it is more than likely because there is doubt as to liability in the offline world as well.[55] In view of this fact, calls are increasing for the development of accessory liability into a single well-grounded doctrine of modern tort law.[56] In the meantime, accessory liability in Europe is probably best described as a 'cluster concept', i.e. a doctrine that is recognisable only from the function it performs within the legal system in question. In order to account for this reality, this book shall select its areas of study by reference to that function – i.e., it shall focus not on how a liability is conventionally classified in national law, but on whether or not the material act that brought it about consisted of a participation by an internet intermediary in a copyright infringement committed by a third party.

It should be noted that, crucially, accessory liability ought not be confused with another kind of 'liability for others',[57] that of vicarious liability.[58] While vicarious liability is a strict kind of liability that arises, regardless of fault, on the basis of the relationship between the primary

53. J Riordan, *The Liability of Internet Intermediaries* (PhD thesis, University of Oxford 2013, forthcoming Oxford University Press 2016) 25. See, for example, *Football Dataco Ltd & Ors v. Stan James Plc & Ors* [2013] EWCA Civ 27 (06 February 2013) at 100.

54. C McIvor, *Third Party Liability in Tort* (Hart Publishing 2006) 1.

55. R Bagshaw, 'Downloading Torts: An English Introduction to On-Line Torts' in H Snijders & S Weatherill, *E-Commerce Law: National and Transnational Topics and Perspectives* (Kluwer Law International 2003) 59.

56. See e.g., P S Davies, *Accessory Liability* (Hart Publishing 2015) 1.

57. K Zweigert & H Kötz, *An Introduction to Comparative Law* (3rd ed., Clarendon Press 1998) 629; W van Gerven et al., *Tort Law* (Hart Publishing 2000) 467.

58. As McBride and Bagshaw stress, '[v]icarious liability is not accessory liability'. According to the definition they give, the difference lies in whether or not the person whose liability is at issue is understood as having in fact committed the tort: if she has not, but is nonetheless held liable for the tort of another as though she had committed it along with that other, her liability is vicarious. Thus, in contrast to accessory liability which is based on one's actual wrongdoing, vicarious liability presupposes an obligation on the part of the person held vicariously liable to compensate the victim of the damage that from the conduct of other persons, usually resulting from the relationship that binds the person whose conduct caused the damage and the person whose liability is being examined (N McBride & R Bagshaw *Tort Law* (4th ed, Pearson 2012) 865 et seq). So, if D is to be held vicariously liable for a tort committed by A, what 'is required is that D should stand in a particular relationship to A and that A's tort should be referable in a certain manner to that relationship'. (W V H Rogers, *Winfield & Jolowicz on Tort* (18th ed., Sweet & Maxwell 2010) 944). The law of vicarious liability is complicated, but it can generally be said to rest on 'how much control' the person in question exerted over the primary tortfeasor (see Supreme Court of Canada, *KLB v. British Columbia* [2003] 2 SCR 403. Typically, this will encompass the liability of an employer for the wrongdoings of an employee acting at his request. The usual civilian terminology is 'liability for the acts of

wrongdoer and the secondary party,[59] accessory liability requires the personal wrongdoing of the accessory.[60] Although this book shall focus primarily on accessory liability, on a secondary level, vicarious liability, along with its polar opposite of immunity, shall, in the final conclusion, be considered as possible alternatives where the rules of fault fail to provide satisfactory solutions.[61] Fault is always the default:[62] once a robust doctrinal framework is established for that, the possibility of deviations by reference to political objectives in the direction of more or less liability may be addressed on an exceptional basis.

1.3.2 INTERNET INTERMEDIARIES

The accessory liability that will be examined in this book will be specifically that of internet intermediaries. This gives rise to the next question: what are internet intermediaries? An intermediary generally is 'any entity that enables the communication of information from one party to another'.[63] An internet intermediary therefore is an entity that enables such communications on the internet. The Organisation for Economic Co-operation and Development (OECD) proposes the following definition:

> 'Internet intermediaries' bring together or facilitate transactions between third parties on the Internet. They give access to, host, transmit and

---

others' (P Giliker, 'Vicarious Liability or Liability for the Acts of Others in Tort: A Comparative Perspective' (2011) 2(1) Journal of European Tort Law 31.

59. For the avoidance of confusion, it should be noted that this is no longer the case with US vicarious liability, which, especially after the *Grokster* ruling (*Metro Goldwyn Mayer Studios Inc. v. Grokster* (2005) 545 U.S. 913), has been repositioned from strict to fault liability, see A Yen, 'Third-Party Copyright Liability after Grokster' (2007) 16(3) Information & Communications Technology Law 233.
60. C McIvor, *Third Party Liability in Tort* (Hart Publishing 2006) 1. See also, D Cooper, *Secondary Liability for Civil Wrongs* (unpublished PhD thesis, University of Cambridge 1995) 3; P S Davies, *Accessory Liability* (Hart Publishing 2015) 58.
61. R MacKinnon et al., 'Fostering Freedom Online: the Role of Internet Intermediaries' (UNESCO/Internet Society 2014) 19 and 40. See also: 'Manila Principles on Intermediary Liability – Background Paper', 30 May 2015, p. 6, available at: www.manilaprinciples.org.
62. M Vivant et al., *Lamy – Droit du Numérique: Informatique, Multimedia, Réseaux, Internet* (Wolters Kluwer France 2012) 1706. See also: European Group on Tort Law, *Principles of European Tort Law – Text and Commentary* (Springer 2005) 64; P Widmer, 'Comparative Report on Fault as a Basis of Liability and Criterion of Imputation (Attribution)' in P Widmer (ed.), *Unification of Tort Law: Fault* (Kluwer Law International 2005) 332; C van Dam, *European Tort Law* (2nd ed., Oxford University Press 2013) para. 801.
63. T F Cotter, 'Some Observations on the Law and Economics of Intermediaries' (2005) 1 Michigan State Law Review 2.

> index content, products and services originated by third parties on the Internet or provide Internet-based services to third parties.[64]

Significantly, this definition is limited to 'pure' intermediaries, thereby excluding service providers that 'give access to, host, transmit or index content or services that they themselves originate'. By this measure, internet publishers, broadcasting providers and other media that produce and disseminate their own content are not to be considered intermediaries.[65] This makes sense: content creators are not middlemen bringing together two isolated communication end points, but constitute the very source of that information.

With this in mind, a very simple and very broad concept of the internet intermediary emerges: internet intermediaries are entities that facilitate in any way the use of the internet by others to access content produced by third parties. Three basic conditions can be identified. The actor must: (a) provide services related to the internet; that (b) involve content produced by somebody else; and (c) are used by third parties.[66] The intermediary itself will most usually be a company of some kind, but conceivably may also be an individual.[67] Depending on the intermediary's business model, both the original content provider and the third parties may be paying customers, mere users or random unaffiliated others. This places the intermediary in-between two other parties. It is precisely this go-between nature that makes internet intermediaries particularly susceptible to accessory liability: internet intermediaries are essentially accessories to all conduct of all third parties that use their services. When that conduct illegally impacts somebody else, the spectre of liability looms.

Depending on the type of service that the intermediary provides, further specifications may be possible. The OECD lists the following types of internet intermediaries:

- internet access and service providers (ISPs);
- data processing and web hosting providers, including domain name registrars;
- internet search engines and portals;

64. K Perset, 'The Economic and Social Role of Internet Intermediaries', OECD Study, STI/ICCP(2009)9/FINAL, March 2010, p. 9.
65. R MacKinnon et al., 'Fostering Freedom Online: the Role of Internet Intermediaries' (UNESCO/Internet Society 2014) 19; European Union Ministers, Declaration 'Global Information Networks: Realising the Potential', Bonn, 6-8 July 1997 ('Bonn Declaration'). See also CJEU, C-291/13, *Papasavvas v. O Fileleftheros Dimosia Etairia,* 11 September 2014, at 39 and 45.
66. B Martinet Farano, 'Internet Intermediaries' Liability for Copyright and Trademark Infringement: Reconciling the EU and US Approaches' (2012) TTLF Working Paper No 14, 100.
67. See e.g., BGH, *Halzband,* 11 March 2009, I ZR 114/06.

- e-commerce intermediaries, where these platforms do not take title to the goods being sold;
- internet payment systems; and
- participative networking platforms, which include internet publishing and broadcasting platforms that do not themselves create or own the content being published or broadcast.[68]

This list is not exhaustive.[69] Indeed, the rapid development of the internet industry, particularly since the emergence of web 2.0 services, has given rise to a vast array of new internet-based business types: social networking sites, news and other data aggregators, online marketplaces, auction websites, peer-to-peer file-sharing platforms, online advertisers, crowdsourced databases, blogs, wikis, apps, while even the manufacturers of hardware – as opposed to services – used for accessing content can be considered to qualify as intermediaries.[70] Significantly, none of these categories will be insular and many intermediaries have a hybrid character, combining a variety of different intermediary activities together, as well as potentially non-intermediary ones as well.[71]

This diversity is significant from a legal perspective: as was noted above, the E-Commerce Directive relies on distinctions between intermediaries to suggest a fragmented and casuistic liability system consisting of specialised sub-regimes dependant on the type of service offered, isolated from the general principles of law.[72] However, while this horizontal

68. K Perset, 'The Economic and Social Role of Internet Intermediaries', OECD Study, STI/ICCP(2009)9/FINAL, March 2010, 9.
69. For a list of various different categorisations of intermediaries, see 'Manila Principles on Intermediary Liability – Background Paper', 30 May 2015, p. 8, available at: www.manilaprinciples.org.
70. N Zingales, 'Internet Intermediary Liability: Identifying Best Practices for Africa' (2013) Association for Progressive Communications (APC); 'Manila Principles on Intermediary Liability – Background Paper', 30 May 2015, p. 7, available at: www.manilaprinciples.org.
71. K Perset, 'The Economic and Social Role of Internet Intermediaries', OECD Study, STI/ICCP(2009)9/FINAL, March 2010, 10; R MacKinnon et al., 'Fostering Freedom Online: the Role of Internet Intermediaries' (UNESCO/Internet Society 2014) 20; N Elkin-Koren, 'After Twenty Years: Copyright Liability of Online Intermediaries' in S Frankel & D J Gervais (eds.), *The Evolution and Equilibrium of Copyright in the Digital Age* (Cambridge University Press 2014) 29.
72. This has encouraged and extension of this break down in the literature. Martinet Farano, for example, groups intermediaries into (a) information location tools; (b) online marketplaces and auction websites; (c) participative networked platforms and (d) peer-to-peer file-sharing platforms, see B Martinet Farano, 'Internet Intermediaries' Liability for Copyright and Trademark Infringement: Reconciling the EU and US Approaches' (2012) TTLF Working Paper No 14, 101. Féral-Schuhl breaks her analysis down to eleven different kinds of intermediaries: *opérateurs, fournisseurs d'accès, fournisseurs d'hébergement, hébergeurs de donnés médicales dématérialisées, fournisseurs de contenus, moteurs de recherché, fournisseurs de liens hypertexts, fournisseurs de liens commerciaux, gestionnaires de forum de discussion, hébergeurs de blogs et*

compartmentalisation that divides the law by subject rather than subject matter might have provided a good foothold for concretising the debate in the early days of mystification at theretofore unknown entities, as the internet comes of age, the idea of internet exceptionalism – including internet intermediary exceptionalism – must be questioned.[73] Although the information lawyer must accordingly certainly familiarise herself with the characteristics of different internet intermediaries in order to be able to accurately understand the facts of each case, this book will proceed from the assumption that the principles that govern those facts should be given a sturdier foundation, capable of transcending the multitude of services online technologies throw its way.[74] This approach is particularly pertinent given that, as Elkin-Koren notes, the distinctions drawn at the dawn of the internet era have been 'blurred in recent years due to the increasing convergence of communication and content in digital markets'.[75] With this in mind, the objective here shall be to reintegrate intermediary copyright liability into the underlying general rules, so as to formulate a clear theory of intermediary accessory copyright liability capable of being adjusted and applied to all kinds of internet intermediaries, regardless of specialisation.[76] For this purpose, in this book, a broad conception of internet intermediaries shall be used that encompasses all sorts of different kinds of providers, as long as they do what internet intermediaries do: facilitate internet-based communications.

---

blogueurs and *plateformes de commerce en ligne*, see C Féral-Schuhl, *Cyberdroit – Le Droit à l'Épreuve de l'Internet* (6th ed., Dalloz 2010) 743-903. Hoeren and Bensinger also use eleven categories, but arranged in a completely different manner: *Access-Provider, Anschluss- und Accountinhaber, der Website-Betreiber, Sharehoster und andere Host-Provider, Suchmaschinen, Blogs, Foren und Bewertungsportale, Affiliate-Marketing, Cloud-Dienste, Domains und Keyword Advertising, Bezahldienste, and Soziale Netzwerke*, see T Hoeren & V Bensinger, *Haftung im Internet – Die Neue Rechtslage* (De Gruyter, Berlin 2014) 101-717. Riordan distinguishes between 'platforms', 'hosts', 'ISPs', 'gateways' and 'marketplaces', see J Riordan, *The Liability of Internet Intermediaries* (PhD thesis, University of Oxford 2013, forthcoming Oxford University Press 2016) 151-163.

73. J Riordan, *The Liability of Internet Intermediaries* (PhD thesis, University of Oxford 2013, forthcoming Oxford University Press 2016) 10 and 29. See also, R J Mann & S R Belzley, 'The Promise of Internet Intermediary Liability' (2005) 47 William and Mary Law Review 239.
74. For a similar conclusion see, S Stalla-Bourdillon, 'Sometimes One Is Not Enough! Securing Freedom of Expression, Encouraging Private Regulation, or Subsidizing Internet Intermediaries or All Three at the Same Time: the Dilemma of Internet Intermediaries' Liability' (2012) 7(2) Journal of International Commercial Law and Technology 154.
75. N Elkin-Koren, 'Making Technology Visible: Liability of Internet Service Providers for Peer-to-Peer Traffic' (2005) 9(1-2) New York University Journal of Legislation and Public Policy 15.
76. M Vivant et al., *Lamy – Droit du Numérique: Informatique, Multimedia, Réseaux, Internet* (Wolters Kluwer France 2012) 1706.

1.3.3 Copyright Law

This book does not seek to harmonise all of tort law, all of accessory liability in tort law or even all the accessory liability of internet intermediaries. Instead, it is limited exclusively to intermediary accessory liability in one single area of law: copyright. Intermediary accessory liability for wrongful acts other than copyright infringement shall therefore not be examined, including the infringement of other IPRs, such as trademarks, other 'speech torts', such as defamation, or online criminal behaviour, such as hate speech.

There are several reasons why this limitation has been made. For one thing, as mentioned above, copyright already enjoys a high level of harmonisation not reproduced in other areas of online wrongdoing. This means that, although the EU copyright *acquis* is by no means yet complete,[77] as opposed to other types of illegality that have no basis in EU law, this is an area in which concrete harmonising groundwork has already been laid. This is particularly important in view of the aforementioned parasitic nature of accessory liability, which depends on the commission of a primary wrong – in copyright, that primary wrong has already received a European definition, opening the door for an extension of harmonisation to the accessory realm as well. Moreover, even in comparison to other, highly harmonised, IPRs, copyright remains of heightened relevancy in the online environment. The low threshold for its protection, requiring no formalities for its institution,[78] has combined well with the easy content dissemination enabled by the internet to turn the information era into the perfect storm of copyright infringement: copyright is simply very readily and, consequently, in fact very commonly infringed online. Although obviously not every copyright infringement will receive the attention of the law and the vast majority will never even make it before a court, the result has nevertheless been an expanding body of case law on accessory copyright liability, both on the national and the EU level. This supplies copyright with sufficient interpretative material on which to build a common European legal edifice, solidifying its harmonisation edge.

Some further limitations of scope should be noted here: the term 'copyright' in this context is used restrictively to cover only the rights of authors in their works. For simplicity's sake, the 'semi-copyright'[79] of related or neighbouring rights has been set aside in this book. The scope of this 'copyright proper' must also be further circumscribed exclusively to the author's economic rights. This is necessary: while certainly the online infringement of the author's moral rights is also possible, moral rights have

77. On this see M van Eechoud et al., *Harmonizing European Copyright Law* (Kluwer Law International 2009).
78. See Art. 5(2) of the Berne Convention.
79. M van Eechoud et al., *Harmonizing European Copyright Law* (Kluwer Law International 2009) 34.

to date not been harmonised on the EU level,[80] meaning that any potential harmonisation of accessory liability for their infringement would be toothless.

Inevitably, this concentration exclusively on copyright *stricto sensu* will influence outcomes. Different torts depend on different requirements. Just as is the case with primary liability, accessory liability too, including intermediary accessory liability, should be formulated not as a monolith, but with due consideration for the individual nature of the wrong committed. Participation in copyright infringement can thus not depend on the same conditions or lead to identical outcomes as participation in defamation or participation in the dissemination of child pornography. Certainly, similarities will often exist, particularly with other IPRs that exercise a similar social function. As a result, analogies will often be possible – indeed, this book will draw from the example of other areas of IP and particularly trademark liability, where appropriate. But caution must be had and it should be emphasised that the conclusions drawn here with regard to accessory copyright liability will by no means be one-on-one translatable to other areas of tort law, much less criminal law.[81]

1.3.4 Remedies

A final question of scope concerns the end-goal of liability: remedies. Liability rules can, after all, only be effective if the law provides a remedy, while remedies furnish the main incentive for right-holders to bring claims against intermediaries.[82] Two main types of remedies relevant to intermediary liability for the copyright infringements of others can be distinguished: damages and injunctions.[83] Damages consist of 'pecuniary compensation,

80. See Recital 19 of the Copyright Directive.
81. The United Nations (UN) Special Rapporteur on Freedom of Opinion and Expression, the Organization for Security and Co-Operation in Europe (OSCE) Representative on Freedom of the Media, the Organization of American States (OAS) Special Rapporteur on Freedom of Expression and the African Commission on Human and Peoples' Rights (ACHPR) Special Rapporteur on Freedom of Expression and Access to Information, 'Joint Declaration on Freedom of Expression and the Internet', 1 June 2011, p. 68.
82. C van Dam, *European Tort Law* (2nd ed., Oxford University Press 2013) para. 1202-2; P S Davies, *Accessory Liability* (Hart Publishing 2015) 255. See also, Art. 13 of the ECHR on the right to an effective remedy, according to which everyone 'whose rights and freedoms as set forth in this Convention are violated shall have an effective remedy before a national authority notwithstanding that the violation has been committed by persons acting in an official capacity'.
83. W van Gerven, et al., *Tort Law* (Hart Publishing 2000) 868-869; C van Dam, *European Tort Law* (2nd ed., Oxford University Press 2013) para. 1202-2; P S Davies, *Accessory Liability* (Hart Publishing 2015) 255.

obtainable by success in action' for the harm suffered.[84] An injunction is a 'court order prohibiting a person from doing something or requiring a person to do something'.[85]

The wording in the E-Commerce Directive gives the impression that liability is irrelevant to injunctions and may result only in damages. So, according to Recital 45, the 'limitations of the liability of intermediary service providers established in this Directive do not affect the possibility of injunctions of different kinds'. If an intermediary is 'not liable' under Article 12, 13 or 14 of the E-Commerce Directive, but may nevertheless be susceptible to injunctive relief, injunctive relief would seem to exist outside of the confines of liability. As a result, discussion has proliferated in Europe on the imposition of injunctions on so-called innocent intermediaries.[86] The CJEU endorsed this perspective in *L'Oréal v. eBay,* where it clarified that Article 11 of the Enforcement Directive 'requires the Member States to ensure that [an intermediary] may, *regardless of any liability of its own* in relation to the facts at issue, be ordered to take' enforcement measures by means of an injunction.[87]

Certainly, the idea of the irrelevancy of injunctions to liability has deep roots: in classic Roman law, the rule was '*omnis condamnatio est pecuniaria*'.[88] In the common law, the same evolution is reflected in the distinction between law and equity. Even today, tort experts are conflicted as to whether injunctions can really be considered part and parcel of tort law, while most legal systems retain a distinction between substantive tort law and procedural matters, which include injunctions. At the same time, from a conceptual point of view, the link between the two is obvious,[89] particularly given that in

84. H McGregor, *McGregor on Damages* (16th ed., Sweet & Maxwell 1997) 3, as quoted in W van Gerven, J Lever & P Larouche, *Tort Law* (Hart Publishing 2000) 739-741 and 868-887; N McBride & R Bagshaw, *Tort Law* (4th ed., Pearson 2012) 771.
85. See the UK Ministry of Justice, Civil Procedures Rules, Glossary.
86. See e.g., M Husovec, 'Injunctions against Innocent Third Parties: the Case of Website Blocking' (2013) 2 Journal of Intellectual Property, Information Technology and Electronic Commerce Law (JIPITEC) 116; M Husovec & M Peguera, 'Much Ado about Little – Privately Litigated Internet Disconnection Injunctions' (2015) 46(1) International Review of Intellectual Property and Competition Law (IIC) 10.
87. CJEU C-324/09, *L'Oréal v. eBay,* 12 July 2011 (emphasis by the author). See also, Report from the Commission to the European Parliament, the Council, the European Economic and Social Committee and the Committee of the Regions on the Application of Directive 2004/48/EC of the European Parliament and the Council of 29 April 2004 on the enforcement of intellectual property rights, COM(2010) 779 final, 22 December 2010 and Commission Staff Working Paper, Analysis of the application of Directive 2004/48/EC of the European Parliament and the Council of 29 April 2004 on the enforcement of intellectual property rights in the Member States, SEC(2010) 1589 final, 22 December 2010.
88. W van Boom, 'Comparative Notes on Injunction and Wrongful Risk-Taking' (2010) 17(1) Maastricht Journal of European and Comparative Law 10.
89. W van Boom, 'Comparative Notes on Injunction and Wrongful Risk-Taking' (2010) 17(1) Maastricht Journal of European and Comparative Law 10.

many cases injunctive relief will protect claimants far more effectively than any award of damages.[90] This will particularly be so in cases of mass copyright infringements, where the concern lies much more heavily on the disruption of future repetition, rather than the punishment of past transgressions. In any case, nowadays it is the rare tort law textbook that leaves injunctions out of the equation.[91] Von Bar opens his detailed exposition of European tort law with an explicit inclusion:

> 'Law of delict' describes the field of private law which determines whether a person who has sustained damage has a right to compensation (or where such damage is impending, to injunctive relief) even if the infliction of the damage forms the only legal bond between the two parties.[92]

As he concludes, '[p]reventive legal protection is [therefore] a necessary component of the law of delict'.[93] What nevertheless does persist into modern European tort law is the partial disconnect between injunctive relief and, not all of tort law, but at least fault, as the former generally does not require proof of the latter: although fault can certainly result in injunctive relief, the causation of damage alone ('*les constantes de la responsabilité*', according to the French)[94] may also suffice.[95] As this is also true of the injunctions of Article 8 of the Copyright Directive and Article 11 of the Enforcement Directive, it is through this lens that they should best be viewed: not as existing outside the ambit of all liability, but simply as (occasionally) extending it beyond personal misconduct.

In conclusion, remedies, in the tort law context, cannot be excised from the concept of liability. Both damages and injunctions may be awarded upon a finding of liability in tort, while the imposition of an injunction implies liability, even if of a limited reach. Of course, the type of remedy might depend on the circumstances accompanying the triggering event.[96] As shall be shown below, remedies are particularly inextricable from the question of accessory liability, as some legal systems approach that issue only obliquely through the lens of apportionment or even limit accessory liability

90. W van Gerven et al., *Tort Law* (Hart Publishing 2000) 869.
91. See e.g., P le Tourneau & L Cadiet, *Droit de la responsabilité et des contrats – Régimes d'indemnisation* (Dalloz-Sirey, 2012) 2437-2482; W V H Rogers, *Winfield & Jolowicz on Tort* (18th ed., Sweet & Maxwell 2010) 1070-1078; N McBride & R Bagshaw, *Tort Law* (4th ed., Pearson 2012) 832-844; W van Gerven et al., *Tort Law* (Hart Publishing 2000) 847-868.
92. C von Bar, *The Common European Law of Torts – Vol. I* (Clarendon Press 2000) para. 1.
93. C von Bar, *The Common European Law of Torts – Vol. I* (Clarendon Press 2000) para. 1, footnote 3.
94. C van Dam, *European Tort Law* (2nd ed., Oxford University Press 2013) para. 1202-2.
95. C van Dam, *European Tort Law* (2nd ed., Oxford University Press 2013) para. 1202-2.
96. W van Gerven et al., *Tort Law* (Hart Publishing 2000) 870.

exclusively to injunctive relief. While this book therefore will concentrate primarily on the question of the conditions for liability, ignoring matters of procedural law, it will nevertheless consider remedies where these are relevant to the determination of the appropriate conditions for liability.[97]

1.4 TERMINOLOGY

The creation of a new legislative order inevitably brings with it the need for appropriate linguistic means with which to formulate its norms.[98] The plurijural nature of Europe in particular goes hand in hand with European multilingualism.[99] As a result, European legal integration requires a parallel multilingual terminological integration for the expression of common ideas originating in linguistically diverse jurisdictions. In the same way, the European harmonisation of intermediary accessory copyright liability cannot limit itself only to the substance of the rules, but must formulate appropriate terminological means to enable the successful communication of that substance.

How can this goal be achieved? A variety of methods exists. One obvious way to handle the terminological conundrums that accompany harmonisation projects is through the introduction of neologisms. Disadvantages do present themselves in this regard however: while neologisms are good for the expression of emergent concepts, they are not always very easy to understand and carry with them the danger of misinterpretation. They are particularly impractical in the comparison of multiple sets of national approaches, especially in an area so strongly integrated into national language as tort law. In this book, this option shall therefore only be used sparingly, when describing original conceptual devices developed specially for it.[100]

As an alternative, semantic repurposing, through which existing legal terms are borrowed from one jurisdiction native in the language used and given distinct European meaning, will instead be heavily relied upon.[101] This

97. On this see also, M Infantino, 'Making European Tort Law: the Game and its Players' (2010) 18(1) Cardozo Journal of International & Comparative Law 45.
98. G Dannemann et al., 'Language and Terminology' in C Twigg-Flesner (ed.), *The Cambridge Companion to European Union Private Law* (Cambridge University Press 2010) 70.
99. R L Creech, *Law and Language in the European Union: The Paradox of a Babel 'United in Diversity'* (Europa Publishing 2005).
100. Examples of original terms developed for this book include the terms 'residual fault' and 'concurrent fault' used to described the two major approached to accessory liability used in the selected national legal systems.
101. G Dannemann et al., 'Language and Terminology' in C Twigg-Flesner (ed.), *The Cambridge Companion to European Union Private Law* (Cambridge University Press 2010) 70.

approach shall be the one primarily used in this book for the labelling of the proposed harmonised solutions put forth for the improvement of European intermediary accessory copyright liability. In that exercise, legal terminology too closely linked to a given national legal system shall be avoided.[102] The lead will instead be taken from prior comparative work in the area of European tort law, so that the terms employed sound natural and do not cause confusion.[103]

Finally, the comparative descriptions of the existing national legal solutions shall rely on local terms given in the national language. This shall be done in order to distinguish properly between the legal devices used in each of the compared jurisdictions and the proposed European solution: although peppering the text with foreign words can arguably make it clunky and pretentious, this approach at least guarantees precision and avoids causing confusion between the different legal approaches of different national jurisdictions, as well as the misrepresentation of national concepts by language crafted for other purposes by foreign lawyers. After all, local terms are by no means obviously inappropriate for the description of local concepts. To the contrary, the exclusive use of English terminology in a harmonisation exercise intended for a supranational jurisdiction counting twenty-four official languages[104] is what would not be quite right.

1.4.1 'Accessory Liability'

Having settled these general questions, it is also worth making a few observations on the use in this book of two specific legal terms that raise particularly difficult issues. The first and most problematic of these is that of 'accessory liability'. It should be noted that, even outside of a harmonisation context, accessory liability is an area of law that faces a terminological problem that is 'more than usually acute'.[105] Indeed, Riordan suggests that much 'of the confusion that has bedevilled [accessory liability] stems from

102. European Communities, 'Joint Practical Guide of the European Parliament, the Council and the Commission for Persons Involved in the Drafting of Legislation within the Community Institutions' (Office for Official Publications of the European Communities 2003).
103. See below, s. 1.5.
104. At present the official languages of the EU are Bulgarian, Croatian, Czech, Danish, Dutch, English, Estonian, Finnish, French, German, Greek, Hungarian, Italian, Irish, Latvian, Lithuanian, Maltese, Polish, Portuguese, Romanian, Slovak, Slovene, Spanish and Swedish.
105. W V H Rogers, 'Comparative Report on Multiple Tortfeasors' in W V H Rogers, *Unification of Tort Law: Multiple Tortfeasors* (Kluwer Law International 2004) 272. See also, P S Davies, *Accessory Liability* (Hart Publishing 2015) 54.

the use of undefined, inconsistent or misleading terminology'.[106] A brief overview of the multitude of terms that are used internationally to refer to the concept is at this point appropriate.

So, the most popular term used to denote this area of copyright law is that of 'secondary liability'. This is the term used in the US, which further subdivides the notion into the two alternatives of 'contributory liability' and 'vicarious liability'.[107] The American terminology has greatly influenced the international debate, making 'secondary liability' common in English-language writings within the EU as well.[108] Nevertheless, for the purposes of this book, 'secondary liability' has to be regarded as unsuitable, as it clashes with the provisions of sections 22-26 of the UK's Copyright, Designs and Patents Act 1988 (CDPA), entitled 'Secondary infringement of copyright', which have much more limited application. The term also runs the risk of giving the impression that the accessory to somebody else's infringement is secondarily liable for the same wrong as the primary wrongdoer, which (as explained above) is not always the case.[109] Finally, although the divisions seem to be gradually shifting, US secondary liability, extending as it does

106. J Riordan, *The Liability of Internet Intermediaries* (PhD thesis, University of Oxford 2013, forthcoming Oxford University Press 2016) 66.
107. J Ginsburg, 'Separating the Sony Sheep from the Grokster Goats: Reckoning the Future Business Plans of Copyright-Dependent Technology Entrepreneurs' (2008) 50(2) Arizona Law Review 577; L Helman, 'Pull Too Hard and the Rope May Break: on the Secondary Liability of Technology Providers for Copyright Infringement' (2010) 19(1) Texas Intellectual Property Law Journal 111; S K Högberg, 'The Search for Intent-Based Doctrines of Secondary Liability in Copyright Law' (2006) 106(4) Columbia Law Review 909; M Bartholomew & J Tehranian, 'The Secret Life of Legal Doctrine: the Divergent Evolution of Secondary Liability in Trademark and Copyright Law' (2006) 21(4) Berkeley Technology Law Journal 1363; C A Grossman, 'From *Sony* to *Grokster*: the Failure of the Copyright Doctrines of Contributory Infringement and Vicarious Liability to Resolve the War between Content and Destructive Technologies' (2005) 53(1) Buffalo Law Review 141; K M Saunders & G Berger-Walliser, 'The Liability of Online Markets for Counterfeit Goods: A Comparative Analysis of Secondary Trademark Infringement in the United States and Europe' (2011) 32(1) Northwestern Journal of International Law & Business 37.
108. D Cooper, *Secondary Liability for Civil Wrongs* (unpublished PhD thesis, University of Cambridge 1995); P Sales, 'The Tort of Conspiracy and Civil Secondary Liability' (1990) 49(3) Cambridge Law Journal 491; M Leistner, 'Common Principles of Secondary Liability?' in A Ohly, *Common Principles of European Intellectual Property Law* (Mohr Siebeck 2012) 117; A Kur, 'Secondary Liability for Trademark Infringement on the Internet: the Situation in Germany and throughout the EU' (2014) 37(4) Columbia Journal of Law & the Arts 525; A Bayer, 'Liability 2.0 – Does the Internet Environment Require New Standards for Secondary Liability? An Overview of the Current Legal Situation in Germany' in M J Adelmann et al., *Patents and Technological Progress in a Globalized World* (Springer 2009) 365; E Smith, 'Lord of the Files: International Secondary Liability for Internet Service Providers' (2011) 68(3) Washington and Lee Law Review 1555; J Riordan, *The Liability of Internet Intermediaries* (PhD thesis, University of Oxford 2013, forthcoming Oxford University Press 2016).
109. See above s. 1.3.1.

into vicarious liability, is not limited to fault-based instruments and therefore transcends the scope of the analysis engaged in here.

An alternative could be found in the term 'indirect liability', which is also common.[110] Ultimately however is equally unappealing: 'indirect liability' has the disadvantage of suggesting a circuitous route to liability that passes through a 'direct' infringer. As such, it is not suitable to describe cases of liability that, although always dependent on the commission of a primary wrong, is technically categorised as a primary liability.

A further possibility is that of 'third party liability'.[111] Yet this term too has a significant disadvantage, as it does not immediately make clear who the 'third party' is: is it the accessory or the principal? The same lack of clarity is presented by other, less widespread terms, such as 'tertiary liability',[112] 'gatekeeper liability',[113] 'participatory liability'[114] or 'joint liability'.[115] To overcome this problem, some texts prefer combining a selection of these terms to convey the appropriate concept without committing to a single moniker.[116]

---

110. B Martinet Farano, 'Internet Intermediaries' Liability for Copyright and Trademark Infringement: Reconciling the EU and US Approaches' (2012) TTLF Working Paper No 14, 47; D Lichtman & W Landes, 'Indirect Liability for Copyright Infringement: An Economic Perspective' (2003) 16(2) Harvard Journal of Law & Technology 395; D Lichtman & W Landes, 'Indirect Liability for Copyright Infringement: Napster and Beyond' (2003) 17(2) Journal of Economic Perspectives 113; P S Menell & D Nimmer, 'Legal Realism in Action: Indirect Copyright Liability's Continuing Tort Framework and Sony's De Facto Demise' (2007) 55(1) UCLA Law Review 143; P S Menell, 'Indirect Copyright Liability and Technology Innovation' (2008) 32 Columbia Journal of Law & the Arts 375; C W Adams, 'Indirect Infringement from a Tort Law Perspective' (2008) 42(3) University of Richmond Law Review 635.
111. C McIvor, *Third Party Liability in Tort* (Hart Publishing 2006); A Yen, 'Third-Party Copyright Liability after Grokster' (2007) 16(3) Information & Communications Technology Law 233; A Yen, '*Sony*, Tort Doctrines, and the Puzzle of Peer-to-Peer' (2005) 55(4) Case Western Reserve Law Review 815; G Pessach, 'An International-Comparative Perspective on Peer-To-Peer File-Sharing and Third Party Liability in Copyright Law: Framing the Past, Present, and Next Generations' Questions' (2007) 40(1) Vanderbilt Journal of Transnational Law 87.
112. B H Glatstein, 'Tertiary Copyright Liability' (2004) 71(4) The University of Chicago Law Review 1605.
113. J Zittrain, 'A History of Online Gatekeeping' (2006) 19(2) Harvard Journal of Law & Technology 255; R H Kraakman, 'Gatekeepers: The Anatomy of a Third-Party Enforcement Strategy' (1986) 2(1) Journal of Law, Economics & Organisation 53.
114. E Lomnicka, '"Knowingly Concerned"? Participatory Liability to Regulators' (2000) 21 Company Lawyer 120.
115. E Lawson, 'Directors Beware' (2002) 13(2) Entertainment Law Review 44.
116. So, for example, in a 2011 paper, the Max Planck Institute for Intellectual Property and Competition Law, in a clear attempt to cover all bases, refers to 'third party liability (contributory or secondary liability; indirect infringement)'. See Max Planck Institute for Intellectual Property and Competition Law, 'Study on the Overall Functioning of the European Trade Mark System' (Munich, 15 February 2011).

More descriptive terminology is also sometimes used, e.g., 'liability for the acts of a third party'[117] or 'liability for the acts of others'.[118] As is to be expected, this option is especially popular with comparative European researchers. Van Gerven, Lever and Larouche, for example, talk of 'multiple tortfeasors' and 'pluralities of established causes',[119] while Von Bar resorts to the even more cumbersome banner of 'liability of independent tortfeasors, accessories and conspirators, and group members'.[120] The European Group on Tort Law (EGTL) is more formalistic still and approaches the issue only sideways through the rules on apportionment as between tortfeasors, referring to the 'solidary liability' of 'multiple tortfeasors'.[121] These solutions clearly have no long-term potential, again risking causing confusion with vicarious liability.

Finally, it should be considered that the above are of course only the terms used by those writing in English. Breaking into works in other European languages opens even broader linguistic horizons.

Clearly, this terminological hodgepodge will not do. Without a standardised cross-border vocabulary, it is very hard to achieve the necessary harmonising clarity. At the same time, the problem is again very much a result of the under-theorised nature of accessory liability: accessory liability faces such a 'systematic failure'[122] that legal experts are unsure not only of its contents, but of its contours and, with that, its very name. It is thus clear that, precisely as with the substance of accessory liability, so with its name, an opportunity exists for the smoother introduction of Europe-wide solutions that can lead the way to clear definitions.

Recent developments from the UK seem to indicate that the biggest English-speaking country in Europe is settling on the term 'accessory liability': after some experimentation by the House of Lords with 'secondary liability' in *Credit Lyonnais,*[123] the Supreme Court in *Sea Shepherd UK v. Fish & Fish Ltd*[124] appears to have unambiguously embraced that term. At

---

117. M Lunney & K Oliphant, *Tort Law – Text and Materials* (3rd ed., Oxford University Press 2007) 465; C McIvor, *Third Party Liability in Tort* (Hart Publishing 2006) 481 or K Horsey & E Rackley, *Tort Law* (4th ed., Oxford University Press 2015) 87.
118. B Martinet Farano, 'Internet Intermediaries' Liability for Copyright and Trademark Infringement: Reconciling the EU and US Approaches' (2012) TTLF Working Paper No 14, 54.
119. W van Gerven et al., *Tort Law* (Hart Publishing 2000) 430-32.
120. C von Bar, *The Common European Law of Torts – Vol. I* (Clarendon Press 2000) para. 50.
121. W V H Rogers, *Unification of Tort Law: Multiple Tortfeasors* (Kluwer Law International 2004) 272.
122. J Riordan, *The Liability of Internet Intermediaries* (PhD thesis, University of Oxford 2013, forthcoming Oxford University Press 2016) 66 and 89.
123. *Credit Lyonnais Nederland NV (now known as Generale Bank Nederland N.V.) v. Export Credits Guarantee Department* [1999] UKHL 9; [2000] 1 AC 486; [1999] 1 All ER 929; [1999] 2 WLR 540 (18 February 1999).
124. *Sea Shepherd UK v. Fish & Fish Ltd* [2015] UKSC 10 (4 March 2015).

the same time, 'accessory liability' is also the term increasingly employed by English tort theoreticians.[125] It thus makes sense to encourage the crystallisation of definitive terminology by accepting the emergent dominant term. And indeed, 'accessory liability' appears to fit the bill: it is simple, straightforward, easily comprehensible, is used for the exact same purpose in criminal law and paints an accurate picture of the doctrine, by conferring the dependence of accessory's liability on the commission of a primary wrong, without necessarily suggesting a triangular liability structure. For these reasons it is the solution opted for in this book.

1.4.2 'Tort Law'

Finally, a second troublesome term worth noting is that of 'tort law'. The reader might have noticed that that is the one used in the text so far over other more jurisdiction-neutral possibilities. It has been argued that the term 'tort' is inextricably intertwined with the common law's casuistic system of multiple nominate heads of liability and that the more neutral alternatives of 'delictual liability' or 'extra-contractual liability' should therefore be preferred in the European realm.[126] In this book however, these have been rejected: while the first risks associations with criminal law, the second is rather unwieldy and therefore not to be preferred in comparative analyses that are liable anyway to become somewhat ungainly. Happily, as opposed to international accessory liability, where confusion continues to reign supreme, in this area a common line is clearly discernible: in comparative European private law the term 'tort law' seems to now have become clearly established as the standard one.[127] Again, this book follows the broader trend.

1.5 METHODOLOGY

In addition to terminology, another practical issue that must be addressed before the analysis can begin in earnest is that of methodology. How shall the research question identified in this book be answered? What methods shall be used to identify a reliable and objective solution? It is now time to tackle this question.

---

125. Indeed, a recent book dedicated to the topic is entitled 'Accessory Liability', see P S Davies, *Accessory Liability* (Hart Publishing 2015). See also, N McBride & R Bagshaw, *Tort Law* (4th ed., Pearson 2012) 860.
126. See e.g., C von Bar, *The Common European Law of Torts – Vol. I* (Clarendon Press 2000) paras 5-6.
127. C van Dam, 'European Tort Law: Features of a Diverse Landscape' in C Twigg-Flesner (ed.), *The Cambridge Companion to European Union Private Law* (Cambridge University Press 2010) 160.

1.5.1 The European Legal Method

The main methodological approach taken in this book will be what is increasingly termed the 'European Legal Method'.[128] Essentially, this refers to the method that should be employed in the interpretation, application and further development of EU law:[129] the 'how' of harmonisation. It is therefore clearly the appropriate methodological tool for any harmonising exercise. While the concept is still evolving, so that it cannot be constricted to a single settled technique,[130] generally speaking, the European Legal Method consists of a comparative analysis with a harmonising objective. As Hesselink puts it, it essentially envisages a 'dialectic relationship between the national and the European level with the explicit aim of overall harmony and convergence [...] legitimised by the European ideal'.[131] In this way, a dynamic

128. M W Hesselink, 'A European Legal Method? On European Private Law and Scientific Method' (2008) 15(1) European Law Journal 20; M W Hesselink, 'How Many Systems of Private Law Are There in Europe? On Plural Legal Sources, Multiple Identities and the Unity of Law' in L Niglia (ed.), *Pluralism and European Private Law* (Hart Publishing 2013) 199; M W Hesselink, 'The Common Frame of Reference as a Source of European Private Law' (2009) 83(4) Tulane Law Review 919; M W Hesselink, 'A Toolbox for European Judges' (2011) 17(4) European Law Journal 441; S Vogenauer, 'Eine gemeineuropäische Methodenlehre des Rechts – Plädoyer und Programm' (2005) 13 *Zeitschrift für Europäisches Privatrecht* 234; J Husa, 'The Method is Dead, Long Live the Methods – European Polynomia and Pluralist Methodology' (2011) 5 Legiprudence 249; R van Gestel & H-W Micklitz, 'Why Methods Matter in European Legal Scholarship' (2014) 20(3) European Law Journal 292; R Brownsword, H-W Micklitz, L Niglia & S Weatherill (eds.), *The Foundations of European Private Law* (Hart Publishing 2011) 323; C Twigg-Flesner (ed.), *The Cambridge Companion to European Union Private Law* (Cambridge University Press 2010); H Collins, *The European Civil Code: The Way Forward* (Cambridge University Press 2008) U Neergaard & R Nielsen, *European Legal Method: Paradoxes and Revitalisation* (Djøf Publishing 2011); U Neergaard & R Nielsen, *European Legal Method: In a Multi-level EU Legal Order* (Djøf Publishing 2012); U Neergaard & R Nielsen, *European Legal Method: Towards a New European Legal Realism?* (Djøf Publishing 2013); K Riesenhüber, *Europäische Methodenlehre: Handbuch für Ausbildung und Praxis* (3rd ed., Walter de Gruyter 2014); H Schepel, 'The European Brotherhood of Lawyers: the Reinvention of Legal Science in the Making of European Private Law' (2007) 32(1) Law & Social Inquiry 183; A Ohly & J Pila (eds), *The Europeanization of Intellectual Property Law: Towards a European Legal Methodology* (Oxford University Press 2013).

129. M W Hesselink, 'How Many Systems of Private Law Are There in Europe? On Plural Legal Sources, Multiple Identities and the Unity of Law' in L Niglia (ed.), *Pluralism and European Private Law* (Hart Publishing 2013) 199.

130. A 'one size fits all' approach would anyway be inappropriate considering both the evolving nature of EU law and the breadth of current and potential harmonisation projects: what works for product liability will not necessarily be helpful in environmental law. A polynomic legal order requires not a single methodological tool, but rather a toolbox of methods. European law's plural ontology must therefore be met with a multi-method methodology. See J Husa, 'The Method is Dead, Long Live the Methods – European Polynomia and Pluralist Methodology' (2011) 5 Legiprudence 249.

131. M W Hesselink, 'The Common Frame of Reference as a Source of European Private Law' 83 (2008-2009) Tulane Law Review 919.

theoretical framework is established that enables a heuristic approach to European rule-making:[132] the identification of pan-EU answers to pan-EU questions.

The starting assumption here is one of European polynomia:[133] the modern European legal landscape is a plural one that combines multiple overlapping sets of normative orders. Within the EU in particular, the interrelationship between the national and supranational (both EU and ECHR-derived) is increasingly a mutually referential one, so that the legitimacy of one is derived from its adherence to the principles set in the other.[134] As such, the traditional '28 model', that views EU law as an aspect of each national legal system, can be seen as giving way to a '28+1 model', that considers the EU legal system as a distinct one that operates on top of the national legal systems or, more radically yet, a 'One Big System model', that conceives of one single EU legal order within which national, international and regional law operate as interconnected sub-systems:[135] the European demoïcracy.[136]

As a result, the construction of a truly European rule necessarily requires multi-level inputs. In this context, comparative law emerges as 'harmonisation's handmaiden'.[137] As Zweigert and Kötz observe, 'unification cannot be achieved by simply conjuring up an ideal law on any topic and hoping to have it adopted'.[138] Instead, 'advantage should be taken of existing national legal orders in order to find possible common denominators, to

132. M W Hesselink, 'A European Legal Method? On European Private Law and Scientific Method' (2008) 15(1) European Law Journal 20.
133. J Husa, 'The Method is Dead, Long Live the Methods – European Polynomia and Pluralist Methodology' (2011) 5 Legiprudence 249.
134. T Koopmans, 'The Birth of European Law at the Cross Roads of Legal Traditions' (1992) 39 The American Journal of Comparative Law 493.
135. R Nielsen, 'Towards an Interactive Comparative Method for Studying the Multi-Layered EU Legal Order' in U Neergaard & R Nielsen, *European Legal Method: In a Multi-level EU Legal Order* (Djøf Publishing 2012) 89. See also, M W Hesselink, 'How Many Systems of Private Law Are There in Europe? On Plural Legal Sources, Multiple Identities and the Unity of Law' in L Niglia (ed.), *Pluralism and European Private Law* (Hart Publishing 2013) 199 and M W Hesselink, 'The Common Frame of Reference as a Source of European Private Law' (2009) 83(4) Tulane Law Review 919.
136. P van Parijs, 'Should the European Union Become More Democratic?' in A Follesdal & P Koslowski, *Democracy and the European Union* (Spinger 1998) 287; K Nicolaïdis, 'Our European Demoi-cracy: Is this Constitution a Third Way for Europe?' in K Nikolaides & S Weatherill, *Whose Europe? National Models and the Constitution of the European Union* (Oxford University Press 2003) 137; K Nicolaïdis, 'The Idea of European Demoicracy*' in J Dickson & P Eleftheriadis, *Philosophical Foundations of European Union Law* (Oxford University Press 2012) 247; K Nicolaïdis, 'European Demoicracy and its Crisis' (2013) 51(2) Journal of Common Market Studies 351.
137. J M Smits, 'European Private Law and the Comparative Method' in C Twigg-Flesner (ed.), *The Cambridge Companion to European Union Private Law* (Cambridge University Press 2010) 33.
138. K Zweigert and H Kötz, *An Introduction to Comparative Law* (3rd ed., Clarendon Press 1998) 24.

develop common principles and, where appropriate, to identify best solutions'.[139] The starting point, both with regard to content and structure, should therefore always be the existing European national laws.[140] This approach allows 'parties to avoid the mistakes and repeat the positive experiences of those who went before'.[141] To this end, national similarities and differences must be investigated, the first to potentially be incorporated in the common solution and the second to be reconciled, through the prevalence of the best variant.

This reveals the central guiding principle of harmonisation, that of 'better law'. The comparison of multiple national legal systems is intended to function as an '*école de vérité*', which can reveal the appropriate solution for the fashioning of a harmonised solution.[142] In cases where no existing national approach is satisfactory (i.e., where adjustments to a changing technological landscape are necessary or an incompatibility the overarching European principles exists) or where fundamental dissimilarities divide the national jurisdictions that cannot be otherwise overcome, the replacement of all by an entirely novel, improved rule should considered.[143] In this way, the harmonisation of law can be combined with the improvement of its substance. This 'better law' principle is generally accepted by harmonising scholars,[144] while that is also the approach taken by the CJEU, as well as the European legislator.[145] As AG Léger stated in *Commission v. CCRE:*

139. Communication from the Commission to the European Parliament and the Council, 'A More Coherent European Contract Law – An Action Plan', COM(2003) 68 final, Brussels, 12 February 2003.
140. B A Koch, 'The "European Group on Tort Law" and its "Principles of European Tort Law"' (2005) 53 American Journal of Comparative Law 189.
141. Communication from the Commission to the European Parliament and the Council, 'European Contract Law and the Revision of the Acquis – The Way Forward', COM(2004) 651 final, Brussels, 11 October 2004.
142. K Lanaerts, 'Le droit compare dans le travail du juge communaitaire' in F R Van de Mensbrugghe, *L'utilisation de la méthode comparative en droit européen* (Presses Universitaires de Namur 2003) 111 as referenced in G Samuel, *An Introduction to Comparative Law and Method* (Hart Publishing 2014) 55.
143. J M Smits, 'Rethinking Methods in European Private Law' in M Adams & J Bomhoff (eds), *Practice and Theory in Comparative Law* (Cambridge University Press 2012) 170.
144. For concrete examples of the application of this working rule in European tort law harmonisation projects, see European Group on Tort Law, *Principles of European Tort Law – Text and Commentary* (Springer 2005) 15 ('In our exercises […] we posed the question whether such a common core would be the best solution for Europe. If the question was answered in the negative, we tried to find a better one') and C von Bar et al. (eds), *Principles, Definitions and Model Rules of European Private Law: Draft Common Frame of Reference (DCFR)*, prepared by the Study Group on a European Civil Code and the Research Group on EC private law (Acquis Group), Outline Edition (Sellier 2009) 38.
145. Communication from the Commission to the European Parliament and the Council, 'A More Coherent European Contract Law – An Action Plan', COM(2003) 68 final, Brussels, 12 February 2003; Communication from the Commission to the European

> to establish the existence of a general principle of Community law, the Court carries out a comparative examination of national legal systems. In this connection, it is unanimously agreed that the Court does not seek to determine the arithmetical average of national laws or to fall into line with the lowest common denominator. On the contrary, the Court takes a critical approach and gives the answer which is most appropriate in relation to the structure and aims of the Community.[146]

Obviously, the search for a 'better solution' naturally raises the epistemological question of how such a solution should be identified.[147] For the purpose of European harmonisation, it is suggested that the interpretative principle to be applied must necessarily be a 'Europe-friendly' one: *favor Europae.*[148] 'Better' in this context should therefore be understood as meaning 'more European' or 'better for European harmonisation'. Existing European law serves as the measuring tape in this regard: if a national approach does not accord with European law, whether in the form of the EU directives, accompanying CJEU case law and the European law of human or fundamental rights, it cannot be 'better' for European purposes. This makes sense: the EU harmonisation of the area may after all be incomplete, but that is no reason to dismiss the advances it has already made, but only to start again from the beginning. Most importantly, the primary rules of the European Convention on Human Rights (ECHR) and the EU Charter can never be ignored. Instead any future principles must be developed in strict conformity with their edicts.

Ultimately, the result is a legal dialogue that reveals the European Legal Method as a self-perpetuating system, a methodological virtuous circle of mutual reinforcement between the national and the supranational, such that each feeds into the other: national law informs the development European law, only to have that reintroduced eventually by the European legislator for its transposition back onto the national level. At the same time, European law helps select the relevant national solutions to be incorporated into the harmonised solution, enhanced with a European interpretation. The objective is a blurring of the lines between the two that allows for the creation of a legal solution shaped by and acceptable to both: a 'cosmopolitan democratic

Parliament and the Council, 'European Contract Law and the Revision of the Acquis – The Way Forward', COM(2004) 651 final, Brussels, 11 October 2004.

146. CJEU, Opinion of Advocate General Léger, case C-87/01 P, *Commission v. CCRE*, 17 September 2002.
147. G Samuel, *An Introduction to Comparative Law and Method* (Hart Publishing 2014) 55. See generally for a criticism of the danger this poses of a devolution into a neo-naturalist '*école de vérité*' approach to comparative law, pages 55 and 42.
148. M W Hesselink, 'A European Legal Method? On European Private Law and Scientific Method' (2008) 15(1) European Law Journal 20.

theory' appropriate for 'an international system which is neither state nor nation'[149] – and particularly fitting for the transnational arena of the internet.

1.5.2 Comparative Law

Given these methodological foundations, a next question arises naturally: if the European Legal Method consists of a comparative analysis with a harmonising objective, what kind of comparative analysis is required? Samuel's 'methodological road map' of comparative law is helpful in this regard.[150] The Europeanising aim sets the tone.

The first choice that must be made in this context concerns the classic divide between Zweigert and Kötz's cardinal decree of *praesumptio similitudinis,* i.e., presumption of similarity, as opposed to Legrand's *praesumptio dissimilitudinis,* a presumption of difference.[151] According to the first, in comparative analyses, similarities rather than differences must be assumed and sought out.[152] As Zweigert and Kötz argue, this approach 'rests on what every comparatist learns, namely that the legal system of every society faces essentially the same problems, and solves these problems by quite different means through very often with similar results'.[153] In other words, once legal doctrine is stripped away, legal systems tend to reach similar practical results. The opposing view prioritises divergences instead. The idea here is that, in the interests of avoiding reductionism and the establishment of 'universalist myths', the comparatist must resist the temptation to identify similarities, as these are likely to be only superficial.[154]

Clearly, from a broader theoretical perspective neither approach is inherently preferable: as Merryman observes, if 'someone asks whether German law is similar to, or different from, American law, the correct answer is, "yes"'.[155] Instead, the pertinent issue will always be that of aim. Given that this book pursues harmonisation and the objective of harmonisation is to hunt out similarities between legal systems in order to use these as

---

149. J M Smits, 'Democracy and (European) Private Law: A Functional Approach' (2009) 2(2) European Journal of Legal Studies 26.
150. G Samuel, *An Introduction to Comparative Law and Method* (Hart Publishing 2014) 173.
151. R Michaels, 'The Functional Method of Comparative Law' in M Reimann & R Zimmermann (eds), *The Oxford Handbook of Comparative Law* (Oxford University Press 2006) 336.
152. K Zweigert & H Kötz, *An Introduction to Comparative Law* (3rd ed., Clarendon Press 1998) 40.
153. K Zweigert & H Kötz, *An Introduction to Comparative Law* (3rd ed., Clarendon Press 1998) 34.
154. G Samuel, *An Introduction to Comparative Law and Method* (Hart Publishing 2014) 54-55.
155. Quoted in G Samuel, *An Introduction to Comparative Law and Method* (Hart Publishing 2014) 55.

drawstrings to pull those systems closer together, it must be concluded that *praesumptio similitudinis* presents a more serviceable starting point. At the same time, effective harmonisation must of course also account for dissimilarities between its object-systems. The idea, after all, is not to deny differences, but to seek out the optimum approach to be employed in the harmonised framework.[156] In this context, it would perhaps be more accurate to say that, in harmonisation, a principle of presumption, not of similarities or dissimilarities, but of harmonising potential should be that to be applied. In the European context, the appropriate rule should thus be '*praesumptio Europae*'. Whether similarities are prominent or not, they can generally be found.[157] If they cannot, as mentioned above, an equivalent novel solution should instead be developed.

In this regard, the second methodological dichotomy between analogical and genealogical comparison is also relevant. Genealogical comparison seeks to relate the objects of the comparison to each other by tracing them back to a common legal ancestor (e.g., Roman law) or otherwise highlighting historical influences between them.[158] By contrast, in an analogical approach, the compared items are examined as such, with the focus lying instead on the differences or similarities of style, mentality and effectiveness that they display. Although an analogical approach shall be taken in this book, it should be understood that a strong genealogical connection does exist between the various legal systems of Europe that makes the analogies between them all the more powerful and their comparative examination all the more pertinent. This is true not only of the civil law jurisdictions, but also of their common law cousins:[159] despite the division of European legal systems' into different legal families, intellectual exchanges across the European continent have been perpetual and potent throughout European history.[160] The result has been the natural emergence of similarities between the national legal systems that greatly facilitate the harmonisation process. In this context, finding a truly European solution is not as difficult a process as

156. G Samuel, *An Introduction to Comparative Law and Method* (Hart Publishing 2014) 42 and 55.
157. M W Hesselink, 'A European Legal Method? On European Private Law and Scientific Method' (2008) 15(1) European Law Journal 20.
158. This is for example the approach taken by Zimmermann in his retrospective analysis of European tort law through the eyes of the Roman *ius commune*, see R Zimmermann, *The Law of Obligations: Roman Foundations of the Civilian Tradition* (Oxford University Press 1996).
159. Indeed, it can be argued that the real divide in European tort law is not between the common law and the civil law, but between the French system and the German 'anti-*Code-civil*' approach, see G Wagner, 'The Project of Harmonizing European Tort Law' (2005) 42 Common Market Law Review 1269; C von Bar, *The Common European Law of Torts – Vol. I* (Clarendon Press 2000) para. 368.
160. R Zimmermann, 'Roman Law and the Harmonization of Private Law in Europe' in A S Hartkamp et al. (eds), *Towards a European Civil Code* (4th ed., Ars Aequi Libri 2011) 21.

a similar exercise between previously entirely isolated legal systems might have been.

Finally, another basic difficulty facing the comparatist is that of perspective. The main choice here is between an internal and an external perspective. At first sight the proper understanding of any legal system would seem to require the adoption of an internal perspective: a complete immersion in the local legal *mentalité*. Yet the simultaneous parallel equal engrossment in multiple different systems will usually be impossible for practical reasons. Moreover, the internal perspective also raises additional intellectually oriented objections: although local informants can be insightful, they can also be misleading.[161] An external perspective grants far greater distance and, with that, objectivity, as well as an improved grounding in comparative context. Again, the interpretative principle of *favor Europae* indicates the appropriate direction: within the European Legal Method, the division between the internal and external perspective loses meaning. By definition, the European harmonisation of private law aims at the gradual integration of the two,[162] with Europeanisation thus pursued as a value in its own right. In this context, the appropriate perspective is one that is neither internal nor external, but a combination perspective that shifts between the two as appropriate. The combined effect can perhaps be described as a perspective that is external to the national legal systems, while remaining internal to a common European law.

On the basis of these three fundamental choices, a basic methodological framework is set. Within this context, a more concrete comparative 'scheme of intelligibility' must be selected. Although other options exist, two main schools of comparative legal thought emerge as relevant from a harmonisation standpoint: functionalism and structuralism. In many ways, the two are complementary. In this book, both shall be combined for a holistic understanding of the relevant issues. What does this mean?

Functionalism is the classic methodological principle of comparative law.[163] As the term suggests, it involves examining the *function* of the disparate laws that form the object of the comparative analysis. The idea here is that, although aiming at similar results, different legal systems will often approach the same legal problem with an entirely different conceptual toolset.[164] Functionalism is especially well suited to exercises of

161. G Samuel, *An Introduction to Comparative Law and Method* (Hart Publishing 2014) 62.
162. M W Hesselink, 'A European Legal Method? On European Private Law and Scientific Method' (2008) 15(1) European Law Journal 20.
163. K Zweigert & H Kötz, *An Introduction to Comparative Law* (3rd ed., Clarendon Press 1998) 34; J M Smits, 'Rethinking Methods in European Private Law' in M Adams & J Bomhoff (eds), *Practice and Theory in Comparative Law* (Cambridge University Press 2012) 170.
164. D Gerber, 'Sculpting the Agenda of Comparative Law: Ernst Rabel and the Façade of Language' in A Riles (ed), *Rethinking the Masters of Comparative Law* (Hart Publishing 2001) 190.

micro-comparison. As opposed to macro-comparison that takes a bird's eye view of whole legal systems, micro-comparison focuses on individual areas of the law.[165] Micro-comparative functionalism seeks out functional equivalents, i.e., the legal mechanisms with which the same function is performed in different legal systems, regardless of the position of these legal mechanisms within their respective systems.[166] That is of course precisely what is pursued in this book: as noted above, intermediary accessory copyright liability – a niche area of tort law if ever there was one – is a cluster concept that does not hold a set place in the national conceptual legal structures, but is best described as a collection of disparate solutions to a particular problem. Its examination therefore requires the gathering of these solutions from across the national tort law landscape for their comparative appraisement.

While micro-comparative functionalism is useful, it cannot be properly executed without a sound grounding in macro-comparative structuralism.[167] As opposed to functionalism, which focuses on the details, structuralism prefers a helicopter view. Structuralism rests on the relativity of meaning that results from the 'shared system of significance' agreed upon by a given community.[168] It thus aims to understand the system in place in each legal jurisdiction by observing the relationship between the elements that comprise it.[169] While structuralism has received relatively little attention within comparative law,[170] this exercise nevertheless has great value: an exclusive focus on the function of individual micro-legal devices does not allow for a conception of the overarching logic that created them or their interrelationship with other surrounding doctrines. As has been pointed out, a playing card has no meaning in itself, but only gains meaning when placed within the system of the pack.[171] This observation is particularly relevant in the context of an EU harmonisation exercise, as the selective, policy-driven instrumentalism that characterises the EU's traditional approach of a patchworked harmonisation-by-directive is particularly susceptible to this effect. So,

165. R Michaels, 'The Functional Method of Comparative Law' in M Reimann & R Zimmermann (eds), *The Oxford Handbook of Comparative Law* (Oxford University Press 2006) 336.
166. M Graziadei, 'The Functionalist Heritage' in P Legrand & R Munday (eds), *Comparative Legal Studies: Traditions And Transitions* (Cambridge University Press 2003) 100, as quoted in G Samuel, *An Introduction to Comparative Law and Method* (Hart Publishing 2014) 67.
167. G Samuel, *An Introduction to Comparative Law and Method* (Hart Publishing 2014) 50.
168. J Bomhoff, 'Comparing Legal Argument' in M Adams & J Bomhoff (eds), *Practice and Theory in Comparative Law* (Cambridge University Press 2012) 84.
169. A Riles, *Rethinking the Masters of Comparative Law* (Hart Publishing 2001) 251.
170. J Bomhoff, 'Comparing Legal Argument' in M Adams & J Bomhoff (eds), *Practice and Theory in Comparative Law* (Cambridge University Press 2012) 84.
171. M-L Izorche, 'Propositions méthologiques pour la comparison' Revue Internationale de Droit Comparé 289, referenced in G Samuel, *An Introduction to Comparative Law and Method* (Hart Publishing 2014) 106.

although the resultant fragmentation of private law into multiple allochthonous *leges speciales* has permitted a kind of 'functional creep',[172] without which the Europeanisation of sensitive areas of law would otherwise undoubtedly have been excessively difficult,[173] it not only poses a danger of *decodificazione* on the national level,[174] but comes at the expense of sound methodology and theory building on the European one.[175] It thus threatens both the inner balance of national European tort systems and the harmonisation process itself. Von Bar warns:

> If directives are treated discretely, rather than as an interconnected body which not only regulates specific matters but also takes responsibility for the creation of an internally consistent system of Community liability law, this can contribute to the disintegration of Community law. What seen in isolation, looks like a success for the approximation of laws can, if seen as part of a whole, prove to the source of retrogressive disunion.[176]

A proper understanding of the position of the micro-area within the macro-whole and the way in which the latter shapes the former to achieve the function at stake can thus help lend the harmonisation of European tort law an *elegantia jurisprudentia*[177] that can not only forward the more suitable harmonisation of particular sub-sections of tort law, but also the creation of an internally coherent common European legal culture. What this means is that, once the functionally equivalent national intermediary accessory liability solutions have been identified, they should also be evaluatively examined as part of the systems to which they belong. In this way, the reasons behind their formation can be identified, thus allowing for the determination of which, from among the various rules under examination, better achieves the purpose they serve, as well as which is best suited to a European structure. In this way, equivalence functionalism can be used as 'a

172. M A Pollack, 'Creeping Competence: The Expanding Agenda of the European Community' (1994) 14(2) Journal of Public Policy 95.
173. A Johnston & H Unberath, 'European Private Law by Directives: Approach and Challenges' in C Twigg-Flesner (ed.), *The Cambridge Companion to European Union Private Law* (Cambridge University Press 2010) 85.
174. C von Bar, *The Common European Law of Torts – Vol. I* (Clarendon Press 2000) para. 372.
175. R van Gestel & H-W Micklitz, 'Why Methods Matter in European Legal Scholarship' (2014) 20(3) European Law Journal 292; H Koziol, 'Comparative Conclusions' in H Koziol, *Basic Questions of Tort Law from a Comparative Perspective* (Jan Sramek Verlag 2015) 690; M Infantino, 'Making European Tort Law: the Game and its Players' (2010) 18(1) Cardozo Journal of International & Comparative Law 45.
176. C von Bar, *The Common European Law of Torts – Vol. I* (Clarendon Press 2000) para. 394.
177. G Samuel, *An Introduction to Comparative Law and Method* (Hart Publishing 2014) 15.

yardstick to determine the "better law"'[178] in intermediary accessory copyright liability and, therefore, as 'a means by which legal change and harmonisation can be achieved in a transparent way', while structuralism determines the framework within which this assessment should be undertaken.[179]

1.5.3 Selection of National Jurisdictions

The next and final step in the methodological process is the selection of the national jurisdictions that shall form the objects of the comparative analysis: if harmonisation relies on the comparison of national legal solutions, which national legal systems will be examined for this purpose must be decided.

Practical considerations mean that not all twenty-eight EU tort law systems can be equally represented within the confines of this book. In view of this obstacle, the analysis below shall concentrate only on three national legal systems: England,[180] France and Germany. These have been chosen as representative of the three major tort law traditions of Europe: England's tort law has had a strong influence on relevant rules in Cyprus, Ireland, and Malta. French tort law has similarly affected the systems of Belgium, Hungary, Italy, Luxembourg, the Netherlands, Poland, Romania and Spain. Finally, Germany's system has close ties with the tort laws of Austria, Bulgaria, the Czech Republic, Greece, Latvia, Portugal, Slovakia and Slovenia.[181]

Other reasons also support the selection of the three jurisdictions. The UK, France and Germany represent over 40% of the total EU population[182] and account for more than half of the EU's gross domestic product (GDP).[183] As a result, the three countries enjoy significant political influence within the EU. As Van Dam observes, 'points of difference and conflict between [them], including those on harmonizing European private law and tort law, will be of major importance for moving the European discussion forward'.[184] The three

178. R Michaels, 'The Functional Method of Comparative Law' in M Reimann & R Zimmermann (eds), *The Oxford Handbook of Comparative Law* (Oxford University Press 2006) 336.
179. J Gordley, 'Comparative Law and Legal History' in P G Monateri (ed), *Methods of Comparative Law* (Edward Elgar 2012) 107, as referenced in G Samuel, *An Introduction to Comparative Law and Method* (Hart Publishing 2014) 67.
180. It should be recalled that the UK encompasses three separate jurisdictions, those of England and Wales, Scotland and Northern Ireland. In the interests of expediency, in this book only the first shall be considered. This shall generally be referred to as 'England'.
181. C van Dam, *European Tort Law* (2nd ed., Oxford University Press 2013) para. 102-2.
182. Eurostat, 'Demography Report – 2015 Edition' (Publications Office of the European Union, Luxembourg 2015) 4-6.
183. See statistics compiled by the World Bank (>Data >Countries >European Union), available at: http://data.worldbank.org/region/EUU.
184. C van Dam, *European Tort Law* (2nd ed., Oxford University Press 2013) para. 102-2.

countries present a crucial starting point for any EU harmonisation project involving an area of tort law.

In addition to these considerations, specifically with regard to intermediary accessory copyright liability, the three jurisdictions' size, population and economic standing has also meant that they have produced the biggest bulk of case law in the area, as well as the largest bodies of accompanying legal theory. Finally, as shall become apparent in the main analysis, England, France and Germany also take divergent approaches to intermediary accessory liability in copyright, in ways that are reflective of the broader differences of their tort systems. The reconciliation of these three can therefore allow for a smoother harmonisation process for in this area of law.

Of course, other tort law traditions also exist within the EU. Most notable are the tort systems of the Scandinavian countries, as well as those of Eastern Europe. Moreover, even within the country groups formed by the influence of the 'big three', there is no blind adherence to a party line: the development of legal systems is not a game of follow-the-leader. Other Member States will hence always have interesting perspectives to contribute. As any future European tort law will have to combine features of both the common law and the civil law, the study of hybrid jurisdictions, such as e.g., those of Scotland or Cyprus or even the non-European Quebec and South Africa, might prove particularly illuminating.[185] While the practical constraints facing this book prohibit a country-by-country examination beyond the three selected jurisdictions, this reality should nevertheless be kept in mind. The understanding of the broader context within which the comparative exercise is executed can add useful perspective: the construction of a harmonised European accessory intermediary copyright liability, like any harmonising exercise, should not be approached as a legal imperialist tug-of-war between the three biggest legal systems of the EU,[186] but as a collaborative process for the identification of truly European solutions. As Von Bar puts it, in 'order to serve justice one must not simply promote 'one's own' law, one must be fully open to foreign ideas'.[187]

1.6 OUTLINE

Having in the above appropriately defined the applicable theoretical framework, how this shall be applied in practice for the harmonisation specifically of European intermediary accessory copyright liability can now be analysed.

185. J M Smits, 'Rethinking Methods in European Private Law' in M Adams & J Bomhoff (eds), *Practice and Theory in Comparative Law* (Cambridge University Press 2012) 170.
186. G Samuel, *An Introduction to Comparative Law and Method* (Hart Publishing 2014) 6 and 17.
187. C von Bar, *The Common European Law of Torts – Vol. I* (Clarendon Press 2000) para. 406.

For this purpose, a preliminary overview of the chapters that follow is given here. What avenue shall the harmonisation of European intermediary accessory copyright liability pursue within this book? A step-by-step description goes as follows.

Chapter 2 will be begin with examining the baseline of European intermediary accessory copyright liability as that is set by the current harmonised rules. The approach taken here shall be an expository one, resting on the tools of classical doctrinal research in the form of grammatical, historical, systematic and teleological interpretation.[188] Three main sources of EU law can be identified at this level: the relevant directives, accompanying CJEU case law and the European law of fundamental rights.

All three are interconnected: as the analysis will show, fundamental rights have been injected into the debate by the case law of the CJEU, in its attempt to properly interpret the provisions of the directives. As a result, fundamental rights, the 'driving force' behind the harmonisation of European tort law more generally,[189] will also be shown to constitute the cornerstone of a European intermediary copyright liability system specifically.[190] With this in mind, existing piecemeal European provisions will be revealed as elaborations on a broader, underlying normative framework of intermediary accessory copyright liability, to which all further substantive development must refer.[191] As well as describing the current state of harmonisation and demonstrating its incompleteness and the consequent need for its further development, Chapter 2 shall therefore lay the groundwork of that development by identifying the parameters within which it must operate.

Subsequently, the comparative analysis will begin. This shall be undertaken in Chapters 3 and 4.

---

188. P Chynoweth, 'Legal Research' in A Knight & L Ruddock (eds.), *Advanced Research Methods in the Built Environment* (Wiley-Blackwell 2008) 28; M W Hesselink, 'A Toolbox for European Judges' (2011) 17(4) European Law Journal 441.
189. C von Bar, *The Common European Law of Torts – Vol. I* (Clarendon Press 2000) para. 410; C van Dam, *European Tort Law* (2nd ed., Oxford University Press 2013) para. 711-4; C van Dam, 'Tort Law and Human Rights: Brothers in Arms on the Role of Tort Law in the Area of Business and Human Rights' (2011) 2(3) Journal of European Tort Law 221; K Oliphant, 'European Tort Law: A Primer for the Common Lawyer' (2009) 62(1) Current Legal Problems 440; M W Hesselink, 'How Many Systems of Private Law Are There in Europe? On Plural Legal Sources, Multiple Identities and the Unity of Law' in L Niglia (ed.), *Pluralism and European Private Law* (Hart Publishing 2013) 199. See also J Pila, 'A Constitutionalized Doctrine of Precedent and the *Marleasing* Principle as Bases for a European Legal Methodology' in J Pila & A Ohly (eds.), *The Europeanization of Intellectual Property Law: Towards a European Legal Methodology* (Oxford University Press 2013) 227.
190. U Gasser & W Schulz, 'Governance of Online Intermediaries: Observations from a Series of National Case Studies' (18 February 2015) Berkman Center Research Publication No. 2015-5, available at: http://ssrn.com/abstract=2566364.
191. For a similar approach see P Savola, *Internet Connectivity Providers as Involuntary Copyright Enforcers – Blocking Websites in Particular* (PhD thesis, University of Helsinki 2015) 9.

Chapter 3 shall be heavily descriptive.[192] A country-by-country approach will be taken. Here, the legal instruments employed to tackle intermediary accessory copyright liability in each of the three selected national jurisdictions of England, France and Germany shall be identified and examined. As we shall see, while England oscillates between the intra-copyright solution of authorisation and the tort-based approach of joint tortfeasance, English legal scholars have begun questioning whether a drastically different approach of negligence liability for the infringements of others should be applied. This latter possibility is precisely the approach currently applied in France. Germany takes an in-between route: while it possesses the theoretical equipment that would allow for the application of both the French negligence-based approach and the English joint tortfeasance solution, for the most part it rejects both in favour of a unique construction it labels 'disturbance liability' (*Störerhaftung*).

The parallel analysis of the national regimes shall reveal the functional inadequacies and doctrinal inconsistencies that undermine them and consequently showcase the need for a new and harmonised solution. At the same time, the strong points of each system shall be highlighted, as will the commonalities between them, both of which can serve as launching pads for a new European scheme. Significant factors that are not currently taken into consideration by extant national law, but arguably should be shall also be investigated. It shall be shown that all three national systems have reached the limits of the accessory liability solutions embedded in their copyright law. Converging in confusion,[193] they are accordingly ready for European guidance.

The functional analysis of Chapter 3 shall give way in Chapter 4 to a structural approach. As Zweigert and Kötz advise, the last step in the comparative process is to 'build a system' with its own 'special vocabulary and syntax'.[194] Accordingly, Chapter 4 shall seek to reposition the evaluative comparative exercise of Chapter 3 within a single, consistent overall concept of European tort law. The objective shall be to seek out the origins of the differing approaches in the national laws to intermediary accessory copyright liability in their underlying general tort structures, as well as investigate the

---

192. As R Cryer et al. explain, descriptive legal positivism of this kind 'is suited to research projects that seek to systematise legal norms, and to understand the relationships between different bodies of legal norms, or to analysing the output of courts and their coherence, or the accuracy of their application of sources of law. Legal research based on positivism is sometimes referred to as analytical, or *doctrinal*, legal research. However it is a prequel to, rather than a substitute for, the making of statements about what the law ought to be.' See: R Cryer, T Hervey, B Sokhi-Bulley & A Bohm, *Research Methodologies in EU and International Law* (Hart Publishing 2011) 38.

193. C Angelopoulos, 'Beyond the Safe Harbours: Harmonising Substantive Intermediary Liability for Copyright Infringement in Europe' (2013) 3 Intellectual Property Quarterly 253.

194. K Zweigert & H Kötz, *An Introduction to Comparative Law* (3rd ed., Clarendon Press 1998) 44.

possibilities for common solutions. This shall signal a shift from a classic doctrinal 'black letter law' focus on existing legal rules to a normative reflection on the law that ought to be.[195] It is here therefore that the search for a European 'better law' paradigm shall begin in earnest.

The break down of the chapter shall be thematic, focusing on the examination of the essential building blocks of a European fault-based liability to the extent that these are relevant to the intermediary accessory copyright liability discussion. These shall be identified as fault, causation and defences. The analysis will draw on the traditional understanding of these notions under the national tort laws of England, France and Germany, but shall also seek to move beyond the national to a broad-gauged European interpretation. For this purpose, inspiration shall be drawn heavily from existing tort harmonisation projects and especially the Principles of European Tort Law (PETL),[196] developed by the EGTL, and the Draft Common Frame of Reference (DCFR),[197] compiled by the Study Group on a European Civil Code and the Research Group on Existing EC Private Law (Acquis Group).[198]

Of course, the comparative exercises of Chapters 3 and 4 are teleological. They are not undertaken out of mere academic curiously, but so as to serve a very specific objective. That objective is the search for a common European future.[199] This shall be the focus of Chapter 5.

Building on the definitions and structures outlined in Chapter 4, in Chapter 5 a harmonised European framework for intermediary liability for copyright infringement shall be proposed. In view of the theoretical approach taken, the structure itself will necessarily be vague. In this context, the obvious risk is that of a re-scattering of the gathered principles along national borders, as national jurists instinctively fall back to national interpretations absent more concrete European guidance.[200] This is inevitable and to some extent the natural condition of tort law even within a single legal system.[201] Greater control can however be achieved by further crystallising the resultant

195. P Chynoweth, 'Legal Research' in A Knight & L Ruddock (eds.), *Advanced Research Methods in the Built Environment* (Wiley-Blackwell 2008) 28.
196. Available at: www.egtl.org. See also European Group on Tort Law, *Principles of European Tort Law – Text and Commentary* (Springer 2005).
197. C von Bar et al. (eds), *Principles, Definitions and Model Rules of European Private Law: Draft Common Frame of Reference (DCFR)*, prepared by the Study Group on a European Civil Code and the Research Group on EC private law (Acquis Group), Outline Edition (Sellier 2009).
198. For more information the website of the Study Group at: www.sgecc.net.
199. R Zimmermann, 'The Europeanization of Private Law' in M Reimann & R Zimmermann (eds), *The Oxford Handbook of Comparative Law* (Oxford University Press 2006) 539.
200. M Infantino, 'Making European Tort Law: the Game and its Players' (2010) 18(1) Cardozo Journal of International & Comparative Law 45.
201. M W Hesselink, 'The Common Frame of Reference as a Source of European Private Law' (2009) 83(4) Tulane Law Review 919.

European framework. Chapter 5 shall accordingly attempt to imbue concrete meaning into the definitions formulated in Chapter 4, while retaining the general structure of a European fault liability. To this end, it will interpret the building blocks of European accessory liability by reference specifically to the issue of intermediary accessory copyright liability. The existing EU *acquis* for intermediary accessory copyright liability already detailed in Chapter 2 shall be heavily relied on for this purpose, as will the disparate national regimes described in Chapter 3. In order to test the resultant framework and examine the outcomes it puts forth, different types of intermediaries will be envisioned positioned within differing circumstances. Where the conclusion is that an intermediary should be held liable, the relevance of remedies shall be examined. Ultimately, a solution shall be sought that allows for fine distinctions and delivers clear definitions tailored to the particularities of the topic at hand.

A final summary and conclusion, in combination with a list of suggestions for the future possible integration of the proposed framework into EU law, will be offered in Chapter 6.

1.7 A BRIEF NOTE ON IDEOLOGY

Of course there will always be those who disagree on principle with any attempt at a European harmonisation in any area of law. The current political climate, rife with talk of 'Brexits' and 'Grexits', deep in the midst of the 'eurocrisis', is conducive to such 'euroscepticism'. Even outside of the context of modern geopolitics, the European tort law community, perhaps with good reason, is often strongly resistant to attempts at the harmonisation of this most nationally bound area of law. In this regard, before moving on to the substantive part of this book a final short note should be made on ideology.

In particular, it must be acknowledged that an obvious ideological dimension exists to both the choice of a harmonising objective of this book and the *favor Europae* methodology adopted to achieve it. The European harmonisation of intermediary accessory copyright liability, like the European harmonisation of private law in general, is after all by its very purpose an ideologically charged question, whose answer depends heavily on the personal belief system of the person examining it.[202] Whether or not harmonisation is appropriate and should be pursued is accordingly, to a large extent, a political,[203] rather than a legal matter and, as such, dependent not

202. M W Hesselink, 'How Many Systems of Private Law Are There in Europe? On Plural Legal Sources, Multiple Identities and the Unity of Law' in L Niglia (ed.), *Pluralism and European Private Law* (Hart Publishing 2013) 199.
203. The European Parliament agrees, see 'Resolution of 23 March 2006 on European Contract Law and the Revision of the *Acquis*: The Way Forward' (2005/2022(INI)

only on the legal possibilities (both harmonisation and non-harmonisation are legally possible), but on the will of the law-maker – and ultimately therefore the European people. That observation can also be extended to the legal methodology adopted to address this issue: as Hesselink observes, it 'seems impossible to define a system of European private law and its boundaries in an objective and static way. It all depends on the conception one has of Europe, of where it is going and, especially, where it *should* be going'.[204] This cannot be surprising: law is after all a normative science and, as such, necessarily builds on normative assumptions, while it is highly unlikely that humanity will come to a conclusive common understanding on these basic assumptions in near future. There are, instead, 'as many legal methods as there are ways of looking at the world'.[205] In this context, the only possible response of the responsible legal theoretician is the open and explicit acknowledgement of her ideological positions.[206]

For this expository purpose, Hesselink suggests a division between six different 'senses of belonging', depending on the individual's outlook towards the prospect of a European private law: the nihilist, nationalist, dualist, pluralist, Europeanist and cosmopolitan views.[207] This book is very

---

Brussels, 23 March 2006 [2006] OJ C 292 E, 109, according to which 'the very decision to opt for a [European Civil] Code is political and its content, albeit legal, is predicated on social and political objectives'.

204. M W Hesselink, 'A European Legal Method? On European Private Law and Scientific Method' (2008) 15(1) European Law Journal 20.
205. M W Hesselink, 'A European Legal Method? On European Private Law and Scientific Method' (2008) 15(1) European Law Journal 20.
206. Hesselink quotes Kelsen, who already at the end of the World War II, talking about the interface between national and international law, made the same observation: 'In our choice [between national and international law], we are obviously guided by ethical and political preferences. A person whose attitude is one of nationalism and imperialism will naturally be inclined to accept the hypothesis of the primacy of national law. A person whose sympathies are for internationalism and pacifism will be inclined to accept the hypothesis of the primacy of international law. From the point of view of the science of law, it is irrelevant which hypothesis one chooses. But from the point of view of political ideology, the choice is important since tied up with the idea of sovereignty. […] Even if the decision between the two is beyond science, science still has the task of showing the relation between them and certain value systems of an ethical or political character. Science can make the jurist aware of the reasons for his choice and the nature of the hypothesis he has chosen, and so prevent him from drawing conclusions which positive law, as given in experience, does not warrant.' See H Kelsen, *General Theory of Law and State* (first published 1945, Transaction Publishers 2007) 388, as quoted in M W Hesselink, 'How Many Systems of Private Law Are There in Europe? On Plural Legal Sources, Multiple Identities and the Unity of Law' in L Niglia (ed.), *Pluralism and European Private Law* (Hart Publishing 2013) 199.
207. M W Hesselink, 'How Many Systems of Private Law Are There in Europe? On Plural Legal Sources, Multiple Identities and the Unity of Law' in L Niglia (ed.), *Pluralism and European Private Law* (Hart Publishing 2013) 199.

clearly inspired by what he terms the 'moderate Europeanist' position:[208] it is 'Europeanist' in that it is 'post-nationalist' within a European context, i.e., it rejects the traditional division of the European continent into distinct and insular jurisdictions and instead favours inter-jurisdictional dialogue with a view to a continuous process of supranational integration. It thus embraces the prospect of an 'ever-closer Union'[209] and in its name a principle of what the German *Bundesverfassungsgericht* (BVerfG) calls *Europarechtsfreundlichkeit* – an openness towards European law.[210] In this spirit, it is untroubled by the concerns of incompatibility between European tort cultures that raise objections among some tort specialists. For one thing, it does not hold with the idea that national culture is inextricably tied in with or exemplified in a meaningful way in national tort law:[211] as Lando has put it, 'law is not folklore'.[212] For another, it does not perceive the gaps that separate European tort laws to be particularly great:[213] as Markesinis observed, any differences

208. M W Hesselink, 'The Common Frame of Reference as a Source of European Private Law' (2009) 83(4) Tulane Law Review 919.
209. See Art. 1 TEU: 'This Treaty marks a new stage in the process of creating an ever closer union among the peoples of Europe, in which decisions are taken as openly as possible and as closely as possible to the citizen.' (Consolidated version of the Treaty on European Union [2012] OJ C326/01). The idea of an 'ever closer union' is first mentioned in the Solemn Declaration on a European Union signed by the then ten Member States in 1983 (19 June 1983, Stuttgard, reproduced from the Bulletin of the European Communities, No. 6/1983). It was subsequently incorporated into EU primary law with the Single European Act in 1987.
210. See BVerfG, 30 June 2009, EuZW 2009, 552 L, quoted in M W Hesselink, 'A Toolbox for European Judges' (2011) 17(4) European Law Journal 441.
211. Much has been written by European tort lawyers about the incompatibilities of national European tort cultures. Van Dam explains this mentality: '[t]he assumption is that national rules in this area are to a great extent the outward manifestation, the body, of the national culture, its soul.' See C van Dam, 'Who is Afraid of Diversity? Cultural Diversity, European Co-operation, and European Tort Law' (2009) 20 King's Law Journal 281. Once the surface has been scratched however these usually dissipate into nothingness.
212. O Lando, 'Optional or Mandatory Europeanisation of Contract Law' (2000) 59(4) European Review of Private Law 69. Regardless, it is fair to suggest that beating heart of national European cultures does not lie in their various intermediary accessory copyright liability laws.
213. Giliker for example ponders: 'Can we realistically guarantee that a judge in Southern Spain will interpret the standard of care in the same way as a judge in Sweden? An English judge to apply the same normative standard as her Greek counterpart?', see P Giliker, 'The Draft Common Frame of Reference and European Contract Law: Moving from the "Academic" to the "Political"' in J Devenney & M B Kenny, *The Transformation of European Private Law: Harmonisation, Consolidation, Codification or Chaos?* (Cambridge University Press 2013) 23. Having grown up between English and Greek cultures, having met a fair number of Spanish and Swedish people and having undertaken a number of comparative European law projects, I am not convinced that this legal culture clash is the acute problem this phrasing suggests. Although indubitably judges are people and people are different, nationality is not the only and not the greatest difference that divides them.

are 'more apparent than real'.[214] At the same time, this pro-Europe approach is also 'moderate' in that it does not seek to either replace traditional nation state-based neo-nationalism with a pan-European variant of the same[215] nor – more relevantly to the topic at hand – to immediately supersede the national European systems. Instead, it promotes the combination of multiple loyalties.

This normative mindset is clearly linked to a specific constitutional conception of the EU. MacCormick explains as follows:

> A pluralistic analysis is in this instance, and on these grounds, clearly preferable to the monistic one that envisages a hierarchical relationship in the rank-order: international law-Community law-Member-State law. Accordingly, the doctrine of supremacy of Community law should by no means be confused with any kind of all-purpose subordination of Member-State law to Community law. Rather, the case is that these are interacting systems, one of which constitutes in its own context and over the relevant range of topics a source of valid law superior to other sources recognized in each of the Member-State systems.[216]

Weiler expresses a similar idea when he states that:

> crucially, [this view] does not extinguish the separate actors who are fated to live in an uneasy tension with two competing senses of the polity's self, the autonomous self and the self as part of a larger community, and committed to an elusive search for an optimal balance of goals and behaviour between the community and its actors.[217]

Taking inspiration from this perspective, this book seeks neither to impose one jurisdiction's notions regarding law on the others nor to replace all individual *iura propria* with a single European *ius commune* uninformed by the national approaches, but, in line with the EU's motto of 'unity in diversity', simply to create something new and truly 'European' that draws from the national systems, while simultaneously bringing them closer together. In this regard, it is worth noting that, even if one does not believe that European integration or the convergence of legal systems more generally is desirable, it seems hard to deny that modern legal theory – even when

---

214. B Markesinis, 'The Not So Dissimilar Tort and Delict' (1977) 93 The Law Quarterly Review 78. See also, G Wagner, 'Comparative Tort Law' in M Reimann & R Zimmermann (eds), *The Oxford Handbook of Comparative Law* (Oxford University Press 2006) 1003.
215. This is the idea of, as it is sometimes referred to, a 'fortress Europe'.
216. N MacCormick, 'Risking Constitutional Collision in Europe?' (1998) 18(3) Oxford Journal of Legal Studies 517.
217. J H H Weiler, 'The Transformation of Europe' in J H H Weiler, *The Constitution of Europe: 'Do the New Clothes Have an Emperor?' and Other Essays on European Integration* (Cambridge University Press 1999) 93.

nationally oriented – relies increasingly on comparative analyses.[218] The EU neither invented polynomia nor has a monopoly over it. Quite to the contrary, legal monism has never been humanity's historical legal norm:[219] '[l]egal pluralism is the fact. Legal centralism is a myth, an ideal, a claim, an illusion'.[220] This inescapable reality has been pushed into high drive by modern globalisation and nowhere is this more obvious than in internet-related debates. Whether expanded to include all of tort law or focused exclusively on intermediary accessory copyright liability, the push for harmonisation is here to stay.

218. R van Gestel & H-W Micklitz, 'Why Methods Matter in European Legal Scholarship' (2014) 20(3) European Law Journal 292.
219. J Husa, 'The Method is Dead, Long Live the Methods – European Polynomia and Pluralist Methodology' (2011) 5 Legiprudence 249.
220. J Griffiths, 'What Is Legal Pluralism?' (1986) 24 Journal of Legal Pluralism and Unofficial Law 1.

Chapter 2

The Need for Reform: The Current EU Legal Framework

The objective of this book is to explore possible avenues for a future substantive European harmonisation of intermediary accessory liability for online copyright infringement. The obvious starting point for this analysis is the existing European legal framework: if harmonisation is the aim, the first step in the process should logically be a proper understanding of its current state. That proper understanding shall be sought in this chapter.[1]

For this purpose, the analysis will begin with a brief examination of the harmonised rules on primary liability in section 2.1, before moving on to the relevant provisions in the secondary law, to be meticulously explored in section 2.2. Section 2.3 shall tackle the legal theoretical and jurisprudential origins of the theory of a 'fair balance' between competing fundamental rights and its application to intermediary liability. Finally, section 2.4 shall pave the way for the country-by-country comparative analysis undertaken in the next chapter.

2.1 A BRIEF OVERVIEW OF THE EU RULES ON COPYRIGHT

Before we examine the rules on accessory liability as they currently exist at the EU level, it is important to first consider those governing primary liability for copyright infringement. This is the case for two main reasons: for one thing, it is possible that an intermediary may be held liable for primary

1. While a short summary was already provided in Ch. 1 (see s. 1.2.), here the analysis will be far more elaborate.

copyright infringement itself, including in cases where there might additionally be some involvement by third parties. If that is the case, there will be no need to examine whether it also acted as an accessory to such infringements as committed by others. For another, before examining the conditions for the imposition of any kind of liability for a wrongdoing, it is important to understand the parameters of the wrong that has been done. This will be true regardless of whether or not the liability is primary or accessory: if the claim is one of primary liability, then the outcome will depend on whether or not the defendant committed the wrongful act in question. To determine that, that wrongful act will have to be defined. If the claim is one of accessory liability, whether the third party primary wrongdoer committed the wrongful act will still be relevant before the link between that act and the accessory may be examined: one person cannot be held liable for the wrongdoing of another unless that other did in fact commit a wrong. As noted in Chapter 1, accessory liability is not inchoate, but derivative, and must be related to the finding of a specific primary wrong.[2] As a result, if accessory liability is to be found, that primary wrong must again be defined. This dependence on primary liability is particularly relevant in the context of this book, as it also has consequences for harmonisation: without a concrete harmonised basis for primary liability, any harmonisation of accessory liability will inevitably fail to produce harmonised outcomes. As a result, the harmonisation of the underlying acts of primary infringement can be seen as part of the process of harmonising accessory liability, including that of intermediaries. In this respect, in copyright, in view of the high level of harmonisation already achieved for primary liability, the EU is off to a comparatively good start.

When does primary liability arise under EU copyright law? For this, the infringement of the exclusive rights of the author of the work will be necessary. As mentioned in Chapter 1, in this book, the focus shall be on copyright in the strictest sense, sidestepping related or neighbouring rights.[3] Moral rights shall also be bypassed, the primary liability for their infringement being as yet untouched by EU law. While the same rules applicable to accessory liability for the infringement of economic rights should arguably also apply to the infringement of moral rights, without a reliable underlying basis in the harmonisation of primary liability, the application of a harmonised accessory liability to the unharmonised concept of moral rights will result in outcomes as fragmented as those of the primary liability for the same, making any such harmonisation ineffectual.

With this in mind, the analysis below shall limit itself only to the economic rights of the author. In the online context, two are the economic rights of the author that are most relevant: the reproduction right and the right

2. See s. 1.4.1. See also P S Davies, *Accessory Liability* (Hart Publishing 2015) 25.
3. See s. 1.4.3. above.

of communication to the public, including making available to the public.[4] On the European level, these have been harmonised by Articles 2 and 3 of the Copyright Directive respectively, thereby providing a concrete basis for the harmonisation of any accessory liability for their infringement as well. The third economic right recognised by the Copyright Directive, the right of distribution, despite recent indications that it might be broadening in the CJEU case law,[5] is for the time being generally understood as limited to tangible copies[6] and is accordingly not relevant to liability in the internet context.

The reproduction right and the right of communication to the public shall be examined in turn below. The objective shall be not to dissect these notions in detail, but merely to investigate their relevance with regard to outlining the scope of the liability of internet intermediaries for infringements of these rights committed online by third parties. This is necessary, as, unhelpfully, the European legislator has not provided a precise definition of either right. Instead, the European harmonisation of copyright has taken its cue from existing international instruments and in particular the Berne Convention for the Protection of Literary and Artistic Works (Berne Convention) and WIPO Copyright Treaty (WCT), while relying on the promise of an eventual harmonising cumulative body of interpretative material as constructed by the CJEU.[7] Consequently, the analysis here shall begin with a brief description of any guidance that can be gleaned from this

---

4. P Savola, 'Blocking Injunctions and Website Operators' Liability for Copyright Infringement for User-Generated Links' (2014) 5 European Intellectual Property Review 279.
5. So, for example, in the recent decision of *Labianca* (CJEU, C-516/13, 13 May 2015), the CJEU interpreted the distribution right expansively to include the online advertisement of protected works or copies thereof, regardless of whether or not such advertising was followed by the transfer of ownership of the protected work or a copy thereof to the purchaser. Similarly, in *UsedSoft* (CJEU, C-128/1, 3 July 2012), the court interpreted the principle of exhaustion of the distribution right as equally applicable in cases where the transfer by the copyright holder to a customer of a copy of a computer programme, accompanied by the conclusion between the same parties of a user licence agreement, took place by means of a download from the right-holder's website as by means of a material medium such as a CD-ROM or DVD. It should be noted that in that case the court was applying Art. 4(2) of the Software Directive (Directive 2009/24/EC), which it explicitly identified as lex specialis in relation to the Copyright Directive. As a result, the same interpretation need not apply to both.
6. Article 4 and Recital 28 of the Copyright Directive. See also: I A Stamatoudi & P Torremans, 'The Information Society Directive' in I A Stamatoudi & P Torremans, *EU Copyright Law* (Edward Elgar 2014) 423; M Walter & S Von Lewinski, *European Copyright Law: A Commentary* (Oxford University Press 2010) 993; S Bechtold in T Dreier & P B Hugenholtz (eds), *Concise European Copyright Law* (Kluwer Law International 2006) 363.
7. S Depreeuw, *The Variable Scope of the Exclusive Rights in Copyright* (Wolters Kluwer 2014) 487.

international '*quasi-acquis*',[8] before moving on to the insights provided by EU-level case law.

2.1.1 The Right of Reproduction

Although a core right covering the oldest form of exploitation of a work, the right of reproduction was initially only tacitly understood to be protected within the framework of the Berne Convention. The Convention's 1967 Stockholm revision changed this with the introduction of Article 9(1).[9] According to this, '[a]uthors of literary and artistic works protected by this Convention shall have the exclusive right of authorizing the reproduction of these works, in any manner or form'. Paragraph 3 clarifies that sound and video recordings are to be considered as reproductions. The WCT does not reproduce these provisions, but does require that Contracting Parties comply with them in its Article 1(4). The Agreed Statement on Article 1(4) of the WCT further confirms that the reproduction right applies fully in the digital environment and in particular to the use of works in digital form. The storage of a protected work in digital form in an electronic medium is moreover recognised as a reproduction of that work. The right to reproduction is therefore a well-established part of copyright's international arsenal, carrying uninterrupted momentum into the internet era.

The EU first tested the harmonisation waters with the introduction of a European reproduction right for software, databases and related rights.[10] Eventually, Article 2(a) of the Copyright Directive proceeded to establish a horizontally harmonised right of reproduction in favour of all categories of works.[11] This grants authors 'the exclusive right to authorise or prohibit direct or indirect, temporary or permanent reproduction by any means and in

8. M van Eechoud et al. 'The Recasting of Copyright and Related Rights for the Knowledge Economy', final report, Institute for Information Law (IViR), University of Amsterdam, November 2006, 31.
9. M Walter & S von Lewinski, *European Copyright Law: A Commentary* (Oxford University Press 2010) 963.
10. See Art. 7 of the old Related Rights Directive (Council Directive 92/100 on rental and lending rights and certain rights related to copyright in the field of intellectual property [1992] OJ L 346/61), Art. 4(a) of the old Computer Programs Directive (Council Directive 91/250 on the legal protection of computer programs [1991] OJ L 122/42) and Art. 5(a) of the Database Directive (Directive 96/9/EC of the European Parliament and of the Council of 11 March 1996 on the legal protection of databases [1996] OJ L 77/20).
11. See in general: S Depreeuw, *The Variable Scope of the Exclusive Rights in Copyright* (Wolters Kluwer 2014) 189-242; I A Stamatoudi & P Torremans, 'The Information Society Directive' in I A Stamatoudi & P Torremans, *EU Copyright Law* (Edward Elgar 2014) 401-405; M Walter & S Von Lewinski, *European Copyright Law: A Commentary* (Oxford University Press 2010) 963-971.

any form, in whole or in part' of their works.[12] The long string of clarifying elements stresses the broad reach of the right. This is in line with the high level of protection granted to copyright in the EU, as required by Recitals 9 and 21 of the Copyright Directive.

The provision makes clear that the right covers both digital and analogue reproductions.[13] Significantly with regard to online infringements, a reproduction will occur even where the form of the work was substantially altered during the copying process: so, for example, a photograph of an artistic work will constitute a copy of that work. In this way, the Directive follows the lead of the WCT in recognising that the digitisation of a work constitutes a reproduction of said work. It is irrelevant whether the copy is made directly on the basis of a tangible original or indirectly, e.g., through the fixation of a broadcast or a communication to the public.

Similarly, not only permanent, but also temporary copies are explicitly encompassed within the scope of the reproduction right, however short-lived or economically irrelevant they might be. This is particularly significant for digital technologies and was the focus of heated debate during the negotiations leading up to the adoption of the WCT. It has been suggested that the breadth of the provision can have the result of an undesirable overextension of protection to include even the *mere use* of a work without the permission of the author, particularly in view of modern technologies with which such use will often require acts of at least temporary reproduction. Indeed, as critics have pointed out, the result could be an unjustified discrimination between the analogue and digital worlds even for similar acts of usage.[14]

This strict stance is tempered on the European level by the mandatory exception introduced by Article 5(1) of the Copyright Directive. According to this, temporary acts of reproduction which are transient or incidental, which constitute an integral and essential part of a technological process, whose sole purpose is to enable either a transmission in a network between third parties by an intermediary or a lawful use of a work to be made and which have no independent economic significance shall be exempted from the reproduction right. The provision likely absolves access providers from direct liability for e.g., proxy caching for the sake of network efficiency or the transient copying necessary in 'store and forward' telecommunications. The services of host providers, on the other hand, are not covered by the

---

12. Article 2 of the Copyright Directive does not apply if the work being reproduced is a computer programme or database, in which case Arts 4 and 5 of the Computer Programmes and Database Directives apply respectively.
13. S Bechtold in T Dreier & P B Hugenholtz (eds), *Concise European Copyright Law* (Kluwer Law International 2006) 357 et seq.
14. M van Eechoud et al., 'The Recasting of Copyright and Related Rights for the Knowledge Economy', final report, Institute for Information Law (IViR), University of Amsterdam, November 2006.

exception, meaning that they may still be liable for direct copyright infringements of the works they store.[15]

In 2014, the CJEU in *Meltwater*[16] assuaged fears of an over-expansive reproduction right[17] by making clear that Article 5(1) of the Copyright Directive applies to any copy on the user's computer screen, as well as copies in the internet cache of that computer's hard disk made by an end-user in the course of viewing a website. These may therefore be made without the authorisation of the copyright holder. This makes clear that online browsing by end-users does not engage the reproduction right. This result incidentally also protects internet intermediaries against potential accessory liability for the technical and automated creation of temporary copies to enable and facilitate such browsing. At the same time, the provision of such hyperlinks might of course still be regarded as a direct communication to the public.[18] In any case, the very existence of an explicit exception underlines Article 2's intention of defining the right of reproduction expansively.[19] Indeed, Walter and Von Lewinski suggest that making clear that the reproduction right extends to temporary copies in order to make the relevant European law fit for the digital age was the very purpose of the express recognition of the right of reproduction in the Copyright Directive.[20]

It should be noted that partial copies of a work are also covered by the right of reproduction, regardless of how small they might be. This is particularly relevant for online aggregators, which rely on snippeting rights. Of course, a partial copy will only be protected if it fulfils the applicable requirements on originality. Like the notion of reproduction itself, originality with regard to works of authorship is undefined in EU law. A first attempt at reconciling Europe's divergent legal traditions with regard to originality was made through the three similar originality standards devised by the European legislator for computer programs, databases and original photographs.[21] Over

---

15. K Koelman, 'Online Intermediary Liability' in P B Hugenholtz (ed.), *Copyright and Electronic Commerce - Legal Aspects of Electronic Copyright Management* (Kluwer Law International 2000) 23.
16. CJEU, C-360/13, *Public Relations Consultants Association Ltd v. Newspaper Licensing Agency Ltd and Others*, 5 June 2014.
17. See e.g., T Hoppner, 'Reproduction in Part of Online Articles in the Aftermath of Infopaq (C-5/08): Newspaper Licensing Agency Ltd v. Meltwater Holding BV' (2011) 33(5) European Intellectual Property Review 331.
18. M Walter & S von Lewinski, *European Copyright Law: A Commentary* (Oxford University Press 2010) 970.
19. S Bechtold in T Dreier & P B Hugenholtz (eds), *Concise European Copyright Law* (Kluwer Law International 2006) 358.
20. M Walter & S von Lewinski, *European Copyright Law: A Commentary* (Oxford University Press 2010) 964.
21. The Computer Programmes Directive demands that a computer programme be 'original in the sense that it is the author's intellectual creation' in order that protection might be recognised. The Database Directive uses the exact same wording. As a result, databases and computer programmes are generally accepted to be subject to the same standard of

time, a certain rapprochement between Member States with a copyright and an author's rights approach to originality can be observed with regard to other copyright works as well, at least in practical outcome, if not in the conceptual tools employed to achieve it.

So, the CJEU in the controversial *Infopaq I,*[22] a case concerning allegations of copyright infringement against a Swedish company operating a media monitoring and analysis business for the unauthorised reproduction of texts of up to eleven words extracted from newspaper articles, relied on the wording and context of Article 2 of the Copyright Directive, as well as the overall objectives of that Directive and of international law, to define the notion of a 'reproduction in part'. On this basis, it concluded that works of authorship should only be protected within the Community legal order if they are original in the sense that they are 'the author's own intellectual creation'. Accordingly, *originality* and not *substantiality* is the test that determines the copyright status of extracted parts of a work. Following this reasoning, the CJEU decided that snippets of eleven words may, depending on national law, be entitled to copyright protection under the European directives, if they can be found to constitute an expression of the intellectual creation of their author. It should be noted that this definition is quite vague and, despite the progress that it represents in crafting a harmonised EU standard, will require further elaboration by national courts in order to be applied in practice.[23] In the 2012 sequel case of *Infopaq II,*[24] the CJEU further noted that the transient copying exception enshrined in Article 5(1) of the Copyright Directive only applies if the act of temporary reproduction does not enable the generation of an additional profit beyond that derived from the lawful use of the protected work and does not lead to a modification of the work. Under this interpretation, the reproduction of news snippets by an automated process would not qualify as a protected use.

Importantly, in *Infopaq I,* the Court indicated the complete nature of the harmonisation of the reproduction right:

> the need for uniform application of Community law and the principle of equality require that where provisions of Community law make no express reference to the law of the Member States for the purpose of determining their meaning and scope, as is the case with Article 2 of [the

---

protection. The Term Directive repeats this standard in Art. 6 in relation to photographs, although it also clarifies in Recital 16 that such an own intellectual creation must also reflect the author's personality. Thus, the European Directives have imposed a vertical harmonisation of the concept of originality at least for these three types of works.

22. CJEU, C-5/08, *Infopaq International A/S v. Danske Dagblades Forening* 16 July 2009.
23. M van Eechoud et al., *Harmonizing European Copyright Law* (Kluwer Law International, 2009) 42.
24. CJEU, C-302/10, *Infopaq International A/S v. Danske Dagblades Forening* 17 January 2010.

> Copyright Directive], they must normally be given an autonomous and uniform interpretation throughout the Community.

This confirms Recital 6 of the Copyright Directive, according to which the objective of the European legislator in adopting that directive was the elimination of legislative differences at the national level, in response to the development of the information society, that can result in a re-fragmentation of the single internal market. The harmonisation of the reproduction right should therefore be understood as a case of maximum harmonisation, setting both a ceiling and a floor to the permissible scope of the right.[25]

2.1.2 The Right of Communication to the Public

The right of communication to the public has a much more complicated relationship with modern technologies. In its first international rendition in the Berne Convention the notion of a communication to the public was given only a very narrow reach.[26] According to Ficsor, within the meaning of that Convention, communication to the public is constricted to:

> a transmission by wire or wireless means, of images or sounds, or both, making it possible for the images and/or sounds to be perceived by persons outside the normal circle of a family and the closest social acquaintances or the family, at a place or places the distance of which from the place where the transmission is started is such that, without the transmission, the images or sounds, or both, would not be perceivable at the said place or places, irrespective of whether the said persons can perceive the images and/or sounds at the same place and at the same time, or at different places and at different times.[27]

Subsequently, the WCT, although adopting a very similar approach in its Article 8, for the sake of accommodating interactive new media, expanded the notion to include the newly crafted right of making available to the public in such a way that members of the public may access the work from a place and at a time individually chosen by them.[28] This broad definition of

25. European Copyright Society, 'Opinion on the Reference to the CJEU in C-466/12 *Svensson'*, University of Cambridge Legal Studies Research Paper Series No. 6/2013, 15 February 2013.
26. See Berne Convention, Arts 11, 11*bis*, 11*ter*, 14(1)(ii) and 14*bis*(1). T Dreier, 'Berne Convention for the Protection of Literary and Artistic Works' in T Dreier & P B Hugenholtz (eds), *Concise European Copyright Law* (Kluwer Law International 2006) 49.
27. Berne Convention, Art. 11*bis* (1). See also M Ficsor, *Guide to the Copyright and Related Rights Treaties Administered by WIPO and Glossary of Copyright and Related Rights Terms* (World Intellectual Property Organization 2003) 275.
28. C Angelopoulos, 'Creative Commons and Related Rights in Sound Recordings: Are the Two Systems Compatible?' in L Guibault & C Angelopoulos (eds.), *Open Content Licensing: From Theory to Practice* (Amsterdam University Press 2011).

communication to the public is then cut back down to size somewhat by the accompanying 'Agreed Statement concerning Article 8'. According to this, 'the mere provision of physical facilities for enabling or making a communication does not in itself amount to communication within the meaning of [the WCT] or the Berne Convention'.

The informal negotiations at the 1996 Geneva Diplomatic Conference reveal that the Agreed Statement was included to mollify non-governmental organisations representing internet service providers and telecommunications companies, which lobbied intensely to include some guarantees in the text of the Treaties immunising them from liability for infringements committed by the users of their services.[29] In this they were unsuccessful: the Statement offers no limitation of liability. Instead it only clarifies that direct liability, at least where the infringement of the right of communication to the public is concerned, should not burden those who did not create, but merely helped distribute unlawful content, while keeping a safe distance from the far more pertinent – and contentious – matter of accessory liability. Later documentation by the International Bureau confirms that accessory liability remains unaffected: 'liability issues', it suggests, are 'very complex; the knowledge of a large body of statutory and case law is needed in each country so that a given case may be judged. Therefore, international treaties on intellectual property rights, understandably and rightly, do not cover such issues of liability'.[30]

In any case, exactly what kind of act would qualify as a 'mere provision of physical facilities' remains open to discussion. A literal interpretation would suggest a limitation only to the provision of hardware, as opposed to acts of installation of the physical facilities or of the provision of services that use them, thus excluding protection for the provision of transmission services that enable the 'pumping' of a signal through a network. Koelman and Hugenholtz have however suggested that the phrase was intended to encompass the services of internet intermediaries as well.[31] The qualifier 'of itself' also raises questions regarding any accompanying circumstances that could be called upon to support assignment of liability. More importantly, the Agreed Statement is limited to the act of communication to the public: there is no equivalent provision regarding the reproduction of copyright-protected works. Indeed, as mentioned above, the Agreed Statement concerning Article 1(4) WCT confirms that the reproduction right applies fully in the digital environment. Consequently, the liability of intermediaries for infringing acts

29. M Ficsor, *Guide to the Copyright and Related Rights Treaties Administered by WIPO and Glossary of Copyright and Related Rights Terms* (World Intellectual Property Organization 2003) 211.
30. International Bureau of WIPO, 'WIPO National Seminar on Digital Technology and the New WIPO Treaties' (WIPO/CNR/SEL/97/1), 22 September 1997.
31. K Koelman & P B Hugenholtz, 'Online Service Provider Liability for Copyright Infringement', Workshop on Service Provider Liability, Geneva, 9 and 10 December 1999.

of reproduction is not addressed in the WCT. This raises the question: if an act of communication to the public also constitutes an act of reproduction, can the provider be held liable despite the Agreed Statement?[32]

The EU copied the WCT approach in Article 3(1) of the Copyright Directive.[33] Recital 23 of the Directive confirms that the right of communication to the public should be understood in a broad sense as covering all communications to the public not present at the place where the communication originates, by wire or wireless means. The decisive factor is whether the public to which the communication is transmitted is located in a place different from the place where the communication originates. As such, it will exclude any local communications, such as public performance, recitation and display, but include broadcasting, cable and – of course – online transmissions. According to Bechtold, even a transmission of a public performance via technical means to an audience in an adjacent room may qualify.[34] Again, this broad definition is circumscribed somewhat by Recital 27 of the Copyright Directive, which repeats the Agreed Statement on Article 8 almost verbatim, thus introducing the WCT's deference for the mere provision of physical facilities to the EU legal landscape.

Significantly, as the wording of Article 3(1) of the Copyright Directive makes clear, the approach of the WCT is also copied with regard to the inclusion, in the area of copyright, of the specialised right of making available to the public, as a subcategory of the general right of communication to the public. Making available differs from other types of communication to the public in that it enables, once it is completed, members of the public to access the work from a place and at a time individually chosen by them, i.e., on demand.[35] Thus, the right of communication to the public covers both so-called linear and non-linear services, while simultaneously distinguishing between the two. The first are those that, along a more traditional paradigm, 'push' content to a user that is not granted individual control over when and where to access the work. This might take the form of, for example, regular television and radio transmissions or their more modern equivalents of webcasting and internet radio services. Non-linear services, by contrast, refer to user-initiated modes of communication, such as offers to download a work from a public website or online streaming services, which allow the consumer to 'pull' content at her convenience. It should be noted that the right of making available to the public only covers

32. K Koelman, 'Liability for On-Line Intermediaries', Imprimatur/Institute for Information Law, Amsterdam, 1997.

33. As with the reproduction right, the right of communication to the public was first harmonised partially for databases in Art. 5(d) of the Database Directive and satellite broadcasters with Art. 2 of the Satellite and Cable Directive.

34. S Bechtold in T Dreier & P B Hugenholtz (eds), *Concise European Copyright Law* (Kluwer Law International 2006) 360 et seq.

35. CJEU, C-135/10, *Società Consortile Fonografici (SCF) v. Marco Del Corso*, 15 March 2012. See also, case C-279/13, *C More Entertainment,* 26 March 2015.

the act of providing the work to the public; if a user subsequently retrieves the work, although his action may constitute a reproduction of the work, it will not be covered by the right of making available. Accordingly, the author's exclusive right applies regardless of whether and when the work is actually accessed – the mere possibility suffices.

The most prominent recent CJEU judgment on the right of communication to the public is *SGAE v. Rafael Hoteles,*[36] a case concerning the use of television sets and the playing of ambient music by a hotelier within individual hotel rooms. Here the CJEU concluded that an act of communication to the public requires an act of intervention: the hotel, it was decreed, was an 'organisation which intervenes, in full knowledge of the consequences of its action, to give access to the protected work to its customers' and in the absence of which 'its customers, although physically within that area, would not, in principle, be able to enjoy the broadcast work'. The Court accepted that under Recital 27 of the Copyright Directive the mere provision of physical facilities for enabling or making a communication does not in itself amount to communication. This could cover, besides the hotel, companies specialising in the sale or hire of television sets. In the Court's view however, the installation of such facilities is a different matter. Therefore, if, by means of television sets installed, the hotel distributes the signal to customers staying in its rooms, then communication to the public takes place, irrespective of the technical means used to transmit the signal.

It is worth recalling that the Opinion delivered by AG Sharpston on the case had reached the opposite conclusion,[37] while the Court's approach has been heavily criticised. In a joint declaration, leading European copyright scholars described it as a 'logical mistake', that converts one of the characteristics of a communication into a redefinition of the act of communication: if every intervention that gave access to a work were to be characterised as a communication, the right of communication to the public would be transformed into an 'access right', covering such acts as the running of a bookshop, a newsagent, art gallery or library that allows members of the public onto its premises. The consequences for online intermediaries would be similarly adverse. Instead, the concept of a 'transmission' was put forth as a correct substitute. This interpretation has the support of the *traveaux préparatoires* for the World Intellectual Property Organisation (WIPO) Internet Treaties, where it is stated that a communication always involves a transmission to such an extent that the two terms can be regarded as synonymous and interchangeable. The national laws of the Member States have also generally understood 'communication to the

36. CJEU, C-306/05, *SGAE v. Rafael Hoteles,* 7 December 2006.
37. CJEU, Opinion of Advocate General Sharpston, case C-306/05, *SGAE v. Rafael Hoteles,* 13 July 2006.

public' to mean 'transmission' in their transpositions of the Copyright Directive.[38]

Rafael Hoteles focuses heavily on the notion of 'the public'. The Copyright Directive itself includes no indication of how many persons are necessary to compose a 'public' or what type of relationship may exist between them. Drawing on its previous case law,[39] as well as interpretative WIPO documents, in that particular case, the CJEU concluded that the term refers to an 'indeterminate number of potential television viewers'. On this basis, it held that the large number of successive viewers in hotel rooms, as well as of those who are present in the common areas of the hotel, suffice to form a 'public' within the meaning of the Directive. 'It matters little', stated the Court, 'that the only recipients are the occupants of rooms and that, taken separately, they are of limited economic interest for the hotel'. Instead, the crucial factor was whether the persons to whom the work is communicated were considered by their author when authorising the broadcast, thereby comprising a 'new' public: 'if reception is for a larger audience, possibly for profit, a new section of the receiving public hears or sees the work and the communication of the programme via a loudspeaker or analogous instrument no longer constitutes simple reception of the programme itself but is an independent act through which the broadcast work is communicated to a new public'. The private nature of the hotel rooms was considered immaterial, the Court considering this to be a separate issue to the characterisation of the recipients of the communication as 'a public'. In addition, the Court observed that the right to authorise a communication to the public under the Directive includes the right of making works available in such a way that members of the public may access them when and where they wish, thus even in places of a private nature, such as hotel rooms.

In a series of later cases the CJEU confirmed its *Rafael Hoteles* doctrine. So, in *Football Association Premier League (FAPL)*,[40] *Divani Akropolis*[41] and *Airfield*[42] the Court re-asserted its opinion that, in order for there to be a 'communication to the public' within the meaning of Article 3(1) of the Copyright Directive, it is necessary for the work broadcast to be transmitted to a new public, that is to say, to a public wider than that taken into account by the authors of the protected works when they authorised the

38. European Copyright Society, 'Opinion on the Reference to the CJEU in case C-466/12 *Svensson*', University of Cambridge Legal Studies Research Paper Series No. 6/2013, 15 February 2013.
39. CJEU, C-89/04, *Mediakabel,* 2 June 2005, para. 30 and case C-192/04 *Lagardère Active Broadcast,* 14 July 2005, para. 31.
40. CJEU, joined cases C-403/08 and C-429/08, *Football Association Premier League v. Karen Murphy,* 4 October 2011, para 197.
41. CJEU, C-136/09, *Organismos Sillogikis Diacheirisis Dimiourgon Theatrikon kai Optikoakoustikon Ergon v. Divani Akropolis,* 18 March 2010, para. 38.
42. CJEU, joined cases C-431/09 and C-432/09, *Airfield,* 13 October 2011, para. 72.

original communication to the public. *FAPL* also acknowledged that it is not irrelevant if a 'communication' is of a profit-making nature.

With these rulings the CJEU is ponderously – and perhaps somewhat haphazardly – pulling together a harmonised European notion of a communication to the public for copyright. The decisive factors that can be identified would be the following: an intervention undertaken deliberately, which is targeted at an indeterminate (i.e., not restricted to a private group), but new public of a certain, not insignificant size, whose members may have access to the work at the same time or in succession of each other and which was not taken into consideration by the author when granting permission to the original audience or where there is a retransmission to the same audience through another technique that is not solely aimed at improving reception. Whether or not a profit is made through the communication is relevant, but not decisive.[43] All of these criteria are best seen as operating interdependently, rather than cumulatively: as the Court noted in *Del Corso,* these 'several complementary criteria [...] are not autonomous and are interdependent. Consequently, they must be applied individually and in the light of their interaction with one another, given that in different specific situations, they may be met to varying degrees'.[44]

On this basis, the Court first edged its way into the area of electronic communications with *ITV Broadcasting and Others*.[45] Here, clarification was requested as to whether right-holders can prohibit communications to the public of their content through live online streaming. The Court held that, given that the making available of works by the retransmission of a terrestrial television broadcast over the internet uses a specific technical means different from that of the original communication, the concept of communication to the public encompasses retransmissions of the works included in a terrestrial television broadcast made by an organisation other than the original broadcaster by means of an internet stream made available to the subscribers, even if those subscribers are within the area of reception of that terrestrial television broadcast and could lawfully receive the broadcast on a television receiver. Thus, the act of streaming was firmly placed in copyright's restricted area.

Interestingly, in this case the CJEU set aside the concept of a 'new public': the defendant, TVCatchup, had contended that no new public was

---

43. D Visser, 'Europees openbaar maken met ketchup' (2013) 2 AMI: Tijdschriftvoorauteurs-, Media- & Informatierecht 41.
44. CJEU, C-135/10 *Società Consortile Fonografici (SCF) v. Marco Del Corso*, 15 March 2012, para. 79. That case concerned an interpretation of communication to the public within the meaning of Art. 8(2) of Directive 92/100, but the criteria listed are clearly harvested from previous case relating to Art. 3(1) of the Copyright Directive (see para. 81) and thus the same approach can confidently be assumed to apply in copyright as well.
45. CJEU, C-607/11, *ITV Broadcasting and Others*, 7 March 2013.

introduced, as the recipients of the retransmission were already legally entitled to follow the televised broadcast, identical in content, by virtue of their television license. The Court however observed that, as opposed to what had been the case in previous rulings, the case at hand involved two separate transmissions that had to be 'authorised individually and separately by the author concerned given that each is made under specific technical conditions, using a different means of transmission for the protected works'. As a result of these different technical means, in *ITV Broadcasting and Others* there was no longer any need to examine the requirement that there be a new public, as each of the two transmissions had to be authorised individually anyway.[46]

The question of making available via hyperlinking came before the Court with *Svensson,*[47] a case involving a journalist objecting to the inclusion of his work on the website of Retriever, a subscription-based online aggregator which provided hyperlinks to articles that were freely available on the websites of third party newspapers. Retriever's own website did not itself contain copies. The Court repeated its previous findings according to which 'the concept of communication to the public includes two cumulative criteria, namely, an 'act of communication' of a work and the communication of that work to a "public"'. With regard to the first of these, the Court found that the act of communication must be construed broadly. The Court noted that 'the provision, on a website, of clickable links to protected works published without any access restrictions on another site, affords users of the first site direct access to those works'. On this basis, it concluded that such linking must be considered to be making available and therefore constitutes an act of communication.

What foiled the finding of an infringement of the right of communication to the public in *Svensson* was instead the second criterion of a 'public'. Again, the Court emphasised that the public in question must be a new one, i.e., one that was 'not taken into account by the copyright holders when they authorised the initial communication to the public'. Yet, making a work available by means of a clickable link to works freely available on another website cannot be viewed as a communication to a new public, as long as the public targeted by the initial communication consists of all potential visitors to the site concerned. That was found to be true in the instant case, given that access to the works on the newspapers' site was not subject to any restrictive measures, so that they were instead freely available to all internet users. Since the public was not a new one, no authorisation was required for a communication to it. The Court also stated that this outcome would by no means be altered if the link were instead an embedded one that gave the impression that the work was appearing on the site on which it was found, while in fact it came from another site. The legality of such 'inline linking'

46. See also CJEU, C-466/12, *Svensson and Others,* 13 February 2014, para. 24.
47. CJEU, C-466/12, *Svensson and Others,* 13 February 2014.

was later confirmed again in the subsequent case of *Bestwater.*[48] It is not as yet clear what the situation would be if the initial communication to the public had not been authorised.[49]

According to the CJEU, what would certainly make a difference would be whether the link makes it possible for users of the site on which it appears to circumvent any restrictions put in place by the site on which the protected work is posted in order to restrict public access to that work to the latter site's subscribers only. In that case, the link would constitute an intervention without which those users would not be able to access the works transmitted, making those users a 'new public', communication to which would require authorisation. Intriguingly, according to the Court, the same would hold true if the work were no longer available to the public on the site on which it was initially communicated or if new restrictions were to be introduced to that site, after it had already been made accessible through linking at another location without the right-holder's authorisation. This adds some uncertainty to the matter, as it suggests that the legality of linking will hang on the right-holder's future actions, placing linkers who have not obtained explicit authorisation in a precarious legal position.

It should be noted that the CJEU's interpretation is controversial. The European Copyright Society in its opinion on the case argued that hyperlinking should not be encased within the right of communication to the public regardless of whether or not the public is a new one, as hyperlinks fail to communicate the work as such. Instead, they merely provide the viewer with information as to the location of a page that the user can then choose to access or not.[50] As such, hyperlinks are more akin to mere citations of a work.[51] The opinion does allow that circumstances are conceivable in which creating a hyperlink might give rise to various kinds of liability. Interestingly for the purposes of this book, among the possibilities listed by the Society is that of accessory liability, particularly in respect of the knowing facilitation of the making of illegal copies. Yet, as the opinion notes, for the most part such cases will not fall within the competence of the Court, as they deal with unharmonised aspects of copyright law and therefore are to be assessed

---

48. CJEU, C-348/13, *Bestwater,* 21 October 2014. It was also confirmed as applying to the related rights of broadcasting organisations in case C-279/13, *C More Entertainment,* 26 March 2015.
49. A preliminary ruling by the CJEU on precisely this question has been requested by the Dutch *Hoge Raad* in pending case C-160/15, *GS Media BV v. Sanoma Media*, as well as by the district court of Midden-Nederland in pending case C-527/15, *Filmspeler*. A similar question is addressed in pending case C-610/15, *Ziggo v. Stichting Brein.*
50. European Copyright Society, 'Opinion on the Reference to the CJEU in Case C-466/12 *Svensson*', University of Cambridge Legal Studies Research Paper Series No. 6/2013, 15 February 2013. For additional criticism of *Svensson,* see E Arezzo, 'Hyperlinks and Making Available in the European Union – What Future for the Internet after *Svensson*?' (2014) 45(5) International Review of Intellectual Property and Competition Law (IIC) 524.
51. T Aplin, *Copyright Law in the Digital Society* (Hart Publishing 2005) 151.

under national law. This observation might do a lot to explain why the Court was so eager to engage in complicated definitions geared at encompassing hyperlinking within the notion of a direct communication to the public: absent a harmonised European accessory copyright liability, that is the only means of achieving some European uniformity on this indubitably cross-border question.

The CJEU concluded *Svensson* by noting that Member States may not provide for a concept of communication to the public that includes a wider range of activities than those referred to in Article 3 of the Copyright Directive. In other words, as with the reproduction right, the harmonisation of the communication right in Article 3 of the Copyright Directive is intended to be full.

Before moving on, it should be noted that, according to Recital 32 of the Copyright Directive, the possible exceptions and limitations to both the reproduction right and the right of communication to the public are exhaustively enumerated in that text. These can be found in Article 5 of the Directive. The only mandatory limitation is that of Article 5(1) mentioned above. Due to the significant latitude left to the Member States with regard to the remaining exceptions, the extent of the harmonisation achieved in this manner is questionable.[52] In any case, this exclusivity confirms the full nature of the European harmonisation of authors' exclusive rights.

2.1.3 Primary and Accessory EU Copyright Liability

The above analysis indirectly offers some important hints as to the nature and scope of European accessory liability for online copyright infringement: in the absence of a harmonised definition of the notion, comparison with primary infringement on the internet can also help form a negative impression of the concept as it applies on the EU level. If communication to the public and reproduction are the ways with which copyright holders' exclusive rights are infringed on the internet, intermediary accessory copyright liability will require participation by the intermediary in somebody else's acts of communication to the public and reproduction.

As established above, the harmonisation of primary liability for the infringement of both the reproduction right and the right of communication the public is full, setting both a ceiling and a floor: the exclusive rights laid down in Articles 2(a) and 3(1) of the Copyright Directive may receive neither a broader nor a narrower interpretation in national law than that prescribed by the European rules. If an act does not qualify under these provisions as a primary infringement of the rights of reproduction or communication to the public, that possibility will also be closed off to the Member States. If it does,

52. S Bechtold in T Dreier & P B Hugenholtz (eds), *Concise European Copyright Law* (Kluwer Law International 2006) 369.

it must be recognised as such in national law. This imposes an important limitation on the scope of the accessory liability of internet intermediaries for these acts: accessory liability may only come into play where an intermediary is not already primarily liable for the same copyright infringement by the same action; in other words, an intermediary may only be liable as an accessory to the copyright infringement of another for acts which do not constitute infringements of the reproduction right or the right of communication to the public in their own right under EU law. By contrast, while Member States, are, for example, post-*Svensson,* unable to rely on a national interpretation that would label the provision of hyperlinks without rightholder authorisation to works freely available on another website an act of primary infringement, they are nonetheless free to approach such provision as an instance of accessory liability. As shall be shown in Chapter 3, this already constitutes a small harmonisation of accessory liability, as it controls, through the rules on direct infringement, the ability of national law to regulate accessory parties.[53]

As yet however, the reverse is not true: accessory liability is almost entirely unharmonised and, as long as EU law does not declare them acts of primary infringement, Member States remain free to designate any acts they wish as acts of accessory copyright infringement. At the same time, accessory liability can only occur where a primary wrong has been committed: accessory liability is parasitic, so that primary liability provides the foundation of accessory liability and accessory liability cannot exist without it. As a result, the full harmonisation of the rights of reproduction and communication to the public necessarily means that the barrier between primary and secondary copyright infringement should be located at the same place across the EU. On the one side of that barrier will be a fully harmonised primary liability; on the other side, a collection of acts that may or may not constitute accessory infringements depending on the prescripts of national law.

In this context, arguably it is precisely the lack of an explicit mandate to harmonise accessory liability that is pushing the CJEU towards what, by the standards of many national European laws, constitutes a very expansive interpretation of the author's exclusive rights.[54] This pressure is especially

53. This method has been popular for example in France, see Ch. 3, s. 3.2.3.1.

54. Again, this tendency is noticeable on the national level as well, particularly in France. *See* below Chapter 3, s. 3.2.3.1. Other forces are also pushing in that direction. Proposals such as that of the French High Council for Literary and Artistic Property are indicative of the trend towards the broadening of primary infringement. This suggests that the online hosting of information be reconstrued as 'giving access to the public to copyright works' and interpreted as a violation of Articles 2 and 3 of the Copyright Directive (*see* P Sirinelli et al., 'Mission to Link Directives 2000/31 and 2001/29 – Report and Proposals', High Council for Literary and Artistic Property, 3 November 2015).

evident with regard to the right to the communication to the public: in the absence of harmonised rules for accessory liability, the EU Court is arguably attempting to substitute primary liability for accessory liability, at least in the area where modern technological developments have enhanced the trans-border importance of the notion: the liability of internet intermediaries for the online copyright infringements of others. In this way, primary liability might be seen as encroaching on the natural territory of accessory liability: a sort of accessory liability by stealth. A much better approach would of course be the open acknowledgement of the actual issue at stake and its head-on confrontation: the further clarification of the details of the current European copyright regime on primary liability, at least it pertains to online activities,[55] supplemented by – crucially – the adoption of European rules on accessory liability.

Of course, according to the principles of subsidiarity and proportionality,[56] as well as Recital 7 of the Copyright Directive, which reflects them, the EU legal framework for the protection of copyright must be harmonised only as far as is necessary for the smooth functioning of the internal market: 'differences not adversely affecting the functioning of the internal market need not be removed or prevented'. As a result, Member States are free to add acts of primary infringement to copyright holders' arsenal, including for acts dependent on an infringement of Article 2(a) and 3(1) of the Copyright Directive by another, as long as those acts are not incorporated within the reproduction right or the right of communication to the public, thus conflicting with their full harmonisation. With this in mind, it should be noted that a similar confusion between the 'primary' and the 'accessory' to that discernible in the CJEU case law can be observed on the national level as well, with acts designated as 'primary' although their function is clearly accessory.[57] Accordingly, as already mentioned in Chapter 1,[58] in this book such designations in national law shall be ignored: the point of reference shall always be functionality rather than formality, so that any infringement by an intermediary that consists of a participation in a copyright infringement committed by a third party will be seen as substantiating accessory liability. Ideally, EU copyright law should be developed in the same direction.

What are the rules that govern such acts of accessory infringement on the EU level? These shall be examined in detail in the next section.

---

55. The adoption of a unified European copyright code might be especially helpful in this regard.
56. See Art. 5 paras 3 and 4 respectively of the TEU (see: Consolidated version of the TEU, OJ C 326, 26.10.2012, p. 13). See also A Ramalho, *The Competence of The European Union in Copyright Lawmaking - A Normative Perspective of EU Powers for Copyright Harmonization* (unpublished PhD thesis, University of Amsterdam 2014) 100-104.
57. This is the case for example for the concept of 'authorisation' in UK copyright law, see Ch. 3 below, s. 3.1.2.
58. See s. 1.4.1.

2.2 THE EU RULES ON INTERMEDIARY ACCESSORY LIABILITY IN COPYRIGHT

The centrepiece of current European intermediary liability legislation is to be found in the E-Commerce Directive. Although this fails to provide substantive rules for the regulation of accessory copyright liability, specifically with regard to online intermediaries, 'to eliminate the existing legal uncertainty and to bring coherence to the different approaches that are emerging at Member State level',[59] it does introduce a cluster of horizontal conditional liability exemptions: the famous safe-harbours. These grant immunity to intermediaries as regards claims for damages from all liability incurred in the provision of three types of services: 'mere conduit' services (Article 12), 'caching' services (Article 13) and 'hosting' services (Article 14).[60] Each

59. Commission Proposal for a European Parliament and Council Directive on certain legal aspects of electronic commerce in the internal market, 18 November 1998, COM (1998) 586 final.
60. In contrast to their US precursors (s. 512 of the Digital Millennium Copyright Act (DMCA), 17 U.S.C. was adopted earlier, on 28 October 1998), the EU regime does not include a safe harbour for information location tools. No explanation for the exclusion of such services is given in the E-Commerce Directive's *traveaux préparatoires*. A number of Member States (specifically Austria, Hungary, Poland, Portugal and Spain and EEA member Liechtenstein) have introduced liability limitations for search engines of their own accord. As these do not form part of the harmonisation of intermediary liability, but merely add a twist to the national law applicable in such cases, these safe harbours shall not be analysed. See J van Hoboken, 'Legal Space for Innovative Ordering: On the Need to Update Selection Intermediary Liability in the EU' (2009) 13 International Journal of Communications Law & Policy 1. Similarly, the DMCA regulates the liability of universities providing online services, another matter ignored by the E-Commerce Directive. According to s. 512(e), non-profit institutions of higher education are classified as service providers and are shielded from liability for the infringing acts of their staff, as long as these were not required or recommended by the university and the university has not received repeated notifications of claimed infringement by the faculty members. The institution must also promote compliance with copyright law. The provision was included in order to protect the independence of thought, word and action that is at the core of academic freedom and which was considered to set the special relationship which exists between universities and their faculty members engaged in teaching or research apart from the ordinary employer-employee relationship. As a result, the principle of *respondeat superior* that would otherwise guide liability in such situations was found to be inappropriate, necessitating a special standard. See House of Representatives, *Digital Millennium Copyright Act,* Rept. 105-796, 8 October 1998. For a comparison between the DMCA and the E-Commerce Directive, see B Martinet Farano, 'Internet Intermediaries' Liability for Copyright and Trademark Infringement: Reconciling the EU and US Approaches' (2012) TTLF Working Paper No 14; M Peguera, 'The DMCA Safe Harbors and their European Counterparts: A Comparative Analysis of some Common Problems' (2009) 32 Columbia Journal of Law & the Arts 481; K Koelman, 'Online Intermediary Liability' in P B Hugenholtz (ed.), *Copyright and Electronic Commerce - Legal Aspects of Electronic Copyright Management* (Kluwer Law International 2000) 27; N Zingales, 'Internet Intermediary Liability: Identifying Best Practices for Africa' (2013) Association for Progressive Communications (APC).

safe harbour is governed by a separate set of conditions that must be met before the intermediary may benefit. Article 15 of the Directive adds a final flourish by prohibiting the imposition of general obligations on intermediaries, when providing these three services, to monitor the information which they transmit or store or to actively seek out facts or circumstances indicating illegal activity (paragraph 1), as well as giving two examples of obligations that may be imposed on them by national law (paragraph 2).

Significantly, the safe harbour provisions take a horizontal approach to intermediary liability.[61] As such, although there are exceptions (notably with regard to data protection and privacy),[62] the immunities are intended to function as holistic tools equally applicable to, aside from copyright infringement, such a diverse array of illegal activities as child pornography, unfair competition, misleading or illegal advertising, fake banking services ('phishing'), incitements to terrorism or violence in general, defamation, hate speech or illegal pharmaceutical offers.[63] In all these areas, the exemptions cover both cases of primary and cases of accessory liability. This horizontality was chosen in view of the fact that, from a technical perspective, the activity carried out by intermediaries in the provision of the three safe harbour services is the same, regardless of the type of content involved. As a result, a single set of rules covering all fields was deemed appropriate by the European legislator.[64] Whether this approach continues to be valid or not is up for discussion: while at the beginning of the internet era it may have made sense to approach intermediary liability as a special case, the traditional approach in law is to examine the consequences of the defendant's behaviour on a case-by-case basis, rather than carve out exceptions based on the rigid classification of wrongdoers.[65] Regardless, as things stand, the

61. This should not be taken from granted. For example the US solution is a vertical one wherein different regimes of liability regulate different kinds of content. In particular, while the aforementioned s. 512 of the DMCA applies to copyright, s. 230(e) of the Communications Decency Act 1996 (47 U.S.C.) (also known as the 'Good Samaritan' defence) grants total immunity from liability to intermediaries in all areas apart from intellectual property law, federal criminal law and communication privacy law. See B Martinet Farano, 'Internet Intermediaries' Liability for Copyright and Trademark Infringement: Reconciling the EU and US Approaches' (2012) TTLF Working Paper No 14, 23-25.
62. See Recital 14 and Art. 1(5)(b) of the E-Commerce Directive.
63. See Commission Staff Working Paper, 'Online Services, Including E-Commerce, in the Single Market', SEC(2011) 1641 final, 11 January 2012. It has been suggested however that the heavy reliance the E-Commerce immunities on the DMCA's safe harbours does indicate a strong leaning towards the copyright perspective, see J van Hoboken, 'Legal Space for Innovative Ordering: On the Need to Update Selection Intermediary Liability in the EU' (2009) 13 International Journal of Communications Law & Policy 1.
64. M Peguera, 'The DMCA Safe Harbors and their European Counterparts: A Comparative Analysis of some Common Problems' (2009) 32 Columbia Journal of Law & the Arts 481.
65. R J Mann & S R Belzley, 'The Promise of Internet Intermediary Liability' (2005) 47 William and Mary Law Review 239.

result of the horizontal approach that should be noted for the purposes of this book is the inevitable lack of nuance that it achieves, excluding calibration to the peculiarities of each case, or even to those of each broader area of law, but treating all potential illegal activity of an intermediary in an identical manner.

As noted in Chapter 1, the safe harbours do not stand alone, but are surrounded by an assortment of other relevant provisions. So, specifically in the area of copyright, an important addition to the European intermediary liability regime is set out in Article 8(3) of the Copyright Directive. This is silent on the question of liability for damages, the specialty of the safe harbours, but requires that Member States ensure the possibility of injunctions against intermediaries whose services are used by a third party to commit an infringement. As opposed to the safe harbours, the rule here is one of positive law, requiring Member States to take appropriate action, rather than informing them of what is out of reach.

Finally, supplementary guidelines can also be sourced from the Enforcement Directive, as well as from EU data protection and privacy laws. These set limitations on the reach of obligations that can be imposed on intermediaries, both for the avoidance of liability and in the form of court orders.

In the sections that follow, this constellation of provisions that forms the current piecemeal EU framework for intermediary accessory copyright liability will be more closely examined. The interpretative case law that accompanies it will be analysed in parallel. Before that is done however, the scope of application of the relevant provisions must first be briefly considered.

2.2.1 Scope: Defining Intermediaries in the Directives

To what kind of providers does the EU framework on intermediary liability apply? Interestingly, the division of the relevant rules into different directives brings with it a fragmentation of their scope of application. A slight discrepancy can be discerned between the reach of the E-Commerce Directive's safe harbours and that of the Copyright Directive's provision on injunctions.

2.2.1.1 Intermediaries in the E-Commerce Directive

While, as noted in Chapter 1, this book takes an expansive approach towards the definition of intermediaries,[66] the E-Commerce Directive is much more cautious. As its full title indicates, the Directive is intended to regulate the

66. See above, s. 1.4.2.

provision of so-called information society services. But what is an 'information society service'? Article 2(a) of the E-Commerce Directive defines the notion by referring back to Article 1(2) of Directive 98/48/EC.[67] **According to this, an '**information society service' is 'any service normally provided for remuneration, at a distance, by electronic means and at the individual request of a recipient of services'. The article goes on to declare that, for the purpose of this definition, 'at a distance' means that the service is provided without the parties being simultaneously present; 'by electronic means' signifies that the service is sent initially and received at its destination by means of electronic equipment for the processing (including digital compression) and storage of data and is entirely transmitted, conveyed and received by wire, by radio, by optical means or by other electromagnetic means; and 'at the individual request of a recipient of services' means that the service is provided through the transmission of data on individual request, excluding television and radio broadcasting services, unless on-demand.[68] Under Article 2(d) of the E-Commerce Directive, the 'recipient of the service' is defined as 'any natural or legal person who, for professional ends or otherwise, uses an information society service, in particular for the purposes of seeking information or making it accessible'.

With regard to the requirement that the service should be 'normally provided for remuneration', Recital 18 of the E-Commerce Directive clarifies that the service may be offered for free to the recipient, as long as it represents an 'economic activity'. This solution mirrors a broader rule: Article 57 of the Treaty on European Union (TEU) also declares that 'services' within the meaning of the Treaties must be 'normally provided for remuneration', while the CJEU has found that this does not mean that the service has to be paid for by those for whom it is performed.[69] In 2014, in *Papasavvas*, this interpretation was confirmed specifically as regards 'information society services'.[70] Given that one of the dominant successful models of e-business consists of providing a service at no charge, with a view to making returns in lateral ways, in particular through advertising, voluntary

67. Directive 98/48/EC of the European Parliament and of the Council of 20 July 1998 amending Directive 98/34/EC laying down a procedure for the provision of information in the field of technical standards and regulations [1998] OJ L217/18.
68. Near-on-demand services are excluded, see Annex V, Directive 98/48/EC.
69. See also C-352/85, *Bond van Adverteerders v. The Netherlands State*, 26 April 1988, referring to Art. 60 of the Treaty establishing the European Economic Community (EEC Treaty), now Art. 57 of the current Treaty on the European Union.
70. CJEU, C-291/13, *Papasavvas v. O Fileleftheros Dimosia Etairia,* 11 September 2014. In pending case C-484/14, *McFadden,* the Munich district court has asked the CJEU to clarify whether the expression means that the person specifically concerned, claiming the status of service provider, must be the one to normally provide the specific service for remuneration, that there are on the market any providers at all who provide this service or similar services for remuneration or that the majority of these or similar services are provided for remuneration.

donations or by application of the so-called freemium business model,[71] a restrictive interpretation would in any case make little sense: as long as the provider is making economic gains through the activity, that should be sufficient, while any type of consideration for an economic activity should be allowed to qualify as 'remuneration'.[72]

An indicative list of services not covered by the definition of information society services is set out in Annex V of Directive 98/48/EC. Thus, telephony services are, for example, excluded. Arguably, the same should be said of VoIP (Voice over IP).[73] According to Recital 18 of the E-Commerce Directive, television and radio broadcasting also fail to qualify as information society services because they are not provided at individual request. The effect of these limitations is however small, leaving the E-Commerce liability regime applicable to a wide range of activities. Recital 18 confirms this, explicitly citing as examples of activities that constitute information society services the selling of goods online, the offering of online information or commercial communications, the provision of tools allowing for search, access and retrieval of data, the provision of access to a communication network or hosting information provided by a recipient of the service, as well as services which are transmitted point to point, such as video-on-demand or the provision of commercial communications by electronic mail, and services consisting of the transmission of information via a communication network.

In addition, although the Directive was adopted long before the emergence of the current generation of internet-related services, nothing in its provisions would seem to screen out web 2.0 service providers from this definition.[74] The CJEU has offered further insights in this regard: in *L'Oréal*

71. According to this model, the majority of users are offered free access to the service, while a small minority are relied on to pay a premium for additional services. The first ensure the necessary popularity of the service and the second provide the actual financing. See Wikipedia entry on 'freemium', available at: https://en.wikipedia.org/wiki/Freemium.
72. So, for example, free-access online encyclopaedia, Wikipedia, would be included. See: L Edwards, 'Role and Responsibility of Internet Intermediaries in the Field of Copyright and Related Rights' WIPO Study (2011) and DLA Piper, 'EU Study on the Legal Analysis of a Single Market for the Information Society – New Rules for a New Age?', November 2009, available at: http://ec.europa.eu/information_society/newsroom/cf/itemdetail.cfm?item_id=7022.
73. P Valcke & E Dommering, 'E-Commerce Directive' in O Castendyk, E Dommering & A Scheuer, *European Media Law* (Kluwer Law International 2008) 1087-1088.
74. M Peguera, 'The DMCA Safe Harbors and their European Counterparts: A Comparative Analysis of some Common Problems' (2009) 32 Columbia Journal of Law & the Arts 481. On the other hand, respondent right-holders in the Commission's 2012 consultation on the application of the E-Commerce Directive argued that the providers of new services such as auction sites, blogs, social media, video sharing sites and paid referencing systems not foreseen during the adoption of the Directive were unjustly 'hiding' behind safe harbours not intended for their protection, see: European Commission, 'Summary of the results of the Public Consultation on the future of electronic commerce in the Internal Market and the implementation of the Directive on electronic commerce (2000/31/EC)'.

v. eBay the Court confirmed that the operation of an online marketplace is, in principle, an information society service,[75] while in *Netlog*[76] the Court found that a social networking site may qualify as an information society service provider. Similarly, in *Google France*[77] the Court accepted that the prominent search engine's advertising service 'Adwords' can also rely on the hosting safe harbour, likewise making it an information society service provider. Whether Google in its search engine capacity would qualify remains open for debate.[78] It is worth noting that a number of national European courts have accepted an expansive interpretation of the hosting exemption that would encompass information location tools. This is also the position in favour of which AG Poiares Maduro came down in his opinion in *Google France*.[79]

Thus, the notion of an 'information society service' in the meaning of the E-Commerce Directive would seem to be a rather broad one. Nevertheless, the Directive's provisions on liability do not apply to all such services indiscriminately.

One way in which a limitation occurs is through the specialisation of the E-Commerce Directive's liability exemptions regime to only three types of services. Providers of services other than hosting, caching and mere conduit, although arguably still 'information society service providers' for the purposes of the rest of the Directive, remain out of the ambit of its provisions on liability – their liability remains entirely unharmonised. In this regard, it is important to stress that the safe harbours apply, not to providers per se, but only to relevant activities.[80] Advocate General Jääskinen in his Opinion on *L'Oréal* was adamant on this point: '[t]he three articles intend to create exceptions to certain *types of activity* exercised by a service provider. To my understanding, it is inconceivable to think that they would purport to exempt a *service provider type* as such'.[81] As a result, a single company can at the

75. CJEU, C-324/09, *L'Oréal v. eBay International,* 12 July 2011, para. 109.
76. CJEU, C-360/10, *Belgische Vereniging van Auteurs, Componisten en Uitgevers CVBA (SABAM) v. Netlog NV*, 16 February 2012, para. 27.
77. CJEU, joined cases C-236/08 and C-237/08 *Google France v. Louis Vuitton et al,* 23 March 2010.
78. L Edwards, 'Role and Responsibility of Internet Intermediaries in the Field of Copyright and Related Rights', WIPO Study (2011), p. 7.
79. The Advocate General takes the position that the reference to information location tools in Art. 21 of the E-Commerce Directive, far from indicating that such services are not covered by the Directive and the Commission should in the future assess whether there is a need to bring them within its ambit, instead confirms that such services are already included, but that the necessity of specific provisions catering to their specific needs might have to be considered. See Opinion of AG Poiares Maduro, joined Cases C-236/08 and C-237/08, *Google France v. Louis Vuitton et al,* 22 September 2009.
80. Commission Staff Working Paper, 'Online Services, Including E-Commerce, in the Single Market', SEC(2011) 1641 final, 11 January 2012.
81. CJEU, Opinion of Advocate General Jääskinen, case C-324/09, *L'Oréal v. eBay International,* 9 December 2010, para. 147.

same time act as a host, cache provider and mere conduit, as well as providing other unimmunised services, such as search: each action of the company must be assessed individually. The AG applies this logic to eBay: 'the hosting of the information provided by a client may well benefit from an exemption if the conditions of Article 14 of Directive 2000/31 are satisfied. Yet the hosting exception does not exempt eBay from any potential liability it may incur in the context of its use of a paid internet referencing service'.

An additional – and much more controversial – limitation to the scope of the E-Commerce Directive's provisions on liability is introduced by the title of section 4 of the Directive. This makes clear that the immunities are intended to apply, not to all 'information society service providers', but specifically to 'intermediary service providers'. In *Papasavvas,* the CJEU interpreted the notion of an 'intermediary' by linking it to the notion of 'neutrality'.[82] The latter concept was first explored by the CJEU in *Google France.* In that case, the Court had relied on Recital 42 of the E-Commerce Directive to impose neutrality as a pre-condition of safe harbour protection. On this basis, it then interpreted neutrality as requiring that, in order for an intermediary to benefit from immunity, its relevant activity be 'of a mere technical, automatic and passive nature', such that the service provider 'has neither knowledge of nor control over the information which is transmitted or stored'. The Court saw this condition as a necessary prerequisite for cases of hosting, as much as of caching and mere conduit services.[83]

AG Jääskinen expressed vehement opposition to this reading in his later Opinion on *L'Oréal*, going as far as to describe it as seriously endangering the objectives of the E-Commerce Directive.[84] The AG supported the view that sees Recitals 42 to 44 as limited to only mere conduit and caching providers. Instead, he claimed that it is Recital 46, which explicitly mentions the providers of services 'consisting of the storage of information' and confirms the requirement of expeditious take-down, that is intended to apply to hosts. According to the AG, '"neutrality" does not appear to be quite the right test' for host service providers. He voices his criticism in strong terms: 'I would find it surreal that if eBay intervenes and guides the contents of listings in its system with various technical means, it would by that fact be deprived of the protection of Article 14 regarding storage of information uploaded by the users.'[85] Van Eecke agrees, noting that hosting providers

82. CJEU, C-291/13, *Papasavvas v. O Fileleftheros Dimosia Etairia,* 11 September 2014, paras 39, 41 and 45.
83. CJEU, joined cases C-236/08 and C-237/08 *Google France v. Louis Vuitton et al,* 23 March 2010, paras 113-114.
84. CJEU, Opinion of Advocate General Jääskinen, case C-129/14 PPU, *Zoran Spasic,* 2 May 2014, paras 139 et seq.
85. CJEU, Opinion of Advocate General Jääskinen, case C-324/09, *L'Oréal v. eBay International,* 9 December 2010, para. 146.

will almost necessarily have some degree of involvement in the information stored, at least in the form of making available tools for its uploading, categorisation and display.[86] As he points out, any other interpretation would result in a 'Good Samaritan paradox', whereby a hosting intermediary would be disincentivised from taking precautions against infringement for fear of losing safe harbour protection.[87]

The issue is a tricky one. The wording of the Directive's recitals do not offer concrete guidance: Recital 42 does indeed talk vaguely of 'the exemptions from liability established in this Directive', as does Recital 45. This can be contrasted to e.g., Recitals 43 and 44, which explicitly refer to mere conduit and caching, and Recital 46, which openly limits itself to hosting. This could suggest that Court's interpretation might indeed have been the one intended by the legislator. Regardless, in *L'Oréal,* the CJEU sidestepped the pitfalls envisioned by the AG by loosening the definition of neutrality in order to allow hosts the necessary breathing space. So, according to the Court, 'the mere fact that the operator of an online marketplace stores offers for sale on its server, sets the terms of its service, is remunerated for that service and provides general information to its customers cannot have the effect of denying it the exemptions from liability'. Instead, in order to be deemed non-neutral, the host would have to engage in activities such as 'optimising the presentation of the offers for sale in question or promoting those offers'.[88] Under this interpretation, neutrality does not demand complete passivity from the intermediary and certainly is not intended to exclude actions on its part for the detection and removal or blocking of unlawful content.[89] Precisely where the borderline that turns a neutral host into an active content provider should be placed remains however up for discussion.[90] *Papasavvas* itself concerned the obvious case of a newspaper published company operating a website on which an online version of its paper is posted. According to the Court, such a company has, in principle, knowledge of the information which it posts and exercises control over that information. As a result, it is not neutral in the sense of Recital 42 of the E-Commerce Directive and cannot therefore be considered to be an 'intermediary service provider'.

86. P van Eecke, 'Online Service Providers and Liability: A Plea for a Balanced Approach' (2011) 48 Common Market Law Review 1455.
87. P van Eecke, 'Online Service Providers and Liability: A Plea for a Balanced Approach' (2011) 48 Common Market Law Review 1455.
88. CJEU, C-324/09, *L'Oréal v. eBay International,* 12 July 2011, paras 115 and 116.
89. T-E Synodinou, 'Intermediaries' Liability for Online Copyright Infringement in the EU: Evolutions and Confusions' (2015) 31 Computer Law & Security Review 57.
90. M Peguera, 'The DMCA Safe Harbors and their European Counterparts: A Comparative Analysis of some Common Problems' (2009) 32 Columbia Journal of Law & the Arts 481.

The connection of neutrality, under CJEU case law, with the function of intermediation and its dependence on the notions of knowledge and control would suggest that what the Court is in fact attempting through its introduction is a differentiation between 'true intermediaries', which remain uninvolved in the third party wrong despite the use of their services for the commission of that wrong (and which therefore should enjoy immunity) and service providers which, to a greater or lesser extent, are involved in the wrong in such a way that it might be understood to be their own (which therefore do not deserve protection). Seen under this lens, the CJEU's bid for neutrality is probably best interpreted as an attempt to depend liability on the mental attitude of the intermediary towards the primary wrong. The description of neutrality as the status of being 'of a mere technical, automatic and passive nature' suggests that what is important is, not so much what the intermediary does, but the way in which it goes about doing it: passively, through an automatic technical process set in place prior to the infringement, offered to all indiscriminately and exploited by the direct infringer, or as a result of a conscious decision to take part in somebody else's wrongdoing. This is the first indication that not only conduct, but also mental state is relevant to the liability of online service providers. As we shall see below, national rules on accessory liability confirm the relevance of the mental element to the diagnosis of liability-carrying participation.

2.2.1.2 Intermediaries in the Copyright Directive

Beyond the E-Commerce Directive, the Enforcement and Copyright Directives, which govern injunctions against intermediaries, take a much laxer approach, applying themselves freely to all 'intermediaries whose services are used by a third party to infringe'. No further distinction is made with regard to the type of service provided. Although the wording of the provisions suggests expansion beyond the internet to the offline world as well, Recital 59 of the Copyright Directive backtracks to only intermediaries that carry infringements 'in a network',[91] while justifying the obligatory introduction of the possibility of injunctions against them in its Article 8(3) by reference to the increased use of such actors by third parties for infringing activities in the 'digital environment'.[92] In *Telekabel,* the Court stated that the

91. The CJEU is set to examine whether or not 'offline' intermediaries are covered by Art. 11 of the Enforcement Directive in C-494/15, *Tommy Hilfiger Licensing and Others,* a case recently referred for a preliminary ruling by the Supreme Court of the Czech Republic and which concerns persons with a lease on premises in a market who provide stalls and pitches on which stalls may be placed to individual market-traders for their use.
92. Certainly, in CJEU, C-557/07, *LSG-Gesellschaft zur Wahrnehmung von Leistungsschutzrechten GmbH v. Tele2 Telecommunication GmbH*, 19 February 2009, it was confirmed that internet access providers qualify as 'intermediaries' in the sense of Art. 8 of the Copyright Directive.

term 'intermediary' in the sense of Article 8(3) of the Copyright Directive covers any person who carries a third party's infringement of a protected work or other subject matter in a network.[93] Even given this restriction, the resulting reach remains quite broad. Certainly, as opposed to what is the case for the E-Commerce safe harbours, no condition of neutrality seems to limit the application of the Copyright Directive.

These divergent scopes of application are important. What they seem to indicate is the differing attitude of EU law towards different types of liability and their pairing with different types of intermediary activity. Essentially, the EU legislator seems to be aiming at is a system wherein, while injunctive relief should be imposed on any intermediary well-placed to provide assistance in the enforcement of copyright regardless of their blameworthiness, liability for damages should be reserved for only those particularly culpable providers that took a non-neutral attitude towards the infringement. Neutral versus non-neutral, culpable versus non-culpable thus emerges as the backbone of the EU's current intermediary liability regime – the dividing line between two very different legal treatments of internet intermediaries.

As noted in Chapter 1, the broader definition of the Copyright Directive is what will be preferred in this book, at least when not focusing specifically on the regime of the E-Commerce Directive: instead of examining intermediary third party liability as a special kind of liability that centres around the type of service provided by the intermediaries to which it applies or the 'neutrality' of the provider, the approach taken shall be one of a simple application of the rules that govern accessory copyright infringement in general to internet intermediaries. This solution is intended to help avoid the classification problems that accompany service-driven definitions, while also resulting in a scheme that embraces all kinds of intermediary involvement in third party liability, through connecting the right type of involvement to the right type of remedy: the overall objective is to understand the liability position of both neutral and non-neutral providers and the differences that separate them.

Having established the scope of the relevant directives with regard to the subjects whose liability they govern, we shall now proceed with a detailed provision-by-provision analysis of the full EU regime for the accessory liability of internet intermediaries in copyright. The analysis with begin with the three safe harbours and move on to all relevant accompanying provisions.

---

93. This conclusion will hold true regardless of the relationship between that third party and the intermediary. See CJEU, C-314/12, *UPC Telekabel Wien GmbH v. Constantin Film Verleih GmbH,* 27 March 2014, para. 30.

2.2.2 Article 12 of the E-Commerce Directive: The Mere Conduit Safe Harbour

The first EU safe harbour provision for internet intermediaries is found in Article 12 of the E-Commerce Directive. According to this, any intermediary acting as a 'mere conduit' may not be held liable for the information it transmits. Two distinct activities qualify as 'mere conduit' services under this safe harbour: the provision of a service 'that consists of the transmission in a communication network of information provided by a recipient of the service' and 'the provision of access to a communication network'. By contrast, a service provider may not be considered as performing an intermediary 'conduit' activity when transmitting its own information[94] – as has already been established, content providers are not intermediaries.[95]

In order to qualify for the exemption the intermediary must not:

(a) Initiate the transmission. The Explanatory Memorandum makes clear that automatically initiating a transmission at the request of a recipient of the service will not mean that the service provider initiated the transmission in the sense of Article 12.[96]

(b) Select the receiver of the transmission. Again, the Explanatory Memorandum states that a provider will not be disqualified for selecting receivers as an automatic response to a request from the person initiating the transmission.[97]

(c) Select or modify the information contained in the transmission, i.e., exercise any editorial control over the information. Such selection or modifications of the information will requalify the content from that of the recipient of the service to the intermediary's own, thus stripping the intermediary of 'mere conduit' status.[98] Recital 43 states that manipulations of a technical nature which take place in the course of the transmission that do not alter the integrity of the information contained in the transmission should not be considered to be 'modifications' of the information.

94. Explanatory Memorandum to the Proposal for a European Parliament and Council Directive on certain legal aspects of electronic commerce in the internal market, COM(1998) 586 final, 18 November 1998.
95. See Ch. 1, s. 1.4.2.
96. Explanatory Memorandum to the Proposal for a European Parliament and Council Directive on certain legal aspects of electronic commerce in the internal market, COM(1998) 586 final, 18 November 1998.
97. Explanatory Memorandum to the Proposal for a European Parliament and Council Directive on certain legal aspects of electronic commerce in the internal market, COM(1998) 586 final, 18 November 1998.
98. Explanatory Memorandum to the Proposal for a European Parliament and Council Directive on certain legal aspects of electronic commerce in the internal market, COM(1998) 586 final, 18 November 1998.

Qualifying providers cannot be subjected to either civil liability for monetary relief or prosecution in a criminal case. Article 12 does not exclude, however, the possibility of an action for injunctive relief.[99]

Paragraph 2 of Article 12 specifies that the automatic, intermediate and transient storage of the information transmitted does constitute an act of transmission or of provision of access capable of qualifying for protection, as long as it takes place for the sole purpose of carrying out the transmission in the communication network and does not last longer than is reasonably necessary for the transmission. The term 'automatic' here means that act of storage must occur through the ordinary operation of the technology; the term 'intermediate' that the storage of the information must be made in the course of the transmission; and the term 'transient' that the storage must be for a limited period of time only. It should be clear that the information cannot be stored beyond the time that is reasonably necessary for the transmission. In the context of copyright, this will mean that the intermediary will be exculpated for any infringement (direct or accessory) of the reproduction right necessary for the provision of mere conduit services. Acts of storage benefiting from Article 12 protection may not include copies made by the provider for the purpose of making the information available to subsequent users. This possibility is instead addressed in Article 13 of the E-Commerce Directive.[100]

2.2.3 Article 13 of the E-Commerce Directive: The Caching Safe Harbour

According to Article 13 of the E-Commerce Directive, where an information society service is provided that consists of the transmission in a communication network of information provided by a recipient of the service, the service provider may not be held liable for the automatic, intermediate and temporary storage of that information, where that storage is performed for the sole purpose of making more efficient the information's onward transmission to other recipients of the service upon their request. This is the so-called caching safe harbour. In computing, a cache is a component that stores data with the objective of serving future requests for that data faster:[101] 'cached' copies of such data, made available online and transmitted by third parties, are temporarily kept in the operator's system or network for the purpose of facilitating the access of subsequent users to such information.

99. Explanatory Memorandum to the Proposal for a European Parliament and Council Directive on certain legal aspects of electronic commerce in the internal market, COM(1998) 586 final, 18 November 1998.

100. Explanatory Memorandum to the Proposal for a European Parliament and Council Directive on certain legal aspects of electronic commerce in the internal market, COM(1998) 586 final, 18 November 1998.

101. See Wikipedia entry on 'Cache (computing)'.

Caching is accordingly a form of information storage used to limit the need for the retransmission of information from its point of origin, so as to reduce network congestion and enhance the performance and the speed of digital networks.[102] Caches are similar to the transmission copies dealt with in Article 12 in that they are the result of a technical and automatic process and are intermediate between the original making available of the information and its receipt by the final user. As such, like transmission copies, they do not constitute a separate exploitation of the information transmitted.[103] The difference between caching and mere conduit relates instead to the actions' time frame and purpose: in case of mere conduit services, the storage only serves the purpose of carrying out the communication and lasts for a limited amount of time. Caching by contrast refers to temporary copies made for purposes of efficiency and remaining in place for longer periods of time.[104]

Stricter conditions attach to the caching safe harbour than to the mere conduit safe harbour. In order to benefit from the latter the intermediary must:

(a) not modify the information – once again, only real intermediaries may qualify. As with the mere conduit safe harbour however, manipulations of a technical nature which take place in the course of the transmission that do not alter the integrity of the information contained in the transmission do not qualify as 'modifications', as they do not alter the integrity of the information contained in the transmission;[105]
(b) comply with any conditions on access to the information. For the purposes of this analysis, this would include, for example, those applicable under a copyright license;
(c) comply with any rules regarding the updating of the information as widely recognised and used by industry. These could concern such matters as e.g., the frequency with which updating should occur;
(d) not interfere with the lawful use of technology widely recognised and used by industry, to obtain data on the use of the information (e.g., cookies or DRM technology); and
(e) act expeditiously to remove or to disable access to the information it has stored upon obtaining actual knowledge of the fact that the information at the initial source of the transmission has been

102. I Walden, 'Directive 2000/31/EC – Directive on Electronic Commerce' in A Büllesback, Y Poullet & C Prins (eds), *Concise European IT Law* (Kluwer Law International 2006) 251.
103. Explanatory Memorandum to the Proposal for a European Parliament and Council Directive on certain legal aspects of electronic commerce in the internal market, COM(1998) 586 final, 18 November 1998.
104. P Valcke & E Dommering, 'E-Commerce Directive' in O Castendyk, E Dommering & A Scheuer, *European Media Law* (Kluwer Law International 2008) 1101.
105. See Recital 43, E-Commerce Directive.

> removed from the network or access to it has been disabled or that a court or an administrative authority has ordered such removal or disablement. This provision incorporates a kind of 'notice-and-take-down' regime into the caching safe harbour. It is important to note however that, in contrast to the similar system contained in Article 14 hosting safe harbour, the 'actual knowledge' here does not relate to the illegal character of the information, but merely to its removal from the original source.

The five conditions of the caching immunity apply cumulatively. As with the mere conduit safe harbour, qualifying providers cannot be subjected to either civil liability for monetary relief or criminal prosecution, but remain fully susceptible to injunctive relief.

It is notable that, as with the mere conduit safe harbour, a number of these requirements, whether they were intended that way by the legislator or not, have tangible benefits for the originator of the material as well. This could also potentially include the operator of a cached website that infringes copyright – in other words the primary copyright infringer. So, while the condition according to which the intermediary may have had no editorial input into the content helps indicate that it is not at the source of the infringement and thus is indeed a true intermediary, it also safeguards the content provider against unwanted interferences from the caching intermediary. Likewise, the intermediary's obligations to comply with the accepted standards on refreshing its caches and any conditions set on accessing the content, as well as its obligation to avoid interference with technology used to send back data to the website operator, not only establish the disinterested status of the intermediary, but ultimately also serve the interests of the content provider.[106]

Finally, it is worth noting that, given that it imposes an obligation regarding the post-caching treatment of the cached information, not simply the circumstances surrounding the caching process itself, the fifth condition of the caching safe harbour could be seen as implying a duty of care incumbent on the intermediary – albeit one that affects only the accessibility of the safe harbour, not liability per se.[107] In this regard, the immunity regime for caching is harsher than the one for mere conduit services. In its turn however, the caching safe harbour imposes more permissive conditions for protection than the next and final safe harbour, the one for hosting, set out in Article 14.

---

106. K Koelman, 'Online Intermediary Liability' in P B Hugenholtz (ed.), *Copyright and Electronic Commerce - Legal Aspects of Electronic Copyright Management* (Kluwer Law International 2000) 29.
107. P Valcke & E Dommering, 'E-Commerce Directive' in O Castendyk, E Dommering & A Scheuer, *European Media Law* (Kluwer Law International 2008) 1102.

2.2.4 Article 14 of the E-Commerce Directive: The Hosting Safe Harbour

Without a doubt the bulk of the discussion surrounding the safe harbours has concentrated on the third provision on hosting services: this is where things get interesting. This is arguably due to the broad reach acquired over the years by the notion of hosting. Although initially intended to refer only to hosting in a strict sense, i.e., the provision of disk-space and processors on a server that allows a client to serve content to the internet,[108] the concept has subsequently expanded to incorporate any storage of third party content – thus encompassing the services of modern web 2.0 operators which, characterised as they are by user participation, interactivity and mass collaboration, emphasise precisely the creation of information, its dissemination and, for these purposes, storage capabilities.[109] Admittedly, while the US courts shifted smoothly towards this second, wider definition, European judges have had some difficulty jumping on the bandwagon: the initial French inclination to classify online interactive services as 'editors' instead of host providers is indicative.[110] Nevertheless, as explained above, the CJEU seems to be coming down in favour of the more expansive approach (provided the intermediary can prove that it restricts itself to a sufficiently 'neutral' involvement), thus undercutting all national qualms. The broader definition must therefore be accepted as applicable in Europe as well and it is that that shall be assumed below.

What are the conditions of the hosting safe harbour? Like the caching safe harbour, the hosting safe harbour also incorporates a notice-and-take-down regime. While for caching however this is just one condition among many, for hosting, notice-and-take-down forms the main body of the safe harbour. Moreover, rather than attaching to the knowledge of the removal of the information from its source, in hosting notice-and-take-down is instead

---

108. See Wikipedia entry on 'internet hosting service'. According to this, the traditional notion of 'hosting' would include such services as 'web hosting', 'email hosting' or 'DNS hosting'. The Explanatory Memorandum to the Proposal for the Directive suggests that Art. 14 applies to the activity of storage of information provided by recipients of the service and at their request and provides the following examples: 'the provision of server space for a company's or an individual's web site, for a BBS, a newsgroup, etc.' See Explanatory Memorandum to the Proposal for a European Parliament and Council Directive on certain legal aspects of electronic commerce in the internal market, COM(1998) 586 final, 18 November 1998.
109. B Martinet Farano, 'Internet Intermediaries' Liability for Copyright and Trademark Infringement: Reconciling the EU and US Approaches' (2012) TTLF Working Paper No 14; M Peguera, 'The DMCA Safe Harbors and their European Counterparts: A Comparative Analysis of some Common Problems' (2009) 32 Columbia Journal of Law & the Arts 481; P van Eecke, 'Online Service Providers and Liability: A Plea for a Balanced Approach' (2011) 48 Common Market Law Review 1455.
110. R Matulionytė & S Nérisson, 'The French Route to an ISP Safe Harbour, Compared to German and US Ways' (2011) 42(1) International Review of Intellectual Property and Competition Law (IIC) 55. For more details see also Ch. 3 of this book.

triggered by knowledge of unlawfulness. Other than this, little information is provided in the Directive on the proper interpretation of the provision. In particular, no specific harmonised procedure is set up, leaving intermediaries and Member States unsure of the appropriate modalities.[111]

2.2.4.1 The Knowledge Standard

According to Article 14 of the E-Commerce Directive, a service provider may not be held liable for storing illegal third party content, if it neither: (a) has 'actual knowledge' of its illegal character nor (b) is 'aware of facts or circumstances' from which that character is apparent. The latter of the two knowledge thresholds – often referred to as 'constructive' or 'construed' knowledge[112] – applies only 'as regards claims for damages'.[113] The Explanatory Memorandum to the Directive makes clear that the distinction is intended to institute a divergent knowledge standard for criminal and civil liability, the latter of which should only become possible in cases of actual knowledge.[114] The wording of Article 14 itself confirms this interpretation, by first requiring without any qualification that the provider have no actual knowledge of illegal activity or information, but then clarifying that, specifically 'as regards claims for damages', awareness of facts or circumstances from which the illegal activity or information is apparent will also exclude immunity. For civil liability therefore, it must be accepted that the lower threshold of awareness applies.[115] What does this mean?

The EU documents provide little interpretative guidance in this regard. The 2011 consultation on the E-Commerce Directive indicates the resultant broad disagreement on the correct interpretation between the main stakeholders. Three main schools of thought can be identified: according to one, an intermediary can only obtain the necessary level of knowledge through a court order; according to another, an intermediary can only obtain the necessary knowledge through notification (although here again opinions may differ with regard to the level of detail necessary or the need to abide by a formal procedure); according to the third, an intermediary can obtain the

---

111. In comparison, the US DMCA provides directions in glorious detail. See DMCA, s. 512 (c), (d) and (g).
112. L Bently and B Sherman, *Intellectual Property Law* (3rd ed., Oxford University Press 2009) 198.
113. Others however disagree, see J Riordan, *The Liability of Internet Intermediaries* (PhD thesis, University of Oxford 2013, forthcoming Oxford University Press 2016) 85.
114. Explanatory Memorandum to the Proposal for a European Parliament and Council Directive on certain legal aspects of electronic commerce in the internal market, COM(1998) 586 final, 18 November 1998.
115. M Peguera, 'The DMCA Safe Harbors and their European Counterparts: A Comparative Analysis of some Common Problems' (2009) 32 Columbia Journal of Law & the Arts 481.

necessary knowledge even in the absence of any notification if, for instance, it has a 'general awareness' that its site hosts illegal information.[116]

Inspiration as regards the correct meaning of the knowledge requirement can be derived from the US experience. The US approach to 'awareness' rests on the concept of the 'red flag test' mentioned in the Senate Report on the Digital Millennium Copyright Act 1998 (DMCA). This contains, in its section 512, the US equivalents of the safe harbours.[117] The 'red flag test' explains that intermediaries need not monitor their services or affirmatively seek facts indicating infringing activity, but will lose the limitation of liability if they had a special reason to suspect that infringing activities were taking place and yet remained inactive.[118] So, while 'actual knowledge' is only triggered by an appropriate notification, 'awareness' may be triggered by any other circumstance constituting a 'red flag'.[119] Such 'red flags' are assessed on a dual subjective and objective basis: first the subjective element of the awareness on the part of the service provider of the facts or circumstances is taken into account. The US House of Representatives suggests that a notice of the infringement will establish this, as well as 'in appropriate circumstances [...] the absence of customary indicia of ownership or authorization, such as a standard and accepted digital watermark or other copyright management information',[120] although this might be setting the bar a bit low. Further than this, in deciding whether those facts or circumstances of which the intermediary might have been aware constitute a 'red flag', an objective standard is used. This assesses 'whether the infringing activity would have been apparent to a reasonable person operating under the same or similar circumstances'. Providers are under no obligation to seek out red flags, but if they choose to ignore a red flag once they become aware of it, they will cease to qualify for the safe harbour.

In practice, US courts have tended to adopt such a high standard of 'awareness' that it arguably often in fact coincides with 'actual knowledge'.[121] General knowledge of rampant user infringement is not usually understood to furnish the intermediary with sufficient knowledge of specific

116. Commission Staff Working Paper, 'Online Services, Including E-Commerce, in the Single Market', SEC(2011) 1641 final, 11 January 2012, p. 33.
117. For more information on the red flag test, see K Koelman, 'Online Intermediary Liability' in P B Hugenholtz (ed.), *Copyright and Electronic Commerce - Legal Aspects of Electronic Copyright Management* (Kluwer Law International 2000) 30.
118. US Senate, *The Digital Millennium Copyright Act of 1998*, S. Rpt. 105-190, 11 May 1998.
119. B Martinet Farano, 'Internet Intermediaries' Liability for Copyright and Trademark Infringement: Reconciling the EU and US Approaches' (2012) TTLF Working Paper No 14, 79.
120. US House of Representatives, *WIPO Copyright Treaties Implementation and On-Line Copyright Infringement Liability Limitation*, Rept. 105-551, 22 May 1998.
121. B Martinet Farano, 'Internet Intermediaries' Liability for Copyright and Trademark Infringement: Reconciling the EU and US Approaches' (2012) TTLF Working Paper No 14, 79-80.

acts of infringement such that it can require the intermediary to remedy the situation, unless the intermediary can be shown to have exhibited 'wilful blindness'. The standard for wilful blindness is rather strict, requiring that the defendant both knew of a high probability of illegal conduct and purposefully avoided, by taking affirmative steps, more concrete information on a specific infringement.[122] As a result, under US law an intermediary will generally be liable only where it either had actual knowledge of a specific infringement, as acquired through notification, or where it took affirmative steps to avoid the receipt of such notifications.[123]

The main source of information on the European level comes from the CJEU's decision in *L'Oréal v. eBay*.[124] It is indicative of the level of confusion surrounding the issue that Advocate General Jääskinen gets his Opinion on the case off on a wrong footing with a fundamentally fallacious approach to the knowledge standard: the AG appears to treat the notions of 'actual knowledge' and 'awareness of facts or circumstances' as synonymous and revolves his entire analysis around the former.[125] The Court corrects this by reverting to 'awareness' – as noted above, the actually applicable knowledge standard for cases of private law.

What does awareness mean? The CJEU limits itself to observing that the precise definition of this notion is for the domestic courts to decide. It does however provide one very important clue: according to the Court, facts or circumstances of which the intermediary is aware will make illegal activity or information 'apparent', if 'a diligent economic operator should have identified the illegality in question' on the basis of the same information. Intermediaries' knowledge should therefore be assessed in view of the behaviour of a hypothetical 'diligent' example of the same type. Thus, as with the US, in the EU as well, it would seem that a combination subjective/objective standard is set: while the intermediary must have individually, subjectively been 'aware of fact or circumstances', the

---

122. See *Tiffany. v. eBay*, 600 F.3d 93, 107 (2d Cir. 2010), where it was held that 'a service provider must have more than a general knowledge or reason to know that its service is being used to sell counterfeit goods … [s]ome contemporary knowledge of which particular listings are infringing or will infringe in the future is necessary'); *In re Aimster Copyright Litigation*, 334 F.3d 643 (2003) (United States Court of Appeals, 7th Circuit.). See also: B Martinet Farano, 'Internet Intermediaries' Liability for Copyright and Trademark Infringement: Reconciling the EU and US Approaches' (2012) TTLF Working Paper No 14, 79-80; R N Agrees, 'Is There Ever a Reason to Know? A Comparison of the Contributory Liability 'Knowledge' Standard for Websites Hosting Infringed Trademarked Content versus Infringed Copyrighted Content' (2011) 5(1) Journal of Business Entrepreneurship and the Law 179.
123. B Martinet Farano, 'Internet Intermediaries' Liability for Copyright and Trademark Infringement: Reconciling the EU and US Approaches' (2012) TTLF Working Paper No 14, 79-82.
124. CJEU, C-324/09, *L'Oréal v. eBay International*, 12 July 2011.
125. CJEU, Opinion of Advocate General Jääskinen, case C-324/09, *L'Oréal v. eBay International*, 9 December 2010, paras 154 et seq.

knowledge-making power of those facts or circumstances is to be assessed objectively, according to the benchmark of the 'diligent economic operator'.

What kind of facts or circumstances would make an infringement 'apparent' to a diligent economic operator? The introduction of the 'diligent economic operator' metric clearly refers directly back to the non-harmonised national tort laws and in particular the familiar figure of the 'reasonable person'.[126] As Synodinou observes, this might create more questions than it answers, as it risks the re-fragmentation of hosting liability along the lines of each Member State's traditional national definitions of diligence.[127] At the same time, this solution does provide the most logical answer consistent with the usual legal patterns governing such issues[128] and – although the *L'Oréal* Court seemed happy to avoid further elaboration in that particular case – it also establishes a solid basis for the future introduction of a substantive harmonised rule of liability that draws its validity from its integration into the general norms on extra-contractual legal relationships.

In any case, a number of suggestions are made by the CJEU. So, the Court first makes clear that 'every situation in which the provider concerned becomes aware, in one way or another, of such facts or circumstances' is relevant. 'The situations thus covered include', it continues, 'in particular, that in which the operator of an online marketplace uncovers, as the result of an investigation undertaken on its own initiative, an illegal activity or illegal information, as well as a situation in which the operator is notified of the existence of such an activity or such information'. Accordingly, the Court seems to dismiss the strict interpretation according to which a court order is necessary to provide reliable knowledge of an infringement of an IPR. At the same time, it also concedes that receipt of a notification cannot automatically preclude immunity under the hosting safe harbour, as such notification may be 'insufficiently precise or inadequately substantiated'. Nevertheless, notice will definitely constitute 'a factor of which the national court must take account' when assessing the awareness of the intermediary.

It is particularly interesting to note the Court's acceptance of independent observations by the intermediary as sufficient to substantiate the necessary 'awareness'. Arguably, this makes sense, as it does not allow an intermediary that has received no notice, but has become independently aware of an infringement, to hide behind the lack of right-holder mobilisation. It may also be an indication that a general awareness of illegality must have legal consequences of some kind. At the same time, it is important not to overstate the deductive abilities of the paragon provider: as the AG puts it, 'is not enough that the service provider ought to have known or has good reasons to suspect illegal activity' and 'mere suspicion or assumption' will

126. For more on this see Chs 4 and 5 of this book.
127. T-E Synodinou, 'Intermediaries' Liability for Online Copyright Infringement in the EU: Evolutions and Confusions' (2015) 31 Computer Law & Security Review 57.
128. For more on this, see below Ch. 4, s. 4.2.2.

not suffice: the intermediary, as shall be shown below, cannot be forced to research infringements, even while the results of any research is does undertake can establish sufficient knowledge. Mere negligence, assessed on a purely objective basis, is not enough – a subjective element of some kind must be inserted.[129]

In addition to these suggestions, it is worth noting that a key interpretative concept in this regard, increasingly used in relevant EU analyses, is that of 'manifest illegality'.[130] According to this, the necessary knowledge may safely be assumed where the intermediary is aware of the existence of content which is obviously unlawful.[131] However, while the concept of 'manifest illegality' can be very useful in areas of law dealing with strongly objectionable information whose illegality is readily apparent, such as child pornography or otherwise criminal information, it is questionable how helpful it can be in copyright. Arguably, copyright-infringing content may never be considered 'manifestly' illegal, since the assessment of a particular piece of information as constituting a copyright infringement will depend on the circumstances at play.[132] For example, the same digital copy of a film may simultaneously be illegal for one user to post online, while entirely legal for another, depending on such considerations as the position taken by the right-holder, whether the user was obliged to obtain a license and any relevant exceptions or limitations to the copyright.[133]

A final difficult question with regard to the knowledge standard concerns the possibility of awareness of future infringements. In his Opinion, the Advocate General attempts to grapple with this tricky question. According to the AG, legally speaking, knowledge may refer exclusively to past or present occurrences, but not to the future: 'the object of knowledge must be a concluded or ongoing activity or an existing fact or circumstance'. This strict position is loosened by the recognition that the repetition of the same infringement by the same actor should be taken to constitute, not two separate events, but a single 'ongoing activity' that 'covers past, present and future'. On this basis, the AG concludes that the 'exemption from liability does not apply in cases where the [provider] has been notified of infringing use […], and the same user continues or repeats the same infringement'. Thus, a kind of knowledge or awareness limited only to future infringements

129. P van Eecke, 'Online Service Providers and Liability: A Plea for a Balanced Approach' (2011) 48 Common Market Law Review 1455.

130. Commission Staff Working Paper, 'Online Services, Including E-Commerce, in the Single Market', SEC(2011) 1641 final, 11 January 2012, 34.

131. N Zingales, 'Internet Intermediary Liability: Identifying Best Practices for Africa' (2013) Association for Progressive Communications (APC).

132. For a similar assertion regarding trademarks see, OECD, 'The Role of Internet Intermediaries in Advancing Public Policy Objectives, OECD Publishing' (2011), available at: http://dx.doi.org/10.1787/9789264115644-en.

133. P van Eecke, 'Online Service Providers and Liability: A Plea for a Balanced Approach' (2011) 48 Common Market Law Review 1455.

that are likely to occur is indeed possible. According to this exegesis, the hosting exemption from liability will not apply where the same user continues or repeats the same act of infringement after actual knowledge or awareness of that infringement has been acquired by the intermediary and it nonetheless fails to act. The AG would thus seem to favour the right-holder push for a so-called notice-and-*stay-down* interpretation[134] of the hosting safe harbour, whereby a single notification would amount to actual knowledge or awareness of facts or circumstances that could nullify immunity for all potential future infringements that are similar to the notified infringement.[135]

Be that as it may, the consequences attached to the acquisition of knowledge cannot be ignored. While it may be argued that previous infringements might serve as facts or circumstances that would make a future similar infringements apparent to a diligent intermediary, awareness of such past infringements will not necessarily translate into awareness of the precise location of their future reincarnations without further research, potentially impeding their removal or the disablement of access to them. If knowledge of the future is accepted as a possibility, it must be coupled with appropriate reactive obligations: the hosting safe harbour cannot be turned into a trap that imposes conditions no intermediary can realistically satisfy. This difficulty shall be examined in detail below, in the context of the prohibition on general monitoring obligations.

2.2.4.2 Post-knowledge Reaction

Acquiring knowledge or awareness of facts or circumstances indicating illegal activity is not the end of the game for hosting providers. The exemption from liability will still apply if, after obtaining such actual or constructive knowledge, the intermediary acts expeditiously to remove or to disable access to the illegal information. This constitutes the second step of the hosting immunity's 'notice-and-take-down' regime. As with the equivalent condition for the caching safe harbour, here again this requirement could be viewed as an adjusted, immunity-oriented duty of care.[136]

Significantly, both the removal of the information and the disabling of access to it (often termed 'blocking') are valid options open to the

134. Notice-and-stay-down enjoys some popularity in the Member States, particularly France and Germany, as shall be shown in Ch. 3. The Commission also seems to be considering the advantages of a stay-down regime, see Communication from the Commission to the European Parliament, the Council, the European Economic and Social Committee and the Committee of the Regions, 'Towards a modern, more European copyright framework', COM(2015) 626 final, 9 December 2015.
135. Commission Staff Working Paper, 'Online Services, Including E-Commerce, in the Single Market', SEC(2011) 1641 final, 11 January 2012, 43.
136. P Valcke & E Dommering, 'E-Commerce Directive' in O Castendyk, E Dommering & A Scheuer, *European Media Law* (Kluwer Law International 2008) 1103.

intermediary wishing to retain safe harbour protection. Other possible responses to illegal content, such as the posting of warnings informing the public authorities or communicating information enabling the identification of the primary infringer to the right-holders are likewise not listed as capable of preserving the immunity. Other than this, the only hint as to the appropriate parameters of the post-knowledge reaction is given by Recital 46 of the E-Commerce Directive, which, rather vaguely, warns that any removal or disabling of access has to be undertaken in the observance of the principle of freedom of expression; on this basis, AG Jääskinen surmises that the right protection may not take forms that would infringe the rights of innocent users or leave alleged infringers without due recourse to opposition and defence.[137] While certainly an important conclusion, this does not give intermediaries much information with which to work. Rather ominously, it also seems to indicate that failure to properly respect freedom of expression will be attributed to the intermediary, rather than the State that depended its liability on take-down without offering further guidance.

No indication is given in the Directive as to what exactly counts as an 'expeditious' reaction. While this omission provides a flexibility that can allow for adaptation to each individual case, it also causes a fair amount of uncertainty for European hosts. Too short a time frame might increase pressure on hosts to remove or disable access to content too easily. National legislative provisions vary, requiring between twelve hours and three days.[138] This might seem excessively constricted, especially if it is accepted that time should be factored in for fact-checking or consulting legal counsel: small intermediaries might have difficulty identifying an informed member of staff, while in larger companies it may take time for the notice to reach the appropriate department. Again, the extent to which content may be described as 'manifestly' illegal might be relevant in this regard, as the assessment of the legality of information must be factored in to the time allocated. It should also be noted that it is often unclear when the relevant time begins to run: at the moment of receipt of the knowledge or awareness or after the legality of the information has been assessed?

2.2.4.3 Absence of Authority or Control

One final condition for the hosting safe harbour is given by paragraph 2 of Article 14. According to this, the immunity is not available where the recipient of the service was acting under the authority or the control of the provider. This makes clear that the hosting safe harbour is not intended to

137. CJEU, Opinion of Advocate General Jääskinen, case C-324/09, *L'Oréal v. eBay International*, 9 December 2010, para. 158.
138. Commission Staff Working Paper, 'Online Services, Including E-Commerce, in the Single Market', SEC(2011) 1641 final, 11 January 2012, 44.

protect from vicarious, as opposed to accessory, liability.[139] Precisely what level of control is necessary is unclear. The condition has not received great attention either in the literature or by the courts and arguably its practical effect is limited, vicarious liability not generally being relied upon by the European legal systems to hold intermediaries accountable for the wrong-doings of their users.

It is worth noting that, in contrast to the US provision, Article 14 does not prohibit the host provider from receiving financial benefit directly attributable to the infringing activity. Nevertheless, European courts have often added a similar requirement in practice, often through reasoning that, if an intermediary was reaping financial benefit, it must have exercised control over the user.[140] This possibility however would now seem to be locked off by the CJEU approach to neutrality, halting conflicting national interpretations.

2.2.4.4 Notice-and-Action

The notice-and-take-down system of the hosting safe harbour is particularly significant in the context of copyright infringement, given the attachment of the triggering knowledge to the illegality of the content. It is clear that in introducing this system the legislator was hoping that more detailed procedures could be established by the Member States in national law to fill in the rudimentary framework the Directive sketches. So, after noting the need for 'the development of rapid and reliable procedures for removing and disabling access to illegal information' and reflecting that such procedures would be 'in the interest of all parties involved', Recital 40 of the E-Commerce Directive suggests that voluntary codes of conduct could be developed by the industry under the encouragement of the Member States. Recital 46 of the E-Commerce Directive gives the matter an extra nudge by stating clearly that the Member States are free to establish specific requirements which must be fulfilled expeditiously prior to the removal or disabling of information for the enjoyment of the hosting safe harbour. These hints would seem to suggest that the EU was hoping for quite elaborate procedures, ideally containing appropriate guarantees for the interests of content providers. Article 14 *in fine* further urges Member States in this direction by permitting the establishment of procedures governing the removal or disabling of access to information from host providers, a clear invitation for the introduction of national notice-and-take-down regimes. Finally, Article 16 lays the cornerstone by expressly instructing both the Member States and the Commission to encourage self-regulation through the

---

139. For more on the difference between the two notions see above s. 1.4.1.
140. B Martinet Farano, 'Internet Intermediaries' Liability for Copyright and Trademark Infringement: Reconciling the EU and US Approaches' (2012) TTLF Working Paper No. 14, 95-96.

drawing up of codes of conduct at Community level by trade, professional and consumer associations or organisations, designed, among other things, to contribute to the proper implementation of the safe harbours.[141] Along similar lines, Recital 41 explains that the Directive is intended to establish principles upon which industry agreements and standards can be based.

Given the Directive's clear enthusiasm for the idea of notice-and-take-down as a solution to intermediary liability, one has to wonder why the EU legislator didn't forge forward with the establishment of a proper procedure at the time – or at least provide more concrete guidance with regard to the meaning of key terms. Indeed, the lack of harmonised European notice-and-take-down procedure has generally been agreed to constitute one of the Directive's weakest points.[142] Despite the legislator's optimism, most Member States have failed to introduce formal notification procedures, relying instead on the crawling development of criteria through case law.[143] This has resulted in conflicting jurisprudence and legal uncertainty. Even where adequate national solutions have been developed, absent European guidance, the fragmentation of notice-and-take-down systems across the EU into a multitude of often very disparate solutions hampers innovation and growth.[144] This confusion is made worse by the introduction of individualised internal procedures by each separate intermediary wanting to abide by the conditions of Article 14, but unsure of their precise parameters. This privatised enforcement, intended to cover the regulatory gap, additionally suffers from a lack of transparency, particularly worrisome in situations involving fundamental rights.[145] Finally, while other areas have been quicker

141. In comparison, the US DMCA provides directions in glorious detail. See DMCA, s. 512 (c), (d) and (g).
142. Commission Staff Working Paper, 'Online Services, Including E-Commerce, in the Single Market', SEC(2011) 1641 final, 11 January 2012, 25; DLA Piper, 'EU Study on the Legal Analysis of a Single Market for the Information Society – New Rules for a New Age?', November 2009, available at: http://ec.europa.eu/information_society/newsroom/cf/itemdetail.cfm?item_id=7022.
143. Commission Staff Working Paper, 'Online Services, Including E-Commerce, in the Single Market', SEC(2011) 1641 final, 11 January 2012, see 42 and Annex II.
144. Commission Staff Working Document, 'A Digital Single Market Strategy for Europe - Analysis and Evidence', SWD(2015) 100 final, 6 May 2015, 55-56.
145. P B Hugenholtz, 'Codes of Conduct and Copyright Enforcement in Cyberspace' in I A Stamatoudi (ed.), *Copyright Enforcement and the Internet* (Kluwer Law International 2010) 303; P B Hugenholtz, 'Codes of Conduct and Copyright: Pragmatism v. Principle' (2008) 6 International Review of Intellectual Property and Competition Law (IIC) 635; European Commission, 'Initiative on procedures for notifying and acting on illegal online content', last modification: June 2012; Commission Staff Working Paper, 'Online Services, Including E-Commerce, in the Single Market', SEC(2011) 1641 final, 11 January 2012, 42; DLA Piper, 'EU Study on the Legal Analysis of a Single Market for the Information Society – New Rules for a New Age?', November 2009, available at: http://ec.europa.eu/information_society/newsroom/cf/itemdetail.cfm?item_id=7022; T Verbiest et al., 'Study on the Liability of Internet Intermediaries', EU Commission study (MARKT/2006/09/E), 12 November 2007.

to attract coordinated industry-wide attention,[146] in copyright, the cross-border self- and co-regulatory codes of conduct that could have mitigated the problem have mostly failed to materialise.[147] The most prominent cross-border exception to this rule has only very recently (fifteen years after the adoption of the E-Commerce Directive) emerged in the form of the Manila Principles on Intermediary Liability,[148] proposed in March 2015 by a forum of non-governmental organisations from around the world active in the area of digital rights. These do contain more detailed procedural guidelines, also applicable to cases of copyright infringement.[149] At the same time however, although arguably gaining momentum, the Manila Principles only present the position of civil society on the matter and cannot yet be said to have acquired a broader consensus across the board of all relevant stakeholders.

Article 21 of the E-Commerce Directive does foresee the possibility of a future amendment of the Directive for the introduction of a harmonised notice-and-take-down procedure at the European level.[150] Following a consultation in which stakeholders indicated that a more streamlined solution would be welcome as enabling a quicker take-down of illegal content, better respect for fundamental rights and increased legal certainty for online intermediaries,[151] in its 2011 Communication on e-commerce and other online services, the Commission signalled its intention to introduce a

146. This is almost always single-nation-oriented however. See, for example, s. 5 of the Code of Practice adopted by ISPA, the Internet Service Providers Association, a British body representing providers of internet services, on illegal child abuse images (available at: ispa.org.uk); the collection of Voluntary Commitments of Business in youth protection for various areas of the online world (search engines, chat providers, mobile communications providers, social communities and teletext providers) developed by the German *Freiwillige Selbstkontrolle Multimedia-Diensteanbieter e.V.* (available at: fsm.de); or the *Charte des prestataires de services d'hébergement en ligne et d'accès à Internet en matière de lutte contre certains contenus spécifiques* on child pornography and the incitement of racial hatred of the French *Association des Fournisseurs d'Accès et de Services Internet* (AFA) (available at: afa-france.com).
147. Any codes that do exist in Europe tend to be anchored to national jurisdictions (see, for example, the code of conduct defining the conditions of voluntary website blocking by Danish internet access providers adopted on 24 September 2014 by the Danish Telecommunications Industry Association, *Teleindustrien* (available at: teleindu.dk/wp-content/uploads/2014/10/TI-code-of-conduct-blokeringer.pdf)). Even these are few and far between. The one initiate of international breadth that stands out is the Principles for User Generated Content Services, available at: www.ugcprinciples.com. These are quite strict, going so far as to oblige signatory providers to implement filtering technology in the interests of copyright enforcement. However, the Principles have only been signed by a handful of providers (albeit very big ones) and are mostly US-oriented.
148. Available at: www.manilaprinciples.org.
149. See in particular Manila Principles III-VI.
150. Article 21(2) of the E-Commerce Directive.
151. See European Commission, 'Summary of the results of the Public Consultation on the future of electronic commerce in the Internal Market and the implementation of the Directive on electronic commerce (2000/31/EC)'.

regulated horizontal European framework for notice-and-action procedures.[152]

Many applauded this move on the logic that it is more effective, efficient and fair than the EU's current un-system, but others are more dubious. As multiple authors have pointed out, notice-and-take-down may, depending on the precise contours of the regime, carry with it severe disadvantages.[153] So, for example, although the US's much more detailed DMCA procedure does build in a number of safeguards against misuse that could conceivably help improve the European regime,[154] it has been criticised for the one-sided incentives it provides to take down content to entities that have neither the constitutional authority and legal expertise of a court nor, as a general rule, the desire to assume such responsibility.[155] Especially striking in the US regime is the requirement that notification of claimed infringements need only contain a statement that the information in the notification is accurate, but counter-notifications by content providers must be under penalty of perjury.[156] Arguably, at least in cases that do not involve manifestly illegal content, as will happen with a good percentage of copyright claims, content should remain in place until it has been proven illegal by a courts, without any threat of liability for the intermediary.[157]

Of course, the Communication's use of the term 'notice-and-action' might indicate awareness of these difficulties. It is worth noting that, in reaction to the shortcomings of notice-and-take-down, a number of variations on the theme have emerged across the globe. So, in Japan a system of so-called notice-wait-and-take-down requires intermediaries to forward notices to the content provider and then wait a week before proceeding with any removal or blocking. If the provider either consents or does not respond, the

---

152. Commission Communication to the European Parliament, the Council, the Economic and Social Committee and the Committee of the Regions, 'A Coherent Framework for Building Trust in the Digital Single Market for E-Commerce and Online Services' COM(2011) 942 final/2, 6 February 2012.
153. G R Hagen, '"Modernizing" ISP Copyright Liability' in M Geist (ed.), *From 'Radical Extremism' to 'Balanced Copyright': Canadian Copyright and the Digital Agenda* (Irwin Law 2010) 385; C Ahlert et al., 'How "Liberty" Disappeared from Cyberspace: The Mystery Shopper Tests Internet Content Self-Regulation', available at: http://pcmlp.socleg.ox.ac.uk/sites/pcmlp.socleg.ox.ac.uk/files/liberty.pdf; J Urban & L Quilter, 'Efficient Process or "Chilling Effects"? Takedown Notices under Section 512 of the Digital Millennium Copyright Act' (2006) 22(4) Santa Clara Computer & High Technology Law Journal 621.
154. L Edwards, 'Role and Responsibility of Internet Intermediaries in the Field of Copyright and Related Rights', WIPO Study (2011) 11.
155. DLA Piper, 'EU Study on the Legal Analysis of a Single Market for the Information Society – New Rules for a New Age?', November 2009, available at: http://ec.europa.eu/information_society/newsroom/cf/itemdetail.cfm?item_id=7022.
156. N Zingales, 'Internet Intermediary Liability: Identifying Best Practices for Africa' (2013) Association for Progressive Communications (APC).
157. Article 19, 'Promoting Free Expression and Access to Information' (2010) Implementation Report.

intermediary may proceed with the take-down. Canada implements a system of so-called notice-and-notice that simply requires that the intermediary forward notices to content providers. Another approach pioneered in France is 'notice-and-disconnection' (otherwise known as 'graduated response' or 'three strikes'), whereby infringers are sent warning messages by a public authority, which, if repeatedly ignored, culminate in the enforcement of sanctions in the form of the termination of internet subscriptions.[158] A further possibility of 'notice-and-judicial-take-down' is encountered in Chilean law, which requires the complaining party to obtain a court order before take-down can proceed. All of these could be considered as possible alternatives for Europe.

Regardless, the controversy surrounding the question has unsurprisingly resulted in delays. A draft directive on notice-and-action was initially floated in 2013. This, according to a leaked version, proposed a horizontal notice-and-take-down procedure for hosting providers based on Article 14 of the E-Commerce Directive that intended to combine a binding instrument with guidance from the European Commission.[159] The proposal was withdrawn unpublished,[160] following – rumour has it – a conflict between interest groups over the inclusion of the counter-notice provision.[161] Nevertheless, the Commission's intention to pursue notice-and-action was subsequently re-affirmed in December 2015 in its Communication on 'a modern, more European copyright framework'.[162]

In view of the comparatively high demands the surrounding European framework imposes for the protection of counterbalancing concerns that limit the permissible reactive measures, such a scheme will in any case have to be carefully formulated to avoid interference with other protected rights. A better alternative might be for the liability to arise, not on a strict basis, after the intermediary fails to abide by a formalised set of conditions, but only according to the general rules of tort, after it has failed to live up to an applicable duty of care. In 2015, in its Digital Single Market Communication the Commission announced its intention to launch a comprehensive assessment of the role of intermediaries with regard to illegal content on the internet and suggested just that:

---

158. N Zingales, 'Internet Intermediary Liability: Identifying Best Practices for Africa' (2013) Association for Progressive Communications (APC).
159. Leaked draft Proposal for a Directive of the European Parliament and of the Council on procedures for notifying and acting on illegal content hosted by online intermediary service providers ('Directive on notice-and-action procedures') [...] (2013) XXX draft.
160. See letter by nine MEPs to European Commissioner for Internal Market and Services Michel Barnier on the matter, 3 July 2013, available at: http://ameliaandersdotter.eu.
161. See M Horten, 'Notice of Action! EU Commission to Revive Take-Down Directive', 6 February 2014, available at: www.iptegrity.com.
162. Communication from the Commission to the European Parliament, the Council, the European Economic and Social Committee and the Committee of the Regions, 'Towards a modern, more European copyright framework', COM(2015) 626 final, 9 December 2015.

> the Commission will analyse the need for new measures to tackle illegal content on the Internet, with due regard to their impact on the fundamental right to freedom of expression and information, such as rigorous procedures for removing illegal content while avoiding the take down of legal content, and whether to require intermediaries to exercise greater responsibility and due diligence in the way they manage their networks and systems – a duty of care.[163]

2.2.4.5 Duties of Care

Although only contained in its preamble and not its main text, in the analysis of the hosting immunity it is worth taking particular note of Recital 48 of the E-Commerce Directive, as this, in attempting to illuminate the scope of Article 14, casts light on the surrounding framework as well.

According to Recital 48, the provisions of the Directive (including therefore the hosting safe harbour) should not be interpreted as prohibiting Member States from requiring 'service providers, who host information provided by recipients of their service, to apply duties of care, which can reasonably be expected from them and which are specified by national law, in order to detect and prevent certain types of illegal activities'. No similar clarification is made with regard to caching or mere conduit providers. The concession is rather befuddling: given that, as we shall see in Chapter 3, a number of Member States take a negligence-based approach to accessory liability that rests precisely on the imposition of duties of care on intermediaries with regard to the copyright infringements of third parties, any distinction between the notions of 'liability' (i.e., excluded by the hosting safe harbour) and of 'duties of care' (permitted by Recital 48) is an artificial one that could result in a rather curious – and, moreover, fragmented – negation of the very spirit of Article 14 of the E-Commerce Directive. Indeed, arguably fault liability in general arises from nothing else but the violation of a duty to avoid certain proscribed behaviours. Moreover, given that the hosting safe harbour itself is predicated on the idea that, upon receiving 'actual knowledge' or 'awareness of facts or circumstances' of an infringement, the host must 'act expeditiously to remove or to disable access' to it, it arguably incorporates one of the most obvious duties of care that might burden intermediaries into itself. If intermediaries may be placed under a duty of care to prevent infringement in the first place, where would that leave notice-and-take-down regimes that impose merely responsive, *ex post* obligations? As Edwards observes, the extension of the permission granted by Recital 48 beyond mere removal and disabling duties to potential

163. Communication from the Commission to the European Parliament, the Council, the European Economic and Social Committee and the Committee of the Regions, 'A Digital Single Market Strategy for Europe', COM(2015)192 final, 6 May 2015.

obligations to *ex ante* 'prevent' illegality is particularly questionable, as it would 'drive a coach and horses through the notice and take down' (NTD) limited liability paradigm'.[164] The uneasy relationship between preventive obligations and Article 15's general monitoring obligation (to be explored below) is further cause for concern.[165] Bagshaw explains this well: 'a duty to detect illegality makes little sense unless it *precedes* awareness of facts which already make illegality apparent', while 'it is difficult to understand a duty to detect which is not a duty to seek facts'.[166] Even if AG Jääskinen's preventive approach to Article 14's notice-and-take-down regime is favoured, both the added value of separate duties of care and their compatibility with the notion of immunity is questionable.

Precisely for this reason it has been argued that the duties of care in question should be read as extending only to public law, e.g., in aid of crime prevention or national security, and not private law (including copyright law).[167] Perhaps a more convincing approach would involve a constrictive interpretation of the provision that limits it only to duties to take measures other than the removal or disabling of access to infringing information, these possibilities being available only within the safe harbour scheme. In other words, while Member States should be free to impose duties of care of any kind on intermediaries, as long as the conditions of Article 14 have been abided by, no liability can result for information stored per se, even if the intermediary can be held liable for e.g., not informing the competent authorities of an infringement brought to their attention.[168] In that regard it is worth noting that Recital 40 also mentions that 'service providers have a duty to act, under certain circumstances, with a view to preventing or stopping illegal activities' – although given the context, this statement should probably instead be taken as part of the Directive's push for the adoption of voluntary notice-and-take-down procedures and the mention of 'prevention' interpreted restrictively, as per *L'Oréal*.

---

164. L Edwards, 'The Fall and Rise of Intermediary Liability Online' in L Edwards & C Waelde (eds.), *Law and the Internet* (3rd ed., Hart Publishing 2009) 65.
165. Commission Staff Working Paper, 'Online Services, Including E-Commerce, in the Single Market', SEC(2011) 1641 final, 11 January 2012, 47. See also Submission of the Electronic Frontier Foundation on the Consultation on the EU E-Commerce Directive (2000/31/EC), 8, available at: www.eff.org.
166. R Bagshaw, 'Downloading Torts: An English Introduction to On-Line Torts' in H Snijders & S Weatherill, *E-Commerce Law: National and Transnational Topics and Perspectives* (Kluwer Law International 2003) 72.
167. L Edwards, 'The Problem of Intermediary Service Provider Liability' in L Edwards, *The New Legal Framework for e-Commerce in Europe* (Hart Publishing 2005) 114-115. See also: R Bagshaw, 'Downloading Torts: An English Introduction to On-Line Torts' in H Snijders & S Weatherill, *E-Commerce Law: National and Transnational Topics and Perspectives* (Kluwer Law International 2003) 72; L Edwards, 'The Fall and Rise of Intermediary Liability Online' in L Edwards & C Waelde (eds.), *Law and the Internet* (3rd ed., Hart Publishing 2009) 65.
168. On this see Art. 15(2) of the E-Commerce Directive.

Naturally, it should be understood that similar duties of care may be freely imposed by the Member States on intermediaries not protected by any of the three safe harbours.

2.2.5 Article 8 of the Copyright Directive: Injunctive Relief

The liability rules of the E-Commerce Directive are exclusively confined to claims by right-holders for monetary relief pursued against internet intermediaries. The imposition of any kind of injunction by a court or administrative authority is expressly permitted by the final paragraph of each of the safe harbours of Articles 12-14.[169] These enable 'courts and administrative authorities' to order information society services to 'terminate or prevent an infringement'.

In the area of copyright, this possibility is turned into a requirement: Recital 59 of the Copyright Directive observes that in many cases online intermediaries are best placed to bring infringing activities occurring on their digital premises to an end. On this basis, Article 8(3) of the Copyright Directive explicitly instructs Member States to 'ensure that right-holders are in a position to apply for an injunction against intermediaries whose services are used by a third party to infringe a copyright or related right'. Crucially, the possibility of injunctions for intermediaries is independent not only of their liability for monetary relief, but also of any wrongdoing: according to the Commission, injunctions are not intended to act as a penalty against intermediaries, but result simply from their optimal placement to take action against infringements.[170] This explains the lack, noted above, of a neutrality requirement equivalent to that of Recital 42 of the E-Commerce Directive in the Copyright Directive, reinforcing the conclusion that – to the extent that existing provisions can be relied upon to paint a complete picture – the EU law's answer to intermediary accessory copyright liability is a gradient one: injunctive relief with no obligation for monetary compensation for 'neutral' intermediaries whose services are used by third parties to commit copyright infringements, but full liability for both damages and injunctions for 'non-neutral' intermediaries.

The Enforcement Directive reinforces the injunctions obligation in its Article 11. This refers to the Copyright Directive and repeats the order,

169. See also Art. 18 and Recital 52 of the E-Commerce Directive.

170. See Report from the Commission to the European Parliament, the Council, the European Economic and Social Committee and the Committee of the Regions on the Application of Directive 2004/48/EC of the European Parliament and the Council of 29 April 2004 on the enforcement of intellectual property rights, COM(2010) 779 final, 22 December 2010 and Commission Staff Working Paper, Analysis of the application of Directive 2004/48/EC of the European Parliament and the Council of 29 April 2004 on the enforcement of intellectual property rights in the Member States, SEC(2010) 1589 final, 22 December 2010.

expanding it to include all IPRs. In addition to the permanent ones governed by Article 11 of the Enforcement Directive, Article 9(1)(a) also allows interlocutory injunctions against intermediaries. The provision was inserted into the Enforcement Directive in response to the restrictive interpretation that Article 8(3) of the Copyright Directive found in a number of Member States that excluded provisional measures.[171] Interlocutory injunctions may be used to prevent any imminent infringement, by forbidding the continuation of an infringement or making such continuation subject to the lodging of guarantees intended to ensure the compensation of the right-holder. Under Article 9(4), such interlocutory injunctions may be issued without the intermediary defendant being heard, especially where any delay would cause irreparable damage to the right-holder. At the same time, an interlocutory injunction may be revoked if the right-holder does not initiate proceedings on the merits within a reasonable time period, while appropriate compensation may be provided by the right-holder to the intermediary if it is shown that the measures taken were unnecessary.[172]

It should be noted that, while the harmonisation of injunctive relief against intermediaries whose services are used in third party copyright infringements was arguably necessary in view of the differentiated approaches of the Member States with regard to the conditions for injunctive relief and in particular as concerns the possibility of its imposition on bona fide third parties,[173] whether injunctive relief may really be interpreted as a less burdensome remedy suitable for sympathetic, uninvolved, 'innocent' intermediaries is questionable. It is arguable that, in view of the often disproportionate restriction of liberty of action it entails,[174] not only for the intermediary itself, but also for its users, in practice the imposition of injunctive relief can prove a wolf in sheep's clothing that wreaks more far-reaching havoc on the intermediary's business model, ultimately imposing a greater financial burden than any obligation to foot a bill. This effect is accentuated in view of the exclusion of punitive damages for copyright infringement by the Enforcement Directive, thus minimising the difference between the position of neutral and non-neutral providers.[175] The practical

171. Commission Staff Working Paper, Analysis of the application of Directive 2004/48/EC of the European Parliament and the Council of 29 April 2004 on the enforcement of intellectual property rights in the Member States, SEC(2010) 1589 final, 22 December 2010.
172. See paras 5 and 7 of Art. 9 of the Enforcement Directive.
173. For a brief comparison of the fragmented situation previous to the adoption of the Enforcement Directive, see the Explanatory Memorandum accompanying the proposal for the Enforcement Directive in Proposal for a Directive of the European Parliament and of the Council on measures and procedures to ensure the enforcement of intellectual property rights, COM(2003) 46 final.
174. N McBride & R Bagshaw, *Tort Law* (4th ed., Pearson 2012) 833.
175. Recital 26 of the Enforcement Directive notes that, even in cases of infringers who engaged in an activity with knowledge or with reasonable grounds for knowing that it would give rise to an infringement, the aim 'is not to introduce an obligation to provide

consequences of an injunctive order will be particularly serious in cases of orders to prevent, rather than merely to terminate an infringement – the same concerns touched upon above with regard to preventive duties of care and future-orientated notice-and-take-down interpretations resurface here. In view of these concerns, Article 12 of the Enforcement Directive does permit Member States to revert, in appropriate cases and at the request of the defendant, to 'pecuniary compensation to be paid to the injured party' instead of injunctions, 'if that person acted unintentionally and without negligence, if execution of the measures in question would cause him/her disproportionate harm and if pecuniary compensation to the injured party appears reasonably satisfactory'.

In any case, it is worth noting that, their deleterious effect relative to damages aside, injunctions will at least represent a lesser threat to the interests of intermediaries than duties of care, given that these can be used to impose the same disruptive obligations on intermediaries without the added procedural obstacle of a court order. At the same time, in both areas, any real guidance on the permissible parameters of the measures that may be imposed is conspicuous by its absence. Indeed, while Recital 47 of the E-Commerce Directive at least limits the potential duties of care of host service providers to the detection and prevention of illegality, in Recital 59 the Copyright Directive – after demanding and not simply permitting their positive introduction – relinquishes all responsibility, simply stating that the 'conditions and modalities relating to [injunctions against intermediaries who carry third party copyright infringements] should be left to the national law of the Member States'.

Do the EU directives provide no guidance at all on the permissible scope of the obligations that can be imposed on internet intermediaries? Two provisions within the EU's written framework break this silence: Article 3 of the Enforcement Directive and Article 15 of the E-Commerce Directive. The first is both much broader and vaguer than the second, which should therefore, despite being adopted earlier, be understood as an elaboration on the general principles ensconced within it. The two articles must therefore be read in conjunction. This is what shall be done below.

2.2.6 Article 3 of the Enforcement Directive: General Limitations

As the above analysis makes clear, there are two main ways in which obligations can be imposed on internet intermediaries for the enforcement of other people's copyright: through injunctions ordered against them by a court

for punitive damages but to allow for compensation based on an objective criterion while taking account of the expenses incurred by the right-holder, such as the costs of identification and research'.

and through duties of care imposed upon them by the legislator. The latter category might be seen as including any notice-and-action schemes, to the extent that these impose duties on intermediaries that must be abided by if immunity is to be attained and liability therefore avoided.

But what shape may such obligations take? What measures might intermediaries be obliged to adopt for the protection of copyright? According to Article 3 of the Enforcement Directive, any 'measures, procedures and remedies necessary to ensure the enforcement of intellectual property rights' shall be 'fair and equitable and shall not be unnecessarily complicated or costly, or entail unreasonable time-limits or unwarranted delays'. Paragraph 2 elaborates further: 'Those measures, procedures and remedies shall also be effective, proportionate and dissuasive and shall be applied in such a manner as to avoid the creation of barriers to legitimate trade and to provide for safeguards against their abuse.'

Peguera and Husovec suggest that these instructions are intended to implement the overarching principles of proportionality and reasonableness.[176] Unhelpfully of course, the web of conflicting requirements they set out, despite sounding sensible in theory, doesn't offer any great foothold for application into practice. It does however narrow the scope of the possible obligations somewhat, by indicating the golden mean that any measures in pursuit of copyright enforcement should strive to abide by – even while failing to help actually locate that mean. Husovec interprets:

> EU Member States are free to create their own requirements for injunctions against intermediaries only within a certain room that is limited by the *minimal standard* of 'effective and dissuasive measures' and the *maximal ceiling* set by [the remaining requirements of] Article 3 of the Enforcement Directive. It remains to be seen how big this room for the Member States is and how close the minimal standard and maximal standard actually are.[177]

If no other help is provided, then greater legal certainty on the precise parameters of permissible injunctions can at least gradually be achieved through interpretative case law. The same conclusion should hold true of obligations imposed through duties of care, including in particular notice-and-take-down schemes.

Of course, this is precisely how the evolution of the EU rules in the area has proceeded: through the case law of the CJEU. Before we move on to examine this however, one very significant source of guidance provided by

176. M Husovec & M Peguera, 'Much Ado about Little: Privately Litigated Internet Disconnection Injunctions' (2015) 46(1) International Review of Intellectual Property and Competition Law (IIC) 10.
177. M Husovec, 'Injunctions against Innocent Third Parties: The Case of Website Blocking' (2013) 4(2) Journal of Intellectual Property, Information Technology and Electronic Commerce Law (JIPITEC) 116.

the legislator for the elucidation of the opaque commands on Article 3 must be analysed: Article 15 of the E-Commerce Directive, by far the most important provision in the current EU legal framework on the permissible scope of the obligations of internet intermediaries.

2.2.7 Article 15 of the E-Commerce Directive: More Concrete Guidance

Article 15 of the E-Commerce Directive comprises two main provisions. The first, and most important, contains a limitation on the permissible scope of obligations that may be imposed by the Member States on internet intermediaries. This helps give concrete meaning to the vaguer edicts of Article 3 of the Enforcement Directive. The second gives two examples of measures that may be required of intermediaries.

2.2.7.1 No General Obligation to Monitor

A significant limitation to the permissible scope of the measures that can be imposed on intermediaries for the enforcement of copyright is introduced by Article 15(1) of the E-Commerce Directive. This prohibits Member States from imposing general obligations on intermediaries, when providing the services covered by the three safe harbours of Article 12 to 14, to monitor the information which they transmit or store or general obligations actively to seek facts or circumstances indicating illegal activity. In this way, an exception (with regard to the type of measure) to the exceptions (concerning injunctive relief and duties of care) to the exceptions represented by the safe harbours is introduced.

The key term in this provision is the word 'general'. Recital 47 of the E-Commerce Directive indicates what might qualify as a 'general monitoring obligation', by contrasting such obligations with monitoring obligations imposed in a 'specific case' that are issued 'by national authorities in accordance with national legislation'.

What does this mean for Member States seeking to impose obligations on intermediaries for the enforcement of copyright? At which point does a monitoring obligation cross the line from 'specific' into 'general'? Riordan suggests that '[m]onitoring is "general" when it is a systematic arrangement requiring random or universal inspection, rather than relating to individual notified instances — for example, judicial or administrative orders requiring monitoring of "a specific site during a given period of time" to prevent "specific" tortious activity'.[178] This offers a good starting point, but for practical implementation greater granularity is necessary. The challenge here

178. J Riordan, *The Liability of Internet Intermediaries* (PhD thesis, University of Oxford 2013, forthcoming Oxford University Press 2016) 85.

relates to the achievement of a balance between too aggressive and too lax an enforcement of IPRs. Balefully, Advocate General Jääskinen compared solving this problem to 'Odysseus' journey between the two monsters of Scylla and Charybdis'.[179]

The CJEU first applied itself to this juridical conundrum in *L'Oréal v. eBay.*[180] The case tackled the tricky question of the permissible scope of measures intended to prevent future infringements of IPRs. As indicated above, this is a huge bone of contention within the intermediary liability debate. While *L'Oréal* itself concerned trademarks, the conclusions it reached would apply in cases of copyright as well.

In its judgment, the Court, referring back to Article 18 of the E-Commerce Directive and Recital 24 of the Enforcement Directive, accepted that preventive measures are certainly, in the abstract, permissible. At the same time, it cautioned that such measures 'must also observe the limitations arising from [the Enforcement Directive] and from the sources of law to which that directive refers'. Two main such limitations exist. For one, in view of Article 3 of the Enforcement Directive, the court issuing the injunction must ensure that the measures laid down do not create barriers to legitimate trade. This means that it cannot 'have as its object or effect a general and permanent prohibition on the selling' of IP-protected items.[181] For another, Article 15 of the E-Commerce Directive[182] means that measures imposed on intermediaries 'cannot consist in an active monitoring of all the data of each of its customers in order to prevent any future infringement of intellectual property rights via that provider's website'. According to the Court, this also accords with the demands of Article 3 of the Enforcement Directive, as a general monitoring obligation would not respect the conditions of fairness, proportionality and affordability. The decision shows the way in which the provisions of Article 3 of the Enforcement Directive and Article 15 of the E-Commerce Directive are entangled, with the latter providing an elaboration on the more general provisions of the former.

The *L'Oréal* court provides two examples of measures that fit this rather tight bill: the suspension of the perpetrator of the infringement of IPRs in order to prevent further infringements of that kind by the same person in respect of the same right and the adoption of measures to make it easier to identify users. The Court states that these suggestions are non-exhaustive.

In identifying these two possible solutions, the Court drew clear inspiration from the analysis of the case provided by AG Jääskinen. In his Opinion and in keeping with his interpretation concession as to the possibility of a limited kind of 'future knowledge', the AG made a

---

179. Opinion of Advocate General Jääskinen, C-129/14 PPU, *Zoran Spasic,* 2 May 2014, para. 171.
180. CJEU, C-324/09, *L'Oréal v. eBay International,* 12 July 2011.
181. CJEU, C-324/09, *L'Oréal v. eBay International,* 12 July 2011, paras 138-140.
182. See also Art. 2(3) of the Enforcement Directive.

distinction between 'an injunction against the intermediary to prevent any further infringements of a trade mark', which should be excluded, and 'injunctions against the intermediary requiring not only the prevention of the continuation of a specific act of infringement but also the prevention of repetition of the same or a similar infringement in the future', which do not challenge EU law. The AG suggested a rule of thumb for identifying the limit to the scope of permissible injunctions in what he called a 'double requirement of identity'. According to this, injunctions should be permissible where they are targeted at the prevention of an infringement of the same IPR by the same infringing third party. Such a confinement is achieved by the first measure of suspension. The AG follows this suggestion up by noting that 'reasonable measures to reveal the true identity of a user hiding behind several user identifications may be required from the service provider: this would not constitute an obligation of general monitoring forbidden by Article 15(1) of [the E-Commerce Directive] but an acceptable obligation of specific monitoring'. This stipulation translates into the Court's second proposed measure concerning identification. Here, caution is necessary however, given that, as the Court acknowledges, such identification measures might conflict with the EU's data protection rules. With this in mind, the Court observes that the case at hand concerns customer-sellers operating in the course of trade, who must be clearly identifiable. The same measures would therefore logically be ruled out in cases where end-users' activity is limited to private matters.[183] In either case, measures necessitating general monitoring that could run afoul of Article 15 of the E-Commerce Directive should be excluded.[184] For example, requiring that the intermediary proactively attempt to hunt out cases of such 'double identity' would require monitoring innocent bystanders and thereby clearly also tip the scales into the realm of 'unfair'.

In this way, two types of measures that may – depending on circumstances – be imposed on intermediaries are provided. What kind of measures would be excluded? In the subsequent twin *SABAM* cases, *Scarlet*[185] and *Netlog*,[186] the CJEU examined the question of injunctions ordering the implementation of filtering technology.[187] While *Scarlet* concerned an internet access provider, *Netlog* was about a hosting intermediary. In both

183. CJEU, C-324/09, *L'Oréal v. eBay International,* 12 July 2011, para. 142.
184. B Clark & M Schubert, 'Odysseus between Scylla and Charybdis? The ECJ Rules in *L'Oréal v eBay*' (2011) 6(12) Journal of Intellectual Property Law & Practice 880.
185. CJEU, C-70/10, *Scarlet Extended SA v. Société belge des auteurs, compositeurs et éditeurs SCRL (SABAM)*, 24 November 2011.
186. CJEU, C-360/10, *Belgische Vereniging van Auteurs, Componisten en Uitgevers CVBA (SABAM) v. Netlog NV*, 16 February 2012.
187. In general, the term filtering may be said to apply to content-control software applications designed to automatically block the display or downloading of selected material on a web browser or other internet application. See: Council of Europe, 'Report by the Group of Specialists on human rights in the information society (MC-S-IS) on the use and impact of technical filtering measures for various types of content in the online environment', CM(2008)37 add, 26 February 2008.

cases, the Court concluded that the filtering system requested would require the active monitoring of all the data relating to all the intermediary's users in order to prevent any future infringement of copyright. It therefore found that any such injunction would necessitate general monitoring and would therefore be prohibited under Article 15(1) of the E-Commerce Directive.

What this means for filtering has engendered some doubt. Both the *Scarlet* and *Netlog* injunctions required the installation of a filtering mechanism 'for all [the intermediary's] customers, in abstracto and as a preventive measure, exclusively at the cost of that ISP and for an unlimited period, a system for filtering all electronic communications, both incoming and outgoing, passing via its services'. There were strikingly broad: as the AG put it they would have applied 'systematically and universally, permanently and perpetually'. As such, their scope of both was very general with regard to three different perspectives: *ratione temporis* ('… for an unlimited period …'), *ratione materiae* ('… all electronic communications, both incoming and outgoing …') and *ratione personae* ('… for all its customers …').[188]

Commentators have questioned whether narrowed filtering mechanisms might be permissible.[189] The Commission has in fact opined that 'if filtering techniques had become flawless and costless, the need for a prohibition on imposing a general monitoring obligation would have become obsolete'.[190] Yet this seems unconvincing: although improved filtering technology would certainly help bring filtering better into line with some the guidelines of Article 3 of the Enforcement Directive, especially as concerns the mitigation of costs, delays and over- and under-blocking affecting fairness and effectiveness, these matters should be seen as separate to the more exacting general monitoring prohibition.

In that regard, it should be noted that the Court's analysis in *Scarlet* and *Netlog* largely ignored the temporal generality of the discussed injunctions, focusing instead on the identification of infringements among all of the electronic communications (in the *Scarlet* case on mere conduits) or all of the files stored on its servers (in the *Netlog* case on hosting) of all the intermediaries' users. And indeed, by the very definition of its functionality, no filtering mechanism can shake off its quintessential generality *ratione materiae* and *ratione personae*: as AG Villalón Cruz noted in his Opinion on *Scarlet*, filtering is of a dual character, combining monitoring with the blocking or removal of content. In simple terms, filtering consists of the processing a stream (i.e., a sequence of data elements) in order to produce

188. CJEU, Opinion of AG Cruz Villalón, case C-70/10, *Scarlet Extended SA v. Société belge des auteurs, compositeurs et éditeurs SCRL (SABAM)* 14 April 2011, paras 53-59 and 106.
189. S Kulk & F Borgesius, 'Filtering for Copyright Enforcement in Europe after the Sabam Cases' (2012) 34(11) European Intellectual Property Review 791.
190. Commission Staff Working Paper, 'Online Services, Including E-Commerce, in the Single Market', SEC(2011) 1641 final, 11 January 2012, 50.

another stream:[191] the separation of the chaff of infringing content among the grain of lawful information. The monitoring involved, therefore, must at least be general enough to affect some non-infringing content or users – usually indeed more than the infringing ones. In the words of the AG, in order to 'be effective, a filtering system has to be systematic, universal and progressive'.[192] This would suggest that, at most, the only truly 'narrower' filtering measure that might be permissible under Article 15(1) of the E-Commerce Directive would be filtering that is limited to the submissions of a pre-identified sub-group from among all of an intermediary's users, e.g., users somehow labelled as particularly likely to post infringing material.

If filtering is mostly excluded, but the suspension of the perpetrator and the imposition of measures for the identification of the perpetrator are permitted, are there any other measures in between these two options that would be permissible? If the objectionable part of filtering is the monitoring it necessarily entails, logically, duties to suppress specific and clearly pre-identified content that has been found to contain illicit information should be deemed acceptable. Indeed, this conclusion should follow naturally for the requirement of the removal or the blocking of content as part of the notice-and-take-down scheme of Article 14 of the E-Commerce Directive. Insightfully, in *Scarlet,* AG Cruz Villalón pointed out that filtering and blocking mechanisms, although closely related to each other as to the objectives they pursue, differ essentially as to their nature and consequently carry very different legal implications.[193] It should also be noted however that a clear distinction between the mere blocking and removal of content and general monitoring cannot be made, given that even cases of targeted and therefore 'specific' blocking will often necessitate general monitoring in order that the relevant content be located and differentiated from other material. Great care is therefore needed in establishing that measures that might at first sight appear to be sufficiently 'specific' are indeed so.

A final example of a 'specific' monitoring obligation is given by the Directive's own Explanatory Memorandum. This suggests that the prohibition of general monitoring obligations would not affect the 'possibility of a court or law enforcement agency requesting a service provider to monitor, for instance, a specific site during a given period of time, in order to prevent or [fight] specific illegal activity'.[194] This suggestion is however of controvertible logic. At the very least the general or specific nature of such monitoring

191. See Wikipedia entry on 'Filter (software)'.

192. CJEU, Opinion of AG Cruz Villalón, case C-70/10, *Scarlet Extended SA v. Société belge des auteurs, compositeurs et éditeurs SCRL (SABAM)* 14 April 2011, para. 48.

193. CJEU, Opinion of AG Cruz Villalón, case C-70/10, *Scarlet Extended SA v. Société belge des auteurs, compositeurs et éditeurs SCRL (SABAM)* 14 April 2011, para. 46.

194. Explanatory Memorandum to the Proposal for a European Parliament and Council Directive on certain legal aspects of electronic commerce in the internal market, COM(1998) 586 final, 18 November 1998.

would depend on the circumstances: if the 'specific site' in question were to be a blog of a single suspected infringer that probably should be considered sufficiently targeted. However, if e.g., an entire social networking site, such as reddit, Pinterest or Facebook, where to be placed under such scrutiny, it is unclear how that could qualify as anything but 'general'.

2.2.7.2 Notification to the Authorities

Monitoring obligations are not the only kind of measures that can be imposed on intermediaries for the termination or prevention of third party copyright infringement. The second paragraph of Article 15 makes another suggestion, in the form of notification of suspected infringements using their services to the authorities. According to that provision, obligations may be imposed on intermediaries that require them to: a) promptly inform the competent public authorities of alleged illegal activities undertaken or information provided by recipients of their service; or b) to communicate to the competent authorities, at their request, information enabling the identification of recipients of their service with whom they have storage agreements. This sits well with Article 8(1)(d) of the Enforcement Directive, according to which, in the context of proceedings concerning an infringement of an IPR and in response to a justified and proportionate request of the claimant, Member States must ensure that the competent judicial authorities may order that information on the origin and distribution networks of services which infringe copyright be provided by any person who was found to be providing services used in infringing activities on a commercial scale – thus also potentially including internet intermediaries.

Significantly, in the search for such information, particular caution should be had as regards the handling of personal data: in accordance with Article 1(5) of the E-Commerce Directive, that Directive (including therefore Article 15(2)) exceptionally does not apply to matters of privacy and data protection. These are instead solely governed by the Data Protection Directive[195] and the E-Privacy Directive.[196] Accordingly, as stated in Recital 14 of the E-Commerce Directive, the implementation and application of the Directive should be undertaken 'in full compliance with the principles

195. Directive 95/46/EC of the European Parliament and of the Council of 24 October 1995 on the protection of individuals with regard to the processing of personal data and on the free movement of such data [1995] OJ L281/31 (Data Protection Directive).

196. Directive 2002/58/EC of the European Parliament and of the Council of 12 July 2002 concerning the processing of personal data and the protection of privacy in the electronic communications sector (Directive on privacy and electronic communications) [2002] OJ L 201/37 (E-Privacy Directive). This directive replaced Directive 97/66/EC of the European Parliament and of the Council of 15 December 1997 concerning the processing of personal data and the protection of privacy in the telecommunications sector ([1998] OJ L24/1), subsequently repealed, which is the directive mentioned in the E-Commerce Directive.

relating to the protection of personal data, in particular as regards […] the liability of intermediaries'. Recital 40 brings this point home by encouraging 'the development and effective operation, by the different interested parties, of technical systems of protection and identification and of technical surveillance instruments made possible by digital technology' – but only within the limits laid down by data protection and privacy law. The same limitations apply to the provisions of the Copyright Directive under its Article 9 and Recital 60 and those of the Enforcement Directive under its Article 8(3)(e) and Recitals 2 and 15.

On this basis, in *Promusicae,*[197] the Court confirmed that Article 15(2) of the E-Commerce Directive cannot be interpreted as requiring that the Member States lay down an obligation to communicate personal data in order to ensure the effective protection of copyright in the context of civil proceedings.[198] At the same time however, it also stated that Article 8(3) of the Enforcement and the data protection rules to which it refers[199] do not per se preclude national law from laying down an obligation to disclose personal data either. Indeed, Article 15(1) of the E-Privacy Directive and Article 13(1) of the Data Protection Directive, to which this refers, contain an express exception in favour the protection of the rights and freedoms of others. In the absence of further specifying data, it must be concluded that this would include situations in which protection is sought in civil proceedings – and therefore also in copyright.[200] In the follow-up case of *LGS-Gesellschaft,* it was confirmed that the same conclusions apply, not only where the measures in question are ordered by a court, but also where they are imposed by national legislation in the form of duties of care triggered by an application in writing to the intermediary on the part of the right-holder.[201] It would therefore seem that EU data protection law does not provide sufficient guidance in this area.

2.2.7.3 Injunctions versus Duties of Care

It should be noted that, although the relevant CJEU case law, limited as it is by the context of the questions referred, focuses primarily on obligations imposed by courts by means of injunctive orders,[202] Article 15(1) of the E-Commerce Directive applies to measures imposed through any kind of

197. CJEU, C-275/06, *Promusicae*, 29 January 2008, para. 58.
198. CJEU, C-275/06, *Promusicae*, 29 January 2008, paras 58-59.
199. Especially important to consider in this regard are Art. 15(1) of the E-Privacy Directive and Art. 13(1) of the Data Protection Directive.
200. CJEU, C-275/06, *Promusicae*, 29 January 2008, paras 50-55.
201. CJEU, C-557/07, *LSG-Gesellschaft zur Wahrnehmung von Leistungsschutzrechten GmbH v. Tele2 Telecommunication GmbH*, 19 February 2009, paras 14, 27 and 29.
202. *LGS-Gesellschaft* is the only case to date that refers to duties imposed by statute.

legal device. At least with regard to host service providers therefore, in addition to injunctions, obligations can come into play through the duties of care mentioned in Recital 48, as well as through the take-down condition required for the enjoyment of the immunity ensured by Article 14.

As a result of this broad applicability, the same conclusions drawn above as to the dividing line between general and specific monitoring in injunctive relief should, for the most part, be understood as applying to duties of care as well. So, intermediaries protected by the safe harbours cannot be held liable for monetary compensation for failing to implement general monitoring measures.[203] Indeed, in this way, Article 15 should be seen as complementing Article 14 of the E-Commerce Directive, as the possibility of imposing general monitoring obligations would hollow out the notice-and-take-down regime foreseen in that provision: if a hosting provider were obliged to actively monitor its systems, it would be assumed to be aware of all illegal activity occurring on them and notice-and-take-down would be reduced to an immediate take-down obligation.[204] As a result, as already noted above, care should be taken in interpreting notice-and-take-down expansively as a notice-and-stay-down regime that creates ongoing obligations for the intermediary. This interaction between Article 15 and Article 14 also explains the hybrid subjective/objective knowledge standard of Article 14(1)(a): while the basic standard should be an objective one in line with the rules generally applicable in tort law, specifically as concerns the hosting safe harbour, limits are set by the prohibition of general monitoring obligations, such that an intermediary cannot be asked to actively seek out infringements, but may only be obliged to take down those infringements of which it has otherwise acquired awareness.

At the same time, the wording of Article 15(2) of the E-Commerce Directive does indicate that the difference in nature between injunctive orders and duties of care might mean that not all measures that may be ordered by a court or other competent authority may be imposed *ex ante* as an obligation to adopt certain behaviour proactively in the form of a condition for the avoidance of liability: the more stringent procedural guarantees offered by the former will allow measures that cannot be imposed through the latter. So, while intermediaries may be required to inform the competent authorities at their own initiative of their users' possibly illegal conduct for them to investigate, the provision of information enabling the identification of users may only be required following the request of a competent authority.[205]

203. P van Eecke, 'Online Service Providers and Liability: A Plea for a Balanced Approach' (2011) 48 Common Market Law Review 1455.
204. P van Eecke, 'Online Service Providers and Liability: A Plea for a Balanced Approach' (2011) 48 Common Market Law Review 1455.
205. C Angelopoulos, 'Filtering for Copyrighted Content in Europe' (2009) (4) IRIS plus 1.

2.3 A 'FAIR BALANCE' BETWEEN COPYRIGHT AND OTHER FUNDAMENTAL RIGHTS

What does the above framework suggest as regards European intermediary liability? The safe harbours provide definite answers, but only within the limited parameters of their conditions, while they are moreover subject to interpretation. Beyond them, the provisions on the permissible scope of obligations are the only available additional source. Yet, the general monitoring prohibition of Article 15(1) of the E-Commerce Directive only applies in favour of 'providers, when providing the services covered by Articles 12, 13 and 14'. Injunctive orders and duties of care directed against intermediaries when offering services other than mere conduit, caching and hosting accordingly stand outside the reach of the prohibition of general monitoring obligations. At the same time, the normative guidance that arises from the surrounding provisions of Articles 15(2) of the E-Commerce Directive, Article 8(3) of the Copyright Directive and Articles 3 and 11 of the Enforcement Directive, although not restricted in the same way in terms of scope, has the opposite problem of being excessively ill-defined.

In the absence of helpful input from these secondary sources of law, the CJEU has taken a step back and turned instead to the only remaining tool in its interpretative arsenal: primary EU law and in particular the law of fundamental rights. As the resultant case law has demonstrated, far broader limitations on the obligations that national law may impose on intermediaries than those that arise from the directives emerge directly from the Charter.[206]

2.3.1 Balancing Intermediary Liability in the EU

As mentioned above, in its seminal *Promusicae*[207] decision, the CJEU was called upon to clarify the EU law governing the imposition of obligations on internet intermediaries for the communication of their users' personal data for the purpose of copyright enforcement. After finding that, as already detailed, the relevant provisions in the directives did not take a position either way, the Court turned instead to the EU law of fundamental rights. On this basis, it noted that, in the circumstances of the case at issue, four fundamental rights were implicated: on the one hand, the right-holders' right to copyright, protected under Article 17(2) of the Charter as part of the fundamental right to property, as well as their right to an effective judicial protection, protected by Article 47 of the Charter; and on the other, end-users' right to the

206. It should be noted that the contents of s. 2.3 have been partly previously published in the following article: C Angelopoulos, 'Sketching the Outline of a Ghost: the Fair Balance between Copyright and Fundamental Rights in Intermediary Third Party Liability' (2015) 17(6) Info - The Journal of Policy, Regulation and Strategy for Telecommunications, Information and Media 72.

207. CJEU, C-275/06, *Promusicae*, 29 January 2008.

protection of their personal data under Article 8 of the Charter, as well as their right to a private life under Article 7 of the Charter. Given the conflicting demands of these two sets of rights, the question of how best to reconcile the requirements of their protection was brought to the fore. According to the Court, the appropriate solution lies in the pursuit of what it named a 'fair balance': where several rights and interests that stand in opposition to each other are at stake and the relevant EU law is generally stated, so that domestic courts and legislators enjoy considerable discretion in its transposition, 'the Member States must […] take care to rely on an interpretation of the directives which allows a fair balance to be struck between the various fundamental rights protected by the Community legal order'.

From this nebulous starting point, the fair balancing principle was subsequently applied to a series of intellectual property cases. Notably, this was the case even where Article 15(1) of the E-Commerce Directive would arguably have sufficed.

So, in 2012, in *Bonnier Audio*,[208] the CJEU once again went down the 'fair balance' route. The case concerned the same issue encountered in *Promusicae* and *LGS-Gesellschaft,* i.e., the legality of obligations on intermediaries to communicate end-users' personal data in the service of copyright enforcement. The Court reiterated the previous rulings' call for a fair balance – this time however it proceeded to offer a bit more interpretative substance.

Relevant in the case was the fact that the national legislation in question required, *inter alia*, that, for an obligation for the disclosure of the data in question to be imposed, there must be clear evidence of copyright infringement, the provision of the information must be likely to facilitate the investigation into that infringement and the reasons for the disclosure must outweigh any harm it might entail for others. Furthermore, the obligation was to be imposed in the Member State in question by means of a court order. On this basis, the CJEU declared that the relevant national legislation:

> 'enables the national court seised of an application for an order for disclosure of personal data, made by a person who is entitled to act, to weigh the conflicting interests involved, on the basis of the facts of each case and taking due account of the requirements of the principle of proportionality' and therefore 'must be regarded as likely, in principle, to ensure a fair balance'.

Significantly, the decision confirms the importance of judicial oversight, as well as the need for balancing to be grounded in a case-by-case appraisal.[209] While still therefore far from a complete rule on the

208. CJEU, C-461/10, *Bonnier Audio,* 19 April 2012.
209. This conclusion is also in line with Recital 17 of the Enforcement Directive, according to which '[t]he measures, procedures and remedies provided for in this Directive should

circumstances under which injunctions may be ordered that demand the provision by an intermediary of its users' personal data and although clearly offering no guidance as to the legal standing of similar obligations imposed not as injunctions, but as duties of care, the ruling nevertheless reveals important additional pieces of the intermediary liability puzzle.

The notion of a 'fair balance' has also been applied by the European court to investigate measures for the termination or prevention of infringements. The CJEU first tiptoed in this direction in *L'Oréal.* Notably here, fair balance was only mentioned incidentally, as an additional limitation that must be considered: as explained above, the main bulk of the analysis in the ruling rested instead on Article 15 of the E-Commerce Directive. At the same time, after the two measures of end-user suspension and facilitation of the identification of the primary infringer that the Court concluded respected Article 15 had been identified, the judgment also referred briefly to *Promusicae* to note that both those and any other measure which may be ordered in the form of an injunction against an internet intermediary under the third sentence of Article 11 of the Enforcement Directive must strike a fair balance between the various rights and interests involved before it can be imposed.[210] No guidance was given on how such a fair balance might be achieved.

The subsequent *SABAM* cases provided a bit more detail. Here, after observing that the burdensome filtering injunctions in question would constitute a violation of Article 15 of the E-Commerce Directive, the Court focused primarily on exploring their implications for fundamental rights. In both cases, it was acknowledged that copyright is protected as an IPR under Article 17(2) of the Charter. At the same time, the Court stressed that that does not mean that it is inviolable and must it be absolutely protected.[211] To the contrary, the CJEU again noted that, in the context of measures adopted to protect copyright holders, national authorities and courts must strike a fair balance between the protection of that right and the protection of the fundamental rights of individuals who are affected by its enforcement.[212] In both *Scarlet* and *Netlog,* three such opposing rights were identified: the

be determined in each case in such a manner as to take due account of the specific characteristics of that case, including the specific features of each IPR and, where appropriate, the intentional or unintentional character of the infringement.'

210. *CJEU, C-324/09, L'Oréal v. eBay International*, 12 July 2011, para. 143.
211. In this regard, Art. 54 of the Charter on the prohibition of the abuse of rights is worth considering.
212. CJEU, C-70/10, *Scarlet Extended SA v. Société belge des auteurs, compositeurs et éditeurs SCRL (SABAM)*, 24 November 2011, para. 45 and case C-360/10, *Belgische Vereniging van Auteurs, Componisten en Uitgevers CVBA (SABAM) v. Netlog NV*, 16 February 2012, para. 43.

freedom of the intermediary itself to conduct a business (Article 16 of the Charter) and the rights of its customers to the protection of their personal data (Article 8 of the Charter) and their freedom to receive and impart information (Article 11 of the Charter).

On this basis, the Court went on to find that the injunctions requested in those two cases would result in a serious infringement of the Article 16 rights of the intermediaries in question, since they would require that the companies install complicated, costly and permanent computer systems at their own expense. Likewise, infringements of the end-users' rights were also substantiated. So, in *Scarlet,* the installation of the contested filtering system was found to require the systematic analysis of all content passing through the access provider's networks and the collection and identification of any users' IP (Internet Protocol) addresses from which unlawful content was sent. Those addresses were deemed by the Court to be protected personal data, as they allow those users to be precisely identified. In *Netlog,* it was the identification, systematic analysis and processing of information connected with the profiles created by its users on the host service provider's social network that would have instead been necessary. That information was also found to constitute protected personal data, as it too in principle allows those users to be identified.[213] Finally, in both cases, the filtering injunctions were found to potentially undermine end-users' freedom of information, since they could not guarantee that they could adequately distinguish between lawful and unlawful content, with the result that their introduction could lead to the blocking of perfectly legal communications. In this regard, the Court emphasised the intricate copyright rules that make it difficult for laypersons to differentiate between works that are in the public domain and those that are not, as well as the possibility that a work might have been posted online free of charge by its authors.

Finally, in 2014, in *UPC Telekabel Wien,*[214] the CJEU went one step further. The case, referred to the Luxembourg Court by the Austrian *Oberster Gerichtshof,* concerned the imposition of a so-called *Erfolgsverbot* or 'outcome prohibition'. This is a type of injunctive remedy peculiar to Austrian law that allows the courts to order the defendants to achieve a certain result without specifying the measures that should be taken for that purpose. In the material case, the injunction in question was directed against an internet access provider. This was ordered to block access for its

213. This conclusion is in complete compatibility with the definition provided in Art. 2(a) of the Data Protection Directive (Directive 95/46/EC), according to which 'personal data' shall mean any information relating to an identified or identifiable natural person, while an identifiable person is 'one who can be identified, directly or indirectly, in particular by reference to an identification number or to one or more factors specific to his physical, physiological, mental, economic, cultural or social identity'.

214. CJEU, C-314/12, *UPC Telekabel Wien GmbH v. Constantin Film Verleih GmbH,* 27 March 2014.

customers to *kino.to*, a website predominantly used to stream or download a wide range of copyright-protected films.

As the measures examined did not involve general monitoring, Article 15 was not mentioned in the judgment. Instead, referring back to Recital 3 of the Copyright Directive, which grounds the rules of copyright in the fundamental principles of law requiring the protection of property, freedom of expression and the public interest, the CJEU for the first time relied exclusively on the notion of a fair balance. That principle was here moreover explicitly identified as emanating from Article 52(1) of the Charter and the principle of proportionality.

On this basis, the fair balance schematic applied in previous cases was mapped in far greater detail. The Luxembourg Court observed that injunctions requiring the blocking of content by an internet access provider result in a conflict between three fundamental rights: (a) the right-holders' copyright; (b) the intermediary's freedom to conduct a business; and (c) the end-users' freedom of expression and information. In this context, the Court held that blocking injunctions imposed on an intermediary in the enforcement of copyright that leave the decision as to the specific measures to be employed to the intermediary itself would not involve 'unbearable sacrifices' and are therefore not precluded by EU law, as long as the intermediary is given the opportunity to avoid coercive penalties for breach of the injunction by showing that it has taken all reasonable measures. The flexibility afforded to the intermediary by the device of an 'outcome prohibition', was seen as friendly to the access provider, as it allowed it, in aiming at the desired objective, to select the measures better adapted to its resources and abilities and more compatible with other obligations or challenges that might arise.

At the same time, the CJEU also emphasised that, in choosing such a reasonable measure with which to comply with the injunctive order, the intermediary must ensure compliance with the fundamental right of internet users to freedom of information. In this regard, the Court repeated that copyright is not inviolable and warned that it is possible that measures that can achieve complete cessation of the copyright infringement while also respecting user rights might not exist. With this in mind, it concluded that a fair balance must be understood to have been struck, if the measures applied: (i) 'do not unnecessarily deprive internet users of the possibility of lawfully accessing the information available' and (ii) 'have the effect of preventing unauthorised access to protected subject-matter or, at least, of making it difficult to achieve and of seriously discouraging internet users who are using the services of the addressee of that injunction from accessing the subject-matter that has been made available to them in breach of the intellectual property right'. Whether these goals are achieved in practice was found to be a matter for the national authorities and courts to establish. Arguably, where no other fair result can be found, it must be assumed that the intermediary must opt for no action at all.

The case was a peculiar one, arising as it did from the national legal idiosyncrasy of outcome prohibitions; its effects will accordingly most likely not easily be reproduced in jurisdictions other than Austria. Even accounting for this however, the decision remains a remarkable one, if only for the ease with which it moved from requiring that a fair balance be struck by the referring court when ordering the injunction to requiring that the intermediary *itself* guarantee the protection of all involved fundamental rights, a very curious horizontal application of fundamental rights directly to a relationship between private parties.[215]

Regardless, one conclusion seems inescapable from this line of case law: helpful as all these judgments certainly are, they only shed light on the individual cases handled. For all the crisp repetition of the vague maxim of 'fair balance', no tools are provided to help identify where this balance should lie or how to find it – although in each of the above cases the Court reached a result which it proclaimed it had achieved the coveted 'fair balance', it did not provide a proper explanation as to why that was so. As Griffiths observes, it 'is difficult to escape the impression that the Court's application of the Charter […] is little more than window dressing, functioning primarily to bolster [a] prior conclusion'.[216] Consequently, currently, no common standard is discernible, leaving all intermediaries except those whose case is identical to those already adjudicated in the dark concerning their rights and obligations:[217] beyond the safe harbours, the law remains shrouded in mystery. Given the very basic nature of the primary rules this case law rests on, this is perhaps unsurprising and maybe even, for the time being, unavoidable: as AG Mazák noted in Case C-47/07 *Masdar* on an entirely different area of extra-contractual liability, 'as is generally the case with general principles of law as a legal source, until there is settled case-law on the matter discussing the concrete content of such a principle can be very much like discussing the shape of a ghost'.

How can the ghost of fair balance begin to take more concrete shape? AG Mazák's quote indicates the answer. Before turning to a detailed investigation however, below an attempt shall first be made to track the doctrine of 'fair balance' back to its legal theoretical and jurisprudential origins, in order to investigate what it might look like and where it can be found.

---

215. C Angelopoulos, 'Are Blocking Injunctions against ISPs Allowed in Europe? Copyright Enforcement in the Post-Telekabel EU Legal Landscape' (2014) 9(10) Journal of Intellectual Property Law & Practice 812.
216. J Griffiths, 'Constitutionalising or Harmonising? The Court of Justice, the Right to Property and European Copyright Law' (2013) 38(1) European Law Review 65.
217. M Husovec, 'Injunctions against Innocent Third Parties: Case of Website Blocking' (2013) 4(2) Journal of Intellectual Property, Information Technology and Electronic Commerce Law (JIPITEC) 116.

2.3.2 The Origins of Fair Balance: Balancing in Legal Theory, the CJEU and the ECHR

In the face of the considerable dismay exhibited by copyright lawyers in the wake of *Promusicae* and its spawn and the criticism they have levied against the CJEU's retreat to fundamental rights and the accompanying vagaries of fair balance, Groussot, taking a constitutional law perspective, suggests that there was nothing either surprising or obscure about the way the case was decided:[218] instead it constitutes the logical application of decades of CJEU jurisprudence. *Promusicae* might have been the first case in which IPRs were approached as fundamental rights that need to be balanced against others of their kind, but, he notes, a balancing approach has long being applied to reconcile similar conflicts.[219]

Indeed, although it does not always mean the same thing in different jurisdictions, [220] the theory of balancing enjoys near universal hegemony in contemporary fundamental rights law.[221] The notion originated in German constitutional law, before 'migrating' across the globe after World War II.[222] According to the German understanding, balancing forms part of the more comprehensive principle of proportionality (*Verhältnismässigkeitsgrundsatz*). This consists of the three sub-principles: those of (a) suitability; (b) necessity and (c) proportionality *stricto sensu* or 'balancing' (*Güterabwägung*). German legal philosopher Robert Alexy, one of the balancing's primary champions, defines the final principle of proportionality *stricto sensu* as a rule according to which 'the greater the degree of non-satisfaction of or detriment to one principle, the greater the importance of satisfying the other'.[223] This Alexy dubs the 'Law of Balancing'.[224] While necessity and suitability are concerned with what is factually possible, according to Alexy, balancing focuses on the legal possibilities. Thus, although proportionality, at least in its German conception, consists of three separate tests, balancing may be understood to constitute its essence,[225] the heart of the legal optimisation discourse.

---

218. X Groussot, 'Rock the KaZaA: Another Clash of Fundamental Rights' (2008) 45 Common Market Law Review 1745.
219. I Kisieliute, 'A "Fair Balance" between Intellectual Property Rights and Other Fundamental Rights' (Master's Thesis, Lund University 2012) 23.
220. J Bomhoff, *Balancing Constitutional Rights: the Origins and Meanings of Postwar Legal Discourse* (Cambridge University Press 2013) 6.
221. S Gardbaum, 'Limiting Constitutional Rights' (2007) 54(4) UCLA Law Review 789.
222. A Barak, *Proportionality – Constitutional Rights and their Limitations* (Cambridge University Press 2010) 185. For a table depicting the consecutive migrations of proportionality till its current world-wide popularity, see 182.
223. R Alexy, 'Balancing, Constitutional Review, and Representation' (2005) 3(4) International Journal of Constitutional Law 572.
224. R Alexy, *A Theory of Constitutional Rights* (Oxford University Press 2002) 102.
225. W Sauter, 'Proportionality in EU Law: A Balancing Act?' TILEC Discussion Paper No. 2013-003, 25 January 2013; X Groussot, 'Rock the KaZaA: Another Clash of Fundamental Rights' (2008) 45 Common Market Law Review 1745.

It should be emphasised that in legal theoretical circles balancing remains a controversial notion. Greer summarises the considerable harsh criticism hurled against it: balancing, he explains, is viewed as 'an irrational and illegitimate renunciation of law in favour of a largely arbitrary judicial discretion, difficult to justify according to the ideals of democracy, respect for human rights, and the rule of law and therefore, ripe for elimination from the legal process'.[226] Put plainly, the argument is that balancing is incapable of consistent application. Habermas leads the opposition, opining that '[b]ecause there are no rational standards here, weighing takes place either arbitrarily or unreflectively, according to customary standards and hierarchies'.[227] According to this view, the very concept of 'rights' is incompatible with the idea that they might be outweighed by counterbalancing factors: rights must be absolute or they are deprived of their normative strength, reduced to mere factors among many others that decision-makers must consider.[228] Habermas again: '[f]or if in cases of collision *all* reasons can assume the character of policy arguments, then the fire wall erected in legal discourse by a deontological understanding of legal norms and principles collapses'.[229]

Despite these considerations, balancing shall be the approach espoused in this book. For one thing, given that both the CJEU and the ECHR have embraced the notion of a 'fair balance' as the solution to the problems of intermediary liability, from a purely doctrinal point of view, the academic disagreements surrounding the suitability of the doctrine are immaterial: it is not the purpose of this book to second-guess existing harmonising doctrine, but simply to identify a solution for European intermediary liability that respects the current guidelines as carved out to date by Europe's highest courts. After all, some pragmatism is necessary here: while concerns regarding the normative value of human rights might be relevant when these are pitted against the public interest, when they conflict with each other, a way out must somehow be found. Moreover, specifically from the perspective of the substantive harmonisation of intermediary accessory copyright liability, balancing has another advantage: as shall be shown in Chapter 4, the language of balancing is also employed in the national tort law systems of Europe to resolve legal conflicts between private individuals. By moving towards a balance-based solution therefore, the CJEU is arguably, not merely aiming at the enforcement of fundamental rights within EU law, but

226. S Greer, '"Balancing" and the European Court of Human Rights: A Contribution to the Habermas-Alexy Debate' (2004) 63(2) Cambridge Law Journal 413.
227. J Habermas, *Between Facts and Norms* (Polity Press 1996) 259.
228. E Barendt, 'Balancing Freedom of Expression and Privacy: The Jurisprudence of the Strasbourg Court' (2009) 1 Journal of Media Law 49.
229. J Habermas, *Between Facts and Norms* (Polity Press 1996) 258.

indirectly inching towards the formulation of European tort norms, at least as regards application to this one well-confined area of law.[230]

2.3.2.1 'Fair Balance' in CJEU Case Law

From its national law origins, the principle of proportionality eventually jumped into the European arena, where it has evolved into one the core general principles of EU law. After some tentative exploration of the concept in a series of CJEU judgments in the 1950s and 1960s, the main breakthrough occurred in the 1970 case *Internationale Handelsgesellschaft* (also known as *Solange I*).[231] This involved a challenge by the German Federal Constitutional Court to the supremacy of EEC law that allegedly violated a human right protected on the national level by the German Constitution. There, AG Dutheillat de Lamonthe demonstrated, by making reference to the Treaty and to preceding CJEU case law, that the principle of proportionality had roots in Community law. The Court subsequently followed suit. By means of this approach, proportionality testing emerged, alongside the recognition of fundamental rights as general principles of the EU, as a legal mechanism that allows EU law to avoid national constitutional review, through the reconciliation of fundamental rights with the principle of supremacy.[232] Significantly, these origins indicate proportionality's dual objective both as an instrument of internal market integration and as a tool for the protection of individual fundamental rights.[233]

Eventually, with the adoption of the Charter, the principle of proportionality was officially enshrined in Article 52:

> Any limitation on the exercise of the rights and freedoms recognised by this Charter must be provided for by law and respect the essence of those rights and freedoms. Subject to the principle of proportionality, limitations may be made only if they are necessary and genuinely meet objectives of general interest recognised by the Union or the need to protect the rights and freedoms of others.

The provision confirms that fundamental rights are not envisioned by the European legislator as absolute, but may be limited, and that proportionality testing is the correct tool with which to assess whether such limitations are justified.[234] Stone Sweet and Matthews note the significance of the integration of the principle of proportionality into EU law:

---

230. This question shall be revisited below, see Ch. 4, para. 4.6.
231. CJEU, C-11/70, *Internationale Handelsgesellschaft mbH v. Einfuhr- und Vorratsstelle für Getreide und Futtermittel*, 17 December 1970.
232. W Sauter, 'Proportionality in EU Law: A Balancing Act?' TILEC Discussion Paper No. 2013-003, 25 January 2013.
233. J Jans, 'Proportionality Revisited' (2000) *Legal Issues of Economic Integration* 239.
234. S de Vries, 'Balancing Fundamental Rights with Economic Freedoms According to the European Court of Justice' (2013) 9(1) Utrecht Law Review 169.

> After the consolidation of the ECJ's 'constitutional' doctrines of supremacy and direct effect, the emergence of proportionality balancing as a master technique of judicial governance is the most important institutional innovation in the history of European legal integration.[235]

How does Article 52 approach the imposition of limitations on rights? The provision contains three different elements: (a) a procedural requirement ('must be provided for by law'); (b) two possible categories of justification ('objectives of general interest recognised by the Union or the need to protect the rights and freedoms of others'); and (c) three interlinked substantive justification tests on the balancing between rights and their limitations ('principle of proportionality', 'respect the essence of those rights and freedoms', 'made only if they are necessary').[236]

What is the reach of the provision at the EU level? Importantly, Article 51(1) of the Charter complements Article 52 by limiting the fundamental rights review of Member States' action to areas within the scope of EU law:

> 1. The provisions of this Charter are addressed to the institutions and bodies of the Union with due regard for the principle of subsidiarity and to the Member States only when they are implementing Union law. They shall therefore respect the rights, observe the principles and promote the application thereof in accordance with their respective powers.
> 2. This Charter does not establish any new power or task for the Community or the Union, or modify powers and tasks defined by the Treaties.

This limitation should be properly appreciated: the Lisbon treaty has not transformed fundamental rights into free-standing tools that can be used to review national law in all situations, but keeps them carefully fettered to EU competence.[237]

In the meantime, the case law has continued to flesh out the relevant concepts. In the 1988 *Wachauf* judgment, the Court ruled that the Member States must respect fundamental rights when enacting legislation in transposition of Community law or, more generally, when they deal with subject matter governed by EU law.[238] This clearly plants the seeds of fundamental rights review that later resurfaced in *Promusicae*. The CJEU elaborated:

235. A Stone Sweet & J Matthews, 'Proportionality Balancing and Global Constitutionalism' (2009) 47 Columbia Journal of Transnational Law 72.
236. S Peers & S Prechal, 'Article 52 – Scope and Interpretation of Rights and Principles' in S Peers, T Hervey, J Kenner & A Ward, *The EU Charter of Fundamental Rights: A Commentary* (Hart Publishing 2014) 1470-1486.
237. X Groussot, L Pech & G Thor Petursson, 'The Reach of EU Fundamental Rights on Member State Action after Lisbon' in S de Vries, U Bernitz & S Weatherill, *The Protection of Fundamental Rights after Lisbon* (Hart Publishing, Oxford 2013) 97.
238. CJEU, C-5/88, *Wachauf v. Bundesamt für Ernährung und Forstwirtschaft*, 13 July 1989.

> [t]he fundamental rights recognised by the Court are not absolute […], but must be considered in relation to their social function. Consequently, restrictions may be imposed on the exercise of those rights […] provided that those restrictions in fact correspond to objectives of general interest pursued by the Community and do not constitute, with regard to the aim pursued, a disproportionate and intolerable interference, impairing the very substance of those rights.

Thus, fundamental rights, being non-absolute,[239] can be restricted as long as proportionality is respected. But how may a right be limited while its substance is left unaffected? The only conclusion can be that the answer must lie within the right itself: in the investigation of that very substance.[240]

The 2003 *Schmidberger* case confirmed this introspective focus, whilst shifting towards a balancing terminology. The case concerned a clash between the principle of the free movement of goods and the constitutional right of freedom of expression and assembly. The Court, after accepting the non-absoluteness of the latter two freedoms, concluded that:

> the exercise of those rights may be restricted, provided that the restrictions in fact correspond to objectives of general interest and do not, taking account of the aim of the restrictions, constitute disproportionate and unacceptable interference, impairing the very substance of the rights guaranteed.

On this basis, it then declared that 'the interests involved must be weighed having regard to all the circumstances of the case in order to determine whether a fair balance was struck between those interests'.[241] Thus, the Court seems to pass over the first and second elements of proportionality (presumably assuming the suitability and necessity of the measure) to focus exclusively on the final element of proportionality *sensu stricto*: the achievement of a fair balance.[242] Proportionality, always a

---

239. Under the ECHR, four rights exist which are absolute in the sense that their restriction or suspension can never be justified, even in a state of emergency: the prohibition of torture under Art. 3; the prohibition of slavery and forced labour under Art. 4; the right not to be convicted for conduct which was not an offence at the time it occurred under Art. 7; and the right not to have a heavier penalty imposed for an offence than the one applicable at the time the offence was committed, also under Art. 7. See S Greer, *The Margin of Appreciation: Interpretation and Discretion under the European Convention on Human Rights* (Council of Europe Publishing 2000) 27. Arguably, although the set-up of the EU's Charter is such that these rights are formally also subject to the limitations provision of Art. 52(1) of the Charter, in view of the need to interpret the Charter in compliance with the Convention, they should be understood as absolute in that context as well. No absolute rights are relevant however to the topic of this book.
240. I Kisieliute, 'A 'Fair Balance' between Intellectual Property Rights and Other Fundamental Rights' (Master's Thesis, Lund University 2012) 23.
241. CJEU, C-112/00, *Schmidberger,* 12 June 2003.
242. A similar approach had been taken much earlier in CJEU, C-44/79, *Hauer v.* Land Rheinland-Pfalz, 13 December 1979, para. 30. See for an analysis, W van Gerven, 'The

flexible tool,[243] is in this way parsed down in fundamental rights cases to a mere balancing exercise. This also seems to be precisely the approach favoured in the copyright case law: in *Telekabel,* for example, the Court mentioned 'the requirement that a fair balance be found, in accordance with Article 52(1), in fine, of the Charter', thus apparently equating 'fair balance' with the 'principle of proportionality' mentioned in that provision.

More importantly, in *Schmidberger,* the CJEU also indicated how the investigation of the substance of fundamental rights and therefore the location of the fair balance between them should take place: on a case-by-case basis so that due regard can be given to the individual circumstances at hand. According to the Court, 'the interests involved must be weighed having regard to all the circumstances of the case in order to determine whether a fair balance was struck between those interests'. Fair balance, it would seem, may not be precisely diagnosed on an abstract theoretical level: the centre of balance will differ from case to case. This conclusion is in perfect accordance with the non-absolute nature of the rights in conflict and their equal normative power: no fundamental right may be said to outflank another in absolute terms,[244] but, instead, either may take precedence over the other, depending on the particular circumstances of the case. There is no stable hierarchy of fundamental rights.

An informative summary of the Court's approach to the question of limitations on fundamental rights and the principle of fair balance was given more recently by the Advocate General in his Opinion on *Zoran Spasic,* as follows:

> with certain exceptions, fundamental rights do not constitute unfettered prerogatives and may be restricted, provided that the restrictions in fact correspond to objectives of general interest pursued by the measure in question and that they do not constitute, with regard to the objectives

---

Effect of Proportionality on the Actions of Member States of the European Community: National Viewpoints from Continental Europe' in E Ellis (ed.), *The Principle of Proportionality in the Law of Europe* (Hart Publishing 1999) 37.

243. It should be noted that in general the principle proportionality has no fixed substantial form within the case law of the Court. Van Gerven observes that proportionality in CJEU case law sometimes presents as a three-pronged test and sometimes is pruned back to a two-pronged one, skipping on the balancing element. (See: W van Gerven, 'The Effect of Proportionality on the Actions of Member States of the European Community: National Viewpoints from Continental Europe' in E Ellis (ed.), *The Principle of Proportionality in the Law of Europe* (Hart Publishing 1999) 37). Jacobs in another essay in the same edited collection, concludes that this flexibility is precisely one of proportionality's advantages as a tool of judicial review. See F G Jacobs, 'Recent Developments in the Principle of Proportionality in European Community Law' in E Ellis (ed.), *The Principle of Proportionality in the Law of Europe* (Hart Publishing 1999) 21.

244. S Peers & S Prechal, 'Article 52 – Scope and Interpretation of Rights and Principles' in S Peers, T Hervey, J Kenner & A Ward, *The EU Charter of Fundamental Rights: A Commentary* (Hart Publishing 2014) 1479.

> pursued, a disproportionate and intolerable interference which infringes upon the very substance of the rights guaranteed. The Court therefore seeks, in its case-law, to strike a fair balance between, on the one hand, the various rights and interests and, on the other, the fundamental rights and economic freedoms, and in carrying out that balancing, it also takes into account the objectives underlying the limitation of a fundamental right.[245]

Moving on, it should be noted that traditional CJEU balancing jurisprudence mainly concerned conflicts between fundamental rights and other provisions of EU law. This changed with the 2003 *Lindqvist* judgment, which applied a similar logic to a conflict between different fundamental rights that stood in opposition to each other – in that case the freedom of expression and freedom of religion of Mrs Lindqvist, as against the right to privacy of others. After confirming once again that domestic authorities must interpret their national rules in a manner consistent with the provisions of EU law and, in so doing, avoid interpretations which would be in conflict with fundamental rights or other general principles of EU law, including the principle of proportionality, the Court went on to specify that domestic authorities and courts responsible for applying the national legislation implementing EU directives must ensure a 'fair balance between the rights and interests in question, including the fundamental rights protected by the Community legal order'. The Court moreover specified that:

> Thus, it is, rather, at the stage of the application at national level of the legislation implementing [Data Protection Directive] in individual cases that a balance must be found between the rights and interests involved.[246]

This not only recognises that a fair balance must be struck between conflicting fundamental rights, but allocates the investigation of that balance to the national authorities: it is not enough that national authorities implement and apply the provisions of the directives, they must also make sure not to violate higher legal norms in so doing. This is in line with Article 51 of the Charter mentioned above. In this regard, it is worth noting that the recognition of national discretion in applying a fair balance is remarkably similar to the 'margin of appreciation' doctrine of the European Court of Human Rights (ECtHR) that will be explored below. Accordingly, it would appear that, in adopting the fair balance doctrine, the CJEU is attempting to provide guidelines to its domestic counterparts, while staying within the bounds of its jurisdiction as a supranational court that mean that it cannot do the work of the national courts work for them.

245. Opinion of Advocate General Jääskinen, C-129/14 PPU, *Zoran Spasic,* 2 May 2014.
246. CJEU, C-101/01, *Lindqvist,* 6 November 2003.

In *Sky Österreich*, the CJEU recently confirmed the principle of fair balance as the form that the principle of proportionality takes when faced with conflicting fundamental rights and the appropriate conflict resolution mechanism for such cases:

> Where several rights and fundamental freedoms protected by the European Union legal order are at issue, the assessment of the possible disproportionate nature of a provision of European Union law must be carried out with a view to reconciling the requirements of the protection of those different rights and freedoms and a fair balance between them.[247]

In view of this, it becomes clear that, in calling for a fair balance in copyright in *Promusicae* and its progeny, the CJEU is indeed applying its settled fundamental rights case law: the pedigree of fair balance must therefore certainly be conceded. Moreover, a picture of balancing's purpose and origins as a judicial tool in the context of CJEU case law is now beginning to take shape: balancing constitutes the application of the principle of proportionality to cases of clashes between fundamental rights – it is thus revealed as the appropriate resolution mechanism for such cases of conflict and should cause no greater consternation than references to that underlying principle. It is in addition clear that, notwithstanding the perhaps impractical objections of many legal theorists, the Luxembourg Court, as well as the EU legislator, subscribe firmly to the theory of the non-absoluteness of fundamental rights, thus relegating the investigation of fair balance to the level of their application – however this non-absoluteness is not intended to take away from the normative strength of fundamental rights, but to reinforce it, by allowing for the preservation of all fundamental rights, while enabling practical solutions to their incompatibilities. Balancing is thus revealed as the process through which non-absolute rights are shuffled against each other, so that they can settle into their natural resting place, which will change in each instance depending on the particular circumstances of the individual case.

Is this conclusion sufficient? Harbo criticises the mutability of proportionality in the case law of the CJEU:

> [t]he dissection of the principle reveals that the principle has no clear or fixed substantial meaning. Given that the reason why courts adapt (*sic*) principles of law, and the proportionality principle, in particular, is to secure some kind of predictability, objectivity and thus legitimacy for their decision (and not only to fill out wholes in statutory law), this revelation is surely disturbing.[248]

---

247. CJEU, C-283/11, *Sky Österreich*, 22 January 2013.
248. T Harbo, 'The Function of the Proportionality Principle in EU Law' (2010) 16(2) European Law Journal 158.

Objections of ambiguity may thus arise as a result of the vaguely defined relationship between balancing and proportionality. Moreover, lack of consistent application also plagues balancing itself: even if it is clear what balancing is intended to achieve in the CJEU's jurisprudence, little indication is given of how it reaches its goals. Griffiths is blunt: 'the concept of the "fair balance" is, without further elucidation, vacuous and unhelpful'.[249] The enigma remains steadfast: the mere statement that a fair balance must be sought offers no information as where that balance might lie. If fair balance may only be struck in practice, how does one go about doing so?

Van Gerven suggests that, to the extent that proportionality is about weighing conflicting interests, these interests must be inventoried, whether they are legitimate or not must be determined and, to this purpose, an order of priority amongst them must be established.[250] This points the way forward. To further investigate this suggestion we shall now dig deeper into balancing's European origins in the case law of the ECtHR. This is particularly pertinent in view of the clear inspiration that the CJEU has derived from that source: not only do the Treaties,[251] as subsequently confirmed in the Charter,[252] explicitly reference the ECHR, unambiguously embracing as part of the EU *acquis*, but, also, more specifically, the concept of 'fair balance' itself can be traced back to the jurisprudence of that Court. Indeed, in *Varec,* the CJEU made the link clear itself, by referring back to the Strasbourg court: 'The European Court of Human Rights has consistently held that the adversarial nature of proceedings is one of the factors which enables their fairness to be assessed, but it may be *balanced* against other rights and interests'.[253]

Admittedly, like the CJEU, it is apparent from the case law of the ECtHR that it too is struggling to find the right formulation of the principle of proportionality and, even more so, a workable definition of balancing. It is however slightly more advanced in its analysis.

---

249. J Griffiths, 'Constitutionalising or Harmonising? The Court of Justice, the Right to Property and European Copyright Law' (2013) 38(1) European Law Review 65.
250. W van Gerven, 'The Effect of Proportionality on the Actions of Member States of the European Community: National Viewpoints from Continental Europe' in E Ellis (ed.), *The Principle of Proportionality in the Law of Europe* (Hart Publishing 1999) 37.
251. According to Art. 6(3) of the TEU, '[f]undamental rights, as guaranteed by the European Convention for the Protection of Human Rights and Fundamental Freedoms and as they result from the constitutional traditions common to the Member States, shall constitute general principles of the Union's law.'
252. According to Art. 52(3) of the Charter, in so far as the rights protected by the two documents overlap, 'the meaning and scope of those rights shall be the same as those laid down by the said Convention'. Art. 53 of the Charter further clarifies that the Charter shall not be interpreted as restricting or adversely affecting human rights and fundamental freedoms as recognised by international agreements to which the Union, the Community or all the Member States are party, including the ECHR.
253. CJEU, C-450/06, *Varec*, 14 February 2008.

2.3.2.2 'Fair Balance' in ECtHR Case Law

Proportionality is central to the ECtHR approach to the limitations of human rights. Like the CJEU, the ECHR recognises that, under certain conditions, deviation from the rights and freedoms it guarantees may be acceptable, provided that the principle of proportionality is observed. Indeed, in *Soering v. UK,* the Strasbourg Court declared that 'inherent in the whole of the Convention is a search for a fair balance between the demands of the general interest of the community and the requirements of the protection of the individual's fundamental rights'. As in CJEU jurisprudence, in the case law of the ECtHR, the precise contours of the relationship between the principle of proportionality and the principle of fair balance remain somewhat obscure. Mowbray suggests that 'fair balance' is used by the Strasbourg Court as a 'basis for assessing the proportionality of respondents' interferences with the Convention rights of applicants',[254] confirming the conclusions reached above in the EU context.

In any case, here too proportionality and fair balance take, in cases of limitations imposed on human rights, centre stage. As opposed to the Charter however, which adopts a one-size-fits-all approach to limitations in its Article 52, the ECHR addresses the question of the limitations to each right individually the body of its respective articles. Different approaches to limitations thus apply depending on the right examined. Significantly, the ECHR does not regard all its rights as non-absolute; however, it should be noted that the principle of proportionality has been used exceptionally to limit even unqualified rights.[255] Below we shall be examining the relevant jurisprudence with regard to freedom of expression and information, the right to privacy and the right to property (including copyright),[256] these being the main rights relevant to the discussion on intermediary copyright liability, as

---

254. A Mowbray, 'A Study of the Principle of Fair Balance in the Jurisprudence of the European Court of Human Rights' (2010) 10 Human Rights Law Review 289.
255. ECtHR, *Kozacioğlu v. Turkey*, application no. 2334/03, 19 February 2009.
256. As opposed to the Charter, the ECHR does not mention intellectual property, but recent case law of the Strasbourg Court makes clear that Art. 1 of Protocol 1 to the Convention should be interpreted as encompassing it. So, in *Anheuser-Busch Inc v. Portugal* (application no. 73049/01, 11 January 2007), the Court stated that, 'intellectual property as such undeniably attracts the protection of Art. 1 of Protocol No.1'. That case was relevant to trademark protection, but the idea was then repeated with regard to copyright in *Balan v. Moldova,* application no. 19247/03 29 January 2008 and *Neij and Sunde Kolmisoppi v. Sweden,* application no. 40397/12, 19 February 2013. See also L R Helfer, 'New Innovation Frontier - Intellectual Property and the European Court of Human Rights' (2008) 49 *Harvard International Law Journal* 1 and E Barendt, *Freedom of Speech* (2nd ed., Oxford University Press 2007) 247 et seq.

identified in the CJEU case law analysed above.[257] Notably, all of these are non-absolute rights, in the ECHR context as well.

How does the ECHR handle the issue of the imposition of limits on the identified rights? Article 10 of the ECHR on freedom of expression and information and Article 8 on the right to respect for private and family life are strikingly similar in their approach in this regard:[258] when an interference with either right is identified, no violation may be found subject to three standards explicitly laid down in the two provisions and subsequently developed in the case law: the interference must (i) be *prescribed by law*; (ii) pursue a *legitimate aim* (corresponding to one of those exhaustively listed in the provision);[259] and (iii) be *necessary in a democratic society*. These conditions are examined in sequence by the Court in its judgments and, with few exceptions, the breach of any will mark a violation of the Convention. As a general rule, the emphasis in the case law lies heavily on the third standard of 'necessary in a democratic society'. The Court has settled the meaning of this phrase as requiring proportionality: according to the ECtHR's established case law, the notion of necessity implies that an interference 'corresponds to "a pressing social need" and is "proportionate to the aim pursued" and [that] "the reasons given were relevant and sufficient"'.[260]

The principle of proportionality is also applied in the examination of restrictions on the protection of property under Article 1 of Protocol No. 1 of the ECHR. Paragraph 1 of that provision guarantees that '[n]o one shall be deprived of his possessions except in the public interest and subject to the conditions provided for by law and by the general principles of international law'. Paragraph 2 then goes on to state that this should not be understood as impairing, 'the right of a State to enforce such laws as it deems necessary to

257. The ECHR does not include an equivalent of the Charter's Art. 16 'freedom to conduct a business'. The right to an effective remedy shall also not be analysed here, as it was only mentioned in *Promusicae* and omitted in the later CJEU rulings under examination in this article.

258. P van Dijk et al., *Theory and Practice of the European Convention on Human Rights* (4th ed., Kluwer Law International 2006) 334.

259. In the case of Art. 8(2) of the Convention these may be 'national security, public safety or the economic wellbeing of the country, for the prevention of disorder or crime, for the protection of health or morals, or for the protection of the rights and freedoms of others', while in the case of Art. 10(2), 'national security, territorial integrity or public safety, for the prevention of disorder or crime, for the protection of health or morals, for the protection of the reputation or rights of others, for preventing the disclosure of information received in confidence, or for maintaining the authority and impartiality of the judiciary'.

260. See Concurring Opinion of Judge Loucaides in ECtHR, *Lindon, Otchakovsky-Laurens and July v. France,* applications nos. 21279/02 and 36448/02, 22 October 2007; See also, ECtHR, *Olsson v. Sweden,* application no. 10465/83, 24 March 1988; *Leander v. Sweden,* application no. 9248/81, 26 March 1987; *Berthold v. Germany*, application no. 8734/79, 25 March 1985; *Sunday Times v. the UK*, application no. 6538/74, 26 April 1979; *Handyside v. the UK*, application no. 5493/72, 7 December 1976.

control the use of property in accordance with the general interest'. In this context, the Strasbourg Court has maintained that 'a reasonable relationship of proportionality between the means employed and the aim sought to be realised' is required, meaning that 'fair balance [must be] struck between the demands of the general interest in this respect and the interest of the individual or individuals concerned'.[261] It therefore seems that, with regard to the right to property, proportionality dispenses of the first two standards of necessity and suitability and concentrates exclusively on the more substantial fair balance test.

Significantly, in the context of the ECHR, the application of the principle of proportionality is tempered by the complementary principle of the margin of appreciation.[262] Under this, Contracting States are given a certain amount of discretion in how they protect human rights. This is usually explained by the absence of any pan-European consensus on how such matters should be regulated. In particular, it has been found that Contracting States must have a broad margin of appreciation with regard to the balancing of conflicting individual interests, since such cases are delicate ones for which the ECtHR cannot provide a definitive answer.[263] In *Chassagnou*, the Court stated that:

> The balancing of individual interests that may well be contradictory is a difficult matter, and Contracting States must have a broad margin of appreciation in this respect, since the national authorities are in principle better placed than the European Court to assess whether or not there is a 'pressing social need' capable of justifying interference with one of the rights guaranteed by the Convention.[264]

However, even allowing for the margin of appreciation, the principle of proportionality will be violated where the requirements for its application in a particular case are so high as to not allow for a meaningful balancing process.[265] Accordingly, the scrutiny to which the Court will subject Contracting States will depend on the breadth of the margin of appreciation granted to them: if it is wide, the Court will be less exacting, if it is narrow, the Court will be stricter.

---

261. ECtHR, *Sporrong and Lönnroth v. Sweden*, application no. 7151/7523, 23 September 1982; *James and others v. the UK*, application no. 8793/79 21 February 1986; *AGOSI v. the UK*, application no. 9118/80, 24 October 1986.
262. ECtHR, *Handyside v. UK*, application no. 5493/72, 7 December 1976.
263. ECtHR, *Chassagnou and Others v. France [GC]*, application nos. 25088/94, 28331/95 and 28443/95, 29 April 1999; *MGN Limited v. the United Kingdom*, application no. 39401/04, 18 January 2011.
264. ECtHR, *Chassagnou and Others v. France* [GC], application nos. 25088/94, 28331/95 and 28443/95, 29 April 1999.
265. D J Harris et al., *Harris, O'Boyle & Warbrick – Law of the European Convention on Human Rights* (3rd ed., Oxford University Press 2014) 13.

How does the above framework apply to cases of opposing human rights? Barendt observes that the traditional proportionality analysis was developed in the ECHR's early case law for the resolution of challenges by applicants against limitations imposed by the State on human rights, so that the presumption is that the human rights should be respected unless one of a narrowly construct set of exceptions can be established. By contrast, in cases of conflicts of rights it is the fair balance test that is best instead applied.[266] This again is in line with the conclusions reached above with regard to EU law. The idea was first put forth by the Court in *Von Hannover,*[267] where is was found that competing non-absolute human rights have to be balanced against each other. Significantly, this case originated once again in Germany, where the national courts attempted to address the conflict between the applicant's privacy and the freedom of expression of the publishers circulating intrusive photographs of the applicant through balancing.

Is this conclusion helpful? Like the EU commentators, Barendt has called for a clarification of the circumstances in which a fair balance might be said to have been struck.[268] In the follow-up judgment of *Von Hannover (No. 2),*[269] the Court delivered. Here, the Court began by first confirming that fair balance is the right tool with which to address the matter. On this basis and in view of the fact that non-absolute rights 'deserve equal respect', the Court then observed that the outcome of an application should not, in theory, vary depending on the right with which it has been lodged with the Court. Most importantly, the Court went on to state that '[w]here the right to freedom of expression is being balanced against the right to respect for private life, the criteria laid down in the case-law that are relevant to the present case are set out below'. For this purpose, it identified the following factors: the contribution to a debate of general interest; how well known the person concerned is, the subject of the report; the prior conduct of the person concerned; the content, form and consequences of the publication; and the circumstances in which the photos were taken. This listing of factors represents a huge insight into the ECtHR's reasoning in balancing cases and an immensely helpful indication of how such weighing should be undertaken.

---

266. He contrasts such cases to those of conflicting rights of equal value, where a test that assesses the importance and scope of each right in the context of the circumstances of case is more appropriate, see E Barendt, 'Balancing Freedom of Expression and Privacy: The Jurisprudence of the Strasbourg Court' (2009) 1 Journal of Media Law 49.
267. ECtHR, *Von Hannover v. Germany,* application no. 59320/00, 24 June 2004.
268. E Barendt, 'Balancing Freedom of Expression and Privacy: The Jurisprudence of the Strasbourg Court' (2009) 1 Journal of Media Law 49.
269. ECtHR, *Von Hannover v. Germany (No. 2),* application nos. 40660/08 and 60641/08, 7 February 2012.

In *Von Hannover (No. 2)'s* sister judgment of *Axel Springer,*[270] delivered on the same day, the Court solidified this new line of case law, by following the same approach and listing a second group of criteria, strikingly similar to the first, though, intriguingly, not identical. This time included were the contribution to a debate of general interest; how well known the person concerned is; the subject of the report; the prior conduct of the person concerned; the method of obtaining the information and its veracity; the content, form and consequences of the publication; and the severity of the sanction imposed. In keeping with the principle of the margin of appreciation, in both cases the Court concluded that where 'the balancing exercise has been undertaken by the national authorities in conformity with the criteria laid down in the Court's case-law, the Court would require strong reasons to substitute its view for that of the domestic courts'.

It should always be understood that in such cases, it will not be the rights and interests themselves in abstract terms undergoing the balancing process, but the circumstances of the case under examination.[271] As a result, as in the CJEU case law, here too definitional balancing is clearly rejected:

> [t]he test of whether an interference was necessary in a democratic society cannot be applied in absolute terms. On the contrary, the Court must take into account various factors, such as the nature of the competing interests involved and the degree to which those interests require protection in the circumstances of the case.[272]

What does the above analysis tell us about ECHR balancing? The two cases represent a huge step in the right direction. As Barendt notes, through this criteria-based approach, balancing, contrary to its detractors' accusations, need not be unpredictable. Instead, it is transformed into a tool for cogent practical discourse that enables a detailed and coherent comparative exercise between the requirements of conflicting rights that can lead to an ultimate a rational concluding judgment on the facts of the case.[273] If it is sometimes difficult to follow the reasoning of a ruling, that must be attributed to bad application of the test, not to the insufficiencies of the test itself.[274]

---

270. ECtHR, *Axel Springer v. Germany*, application no. 39954/08, 7 February 2012.
271. D J Harris et al., *Harris, O'Boyle & Warbrick – Law of the European Convention on Human Rights* (2nd ed., Oxford University Press 2009) 354-355.
272. ECtHR, *Neij and Sunde Kolmisoppi v. Sweden,* application no. 40397/12, 19 February 2013.
273. R Alexy, 'Constitutional Rights, Balancing and Rationality' (2003) 16(2) Ratio Juris 131; J Griffiths, 'Constitutionalising or Harmonising? The Court of Justice, the Right to Property and European Copyright Law' (2013) 38(1) European Law Review 65. See also, S Smet, *Resolving Conflicts between Human Rights: A Legal Theoretical Analysis in the Context of the ECHR,* (unpublished PhD thesis, Ghent University 2014) 118.
274. E Barendt, 'Balancing Freedom of Expression and Privacy: The Jurisprudence of the Strasbourg Court' (2009) 1 Journal of Media Law 49.

2.3.3 Balancing Intermediary Liability in the ECHR

What does all of the above mean for intermediary liability? On the 20 October 2013 the ECtHR applied its new factor-infused balancing to the area of intermediary liability. The case concerned the liability of Delfi,[275] one of the most popular internet news platforms in Estonia, for defamatory comments posted by its readers on its website beneath one of its news articles. Following a complaint by the victim, Delfi removed the offensive comments, but refused to pay damages. It should be noted that, at the material time, Delfi had three mechanisms in place for dealing with inappropriate comments: a notice-and-take-down system that allowed users to flag inappropriate comments for deletion; a filtering system that automatically deleted comments that included certain obscene words; and the occasional proactive removal of comments by human agents. In addition, 'rules of comment' warned that insulting or vulgar comments would be removed. Users uploaded comments themselves, without editing or moderation by Delfi. The ECtHR was called upon to decide whether the imposition on Delfi of an obligation to take further measures to ensure that comments posted on its internet portal did not infringe the personality rights of third persons was in accordance with the guarantees set out in Article 10 of the Convention. Although the case did not concern copyright, it is worth detailed examination, as it constitutes the only instance of an elaborate application of the celebrated fair balance doctrine to intermediary liability that makes use of the ECHR new factor-based approach.

As is usual, the bulk of the Court's focus in the case rested on the familiar notion of 'necessity in a democratic society'. The Court noted that, in this context, the domestic authorities were under an obligation to strike a fair balance in the resolution of the conflict between freedom of expression and the right to respect for private life: both rights deserve equal respect and the outcome of an application should not, in principle, vary according to whether it has been lodged with the Court under Article 10 of the Convention by the publisher of an disputed article or under Article 8 of the Convention by the person who has been the subject of that article. The margin of appreciation should therefore in principle always be the same.

In this context, the Court outlined four criteria to be taken into consideration where the right to freedom of expression is balanced against the right for private life. These were:

- the context of the comments;
- the measures applied by the applicant company in order to prevent or remove defamatory comments;

275. ECtHR, *Delfi v. Estonia,* application no. 64569/09, 10 October 2013.

- the liability of the actual authors of the comments as an alternative to the applicant company's liability; and
- the consequences of the domestic proceedings for the applicant company.

A detailed analysis followed. As concerns the context of the comments, the Court noted that, in view of the intense public interest in the topic of the news article it had published and the above average number of responding comments, Delfi was expected to exercise a high degree of caution, as the context was such that there was a higher than average risk that the comments would go beyond the bounds of acceptable speech and reach the level of gratuitous insult or hate speech. The fact that Delfi was a professionally managed news portal was also seen as relevant in this regard.

As concerns the measures taken by Delfi in order to prevent or remove defamatory comments, the Court found that, while Delfi could not be said to have wholly neglected its duty to avoid causing harm to third parties, the word-based filter was easy to circumvent, meaning that, even though some of the insults or threats were deleted, others were allowed through. Likewise, while the notice-and-take-down system did result in the successful removal of defamatory comments after the victim had brought them to the attention of the applicant company, that occurred only after they had already been published. The system in place was therefore deemed insufficient to prevent harm to others. This conclusion seems to imply that if a system is not infallible, it is not sufficient, a rather curious result. In this respect, the wide audience of the comments and Delfi's dependence on advertising revenue, as well as the control Delfi exercised over the comments published were all considered to be pertinent: it was Delfi and not the victim that was in the better position to know about an article to be published, to predict the nature of the possible comments prompted by it and, above all, to take technical or manual measures to prevent defamatory statements from being made public. It was also noted, in echo of the CJEU *Telekabel* case, that Delfi could choose which measures to apply in satisfying its duty of diligence with regard to the protection of the rights of others – again, this was viewed as an important factor in reducing the severity of the interference with its freedom of expression.

The ECtHR proceeded to acknowledge that the victim could take action against the actual authors of the comments, but noted that their identity would be difficult to establish. It was therefore not convinced that measures allowing an injured party to bring a claim only against the authors of defamatory comments would have guaranteed an effective protection of the injured person's right to private life. In any case, the applicant company's choice to allow comments by non-registered users must be considered to entail an assumption of a certain responsibility for these comments. Finally, the Court observed that the applicant company was obliged to pay the affected person the equivalent of only EUR 320 in non-pecuniary damages and that this sum, in view of the fact that that the applicant was a professional operator of one of the largest internet news portals in Estonia, could by no means be considered disproportionate to the breach established by the domestic courts.

In summary, the Court found that 'the insulting and threatening nature of the comments, the fact that the comments were posted in reaction to an article published by the applicant company in its professionally-managed news portal run on a commercial basis, the insufficiency of the measures taken by the applicant company to avoid damage being caused to other parties' reputations and to ensure a realistic possibility that the authors of the comments will be held liable, and the moderate sanction imposed on the applicant company' meant that restriction on the applicant company's right to freedom of expression was justified and proportionate.

Two years later this decision was affirmed by the Grand Chamber of the ECtHR in June 2015, despite vociferous objections by the dissenting judges.[276] The Grand Chamber confirmed not only the outcome of the case, but – more importantly for our purposes – also the criteria identified by the First Section for the assessment of whether or not a fair balance has been achieved. This is the most pertinent consequence of the case: the *Delfi* results, going as they do in the complete opposite direction of Article 15 of the E-Commerce Directive and the jurisprudence of the CJEU in the *SABAM* cases, cannot be reproduced in other EU Member States without breaking EU law. However, the criteria it applies and the insights these offer to the jurisprudential method underlying fair balance that the Court took remain relevant to the analysis of the obligations of intermediaries with regard to third party copyright infringement even within the EU.

The inapplicability of the *Delfi* result to the EU is particularly evident, given that the only fundamental rights examined in the case were the right of the claimant to respect for their private life under Article 8 and the opposing freedom of impart information under Article 10 of the ECHR of the intermediary thus affected: in contrast to the CJEU case law, nothing was said about the rights of the intermediary's users, who were not represented in the dispute. More importantly yet, the case also did not concern copyright, but the much more serious wrongdoing of hate speech, a fact which cannot but have an impact on the outcome of the balancing process. Indeed, it is worth noting that the Grand Chamber accepted that notice-and-take-down schemes, if accompanied by effective procedures allowing for rapid response, can indeed in many cases function as an appropriate tool for balancing the rights and interests of all those involved. That system was

276. ECtHR, *Delfi v. Estonia* [GC], application no. 64569/09, 16 June 2015.

simply deemed inappropriate in *Delfi,* because the third-party comments under examination contained hate speech and direct threats to the physical integrity of individuals, thus tipping, due to their extreme nature, the balance in favour of the legality of the imposition of an obligation to for their removal, even without notice from the alleged victim or from third parties.[277] Finally, the moderate amount of damages that were imposed by the Estonian courts is another factor that can also not be ignored: arguably, if the ECtHR were to be faced with a case concerning a much higher penalty for the intermediary, the balance would tip the other way.

It has been suggested that the divergence between the ECtHR's ruling in *Delfi* and EU law as enshrined in the E-Commerce Directive and interpreted by the CJEU, in particular in *L'Oréal* and *Scarlet*, marks a conflict between Europe's two highest courts, awkward in view of Article 52(3) of the Charter.[278] However, it is important in this regard to remember that the in-built flexibility of the margin of appreciation recognised by the ECtHR to Contracting Parties need not be afforded by the CJEU to EU Member States in a harmonisation context. The margin of appreciation doctrine is designed for an international court called upon to take account of diverse legal and cultural traditions.[279] By contrast, the Charter should be seen as applying to the single jurisdiction of the EU, leaving no room for such a comparative perspective. As mentioned above, the EU has other mechanisms of dealing with Member State individuality, in particular the principle of subsidiarity.[280] In this regard, it should be recalled that Article 52(3) of the Charter specifically accepts that EU law may provide more extensive protection than the ECHR.[281]

---

277. Indeed, to date, no case brought before the ECtHR has examined the question of a fair balance between the protection of property and the right to freedom of expression or the privacy of end-users. The closest the Strasbourg Court has come to examining such matters was in *Neij and Sunde Kolmisoppi v. Sweden* (application no. 40397/12, 19 February 2013), where it identified a clash between the right to copyright, as protected as a property right, and the right to freedom of expression of the founders of the file-sharing website 'The Pirate Bay'. That case however did not examine users' rights. Moreover, although Sweden was found to have struck a fair balance within its margin of appreciation, factors detailing the Court's thought-process in that conclusion were not identified. As a result, the *Delfi* judgment remains the closest – although severely lacking – approximation currently available in the ECtHR case law to the balancing of intermediary obligations, as this has been approached by the CJEU.
278. G Smith, 'Who Will Sort Out the Delfi Mess?' Inforrm's Blog, 17 October 2013.
279. It is worth perhaps noting that, as a general rule, the ECtHR talks not of *the* correct balance, but 'an appropriate balance'.
280. S Peers & S Prechal, 'Article 52 – Scope and Interpretation of Rights and Principles' in S Peers, T Hervey, J Kenner & A Ward, *The EU Charter of Fundamental Rights: A Commentary* (Hart Publishing 2014) 1481.
281. S Peers & S Prechal, 'Article 52 – Scope and Interpretation of Rights and Principles' in S Peers, T Hervey, J Kenner & A Ward, *The EU Charter of Fundamental Rights: A Commentary* (Hart Publishing 2014) 1469 and 1498-1503.

2.3.4 Balancing as Legal Discourse

As Smet observes, the listing of relevant criteria in *Axel Springer, Hannover (No.2)* and *Delfi* has the advantage of providing some much needed structure to the Court's previously abstract balancing test. At the same time however, it is not easy to ignore the fact that the lists supplied differ between the three judgments, despite the great similarity in the cases examined. Moreover, in all three cases, the criteria are customised to conflicts between the freedom of the press and privacy and are inapplicable in other contexts.[282] They therefore offer little guidance as to how other human rights conflicts should be resolved: presumably the Court would pull another list of doubtless relevant, but entirely unpredictable criteria out of its judicial hat. As a result, it is not easy to derive clear conclusions, let alone construct a coherent theoretical framework on this inscrutable basis.[283] Aside from the changeable nature of the selected criteria, the mode of their application is also unclear. Van Dijk and Van Hoof express their dismay at this state of affairs: '[j]udgments typically contain a (sometimes extensive) listing of the factors to be taken into account, but then somewhat abruptly – without additional arguments as to the weight of the factors concerned – concluded, for instance, that … "a proper balance was not achieved"'.[284] This is one of the most common criticisms against balancing. From across the Atlantic, Coffin laments: '[a]ll too commonly in judicial opinions, lip service is paid to balancing, a cursory mention of opposing interests is made, and, presto, the 'balance' is arrived at through some unrevealed legerdemain'.[285]

Certainly, some degree of flexibility may not necessarily be avoidable. Indeed, as noted above, proportionality as a legal tool is generally agreed to be determinable only on a case-by-case basis in light of the particular circumstances at issue.[286] In *EMI Records v. British Sky Broadcasting,* British judge Arnold J. noted that 'the proportionality of a blocking order is bound to be a context-sensitive question'.[287] Mowbray comments that when 'assessing if a fair balance has been achieved in specific cases the Court has had to take account of a myriad of competing individual and community

282. S Smet, *Resolving Conflicts between Human Rights: A Legal Theoretical Analysis in the Context of the ECHR*, (unpublished PhD thesis, Ghent University 2014) 170.

283. D J Harris et al., *Harris, O'Boyle & Warbrick – Law of the European Convention on Human Rights* (2nd ed., University Press 2009) 511.

284. Van Dijk & Van Hoof, as found in S Smet, *Resolving Conflicts between Human Rights: A Legal Theoretical Analysis in the Context of the ECHR,* (unpublished PhD thesis, Ghent University 2014) 162.

285. F M Coffin, 'Judicial Balancing: The Protean Scales of Justice' (1988) 63 New York University Law Review 16.

286. O Fischman Afori, 'Proportionality – A New Mega Standard in European Copyright Law' (2014) International Review of Intellectual Property and Competition Law (IIC) 889.

287. *EMI Records Ltd & Ors v. British Sky Broadcasting Ltd & Ors* [2013] EWHC 379 (Ch), 28 February 2013.

interests'.[288] It may therefore be argued that the list of relevant factors will never be capable of abstract or exhaustive remuneration.

This realisation indicates the real value of the listing of factors by the courts: it lies not in the identified criteria themselves, but in the ensuing analysis. This moves us closer to a real understanding of how to approach the concept of a 'fair balance', not as a myth applied by the courts to obfuscate their subjective assessments or as a scientific method capable of providing definitive answers, but as a metaphor for the exercise of a detailed dissection, comparison and ordering of the available options with a view to identifying the optimal outcome: a call for rational discourse. Greer suggests: '[l]ittle hinges on whether this process is called "defining", "interpreting", or "balancing". The important point is that, since it involves applying, and giving greater precision to, vague norms, judicial discretion is inescapable, although the structure, terms and underlying values of the Convention provide a framework of constraint'. In *Chassagnou,* the ECtHR in fact located the very essence of democracy in this evaluative deliberation: '[i]t is precisely this constant search for a balance between the fundamental rights of each individual that constitutes the foundations of a "democratic society"'.[289] From this perspective, accusations according to which balancing is merely a rhetorical device, 'window-dressing' employed by courts incapable of actually providing real answers, but only reframing conclusions reached through elliptical thinking, miss the central point: choosing between options on the basis of subjective assessment is often the job of the courts, particularly in difficult cases. As Frantz put it, as 'soon as he finishes measuring the unmeasurable, the judge's next job is to compare the incomparable'.[290] What is necessary is that judges lay bare their reasoning and the factors that led them through it to their ultimate decision. As Barendt insightfully argues, courts 'must give coherent and consistent reasons for their decisions. […] Rulings on fundamental rights need not be arbitrary and are no more unreasonable than they are in other areas of law such as the law of negligence or charitable trusts'.[291]

From this perspective, it becomes clear that balancing is inextricably intertwined with the deliberative acceptance of a system of principles to guide decisions and achieve rational outcomes. The outcomes of balancing are not so much 'arbitrary' as dictated by the values of the society within which the exercise occurs. Identifying those values requires investigation

---

288. A Mowbray, 'A Study of the Principle of Fair Balance in the Jurisprudence of the European Court of Human Rights' (2010) 10 Human Rights Law Review 289.
289. *Chassagnou and Others v. France*, application nos. 25088/94, 28331/95 and 28443/95, 29 April 1999.
290. L B Frantz, 'Is The First Amendment Law? A Reply to Professor Mendelson' (1963) 51(4) California Law Review 729.
291. E Barendt, 'Balancing Freedom of Expression and Privacy: The Jurisprudence of the Strasbourg Court' (2009) 1 Journal of Media Law 49.

through social dialogue. As the ECtHR emphasised, the essence of democratic governance is in the assessment and re-assessment of tough judgment calls between the basic cornerstones of societal organisation, in the constant re-shuffling of values and the unpacking of ideals: ultimately, in constitutional discourse.

It could of course be argued that the courts are not the appropriate venue for such assessments. Jacobs questions whether the judiciary is well-situated to evaluate social, economic or political choices and suggests that that might instead be a task best performed by the executive within the limits laid down by the legislature.[292] Van Gerven agrees that the basic issues must be solved by the constitutional legislator proper, with the courts limiting themselves to an interpretative and implementational role.[293]

Consequently, and now moving back to the EU context, if further guidance is to be provided, it should perhaps be formulated not by the CJEU, but by the EU legislator. This could explain the CJEU's reluctance to delve into the details of its balancing thought-process, preferring to let the national legislator fill in the gaps as it sees fit. Until a harmonised substantive intermediary liability is adopted on the European level, national tort law must continue to govern the area. Synodinou, pointing out that 'the standards of duty of care imposed by national courts continue to differ significantly from jurisdiction to jurisdiction', submits: '[n]ational legal orders balance those rights in a manner that reflects their national values, so any alternative approach of the CJEU is problematic'.[294] On that note the principle of subsidiarity that binds the EU and the limited scope of application of the Charter are particularly relevant. As Lind and Strand argue:

> [t]he closer we move toward the core values of the EU, the more intense and present is thus the question of how the Court respects the separation of powers and a potential hierarchy of norms. With the Charter now being legally binding, and the succession of the EU to the ECHR pending (further complicating an already complicated relationship to the human rights regime of the Council of Europe), these questions will not cease to gain importance.[295]

---

292. F G Jacobs, 'Recent Developments in the Principle of Proportionality in European Community Law' in E Ellis (ed.), *The Principle of Proportionality in the Law of Europe* (Hart Publishing 1999) 21.
293. W van Gerven, 'The Effect of Proportionality on the Actions of Member States of the European Community: National Viewpoints from Continental Europe' in E Ellis (ed.), *The Principle of Proportionality in the Law of Europe* (Hart Publishing 1999) 37.
294. T-E Synodinou, 'Intermediaries' Liability for Online Copyright Infringement in the EU: Evolutions and Confusions' (2015) 31 Computer Law & Security Review 57.
295. A Lind & M Strand, 'A New Proportionality Test for Fundamental Rights? The Joined Cases C-92/09 and C-93/09 Volker und Markus Schecke GbR (C-92/09) and Hartmut Eifert (C-93/09) v. Land Hessen' (2011) 7 European Policy Analysis 1.

Alexy contemplates this question by reflecting on the interconnection of constitutional judicial review and democratic governance as a guarantor of *tranquillitas publica*:

> The existence of good or plausible arguments is enough for deliberation or reflection, but not for representation. For this, it is necessary that the court not only claim that its arguments are the arguments of the people; a sufficient number of people must, at least in the long run, accept these arguments for reasons of correctness. Only rational persons are able to accept an argument on the ground that it is correct or sound. […] Constitutional review can be successful only if the arguments presented by the constitutional court are sound and only if a sufficient number of members of the community are able and willing to exercise their rational capacities.[296]

Regardless of the conclusion, what is clear is that, if fragmentation is to be avoided, the debate should occur on the European level. Interestingly, this was precisely the concern that motivated the Austrian *Oberster Gerichtshof* in its submission of a request for a preliminary ruling in *Telekabel.* Observing that the courts in different Member States were reaching different conclusions on the proportionality of blocking orders, the Austrian court called for 'guidelines for assessing the proportionality of specific blocking measures' to be laid down by the CJEU, so that the question may 'be judged in a uniform manner throughout Europe'.[297] The identification of criteria capable of guiding the discussion on intermediary obligations for copyright enforcement along the lines of the example set by the ECtHR can and should be provided by the EU. A national approach to an internet – and therefore international – problem is not going to supply an adequate solution.[298]

In this regard, it is worth noting the evolution that occurs in the CJEU's intermediary liability case law: while in *Promusicae* the Luxembourg court limited itself to noting that a fair balance must be struck and deferred the actual balancing operation to the national level, in *L'Oréal* it repeated that edict, but now added guidance as to how to achieve that balance; finally in *Scarlet Extended* and *Netlog,* although again low on the guidelines, the Court delved into the substantive questions and provided a concrete answer with regard to whether the measure in question struck a fair balance or not. Although the CJEU's reasoning is inscrutable, its concrete rejection of the

296. R Alexy, 'Balancing, Constitutional Review, and Representation' (2005) 3(4) International Journal of Constitutional Law 572.
297. *EMI Records Ltd and others v. British Sky Broadcasting Ltd and others*, [2013] EWHC 379 (Ch), para. 99.
298. C Kuner, 'Data Protection and Rights Protection on the Internet: the Promusicae Judgment of the European Court of Justice' (2008) 30(5) European Intellectual Property Review 199.

filtering mechanism under discussion is noteworthy.[299] This different treatment can likely be attributed to the limits to the Court's jurisdiction and the different type of rule under examination in each case: in *Promusicae,* the Court was simply reminding its national counterparts of their obligations under EU primary law, while in the *SABAM* cases, it was called upon to interpret specific provisions of the copyright directives. Similarly, if in *Telekabel* the Court then took two steps back to pass the hot potato of 'fair balance' further down the line, not even to the national authorities, but to the service providers themselves, this can be attributed to the nature of the submitted question that focused on the Austrian 'outcome prohibition' peculiarity. What is of course missing in this line of case law is a decision outlining guidelines for the application of a balancing test and subsequently applying these in a coherent manner that can reveal the appropriate rationale – but that would be making law.

2.4 CONCLUSION

The above analysis reveals the shortcomings of the current shallow European regulation of intermediary accessory liability. As opposed to primary liability, accessory liability in copyright remains almost entirely unharmonised. This discrepancy itself is awkward, as the distinction between the two areas is not straightforward: absent a clear line distinguishing the two, the harmonisation of primary liability ends up impinging on the national rules on accessory liability, while the lack of harmonisation of accessory liability encourages an expansion of the rules of primary liability to unreasonable breadth by European judges searching for cross-border solutions for the liability issues presented by intermediaries.

To the extent that a harmonised European regime for intermediary accessory liability does exist, its main thrust lies in the safe harbours. Yet these are negatively stated and their reach is restricted: they only apply in the provision of certain services; they are conditional, so that do not always apply in the provision of those services; they do not protect intermediaries from injunctions ordered against them; and more importantly, they do nothing to change existing substantive national law on accessory copyright infringement. Instead, as the Explanatory Memorandum of the E-Commerce Directive emphasised, the safe harbours are mere 'limitations on liability' that might oust national law under certain circumscribed circumstances, but do not amend it. As a result, if a service provider fails to qualify for the protection of any of the three immunities, this will not automatically signify its liability, but merely the loss of an additional layer of protection, whose only effect will be to bring national substantive provisions into play that,

299. G González Fuster, 'Balancing Intellectual Property against Data Protection: A New Right's Wavering Weight' (2012) 14 IDP: Revista de Internet, Derecho y Política 34.

depending on their prescripts, may or may not result in an ultimate finding of liability.[300]

This situation makes the clear delineation of the conditions for the application of the safe harbours particularly important. Yet, while the mere conduit and caching safe harbours seem to be simply stated and well-understood, the requirements of the hosting immunity – the most widely applicable of the three – are steeped in ambiguity: what constitutes actual and what construed knowledge? What facts or circumstances will make a copyright infringement apparent to a diligent economic operator? What qualifies as a removal or a disabling of access to an infringement and do these notion encompass the prevention of future infringements? When will an intermediary's reaction qualify as 'expeditious'? Article 15 of the E-Commerce Directive is equally troublesome: what is the difference between 'general' and 'specific' monitoring obligations? How does the distinction impact obligations to prevent future infringement? These questions must either be dealt with at the Community level or will default for answers to national tort rules, muddying the division between the safe harbours and the law against which they are intended to insulate. The streamlined notice-and-action procedure currently being contemplating by the Commission could provide a clear, usable procedural model to help alleviate some of the legal uncertainly at least in this one crucial area, but the proposal remains contentious.

In any case, what would offer an even better solution would be a comprehensive European regime of intermediary accessory copyright liability. Yet currently, the one positive demand made by the European legal framework with regard to intermediaries is limited to injunctive relief.[301] The expansive breadth afforded to this provision in comparison to the carefully circumscribed safe harbours indicates a desire on the part of the European legislator to establish two separate liability regimes for 'neutral' and 'non-neutral' intermediaries: the first – provided they qualify under the other numerous conditions – may, under this scheme, be exposed only to injunctive orders, while the second are liable for both monetary and injunctive relief. At the same time, the scope of any obligations that may be imposed through injunctive means remains entirely unclear. Article 15 of the E-Commerce Directive is helpful in this regard, but its applicability is restricted only to safe harbour activities, while it anyway reaches its limits at the ambiguous intersection between the 'general' and the 'specific'. Other provisions scattered across the legal landscape provide occasional additional guidance,

300. Commission Proposal for a European Parliament and Council Directive on certain legal aspects of electronic commerce in the internal market, 18 November 1998, COM (1998) 586 final.

301. M Leistner, 'Common Principles of Secondary Liability?' in A Ohly, *Common Principles of European Intellectual Property Law* (Mohr Siebeck 2012) 117.

but this too is incidental, incomplete and, for the most part, excessively vaguely worded to be of great use.

The CJEU has attempted to overcome this problem by backtracking to the underlying norms on a 'fair balance' between conflicting fundamental rights. So, according to the Court, copyright, as a fundamental right protected under Article 17(2) the EU's Charter of Fundamental Rights, must be weighed against all opposing fundamental rights of equal normative value. In cases of intermediary liability, these will usually consist of the right of the intermediary to conduct a business (Article 16 of the Charter) and the rights of its users to the protection of their privacy and personal data (Articles 7 and 8 of the Charter) and their freedom of expression (Article 11 of the Charter). This approach, in addition to providing a legal basis for a European regulation of the responsibilities of intermediaries with regard to third party copyright infringements beyond the limited scope of the existing directives, has also elevated the discussion on intermediary liability to hierarchically higher legal planes: the driving force behind the harmonisation of European intermediary liability have been revealed to lie in fundamental rights. The solution is not inappropriate. After all, by its very nature as a newly emergent area of high legal controversy, intermediary liability demands a balanced assessment. Unsurprisingly, the logic of balancing pervades the relevant directives,[302] while, as *Promusicae* confirms, these are moreover intended precisely to provide the mechanisms that allow for a correct balancing of fundamental rights to be procured in practice.[303] As a result, the existing European provisions can be viewed as elaborations on a broader, underlying, unwritten and unified normative framework of intermediary accessory copyright liability, to which any further substantive development must refer. Where the relevant secondary legislation does not sufficiently achieve this effect, the need for balance must be understood as persisting, meaning that it can then be invoked in its own right for the regulation of intermediary liability.

What is the significance of this 'constitutionalisation', as it has been termed, of the intermediary liability debate? McCormick has posited that, in the multi-level pluralistic legal order of a united Europe, principles reflecting

302. For example, Recital 41 of the E-Commerce Directive explicitly states that that 'directive strikes a balance between the different interests at stake', while Recital 31 of the Copyright Directive declares that a 'fair balance of rights and interests between the different categories of right-holders, as well as between the different categories of right-holders and users of protected subject-matter must be safeguarded'.

303. Indeed, where a directive insufficiently achieves this result, it will constitute bad law that should be revoked, as was the case with the annulment of the Data Retention Directive by the CJEU in joined cases C-293/12 and C-594/12, *Digital Rights Ireland and Seitlinger and Others,* 8 April 2014. The Data Retention Directive was Directive 2006/24/EC of the European Parliament and of the Council of 15 March 2006 on the retention of data generated or processed in connection with the provision of publicly available electronic communications services or of public communications networks and amending Directive 2002/58/EC [2006] OJ L105/4.

the common tradition of ideas of EU Member States and securing the compatibility of partially overlapping systems are necessary.[304] He has accordingly suggested that fundamental rights law, alongside the principles of proportionality, subsidiarity and natural justice, might successfully serve that function. In copyright law, probably currently the most extensively harmonised area of private law in the EU, we can see this suggestion beginning to take practical effect. This was the main offering of the application of 'fair balance' to EU copyright case law: the establishment of fundamental rights – only vaguely nodded at in text of the copyright directives themselves – as an essential component of the discussion on intermediary liability and relevant factors in solving the tensions between copyright and other rights and interests. In this way, the limits of enforcement are no longer identified exclusively in the secondary legislation, but in the primary sources that underpin them, which are thus used to pull diverse national tort systems closer together.

Ultimately, in this way, as Griffiths suggests, constitutionalisation is employed as a method of harmonisation:[305] through the injection of fundamental rights into the intermediary liability debate, the Europeanising of what would otherwise be a national discussion is unlocked. This should not be seen as in any way paradoxical or undesirable, but rather the natural function of fundamental rights and the obvious jurisdiction of any court that oversees their application. Once fundamental rights have been acknowledged as carrying European authority, a cross-fertilisation of the private and public law spheres will necessarily follow: absent a European substantive intermediary liability regime, let alone a unified tort law, fundamental rights become the only resource to which the CJEU can turn for answers. And although fundamental rights and tort law differ drastically as to their mechanisms of enforcement, in their parallel pursuit of a basic standard of decent human behaviour, they constitute two sides of the same coin. Indeed, tort law (including intermediary liability, whether for monetary compensation or injunctive relief) is often the tool through which the State discharges its duty to provide for an effective remedy against a violation of a fundamental right, while, conversely, fundamental rights law determines the cadre within which States must remain when constructing their tort rules. In creating and enforcing its tort law regime, therefore, the State may not overstep the boundaries of fundamental rights either by acting in a way that would violate the fundamental rights of private parties or by omitting to put in place guarantees for the practical and effective protection of those rights that – as

---

304. N McCormick, 'Beyond the Sovereign State' (1993) 56 Modern Law Review 1, as discussed in particular reference to intellectual property in J Pila, 'Intellectual Property as a Case Study in Europeanization: Methodological Themes and Context' in A Ohly & J Pila (eds), *The Europeanization of Intellectual Property Law: Towards A European Legal Methodology* (Oxford University Press 2013) 23.
305. J Griffiths, 'Constitutionalising or Harmonising? The Court of Justice, the Right to Property and European Copyright Law' (2013) 38(1) European Law Review 65.

the 'ultimate guarantor of pluralism'[306] – are expected of it. This interconnection means that the standard of care that can be imposed on private individuals by State-enacted legal provisions or court-ordered mandates may be illuminated by the underlying fundamental rights obligations of that State: the duties incumbent upon individuals are reflections of the duties incumbent on the State with regard to the regulation of the conduct of those individuals. As Van Dam puts it, 'tort rights are human rights'.[307]

In the EU context, this means that, in transposing and interpreting EU rules on intermediary liability, EU Member States must take care to respect fundamental rights.[308] More importantly for the purposes of this book, it also means that the EU itself, in the construction of its harmonising law, must be equally respectful. This conclusion will hold true for all areas of European law, thus including intermediary liability: obligations may be imposed on intermediaries by EU law, as long as the EU legislator and courts respect, in their selection, the EU Charter and the 'fair balance' that should be achieved between the rights that it protects. In effect, the result is a very traditional conception of the role of fundamental rights, but with a modern, Europeanising outlook that employs fundamental rights to govern – albeit in very broad strokes – a matter that according to the usual divisions ought to be delegated to tort law. In this way, the concept of a 'fair balance' opens the door for a reverse-engineering of intermediary liability – and thus, ultimately, offers as the first obvious inroad into the establishment of a European substantive law for intermediary liability.[309]

In the meantime, it is important for commentators and policy-makers to properly understand the jurisprudential *status quo*. To this end, in the text above the concept of a 'fair balance' has been traced back to its origins in legal theoretical debate and the interconnected jurisprudence of the CJEU and ECtHR. In this way, an understanding of exactly what the principle 'fair balance' is intended to achieve and how it should be employed to reach those ends can be assembled. The conclusion is that balancing would appear to be nothing more or less than the idea that fundamental rights are not, *pace* Habermas, to be conceived of as absolute, but simply as deserving equal protection, each, in this way, forming the natural limit of the other. This in turn means that the resolution of clashes between them may only be decided

306. ECtHR, *Manole and others v. Moldova*, application no. 13936/02, 17 September 2009, para. 107.
307. C van Dam, *European Tort Law* (2nd ed., Oxford University Press 2013) para. 711-4.
308. At least, in the EU context, as concerns areas relevant to EU competence, such as copyright.
309. Indeed, Pila implies that copyright might show the way forward for the European harmonisation of other areas of private law as well, as the title of her chapter suggests, see: J Pila, 'Intellectual Property as a Case Study in Europeanization: Methodological Themes and Context' in A Ohly & J Pila (eds), *The Europeanization of Intellectual Property Law: Towards A European Legal Methodology* (Oxford University Press 2013) 23.

on a case-by-case basis, the individual circumstances at hand being the factors that tilt the judgment one way or another: it can never absolutely be said that the right to property deserves greater protection than the right to freedom of expression and should therefore always prevail or *vice versa*. Instead, both will, from time to time and depending on the circumstances, be used to force the other into its proper place, coming together in this way to form a virtuous circle of optimal fundamental rights protection.

But if balancing is case-by-case weighing, what is that is being weighed? If weighing is what is being done, where are the scales? Currently in CJEU case law they are entirely missing: the Luxembourg Court has, for the time being, limited itself to simply observing that a fair balance must be struck or, at most, rejecting specific possibilities as not fairly balanced. This is perhaps unsurprising given the subsidiarity barriers that control its jurisdiction. At the same time, mere reference to fair balance with no indication of how the concept should be approached is unhelpful and risks fragmentation across Member State borders. As a result, while fair balance offers good possibilities for a rational fundamental rights adjudication, more concrete guidance regarding its requirements needs to be formulated. A pan-European framework for fair balance, whether applicable to every instance of a fundamental rights conflict or at the very least specifically to the rights of copyright holders and users in the intermediary liability context would be immensely helpful. The ECtHR appears to be making strides in that direction: acknowledging both proportionality and the margin of appreciation that Contracting States enjoy, the Strasbourg Court has, in its recent case law, attempted to trace out the factors that govern the balancing process. It has thus provided invaluable insights into its judicial reasoning. The CJEU should, if it wishes to achieve greater clarify, follow its lead. In any case, in either court, such judicial analyses should, if the outcome is to claim real legitimacy, make sure to always account for the societal discourse surrounding the object of the balancing and clearly embed this in their reasoning. In this way, as long as the debate, both within and without the courts, perseveres, the notion of a fairly balanced intermediary liability framework can continue to take ever more concrete shape.

Of course, the above being said, it must be also admitted that fundamental rights balancing does seem to be a very circuitous way to go about regulating relationships between private parties – the kinship between the two bodies of law does not mean that a complete tort law system can be derived from the fundamental rights framework. To the contrary, Western legal culture is predicated on the idea of a distinction between private law and public law.[310] And indeed, the constitutionalisation of private law through the increased influence of fundamental rights on relationships

---

310. A Barak, 'Constitutional Human Rights and Private Law' in D Friedman & D Barak-Erez (eds), *Human Rights in Private Law* (Hart Publishing 2001) 13.

between private parties has been criticised as doctrinally unsound: relationships between private parties are best governed by rules designed for that purpose. Fundamental rights are, far from this, originally intended to set standards regarding the relationship between private parties and the State. Smits reflects:

> Private law can be interpreted in the light of fundamental rights, but can in the end *not* be absorbed by these rights: the private law rules remain decisive for deciding the case. A different view would be counterproductive as the existing knowledge about the best way how to solve an issue would be thrown away. What would be the use of replacing the existing private law on protection of property by new rules based on the constitutional protection of this right? If there is a conflict between two neighbours, one can certainly solve this conflict by reference to their fundamental rights to property. But this would be a step back because one would then neglect the well-developed rules about nuisance and the rules on how neighbours should behave.[311]

This once again brings forth the question of vagueness: by their very nature as general principles, fundamental rights are too abstract for the definitive solutions suitable for the finicky area of private interpersonal relationships. Instead, it is the law of tort that is dedicated to the detailed regulation of the minutiae of human relationships. Indeed, tort law has centuries of development behind it shaping it precisely for the optimum governance of human extra-contractual interactions. The balancing of conflicting rights and interests of two private parties is consequently typically a private law exercise and it is in this area that it should be located.[312] This should hold true of intermediary liability just as it would for any other area of private law. What does this realisation mean for the European harmonisation of intermediary liability in copyright? Instead of ignoring tort law and leaving the hapless courts to attempt to interpret the applicable higher principles themselves, the EU legislator ought to intervene at the appropriate level and designate a sanctioned tort-based solution a priori designed to satisfy fundamental rights requirements. In other words, if the EU really wishes to formulate a European standard for intermediary accessory copyright liability, it should do just that: formulate a standard. Preferably, this should be done explicitly, rather than through hinting at upper limits enshrined in primary EU law, but only revealed through CJEU interpretation each time a Member State steers too far off a course.

In order to achieve this result, the law must move past both the safe harbours and fundamental rights and dig into the substance of tort law. How

311. J M Smits, 'Private Law and Fundamental Rights: A Sceptical View' in T Barkhuysen & S Lindenbergh, *Constitutionalisation of Private Law* (Brill 2005) 9.
312. J M Smits, 'Private Law and Fundamental Rights: A Sceptical View' in T Barkhuysen & S Lindenbergh, *Constitutionalisation of Private Law* (Brill 2005) 9.

can this be done? The first necessary step in the process should be the careful comparative investigation of the existing disparate national European systems for intermediary accessory liability – beyond the safe harbours of the E-Commerce Directive stretches the deep blue sea of national law. In the next chapter we shall navigate across this to explore the English, French and German tort rules for intermediary accessory copyright liability.

Chapter 3

Digging Deeper: The National Norms on Intermediary Accessory Liability

As noted in the previous chapter, following the adoption of the E-Commerce Directive in 2000, the architecture set up for intermediary liability in Europe has become two-tiered: at a first stage, it is necessary to examine whether a given intermediary attracts, in its pursuit of a certain activity, civil liability according to the standards ensconced in the Member States' legislation and only then, in the second instance, must the inapplicability of any immunity be established.[1] Yet this structure is sometimes questioned. In *L'Oréal v. eBay*, AG Jääskinen suggested that the substantive national rules on liability would exclude liability for intermediaries that act in a way that respects the safe harbours:

> It could be argued that provisions concerning liability in Articles 12, 13 and 14 of Directive 2000/31 should be construed as exceptions to liability and thus be interpreted narrowly. In my opinion this is not necessarily the case, because in many Member States the liability of a service provider in the situations referred to in these articles would be excluded because of the lack of subjective fault. Thus these provisions are better qualified as restatements or clarifications of existing law than exceptions thereto.[2]

---

1. W Duhen, *La responsabilité extra-contractuelle du fournisseur d'accès à Internet* (Presse universitaires d'Aix-Marseille 2013) 64.
2. CJEU, Opinion of AG Jääskinen, case C-324/09, *L'Oréal v. eBay,* 9 December 2010, para. 136.

This is a common perception[3] – but is it really the case? In this chapter the rules in place in the three national jurisdictions of England, France and Germany shall each be investigated in turn to determine exactly that.[4] As noted in Chapter 1 (see section 1.4.1), accessory liability is a cluster concept, recognisable not from its set position within the national conceptual legal structures, but only from the function it performs. In order to conduct its country-by-country analysis therefore, this chapter will collect, from across each national legal landscape, the disparate solutions that comprise it. Section 3.1 will set the ball rolling with an analysis of the English regime on intermediary accessory copyright liability, section 3.2 will move on to France and section 3.3 will take on Germany. Each section will begin with an examination of relevant provisions enshrined in national statute, before moving on to an analysis of the relevant general tort law. A comparative overview will be provided in section 3.4.

3.1 ENGLAND

The E-Commerce Directive was transposed into UK law with the Electronic Commerce (EC Directive) Regulations 2002. Sections 17-19 implement the safe harbours. No implementation of Article 15 of the E-Commerce Directive seems to have been adopted by the British legislator, but this perhaps is unsurprising given that the provision offers guidance to Member States only on what they cannot do (section 1) or what they may, but are not obliged, to do (section 2).[5] Other than that, the Regulations reproduce their EU originators almost verbatim. A special rule on injunctions, implementing Article 8(3) of the Copyright Directive, has been introduced with section 97A of the UK's CDPA. Beyond these provisions, national law applies. This derives from two main sources: provisions dedicated to accessory liability specifically in copyright contained in the CDPA and, where these offer no solution, the English common law. The relevant rules shall be examined below.

3.1.1 Secondary Infringement

The CDPA dedicates sections 22-26 to what the heading proclaims to be the 'secondary infringement of copyright'. The scope given to this 'secondary

3. See for example: J Riordan, *The Liability of Internet Intermediaries* (PhD thesis, University of Oxford 2013, forthcoming Oxford University Press 2016) 82.
4. It should be noted that the contents of this chapter have been partly previously published in the following article: C Angelopoulos, 'Beyond the Safe Harbours: Harmonising Substantive Intermediary Liability for Copyright Infringement in Europe' (2013) 3 Intellectual Property Quarterly 253.
5. Its constraints are certainly not ignored by British judges, see e.g., *Cartier International AG & Ors v. British Sky Broadcasting Ltd & Ors* [2014] EWHC 3354 (Ch) (17 October 2014) (*Cartier v. Sky*), paras 139-141.

infringement' is very limited. The provisions are restricted to five very specific acts concerning the importation of infringing copies, the possession or dealing with infringing copies, the provision of means for making infringing copies, the permitting of the use of premises for infringing performances or the provision of apparatus for infringing performances. They are not therefore relevant with regard to the accessory liability of internet intermediaries for online copyright infringement.[6]

Regardless, the provisions are worth considering for the knowledge requirements they attach to 'secondary liability'. This is to be contrasted to the strict rules on primary infringement, giving us a first insight into the British thinking on the different conditions for direct and indirect infringement. In all cases, the provisions of sections 22-26 require that the secondary infringer 'knew or had reason to believe' that infringements were occurring. The applicable knowledge test thus appears to be an objective one.[7] As such, if the defendant had knowledge of the relevant facts, it is not important whether or not he in fact believed that his behaviour was wrongful, as long as a reasonable person would have reached that conclusion. In addition, the defendant must have been in a position that enabled him to properly evaluate the situation; as a result, an appropriate amount of time to consider the information must have been allowed.[8] The normal period is fourteen days,

6. A possible basis for the secondary liability of internet intermediaries might conceivably be provided by s. 24(1), which imposes liability on persons who, without the licence of the copyright owner, *inter alia*, make, possess in the course of business, sell or let for hire articles specifically designed or adapted for making copies of a work. However, although important in preventing commercial piracy, the provision only encompasses articles such as photographic negatives, moulds, master recordings or templates, which are specifically designed or adapted for copying a particular work; it accordingly does not extend to articles such as photocopiers, tape-to-tape recorders or, presumably, their digital equivalents, which merely have the potential to copy in the abstract. More importantly, the narrow confines of the term 'article' not do not lend it to easy application to the facilities and services of internet intermediaries. The same issue hampers a broader application of ss 22 and 23, while in a similar way, s. 26 limits itself to liability arising from the provision of 'apparatus', another term that does not comfortably describe the services of internet intermediaries. Finally, while s. 24(2) decrees that the transmission of a work by means of a telecommunications system without licence constitutes an infringement, it explicitly excludes communication to the public from its ambit. Accordingly, while it affects such acts as transmissions by fax, it is most likely inappropriate for application to online copyright infringement. See L Bently & B Sherman, *Intellectual Property Law* (3rd ed., Oxford University Press 2009) 195-198; H MacQueen et al., *Contemporary Intellectual Property – Law and Policy,* (2nd ed., Oxford University Press 2011) 166-168; D Seng, 'Comparative Analysis of the National Approaches to the Liability of Internet Intermediaries', WIPO study, available at: www.wipo.int/copyright/en/internet_intermediaries.
7. L Bently & B Sherman, *Intellectual Property Law* (3rd ed., Oxford University Press 2009) 198; H MacQueen et al., *Contemporary Intellectual Property – Law and Policy* (2nd ed., Oxford University Press 2011) 167. See also, *Copinger and Skone James on Copyright*, quoted in *L.A. Gear Inc. v. Hi-Tec Sports Plc* [1992] FSR 121.
8. *Hutchinson Personal Communications v. Hook Advertising* [1995] FSR 365.

although this might vary with the facts.[9] The information provided on the infringement must also have been sufficiently detailed: general allegations of infringement will not suffice. Finally, the courts have made it clear that facts from which the reasonable man might simply suspect infringement are not enough.[10] Copinger and Skone James therefore suggest that where the defendant is not aware of the infringement, he must be given notice, commonly by letter, before he can be found to be a secondary infringer.[11]

Interestingly, as with the knowledge standard of the hosting safe harbour, here too the objectivity of the test is diluted with a small element of subjectivity, in that the knowledge must be personal to the defendant: the belief of wrongfulness must have been reasonable not only to the reasonable person, but to the defendent himself. Thus, account must be taken of his subjective knowledge and experience.[12] This will especially be the case, where the defendant was in possession of contradictory information. So, Laddie, Prescott and Vitoria suggest that if 'the defendant can convince the court that he genuinely did not have reason to believe despite the fact that others, more worldly or more wisely in his position would have done so, then he should be able to avail himself of the defence'.[13] Mere denial would not be sufficient in this regard: the defendant must be able to establish that, for example, he was aware of facts which negated or cast doubt on the allegations of the claimant.

Limited as they are, these provisions on secondary infringement by no means exhaust the possibilities offered by the CDPA for liability for copyright infringements committed by others. A further solution is introduced in the act in the form of the famous doctrine of 'authorisation'.

3.1.2 Authorisation of Infringement

Absent other appropriate mechanisms, the legal tool primarily relied upon by the English courts for findings of liability by internet intermediaries is that of authorisation. Under section 16(1) of the UK's CDPA, the owner of a copyrighted work is granted the exclusive right to undertake a set of six restricted acts in relation to the work.[14] Under section 16(2), those rights will be infringed by any person who not only does any of these acts without the

9. *Monsoon v. Indian Imports* [1993] FSR 486; *L.A. Gear Inc. v. Hi-Tec Sports Plc* [1992] FSR 121.
10. *L.A. Gear Inc. v. Hi-Tec Sports Plc* [1992] FSR 121; *ZYX Music GmbH v. King* [1997] 2 All ER 129; *Pensher Security Door Co Ltd v. Sunderland City Council*, [2000] R.P.C. 249; *Vermaat and Powell v. Boncrest (No 2)* [2002] FSR 21.
11. *Copinger and Skone James on Copyright*, quoted in *L.A. Gear Inc. v. Hi-Tec Sports Plc* [1992] FSR 121.
12. C Colston, *Principles of Intellectual Property Law* (Cavendish Publishing 1999) 232.
13. Laddie, Prescott & Vitoria quoted in *L.A. Gear Inc. v. Hi-Tec Sports Plc* [1992] FSR 121.
14. These rights are six: to copy the work; to issue copies of the work to the public; to rent or lend the work to the public; to perform, show or play the work in public; to

licence of the copyright owner, but who also authorises another person to do them. The wording of the section is reminiscent of the European directives and international treaties, which generally accompany descriptions of an 'exclusive right' with the explication 'to authorise or to prohibit',[15] albeit without seeing the need for an express reference to the actual 'doing' of the restricted act.[16]

According to Bently and Sherman, when the right of authorisation was first introduced to the Copyright Act 1911, it was dismissed as tautologous to the act itself and therefore superfluous.[17] Over time however, the concept of authorisation has widened in the UK to exact liability beyond the primary infringer. In this way, despite its statutory provenance, authorisation has been primarily shaped by the common law.[18] *Falcon v. Famous Players Film Company Ltd* set the tone in 1926, when Bankes LJ accepted that to 'authorise' means to 'sanction, approve and countenance'. A concurring Atkin LJ defined the notion as to 'grant or purport to grant to a third person the right to do the act complained of, whether the intention is that the grantee shall do the act on his own account, or only on account of the grantor'. On this basis, authorisation, although strictly speaking categorised as an act of direct infringement,[19] has developed in the UK into one of the main sources of accessory liability for copyright infringement. Importantly, each of the two *Falcon* judges' interpretations has given rise to a different line of case law. How have these developed?

3.1.2.1 The Evolution of Authorisation

In *Monckton v. Pathé Frères,*[20] Buckley LJ stated that the 'seller of a record authorizes, I conceive, the use of the record, and such user will be a

---

communicate the work to the public; to make an adaptation of the work or do any of the above in relation to an adaptation.

15. See for example, Arts 2, 3 and 4(1) of the Copyright Directive, Arts 6 and 8 of the WCT and Arts 9, 11 and 11*ter* of the Berne Convention, as well as Art. 4.1 of the Wittem Group's European Copyright Code.
16. Gendreau points out that the authorisation right of the international treaties should be seen as corresponding to the 'main' right of the Commonwealth tradition (the actual 'doing' of the acts restricted by copyright), with the Commonwealth authorisation right being understood as at best subsumed into the main right, see Y Gendreau, 'Authorisation Revisited' (2001) 48 Journal of the Copyright Society of the U.S.A. 341.
17. This will have been particularly so, given the recognition of authorisation by the common law as a 'participation link' leading to joint tortfeasance. See, L J Scrutton, *Performing Right Soc'y, Ltd. v. Ciryl Theatrical Syndicate, Ltd.* [1924] 1 K.B. 1 and *Falcon v. Famous Players* [1926] 2 KB 474.
18. R Giblin, 'Authorisation in Context – Potential Consequences of the Proposed Amendments to Australian Secondary Liability Law' Australian Digital Alliance, August 2014.
19. E D Ventose & J J Forrester, 'Authorisation and Infringement of Copyright on the Internet' (2010) 14(6) Journal of Internet Law, 3 and Y Gendreau, 'Authorisation Revisited' (2001) 48 Journal of the Copyright Society of the U.S.A. 341.
20. *Monckton v. Pathé Frères Pathephone Ltd* [1914] 1 KB 395.

performance of the musical work'. This makes clear that, as had been since repeatedly confirmed by the courts, authorisation may be express or implied from all the relevant circumstances. Implied authorisation will require that the infringement is a necessary consequence of the act expressly allowed. So, in *Evans v. Hulton,* it was held that 'where a man sold the rights in relation to a manuscript to another with a view to its production, and it was in fact produced, both the English language and common sense required him to hold that this man had 'authorised' the printing and publication'.[21]

A different treatment was reserved for blank tapes: in *A&M Records,*[22] it was held that the manufacturer of blank cassette tapes could not be understood as having authorised infringing home-taping by their customers. Here, Foster J was clear on the strong link that must connect the authorisation and the act of infringement:

> It is, I think, clear from the authorities that the plaintiffs must plead some specific authorisation of an actual breach of copyright affecting a particular plaintiff. It is not, I think, sufficient to allege authorisation at large. Authorisation meant sanctioning, express approval or countenancing of an actual breach of copyright by some act directly related to that breach.

Along similar lines, in *C.B.S. Inc. v. Ames Records & Tapes Ltd,*[23] it was found that a chain of record libraries that lent out records and at the same time provided blank tapes for sale, thus facilitating their copying, was not liable for authorisation of copyright infringement. Whitford J asserted that the commonly understood meaning of the term 'authorisation' excludes mere facilitation of copyright infringement and requires the assumption of some degree of *authority*:

> [a]ny ordinary person would, I think, assume that an authorisation can only come from somebody having or purporting to have authority and that an act is not authorised by somebody who merely enables or possibly assists or even encourages another to do that act, but does not purport to have any authority which he can grant to justify the doing of the act.

Thus, what is necessary for authorisation is what Gendreau calls 'holding out': conduct that can reasonably give the impression to the person being authorised that they have received permission from somebody who actually has the copyright prerogative at stake.[24] Mere facilitation is not sufficient, because it does not in and of itself create this effect. This

21. *Evans v. Hulton* (1924) 131 LT 534.
22. *A&M Records Inc v. Audio Magnetics Inc. (UK) Ltd* [1979] FSR 1.
23. *CBS Inc v. Ames Records and Tapes* [1981] 2 All ER 812.
24. Y Gendreau, 'Authorisation Revisited' (2001) 48 Journal of the Copyright Society of the U.S.A. 341.

restriction was tempered by *Ames's* willingness to treat indifference as capable of signalling authorisation, although the circumstances established in evidence in each case will be essential in this regard. Relying on precedent, Whitford J put forth that the 'indifference of one who did not consider it his business to interfere, who had no desire to see another person's copyright infringed, but whose view was that copyright and infringement were matters in this case not for him, but for the owners of the copyright' will not be enough to signify authorisation, as opposed to the indifference that denotes that the person in question does not care whether copyright is infringed or not. Burrell and Weatherall make the useful distinction between 'granting permission' to the primary infringer and simply 'permitting' an infringement in the sense of 'letting it happen'.[25]

The dividing line was finally settled by the seminal case of *CBS v. Amstrad.*[26] The appellants, BPI Ltd, accused Amstrad of authorising copyright through the manufacture and advertisement of a double-spin twin-tape recorder capable of copying protected material at high speed. Lord Templeman, speaking for a unanimous House of Lords, confirmed the *Ames* distinction between authorisation and mere facilitation and stated categorically that copying apparatus is only capable of the second:

> no manufacturer and no machine confers on the purchaser authority to copy unlawfully. Blank tapes are capable of being used for recording or copying, but such copying might be lawful or unlawful. The purchaser or other operator of the recorder determines whether he shall copy and what he shall copy. By selling the recorder, Amstrad may facilitate copying in breach of copyright but do not authorise it.

In this way, after considering both *Falcon* authorisation formulations, Lord Templeman came down in favour of the narrower Atkin LJ approach: to 'authorise' is to 'grant or purport to grant to a third person the right'. Although it was acknowledged that authorisation may be express or implied, Lord Templeman observed that a distinction must be made between conferring the *power to copy* upon the purchaser and purporting to grant the *right to copy*. In this context, a crucial factor in the finding of no authorisation in the case at hand was the footnote that accompanied Amstrad's advertisements of its machines which warned users that copying may require prior permission by a copyright owner and made clear that Amstrad did not have the authority to grant such permission. Although the ads were therefore described by the House of Lords as 'open to severe criticism', 'cynical' and even 'deplorable', it was recognised that no purchaser of an Amstrad model could reasonably have deduced from either

25. R Burrell & K Weatherall, 'Before the High Court – Providing Services to Copyright Infringers: *Roadshow Films Pty Ltd v. iiNet Ltd*' (2011) 33 Sydney Law Review 801.
26. *CBS Songs v. Amstrad* [1988] UKHL 15 (12 May 1988).

the facilities incorporated in the recorder itself or from the advertisements that Amstrad possessed or purported to possess the authority to grant the permission required for a record to be copied.

It is worth noting that, in his ruling, Lord Templeman cited and then rejected as:

> 'stated much too widely' the view given in Laddie, Prescott and Vitoria, according to which 'a person may be said to authorise another to commit an infringement if the one has some form of control over the other at the time of infringement or, if he has no such control, is responsible for placing in the other's hands materials which by their nature are almost inevitably to be used for the purpose of infringement'.

In the view of the Court, the lack of control is in itself decisive. In *Amstrad* itself, for example, the final decision as to which material was to be recorded lay with the operator of the machine alone, not with the manufacturers:

> The purchaser will not make unlawful copies because he has been induced or incited or persuaded to do so by Amstrad. The purchaser will make unlawful copies for his own use because he chooses to do so. Amstrad's advertisements may persuade the purchaser to buy an Amstrad machine but will not influence the purchaser's later decision to infringe copyright.

This stresses the independence of decision-making by autonomous persons. The Court pointed out that a variety of materials are 'by their nature almost inevitably to be used for the purpose of an infringement', yet their invention, manufacture, sale and advertisement is nonetheless not inhibited by the law and cannot be convincingly interpreted as authorisation of infringement.

In order that unlawful authorisation may be found, primary infringement by the person to whom 'authorisation' was illegitimately given must have taken place.[27] MacQueen et al., for example, comparing cases where authorisation was established with those where it was rejected, suggest that a 'direct and immediate link' between an act of primary infringement and the actions of the third party accused of authorising the infringement has in most cases proven to be the turning factor. They note that, where the core of the complaint is the fact that the defendant had created an opportunity for others to infringe, which had been probably, or even certainly, taken up, but the claimants failed to document any specific instances of infringement, claims of authorisation are likely to strike out. By contrast, where the creation of such an opportunity has been substantiated by specific instances of

27. H MacQueen et al., *Contemporary Intellectual Property – Law and Policy* (2nd ed., Oxford University Press 2011) 159.

infringement, findings of authorisation are more common.[28] This being said, as we shall see below, in recent cases the courts seem to have taken a turn towards a more relaxed approach to identifying the primary wrong.[29] In this they have been greatly influenced by the debate on the correct interpretation of authorisation in other Commonwealth jurisdictions. It is worth taking a moment to examine this here.

3.1.2.2 Authorisation Abroad: Divergent Interpretations

How has the nuanced notion of authorisation been treated in other common law countries? Interestingly, no unified interpretative line has emerged, with national jurisprudential evolutions instead heading, from the single starting point of *Falcon,* in completely opposite directions. The main divide is between the hard-liner Australian approach, as opposed to the more user-friendly Canadian one. This cross-jurisdictional debate has naturally had a strong influence the evolving English case law.

So, in *Moorhouse v. University of New South Wales*[30] the High Court of Australia, citing the broader 'sanction, approve, countenance' *Falcon* test of Bankes LJ, held that a university library was liable for authorising copyright infringement by providing photocopying machines without offering adequate supervision of what was being copied. In direct contrast to the *Amstrad* school of thought, a notice posted above the photocopiers warning against copyright infringement was deemed to be an insufficient safeguard. Specific instances of infringement were established and the Court found that, although there was no express permission given to students to copy protected material, the indifference exhibited by the university towards the possibility of infringement contained an implied invitation. The university was said to have had the power to control infringement by the students, either by not providing photocopying facilities or by ensuring adequate supervision of any copying. Making available the means by which an infringement of copyright may be committed, while knowing or having reason to suspect that it was likely to be used for the purpose of committing infringement, without taking reasonable steps to limit is use to legitimate purposes was thus considered to constitute a form of authorisation.

In reaction to the decision, in 1980, section 39A was inserted to the Australian Copyright Act 1968 giving libraries a limited immunity from the authorisation of copyright infringement; under the new provision, libraries offering photocopying services would not be liable for authorisation of

---

28. H MacQueen et al., *Contemporary Intellectual Property – Law and Policy* (2nd ed., Oxford University Press 2011) 161.
29. P S Davies, 'Accessory Liability Protecting Intellectual Property Rights' (2011) 4 Intellectual Property Quarterly 390.
30. *Moorhouse v. University of New South Wales* [1976] RPC 151 (HCA).

copyright infringement as long as they, as the UNSW library had done, had put up a notice warning users of the provisions of the act near the machine.[31] This would suggest an initial legislative disapproval of the outcome in *Moorhouse*. Nevertheless, in more recent years, the *Moorhouse* formulation became firmly entrenched in Australian law through codification in statute.[32] Section 36(1A) of the Copyright Act,[33] which was inserted with section 39 of the Copyright Amendment (Digital Agenda) Act 2000, provides that:

> In determining, for the purposes of subsection (1), whether or not a person has authorised the doing in Australia of any act comprised in a copyright subsisting by virtue of this Part without the licence of the owner of the copyright, the matters that must be taken into account include the following:
>
> - the extent (if any) of the person's power to prevent the doing of the act concerned;
> - the nature of any relationship existing between the person and the person who did the act concerned;
> - whether the person took any other reasonable steps to prevent or avoid the doing of the act, including whether the person complied with any relevant industry codes of practice.

The codification is partial only and courts must also take into account other relevant circumstances.[34] The *Moorhouse* principles have subsequently been applied by the Australian courts to find internet intermediaries liable for authorising online copyright infringements by their users.[35]

The Australian understanding of authorisation has been criticised as vague and overly broad. Vaver has described the formulation as an attempt to turn passivity into authorisation: he notes that 'authorise', 'sanction', and 'approve' 'may be close paraphrases, but 'countenance' is too wide since it connotes condonation, and to condone is not to authorise'.[36] From this perspective, the acceptance of the broader 'approve, sanction and countenance' definition of authorisation extends past the commonplace understanding of the word and does not allow for a dependable distinction between

31. M Rimmer, 'Canadian Rhapsody: Copyright Law and Research Libraries' (2004) 35(3) Australian Academic & Research Libraries 193.
32. The Parliament of the Commonwealth of Australia, Revised Explanatory Memorandum to the Copyright Amendment (Digital Agenda) Bill 2000.
33. Australian Copyright Act 1968 (consolidated as of 1 June 2011).
34. R Giblin, 'Authorisation in Context – Potential Consequences of the Proposed Amendments to Australian Secondary Liability Law' Australian Digital Alliance, August 2014.
35. *Universal Music Austl. Pty. Ltd v. Cooper* [2005] FCA 972 and *Universal Music Austl. Pty. Ltd v. Cooper* [2006] FCAFC 187 and *Universal Music Austl. Pty Ltd v. Sharman Licence Holdings Ltd* [2005] FCA 1242 (also known as '*Kazaa*').
36. D Vaver, *Copyright Law: Essentials of Canadian Law* (Toronto Irwin Law 1997) 142-143.

authorisation and mere facilitation.[37] Gendreau traces the broad Australian construction back to the lack of a provision in Australian law corresponding the CDPA rules on secondary liability. This results, she suggests, in a different relationship in Australia between acts of primary and of secondary infringement:

> When the distinction between the two types of infringements is maintained and authorization sits firmly in the camp of 'primary' infringements, as in Canada and the United Kingdom, it is easier to confine the concept of authorization to situations where the would be infringer is 'holding out' as the copyright owner; […] However, when the difference is obfuscated, as in Australia, it becomes possible to entertain as possible 'authorizers' persons who would not likely be regarded as actual copyright owners.[38]

This illustrates the confusion that is engendered when general principles stand in for more tailored specific provisions, resulting in fuzzy definitions that fail to adequately confine and thereby differentiate between different copyright concepts – in this case primary infringement, secondary infringement and authorisation.

In *Amstrad,* Lord Templeman briefly considered the Australian view, but (albeit somewhat non-committedly) seemed to dismiss it.[39] A more vociferous condemnation of the *Moorhouse* approach has come from the Supreme Court of Canada. *CCH*,[40] a case featuring very similar facts, concerned the provision by the Law Society of Upper Canada of a self-service photocopying machine for the use of its patrons in its Great Library at Osgoode Hall in Toronto. A notice was posted over the photocopiers warning that the library would not be responsible for any copyright-infringing copies made by means of the machine. McLachlin CJ, noting that no actual infringement had been documented, held that, although authorisation could be inferred from indirect acts and omissions, the authorisation of the use of equipment capable of infringing copyright did not constitute authorisation of such infringement. In this, he seems to be following the UK House of Lord's distinction between the concepts of the power to copy and the right to copy. While interestingly the Canadian court then opted for the broader Bankes LJ formulation of authorisation as 'to sanction, approve and countenance', it followed this interpretation up by insisting that 'countenance' must be understood in its strongest dictionary meaning of '[g]ive approval to; sanction, permit; favour, encourage'. The court acknowledged

37. E D Ventose & J J Forrester, 'Authorisation and Infringement of Copyright on the Internet' (2010) 14(6) Journal of Internet Law 3.
38. Y Gendreau, 'Authorisation Revisited' (2001) 48 Journal of the Copyright Society of the U.S.A. 341.
39. *CBS Songs v. Amstrad* [1988] UKHL 15 (12 May 1988), para. 605.
40. *CCH Canadian Ltd v. Law Society of Upper Canada* [2004] 1 SCR 339.

that authorisation can be inferred from acts that are less than direct and positive, including a sufficient degree of indifference, but noted that a person does not authorise infringement by simply authorising the use of equipment that could be used to infringe copyright. Instead, courts should presume that a person who authorises an activity does so only in so far as such activity is in accordance with the law, this assumption being rebuttable if a relationship or degree of control exists between the authoriser and the primary infringers. In the case at hand, the posting of a notice warding off responsibility for potential infringement could not be taken as express acknowledgement that the machines could be used for unlawful purposes, but instead was a reminder that no authorisation was given, while the Law Society could not be said to have no real control over its patrons. In the final analysis, the judge roundly condemned the Australian approach as inconsistent with what he identified as a united front of Canadian and British jurisprudence on the matter and bluntly criticised the liberal *Moorhouse* definition of authorisation as having shifted 'the balance in copyright too far in favour of the owner's rights and unnecessarily interfere[d] with the proper use of copyrighted works for the good of society as a whole'.

Interestingly, in that case there was no evidence that the photocopiers had been used in a manner inconsistent with copyright law. Instead, the Court of Appeal had simply assumed that that was the case. The Supreme Court disagreed with this approach, accepting that 'it is equally plausible that the patrons using the machines were doing so in a lawful manner'. This confirms the derivative nature of authorisation: 'a person does not authorize copyright infringement by authorizing the mere use of equipment (such as photocopiers) that could be used to infringe copyright'.

3.1.2.3 Authorisation Online

How have these foreign evolutions impacted English law? Before the English courts, the Australian argument of facilitation as a form of authorisation has been gaining more traction in recent years. Faced with rampart online infringement, right-holders have been putting forth claims that making available facilities in the knowledge that they will probably be used to infringe should qualify as 'authorising' them.[41] In response, UK judges have attempted to introduce a bit more flexibility to the traditionally restrictive interpretation of authorisation by backpedalling to the broader Bankes LJ definition.

So, in *Newzbin (No. 1)*,[42] a case involving the liability of a Usenet indexer liable for locating, categorising and reassembling for download binary files containing copies of protected films, Kitchin J initially reaffirmed

41. L Bently & B Sherman, *Intellectual Property Law* (3rd ed., Oxford University Press 2009) 154.
42. *Twentieth Century Fox Film Corporation & Anor v. Newzbin Ltd* [2010] EWHC 608 (Ch).

the traditionally restrictive English approach to authorisation: according to the judge 'it is clear […] that 'authorise' means the grant or purported grant of the right to do the act complained of. It does not extend to mere enablement, assistance or even encouragement'. However, after noting that authorisation may be express or implied from all the relevant circumstances, the judge proceeded to recite a checklist of circumstances with the potential to imply 'authorisation by supply':

(1) the nature of the relationship between the alleged authoriser and the primary infringer;
(2) whether the equipment or other material supplied constitutes the means used to infringe;
(3) whether it is inevitable that it will be used to infringe;
(4) the degree of control which the supplier retains; and
(5) whether the supplier has taken any steps to prevent infringement.

The judge made it clear that this list is not intended to be exhaustive, while individual items may or may not be determinative depending upon all other circumstances. In application to the case before him, Kitchen J found a number of factors relevant, including the provision by Newzbin of sophisticated tools facilitating infringement, the large number of commercial content hosted, the payment of a weekly fee by the site's premium members, the lack of a filtering system and the fact that Newzbin had actively encouraged its editors to make reports on films, had rewarded them for doing so and had instructed and guided them to include URLs in their reports, while also failing to take any steps to remove editors who had, to its knowledge, posted reports on infringing material. It was also noted that, although contractual restrictions were imposed on editors and members in relation to infringing activity, these were inconsistent with the structure and operation of the Newzbin system and the advice given to editors. They were therefore clearly window dressing.

As a result of all the above, Newzbin was found to be liable for purporting 'to possess the authority to grant any required permission to copy any film that a member may choose from the Movies category on Newzbin', having 'sanctioned, approved and countenanced the copying of the claimants' films, including each of the films specifically relied upon in these proceedings'.

The case is particularly interesting in its treatment of the relationship of authorisation to the establishment of primary infringements: Kitchin J, although accepting that a copyright infringement by Newzbin's premium members must first be found before he can proceed to considering Newzbin's accessory liability, glibly substantiated such liability only on the *overwhelming likelihood* that infringement had occurred. The court relied in this reasoning on the substantial number of active premium members, the evident interest of these members in films, as well as the popularity of the titles suggested by the claimants. The judge noted that the reason why greater accuracy was not possible in the identification of the particular films downloaded by premium members was the decision on Newzbin's part to avoid recording the details of the files downloaded via its system.

The Newzbin case law was replicated two years later in *Dramatico Entertainment,*[43] a case described by its judge as '[i]f anything, [...] stronger' than *Newzbin (No. 1). Dramatico* examined two preliminary issues with regard to the imposition of a section 97A CDPA injunction requiring six UK main retail internet service providers to take measures to block or at least impede access by their customers to the well-known peer-to-peer file-sharing website 'The Pirate Bay' (TPB): whether (a) the users of TPB and (b) the operators of TPB have infringed the claimant right-holder's copyrights. Referring back to *Newzbin (No. 1),* Arnold J proceeded to apply, in a much more systematic fashion, the criteria relevant to a finding of authorisation by supply as previously identified by Kitchin J. The findings of the Court in this regard were as follows:

(1) The nature of the relationship: TPB provided a sophisticated and user-friendly environment in which its users were able to search for and locate content. TPB was in no sense a passive repository of torrent files. By contrast, it went to great lengths to facilitate and promote the download of torrent files by its users.
(2) The means used to infringe: The torrent files indexed, arranged and presented by TPB were precisely the means employed by end-users to infringe in the downloading and making available to others of protected works.
(3) The inevitability of infringement: According to the Court, infringement was not merely an inevitable consequence of the provision of torrent files by TPB. Instead, it was the operators' objective and intention, as evidenced by, among other elements, the name of the site, the pirate ship logo, the fact that it was founded by a Swedish anti-copyright organisation, statements by its founders to the effect that its purpose entailed pirate copying and the site's embroilment in numerous court cases across Europe, which should have made clear to its operators that it was engaged in copyright infringement, as well as the derisive attitude taken by its operators towards the legal proceedings begun against them.[44]

---

43. *Dramatico Entertainment Ltd & Ors v. British Sky Broadcasting Ltd & Ors* [2012] EWHC 268 (Ch).
44. So, for example, as the judge noted, the 'about' page of TPB contained comments such as the following: '[a]ny complaints from copyright and/or lobby organisations will be ridiculed and published at the site' or '[n]o action (except ridiculing the senders) has been taken by us because of these.:-) Nice graphs for the law firms who don't get the hint above: (we used to have a nice graph here, but it's simpler to just say: 0 torrents has been removed, and 0 torrents will ever be removed.)'

(4) The degree of control: Should the operators have wished to do so, it would have been be possible to remove infringing torrents from TPB website. Such removals were effected in other circumstances, such as e.g., where the name of a file did not correspond to its content or in cases of child porn, fakes, malware, spam and miscategorised torrents. The rights of copyright owners were excluded from the criteria by which the operators of the TPB choose to exercise this power as a matter of policy.

(5) Steps taken to prevent infringement: The operators of TPB did not take any steps to prevent infringement, despite their ability to do so and the judicial findings against them – indeed they encouraged infringement and treated attempts to curb it with contempt.

In conclusion, the Court found that TPB operators went 'far beyond merely enabling or assisting. On any view, they 'sanction, approve and countenance' the infringements of copyright committed by its users'. They were also found to purport to grant users the right to do the acts complained of. The judge further noted that it was 'no defence that they openly defy the rights of the copyright owners'. It is worth noting that neither *Newzbin (No. 1)* nor *Dramatico* make mentioned of the E-Commerce safe harbours, although these would likely not apply anyway, in view of the operators disregard for notices of infringement. The omission is nevertheless curious, as the safe harbours would at least seem to suggest that a stronger claim for the existence of a primary wrong than mere 'likelihood' – however overwhelming – must exist.

Strangely, both rulings seem more compatible with the broader Australian notion of authorisation than the more stringent English test. The judges, although paying lip-service to Lord Templeman's understanding of authorisation as 'the granting or purporting to grant of a right' and accepting that authorisation 'does not extend to mere enablement, assistance or even encouragement', then unaccountably revert to the 'sanction, approve and countenance' test, ignoring its dismissal by the House of Lords. Indeed, although Kitchin J's list of circumstances substantiating 'authorisation by supply' is ostensibly derived by an extensive excerpt quoted from *Amstrad,* upon examination this does not in fact seem to offer a strong foothold for their selection, given that two of the five criteria listed (whether the equipment constituted the means used to infringe and whether it was inevitable that it would be used to infringe) are circumstances that Lord Templeman explicitly rejected and a further two (the degree of control retained by the supplier and whether they had taken any steps to prevent infringement) circumstances about which he was at best ambivalent. Instead, the list appears to derive clear inspiration from the Australian 'sanction, approve and countenance' test, to which the decision then turns, with three out of the five listed factors eerily reminiscent of section 36(1A) of the Australian Copyright Act and the rest taken straight out of the Australian case law denounced by Lord Templeman. The *Newzbin (No. 1)* judge in fact concludes that '[i]n my judgment [the Australian] decisions are entirely consistent with the principles which I have summarised and which I believe I must apply' – given that they are the only real basis offered in the ruling for their introduction this is perhaps unsurprising.[45]

The British judges' preference for foreign case law over that of their own jurisdiction's highest court can be explained by the fact that a faithful application of Lord Templeman's reasoning would most likely have led to a finding of no liability.[46] Arguably, neither Newzbin nor TPB 'purport to authorise' copyright infringement by their users; rather, their users download copyright-protected material from their sites in full knowledge of the illegality of their actions and with the intent to engage in them as such. The founders of the TPB in particular, vocal anti-copyright advocates who openly support users' right to copy without having to request right-holder authorisation, cannot be said to assume any authority to grant a right, as it is quite clear from their statements that they object to the very existence of copyright. As Laddie, Prescott and Vitoria have observed, 'the reference to granting or purporting to grant the right to do something cannot properly be construed as a reference to the purported grant to the 'right' to sue the copyright work, for this does not occur where both parties know perfectly well that a piratical use is intended'.[47] If both parties know that the intended copying is illegal, it is misleading to talk about the purported grant of a right.[48] Quite to the contrary, what the sites in question encourage is precisely unauthorised copying; if anything, therefore, they can be accused of superseding, not the right-holder in her prerogatives, but the legislator in his. The distinction is significant as it highlights the limits of the authorisation doctrine and the extent to which the term is being distorted beyond its natural meaning in an effort to adapt outdated liability rules to a changing landscape.

Interestingly, in the meantime, the Australian approach to authorisation has been somewhat mitigated.[49] In 2010, in *iiNet,*[50] the Federal Court of Australia decided a case brought against Australia's second largest internet access provider, for failing to prevent their customers from downloading and sharing infringing copies of protected works using BitTorrent. Cowdroy J

45. Riordan reaches the same conclusion, see J Riordan, *The Liability of Internet Intermediaries* (PhD thesis, University of Oxford 2013, forthcoming Oxford University Press 2016) 152.
46. Cf. a pre-Newzbin analysis of a hypothetical outcome of *Cooper* under UK law, L Bently & B Sherman, *Intellectual Property Law* (3rd ed., Oxford University Press 2009) 156.
47. H Laddie et al., *The Modern Law of Copyright and Designs* (3rd ed., Butterworths 2000) 1776.
48. E D Ventose & J J Forrester, 'Authorisation and Infringement of Copyright on the Internet' (2010) 14(6) Journal of Internet Law 3.
49. D Seng, 'Comparative Analysis of the National Approaches to the Liability of Internet Intermediaries', WIPO study, available at: www.wipo.int/copyright/en/internet_intermediaries.
50. *Roadshow Films Pty Ltd v. iiNet Limited (No 3)* [2010] FCA 24.

reread *Moorhouse* to hold that, before it can be said to have authorised infringement, an internet intermediary has to be found to have provided 'the true "means" of infringement' by extending an implied or express invitation to use its facilities infringe. This must be done in a *calculated* way so as to bring about the infringements that resulted. A subsequent appeal to the High Court of Australia was unanimously dismissed. The court concluded that 'the concept and the principles of the statutory tort of authorisation of copyright infringement are not readily suited to enforcing the rights of copyright owners in respect of widespread infringements occasioned by peer-to-peer file sharing, as occurs with the BitTorrent system'.[51]

Back in the UK, there has been no halt yet in the expansive interpretation of authorisation – indeed, recent developments have, if anything, headed in the opposite direction. So, in *EMI v. Sky,* Arnold J (again applying five *Newzbin (No. 1)* criteria) established the liability for the authorisation of infringement of three peer-to-peer file-sharing websites, KAT, H33T and Fenopy, on the back of the insufficiencies of their notice-and-take-down regime:

> A 'provision of URL' policy might work for a website which generally hosts legal content, but which suffers from isolated instances of infringing content. It is entirely unworkable where the website is geared towards offering a constantly replenished stock of infringing content. […] BPI wrote to the operators of each of the Websites explaining to them the impracticality of a 'provision of URL' policy for removal of content and asking them to remove all listings and links relating to a sample list of 533 recordings from 40 albums and to confirm that they would remove any further listings and links that were notified to them from time to time. As is explained by Mr Whitehead, the responses have either been obstructive (in the cases of KAT and H33T) or non-existent (in the case of Fenopy). None of the listings or links relating to the sample recordings was taken down by any of the Websites.[52]

Once again, whether refusal to combat infringement can properly be said to represent an appropriation of authority can be disputed. More troublingly, the reasoning here indicates a belief that the websites in question were not only liable for notified content that was not taken down, but should have implemented notice-and-*stay-down* procedures, incorporating permanent filtering measures such as to necessarily require the monitoring of all content posted by all users, as a preventive measure and exclusively at the cost of the intermediary – i.e., general monitoring of the *Netlog* type. As

---

51. *Roadshow Films Pty Ltd & Ors v. iiNet Ltd* [2012] HCA 16.
52. *EMI Records Ltd & Ors v. British Sky Broadcasting Ltd & Ors* [2013] EWHC 379 (Ch) (28 February 2013).

explained above, this interpretation is of exceedingly dubious legality under EU law.[53]

The decisions of the High Court cannot of course be said to mark a departure in English law from the precedent laid down in *Amstrad* – such a development would be a task for the Supreme Court of the United Kingdom (UK).[54] What they do reveal is bewildered lower courts struggling to identify a sound jurisprudential basis on which to ground the liability of third parties whose blameworthiness the judges instinctively accept. The result is legal gymnastics that fail to convince. As an alternate route, given that the infringement of copyright is a tort,[55] a more sensible and straightforward approach to the issue of intermediary liability can be identified in the general theory of tort law and more specifically in the common law doctrine of joint tortfeasance.[56] After all, this is where the codified notion of authorisation finds its roots, while joint tortfeasance has also been described as the English equivalent of the American intermediary liability solutions of 'contributory liability'[57] and 'inducement'.[58]

3.1.3 Return to Tort Law Basics: Joint Tortfeasance

The doctrine of joint tortfeasance is the legal tool through which English tort law is allowed to hold multiple persons liable for a single tort that results in a single damage occasioned by all of them.[59] It applies equally to statutory torts, such as copyright infringement, as it does to common law torts.[60] Joint tortfeasance is a subcategory of 'concurrent tortfeasance', i.e., the liability of

53. See Ch. 1, especially ss 2.2.4.1., 2.2.4.5., 2.2.7. and 2.3.1.
54. M Shillito & D Meale, 'Twentieth Century Fox Film Corp v Newzbin Ltd – Copyright – Online Service Provider Held Liable for Copyright Infringements of Its Users' (2010) 32(8) European Intellectual Property Review 67.
55. In *Credit Lyonnais Bank Nederland,* Hobhouse LJ was clear: 'These are cases which arise out of the law of intellectual property but the principles applied are drawn from the general law of tort. Infringement of a patent or copyright is a tort.' *Credit Lyonnais Bank Nederland NV (now Generale Bank Nederland NV) v. Export Credits Guarantee Department* [1999] C.L.C. 823.
56. E D Ventose & J J Forrester, 'Authorisation and Infringement of Copyright on the Internet' (2010) 14(6) Journal of Internet Law 3; L Bently & B Sherman, *Intellectual Property Law* (3rd ed., Oxford University Press 2009) 157; H Laddie, P Prescott, M Vitoria & A Speck, *The Modern Law of Copyright and Designs* (3rd ed., Butterworths 2000) 1777.
57. P S Davies, 'Accessory Liability Protecting Intellectual Property Rights' (2011) 4 Intellectual Property Quarterly 390.
58. L Bently & B Sherman, *Intellectual Property Law* (3rd ed., Oxford University Press 2009) 157.
59. H Carty, 'Joint Tortfeasance and Assistance Liability' (1999) 10 Legal Studies 489; J Dietrich, 'Accessorial Liability in the Law of Torts' (2011) 31(2) Legal Studies 231; G Williams, *Joints Torts and Contributory Negligence* (Stevens & Sons Ltd 1951) xxxix.
60. J Riordan, *The Liability of Internet Intermediaries* (PhD thesis, University of Oxford 2013, forthcoming Oxford University Press 2016) 149.

two or more persons who act to produce a single injury.[61] 'Joint (concurrent) tortfeasors' are thus to be distinguished from another kind of concurrent tortfeasors, 'several concurrent tortfeasors', i.e., two or more persons whose separate, independent torts combine to produce a single damage to the plaintiff.[62]

Joint tortfeasance may arise in any of three basic ways.[63] Either through: (a) the breach of a duty imposed jointly on multiple persons; (b) through a 'relationship link' binding the tortfeasors to each other (the result here is what is termed 'vicarious liability');[64] or c) through a 'participation link' binding the joint tortfeasors to the tort.[65] This book is primarily concerned with this final category, increasingly identified in the literature as 'accessory liability'. It should be noted that, the term 'participation link' was coined by Carty in her leading exposition of the topic,[66] but other terms are also employed by legal scholars: Cooper refers to the same concept as 'modes of participation';[67] Riordan talks about 'connecting factors',[68] while the more common term nowadays is probably 'conduct element'.[69]

Significantly, it is not any 'participation link' that will be sufficient to render a person an accessory to a tort; the participation of each joint tortfeasor must be significant enough to justify the imposition of liability. As Peter Gibson LJ's oft-repeated aphorism in *SABAF SpA v. MFI Furniture* would have it, each joint tortfeasor must be 'so involved in the commission of the tort as to make the infringing act their own'[70] – although, as Neuberger LJ objects in *Sea Shepherd v. Fish & Fish*, this is circular reasoning that isn't ultimately very illuminating.[71] Carty identifies three participation links or conduct elements that are generally acknowledged: authorisation, procurement and combination. A fourth possibility of assistance or facilitation is controversial, however the Supreme Court seems very recently to have given it the green light, albeit with a certain reconfiguration of the surrounding

61. G Williams, *Joints Torts and Contributory Negligence* (Stevens & Sons Ltd 1951) xxxix.
62. 'The *damnum* is single, but each commits a separate *injuria'* notes Williams; see, G Williams, *Joints Torts and Contributory Negligence* (Stevens & Sons Ltd 1951) 16. See: *The Koursk* [1924] P 140 (CA).
63. G Williams, *Joints Torts and Contributory Negligence* (Stevens & Sons Ltd 1951) 1.
64. P S Davies, *Accessory Liability* (Hart Publishing 2015) 59; L Bently & B Sherman, *Intellectual Property Law* (3rd ed, Oxford University Press 2009) 1075.
65. H Carty, 'Joint Tortfeasance and Assistance Liability' (1999) 10 Legal Studies 489.
66. H Carty, 'Joint Tortfeasance and Assistance Liability' (1999) 10 Legal Studies 489.
67. D Cooper, *Secondary Liability for Civil Wrongs* (unpublished PhD thesis, University of Cambridge 1995) 6.
68. J Riordan, The Liability of Internet Intermediaries (PhD thesis, University of Oxford 2013, forthcoming Oxford University Press 2016) 65-82.
69. P S Davies, *Accessory Liability* (Hart Publishing 2015) 7.
70. *Sabaf Spa v. MFI Furniture Centres and Another* [2002] EWCA Civ 976 (11 July 2002) paras 58-59.
71. *Sea Shepherd UK v. Fish & Fish Ltd* [2015] UKSC 10 (4 March 2015) para. 59.

theory. It is worth noting that, while this break down into 3+1 participation links is the one most commonly used in the literature, it is by no means universally adhered to: for example, McBride and Bagshaw list a fifth possibility of 'ratification',[72] while Sales limits himself to procurement and assistance[73] and Griffiths et al. opt for only procurement and common design.[74] The division adopted has little effect as, in any case, the enumerated participation links are non-exhaustive,[75] while the boundaries between the various links are exceedingly indistinct. As Bankes LJ observed in *The Koursk,* it would 'be unwise to define the necessary amount of connection. Each case must depend upon its own circumstances'.[76] This point is especially significant in view of the reformulation of the doctrine with the acceptance of assistance liability and shall thus be elaborated on in later sections.

Below, only the two 'participation links' of procurement and combination shall be examined. Enough has already been said about the authorisation of copyright infringement under its statutory guise above and there is no reason why the concept should have a different meaning in common law than in the CDPA.[77] The emerging participation link of assistance shall subsequently also be considered.

3.1.3.1 Procurement or Inducement

In *John Hudson v. Oaten*, Oliver LJ explained that a person who procures or induces the commission by another of a tortious act will be liable as a principle in the commission of the act: 'It is his tort'.[78] In extreme cases it is

72. N McBride & R Bagshaw *Tort Law* (3rd ed., Pearson 2012) 645. Riordan sees ratification as simply a 'retrospective version of authorisation', see J Riordan, The Liability of Internet Intermediaries (PhD thesis, University of Oxford 2013, forthcoming Oxford University Press 2016) 79.
73. P Sales, 'The Tort of Conspiracy and Civil Secondary Liability' (1990) 49(3) Cambridge Law Journal 491.
74. J Griffiths et al., 'United Kingdom' in L Bently, P Geller & M Nimmer, *International Copyright Law and Practice* (Matthew Bender/LexisNexis 2013) § 8[1][c][i][A].
75. J Riordan, The Liability of Internet Intermediaries (PhD thesis, University of Oxford 2013, forthcoming Oxford University Press 2016) 70-71.
76. *The Itria v. The Koursk* [1924] P 140 (22 February 1924).
77. P S Davies, 'Accessory Liability for Assisting Torts' (2011) 70(2) Cambridge Law Journal 353. Indeed, it has been suggested that Parliament's express inclusion of the tort of authorising infringement in the Copyright Act 1911 was simply a reaction to the undesirable judicial interpretation in *Karno v. Pathé Fréres* (*Karno v. Pathé Fréres* (1909) 100 LT 260), in which it was held that a defendant who gave permission to a third person to represent a play in breach of the right-holder's copyright did not 'cause it to be represented', as earlier statutes required, unless the person so representing it was the servant or agent of the defendant. Thus, the creation of the statutory tort was intended to re-establish the correct effect in copyright of the common law in joint tortfeasance. As a result, the two concepts should perfectly align.
78. *John Hudson & Co Ltd v. Oaten,* 1980 WL 612807.

indeed conceivable that the inducer may be the primary moving force behind the tortious act, controlling the actions of another, who is merely acting as his 'tool or cat's paw'. This could, for example, be the case where a legal person commits a wrong under the instructions of its director.[79] Similarly, if a person sells an article with instructions which, if followed, will result in the commission of a wrong, this can qualify as inducement.[80] In *Innes v. Short and Beal*, Bingham J, discussing the defendant's liability for selling powdered zinc with accompanying instructions that enabled the purchaser to infringe a patent, remarked that, although 'there is no reason whatever why Mr. Short should not sell powdered zinc […] though he may know or expect the people who buy it from him are going to use it in such a way it will amount to an infringement of Mr. Innes' patent rights', the defendant could not ask anyone to use his product in that way in order to induce them to buy it.[81] In *Dunlop Pneumatic*, another patent case, Swinfen Eady LJ, foreshadowing the US principle of substantial non-infringing uses,[82] found that the defendants did not infringe, despite the fact that most of their tyre covers would probably ultimately be used in one or the other of the claimant's patented methods, as they 'do not exhaust the purposes to which the covers may be put, and […] they would be useful for other purposes in connection with other tyres'.

Three points must be made with regard to inducement: a) an inducer can only be held liable for another's tortious actions if his inducement, incitement or persuasion played some part in the other's decision to infringe (although it should be noted that it has been found excessive to demand that it be shown that the principal tortfeasor would not have acted without the second party's involvement); b) the inducer can only be held to be a joint tortfeasor if he or she intended to encourage the other infringe;[83] c) finally, as Lord Templeman noted in *Amstrad,* generally speaking, for inducement, incitement or persuasion to infringe to establish joint tortfeasance to be found, they must be by a defendant to an individual infringer and must identifiably procure a particular infringement.[84]

3.1.3.2 Combination or Common Design

The leading authority on combination is *The Koursk*, a 1924 Court of Appeals case examining the liability of the navigators of two ships for damage caused to a third. Here Scrutton LJ commented that '[p]ersons are

79. L Bently & B Sherman, *Intellectual Property Law* (3rd ed., Oxford University Press 2009) 1075.
80. L Bently & B Sherman, *Intellectual Property Law* (3rd ed., Oxford University Press 2009) 1075; *Rotocrop International v. Genbourne* [1982] FSR 241.
81. *Innes v. Short and Beal* [1898] 15 RPC 449.
82. See *Sony Corp. v. Universal City Studios*, (1984) 464 U.S. 417.
83. N McBride & R Bagshaw *Tort Law* (4th ed., Pearson 2012) 700.
84. *CBS Songs v. Amstrad* [1988] UKHL 15 (12 May 1988).

said to be joint tortfeasors when their respective shares in the commission of the tort are done in furtherance of a common design'.[85] Significantly, mere similarity of design on the part of independent actors, causing independent damage, is not enough; there must be concerted action to a common end.[86] In other words, if two or more people agree on a plan of action in pursuance of which one of the group commits a tort, this will be treated as having been committed on behalf of and in concert with the rest, who will be considered to be accessories to the wrongdoing. It is not necessary that the secondary party have mapped out a plan with the primary offender: tacit agreement will suffice. Moreover, there need not be explicit common design to infringe, as long as the parties combine to secure the doing of acts which in the event prove to be infringements.[87] It also does not matter whether or not all parties knew they were infringing or believed e.g., that permission to copy the infringed goods had been given.[88] In *Amstrad*, control emerged as a dividing factor: once a model was sold by Amstrad, the company lost all control over its future use, eliminating the possibility of a common design. Lord Templeman instead concluded that, given that Amstrad lacked control over the actions of the purchasers of their machines or other users or in fact any interest in the use to which they put them, Amstrad could not be said to have acted in concert with the primary infringers on the mere fact that their machines could be used for unlawful as well as lawful purposes once sold. According to his Lordship, '[a]ll recording machines and many other machines are capable of being used for unlawful purposes but manufacturers and retailers are not joint infringers if purchasers choose to subsequently break the law'.

It should be noted that it is currently uncertain whether procurement and combination form two distinct ways of infringing or are different aspects of one single one. In *Unilever v. Gillette*, Mustill LJ leaned in favour of the former view, although noting that procurement may lead to combination and therefore qualify under both heads.[89] This interpretation, however, can certainly be disputed: so, for example, while it has been suggested that common design is narrower than procurement, in that in the former the accessory must actually take part in executing the plan,[90] it is not clear why encouragement would not qualify as 'taking part'. Similar question marks hang over the separation of authorisation from both procurement and

85. In the event the parties were found to be several concurrent tortfeasors. See *The Itria v. The Koursk* [1924] P 140 (22 February 1924).
86. Clerk and Lindsell on Torts, cited by Scrutton LJ in *The Itria v. The Koursk* [1924] P 140 (22 February 1924).
87. *Unilever plc v. Gillette (UK) Ltz* [1989] RPC 583.
88. L Bently & B Sherman, *Intellectual Property Law* (3rd ed., Oxford University Press 2009) 1076.
89. *Unilever plc v. Gillette (UK) Ltz* [1989] RPC 583.
90. J Riordan, The Liability of Internet Intermediaries (PhD thesis, University of Oxford 2013, forthcoming Oxford University Press 2016) 74.

combination, particularly in view of its codification in copyright law. Carty sees procurement as differing from authorisation in that the first refers to persuasion and the second to permission or command;[91] but if so, the line is very fine line indeed. Given how we have already seen above the difficulty that the courts face in properly separating authorisation from other types of involvement, the different treatment in the theory might not translate well into real world situations. Carty herself agrees that it is possible for both the permission or command elements that indicate authorisation and the persuasion necessary for procurement to accrue on the facts of a single case, allowing liability to be extended under both heads.[92]

3.1.3.3 Assistance or Faciliation

Until very recently it was understood that providing assistance or faciliation[93] to commit a tort could not substantiate joint tortfeasance. Carty, for example, is adamant: '[t]he doctrine of joint tortfeasance does not include liability for facilitators'.[94] McBride and Bagshaw reach the same conclusion: 'there is no accessory liability for assisting somebody to commit a tort'.[95] Winfield and Jolowicz state that 'there is no tort of 'knowing assistance' or any direct counterpart of the criminal law concept of aiding and abetting'.[96] A long line of case law supports these assertions: Aldous J in *PLG* stressed that 'a person who only facilitates a tort is not liable as a joint tortfeasor'.[97] In *Credit Lyonnais,* Stuart-Smith LJ stated that 'it is not enough that [the defendant] merely facilitates the commission of the tort unless his assistance is given in pursuance and furtherance of the common design'.[98] Hobhouse LJ was clearer still: 'knowing assistance is not enough to found tortious liability'; and later: '[a]cts which facilitate the commission of a crime amount to the crime of aiding and abetting but they do not amount to a tort or make the aider liable as a joint tortfeasor'.[99] As noted above, Lord Templeman rested the main thrust of his speech in *Amstrad* on a clear

91. H Carty, 'Joint Tortfeasance and Assistance Liability' (1999) 10 Legal Studies 489.
92. H Carty, 'Joint Tortfeasance and Assistance Liability' (1999) 10 Legal Studies 489.
93. The terms 'assistance', 'facilitation', 'aiding' and 'helping' should be understood as synonymous, see D Cooper, *Secondary Liability for Civil Wrongs* (unpublished PhD thesis, University of Cambridge 1995) 7.
94. H Carty, 'Joint Tortfeasance and Assistance Liability' (1999) 10 LS 489. Carty also rejects the idea of a theory of secondary liability for facilitation or assistance that applies separate to joint tortfeasance.
95. N McBride & R Bagshaw *Tort Law* (4th ed., Pearson 2012) 862.
96. W V H Rogers, *Winfield & Jolowicz on Tort* (18th ed., Sweet & Maxwell 2010) 993.
97. *PLG Research Ltd v. Ardon International Ltd* [1993] FSR 197.
98. *Credit Lyonnais Bank Nederland NV v. Export Credit Guarantee Department* [1999] CLC 823.
99. *Credit Lyonnais Bank Nederland NV (now Generale Bank Nederland NV) v. Export Credits Guarantee Department* [1999] CLC 823.

distinction between the legal treatment of facilitation and that of authorisation, procurement and common design. At first instance, Lawton LJ had been even more emphatic, when he stated that 'mere supplying with knowledge and intent will not be enough to make the supplier himself an infringer or a joint tortfeasor with someone who is'.[100]

Yet, the denial of assistance liability in English tort law was always somewhat puzzling: liability for aiding and abetting the commission of a crime is well established in penal law, while it is also agreed upon that dishonestly assisting someone to commit a breach of trust constitutes an equitable wrong.[101] The obvious reason for the juridical reluctance to recognise assistance liability in tort lies in the broad array of legitimate acts that would be implicated by such a measure.[102] Lord Templeman's discomfort with the idea of outlawing the manufacture and sale of recording devices is indicative. As McBride and Bagshaw opine, not 'holding A liable in a case where he throws a knife to B, which is then used to stab C, is a price we have to pay in the interests of legal certainty and public welfare'.[103] In order to appropriately circumscribe any potential assistance liability, the courts would have to limit its scope to either those who unreasonably do something that has the effect of assisting an infringement or those who intend their actions to assist in the commission of an infringement. But identifying the defendant's frame of mind – why she did what she did – is an exceedingly difficult task. McBride and Bagshaw advise: 'As we are not blessed with the ability to peer inside other people's souls, we would do well to steer clear of legal rules that require us to do this'.[104]

Nevertheless, English legal scholars have increasingly been questioning this logic. Most notably, Davies, as part of his broader proposal for a single, unified principle of civil accessory liability, has argued for the recognition of assistance liability both generally in tort and in particular for IPRs.[105] Davies criticises the rejection of facilitation as a participation link, noting that it

100. *Amstrad Consumer Electronics plc v. The British Phonographic Industry Ltd* [1986] FSR 159.
101. N McBride & R Bagshaw *Tort Law* (4th ed., Pearson 2012) 862-863.
102. N McBride & R Bagshaw *Tort Law* (4th ed., Pearson 2012) 863.
103. N McBride & R Bagshaw *Tort Law* (4th ed., Pearson 2012) 864.
104. N McBride & R Bagshaw *Tort Law* (4th ed, Pearson 2012) 659.
105. P S Davies, 'Accessory Liability for Assisting Torts' (2011) 70(2) Cambridge Law Journal 353; P S Davies, 'Accessory Liability: Protecting Intellectual Property Rights' (2011) 4 Intellectual Property Quarterly 390; P S Davies, 'Aid, Abet, Counsel or Procure?' in S Pitel, J Neyers, E Chamberlain (eds), *Tort Law: Challenging Orthodoxy* (Hart Publishing 2013) 413; P S Davies, *Accessory Liability* (Hart Publishing 2015). See also, P Sales, 'The Tort of Conspiracy and Civil Secondary Liability' (1990) 49(3) Cambridge Law Journal 491; J Dietrich, 'Accessorial Liability in the Law of Torts' (2011) 31(2) Legal Studies 231 and P Birks, 'Civil Wrongs: A New World' in *Butterworth Lectures 1990-91* (Butterworths 1992) 100.

seems inconsistent with pre-*Amstrad* case law.[106] He instead suggests the adoption of a widely defined conduct element, restrained by a narrow mental element, all anchored upon the premise of the commission of a primary wrong.

Davies puts forth a number of arguments in favour of this proposal, but one is particularly relevant for the purposes of this book. This relates to the practical difficulty of transposing into real life the theoretically unambiguous distinction between authorisation, inducement and common design on the one hand and assistance on the other: as Sales had earlier worried, in 'many cases, the dividing line between inducing a third party to commit a wrong and assisting him in its commission is so fine as to be non-existent'.[107] As an alternative, Davies suggests that 'both might better be viewed as points on a spectrum of participation which establish that the accessory bears some responsibility for the wrong committed'.[108] Rather than attempting to categorise types of participation, the focus should instead lie on whether or not the defendant's actions had a 'substantial impact' on the infringement. Thus, a *de minimis* rule equally applicable to all conduct elements that requires that the accessory have done more than negligibly contribute to a wrong committed by another would be better suited to the task of separating adequately tortious from inadequately tortious behaviour.[109] With regard to the mental element, Davies suggests a threshold of actual knowledge or at least of the constructive knowledge involved in 'turning a blind eye'. Helpfully, this corresponds to the knowledge test under the E-Commerce

---

106. Sales reports a long line of relevant case law in P Sales, 'The Tort of Conspiracy and Civil Secondary Liability' (1990) 49(3) Cambridge Law Journal 491, see footnote 39. Conventional legal theory also supported the idea. For example, in the 1960s, Atiyah wrote that just 'as in the criminal law relating to misdemeanours any person who 'aids or abets' the commission of the offence is guilty as a secondary party, so it is clear that in the law of torts any one who assists the commission of a tort is liable as a secondary party', see P S Atiyah, *Vicarious Liability in the Law of Torts* (Butterworth 1967) 195. According to Fleming, '[k]nowingly assisting, encouraging or merely being present as a conspirator at the commission of the wrong would suffice', see J Fleming, *The Law of Torts* (8th ed., Law Book Co 1992), 256. Similarly, Williams stated that if 'A claps C in irons and B assists by threatening to strike C if he resists, B is liable as a joint tortfeasor'. Where Williams does draw the line is instead at 'mere presence': 'mere presence will not make a person a joint tortfeasor any more than it makes him a party to a crime […] [He] did not assist (save in the Gallic sense), and therefore [is not party] to a tort', see G Williams, *Joints Torts and Contributory Negligence* (Stevens & Sons 1951), 11-14.
107. P Sales, 'The Tort of Conspiracy and Civil Secondary Liability' (1990) 49(3) Cambridge Law Journal 491.
108. P S Davies, 'Aid, Abet, Counsel or Procure?' in S Pitel, J Neyers, E Chamberlain (eds), *Tort Law: Challenging Orthodoxy* (Hart Publishing 2013) 413.
109. P S Davies, *Accessory Liability* (Hart Publishing 2015) 24, 39. This suggestion seems to be inspired by criminal law: according to Williams, as 'a matter of common sense a person who gives very minor assistance ought not to be held liable as an accessory', see G Williams, *Criminal Law: The General Part* (Stevens & Sons 1953) 294.

Directive's hosting safe harbour; and indeed, Davies locates in the harmonising influence of the EU a potential catalyst for the acceptance of a conduct element of assistance in England, at least as regards intellectual property law.[110]

In a dramatic twist, in its recent decision in *Sea Shepherd v. Fish & Fish*[111] the UK's Supreme Court seems to have moved in precisely this direction, thus accepting facilitation into the participation link fold. Already at first instance and in a break from conventional wisdom, Hamblen J had stated that the 'joint tortfeasor needs to join or share in the commission of the tort which generally means some act which at least facilitates its commission'.[112] In this conclusion, the judge seems to have relied on the following statement by Hobhouse LJ *Credit Lyonnais:*[113]

> Mere assistance, even knowing assistance, does not suffice to make the 'secondary' party jointly liable as a joint tortfeasor with the primary party. What he does must go further. He must have conspired with the primary party or procured or induced his commission of the tort […] or he must have joined in the common design pursuant to which the tort was committed.

Hamblen J interpreted this pronouncement to conclude that, in order to establish joint tortfeasance, what is required of the accessory joint tortfeasor will be 'some act which at least facilitates its commission'. The Supreme Court seems to have by and large agreed: Lord Sumption identified three requirements of joint tortfeasance: 'the defendant will be liable as a joint tortfeasor if (i) he has assisted the commission of the tort by another person, (ii) pursuant to a common design with that person, (iii) to do an act which is, or turns out to be, tortious'.[114] The Court uses the term 'accessory liability' to describe this type of joint tortfeasance.

At first sight, this seems to turn the traditional wisdom with regard to joint tortfeasance on its head. Upon closer inspection, it is clear that it instead represents an eminently coherent conclusion that remains fully in line with precedent, while demonstrating the wrong-headedness of the usual assumptions about, not only the relationship of facilitation to joint tortfeasance, but the very structure of joint tortfeasance and its dependence on identified 'participation links'. Indeed, according to the judge's interpretation, 'mere' facilitation remains incapable of substantiating liability. As is usually said, 'something more is needed'. That something more is provided by the primary

110. P S Davies, *Accessory Liability* (Hart Publishing 2015) 201.

111. *Sea Shepherd UK v. Fish & Fish Ltd* [2015] UKSC 10 (4 March 2015).

112. *Fish & Fish Ltd v. Sea Shepherd UK & Anor* [2012] EWHC 1717 (Admlty) (25 June 2012).

113. *Credit Lyonnais Bank Nederland NV v. Export Credits Guarantee Department* [1998] 1 Lloyd's Rep 19.

114. *Fish & Fish Ltd v. Sea Shepherd UK & Anor* [2012] EWHC 1717 (Admlty) (25 June 2012) para. 37.

wrong and, as case law had repeatedly informed us, 'a common design'. The first confirms the nature of accessory liability as 'parasitic' upon the tort of the primary tortfeasor. Much more importantly, the second reveals that, instead of functioning, as has been assumed, as a conduct element and thus an alternative to 'mere facilitation', common design is instead an additional condition of joint tortfeasance to be added to facilitation: the facilitation of a tortious act cannot be 'mere', not because it doesn't offer a strong enough participation link binding the facilitator to the tort, but because it is only one among three conditions for a finding of joint tortfeasance as an accessory. The judge explains the formulation of the law as a result of its concern with recognising 'a liability for assisting the commission by the primary actor of a tort, while ensuring that the mere facilitation of the tort will not give rise to such a liability, even when combined with knowledge of the primary actor's intention'.

This interpretation makes 'common design' sound much less like a description of the type action that the accessory must engage in (which is instead permitted to remain at 'mere facilitation') and much more as a reference to the joint tortfeasor's state of mind. Indeed, Lord Sumption compares the function of 'common design' to that of *mens rea* in criminal law. This confirms the break down of participation links into a 'conduct element' and a 'mental element', as often suggested in the literature.[115] What should the threshold for satisfying this mental element be? Importantly, the Court does not agree to the same standard for accessory liability in tort law as that accepted by its criminal law counterpart. While in criminal law an act of assistance may lead to liability if accompanied by knowledge that the primary offence is being aided and abetted, in tort law the need to limit interference with peoples' right to do things which are in themselves entirely lawful makes this possibility excessive. Thus, the idea advocated in recent scholarship of the recognition of liability in tort law for knowing assistance is rejected.[116]

Instead, in a ground-breaking pronouncement, Lord Sumption, goes on to equate 'common design' with 'intent'. Referring to Lord Templeman's declaration in *Amstrad* that 'joint tortfeasors are two or more persons who act in concert with one another pursuant to a common design', he states:

> I do not think that in this passage Lord Templeman was seeking to limit liability as a joint tortfeasor to cases of inducement or procurement, as opposed to assistance. When read with his general statement of the elements of liability as a joint tortfeasor, it is clear that he was intending to limit it to cases of common intent. Inducing or procuring a tort necessarily involves common intent if the tort is then committed. Mere

115. See e.g., P S Davies, *Accessory Liability* (Hart Publishing 2015) 21 et seq and 40 et seq.
116. J Dietrich, 'Accessorial Liability in the Law of Torts' (2011) 31(2) Legal Studies 231; P S Davies, 'Accessory Liability for Assisting Torts' (2011) 70(2) Cambridge Law Journal 353; P S Davies, *Accessory Liability* (Hart Publishing 2015) 177-222.

> assistance may or may not do so, depending on the circumstances. The mere supply of equipment which is known to be capable of being used to commit a tort does not suggest intent. Other circumstances may do so.

In this way, common design appears to make a quantum leap[117] from conduct element to mental element. At the same time, although repositioned within joint tortfeasance, 'common design' remains the key to its substantiation: the essence of joint tortfeasance resides, not so much in the defendant's behaviour, but rather in a need to establish an intention to cause harm through that behaviour. It is indicative that, although *Sea Shepherd* is not even a copyright case, Lord Sumption refers to the US case of *Grokster,*[118] citing with approval the American doctrine of inducement and observing that it makes 'the same distinction between mere knowledge at the point of sale and action combined with common intention'.

Curbs on the breadth of the conduct element are also foreseen: not all facilitation indiscriminately will be able to satisfy the first hurdle of joint tortfeasance. Says Lord Neuberger:

> the assistance provided by the defendant must be substantial, in the sense of not being *de minimis* or trivial. However, the defendant should not escape liability simply because his assistance was (i) relatively minor in terms of its contribution to, or influence over, the tortious act when compared with the actions of the primary tortfeasor, or (ii) indirect so far as any consequential damage to the claimant is concerned. Nor does a claimant need to establish that the tort would not have been committed, or even that it would not have been committed in the precise way that it was, without the assistance of the defendant. I agree with Lord Sumption that, once the assistance is shown to be more than trivial, the proper way of reflecting the defendant's relatively unimportant contribution to the tort is through the court's power to apportion liability, and then order contribution, as between the defendant and the primary tortfeasor.

De minimis non curat lex: the law does not concern itself with trifles. Facilitations so small as to be legally equivalent to nothing do not suffice to satisfy the first step of joint tortfeasance.[119]

The above analysis is confirmed by the rest of the court. Indeed, although the judges are split 3 to 2 as to the outcome of the case, they declared their broad agreement as to the legal principles, their differences of

117. That is to say, a shift that is in fact very small, while being commonly assumed to be monumental, see Z Weiner, 'Saturday Morning Breakfast Cereal', available at: http://smbc-comics.com/?id=2628.
118. *Metro-Goldwyn-Mayer Studios Inc v. Grokster Ltd,* 545 US 913 (27 June 2005).
119. See in this regard also earlier suggestions in legal scholarship: D Cooper, *Secondary Liability for Civil Wrongs* (unpublished PhD thesis, University of Cambridge 1995) 8-9; P S Davies, *Accessory Liability* (Hart Publishing 2015) 34-39.

opinion instead relating only on the application of these to the facts of the case at hand. Lord Neuberger for example, although disagreeing with him as to their application, repeats Lord Sumption's 'three-step test' almost verbatim.[120] Lord Toulson also agrees that assistance is the 'first element of accessory liability' and common design the 'second element'.[121] Lords Kerr and Mance focus more on the minimal or non-minimal nature of the assistance given, but both accept that non-minimal assistance should be enough to lead to liability.

The ultimate result is eminently satisfactory. Assistance liability in English tort law is finally recognised. Accessory liability is also recognised, named as such and given a definition: it is 'assistance in furtherance of a common design' to commit a tort, i.e., essentially joint tortfeasance by common design.[122] Moreover, these developments are achieved while keeping the judgment in perfect alignment with previous precedent and deftly crafting a coherent principle out of a historically notoriously troublesome area of tort law. Indeed, it could be argued that the House of Lords at least, always understood this to be the theory of accessory liability: in *Credit Lyonnais*, Hobhouse LJ contrasts 'mere assistance' with 'knowing assistance', indicating that the word 'mere' refers to a lack of a mental element. In 2008, in *Total Network SL v. Revenue and Customs,*[123] Lord Neuberger tellingly referred in passing to 'the well-established principle that, where two or more parties join together in some way with a view to assisting or enabling one or more of them to commit a tort, all are liable for the tort as joint tortfeasors' – a rather incongruous statement perhaps in view of the common assumptions as to the standing of assistance liability in English law at the time, but one whose validly is revealed by the later analysis of *Sea Shepherd.*

If the Court does take one false turn then that relates to the precise positioning of accessory liability within the broader structure of joint tortfeasance. Lord Toulson seems to see English accessory liability as limited to cases exhibiting a conduct element of assistance, while forming a forth branch on the joint tortfeasance tree alongside the joint breach of duty, vicarious liability and 'procuring the commission of a tort by inducement, incitement or persuasion'.[124] This would indicate that 'accessory liability' is a separate category to joint tortfeasance by procurement. It is submitted that this is a pointless distinction. The issue brings back the tricky question of fine lines and their elusive translation from theory into practice. The nature of procurement is relevant in this regard is that also capable of being broken down into a conduct and mental element? If so, how is its conduct element different from assistance and its mental element from intention? Dietrich

120. At para. 55.
121. At para. 27.
122. Lord Sumption at para. 49.
123. *Total Network SL v. Revenue and Customs* [2008] UKHL 19 (12 March 2008).
124. At paras 19-20.

observes that where one person induces another to commit a tort, they clearly intend that the tort be committed.[125] But if the mental element is contained within the procurement itself, how is that procurement different to assistance combined with common design? In *Belegging-en Exploitatiemaatschappij Lavender v. Witten Industrial Diamonds,* Buckley LJ agreed that 'facilitating the doing of an act is obviously different from procuring the doing of an act'.[126] This might be so, but does that difference rest in anything other than the existence mental element of intent? If not, then it evaporates as soon as intent is added to assistance following the 'common design' recipe of *Sea Shepherd.* Riordan breaks down both 'procurement' and 'participation in a common design' into a 'physical element' and 'mental element', the latter being intention for both categories. He then suggests that the 'physical element' of procurement must exert on the primary wrongdoer a 'material causal influence', which he submits imposes a significantly higher threshold than the mere facilitation that forms the conduct element of common design or (in the terminology of *Sea Shepherd*) 'accessory liability'.[127] But, as was mentioned above, an encouragement to commit a tort might well take the form of assistance and *vice versa.*[128] The particular focus of this book, the supply of means by internet intermediaries to copyright infringers, reveals this well, as it could conceivably be viewed as both assistance and as encouragement to commit a tort, while (as was seen above) the courts have gone as far as to suggest it also amounts to authorisation.

It is not clear how the other judges feel about Lord Toulson's compartmentalisation. The only hint is given by Sumption LJ's statement that '[i]nducing or procuring a tort necessarily involves common intent if the tort is then committed'. This indicates that he sees inducement as a conduct that contains within itself proof of the necessary mental element. This seems much more reasonable. Indeed, it is suggested that what would make for a much better solution would be a single wider principle according to which a party that intentionally participates in a tort in any way will be liable as an accessory to that tort: this would both provide a more accurate description of the standard the courts seem to be driving at, as well as a considerably more workable test. Along similar lines of thinking, Dietrich expresses his dislike for the break down into multiple, separate 'participation links' arguing that they conflate the real dependence of accessory liability in all cases on two basis conditions: the finding of a conduct element and the finding of a mental element.[129] Davies has also suggested that '[a]ll forms of participation that

125. J Dietrich, 'Accessorial Liability in the Law of Torts' (2011) 31(2) Legal Studies 231.
126. *Belegging-en Exploitatiemaatschappij Lavender BV v. Witten Industrial Diamonds Ltd,* [1979] FSR 59.
127. J Riordan, The Liability of Internet Intermediaries (PhD thesis, University of Oxford 2013, forthcoming Oxford University Press 2016) 71.
128. P Sales, 'The Tort of Conspiracy and Civil Secondary Liability' (1990) 49(3) Cambridge Law Journal 491.
129. J Dietrich, 'Accessorial Liability in the Law of Torts' (2011) 31(2) Legal Studies 231.

create a link between the defendant and the infringement of the claimant's right by contributing in a more than minimal way to the primary wrong should be sufficient for accessory liability'.[130] As mentioned above, it is already anyway acknowledged that the participation links currently identified in the case law and scholarship are non-exhaustive.[131] It is therefore time that English law fully accept this fact instead of searching for ways to mask it and adopt a broadly stated general principle that does not rely on the identification of limited 'links'. At the same time, it is of course true that little of relevance rests on the precise categorisation of accessory liability, procurement and assistance liability. These are matters much more relevant in theory than in practice. For this same reason, the judges' statements on the topic should probably anyway be seen as *obiter*.

3.1.3.4 Joint Tortfeasance and Intermediary Liability

In any case, regardless of its precise formulation, for the assessment of the liability of internet-based intermediaries for copyright infringements committed by others, joint tortfeasance has a pronounced advantage over the overworked and outdated concept of authorisation. Not least among its advantages is the fact that it provides solid legal grounds for the introduction of a component of blameworthiness to the liability standard, i.e., of precisely that mental element of malevolence as to the commission of the tortious act that the courts seem to be so intent on injecting into the discussion. This is strengthened by *Sea Shepherd's* emphasis of intention as a condition for a finding of accessory liability. Under such an approach, while Lord Templeman's suggestion that no common design to infringe can be deduced in cases such as *Amstrad* would remain entirely valid, cases involving malicious file-sharing providers could, without any incongruity, lead to the exact opposite result, at least where the operators of the site make their anti-copyright sentiments public, thereby allowing the courts sturdy footing for condemning excessive involvement in the infringements of others.[132]

Indeed, the principles of joint tortfeasance have already been applied (alongside authorisation) by the judges in both *Newzbin (No. 1)* and *Dramatico*. Admittedly, there still seems to be some confusion on the part of the courts, as demonstrated by Kitchin J's reference to assistance and the provision of means as evidence in favour of the establishment of joint tortfeasance. This approach was five years ahead of its time, a fact evident from the confused coupling of that conduct element with a muddle of words

130. P S Davies, *Accessory Liability* (Hart Publishing 2015) 39-40.
131. J Riordan, The Liability of Internet Intermediaries (PhD thesis, University of Oxford 2013, forthcoming Oxford University Press 2016) 70-71.
132. E D Ventose & J J Forrester, 'Authorisation and Infringement of Copyright on the Internet' (2010) 14(6) Journal of Internet Law, 3. Although, see Davies's suggestion that Amstrad did in fact have intent to infringe, P S Davies, *Accessory Liability* (Hart Publishing 2015) 221.

indicating very different levels of mental involvement ('well knows', 'intended', 'promote', 'guide', 'induced', 'encouraged'). It is likewise unclear why Newzbin's profit from its operations should be considered relevant, as implied in the judgment,[133] given that the accusation is one of accessory, not vicarious liability. That said, even if the judgment's reasoning is objectionable, the result is not inappropriate, while the under-developed condition of the theory, especially at the time, goes a long way towards explaining any incoherence. More worrying is the way in which the *Newzbin (No. 1)* judge breezes over Lord Templeman's instructions as to the significance of the identification of an individual primary offender and a specific primary infringement, by interpreting this simply as 'one of the matters to be taken into account' – surely a strange take on a sentence that contains the word 'must' twice. Riordan suggests that the decision 'reflects a pragmatic concession to the traditional rule' – a very diplomatic way of saying it goes entirely against it.[134] In any case, Lord Templeman's dictum clearly refers exclusively to the participatory nexus of procurement and leaves common design unaffected. Again, although it would have been preferable if the judge had taken some time to properly tease out the applicable rules, it is understandable if the out-of-shape precedent did not make that task an easy one.[135]

These discrepancies are likely to be ironed out over time. It is indicative that, in *L'Oréal v. eBay*[136] Arnold J, while acknowledging that eBay (a much more sympathetic defendant) facilitate the infringement of third parties' trademarks by sellers, know in a general sense that such infringements have occurred and are likely to continue to occur and make profit from such infringements, ultimately stated (albeit 'not without considerable hesitation') that this is not enough to confirm eBay's liability: knowing participation cannot establish joint tortfeasance. Interestingly, the judge did rely on the lack of any specific acts of infringement by particular infringers that could be said to have been procured by the defendant. Of course, this ruling too is characteristically nebulous: with regard to common design, Arnold J pointed out that eBay could not be held liable as, under the provisions of the CDPA, although it owed a duty to not participate in a common design to infringe copyright, it was under no duty or obligation to prevent infringement of third parties' registered trademarks. The judge dismissed the suggestion that this was not the case as a circular argument: 'eBay Europe are under a duty to prevent third parties from infringing because they are under a duty not to

133. Arnold J also mentions profit as an indication of joint tortfeasance in *Dramatico*.
134. J Riordan, The Liability of Internet Intermediaries (PhD thesis, University of Oxford 2013, forthcoming Oxford University Press 2016) 153.
135. Indeed, Lord Templeman's reasoning is a rather confused itself, as he seems, under the influence of the corresponding principles of accessory liability in contract law, to mix the issue of procurement as a connecting factor leading to joint tortfeasance with the separate tort of 'incitement to commit a tort'.
136. *L'Oreal S.A v. eBay International AG* [2009] EWHC 1094 (Ch).

participate in a common design to infringe and they have participated in a common design to infringe because they have failed to prevent third parties from infringing'. But this reasoning avoids the central question: does failing to prevent infringement by one's users amount to participation in a common design to infringe? Accessory liability is by definition an exception to the general principle according to which one person will not ordinarily be responsible for the voluntary behaviour of others.[137] Simply reverting to the rule this deviates from in an attempt to define its reach is a different kind of circular reasoning that responds to an inquiry as to the existence of an exception to a rule by a restatement of the rule.

Indeed, one has to wonder from where TPB and Newzbin's duty arose that did not create a similar effect for eBay. The obvious answer here can once again be found in intention. And although this is not stated as such *in L'Oréal*, the judge does seem to rest the main thrust of his argument on observations that clearly head in this direction: thus, he observes that eBay's systems and policies contained no in-built bias or tendency in favour of infringement, while it could not be said that its facilities inherently lead to infringement. The most dubious of eBay's activities was the encouragement of and the provision of specific facilities for the promotion of cross-border trade, which translated in practice into assistance for the listing and sale of goods from outside the EEA to buyers in the United Kingdom. But, even in such cases, it not could be said that the services provided by eBay, given that they were capable of being used by sellers in a manner which does not infringe third party trademarks, were such as to inherently lead to infringement.[138] Instead, infringement depended on the autonomous actions of others. On this basis, we can extrapolate the conclusion that that neutrality and impartiality indicate a lack of intention and thus of duty and that they are to be measured against the benchmark of substantial non-infringing uses – but this could have been more clearly stated. In the end, Arnold J concludes that 'facilitation with knowledge and an intention to profit is not enough' to establish joint tortfeasance. Of course, depending on whether intention to profit can be equated with intention to cause, *Sea Shepherd* would of course cast serious doubt on this statement. Nevertheless, just as with *Newzbin (No 1)* and *Dramatico*, the lower courts cannot be blamed for not identifying clearly principles only later elucidated by higher authorities.

---

137. J Riordan, The Liability of Internet Intermediaries (PhD thesis, University of Oxford 2013, forthcoming Oxford University Press 2016) 88.
138. In this context, it is worth contemplating that, according to uncontested evidence supplied by *L'Oréal*, 202 out of 287 (70%) products delivered as part of investigatory purchases were not intended for sale in the EEA. 250 test purchases were conducted by L'Oréal out of which only one listing was removed by eBay before the transaction was completed. The bar for substantial non-infringing uses thus seems to be set remarkably low.

A much more straightforward case was presented by *Football Dataco v. Sportradar.*[139] This involved a pop-up box which, when clicked upon by a user, revealed data from a database protected by the *sui generis* database right. Here, Floyd J held that the website operator was not 'a mere intermediary, like eBay', whose services are used by a third party to infringe a right. Rather, the defendants 'adopt the acts of extraction which their customers will perform and make them their own'. Along similar lines, in a preliminary ruling on the liability of the primary infringers, the CJEU had noted that 'it may be concluded that the act discloses an intention on the part of the person performing the act to target members of the public'.[140] These observations reveal the connection between the language of 'making the tort one's own' and the question intention: supplying a service with no lawful uses suggests an obvious intention to engage in infringement through the vehicle of the actions of others,[141] while if there is intention to commit a tort, it matters little if the tortfeasor commits it by her own acts or by using another as a pawn. This is also why instances of 'accessory liability' are classified as a form of 'joint tortfeasance' under English law, as well as why knowing assistance – sufficient for secondary liability under sections 22-26 of the CDPA – cannot, as *Sea Shepherd* confirmed, be allowed to be enough to substantiate joint tortfeasance. As the Court of Appeal later stated, '[t]his is not a case of secondary liability but one of primary liability along with another'.[142] As Riordan observes, this is all the doctrine was ever supposed to do: not offer precise tests, but furnish conceptual structures for analysing the causal and relational culpability of secondary actors in particular cases.[143] The distinction between joint tortfeasance and secondary liability is an important part of that structure.

Football Dataco v. Sportradar was obviously an extreme case as no non-infringing uses were possible for the end-user, substantiating absolutely the intention of the website to infringe. Subsequently, Arnold J endorsed its reasoning in *EMI v. Sky,* this time involving copyright. A much less simple case, this involved peer-to-peer websites, the use of which was not inevitably infringing, even if in practice that was overwhelmingly often the case. The judge nevertheless concluded that the operators of websites in question 'induce, incite or persuade their users to commit infringements of copyright, and that they and the users act pursuant to a common design to infringe'. The judge did not elaborate greatly on his reasoning. Certainly, a strong argument

---

139. *Football Dataco Ltd & Ors v. Sportradar GmbH & Anor* [2012] EWHC 1185 (Ch) (8 May 2012).
140. CJEU, C-173/11, *Football Dataco and Others*, 18 October 2012.
141. J Riordan, The Liability of Internet Intermediaries (PhD thesis, University of Oxford 2013, forthcoming Oxford University Press 2016) 151.
142. *Football Dataco Ltd & Ors v. Stan James Plc & Ors* [2013] EWCA Civ 27 (6 February 2013).
143. J Riordan, The Liability of Internet Intermediaries (PhD thesis, University of Oxford 2013, forthcoming Oxford University Press 2016) 161.

can be made that the websites' refusal to take specifically identified content down indicated an intention to support the infringement and in that way substantiated joint tortfeasance.

The ultimate conclusion would seem to be that, although joint tortfeasance does indeed offer more promising grounds for a fair determination of the liability of internet intermediaries in comparison to the overwrought concept of authorisation, it is still not without its faults. Riordan suggests that it suffers from four main defects which undermine its ability to demarcate effective and proportionate limits on intermediary liability for internet copyright infringement: 'first, intrinsic ambiguity in the causal and relational thresholds required for liability; second, overlap and incoherence; third, inflexibility; and fourth, the absence of distributive tools needed to apportion responsibility'.[144] The explicit welcoming of a conduct element of facilitation into the joint tortfeasance fold arguably represents a reaction to these faults. If properly utilised, it could allow courts to introduce greater flexibility to the doctrine, while at the same time embracing a stronger, unitary structure, free from the traditional fragmentation into nominally separate, but factually exceedingly similar 'links'.

3.1.4 Injunctive Relief

If a claimant pursues his case to trial and succeeds, the next question that arises is that of remedies. Generally speaking pecuniary awards will be granted by the court, most commonly in the form of damages.[145] The court will usually also grant a permanent injunction for the protection of the claimant's rights.[146] Both of these remedies are available equally against primary and accessory tortfeasors. While this will be the end of the road for damages, injunctive relief may additionally, under certain circumstances, be deployed against otherwise entirely non-liable, neutral parties.[147] Two such possibilities are relevant to English intermediary liability.

3.1.4.1 Section 97A CDPA

According to section 20 of the Electronic Commerce (EC Directive) Regulations 2002, and in line with the E-Commerce Directive, the safe harbours of sections 17-19 are not intended to 'affect the rights of any party

144. J Riordan, The Liability of Internet Intermediaries (PhD thesis, University of Oxford 2013, forthcoming Oxford University Press 2016) 160.
145. See section 97 of the CDPA 1988 on damages for the infringement of copyright.
146. J Griffiths, L Bently & W Cornish, 'United Kingdom' in L Bently, P Geller & M Nimmer, *International Copyright Law and Practice* (Matthew Bender/LexisNexis 2013) § 8[4][a][iii].
147. J Riordan, The Liability of Internet Intermediaries (PhD thesis, University of Oxford 2013, forthcoming Oxford University Press 2016) 77.

to apply to a court for relief to prevent or stop infringement of any rights'. This point is further enforced by section 97A of the CDPA, which implements Article 8(3) of the Copyright Directive. Accordingly, it grants the High Court the power to issue injunctions against service providers whose services are being used by others to infringe copyright. Section 97A needed to be enacted in order to give effect to Article 8(3), as under English law an injunction cannot normally be granted against a person against whom no substantive cause of action exists.[148] The provision was applied for the first time by the English courts in *Newzbin (No. 2).*[149] Later, in *Dramatico v. Sky (No.2),* Justice Arnold set out in a clear manner the four jurisdictional requirements for the imposition of a section 97A injunction:

- the defendants must be service providers;
- the defendants' users must have infringed the claimants' copyright;
- the users must be using the defendants' services to do that;
- the defendants must have had actual knowledge of this.[150]

The last of these conditions is particularly interesting. The requirement of actual knowledge does not exist in Article 8 of the Copyright Directive, but is an innovation of the CDPA, which potentially brings UK law out of line with EU law. According to section 97A CDPA, in determining whether a service provider has actual knowledge, the court should take into account all matters which appear in the particular circumstances to be relevant.

---

148. *Paramount Home Entertainment & Anor v. British Sky Broadcasting & Ors* [2014] EWHC 937 (Ch) (18 February 2014) para. 8. No similar implementation exists in UK law for Art. 11 of the Enforcement Directive, potentially creating obstacles for the issue of injunctions against intermediaries for the enforcement of other IPRs, see *L'Oreal S.A v. eBay International AG* [2009] EWHC 1094 (Ch).
149. *Twentieth Century Fox Film Corp & Ors v. British Telecommunications Plc* [2011] EWHC 1981 (Ch) (28 July 2011) (*Newzbin No.2)*). See also on the form of relief, *Twentieth Century Fox Film Corporation & Ors v. British Telecommunications Plc* [2011] EWHC 2714 (Ch) (26 October 2011) (*Newzbin No.3)*).
150. *Dramatico Entertainment Ltd & Ors v. British Sky Broadcasting Ltd & Ors* [2012] EWHC 1152 (Ch) (2 May 2012) (*Dramatico v. Sky (No.2)*) para. 4. See also the subsequent line of case law issuing 97A injunctions: *EMI Records Ltd & Ors v. British Sky Broadcasting Ltd & Ors* [2013] EWHC 379 (Ch) (28 February 2013) (*EMI v. Sky*) para. 21; *The Football Association Premier League Ltd v. British Sky Broadcasting Ltd & Ors* [2013] EWHC 2058 (Ch) (16 July 2013) (*FAPL v. Sky*) para. 24; *Paramount Home Entertainment International Ltd & Ors v. British Sky Broadcasting Ltd & Ors* [2013] EWHC 3479 (Ch) (13 November 2013) (*Paramount v. Sky (No. 1)*) para. 8. *Paramount Home Entertainment & Anor v. British Sky Broadcasting & Ors* [2014] EWHC 937 (Ch) (18 February 2014) (*Paramount v. Sky (No. 2)*) para. 12; 1967 *Ltd & Ors v. British Sky Broadcasting Ltd & Ors* [2014] EWHC 3444 (Ch) (23 October 2014) (*1967 v. Sky*) para. 9; *Twentieth Century Fox Film Corporation & Ors v. Sky UK Ltd & Ors* [2015] EWHC 1082 (Ch) (28 April 2015) (*Popcorn Time*) para. 25. A similar injunction for the enforcement of trademarks was also issued in 2014: *Cartier International AG & Ors v. British Sky Broadcasting Ltd & Ors* [2014] EWHC 3354 (Ch) (17 October 2014) (*Cartier v. Sky*).

Amongst other things, it should consider whether the service provider has received a notice and, if so, the extent to which such notice includes the full name and address of the sender and details of the infringement in question. Whether the provider has made available a means of contacting it is also relevant.[151]

In *Newzbin (No.2),* Justice Arnold found that actual knowledge should not be interpreted restrictively. Accordingly, all that must be shown is that the intermediary had actual knowledge that one or more persons use its service to infringe copyright. It is not necessary to prove actual knowledge of a specific infringement of a specific work by a specific individual.[152] This closes the gap between UK and EU law considerably, although the disconnect concerning the requirement of notice for the issue of injunctive relief (as opposed to the mere creation of a duty of care to take down as a condition for retaining safe harbour protection) remains. One has to wonder what the purpose of the 'actual knowledge' criterion under the CDPA approach is: if an injunction is being sought against an intermediary, it will always have knowledge that allegations of copyright infringement against its users have been made, while it is unclear why – once it is accepted that injunctions can be issued against non-infringers – it would be important that an applicant issue a notice to that non-infringer informing them that infringement has occurred, before turning to a court to seek an injunction against them. Arnold J speculates that the actual knowledge requirement has been transplanted to section 97A from Articles 13 and 14 of the E-Commerce Directive, but the logic behind this transplantation remains obscure. It is especially unclear why the knowledge standard reserved by the EU directive for criminal matters would be applied for injunctions in civil law. In any case, the flexible understanding of 'actual knowledge' opted for by the judge means that in practice it will probably be impossible to avoid broadening the reach of the injunction back to the breadth it has in the Copyright Directive.

There appears to have been some initial confusion as to whether English law alone, absent an explicit transposition of Article 8(3) of the Copyright Directive, could support injunctions against innocent third parties. The issue came up in *L'Oréal v. eBay,* a trademark case, in view of the fact that the UK had not taken steps to implement into national law Article 11 of the Enforcement Directive, the provision that extends the injunctions against intermediaries made available by Article 8(3) of the Copyright Directive to all IPRs. Arnold J ultimately came down in favour of the idea:

> I consider that, if Article 11 requires that the grant of an injunction against an intermediary who is not an infringer, then that provides a sufficient reason for a court of equity to exercise its power to grant an

151. This is required of service providers under regulation 6(1)(c) of the Electronic Commerce (EC Directive) Regulations 2002 (SI 2002/2013).
152. *Twentieth Century Fox Film Corp & Ors v. British Telecommunications Plc* [2011] EWHC 1981 (Ch) (28 July 2011) (*Newzbin (No.2)*) paras 148 and 157.

injunction to protect an intellectual property which has been infringed. In saying this, I am not treating Article 11 as having direct effect; but as providing a principled basis for the exercise of an existing jurisdiction in a new way. The question then is whether, and if so to what extent, that is what Article 11 requires.

In 2015, in *Cartier,* another trademark case, the judge was much more decisive. He observed that section 37(1) of the Senior Courts Act 1981 allows the courts expansive powers with regard to injunctive relief: 'The High Court may by order (whether interlocutory or final) grant an injunction […] in all cases in which it appears to the court to be just and convenient to do so.' This is supported by the distinction made by Lord Woolf in *Broadmoor Hospital v. Robinson* between the issues of jurisdiction, and the mere common practice of discretion.[153] On this basis, Arnold J concluded that, while the well-settled principles guide the courts in the issue of injunctions, those principles are not immutable. Instead, they have evolved over time in the face of new circumstances. Accordingly, an injunction may issue in the protection of any legal right whatever,[154] while this power is not restricted to injunctions against the infringers of the right.[155] The judge therefore felt comfortable issuing an order against internet service providers requiring them to block access to infringing websites.

Of course, as Arnold J stressed, the discretion of the court is not entirely unfettered, but – beyond the four threshold conditions of section 97A – must be contained within the limits set by interpretative principles of EU law and in particular the requirements of proportionality.[156] Since the *Newzbin* order,[157] injunctions issued under section 97A have allowed claimants to notify intermediaries of additional IP addresses or URLs to be added to the blocking measures.[158] This is intended to allow right-holders to respond to circumvention measures by website operators that involve changing IP addresses or URLs. The courts considered that it would not be proportionate to require that the right-holders identify individual URLs relating to infringing copies of individual copyright works, instead of blocking the entire site. Such a condition would require claimants to expend considerable effort and costs notifying intermediaries on a daily basis. Arnold J did

153. *Broadmoor Hospital Authority & Anor v. R* [1999] EWCA Civ 3039 (20 December 1999) para. 21.
154. I Spry, *Equitable Remedies* (9th ed., Sweet & Maxwell 2014) para. 333.
155. See Arnold J in *Cartier International AG & Ors v. British Sky Broadcasting Ltd & Ors* [2014] EWHC 3354 (Ch) (17 October 2014) para. 105.
156. *Cartier International AG & Ors v. British Sky Broadcasting Ltd & Ors* [2014] EWHC 3354 (Ch) (17 October 2014) para. 140.
157. *Twentieth Century Fox Film Corporation & Ors v. British Telecommunications Plc* [2011] EWHC 2714 (Ch) (26 October 2011) (*Newzbin (No.3)).*
158. *Cartier International AG & Ors v. British Sky Broadcasting Ltd & Ors* [2014] EWHC 3354 (Ch) (17 October 2014) para. 58.

however mention that this would be a possibility worth considering in cases of target websites containing a substantial proportion of non-infringing content.[159]

Although the ability to impose injunctions was therefore acknowledged in *Cartier*, importantly, in the name of proportionality, 'safeguards against abuse' were also incorporated into the decision. So, Arnold J recognised that intermediaries may apply to the courts to discharge or vary the order in case of a change of circumstances. Under the influence of *Telekabel* and its emphasis on the recognition of *locus standi* for third party end-users, that right was also extended to end-users. In addition, it was decided that the page displayed to users who attempt to access blocked websites should not merely state that access to the website has been blocked by court order, but also should identify the claimant which obtained the order and state that affected users have the right to apply to the courts to discharge or vary the order.[160] Finally, the court also agreed that orders should not last longer than necessary and thus incorporated a 'sunset clause', setting a time limit of two years.

3.1.4.2 Norwich Pharmacal *orders*

Finally, in 2012, in *Golden Eye*,[161] a different kind of injunction was granted. Again, the case concerned unauthorised peer-to-peer file-sharing by the customers of an internet access provider. Instead of seeking a section 97A injunction however, the claimants opted for a much more well-established procedure under English law: a *Norwich Pharmacal* order for the disclosure of identifying information of the intermediary's infringing subscribers.[162] It is worth noting that the defendant intermediary did not oppose the order or in fact make any submission. Instead, Consumer Focus, a consumer watchdog, intervened on behalf of the affected subscribers. This indicates what should be obvious: while the interests of intermediaries and end-users will often align in online copyright cases, that is not something that can be relied upon and users require independent representation in the enforcement process.

In his judgment Arnold J, diligently following in the footsteps of the CJEU, applied the 'ultimate balancing test' for the resolution of the

159. *Twentieth Century Fox Film Corp & Ors v. British Telecommunications Plc* [2011] EWHC 1981 (Ch) (28 July 2011) (*Newzbin (No.2)*) para. 201.
160. *Cartier International AG & Ors v. British Sky Broadcasting Ltd & Ors* [2014] EWHC 3354 (Ch) (17 October 2014) para. 264.
161. *Golden Eye (International) Ltd & Anor v. Telefónica UK Ltd* [2012] EWHC 723 (Ch) (26 March 2012).
162. A Norwich Pharmacal order was first granted in 1974 by the House of Lords in *Norwich Pharmacal Co. v. Customs and Excise Commissioners* [1973] UKHL 6 (26 June 1973). For more on Norwich Pharmacal orders, see S Sime, *A Practical Approach to Civil Procedure* (18th ed., Oxford University Press 2015) 496-506 and P Matthews & H M Malek, *Disclosure* (4th ed., Sweet & Maxwell 2012) 63-100.

dispute.[163] To this end, the justifications for interfering with or restricting each of the two conflicting rights were considered. So, on the one hand, the substantial scale of the infringement of the claimants' copyrights was noted, as well as the obvious necessity of the communication of the names and addresses of the end-users involved. On the other hand, the judge observed that the end-users were ordinary consumers, likely on a low income and without ready access to specialised legal advice; that the order sought would by definition invade their privacy and impinge upon their data protection rights; that, due to inevitable errors, they may not be guilty of infringement at all and that the subject matter of the claim (which involved accusations of unauthorised use of pornographic material) was likely to cause embarrassment.

On this basis, the judge opted to grant the order, but concluded that the precise terms of the letter to be sent to end-users were significant. The judge objected to the draft letter submitted before him as, although it took sufficient account of the interests of both the claimant and the ISP, it did not account for the rights of the users themselves, being misleading, one-sided, occasionally incorrect and excessively demanding in terms of the time-frame it established for responses. Additionally, the letter contained a threat of disconnection or of a slowing-down of internet speeds that was unjustified in the circumstances. Finally, it requested the payment of an arbitrary figure of GBP 700 that was insupportable. As an alternative, the judge endorsed the case-by-case approach, finding that the settlement sum should be individually negotiated with each end-user. As with *Cartier*, the question of safeguards was also addressed. This time the judge recommended the adoption of the selection of a suitable set of 'test cases' that could investigate common issues that are likely to arise.

In addition to the above, Arnold J also limited the scope of the order to only two of the claimants, as the claims of the rest were based on agreements for the aggregation of disclosure rights in return for a share in recoveries. According to the judge, this 'would be tantamount to the court sanctioning the sale of the [subscribers'] privacy and data protection rights to the highest bidder'.[164] This indicates the significance of the protection of personal data to the balancing test. Regrettably, the Court of Appeal overturned this restriction, refusing to find any impact by the agreements on the proportionality test.[165] In this way, the appeal judges removed the only effective limitation on large-scale commercial disclosure.[166] Regardless, it is worth

163. *Golden Eye (International) Ltd & Anor v. Telefónica UK Ltd* [2012] EWHC 723 (Ch) (26 March 2012) para. 117.
164. *Golden Eye (International) Ltd & Anor v. Telefónica UK Ltd* [2012] EWHC 723 (Ch) (26 March 2012) para. 146.
165. *Golden Eye (International) Ltd & Ors v. Telefónica UK Litd & Anor* [2012] EWCA Civ 1740 (21 December 2012).
166. J Riordan, The Liability of Internet Intermediaries (PhD thesis, University of Oxford 2013, forthcoming Oxford University Press 2016) 215.

noting that both judgments, considering as they do the circumstances of the case and providing crucial judicial oversight, are likely fully in line with the demands of the CJEU's *Bonnier Audio.*

3.1.5 Duties of Care: The Negligence Approach

Amidst this impressive variety of possible legal tools available for the substantiation of intermediary liability, one possibility that is not considered at all by English law is that of the direct application of the tort of negligence to accessories in tort law. Indeed, the suggestion is usually treated as an anathema by British lawyers. So, for example, although happy to expand the conduct element of accessory liability to include assistance, Davies steers clear of the application of negligence to copyright law:

> It might finally be noted that it is unlikely that an accessory could be liable in negligence, as it is difficult to establish that such an accessory owes any duty of care to the claimant. [... It] seems inappropriate for negligence to trespass upon an area which is already regulated by principles of accessory liability. Negligence has expanded such that it encompasses a huge area of tort law, but it should not cover joint tortfeasance. Accessories are not negligent, but act knowingly and deliberately. If they are not liable under general principles of accessory liability, then it should be concluded that this is a choice the law has made, and that it is not for negligence to disturb that balance struck.[167]

This reluctance has deep roots in the common law. Its basis lies in the idea that no general duty to take affirmative measures to prevent harm to another should be allowed to exist, as to hold otherwise would stretch liability in negligence beyond the established principles and fracture the coherence of the doctrines of joint tortfeasance.[168] In *Amstrad,* Lord Templeman showed his impatience with the notion, decrying the 'fashionable plaintiff' who alleges negligence:

> [t]he pleading assumes that we are all neighbours now, Pharisees and Samaritans alike, that forseeability is a reflection of hindsight and that for every mischance in an accident-prone world someone solvent must be liable in damages.

The judge concludes that the rights of copyright owners are to be found in copyright law and nowhere else: '[u]nder and by virtue of that Act Amstrad owed a duty not to infringe copyright and not to authorise an

---

167. P S Davies, 'Accessory Liability: Protecting Intellectual Property Rights' (2011) 4 Intellectual Property Quarterly 390; See also: P S Davies, *Accessory Liability* (Hart Publishing 2015) 52, 56-57.
168. J Riordan, The Liability of Internet Intermediaries (PhD thesis, University of Oxford 2013, forthcoming Oxford University Press 2016) 148.

infringement of copyright. They did not owe a duty to prevent or discourage or warn against infringement'. Yet this statement is not obviously correct, since – if nothing else – the doctrine of joint tortfeasance certainly applies to copyright, despite being tort law-sourced. Possibly Weir is close to the truth when he suggests that 'by denying that Amstrad owed any duty to the copyright holders, the courts spared themselves the undelightful task of deciding whether what Amstrad did was reasonable or not'.[169] Yet, though edge-case negligence can definitely be tough to call, surely do so is precisely the job the courts are entrusted with undertaking? It is, in any case, not immediately obvious why this task would be any harder than fashioning appropriate rules of joint tortfeasance.

As shall be shown in Chapter 4, the traditional English rejection of the notion of affirmative duties of care to prevent the wrongdoings of others is currently encountering some resistance among tort law scholars. This broader movement is also beginning to find tentative echoes in the intermediary liability debate.[170] Indeed, with regard to intermediary liability a negligence-based construction would have the great advantage of allowing English courts an appropriate opening that they are clearly eager for to impose some liability on intermediaries that do not intent third party infringement, but carelessly occasion them.[171] These developments are unsurprising: as Aldous LJ notes in *One in a Million,* 'the common law [is] evolving to meet changes in methods of trade and communication as it had in the past'.[172] The European harmonisation of intermediary liability might be a good reason for it to evolve a little bit more: as shall be shown below, the negligence approach to intermediary liability is precisely the approach taken in other EU jurisdictions.

---

169. T Weir, 'Liability for Knowingly Facilitating Mass Breaches of Copyright' (1988) 47(3) The Cambridge Law Journal 348.
170. The application of the tort of negligence to intermediary liability for third party copyright infringements was suggested for example by McIvor in a presentation on the topic in Amsterdam in 2015, see C McIvor, 'Liability for the Acts of Third Parties: Tort Lessons for Intermediary Copyright Liability', roundtable discussion on 'The European Harmonisation of Intermediary Accessory Liability for Online Copyright Infringement: at the Intersection of Tort Law and Fundamental Rights', 13 April 2015, Institute for Information Law (IViR), Amsterdam. See also, C McIvor, *Third Party Liability in Tort* (Hart Publishing 2006) 50-65.
171. This is most obvious in *EMI Records Ltd & Ors v. British Sky Broadcasting Ltd & Ors* [2013] EWHC 379 (Ch) (28 February 2013), discussed above under s. 3.1.2.3, where the judge appeared to assume authorisation (a doctrine that should normally require intention) on the basis of a failure to take down notified content, an obligation which essentially amounts to little more than a violation of, precisely, a duty of care, i.e., negligence.
172. *British Telecommunications Plc & Ors v. One In A Million Ltd & Ors* [1998] EWCA Civ 1272 (23 July 1998).

3.2 FRANCE

The safe harbour provisions of the E-Commerce Directive were implemented into French law with the *loi* ***n° 2004-575 du 21 juin 2004 pour la confiance dans l'économie numérique,*** **otherwise known as the LCEN.** The resultant *régime de responsabilité limitée* hinges on two main provisions: under Article 9 of the LCEN, internet access providers that fulfil the appropriate conditions benefit from a safe harbour for both their mere conduit and caching activities,[173] while the immunity of host services providers from civil liability is implemented by Article 6-I-2 LCEN.[174] Article 15 of the E-Commerce Directive has been transposed with Article 6-I-7 LCEN.

Article 6-I-2 LCEN introducing the notice-and-take-down concept was given a strict interpretation by the *Conseil Constitutionnel*. According to this, hosting providers are only under an obligation to remove content notified as illegal when it is: a) manifestly unlawful; or b) its removal has been ordered by a court.[175] No comprehensive definition of 'manifest unlawfulness' has been provided by the courts, but some commentators suggest that it coincides with the list of particularly prejudicial illegality contained in Article 6-I-7. This includes apologia for crimes against humanity, the incitement of and apologia for terrorist acts, the incitement of racial hatred, sexism, homophobia and ableism, violence and in particular violence against women, child pornography, as well as crimes against human dignity. This suggestion is supported by the fact that Article 6-I-7 introduces an obligation for host providers to proactively take measures to fight such content in view of the general interest in its suppression. Significantly for the purposes of this book, the list does not include copyright infringement, while commentators have agreed that content that merely damages private interests should not be understood as capable of being 'manifestly' unlawful.[176] Early rulings by the

---

173. For this purpose two new articles (Arts L.32-3-3 for mere conduit provision and L.32-3-4 for caching provision) were introduced to the *Code des postes et des communications électronique*. It should be noted that, before the introduction of this set of safe harbours, access providers were also considered comparable to telecommunications operators, which already by means of the 1996 law on postal officers and telecommunications (*Loi n°24-96 relative à la poste et aux télécommunications*) were heavily protected from liability due to the informational content they convey, see: J-F Thery & I Falque-Pierrotin, 'Internet et les réseaux numériques: étude adoptée par l'Assemblée générale du Conseil d'Etat le 2 juillet 1998' (La Documentation française 1998).
174. Article 6-I-3 absolves host service providers from criminal liability as well.
175. Conseil Constitutionnel, Décision No 2004-496 DC du 10 juin 2004, Journal officiel du 22 juin 2004, p. 11182.
176. R Hardouin, 'La jurisprudence, les textes, et la responsabilité des hébergeurs' (2008) 39 RLDI 67; R Hardouin, 'La connaissance de l'illicéité par les hébergeurs ou quand etre notifié ne signifie pas nécessairement devoir retirer' (2012) 47 Revue du droit des technologies de l'information 5.

courts support this conclusion, by suggesting that knowledge of copyright infringement requires either notice or a court ruling.[177]

Article 6-I-5 LCEN fleshes out the underdeveloped EU notice-and-take-down regime by providing that knowledge of illegal activity will be presumed to have been acquired by host service providers if they are notified of the following elements: the date of the notification; specific identifying details of the notifying natural or legal person and of its recipient; a description of the alleged illegal information and its precise location; the reason why the content should be removed, including the legal basis for its removal; and a copy of the letter sent to the content provider or publisher requesting the termination of the illegal activity. Under this scheme, just as notice will not necessarily necessitate take-down if the content is not manifestly illegal,[178] absence of a valid notice should not, strictly speaking, be understood as proving lack of knowledge. Regardless, just as they have assumed knowledge where there was proper notification, the courts have tended to treat such notification as mandatory, holding for example that the intermediary that received a notification missing crucial identifying data could not be said to have had knowledge until served with the writ of summons to appear before the court.[179] The Article 6-I-5 LCEN notice-and-take-down obligation, like its European prototype, retains the obligation for an 'expeditious' reaction ('*promptement*'), while the French *juges du font* have interpreted a five-day delay as insufficiently alacritous.[180]

It is worth noting that the LCEN provides slightly more elaborate language with regard to the imposition of general monitoring obligations against safe harbour intermediaries: in its implementation of Article 15 of the E-Commerce Directive, Article 6-I-7 of the LCEN contrasts prohibited general monitoring with 'targeted and temporary' surveillance, as ordered by a judicial authority. This is a slightly higher standard than that required by the E-Commerce Directive, which merely talks of obligations 'in a specific case', with no mention of temporal restrictions. 'Judicial authorities' also suggests greater protection than 'national authorities in accordance with national legislation'.[181]

---

177. See *Omar & Fred et autres c. Dailymotion*, Tribunal de grande instance de Paris (3ème chambre, 1ère section) jugement du 15 avril 2008; *Jean Yves Lafesse c. Dailymotion*, Tribunal de grande instance de Paris (3ème chambre, 1ère section) jugement du 15 avril 2008. See: N van Eijk, C Jasserand, C Wiersma & T M van Engers, 'Moving towards Balance: A Study into Duties of Care on the Internet' (2010) Institute for Information Law & Leibniz Center for Law, University of Amsterdam, 113-114.
178. C Jasserand, 'Régime français de la responsabilité des intermédiaires techniques' (2013) 25(3) Les Cahiers de la propriété intellectuelle 1135.
179. See for example, *Sté Nord-Ouest c. Dailymotion*, Cour de cassation, 1ère chambre civile, Arrêt n° 165 du 17 février 2011 (09-67.896).
180. *S.A. Télévision* Française *1 (TF1) c. Société YouTube LLC*, Tribunal de Grande Instance de Paris (3ème chambre, 1ère section) jugement du 29 mai 2012.
181. Recital 47 of the E-Commerce Directive.

In contrast to the UK, where they have so far only received the occasional nod in the copyright case law, in France the safe harbours have taken centre stage, their introduction restructuring the fundaments of intermediary liability theory and generating a prolific and controversial jurisprudence. As Nérisson puts it, the 'French law regarding the liability of intermediaries on the internet is essentially the implementation of the European E-commerce Directive'.[182] Analysis has focused especially on the immunity for host service providers. Indeed, the thorny question of which type of intermediary should benefit from the hosting safe harbour or, as the French courts approach the matter, what distinguishes a host (*hébergeur*) from a publisher (*éditeur*), has been described by commentators as 'the principle preoccupation of French jurisprudence in recent years'.[183] The result has been the creation of two special liability regimes. Beyond these, the general rules apply. In the paragraphs below the evolution of the relevant case law shall be detailed.[184]

3.2.1 Special Liability Regimes A: The *Hébergeur*

The initial instinct of the French courts – as of many national courts in Europe – seems to have been to deny online host service providers safe harbour protection.[185] This was achieved through a very strict interpretation of the notion of 'hosting'. So, for example, in June 2007 in *Lafesse v. MySpace*, one of the most well-known earlier cases, the Paris High Court of First Instance (*Tribunal de Grande Instance de Paris (TGI Paris)*), deliberating in a summary proceedings, refused to allow the online social networking site MySpace the protection of Article 6-I-5 LCEN.[186] Although the Court agreed that MySpace offers technical hosting services, it noted that it does not limit itself to those services. Instead, the imposition of a pre-designed page set-up for users' personal accounts, in combination with the revenue-generating ads exhibited upon each visit, established MySpace not

182. S Nérisson, 'Intellectual Property Liability of Consumers, Facilitators and Intermediaries: the Position in France' in A Kamperman Sanders & C Heath, *Intellectual Property Liability of Consumers, Facilitators and Intermediaries* (Kluwer Law International 2012) 77.
183. L Thoumyre, 'Etude 464 – La responsabilité pénale et extra-contractuelle des acteurs de l'Internet' (Novembre 2009) Lamy Droit des Médias et de la Communication.
184. It should be noted that the contents of s. 3.2 are partly based on the following article: C Angelopoulos, 'Filtering for Copyrighted Content in Europe' (2009) (4) IRIS plus 1.
185. M Dhenne, 'Hébergeurs et contrefaçons: de l'usage de la loyauté dans un régime de responsabilité limitée' (2009) 51 RLDI 58.
186. *Jean Yves L. dit Lafesse c. Myspace,* Tribunal de Grande Instance de Paris, Ordonnance de référé 22 juin 2007. A subsequent decision of the court of appeal has since also been issued, however this deals mainly with procedural issues (see *MySpace Inc c. Jean-Yves L dit Lafesse, SARL L Anonyme, Monsieur Daniel L, Monsieur Hervé L,* Cour d'appel de Paris, 29 October 2008).

as a host (*hébergeur*), but as a publisher of content – an *éditeur*: So, according to the Court, MySpace 'is a publisher, and must take on the responsibilities of a publisher'. On this basis, the Court ordered the deletion of the disputed video, on pain of a EUR 1,000 daily fine for any delay, as well as the imposition of damages. A series of similar decisions were issued across the country around the same time.[187]

Occasionally, this straightforward rejection was accompanied by an additional twist: in 2006 the Paris Court of Appeal caused uproar by qualifying, in *Tiscali v. Lucky Comics,*[188] the internet website operator Tiscali simultaneously as both a host and a publisher. Tiscali was accordingly held liable under two hats, i.e., both as: a) a host, for failing to comply with the obligation, imposed on host service providers by Article 6-II LCEN, to keep data identifying its users; and b) as a publisher whose services went beyond the merely technical and which was therefore liable for uploaded content.[189] In January 2010, the *Cour de cassation* handed down a much-anticipated decision on the case, which however just serviced to deepen the controversy.[190] Although the Court avoided designating Tiscali an *éditeur* of the objectionable content, it also refused the provider the hosting immunity. After observing that Tiscali offered internet users the possibility of creating personal pages on its site and advertisers the possibility of buying advertising space managed by the company on those pages, the Court claimed that the provider exceeded the simple technical functions of storage and could therefore not be exempt from liability. It should be noted however that the case applied Article 43-8 of the Law of 30 September 1989[191] that contained the French pre-E-Commerce Directive home-grown hosting safe harbour,

---

187. Although from the field of trademarks, the Google Adwords cases, ultimately leading to the CJEU judgement by the same name, are good examples. See: *Louis Vuitton Malletier c. Google,* Tribunal de Grande Instance de Paris, 4 February 2005 and Cour d'appel de Paris, 28 June 2006; *GIFAM c. Google,* Tribunal de grande instance de Paris, 12 July 2006 and Cour d'appel de Paris, 1 February 2008*; Viaticum et Luteciel c. Google,* Tribunal de grande instance de Nanterre, 13 October 2003 and Cour d'appel de Versailles, 10 March 2005*; CNRRH, Pierre Alexis T. c. Google,* Tribunal de grande instance de Nanterre, 14 December 2004 and Cour d'appel de Versailles, 23 March 2006.
188. *Tiscali Media c. Dargaud Lombard, Lucky Comics,* Cour d'appel de Paris, 7 June 2006.
189. S Nérisson, 'Intellectual Property Liability of Consumers, Facilitators and Intermediaries: the Position in France' in A Kamperman Sanders & C Heath, *Intellectual Property Liability of Consumers, Facilitators and Intermediaries* (Kluwer Law International 2012) 77.
190. *Télécom Italia (Tiscali) c. Dargaud Lombard, Lucky Comics,* Cour de cassation, 14 January 2010.
191. *Loi n° 86-1067 du 30 septembre 1986 relative à la liberté de communication (Loi Léotard)* (Law No. 86-1067 of 30 September 1986 on freedom of communication) as amended by the *Loi no 2000-719 du 1er août 2000 modifiant la loi no 86-1067 du 30 septembre 1986 relative à la liberté de communication* (Law No. 2000-719 of 1 August 2000 modifying the law No. 86-1067 of 30 September 1986 on freedom of communication).

since repealed in 2004. As Hardouin points out, as opposed to the subsequent LCEN, the old immunity was limited to providers of hosting services that were '*direct et permanent*', two limitations that indicate a provision clearly tailored to classic Web 1.0 hosts that offer physical, as opposed to virtual, storage.[192] Nevertheless, the judgment received considerable criticism, with commentators noting that nothing in either the Freedom of Communication Act or the LCEN indicated that merely deriving income from a service could in itself be sufficient to deny safe harbour protection. As Nérisson observes, '[c]onsidering that storage capacity is limited and service providers are not all angels living on love alone, the storage carried out free of charge has to be financed by cross-subsidising. This is done mostly by renting advertising space'.[193]

As we saw in Chapter 2, the CJEU clearly rejected the French line of reasoning on this matter in the *Google Adwords* case in 2010.[194] On 13 July 2010 the *Cour de cassation* fell into line, issuing four judgments[195] that adjusted French law to the CJEU's guidance on all points: accordingly, it annulled the lower courts' rulings that rejected immunity as having employed the wrong criterion in examining Google's advertising activities and confirmed that protection from liability as a host service provider depends on whether the intermediary has played an active role of such a kind as to convey knowledge or control over the stored information. The following year, in *Nord-Ouest v. Dailymotion,* the *Cour de cassation* cemented this approach by acknowledging the irrelevance of the commercial exploitation of a site for its eligibility for the new Directive-based set of safe harbours.[196] Here the court explicitly acknowledged that 'the sale of advertising space does not imply the service's ability to act in relation to the uploaded content'. The court also noted that the implementation of technical means ensuring the content's compatibility with the viewing interface and limiting the size of posted files for reasons of optimisation of the server's integration capacity are mere technical operations that are part of the essence of a hosting service and in no way imply that the provider is involved in the selection of uploaded content. The same was said about the provision of presentation frames and of

192. R Hardouin, 'L'hébergeur et la publicité: la neutralité comme condition d'une coexistence' (2010) 62 Revue Lamy Droit de l'Immatériel 2041.
193. R Matulionytė & S Nérisson, 'The French Route to an ISP Safe Harbour, Compared to the German and US Ways' (2011) 42(1) International Review of Intellectual Property and Competition Law (IIC) 55. See also, C Manara, 'Hébergement des contenu: une decision critiquable!' (2010) Recueil Dalloz 260.
194. CJEU, joined cases C-236/08 and C-237/08, *Google France v. Louis Vuitton et al,* 23 March 2010.
195. *Google France c. Louis Vuitton Malletier* (06-20.230), *Google France c. GIFAM* (08-13944); *Google France c. CNRRH* (06-15136); *Google France c. SA Viaticum* (05-14331), Cour de cassation (Chambre commerciale, financière et économique), 13 July 2010.
196. *Sté Nord-Ouest c. Dailymotion* (09-67.896), Cour de cassation, 17 February 2011.

tools for the classification of content, which are necessary for the organisation of the service and in order to facilitate user access to the content.[197]

The decisions reset the liability scene for host service providers in France:[198] the new understanding of the applicable regime, in much better alignment with the EU rules, appears to require a case-by-case inquiry into the circumstances at hand that focuses on any intrusion by the intermediary into the selection of the content. Thus, in 2012, the *Cour de cassation,* while denying eBay protection under the hosting safe harbour, did so on a much sounder analytical basis: this time, in substantiating its conclusion, the court mentioned in particular the provision by eBay of facilities that enable sellers to optimise their sales and of assistance in the definition and description of items for sale, including through the offer of the creation of a personalised marketplace or support by sales assistants. It also highlighted the fact that eBay sends unsolicited emails to buyers encouraging them to purchase items on sale and inviting bidders to bid on similar items.[199] Critically, these facts were found by the court to indicate an 'active role' played by eBay, which provided it with knowledge and control over the information it hosted. This reasoning conforms much more readily with the European provisions.

In the meantime, the lower courts had headed down another path for the disqualification of intermediaries from the hosting safe harbour, this time relying on the notion of general knowledge of infringement. So, in early 2007, upon the discovery of unlawful copies of the film '*Joyeux Noël*' hosted on the video-sharing platform Dailymotion, the producer, director and distributor of the film initiated a lawsuit against the website for copyright infringement.[200] This time, the plaintiffs' claim that Dailymotion functioned as a publisher was rejected – instead, in a decision issued in July 2007, the TGI Paris, foreshadowing the later rulings of the CJEU and the *Cour de cassation,* found that Dailymotion's advertising-based business model did not detract from the fact that the content was uploaded by users, thereby qualifying Dailymotion as a hosting provider. Having said this however, the Court then stated that the hosting immunity does not provide an exemption from liability, but only a limitation. It then went on to hold that the architecture and technical means put in place by Dailymotion enabled illicit activities, while the very success of the website depended on the making

197. See also, *La société Agence des médias numériques (AMEN)* (09-15.857), Cour de cassation, 17 February 2011 and *Olivier Martinez c. Bloobox (Fuzz)* (09-13.202), Cour de cassation, 17 February 2011.

198. Thus, the jurisprudence is often divided into two stages: 'avant Google' and 'après Google', see C Castets-Renaud, 'Le renouveau de la responsabilité délictuelle des intermédiaires de l'internet' (2012) Recueil Dalloz 827.

199. *La société eBay Inc. c. la société Parfums Christian Dior* (11-10.508), Cour de cassation, 3 May 2012.

200. *Christian C., Nord Ouest Production c. Dailymotion, UGC Images,* Tribunal de Grande Instance de Paris, 13 July 2007.

available of copyright-protected material by its users. Given that Article 6-I-2 LCEN requires that, in order to claim protection from liability, a hosting provider must (a) not have had actual knowledge of illegal activity or of facts or circumstances that render such activity apparent; and (b) upon obtaining such knowledge, have acted expeditiously to remove or disable access, Dailymotion was considered ineligible for the application of the safe harbour provision. Dailymotion recalled the proscription of a general obligation to monitor as imposed by Article 6-I-7 LCEN, the Court, however, rejected this reasoning, estimating that the prohibition only applies in cases where the unlawful activities were not generated or induced by the intermediary itself. By contrast, the Court held that intermediaries who provide their users with means for infringing copyright have a duty to carry out prior control for the prevention of such user behaviour. By abstaining from the implementation of equipment preventing access to the film, Dailymotion had breached this obligation. Accordingly, Dailymotion was found liable for copyright infringement and ordered to pay damages.

The ruling gave rise to debate and criticism, in particular surrounding the imposition of a novel duty upon service providers for an *a priori* implementation of technical filtering measures for the prevention of online piracy. The court's reasoning was especially puzzling given that the facts of the case revealed that Dailymotion had failed to withdraw all infringing videos from its site, even after notification on the part of the right-holders – behaviour that would in any case normally have precluded the deployment of Article 14 hosting safe harbour. In view of Dailymotion's breach of its reactive obligation to prevent infringements brought to its attention, the need to impose a proactive duty on hosting intermediaries to block all unlawful content is questionable and difficult to reconcile with Article 15 E-Commerce Directive; indeed, in its strictest interpretation, the innovative obligation did away with most safe harbour benefits, effectively equating the liability of a hosting platform with that of a publisher.[201]

This approach eventually evolved in a slightly more moderate direction. In October 2007, the TGI Paris ruled that another video-sharing service, Google Video, was liable for copyright infringement, due to the multiple unauthorised copies of the documentary '*Les enfants perdus de Tranquility Bay*' present on its website.[202] As in the Dailymotion case, the Court again conceded that Google Video did qualify for the safe harbour extended to hosting services by Article 6-I-2 LCEN. Moreover, the facts of the case revealed that this time the service provider had acted expeditiously to disable access to the infringing copies of the film upon notification by the

---

201. N Jondet, 'The Silver Lining in Dailymotion's Copyright Cloud', as referenced in C Angelopoulos, 'Filtering for Copyrighted Content in Europe' (2009) (4) IRIS plus 1.
202. *SARL Zadig Productions, Jean-Robert Viallet et Mathieu Verboud c. Sté Google Inc. et AFA*, Tribunal de Grande Instance de Paris, 19 October 2007.

right-owners. Nevertheless, each removal of the infringing content was followed by speedy re-postings, forcing the right-owners, website and users into a repetitive game of cat and mouse. The court concluded that, once Google had been informed of the existence of infringing copies of the film, it was under an obligation to implement any means necessary to avoid future dissemination; consequently, although the speedy blocking of access to the unlawful video upon the first notification exonerated Google on that single instance, Google had failed to comply with the conditions of Article 6-I-2 LCEN in respect of every subsequent uploading. Google was therefore deemed to be liable and ordered to pay damages.

Although crafted in more cautious terms than the preceding '*Joyeux Noël*' case – the imposition of a general duty of prior control over all copyrighted content uploaded by users onto the site is sidestepped[203] – the *Tranquility Bay* ruling also gives rise to questions of compatibility with Article 15 E-Commerce Directive: as explained in Chapter 2, a duty to avoid future infringement is difficult to navigate around a ban on general monitoring by the intermediary. As commentators have observed, the Paris court likely rested its interpretation on paragraph 2 of Article 6-I-7 LCEN, which permits the imposition of specific 'targeted and temporary' surveillance charges. Indeed, as the Court reasons, although the multiple postings are attributable to different users, the content is identical, arguably rendering the monitoring obligation specific. However, Google was swift to take down all infringing copies tracked through human observation on the part of the right-holder, while a duty to avoid future infringement is difficult to navigate around a ban on general monitoring by the intermediary. According to the interpretation of the Court, if host service providers wish to avoid liability they are obliged, after receiving notification, to hunt out each and every remaining or reposted unauthorised copy. As notifications are likely to accumulate at a fast rate, the only practical way to achieve this would necessitate the use of fingerprinting or similar automatic filtering technology. This however, can only be achieved by screening all (even non-infringing) content passing through the providers' servers for infringing copies, i.e., practicing general monitoring.

In this way, the prima facie specificity of the obligation is negated by the broad reach of the practical implications: the envisioned blocking of content might be specific, but the monitoring itself remains general. The expansively future-oriented preventive duties spill over into the monitoring of all content, even that which has not yet been created. As a result, the court ends up placing liability-expanding powers with *ex ante* effect in the hands of right-holders, thereby enabling the indefinite suspension of the Article 14

203. R Hardouin, 'Observations sur les nouvelles obligations prétoriennes des hébergeurs' (2007), available at: Juriscom.com.

hosting safe harbour upon right-holder request.[204] Even the requirement of judicial oversight set by Article 6-I-7 LCEN is ignored.

The ultimate effect was the transformation by the French courts of the 'notice-and-take-down' scheme crudely sketched out in Article 14 of the E-Commerce Directive into a judge-made 'notice-and-stay-down' regime, with an obligation to monitor derived directly from Article 14's requirement for the expeditious removal or disabling of access to allegedly infringing information upon obtaining knowledge of awareness.[205] This is arguably a considerable misinterpretation of a provision intended to provide immunity from liability, not add grounds for its establishment.

As was already shown above, the 'notice-and-stay-down' approach eventually caught on in a limited way in the UK as well.[206] The German approach of *Störerhaftung* – although crafted in much more careful terms, being limited only to the issue of injunctive orders by courts and not the imposition of *ex* ante liability for damages – also encounters the same fundamental obstacles.[207] A safer approach, guaranteeing respect of the specificity requirement would have been the issue of individual court orders for measures along the lines of those later suggested by the CJEU in *L'Oréal,* e.g., the deletion of the infringer user's account or the provision of identifying information on that user.

It is worth noting that the strictness of the French 'stay-down' obligation was never definitively determined. Thus, in *YouTube v. Omar et Fred,*[208] the TGI de Paris required that right-holders must also play an active role in the stay-down process, through providing a copy of the original DVD of the show for which protection was claimed and authorisation to create a fingerprint. On 29 May 2012, the TGI Paris in *TF1 v. YouTube*[209] refused to find YouTube liable for postings by users that violated the broadcaster's related rights, in view of YouTube's offer of its 'Content ID' filtering system

204. N Jondet, 'Google Video held liable for the copyright infringement of 'Tranquility Bay' (TGI Paris 19 octobre 2007)', as referenced in C Angelopoulos, 'Filtering for Copyrighted Content in Europe' (2009) (4) IRIS plus 1.
205. A Lucas et al., *Traité de la Propriété Littéraire et Artistique* (4th ed., LexisNexis 2012) 912; P Sirinelli, 'Chronique de Jurisprudence – Mise à la disposition illicite d'oeuvres par l'intermédiaire des réseaux numériques' (2011) 228 Revue Internationale du Droit d'Auteur 287; C Castets-Renaud, 'Le renouveau de la responsabilité délictuelle des intermédiaires de l'internet' (2012) Recueil Dalloz 827; C Jasserand, 'Régime français de la responsabilité des intermédiaires techniques' (2013) 25(3) Les Cahiers de la propriété intellectuelle 1135; R Hardouin, *La responsabilité limitée des prestataires techniques dans la loi pour la confiance dans l'économie numérique* (unpublished PhD thesis, Université de Versailles Saint-Quentin-en-Yvelines 2011) 294.
206. See s. 3.1.2.3.
207. On this see especially s. 3.3.1.3.
208. *ADAMI, Omar S., Fred T. et a. c/ Sté Youtube*, Tribunal de Grande Instance de Paris, 22 September 2009.
209. *S.A. Télévision* Française *1 (TF1) c. Société YouTube LLC*, Tribunal de Grande Instance de Paris, 29 May 2012.

that allowed the identification of protected material for the prevention of its future upload. According to the court, YouTube had in this way provided the right-holders with the means of ensuring the real protection of their content and thus fulfilled its obligation. At the same time, other rulings took a stricter approach, rejecting any requirement of right-holder cooperation.[210] Envisioning a different kind of limitation, in *Magdane v. YouTube* the Paris Court of Appeal[211] ruled that the stay-down obligation could be limited in time for a two-year period in view of the protective character of the measure.

The 'take-down-stay-down' approach was confirmed in January 2011 by the Paris Court of Appeal: in four judgments handed down on the same day, the Court of Appeal held Google Video liable for copyright infringement committed by users with regard to the films '*Le génocide arménien*',[212] '*L'affaire Clearstream*',[213] '*Les dissimulateurs*'[214] and '*Mondovino*'.[215] Interestingly, Google had been absolved from liability at first instance before the *Tribunal de Commerce*, which accepted Google's eligibility for safe harbour protection. The court did however issue an injunction ordering Google to refrain from future reproduction or communication to the public of all or part of the films in question, as well as from referencing any link allowing them to be viewed or downloaded on pain of a fine. Google contested the order before the Court of Appeal, which reverted back to the lower courts' earlier liability-inducing heightened duty of surveillance regime: although accepting the neutral and passive character of Google's activities, the Court refused to delay proceedings till the CJEU could hand down its ruling on the *SABAM v. Netlog* case and found that, in order to benefit from the protection, the host service provider should not have limited itself to the mere withdrawal of the notified content, but also implemented every possible technical measure to render impossible future access to the disputed content through its search engine. The Article 15 prohibition on general monitoring obligations was deemed inoperable, as the obligation was specific to the documentary in question and notice as to its copyright status had already been given. According to the Court of Appeal, as soon as the protected status of the video had been indicated, insisting that each upload by the same or different users constitutes a novel circumstance necessitating separate notification is meaningless. The same logic was redeployed by the same court a month later in *André Rau v. Auféminin* against Google Images, this time with regard to photographs of singer and actor Patrick Bruel that

210. P Sirinelli, 'Chronique de Jurisprudence – Mise à la disposition illicite d'oeuvres par l'intermédiaire des réseaux numériques' (2011) 228 Revue Internationale du Droit d'Auteur 287.
211. *YouTube c. Roland Magdane et autres*, Cour d'appel de Paris, 26 May 2010.
212. *Google Inc. c. Compagnie des phares et balises,* Cour d'appel de Paris, 14 January 2011.
213. *Google Inc. c. Bac Films, The Factory,* Cour d'appel de Paris, 14 January 2011.
214. *Google Inc. c. Bac Films, The Factory,* Cour d'appel de Paris, 14 January 2011.
215. *Google Inc. c. Les Films de la Croisade, Goatworks Films,* Cour d'appel de Paris, 14 January 2011.

were posted without the photographer's authorisation by an online magazine and thereafter reproduced and communicated to the public by Google's image searching engine.[216]

In any case, this extended liability regime was finally put to an end by the *Cour de cassation* with three succinct rulings on '*L'affaire Clearstream*', '*Les dissimulateurs*' and *Auféminin* on 12 July 2012.[217] Following the lead of the CJEU in the two *SABAM* judgments, the court ruled that the judge-made 'stay-down' obligation cannot be observed by online providers without conducting prohibited general monitoring: the obligation would have forced Google to 'seek out illicit uploads', as well as implement a 'blocking mechanism with no limitation in time', which would have been 'disproportionate to the aim pursued'. On this basis, the court concluded that Google should have been allowed to benefit from the LCEN immunity. Copyright holders must instead monitor the content of websites themselves and notify intermediaries of each new infringement of protected content: content re-uploaded after a first round of notice-and-take-down does not have to be taken down again by the intermediary, as long as a new notification is not sent.[218] In this way, in France at least, the 'stay-down' approach was finally put to rest.

3.2.2 Special Liability Regime B: The *Éditeur*

As noted above, the notion of a *hébergeur* is commonly contrasted by the courts to that of a content publisher or, in French, *éditeur*: as Sirinelli notes, the courts seem to define the two notions in reference to each other, so that a provider is essentially considered to be a host when it is not a publisher.[219] The TGI Paris has been blunt, stating that '*la société […] qui n'est pas éditeur a le statut d'hébergeur*'.[220] Yet, to date, no workable definition of a 'publisher' is provided by French law[221] – indeed, no unitary definition could

216. *Google France et Google Inc., Auféminin.com v. H&K SARL, André Rau,* Cour d'appel, 4 February 2011.

217. *La société Google France* c. *la société Bach films (L'affaire Clearstream)* (11-13.669), Cour de cassation, 12 July 2012; *La société Google France c. La société Bac films (Les dissimulateurs)* (11-13666), Cour de cassation, 12 July 2012; *La société Google France c. André Rau* (Auféminin) (11-15.165; 11-15.188) Cour de cassation, 12 July 2012.

218. C Jasserand, 'Régime français de la responsabilité des intermédiaires techniques' (2013) 25(3) Les Cahiers de la propriété intellectuelle 1135.

219. P Sirinelli, 'Chronique de Jurisprudence – Mise à la disposition illicite d'oeuvres par l'intermédiaire des réseaux numériques' (2011) 228 Revue Internationale du Droit d'Auteur 287.

220. *Omar & Fred et autres c. Dailymotion*, Tribunal de grande instance de Paris, 15 April 2008; *Jean Yves Lafesse c. Dailymotion*, Tribunal de grande instance de Paris, 15 April 2008.

221. Article L.132-1 of the CPI does define the publishing contract (*le contrat d'édition*) as the agreement 'by which the author of a work of the mind or his successors in title assign under specified conditions to a person referred to as the editor the right to manufacture

possibly be adopted, as the notion of an '*éditeur*' is a protean[222] one: across the board of French legislation many different categories of publishers can be unearthed, including the publisher of an online press service,[223] the publisher of a media service[224] or the publisher of radio and television services.[225] Of these it is worth singling out as of particular relevant to internet related matters the publisher of online services of communication to the public (*éditeur de service de communication au public en ligne (SCPL)),* a concept introduced by the LCEN. As with the publisher of content, no definition of the SCPL publisher is provided by the law, while the current state of the jurisprudence is insufficiently developed to allow for concrete conclusions.[226]

Absent a concrete definition by the legislator, the notion of a content publisher in French law has been progressively refined through the case law. Older jurisprudence rests on more concrete criteria. So, for example, in *Olivier D. c/ Éric D.*, the *Tribunal de Grande Instance de Nanterre* listed five indications of the editorial character of content aggregators: alongside the sorting of information through the use of an RSS feed and the formation of a comprehensive overview of a given topic through the automatic compilation of information from a variety of sites, the commercial exploitation of the content through the placement of advertisements, the use of a structured display framework and the use of search engine functionalities to assist the user in the collection of material relevant to a certain topic were cited as proof of editorial capabilities.[227] This line of thinking was likely influenced

or have manufactured a number of copies of the work, it being for the latter to ensure publication and dissemination thereof.' Although the focus on the production of physical copies reveals the provision's age, it has been suggested that we can deduce on this basis that an editor should be understood as the person who ensures the publication and distribution of a work, see L Thoumyre, 'Etude 464 – La responsabilité pénale et extra-contractuelle des acteurs de l'Internet' (Novembre 2009) Lamy Droit des Médias et de la Communication.

222. L Thoumyre, 'Etude 464 – La responsabilité pénale et extra-contractuelle des acteurs de l'Internet' (Novembre 2009) Lamy Droit des Médias et de la Communication.
223. *Loi no 2009-669 du 12 juin 2009 favorisant la diffusion et la protection de la création sur internet (hereafter: HADOPI).*
224. *Loi no 2009-258 du 5 mars 2009 relative à la communication audiovisuelle et au nouveau service public de la télévision.*
225. *LCEN, Article 1.III insérant un article 3-1 dans la loi no 86-1067 du 30 septembre 1986.*
226. B Beignier, B de Lamy et E Dreyer, *Traité de droit de la presse et les médias* (Litec 2009) 1168. Thoumyre suggests that an SCPL publisher should be understood as being the person who takes the initiative of creating and managing a platform enabling the publication of content either at her own initiative or at the initiative of a third party. Accordingly, the qualification of SCPL publisher could intersect with e.g. that of a host service provider or even that of a mere internet user. See, L Thoumyre, 'Etude 464 – La responsabilité pénale et extra-contractuelle des acteurs de l'Internet' (Novembre 2009) Lamy Droit des Médias et de la Communication.
227. *Olivier D. c. Éric D.* TGI Nanterre, 23 February 2008.

by the more stringent requirements surrounding the French pre-E-Commerce Directive hosting immunity regime of Article 43-8 of the Freedom of Communication Act of 2000.[228]

In the meantime, the French courts have come round to a broader definition of the *éditeur*: by opposition to host providers, which are considered to *passively* provide the means allowing for the communication of content to the public by others, publishers are understood as performing an *active* role in the collection, evaluation and modification of material prior to knowingly and willingly proceeding to its publication.[229] Thus, in *Tranquility Bay*[230] the TGI Paris refused to categorise Google as a publisher, as it was not 'personally at the origin of the distribution', that activity being performed by the users.[231] In the aforementioned *MySpace* case, the same court described the *éditeur* as 'the person who determines the content which will be communicated to the public on the service that he/she has created or of which he/she is in charge'. In this way, editorial choice, i.e., 'choice over the content of uploaded files' is identified as the hallmark of the publisher. The familiar touchstones of knowledge and control once again rise to the surface: in order to select the material to be put online, the editor must have knowledge of and the capacity to take action over the content and the publication process. In the *Google France* case, the TGI de Paris denied Google categorisation as a publisher, as it was not 'personally at the origin of the distribution', that activity being performed by the users. For the avoidance of confusion, Thoumyre[232] has suggested modifying this 'origin of content' definition to that of 'the person at the initiative of whom the content was placed online': indeed, although the content need not be produced directly by the publisher, she must at a minimum be the one to choose the material to be published and its mode of presentation in a manner that indicates an intellectual intervention.[233] From this perspective, '*éditeur*' in

228. R Matulionytė & S Nérisson, 'The French Route to an ISP Safe Harbour, Compared to the German and US Ways' (2011) 42(1) International Review of Intellectual Property and Competition Law (IIC) 55.
229. L Thoumyre, 'Etude 464 – La responsabilité pénale et extra-contractuelle des acteurs de l'Internet' (Novembre 2009) Lamy Droit des Médias et de la Communication.
230. *SARL Zadig Productions, Jean-Robert Viallet et Mathieu Verboud c. Sté Google Inc. et AFA,* Tribunal de Grande Instance de Paris, 19 October 2007.
231. It has been suggested that the courts have derived this definition of the concept of editor from Art. 6-II LCEN, which refers to 'the person who contributed to the content of an online service of communication to the public', see: P Mimja, 'La Definition de l'Éditeur Était dans la Loi … ' (March 2009), available at: Juriscom.com.
232. L Thoumyre, 'Etude 464 – La responsabilité pénale et extra-contractuelle des acteurs de l'Internet' (Novembre 2009) Lamy Droit des Médias et de la Communication.
233. B Beignier, B de Lamy et E Dreyer, *Traité de droit de la presse et les médias* (Litec 2009) 1176, 1217. Compare also with notion of 'éditeur' in criminal liability, M Vivant *et al., Lamy – Droit du Numérique: Informatique, Multimedia, Réseaux, Internet* (Wolters Kluwer France 2012) 1662.

the hosting jurisprudence seems to simply refer to an '*éditeur de contenu*',[234] i.e., essentially to constitute the term the French courts use to indicate the content provider. In view of this conclusion, it has been suggested that the '*éditeur*', as the notional opposite of the '*hébergeur*', should – most simply – be connected to the reference to 'anyone who contribute to the content of an online service of communication to the public' in Article 6-II LCEN.[235] This seems to be as good a definition as any.

What is the liability regime that attaches to such publishers? Is it a separate, special one in the same way as that which applies to the providers of activities protected by the safe harbours? The question of editorial liability in France is dominated by the analysis of the famous *responsabilité en cascade*.[236] This was introduced by Article 42 of the *loi du 29 juillet 1881 sur la liberté de la presse* and extended to audiovisual services by Article 93-3 of the *loi du 29 juillet 1982 sur la communication audiovisuelle*. The latter was later amended by the LCEN to include online services for communication to the public.[237] These provisions do indeed introduce a special liability scheme, in the form of a liability hierarchy. According to Article 93-3 of the law on audiovisual communication, where a relevant wrong is committed online, in the first instance, the director or co-director of the publication will be held liable. Under Article 93-2 of the same law, every online communication service is obliged to designate a director or co-director of publication to be held liable for offending content.[238] In the absence of a known director or co-director ('*à défaut*'), the author will incur liability and, in his absence, the producer. When the director or co-director is held liable, the author can also be pursued as an accomplice, as well as anybody who provokes or knowingly facilitates the commission of the offence in accordance with the provisions of Article 121-7 of the *Code pénal*. The objective is to guarantee that a defendant can always be identified. Thus, the notion of 'editorial

---

234. P le Tourneau, *Droit de la responsabilité et des contrats – Régimes d'indemnisation* (9th ed., Dalloz 2013) 6787.
235. P Mimja, 'La Definition de l'Éditeur Était dans la Loi … ' (March 2009), available at: Juriscom.com.
236. See, A Lepage, *Libertés et droits fondamentaux à l'épreuve de l'internet* (Litec 2002) 295-297 and M Vivant *et al.*, *Lamy – Droit du Numérique: Informatique, Multimedia, Réseaux, Internet* (Wolters Kluwer France 2012) 1661 et seq.
237. Article 6-V of the LCEN also provides that the relevant provisions of Chs IV and V of the law of 29 July 1982 apply to online services of communication to the public.
238. Although the 1982 law only refers to the director of the publication, as opposed to 'the director of the publication or editor' of the 1881 press law. Strictly speaking, this should signify that there is no concept of 'editorial liability' in the context of online services of communication to the public. However, for the purposes of this analysis the two terms shall be treated as tautologous, as this as been the approach taken by the French courts and legal experts, see: L Thoumyre, 'Etude 464 – La responsabilité pénale et extra-contractuelle des acteurs de l'Internet' (Novembre 2009) Lamy Droit des Médias et de la Communication.

liability' is essentially a specialised scheme of vicarious liability applicable to publishers.

Does the cascading editorial liability regime provide answers relevant to internet intermediaries? In 2009, a new Article 27 added to the law on audiovisual communication adapted the *responsabilité en cascade* to the internet world. Contrary however to what is the case for offences of the printed press under the older 1881 law, here the cascading system only applies under the condition that the unlawful message was subject to fixation prior to its communication to the public (i.e., no liability exists for 'live' transmissions). In addition, the provision requires that, in cases where the offence results from content sent by an end-user made available to the public by a provider of communication the public services in a personalised communication space, the (co-)director cannot be held criminally liable if he was not actually aware of the content before it was put online or if, from the moment he became aware, he acted promptly to remove it. Thus, a different notice-and-take-down regime applies in such cases that spares the director from liability for content communicated to the public during live broadcasts or chats over which he has no knowledge or control. As a result, immediately we see that the interactive character of the web 2.0 tends to disqualify the application of *responsabilité en cascade*.[239] At the same time, if the cascading system does apply, as with the case of the *responsabilité limitée* of the safe harbour regime, it is given primacy over the general rules as lex specialis; so the substantiation of intermediary editorial liability for the offences of others is entirely possible.[240]

None of this however makes *responsabilité en cascade* relevant to intermediary liability specifically in the area of copyright. Importantly, the system only applies to certain specific *infractions de presse*, i.e., criminal abuses of the freedom of expression as enumerated in Chapter IV of the 1881 law. These include such crimes as defamation, the denial of crimes against humanity, incitement of discrimination and racial hatred, incitement to commit a felony or misdemeanour, racist speech and the distribution of violent or pornographic images where a minor is likely to encounter them, but not the infringement of intellectual property. In copyright therefore, no special liability regime is attached to the concept of content publishers.[241]

Similarly, and despite calls for the introduction of an immunity to their benefit, currently no sui generis liability regime is instituted in French law for

239. B Beignier et al., *Traité de droit de la presse et les médias* (Litec 2009) 1234.
240. M Vivant et al., *Lamy – Droit du Numérique: Informatique, Multimedia, Réseaux, Internet* (Wolters Kluwer France 2012) 1663; V P Auvret, 'Application de la loi de 1881 à la communication en ligne: délits de presse' (15 March 2006) JCL Communication, Fasc. 4870.
241. L Thoumyre, 'Etude 464 – La responsabilité pénale et extra-contractuelle des acteurs de l'Internet' (Novembre 2009) Lamy Droit des Médias et de la Communication; J-F Thery & I Falque-Pierrotin, 'Internet et les réseaux numériques: étude adoptée par l'Assemblée générale du Conseil d'Etat le 2 juillet 1998' (La Documentation française 1998) 161.

the SCPL publisher either.[242] Article 6-III of the LCEN instead limits itself to requiring that the SCPL publisher make public identifying information, as well as the name of the director or co-director of publication. Breach of this identification obligation incurs the liability of the SCPL publisher, although the courts have to date been lenient in the application of these rules. Thus, the SCPL publisher does not benefit from a special liability regime, unless it can claim safe harbour protection under the terms of the safe harbours.

The conclusion is that no special liability regime is attached to the concept of content publishers, at least not in intellectual property.[243] The '*éditeur*' should therefore best be understood as the default shorthand term that French courts fall back on when finding somebody liable through applying the general rules in absence of safe harbour protection. In the final analysis therefore, at least in the area of copyright, an *éditeur* could perhaps most accurately be described as the person who, in accordance with general norms and unqualified for an immunity, attracts liability for infringing content. The concept of the *éditeur* thus appears to be somewhat of a red herring, or at least a tautology, in as much as its meaning can, for all intents and purposes, be boiled down to 'the person who is liable for the content'. Essentially, the *éditeur* is the *fournisseur de contenus.*[244] As a result, French commentators have rejected the '*hébergeur – éditeur*' divide as a false dichotomy.[245] For example, Azzi states:

> s'il n'est pas hébergeur ou s'il est plus qu'un hébergeur, il engagera sa responsabilité dans les conditions du droit commun. Peu importe, en ce cas, qu'il soit éditeur ou qu'il ne le soit pas, puisque ce status n'a pas, en lui-même, d'incidence sur la responsabilité en matière de violation des droits de propriété intellectuelle.[246]

The typological binary is rejected and the only pertinent question is whether the provider benefits or not from a safe harbour: not, thus, '*hébergeur ou éditeur?*', but '*hébergeur, fournisseur d'accès, fournisseur de cache ou aucun des trois*?' In view of that conclusion, in the following, we shall be discarding the notion of the *éditeur* as entirely misleading and devoid of real meaning, at least within the context of French copyright law, and simply proceed with an examination of the applicable rules. For

242. B Beignier, B de Lamy et E Dreyer, *Traité de droit de la presse et les médias* (Litec 2009) 1166.
243. L Thoumyre, 'Etude 464 – La responsabilité pénale et extra-contractuelle des acteurs de l'Internet' (Novembre 2009) Lamy Droit des Médias et de la Communication.
244. C Féral-Schuhl, *Cyberdroit – Le Droit à l'Épreuve de l'Internet* (6th ed., Dalloz 2010) 822.
245. M Vivant et al., *Lamy – Droit du Numérique: Informatique, Multimedia, Réseaux, Internet* (Wolters Kluwer France 2012) 1706 and 1729.
246. T Azzi, 'La responsabilité des nouvelles plates-formes: éditeurs, hébergeurs ou autre voie?' in Colloque de l'IPRI, *Contrefaçon sur internet: les enjeux du droit d'auteur sur le WEB 2.0* (Litec 2009) 59-75.

copyright, given the lack of any other special liability regime,[247] this will mean the *droit commun,* i.e., the general tort law principles as enshrined in the French intellectual property act and the civil code.[248]

3.2.3 *Le Droit Commun:* The General Rules of Tort Law

As in the rest of the EU, in France as well the LCEN safe harbours are only exceptional provisions: they are intended to immunise against liability that might arise from any otherwise applicable rules. This is made clear by the wording of the provisions themselves (' … *ne peuvent pas voir leur responsabilité civile engage* … '). The French government confirms:

> ces dispositions n'ont ni pour objet, ni pour effet de déterminer a contrario des cas d'engagement de la responsabilité des prestataires. Dans l'hypothèse où un prestataire ne serait pas en mesure de justifier que les conditions prévues par l'article 6 pour l'exonérer de sa responsabilité sont réunies, sa responsabilité ne serait pas pour autant automatiquement engagée; elle ne pourrait l'être qu'à la condition qu'il soit jugé que les conditions mises par le droit commun à l'engagement de la responsabilité soient remplies.[249]

As Vivant has it therefore, the substantive answer to intermediary accessory liability in French law is to be found in '*le droit commun, encore et toujours!*'[250] – the general law, again and forever. What does *le droit commun* – i.e., the general law[251] – have to say on this particular topic?

In contrast to the casuistic approach of the English law of torts, the French *droit de la responsabilité extracontractuelle* centres around a single heading for civil liability of universal scope. The rules governing this are set out in Articles 1382 to 1386 of the *Code civil* (C.civ.), entitled '*Des délits et des quasi-délits*'. Three possible *faits générateurs* – i.e., circumstances generative of liability – are introduced here: fault, the acts of things and the acts of others. The essential core of this regime focuses on the first of the three resultant types of liability: *la responsabilité pour faute* (also known as

247. T Azzi, 'La responsabilité des nouvelles plates-formes: éditeurs, hébergeurs ou autre voie?' in Colloque de l'IPRI, *Contrefaçon sur internet: les enjeux du droit d'auteur sur le WEB 2.0* (Litec 2009) 59-75.
248. B Beignier et al., *Traité de droit de la presse et les médias* (Litec 2009) 1236.
249. 'Observations du Gouvernement sur les recours dirigés contre la loi pour la confiance dans l'économie numérique', JORF n°143 du 22 juin 2004 page 11193, texte n° 6.
250. M Vivant, 'Conditions de la responsabilité civile des fournisseurs d'hébergement d'un site sur le réseau Internet' (2000) 13 La Semaine Juridique Édition Générale 577. See also: B Beignier, B de Lamy et E Dreyer, *Traité de droit de la presse et les médias* (Litec 2009) 1160.
251. X Amadei, 'Standards of Liability for Internet for Internet Service Providers: A Comparative Study of France and the United States with a Specific Focus on Copyright, Defamation, and Illicit Content' (2002) 35 Cornell International Law Journal 189.

responsabilité du fait personnel and *responsabilité subjective*). This resides in the two *clausulae generalis* of Articles 1382 and 1383. According to the first of these, any person who, when acting with fault, caused prejudice to another is obliged to pay compensation to that other (*responsabilité délictuelle*). Article 1383 expands this obligation to damage caused by negligence or imprudence (*responsabilité quasi-délictuelle*). Own fault, whether in the form of intent or negligence, is therefore one of the possible bases of liability. The rest of the chapter (Articles 1384-1386) handles the notion of liability without fault, analogous to the English concept of vicarious liability. This is divided into two main subcategories: liability for things (*responsabilité du fait des choses*) and liability for other persons (*responsabilité du fait d'autrui*).

No specialised provisions for accessory liability are given. Indeed, France is one of the few European civil law countries that have not explicitly clarified the issue in their civil codes.[252] So, the C.civ. makes no distinction between joint principles, inciters, aiders and abettors, recognising instead only *co-auteurs*.[253] The words of the Belgian *Cour de cassation* hold true also for the French system: it is unnecessary '*de faire une distinction suivant que la participation a été principale ou accessoire, ni suivant la measure dans laquelle les participants one contribué aux divers faits qui ont causé le dommage*'. [254]

How does this system work? Very simply, the rules on direct liability themselves are relied upon to achieve the precise same practical outcome as that achieved in other countries through specialised rules. Thus, in France, the liability of third parties is based, in accordance to the general rules for tortious liability, directly either on their own fault or on their responsibility for objects or persons under their control. As we shall see below therefore, the French liability regime for harm caused by another, as applied in the

252. W van Gerven et al., *Tort Law* (Hart Publishing 2000) 432.

253. By contrast, a notion of accessory liability does exist in French criminal law where, in addition to the primary perpetrator, the person who knowingly provided help or facilitated the preparation or commission of an offence or who by means of a gift, promise, threat, order or an abuse of authority or power provoked the commission of a crime or gave instructions to commit it can incur liability as an accomplice. See: *Code pénal*, Art. 121-7. According to Art. 121-6 of the criminal code, accomplices are punished as perpetrators. Köhler and Burmeister suggest these provisions could help cover the lack of accessory liability in civil law, as civil liability follows automatically where criminal liability can be established. The provision would also have the advantage of making clear the necessity of establishing *mens rea*. To date however, this possibility has not, to the author's knowledge, been applied by the courts. See C Köhler & K Burmeister, 'Copyright liability on the Internet today in Europe (Germany, France, Italy and the E.U.)' (1999) 21(10) European Intellectual Property Review 485. See also X Amadei, 'Standards of Liability for Internet for Internet Service Providers: A Comparative Study of France and the United States with a Specific Focus on Copyright, Defamation, and Illicit Content' (2002) 35 Cornell International Law Journal 189.

254. Quoted in C von Bar, *The Common European Law of Torts – Vol. I* (Clarendon Press 1998) para. 55.

context of third party copyright infringement, is not a true regime of liability for the acts of the other at all, but rather a regime of fault and causation formulated in the same way as any other form of delictual liability. French tort law thus integrates 'accessory liability' into the general regime of causative plurality. As such, in France no hierarchy is established between multiple joint tortfeasors: one is not prime and the other accessory, only seen as participating in the tort of the other.[255] Instead, the indivisible damage is understood as being caused by *plusieurs faits générateurs*. Where all of these multiple attributive causes constitute faults, these are identified as *fautes concurrentes,* i.e., multiple wrongdoings by several concurrent tortfeasors – what English law calls 'several concurrent tortfeasance'.[256] In this way, each co-author is understood as having committed his own *faute,* all of which are at the origin of the indivisible injury.[257] Notably, the C.civ. explicitly rejects joint and several liability (*solidarité*) as a solution in such cases (Article 1202 of the C.civ.) – nevertheless, in order to sidestep the inconvenient consequences of this rule, under French law the multiple co-authors of a single damage are instead seen as liable, as it is said, *in solidum.* What does this mean? *In solidum* liability has essentially the same basic characteristics as joint and several liability, so that, as in England, in France as well each co-author has an obligation to provide full compensation. Subsequently, the co-defendants may settle the issue between themselves.[258] As the *Cour de cassation* explains, '*dans le cas de concours de* responsabilité, *chacun des responsables d'un dommage, ayand concouru* à *le causer en entire, doit* être *condamn*é *envers la victime* à *en assurer l'*entière *réparation, sans qu'il y ait lieu d'envisager l'*éventualité *d'un recours a l'*égard *de l'autre coauteur*'.[259]

Within the logic of French tort law, this approach makes sense: in order for a third party to be held liable for the commission of a tort, the English preoccupation with the detailed analysis of the individual characteristics of each of a collection of idiosyncratic torts dictates the invention and application of an 'accessory' liability concept that captures the involvement of persons who do not fit the profile of primary tortfeasor. In France by contrast, the same effect can easily be achieved simply by expanding the area of applicability of the very broad basic tort norms to encompass behaviour

255. Quoted in C von Bar, *The Common European Law of Torts – Vol. I* (Clarendon Press 1998) para. 55.
256. See above, s. 3.1.3. See also, W van Gerven et al., *Tort Law* (Hart Publishing 2000) 432 and 464.
257. P le Tourneau, *Droit de la responsabilité et des contrats – Régimes d'indemnisation* (9th ed., Dalloz 2013) 1738; C von Bar, E Clive, H Schulte-Nölke et al. (eds), *Principles, definitions and model rules of European private law: Draft Common Frame of Reference (DCFR)*, prepared by the Study Group on a European Civil Code and the Research Group on EC private law (Acquis Group), Outline Edition (Sellier 2009) 3447.
258. P le Tourneau, *Droit de la responsabilité et des contrats – Régimes d'indemnisation* (9th ed., Dalloz 2013) 1733-1772.
259. F H Lawson & B Markesinis, *Tortious Liability for Unintentional Harm in the Common Law and the Civil Law* (Cambridge University Press 1982) 131.

that constitutes an involvement of a person in the tort of another, so that such behaviour is understood as a breach of that fundamental norm and accordingly labelled as *primarily and directly* tortious, giving rise to liability in its own right.

What do these general rules mean for internet intermediaries in the context of third party copyright infringement? The two strict liability options of *responsabilité du fait des choses* and *responsabilité du fait d'autrui* depend on the existence of a relationship with a person or thing. Although attempts have been made to bend the two notions to encompass intermediary accessory liability in copyright, these have not been generally accepted by French lawyers. They are therefore of little interest to the subject and shall not be examined here.[260] The analysis below shall instead concentrate on the remaining broader, and therefore more promising, heading: *faute*.[261]

What qualifies as a *faute* under French law? Le Tourneau and Cadiet explain that '*la faute est un comportement illicite qui contrevient à une obligation ou à un devoir imposé par la loi ou par la coutume*': a *faute* is unlawful behaviour that breaches an obligation or a duty imposed by law or by custom. This formula is characterised by its generality. The resultant regime is one of an exceptionally wide reach, extending protection to the victims of a harm of any kind, however original (including therefore damage resulting from modern technological means), caused by a fault of any

260. It should be noted that the idea of applying the rules of *responsabilité du fait des choses* and *responsabilité du fait d'autrui* to intermediary liability has been suggested by French scholars. As to the first possibility, there is little doubt nowadays that information can constitute a movable object in the sense of Art. 1384 that governs the issue. Theoretically, therefore, intermediaries involved in the dissemination of information could qualify as guardians of that information. Nevertheless, this route has not yet, to the author's knowledge, ever been applied by the courts. The second doctrine of *responsabilité du fait d'autrui* would require that the third party be within the 'sphere of authority' of the defendant. As with the liability for things, this is unlikely to be the case for internet intermediaries and certainly not without control and knowledge that would result in liability for fault anyway. For more on these two theoretical possibilities, see: R Hardouin, *La responsabilité limitée des prestataires techniques dans la loi pour la confiance dans l'économie numérique* (unpublished PhD thesis, Université de Versailles Saint-Quentin-en-Yvelines 2011) 241-247 and 249-250; V L Benabou, 'Quelle(s) responsabilité(s) des intermédiaires techniques sur Internet?' (2006) 61(7-8) Annales Des Télécommunications 865; S Stalla-Bourdillon, 'Responsabilité civile et strategie de regulation – Essai sur la responsabilité civile des prestataires intermédiaires de service en ligne' (PhD thesis, European University Institute, Florence 2010) 493-496; P le Tourneau & L Cadiet, *Droit de la responsabilité et des contrats* (Dalloz-Sirey 2000) 1152-1155.

261. On this see Hardouin: '*Dès lors, il faut convener que le fait générateur de responsabilité de prestataire ne peut être que le fait personnel.* […] *Les principes gouvernant la responsabilité des prestataires s'inscrivent dans une vision classique du droit de la responsabilité. Il s'agit d'une responsabilité du fait personnel fondée sur la faute*', R Hardouin, *La responsabilité limitée des prestataires techniques dans la loi pour la confiance dans l'économie numérique* (unpublished PhD thesis, Université de Versailles Saint-Quentin-en-Yvelines 2011) 250.

kind.[262] There are two main ways of committing a *faute:* through the violation of either a legal provision (such as the intellectual property code) or, more usually, of customary norms. There are two main mechanisms through which such a violation could occur: the application of the *règles spéciales* or 'specialised rules' – in this case the rules of French copyright law – or the application of the *règles générales* or 'general rules', as these emanate from the civil code itself. The main difference between the two approaches comes down to the degree of objectivity with which the fault in question will be considered: while in intellectual property law, as is the case elsewhere, liability is strict, the general rules allow for greater consideration of the personal fault of the infringer.[263] Below, we shall begin with the *règles spéciales.*

3.2.3.1 Règles spéciales: *The Intellectual Property Code*

Chapter II of the French *Code de la propriété intellectuelle* (CPI) covers the economic rights of the author. France takes a synthetic approach to economic rights under Article L.122-1, according to which the 'right of exploitation belonging to the author shall comprise the right of performance and the right of communication to the public'.[264] Article L.122-4 of provides that '[a]ny complete or partial communication to the public or reproduction made without the consent of the author or of his successors in title or assigns is unlawful'. As is the case in all European jurisdictions, reproduction includes digitisation, while communication to the public encompasses the making available right, meaning that the digitisation and online distribution of a protected work on a network will require the express permission of the right-holder.[265]

Articles L.335-2 to 4 repeat the same prohibitions for criminal purposes, establishing that any breach of the economic rights of the author constitutes an infringement: '*une contrefaçon*'.[266] The term *contrefaçon* is a term particular to French intellectual property law. The notion is a unified one that corresponds both to a civil tort and to a criminal offence; thus it is an act to which both civil and criminal sanctions attach – an all-purpose

262. P le Tourneau & L Cadiet, *Droit de la responsabilité et des contrats* (Dalloz-Sirey 2000) 1046.
263. T Azzi, 'La responsabilité des nouvelles plates-formes: éditeurs, hébergeurs ou autre voie?' Colloque de l'IPRI, *Contrefaçon sur internet: les enjeux du droit d'auteur sur le WEB 2.0* (Litec 2009) 59-75.
264. The French text uses the term 'representation', but clarifies in Art. L.122-2 that '*[l]a représentation consiste dans la communication de l'oeuvre au public par un procédé quelconque*'.
265. S Durrande et al., *Code de la Propriété Intellectuelle Commenté* (15th ed., Dalloz 2015) 423.
266. According to Art. L.335-2, '*toute contrefaçon est un délit.*'

remedial tool.[267] In civil law, *contrefaçon* is subject to compensatory damages and injunctive orders. In criminal law it can result in imprisonment and a fine.[268] In practice, the right-holder must choose before which court an action will be brought, however civil suits may be joined with criminal proceedings and criminal sanctions may be supplemented with civil remedies.[269] In any case, it should be kept in mind that *contrefaçon* is perhaps primarily perceived in France as a criminal offence, explaining the common substantiation of civil sanctions with reference to the criminal provisions of the CPI by the civil courts, as well as generally their use of the legal tools of criminal law.[270]

On its face the French CPI does not seem to *a priori* cover the act of facilitating copyright infringement by a third party. Yet the *Code Dalloz* confirms that a communication to the public as prohibited by Article L.122-2 may be 'direct' or 'indirect' and classifies as 'indirect' communication by means of modern technologies, including the internet.[271] As Ginsburg and Gaubiac note, the general provisions have long been interpreted by the courts as applying beyond the material acts of infringement themselves to the provision of means for their commission.[272] It is worth noting that the terminology of the 'provision of means' is strikingly close to English legal expression of 'mere facilitation'.

The two authors refer to older case law on traditional means of reproduction for analogies. They cite *Ranou-Graphie,* a 1984 case concerning the liability of a copy-shop for reproductions created by its customers using its photocopiers.[273] There, the *Cour de cassation* held the copy-shop directly liable as a '*copiste*' within the meaning of the CPI.[274] The Court noted that the business in question had 'ensured the proper function of the machine placed on its premises and kept under its supervision, direction and control'. As a result, no distinction could be made between 'the case where

267. J Ginsburg, 'A Common Lawyer's Perspective on *Contrefaçon*' in L Bently, J Davis & J Ginsburg, 'Copyright and Piracy: An Interdisciplinary Critique' (Cambridge University Press 2010) 80.
268. D Lefranc, 'The Metamorphosis of *Contrefaçon* in French Copyright Law' in L Bently, J Davis & J Ginsburg, 'Copyright and Piracy: An Interdisciplinary Critique' (Cambridge University Press 2010) 55.
269. A Lucas et al., 'France' in L Bently, P Geller & M Nimmer, *International Copyright Law and Practice* (Matthew Bender/LexisNexis 2013) § 8 [4][b].
270. A Lucas et al., *Traité de la Propriété Littéraire et Artistique* (4th ed., LexisNexis 2012) 890.
271. S Durrande et al., *Code de la Propriété Intellectuelle Commenté* (15th ed., Dalloz 2015) 144.
272. J Ginsburg & Y Gaubiac, 'Contrefaçon, fourniture de moyens et faute: perspectives dans les systèmes de *common law* et civilistes à la suite des *arrêts Grokster et Kazaa'* (2006) 228 Revue Internationale du Droit d'Auteur 3.
273. *Ranou-Graphie* (82-17016), Cour de cassation, 7 March 1984.
274. At the time, Arts 40 and 41-2 of the Loi n°57-298 du 11 mars 1957 sur la propriété littéraire et artistique were applied, corresponding to the current Arts L.122-4 and L.122-5, para. 2 of the CPI.

the placement of the pages and the operation of the on-off button was performed by the client in a self-service system and the case where these actions were performed, exceptionally or not, by the entrepreneur himself or one of his employees'. Instead, note Ginsburg and Gaubiac, a kind of '*entreprise commun*' was found to have been established between the copy-shop and its clientele.

Further developments in the area of trademarks subsequently pushed this approach from the analogue into the digital realm. The *Google France* cases are indicative. In *Louis Vuitton Malletier,* at first instance before the TGI Paris, the famous search engine was found liable for the commission of acts of infringement by imitation of the plaintiff's trademarks under Article L.713-3 of the CPI.[275] Notably, the decision does not make a distinction between the acts of infringement themselves and the provision of the means that enabled their commission. Instead, the Court found that Google had itself committed infringement though the imitation of the plaintiff's trademark by means of its active role as indicated by its suggestion of keywords to promote and thus facilitate the consultations of sites whose unlawfulness is uncontested.[276] Later the same year, the TGI Versailles also found Google criminally liable as an 'accomplice in supplying the means' on the basis of three considerations: (a) Google had failed to carry out any preliminary checks regarding the keywords reserved by its clients; (b) it had failed to carry out a serious study of the potential rights of third parties over these words; and (c) it had failed to put an immediate and full stop to such infringement, once it was notified of the unlawful use of the keywords.[277] The court accepted that '*l'intention frauduleuse de la société Google France, laquelle n'est pas l'auteur principal du délit, mais le complice par fourniture de moyens, ne peut résulter du seul fait que l'élément matériel est constitué*'. At the same time, it was established that, according to Article 339 of Law no. 92-1336 of 16 December 1992, for offences substantiated by the material element alone (as is the case for the infringement of trademarks), intent need not be found, but mere evidence of carelessness or negligence is sufficient for a finding of liability. Thus, negligent complicity in the commission of an infringement was treated as a form of trademark infringement. As Ginsburg and Gaubiac note, the same rules should be understood as governing civil liability as well, so that the provision of means may engage civil liability under the CPI.[278]

275. *Louis Vuitton Malletier c. Google Inc et Google France,* Tribunal de Grande Instance de Paris (3ème chambre, 2ème section) jugement du 4 février 2005.
276. J Ginsburg & Y Gaubiac, 'Contrefaçon, fourniture de moyens et faute: perspectives dans les systèmes de *common law* et civilistes à la suite des *arrêts Grokster et Kazaa*' (2006) 228 Revue Internationale du Droit d'Auteur 3.
277. *Google v. Viaticum et Luteciel,* Cour d'appel de Versailles, 10 March 2005.
278. J Ginsburg & Y Gaubiac, 'Contrefaçon, fourniture de moyens et faute: perspectives dans les systèmes de *common law* et civilistes à la suite des *arrêts Grokster et Kazaa*' (2006) 228 Revue Internationale du Droit d'Auteur 3.

As we already know, these cases eventually ended up before the CJEU, to which they were referred by the *Cour de cassation* in 2008.[279] In 2010, the Luxembourg court[280] declared that an internet referencing service provider which stores, as a keyword, a sign identical to a reputable trademark and arranges the display of ads on the basis of that keyword does not use that sign within the meaning of the relevant EU trademark rules.[281] In compliance, the *Cour de cassation* reversed the decisions of the lower courts and aligned itself with the European judges by laconically repeating their refusal to find Google liable.[282] The expansive interpretation of primary acts of infringement favoured by the French courts does not therefore seem to be compatible with the harmonised European definitions. This jurisprudence was diligently followed by the Court of Appeal of Lyon in 2012, in order to reject the liability of Google for trademark infringements. In so holding, the court here noted that Google 'in no way used the trademark in the course of its own commercial communications, but only allowed such use to counterparties'.[283]

There is no reason why the same conclusion should not apply to copyright law as well – yet, in *Tiscali,* the Court of Appeal found that '*la société Tiscali Media a commis des actes de contrefaçon des bandes dessinées Lucky Luke 'Le Daily Star' et Blake et Mortimer 'Le secret de l'Espadon' au préjudice des sociétés Dargaud Lombard et Lucky Comics*'. In other words, Tiscali was liable for a direct infringement of the reproduction right. Similarly, in 2011, the Paris Court of Appeal confirmed the decision of the TGI Paris in *Auféminin,* according to which Google had infringed Article L.335-3 of the CPI through the reproduction of the contested photograph on its image search service ('*les sociétés Google Inc. et Google France [...] ont engagé leur responsabilité pour avoir porté atteinte aux droits patrimoniaux et au droit moral d'André R*'.):[284] the appellate court had found that, given that the relevant content could be viewed directly on the pages of Google Video and Google Images, Google was liable for copyright infringement. And although, as we saw above, the *Cour de cassation* in 2012 agreed to grant Google immunity in view of the provisions of the LCEN, it also refused to reverse the finding according to which the company had in principle

279. *Google v. CNRRH, Google v. Louis Vuitton Malletier, Google v. Viaticum et Luteciel,* Cour de cassation, 20 May 2008.
280. CJEU, joined Cases C-236/08 to C-238/08, *Google France and Google Inc. et al. v. Louis Vuitton Malletier et al,* 23 March 2010.
281. Article 5(1) and (2) of the First Council Directive 89/104/EEC of 21 December 1988 to approximate the laws of the Member States relating to trade marks [1989] OJ L040/1 (Trademark Directive) and Art. 9(1) of Council Regulation (EC) No 40/94 of 20 December 1993 on the Community trade mark [1994] OJ L11/1.
282. *Google c. GIFAM (08-13944), Google c. Louis Vuitton Malletier (06-20.230), Google c. CNRRH (06-15136), Google c. SA Viaticum (05-14331),* Cour de cassation, 13 juillet 2010.
283. *Google France c. Jean-Baptiste D.-V. et autres*, Cour d'appel de Lyon, 22 March 2012.
284. *Google France c. Auféminin et autres*, Cour d'appel de Paris, 4 February 2011.

committed an infringement of copyright.[285] Indeed, in the parallel cases of *L'affaire Clearstream* and *Les dissimulateurs,* the court went even further and declared that Google had implemented an 'active function' which enabled it to take over the content stored on third party sites in order to represent it directly on their own pages for access by their own users. Thus, Google had reproduced the content without authorisation in a manner that is characteristic of copyright infringement. It accordingly appears that Recital 27 and Article 5(1) of the Copyright Directive are not enough to contain direct infringement within appropriate bounds before the national courts – acts of provision of means to third parties are encompassed within their ambit by the French courts. Potentially, a referral to the CJEU could have been beneficial here as well, as the distinction could be relevant for intermediaries that fail to abide by the conditions for safe harbour protection.

Interestingly, the two *Bac films* decisions seem to point towards a concept of 'adoption' of foreign content. Sirinelli notes that, while the rulings are undeniably significant, they cannot be interpreted as condemning all referencing activities. Indeed, the interpretation adopted rested heavily on the specific technical means employed by Google: Google's activity in these cases was not limited to the mere creation of links enabling users to visit infringing sites, but extended to enabling works stored elsewhere to be viewed on its own site, thus 'taking over' third party content. The *Cour de cassation* recognised that the infringing content was stored on third party servers and uploaded by third party infringers, however, as the process used was such that the reproduced remote content was displayed by the intermediary in such a way that the end-user was unaware of having been transferred to another site, the intermediary was to be interpreted as having 'borrowed' or 'adopted' the content. As a result, 'from the moment that the adopted process led to an act that was technically analysed then legally classified as reproduction, Google could incur liability on that score because the act was carried out without the rightholders' authorisation'.[286]

These decisions spell difficulty for online linking to infringing content: although the Court's reasoning cannot easily be transplanted to surface links providing access to the home page of other websites or even 'deep links' that lead to an 'inner page' belonging to another website, arguably it may apply to all cases of framing or 'embedded links'. However, in view of *Svensson*, liability if not for a reproduction, then for a communication to the public could certainly be argued if a link – embedded or not – enables users 'to circumvent restrictions put in place by the site on which the protected work appears in order to restrict public access to that work to the latter site's

---

285. *La société Google France c. André Rau* (11-15.165; 11-15.188) Cour de cassation, 12 July 2012.

286. P Sirinelli, 'Chronique de Jurisprudence – Échanges pair à pair non autorisés d'oeuvres protégées (P2P)' (2012) 231 Revue Internationale du Droit d'Auteur 184.

subscribers only', thus communicating it to a 'new public'.[287] Sirinelli additionally suggests that French case law supports liability where the creator of a link had reason to believe that the linked content was infringing.[288] French sources generally seem to agree that, although in principle the freedom to link must be preserved,[289] hyperlinking to a website containing infringing works may constitute an infringement in its own right, depending on the circumstances.[290]

Court rulings have gone both ways: for example, in 2000, the TGI Épinal found that the creator of links permitting access to other websites offering musical files without the authorisation of the right-holders constituted an infringement of Articles L.335-3 and L.334-5 of the CPI.[291] In 2011, the TGI Paris found that a company that edited two websites which listed and made available to the public audiovisual programmes available as catch-up TV using deep hyperlinks had not infringed Article L. 122-2 of the CPI: '*En mettant les programmes de M6 Replay et W9 Replay à la disposition du public, la société SBDS ne lui communique nullement elle-même les oeuvres, mais ne fait que l'aider en lui indiquant un lien permettant de les visionner directement sur les sites m6replay.fr et w9replay.fr, lesquels sites effectuant alors l'acte de représentation au sens de ce texte*'.[292] This seems perfectly in line with *Svensson*. The Court of Appeal affirmed in 2011, noting that the plaintiffs had not identified specific works they claimed had been infringed and the plaintiff could not collectively claim the infringement of undifferentiated rights.[293]

In conclusion, it is clear that if a provider is involved in the management of the content in such a way as to engage its liability under the regular rules of copyright, it will be liable. This confirms the notion of *éditeur* as essentially indicative in copyright of a liability scheme identical to that of the *fournisseur de contenus* – the content provider. The same criteria and procedures – without the need for e.g., prior notification, as would be the case for an *hébergeur* – apply.[294] Essentially, this is the French interpretation of England's joint tortfeasance: where the accessory has 'adopted' the

---

287. CJEU, C-466/12, *Svensson and Others,* 13 February 2014.
288. P Sirinelli, 'Chronique de Jurisprudence – Échanges pair à pair non autorisés d'oeuvres protégées (P2P)' (2012) 231 Revue Internationale du Droit d'Auteur 184.
289. P le Tourneau, *Droit de la responsabilité et des contrats – Régimes d'indemnisation* (9th ed., Dalloz 2013) 6787.
290. S Durrande et al., *Code de la Propriété Intellectuelle Commenté* (15th ed., Dalloz 2015) 144, 149, 157-158, 424; C Féral-Schuhl, *Cyberdroit – Le Droit à l'Épreuve de l'Internet* (6th ed., Dalloz 2010) 832-842.
291. *MP et SCPP c. Conraud,* Tribunal de grande instance d'Epinal, 24 October 2000.
292. *M6 Web, Metropole Television et autres c. SBDS*, Tribunal de Grande Instance de Paris, 18 June 2010.
293. *Metropole Télévision et autres c. SBDS Active*, Cour d'appel de Paris, 27 April 2011, confirmed by Cour de cassation, (11-20480), 31 October 2012.
294. A Lucas et al., 'France' in L Bently, P Geller & M Nimmer, *International Copyright Law and Practice* (Matthew Bender/LexisNexis 2013) § 8[1][c][ii].

content through sufficiently involved editorial functions, their liability is indistinguishable from the liability of the primary infringer.

It should be noted that liability in copyright in France, as in other jurisdictions, is strict:[295] there is no need to prove the infringer's fault, i.e., either intent or negligence. As opposed to other areas of tortious liability, in copyright, the *Cour de cassation*[296] has declared that, due to the *erga omnes* opposability that results from copyright's nature as an absolute right, i.e., a right which are enforceable against everyone, no fault is required. This holds true both for the imposition of reparative measures (i.e., to say court orders, injunctions and fines intended to prevent the continuation of the infringement and to confirm the exclusivity of the holder's rights) and for claims for the compensatory payment of damages. This is because the hybrid *action en contrefaçon* traditionally affords French judges the discretion to pick and choose from among available remedies.[297]

This approach has been heavily criticised.[298] Lucas and Lucas observe that 'the autonomy of copyright is not such as to justify a self-standing notion of infringement and a fault-independent tort which evades (both dangerously and pointlessly) the general rules of civil liability'.[299] Azzi agrees, noting that there it is one thing to say that a platform has contributed to the development of a *contrefaçon* and another to assimilate them with *contrefacteurs* themselves:[300] while for the primary offender a rule of strict liability appears quite reasonable, it becomes less easy to accept in the case of other parties involved in the distribution of a work,[301] particularly the multiple actors participating in the digital dissemination of works who do not directly

295. S Durrande et al., *Code de la Propriété Intellectuelle Commenté* (15th ed., Dalloz 2015) 158.
296. Cour de cassation, 10 May 1995 (93-14767), Bulletin 1995 I N° 203 p. 145: '*sans avoir à rechercher l'existence d'une faute dès lors que la contrefaçon était établie*', see (1995)166 Revue Internationale du Droit d'Auteur 291; Cour de cassation, 29 May 2001 (99-15284), Bulletin 2001 I N° 154 p. 100: *'la contrefaçon est caractérisée, indépendamment de toute faute ou mauvaise foi, par la reproduction, la représentation ou l'exploitation d'une oeuvre de l'esprit en violation des droits de propriété intellectuelle qui y sont attachés'*.
297. See Y Benhamou, 'Compensation of Damages for Infringements of Intellectual Property Rights in France, Under Directive 2004/48/EC and its Transposition Law – New Notions?' (2009) 40 International Review of Intellectual Property and Competition Law (IIC) 125; A Lucas et al., 'France' in L Bently, P Geller & M Nimmer, International Copyright Law and Practice (Matthew Bender/LexisNexis 2013) § 8[1][c][i].
298. A Lucas et al., *Traité de la Propriété Littéraire et Artistique* (4th ed., LexisNexis 2012) 893.
299. A Lucas et al., *Traité de la Propriété Littéraire et Artistique* (4th ed., LexisNexis 2012) 901 (translation by the author).
300. T Azzi, 'La responsabilité des nouvelles plates-formes: éditeurs, hébergeurs ou autre voie?' in Colloque de l'IPRI, *Contrefaçon sur internet: les enjeux du droit d'auteur sur le WEB 2.0* (Litec 2009) 59-75.
301. A Lucas et al., *Traité de la Propriété Littéraire et Artistique* (4th ed., LexisNexis 2012) 903.

contribute to an infringement and whose fault is harder to take as given.[302] The lower French courts have taken a much more moderate approach: although falling short of expressly accepting a presumption of fault, they generally impose the burden of proving the absence of fault on the defendant, but will absolve from liability defendants who demonstrate that they could not have foreseen the damage.[303]

As we shall see below, the German courts have developed a much more coherent framework, through distinguishing between the imposition of reparative measures against persons acting without fault and the compensation of damages in cases of fault – although here too criticism has been levied against the idea that any kind of sanction should be imposed on innocent intermediaries. It should in any case be noted that the primary liability of intermediaries for copyright infringement – even the infringements of their users – is by no means peculiar only to France. For example, in the UK, Newzbin, in addition to authorisation and joint tortfeasance, was also held liable for the unauthorised communication of the claimants' works to the public.[304] What is particular in France's case is the lack of any well-defined distinction between direct and indirect infringement and the use of different legal tools for each. As a result, in France, direct liability might be more easily attributed to a party that arguably could more plausibly be held liable under some sort of indirect liability.[305] This confirms the need identified in Chapter 2 for an improved European differentiation between the two types of liability[306] – at the same time, it must be acknowledged that, in terms of substance, arguably, the difference is minimal.

In an attempt to address online infringement, the French legislator in 2009 added new criminal provisions to the CPI that introduce sanctions for

302. A Lucas & H-J Lucas, *Traité de la Propriété Littéraire et Artistique* (2nd ed, Litec 2001) 606 et seq.

303. See Y Benhamou, 'Compensation of Damages for Infringements of Intellectual Property Rights in France, Under Directive 2004/48/EC and its Transposition Law – New Notions?' (2009) 40 International Review of Intellectual Property and Competition Law (IIC) 125.

304. See, *Twentieth Century Fox Film Corporation & Anor v. Newzbin* Ltd [2010] EWHC 608 (Ch) (29 March 2010), para. 125. The judge relied on the CJEU's findings in *Rafael Hoteles* to substantiate this conclusion (see C-306/05, *SGAE v. Rafael Hoteles,* 7 December 2006). Nevertheless, the ruling is likely incompatible with the exclusion of the provision of mere physical facilities from the purview of the right of communication to the public under EU copyright law (see Recital 27 of the Copyright Directive) even restrictively interpreted – after all, no 'act of intervention' as demanded by the CJEU existed, as the relevant software was not installed by Newzbin onto end-users' computers and the works were made available by Newzbin's users onto its systems. Some clarification on these matters may be offered by the CJEU in pending case C-610/15, *Ziggo v. Stichting Brein.*

305. A Lucas et al., 'France' in L Bently, P Geller & M Nimmer, *International Copyright Law and Practice* (Matthew Bender/LexisNexis 2013) § 8[1][c][i], see footnote 45.

306. See s. 2.1.3.

specific acts of accessory liability.[307] So, Article L.335-2-1 of the code punishes anyone who 'publishes, makes available or communicates to the public, knowingly and in any form whatsoever, software manifestly intended to communicate unauthorised works or protected objects to the public', as well as a the knowing incitement of the use of such software. The provision was inspired by the US *Grokster* and Australian *Kazaa* rulings and is intended precisely to impose liability on providers whose business model entails the facilitation or the incitement of infringement.[308] Thus, it would effortlessly apply to e.g., peer-to-peer software producers (e.g., BitTorrent clients), as well as online indexes of infringing content (e.g., TPB).[309] The provision rests on the key terms 'knowingly' and 'manifestly' that ensure its insusceptibility to the safe harbours – essentially, therefore, it represents the UK's 'secondary liability' doctrine, reworked for the digital environment. In this way, the specific provisions of the CPI are given the tools they require to impose direct liability on providers in a more convincing manner – although it should also be noted that the provision is not intended to prejudice the application of the theory of *complicité par fourniture de moyens.*[310]

The application of these rules has made the extraction of liability from intermediaries for copyright infringement even easier under French law. So, in 2009, in *Radioblogclub,*[311] both criminal and civil sanctions were imposed on a website for violating Articles L.212-1 et seq on performers rights and L.335-1 et seq of the CPI by reproducing and making available to the public without authorisation unlawful copies of phonograms through the their online application, which enabled internet users to create their own personal audio pages to stream musical works through user-created playlists. At the same time however, the provider was also held liable under Article L.335-2-1.

In May 2012, the TGI Paris rejected the liability of YouTube for the infringement of the rights of broadcaster TF1.[312] The court, referring back to the criteria established by the *Cour de cassation* in *Nord-Ouest* and by the CJEU in *SABAM v. Netlog*, found that YouTube was sufficiently passive to qualify for the LCEN immunity. Nevertheless, the platform was denied protection for failure to abide by the conditions of the safe harbour, as it had

307. See: *Loi n° 2009-669 du 12 juin 2009 favorisant la diffusion et la protection de la création sur internet (1).*
308. S Durrande et al., *Code de la Propriété Intellectuelle Commenté* (15th ed., Dalloz 2015) 421.
309. A Lucas et al., 'France' in L Bently, P Geller & M Nimmer, *International Copyright Law and Practice* (Matthew Bender/LexisNexis 2013) § 8 [4][b].
310. S Durrande et al., *Code de la Propriété Intellectuelle Commenté* (15th ed., Dalloz 2015) 421.
311. *SCPP c. Jean-Louis et Benoît T.*, Tribunal de grande instance de Paris, 3 September 2009; *SPPF, SCPP c. Mubility et autres*, Cour d'appel de Paris, 22 March 2011.
312. *TF1 et autres c. YouTube*, Tribunal de Grande Instance de Paris, 29 May 2012.

only removed notified videos five days after their notification, a lapse which was not considered reasonable. Ultimately however, no liability was found, as the Court considered that the conditions of Article L.216-1 of the CPI dealing with the related rights of broadcasting organisations, on which the claims were based, had not been met. While this outcome initially sounds convincing, it should be noted that the Court based its conclusion on the absence of any entrance fee imposed by YouTube for access to its website. The payment of an entry fee is a condition for protection under Article L.216-1 of the CPI that is not reproduced in the code's provisions on the economic rights of copyright. Indeed, even the application of the condition to the related rights of broadcasters in France is curious, given that no such limitation exists under Articles 2 and 3 of the Copyright Directive.

Three months later a similar decision was handed down in *TF1 v. Dailymotion*, but with a drastically different conclusion.[313] Again, the Court found that, although Dailymotion was not a publisher, but a host and therefore eligible for the safe harbour, it had not abided by the conditions of Article 6-I-2 of the LCEN, as it had left an excessively long period between the notification and the removal. This time the case made it to the Court of Appeal, which confirmed this reasoning, albeit placing it on a sounder legal basis.[314] Here it was found that the failure to promptly remove constituted an act of unfair and parasitic competition that forms a fault, thus engaging the liability of Dailymotion on the basis of Article 1382 of the Civil Code. Helpfully, this points the way to the other major legal basis upon which intermediary liability can be founded under French law, i.e., the characterisation of an intermediary's involvement as a *faute* under the general provisions of civil liability.[315]

3.2.3.2 Règles générales: *Negligence Liability*

As mentioned above, a *faute* may be committed through, not only the violation of a legal provision, but also of customary norms. In this way, fault and, with it, liability can in France further arise from failure to adhere to a duty of care, e.g., to block access to a site carrying infringing material.[316] Le Tourneau emphasises that such customary norms extend to the internet: '*Le monde de l'internet produit ainsi son propre droit, de nature déontologique, la 'nétiquette', sorte de* lex internautica'. These rules are not special or separate from those that regulate offline life: '*l'internet n'a pas besoin d'un droit spécifique [mais] il convenait plutôt d'en appeler au sens des*

313. *TF1 et autres c. Dailymotion*, Tribunal de grande instance de Paris, 13 September 2012.
314. *TF1 et autres c. Dailymotion*, Cour d'appel de Paris, 2 December 2014.
315. J Ginsburg & Y Gaubiac, 'Contrefaçon, fourniture de moyens et faute: perspectives dans les systèmes de *common law* et civilistes à la suite des *arrêts Grokster et Kazaa*' (2006) 228 Revue Internationale du Droit d'Auteur 3.
316. K Koelman, 'Liability for On-Line Intermediaries', Imprimatur/Institute for Information Law, Amsterdam, 1997.

responsabilités du 'citoyen-internaute', pour 'faire des réseaux numériques un espace de civilité mondiale'.[317]

In the case of violation of customary norms, the discretion of the judge is naturally of heightened importance. As a result, the early French regime of internet intermediary liability was the joint creation of legislator and the courts, the lead being taking by the latter.[318] Significantly, the French notion of *faute* implies unlawfulness: as opposed to other legal systems that distinguish between the two notions,[319] in France a *faute* may simply consist of a failure to comply with a rule of conduct, whether laid down in statute or infused in custom. As Viney points out, tort liability in France is also 'devoid of relativity, in that it is not conceived of as a failure of a duty toward this of that person, as is the case of negligence in English law'. It likewise does not follow the German theory of *Schutzzweck der Norm* (referred to in French as *relativité aquilienne*), according to which damage may be recovered only when it is within the scope of protection of the norm which has been infringed. The French judge is satisfied by a mere objective failure to respect the relevant rules of conduct.[320]

As noted above, Article 1382 of the civil code covers *la faute délictuelle.* This describes unlawful behaviour committed with the intent to cause harm. It is not necessary that the specific damage have been envisioned by the tortfeasor as the desired result per se. Article 1382 is complemented by Article 1383, which is dedicated to *la faute quasi-délictuelle*. This consists of a defective behaviour that upsets social harmony, an error committed without malicious intent, through inattention or mistake, which could have been avoided if greater attention had been paid. The distinction between delicts and quasi-delicts corresponds to the difference between intent and negligence.[321] It should be noted that *faute* is always personal – it cannot extend to groups of people, there being no concept of a *faute collective,* exempting cases where it is impossible to ascertain who from among a liable group is in fact responsible – although two or more people may be held liable for the same damage as long as they have all committed an independent *faute.* In addition, *faute* must be proven, it cannot be presumed. At the same time, any *faute* however slight, suffices to engage liability – it need not reflect a special level of seriousness, nor is there any hierarchical organisation of the imposed reparations depending on the degree of fault.[322] Significantly, a

317. P le Tourneau, *Droit de la responsabilité et des contrats – Régimes d'indemnisation* (9th ed., Dalloz 2013) 6784.
318. A Lepage, *Libertés et droits fondamentaux à l'épreuve de l'internet* (Litec 2003) 276.
319. See Ch. 4, s. 4.3.
320. G Viney, 'Tort Liability' in G Bermann & E Picard, *Introduction to French Law* (Walters Kluwer 2008) 238 et seq.
321. G Samuel, 'Western Law of Obligations' in M Bussani & F Werro, *European Private Law: A Handbook (Vol. I)* (Stämpfli 2009) 143.
322. P le Tourneau & L Cadiet, *Droit de la responsabilité et des contrats* (Dalloz-Sirey 2000) 1046 et seq.

faute may also result from mere abstention. As Greuille explains, '*s'il ya a faute ou imprudence, quelque légère que soit leur influence sur le dommage commis, il en est dû réparation*'.[323] Indeed, there has been a 'progressive radical dissociation of civil wrongdoing from moral wrongdoing', to the extent that not only is unnecessary to found a *faute* on any concept of a moral failing, but current case law does not even allow defendants to escape fault by proving unconsciousness, mental illness or young age, except where a specific exception is established by law.[324]

The applicable standard for the finding of a *faute* is the traditional one of the '*bonus pater familias*' or, in French, '*bon père de famille*'. This good family man threshold refers to what English-speaking systems term the 'reasonable person' and is in fact further elaborated as that of an '*homme raisonnable et avisé*'. Such a good family figure would never wish misfortune on another, but always respects moral obligations and comports herself as a diligent, prudent and skilful person ideally would. With this standard in mind, *faute* takes shape as any conduct that deviates from that which an ordinary circumspect person would demonstrate: according to Vivant, '*être responsable, ce n'est pas se comporter comme le "bon père de famille" […] C'est s'écarter du comportement qui aurait dû être idéalement suivi*'.[325] The assessment of an individual's conduct against the *bon père de famille* standard is conducted in an abstract manner, albeit with due regard for the circumstances within which the given individual finds themselves, as well as the nature of the relevant activity.[326]

From the above it is clear that the French notion of fault is very broadly defined. This accounts for its persistent relevance to French tort law: its versatility allows it to act as a stop-gap measure that can impose a duty to compensate in appropriate circumstances which existing specific liability regimes have failed to capture – as is the case, for example, when the rules on copyright liability, as enshrined in the intellectual property code, fail to properly account for the particular and evolving situation of internet intermediaries.

To this extent, the application of the general principles of Article 1382 and 1383 to intermediary copyright liability can perhaps be accurately described as having a 'secondary' function of sorts. But what is probably more relevant in distinguishing a 'secondary' liability regime from a 'primary' one in the French context will be the type and extent of the obligations imposed on tortfeasors that are considered sufficient to keep them

323. B de Greuille, Rapport fait au Tribunal, séance du 16 pluviôse an XII (6 février 1803) in Locré, t.XIII, 57.

324. G Viney, 'Tort Liability' in G Bermann & E Picard, *Introduction to French Law* (Walters Kluwer 2008) 238 et seq.

325. M Vivant, 'La responsabilité des intermédiaires de l'internet' (1999) 45-46 JCP - La Semaine Juridique Edition Générale 2021.

326. P le Tourneau & L Cadiet, *Droit de la responsabilité et des contrats* (Dalloz-Sirey 2000) 1062.

in line with the requisite standard: the application of Articles 1382 and 1383 presupposes the identification of tortious activity. This in turn requires the violation of certain set obligations, which, in conclusion, means that concrete duties that must be respected by law-abiding intermediaries must be articulated and recognised.[327] Here the role of the judiciary cannot be overstated: it is the courts' job to adapt the vague prescriptions of the general tort norms to the specific situation in order to construct a workable rule of 'reasonable' conduct that can be understood as expected of professional players.

Following this system, the general tort obligation has been utilised by the French courts to construct a broadly drafted concept of 'accessory liability' available against internet intermediaries for the unlawful behaviour of third parties. This is essentially the 'duty of care' approach currently rejected by English law. For an intermediary to be found liable three conditions must be fulfilled: the existence of fault or negligence; a resultant damage; and a causal connection between the two first elements.[328] The first and most important of these may be provided by a violation of a general obligation of prudence or vigilance ('*la violation d'une obligation générale de prudence et de diligence*'). In other words, an internet intermediary can be said to have committed a *faute* by intentionally or negligently causing an infringement by a third party through disregarding reasonable duties of care to identify and prevent or terminate direct acts of infringement. If liability can be established, all remedies available in cases of direct copyright infringement also become available against the accessory, including both injunctive relief and joint and several liability for damages.[329]

The pre-E-Commerce Directive case law provides insights into the regime still applicable outside the reach of the immunities.[330] Invoking Articles 1382 and 1383, the jurisprudence of the day formulated a relatively harsh liability scheme. So, in 1998 in the famous *Estelle Hallyday* case,[331] the judge, reasoning that the hosting provider's position permitted it to both ascertain the existence of unlawful content on its pages and discontinue its communication to the public, although refusing to impose damages, did find that the provider was under an obligation to terminate any infringements

327. F Olivier & E Barbry, 'Conditions de la responsabilité civile des fournisseurs d'hébergement d'un site sur le réseau Internet' (2000) 13 JCP - La Semaine Juridique Edition Générale 577.
328. Y Benhamou, 'Compensation of Damages for Infringements of Intellectual Property Rights in France, Under Directive 2004/48/EC and its Transposition Law – New Notions?' (2009) 40 International Review of Intellectual Property and Competition Law (IIC) 125; M Leistner, 'Common Principles of Secondary Liability?' in A Ohly, Common Principles of European Intellectual Property Law (Mohr Siebeck 2012) 117.
329. M Leistner, 'Common Principles of Secondary Liability?' in A Ohly, Common Principles of European Intellectual Property Law (Mohr Siebeck 2012) 117.
330. V L Benabou, 'Quelle(s) responsabilité(s) des intermédiaires techniques sur Internet?' (2006) 61(7-8) Annales Des Télécommunications 865.
331. *Estelle H. c. Valentin L. et Daniel*, Tribunal de grande instance de Paris, 9 June 1998.

brought to its attention. The court accordingly ordered the defendant to take all appropriate measures to make the distribution of the infringing photographic negatives in question impossible from the hosted website on penalty of 100,000 francs per day of non-compliance. This comparatively lenient decision was overthrown on appeal, where the judge imposed 300.000 francs in damages, reasoning that host service providers exceed the technical role of a mere transmitter of information, thus opening themselves up to liability for the infringement of third party rights impinged upon as a consequence of an activity into which they deliberately enter and for which they gain profit.[332] Intermediaries were thus placed under a duty to take all necessary precautions to prevent any breach of the rights of third parties if they were to avoid liability. In a complementary fashion, French courts also refused to hold liable intermediaries who blocked access to or promptly took down unlawful content, thus excluding own fault.[333] This system is strikingly different from the traditional English approach: not only is facilitation explicitly recognised as an association with the primary tort capable of substantiating liability, but the method with which this is achieved takes the form of the imposition of duties of care of a kind explicitly rejected in English law.

In the subsequent *Lacoste* case, the TGI de Nanterre, referring back to Articles 1382 and 1383 of the C.civ., went one step further and identified the three main obligations incumbent on service providers that it declared derive from the general duty of care:

- to bring the need to respect the rights of others to the attention of users (*obligation d'information*);
- to remain vigilant against infringement along a standard of professional care (*obligation de vigilance*); and
- to act against verified infractions by removing the unlawful material and impeding its future re-posting (*obligation de réaction*).[334]

The *Cour d'appel de Versailles* later mitigated the obligation of vigilance by specifying that it should not be understood as requiring a systematic and general examination of all content on all hosted websites, but only due diligence checks (*diligences appropriées*), which must be proactively executed by the intermediary once it acquires knowledge of the unlawful nature of the content on a specific site or once it has reason to

332. *Estelle H. / Valentin L. et Daniel*, Cour d'appel de Paris, 10 February 1999.

333. X Amadei, 'Standards of Liability for Internet for Internet Service Providers: A Comparative Study of France and the United States with a Specific Focus on Copyright, Defamation, and Illicit Content' (2002) 35 Cornell International Law Journal 189; B Beignier, B de Lamy & E Dreyer, *Traité de droit de la presse et les médias* (Litec 2009) 1161; L Thoumyre, 'Etude 464 – La responsabilité pénale et extra-contractuelle des acteurs de l'Internet' (Novembre 2009) Lamy Droit des Médias et de la Communication.

334. *Madame L. c. les sociétés Multimania*, Tribunal de Grande Instance de Nanterre, 8 December 1999. For an analysis see, A Lepage, *Libertés et droits fondamentaux à l'épreuve de l'internet* (Litec 2003) 283-286.

suspect unlawfulness.[335] As a general rule however, these obligations on intermediaries were subject to a broad interpretation: so, for example, in the *Calimero* case of 2000, the judge acknowledged the civil liability, under Article 1382 of the civil code, of a service provider hosting a website dedicated to sadomasochism under the title '*La page francophone de Calimero'* at the domain name 'www.calimero.org'. The provider had earlier decided to terminate the provision of its hosting services due to the unsuitability of the content in question for minors and had asked the owner of the website to relocate to a different server, but had then maintained for a number of months a hyperlink directing users to the new location. On this basis and in view of the fact that the renown of the cartoon character in question made it unlikely that the host, notwithstanding the great number of websites under its control, could claim ignorance of the copyright and brand name infringements that had occurred, the intermediary was found to have tolerated the infringement, thus substantiating its liability under Article 1382 of the C.civ..[336]

The case law imposing *diligences appropriées* after receiving notification of illegal or damaging content was inserted into the primitive French safe harbour provisions of the first draft of the law of 1 August 2000 on the freedom of communication.[337] Notably however, the law only codified the *obligation de reaction*, implicitly rejecting the other two court-created duties of information and vigilence.[338] In any case, even this lax re-interpretation was subsequently struck down by the *Conseil Constitutionnel.*[339] This confirms that notice-and-stay-down obligations would not be valid under French law even absent Article 15 of the E-Commerce Directive. Regardless, the inauspicious fate of the Nanterre court's three *obligations* clearly does not affect the validity of the basic concept of the application of the general principles of tort law to intermediary liability.

Ultimately, through this approach, the *bon père de famille* standard was translated, specifically for the area of intermediary liability, into that of a '*prestataire diligent et avisé*', i.e., a diligent and prudent intermediary.[340] Such an intermediary must take all the reasonable measures that a prudent professional would take to avoid having its services used by third parties to

335. *S.A Multimania Production c. Madame Lynda L.,* Cour d'appel de Versailles, 8 June 2000.
336. C Vier, 'Counterfeit of a Brand-Name and Infringement of Copyright on the Internet' IRIS 2000-5/18.
337. *Loi n° 2000-719 du 1 août 2000 modifiant la loi n° 86-1067 du 30 septembre 1986 relative à la liberté de communication.*
338. A Lepage, *Libertés et droits fondamentaux à l'épreuve de l'internet* (Litec 2003) 287; C Féral-Schuhl, *Cyberdroit – Le Droit à l'Épreuve de l'Internet* (6th ed., Dalloz 2010) 743-901.
339. Conseil Constitutionnel, Décision n° 2000-433 DC du 27 juillet 2000.
340. S Stalla-Bourdillon, 'Responsabilité civile et strategie de regulation – Essai sur la responsabilité civile des prestataires intermédiaires de service en ligne' (PhD thesis, European University Institute, Florence 2010) 491.

infringe the rights of others.[341] The parallel with the CJEU's concept of a 'diligent economic operator' is obvious.[342] According to French case law, these *diligences raisonnables* cannot be such as to impose a disproportionate burden on the intermediary or on third parties – the heart of the discussion is thus located in the determination of what is and what is not proportionate. To find the appropriate balance, Vivant recommends a liability-inducing triptych for the regulation of intermediary liability consisting of three elements: '*pouvoir – savoir – inertie*'. Under this scheme, if an intermediary has the power to intervene to prevent harm and knows that there is infringing material present, but nevertheless does nothing to prevent or remove it, then it is not a 'good family intermediary' and the judge may hold it accountable for any resultant damage incurred to a right-holder.[343] This *faute*-based solution allows for the insertion of a level of nuance into the intermediary liability debate that the strict approach traditional to French copyright law excludes. Vivant calls the ultimate result a '*responsabilité de raison*'[344] – a liability scheme that rests on deliberative reasoning. Importantly, the versatility of the *faute* standard enables different outcomes for different types of intermediary activity, without the need for detailed classifications: focus is instead diverted to the specifics of the intermediary's behaviour in each individual case. In this way, it is left up to the case law to determine the standards of reasonable behaviour that intermediaries should follow, taking pointers from the general wisdom that has developed around each type of provider.[345]

Perhaps unfortunately, this sophistication has been subsequently somewhat eroded, as the development of the legal discussion on the application of the general duty of care to intermediaries in copyright has become inextricably intertwined with that on the safe harbours. This has muddied the waters somewhat: with the gradual evolution of French fault-based intermediary liability through the regular passing of the baton from courts seeking to elaborate the positive rules on intermediary liability to a legislator attempting to hedge those rules in through immunities and fundamental rights, the two seemingly opposing approaches have seemed to become one and the same. As a result, immunities and liability now appear to operate as communicating vessels, with the courts relying on the first to take cues from the legislator as

341. M Vivant, 'Conditions de la responsabilité civile des fournisseurs d'hébergement d'un site sur le réseau Internet' (2000) 13 La Semaine Juridique Édition Générale 577.
342. C Castets-Renaud, 'Le renouveau de la responsabilité délictuelle des intermédiaires de l'internet' (2012) Recueil Dalloz 827.
343. M Vivant, 'La responsabilité des intermédiaires de l'internet' (1999) 45-46 JCP - La Semaine Juridique Edition Générale 2021.
344. M Vivant et al., *Lamy – Droit du Numérique: Informatique, Multimedia, Réseaux, Internet* (Wolters Kluwer France 2012) 1709.
345. J-F Thery & I Falque-Pierrotin, 'Internet et les réseaux numériques: étude adoptée par l'Assemblée générale du Conseil d'Etat le 2 juillet 1998' (La Documentation française 1998) 171-172.

to how to define the second. The ultimate outcome is a system wherein failing to abide by the conditions of the hosting safe harbour will not only deprive hosting providers of their immunity, but engage the liability of all kinds of internet intermediaries. Despite the assertions of the French government to the contrary therefore, for France at least, AG Maduro seems to be perfectly right when he calls the safe harbours a restatement of the substantive norms. So, for example, the *Cour d'appel de Paris* in *L'affaire Clearstream,* approached the violation of its notice-and-stay-down interpretation as constitutive of a *faute:*

> Considérant que, faute pour elles d'avoir accompli les diligences nécessaires en vue de rendre impossible une nouvelle mise en ligue dudit documentaire déjà signalé comme illicite, les sociétés Google ne peuvent se prévaloir du régime instauré par l'article 6.I.2 de la loi du 21 juin 2004 et voient en conséquence leur responsabilité civile engagée de ce chef dans les termes du droit commun de la contrefaçon, sur le fondement des articles L.335-3 et L.335-4 du code de la propriété intellectuelle.

Thus, once an intermediary has received notice, subsequent inaction on its part will not only disqualify it from safe harbour protection, but – more likely than not – further be interpreted as a dereliction of a duty of care, which serves to substantiate its fault and thus its liability. A better distinction between immunities and substantive law is missing and clearly necessary.

3.2.4 *Action en cessation*: Injunctive Relief

Vivant astutely observes that the real effect of liability lies in the remedies.[346] This brings forth the question of injunctions. As noted above, the failure of traditional French jurisprudence to demand fault as a condition for liability results in a hybrid system that applies identical conditions for both monetary compensation and injunctive relief.[347] As in the UK however, recently, a clearer distinction between the requirements for restitutional and compensatory remedies has crept into French law through the transposition of the European directives.

So, in addition to implementing the safe harbours, the LCEN has also tackled the question of injunctions. In particular, Article 6-I-8 enables judicial authorities to prescribe all appropriate measures to prevent or terminate damage caused by the content of an online public communication service to: a) intermediaries offering access to services of online communication to the public; or b) in their default, intermediaries offering hosting

346. M Vivant, 'Conditions de la responsabilité civile des fournisseurs d'hébergement d'un site sur le réseau Internet' (2000) 13 La Semaine Juridique Édition Générale 577.
347. A Lucas et al., *Traité de la Propriété Littéraire et Artistique* (4th ed., LexisNexis 2012) 893.

services.[348] The provision's explicit limitation only to injunctive relief breaks up the hybrid character of the *action en contrefaçon* and impregnates French law with precisely the foreign-inspired *summa divisio* between injunctions and damages it was previously missing.[349] In 2006, Article 6-I-8 of the LCEN was applied in the well-known *AAARGH* case. Here the TGI de Paris, upon petition by eight anti-racist organisations, ordered a number of internet access providers to block access to a website containing revisionist anti-Semitic content hosted abroad.[350] The *Cour de cassation* confirmed the order in 2008.[351] The French Supreme Court's ruling in the case made clear that, notwithstanding the wording of Article 6-I-8, which suggests a hierarchy of defendants ('*à défaut*'), no principle of subsidiarity applies: it is not necessary to first attempt action against the content provider or host, before turning against the access provider. On the other hand, the principle of proportionality was explicitly mentioned as relevant,[352] although the ruling fails to provide any analysis of its application to the case at hand.

Subsequently, with the adoption, on 12 July 2009, of the law on 'Creation and the Internet' (otherwise known as the HADOPI Act), [353] the possible recipients of injunctive orders were further expanded to include any innocent third party – thus, presumably, also any type of internet intermediary. So, Article 10 of the law introduced a new Article L.336-2[354] to the intellectual property code, which explicitly empowers the *tribunal de grande instance*, in the event of an infringement of a copyright or related right caused by the content of an online public communication service and at the request of the right-holder, to order all appropriate measures to prevent or to terminate such infringement against anyone in a position to help remedy the

348. As described in Arts 6-I-1 and 6-I-2 of the LCEN respectively.
349. A Lucas et al., *Traité de la Propriété Littéraire et Artistique* (4th ed., LexisNexis 2012) 892-898.
350. *Tiscali Acces et autres / Free, Uejf et autres*, Cour d'appel de Paris, 24 November 2006.
351. *Association des fournisseurs d'accès et de service internet AFA et autres c. Association l'Union des étudiants juifs de France UEJF et autres* (07-12.244), Cour de cassation, 19 June 2008.
352. P Sirinelli, 'Chronique de Jurisprudence – Mise à la disposition illicite d'oeuvres par l'intermédiaire des réseaux numériques' (2011) 228 Revue Internationale du Droit d'Auteur 287.
353. *Loi n° 2009-669 du 12 juin 2009 favorisant la diffusion et la protection de la création sur internet* (Law No. 2009-669 of 12 June 2009 on Promoting the Dissemination and Protection of Creative Works on the Internet). The act was dubbed the *Loi HADOPI* after the authority it created, the *Haute Autorité pour la Diffusion des Oeuvres et la Protection des Droits sur Internet*.
354. The provision is the successor of Art. L.332-1 of the intellectual property code, according to which the president of the *Tribunal de grande instance* was empowered to order 'the suspension, by any means, of the streaming of on-line public communication services affecting copyright, including by ordering to cease to store the streaming or, failing that, to cease allowing to have access to it. In this case, the time limit provided for under Art. L.332-2 shall be reduced to fifteen days.' This provision was repealed by Art. 7 of HADOPI.

situation. The provision makes no mention of any 'cascade', confirming the *Cour de cassation's* no-subsidiarity approach to injunctions, at least within the confines of intellectual property law. It is worth noting that discussions during the adoption of the amendment gave rise to criticism precisely of the kind also encountered at the European level regarding the compatibility of injunctive relief with the safe harbours of Articles 12-14 of the E-Commerce Directive and the prohibition of Article 15 of general monitoring obligations.[355] Subsequently, in its ruling on the law, the *Conseil Constitutionnel* established that Parliament had not failed to respect freedom of expression in adopting the provision, but noted that it would be incumbent upon courts called upon to hear petitions for such injunctions to abide by the principle of proportionality, by refraining from ordering measures other than those strictly necessary to preserve the rights involved.[356]

Article L.336-2 was relied upon by the *Cour de cassation* in yet another decision of 12 July 2012, this time concerning 'Google Suggest', the Google search engine's suggestion functionality.[357] The problem centred on a complaint by SNEP, the national trade association of record producers, against the automatic suggestion by the search engine, when a user entered an artist's name or the title of a song or music album into the search box, of keywords such as 'Torrent', 'Megaupload' or 'Rapidshare'. The first of these refers to a peer-to-peer file sharing system and the latter two to file-hosting platforms. Both the Court of First Instance and the Court of Appeal had rejected the right-holders' request for an order against Google to remove the keywords in order to prevent further copyright infringements.[358] According to the appeal court, the suggestion of the keywords was not in itself unlawful, while the websites in question contained both legal and illegal files and were thus not necessarily used for infringing purposes only. Consequently, the fact that illegal file-exchanges took place through those websites did not make them illegal in themselves. The appeal court concluded that the removal of the keywords from Google Suggest would not prevent illegal downloading – which instead depended on the voluntary and conscious behaviour of

355. F Riester, 'Rapport fait au nom de la commission des lois constitutionnelles, de la législation et de l'administration générale de la république sur le projet de loi (n° 1240), adopté par le sénat après déclaration d'urgence, *favorisant la* diffusion *et la* protection *de la* création *sur* internet', 18 February 2009. See also: C Geiger, 'Honourable Attempt but (ultimately) Disproportionately Offensive against Peer-to-peer on the Internet (HADOPI) – A Critical Analysis of the Recent Anti-File-Sharing Legislation in France' (2011) 42(4) International Review of Intellectual Property and Competition Law (IIC) 457.

356. *Conseil Constitutionnel,* Decision No. 2009-580 DC, 10 June 2009, *Journal Officiel,* 13 June 2009, 967.

357. *Syndicat national de l'édition phonographique* c. *la société Google France* (11-20.358), Cour de cassation, 12 July 2012.

358. *SNEP c. Google France*, Cour d'appel de Paris, 3 May 2011.

end-users – but merely made it 'less easy', while the infringing content would remain fully available regardless.[359]

The Court of Appeal's analysis seems to misconstrue the purpose of injunctive orders against intermediaries, in particular through failing to properly understand the independence of such orders from the question of the liability of the intermediary for the infringement.[360] Eventually, the *Cour de cassation* reversed, stating that, although Google had not infringed copyright itself, by systematically directing internet users, through keywords suggested in accordance with the number of search queries, to websites containing recordings made available to the public without right-holder consent, it was 'offering the means' to infringe copyright. This placed it in a position to contribute to the termination or prevention of such infringements: by putting in place the requested measures, Google could help inhibit searches for the unlawful websites and thus foil infringement. The Court emphasised that any measures imposed on Google would not need to be completely effective.

At the same time, the *Cour de cassation* seemed unwilling to give up on the relevance of intermediary liability entirely. Instead, it combined its reading of Article L.336-2 of the IP code with Article L.335-4 of the same text, which establishes the criminal sanctions attached to acts of infringement of copyright and neighbouring rights. The application of this provision not to the linked torrenting sites, but to the search engine itself has raised questions, with commentators struggling to understand the relevance of the reference to criminal liability: should this choice of legal basis be seen as a censure of Google by the Court for complicity in the end-users' infringements through the facilitation of their commission? If so, the statement would be a curious one, as without the establishment of intent, the intermediary cannot be found complicit in the criminal sense, while establishing its liability is not necessary for the deployment of Article L.336-2 injunction.[361] Thus, while technically failing to presuppose liability, the *Cour de cassation* returns to eerily similar insinuations in an attempt to justify an injunction that is supposed to be independent of it.

---

359. Interestingly, Google's appeal to the fundamental right to information was dismissed by the Court of Appeal on the mere observation that, under Art. 10 of the ECHR, the exercise of that right carries with it duties and responsibilities and may be subject to limitations relating to the protection of the rights of others. This is indicative of the lack of attention that the fundamental rights dimension of copyright enforcement received in early French case law.

360. P Sirinelli, 'Chronique de Jurisprudence – Mise à la disposition illicite d'oeuvres par l'intermédiaire des réseaux numériques' (2011) 228 Revue Internationale du Droit d'Auteur 287.

361. C Jasserand, 'Régime français de la responsabilité des intermédiaires techniques' (2013) 25(3) Les Cahiers de la propriété intellectuelle, 1135; G Gomis 'Consécration jurisprudentielle de l'Article L.336-3 du code de la propriété intellectuelle' (2012) 87 Revue Lamy Droit de l'Immatériel 2905.

This small glitch aside, the *Cour de cassation's* epexegesis of the question of effectiveness appears to be in line with the decisions of other European courts, those of the CJEU, as well as the logic of the European directives: the injunction solution is not intended to be an 'all or nothing' liability-dependent one. The proposed measure must simply be capable of at least contributing to the enforcement of copyright, even if it does not completely eradicate the problem.[362] This is perfectly in line with the CJEU's 'do something' approach exemplified in *Telekabel*. It is furthermore interesting that the *Cour de cassation* again felt it necessary to depend this regime on the observation that Google 'offered the means' of committing infringement – i.e., on the facilitation of infringement.

Of course, from a factual perspective, it can perhaps be questioned whether the removal of the keywords in this specific case would in fact be capable of achieving even that comparatively modest result: after all, as the Court of Appeal rightly pointed out, users are still left with the possibility of entering the term themselves, while those likely to recognise the suggested keywords will largely coincide with those already familiar with the sites in question. Google Suggest in that regard is nothing more than an auto-complete function specially developed for search operations. Even users not previously familiar with the particular technologies it promotes are always left with the option of simply researching file-sharing websites. With this in mind, one has to wonder: may any explanation of file-sharing or mention of websites offering the functionality lead to an injunction? Manara observes that 'a signpost should not be confused with the place to which it leads'.[363] Some statistical analysis of effects might perhaps have been helpful in this regard – what is the lowest level of ineffectiveness that a measure might display and still be demanded by the courts?[364]

---

362. P Sirinelli, 'Chronique de Jurisprudence – Mise à la disposition illicite d'oeuvres par l'intermédiaire des réseaux numériques' (2011) 228 Revue Internationale du Droit d'Auteur 287 and P Sirinelli, 'Chronique de Jurisprudence – Droit d\'auteur et réseaux numériques' (2012) 234 Revue Internationale du Droit d'Auteur 412.
363. C Manara, 'Les moteurs de recherche, les sites illicites et leurs utilisateurs' Dalloz actualité, 16 July 2012.
364. It is worth noting that a Dutch appeal court recently ruled in the opposite direction, overturning an injunction ordering access providers ZIGGO and XS4ALL to block the Pirate Bay, after studies confirmed minimal effect on the number of downloads from illegal sources. See: *Ziggo & XS4ALL v. BREIN*, Gerechtshof Den Haag, 28 January 2014, NL:GHDHA:2014:88. See also: C Dumitru, J Poort, J Leenheer & J van der Ham, 'Baywatch: Two Approaches to Measure the Effects of Blocking Access to The Pirate Bay' (2014) 4 Telecommunications Policy 383; J Poort & J Leenheer, 'Filesharing 2©12—Downloading from Illegal Sources in the Nederlands', Report by IViR and CentERdata (16 October 2012), available at: www.ivir.nl. Nevertheless, this approach was subsequently rejected by the *Hoge Raad*, the Dutch Supreme Court, which instead referred to *Telekabel* to conclude that the lack of the complete effectiveness of the measure does not preclude a fair balance, before submitting a request for a preliminary ruling to the CJEU. See: *Ziggo & XS4ALL v. BREIN*, Hoge Raad, 13 November 2015, ECLI:NL:HR:2015:3307 and pending case CJEU, C-610/15, *Ziggo v. Stichting Brein*.

Similar cases have followed: on 28 November 2013, the *Tribunal de Grande Instance de Paris* ordered a number of French internet access providers to take all appropriate measures to prevent access to sixteen streaming sites in the so-called Allostreaming galaxy (a group of connected streaming portals), by any effective means and in particular by blocking domain names. Four major search engines were also ordered to dereference the websites.[365] The court began its ruling by noting that the sites in question were 'dedicated or virtually dedicated to the distribution of audiovisual works without the consent of their creators'. The intermediaries tried to argue that blocking the illegal streaming websites would be inefficient, as users can post mirror versions of the sites under different names and use forums to communicate the locations of pirated content, but the court replied that the 'impossibility of ensuring the complete and perfect execution of the decisions should not lead courts to ignore the content creators' intellectual property rights'. The ruling explicitly accounts for the principle of proportionality, noting that the measures 'should only correspond to what appears to be necessary in order to preserve the rights at issue'. The court also stated that the freedom of expression of the operators of the websites did not attract an equal level of protection, in view of its infringing nature, and could be effectively countered by the need to enforce copyright, while the rights of end-users were likewise not limited disproportionately, since there were other options available for accessing the content in question in a lawful manner. Finally, the intermediaries' freedom to conduct a business could not support a rejection of the request, since the order only affected a fraction of the intermediaries' activities: any collateral blocking of legal content would be minimal, while, in view of the low number of non-infringing works (0 non-infringing to 49,577 infringing links with regard to movies and less than 650 non-infringing to 72,354 infringing links with regard to television series, according to a survey analysis provided by the plaintiffs), the risk of harm was not disproportionate. In conclusion, the court found that the measures ordered appeared to be the most appropriate and effective and least likely to cause unwanted side effects and be harmful to other interests. While indirect, they were also capable of achieving a definite result, if taken at the same time by a plurality of service providers in France. At the same time, the court rejected the plaintiff's additional request that it allow new infringing sites to be added automatically to the blocking orders when uncovered by a specially developed software programme – it did however recommend the avenue of self-regulation through cooperation between intermediaries and right-holders for dealing with future problem sites. The injunctions were issued for a limited duration of one year, to avoid obsoletion. The costs of the implementing measures were ordered to be refunded by the plaintiffs.

365. *Association des producteurs de cinema (APC) et autres c. Auchan Telecom et autres*, Tribunal de Grande Instance de, 28 November 2013.

The following year, on 4 December 2014, the same tribunal issued another injunction,[366] this time ordering four big French internet access providers to take every possible means – again in particular through the blocking of domain names – of preventing their subscribers from accessing TPB. A number of specified websites redirecting to that website, three mirror sites (i.e., copies of the original site) and a long list of proxies (computer network services that allow clients to make indirect network connections to other network services) were also included in the order. The court began by noting that TPB's activities are unlawful, since it almost exclusively offers infringing content. The right-holders' request to block access to TPB was then found to be the only effective means available to them to combat the infringement of their copyright-protected content on the internet. Again, no power was given by the court to the right-holders to add to this list: if they wished to request that additional websites be blocked, a new petition before the court would be necessary. The court recognised that the measures would be able to be bypassed by some users, but noted that they were sufficient for the majority, who would not have the time or skills to implement circumvention methods. The court noted in passing that similar orders had been issued by courts in other EU Member States, including the Belgium, Denmark, Finland, Ireland, Italy and the UK. Again echoing *Telekabel,* the access providers were given free reign with regard to the measures to be implemented to achieve the blocking. Recalling the decision of the *Conseil Constitutionnel* of 28 December 2000[367] and the CJEU's judgments in the *Scarlet Extended* and *Telekabel* cases, the court stated that the providers should not be burdened with the cost of implementing the measures ordered and should therefore be able to claim repayment from SCPP of the expense incurred with regard to the measures they already introduced and those undertaken specifically in order to comply with the court's order. The measures were once again foreseen for a period of one year.

In conclusion, as on the European level and in the UK, in France as well the issue of injunctive orders against intermediaries reflects a new tack that, instead of focusing on liability, seeks to oblige providers to prevent, reduce or terminate infringement, while encouraging cooperation between intermediaries and right-holders.[368] Obviously, such injunctive orders cannot overstep the permissible legal boundaries as those have been set up by Article 15 of the E-Commerce Directive and the CJEU's 'fair balance' doctrine. As a result, 'stay-down' obligations cannot be imposed through injunctions any more than they can through the recognition of spontaneous liability-based

366. *La s*ociété civile des producteurs phonographiques (SCPP) c. la société Orange, Tribunal de Grande Instance de Paris, 4 December 2014.
367. This established that the costs of enforcement measures cannot be left to the intermediaries, see *Conseil Constitutionnel,* Decision No. 2000-441 DC, 28 December 2000, Journal Officiel, 31 décembre 2000, 21204.
368. P Sirinelli, 'Chronique de Jurisprudence – Droit d'auteur et réseaux numériques' (2012) 234 Revue Internationale du Droit d'Auteur 412.

obligations. Measures of limited effectiveness will consequently often remain the only legally permissible solution – the only question remains what level of ineffectiveness is still seen as worth the bother. Finally, as before the English courts, guarantees against over-expansive orders are generally also incorporated, in particular in the form of time-limits.

3.2.5 Additional Obligations

Aside from the classical remedies of injunctions and damages, additional obligations not required by the European directives and operating in parallel to liability for infringement are also imposed by French law on intermediaries. All of these are targeted at either warning users against infringement or making the apprehension of direct infringers easier.

So, for example, under Article 6-II LCEN, the providers of safe harbour services are under an obligation to retain information that enables the identification of the primary offender and provide it to the judicial authorities. They must also provide SCPL publishers with the technical capabilities permitting them to abide by their own identification obligations (Article 6-III-1 and 2 LCEN). Mere conduit providers that permit the downloading of files that they have not themselves provided must warn their clients in a clear manner that piracy damages artistic creation (Article 7 LCEN), as well as inform their subscribers of the existence of voluntary private filtering options (Article 6-I-1 LCEN).

Further duties incumbent on access and hosting providers have been more recently introduced with the HADOPI laws. These centre around the new obligation imposed on users with Article L.336-3 of the *CPI* for securing their internet connection against infringement. Under the new rules, mere conduit providers must inform their subscribers of the means of achieving this result (see Article 6-I-1 LCEN *in fine*). At least one efficient technical method included in the list established by the HADOPI Agency in accordance with Article L.331-26 of the same code must be recommended for this purpose. In addition, according to Article L.331-27 of the intellectual property code, the provisions of Article L.336-3 must also be mentioned in internet access providers' subscription contract with users, along with the civil and criminal penalties applicable in cases of copyright infringement.

Finally, as part of the famous graduated response (*riposte graduée*) regime,[369] internet access providers are obligated to assist the HADOPI Agency and the courts in handling copyright infringement, as well as breaches of users' Article L.336-3 duty of surveillance. So, under Article L.331-25 of the *CPI,* the HADOPI Agency can ask access providers to send warning emails to subscribers who do not abide by their duty of surveillance.

369. For more on this see C Jasserand, 'Régime français de la responsabilité des intermédiaires techniques' (2013) 25(3) Les Cahiers de la propriété intellectuelle 1135.

As a last resort, in cases of copyright infringement (Article 335-7 CPI) or of gross negligence linked to the breach of the duty of surveillance (Article 335-7-1 CPI), the courts are also enabled to order the provider to suspend, as a penalty, the user's internet access for a limited period of time. The access provider is then obliged to terminate the user's internet access on pain of a fine.[370] It should be noted that initially the sanction of internet suspension was to be ordered directly by the HADOPI Agency itself, but on 10 June 2009, the *Conseil Constitutionnel* rejected this possibility, noting that the provision of the power to sanction through the suspension of internet access to an independent administrative authority constituted a disproportionate restriction on freedom of expression and communication, as well as an unacceptable presumption of culpability.[371] As a result, the French executive was forced to supplement the text with a new 'HADOPI 2' Act,[372] omitting the section on penalties.

On 19 October 2011, the *Conseil d'Etat* rejected the applications brought by internet access provider FDN and Apple against the two HADOPI Acts which accused the procedure of violating Article 6 of the ECHR on the right to a fair trial. The *Conseil d'Etat* argued that the measures foreseen under the process did not function as sanctions, but were instead intended to inform users of the legal obligations incumbent on them.[373] Finally, on 9 July 2013, in accordance with the recommendations of the Lescure report,[374] the French Ministry of Culture issued a decree lifting the penalty of internet access suspension for persons who failed to secure their access to the network against infringement, allegedly because the graduated response approach had failed to confer the estimated benefit.[375] In future only fines may be issued against internet users for gross negligence in failing to secure their internet connection. Internet suspension may however still be imposed on anyone found guilty of actual infringement.

---

370. For an overview in English, see N van Eijk et al., 'Moving towards Balance: A Study into Duties of Care on the Internet' (2010) Institute for Information Law & Leibniz Center for Law, University of Amsterdam.

371. Conseil Constitutionnel, Décision n° 2009-580 DC du 10 juin 2009, Journal officiel du 13 juin 2009, page 9675, texte n° 3.

372. *Loi n° 2009-1311 du 28 octobre 2009 relative à la protection pénale de la propriété littéraire et artistique, Journal officiel du 29 octobre 2009*, known as HADOPI 2.

373. Conseil d'Etat, *Société Apple Inc et Société I-Tunes Sarl,* 19 October 2011, n° 339154 and French Data Network, 19 October, 2011, n°339279 and n° 342405.

374. P Lescure, 'Mission 'Acte II de l'exception culturelle' – Contribution aux politiques culturelles à l'ère numérique', May 2013.

375. *Décret n° 2013-596 du 8 juillet 2013 supprimant la peine contraventionnelle complémentaire de suspension de l'accès à un service de communication au public en ligne et relatif aux modalités de transmission des informations prévue à l'Article L. 331-21 du code de la propriété intellectuelle, Journal officiel n°0157 du 9 juillet 2013, page 11428, texte n° 60.*

3.3 GERMANY

The E-Commerce safe harbours were implemented into German law with Articles 8 (mere conduit), 9 (caching) and 10 (hosting) of the *Telemediengesetz* (TMG) of 26 February 2007.[376] As in the UK, here too the transposition is almost word-for-word, although Articles 8 and 9 both contain an exception for service providers who intentionally work together with a recipient of their service to commit illegal acts. In practice this apparent deviation is unlikely to result in any real difference in comparison with the application of the conditions already in the E-Commerce Directive provisions – nevertheless, the explicit reference to intent is interesting. Article 15 of the E-Commerce Directive is implemented with Article 7(2) of the TMG, which stipulates that service providers are not required to monitor the information transmitted or stored by them or to search for circumstances indicating an illegal activity. The provision does however go on to warn that this shall be without prejudice to any obligations to remove or disable access to information under general legislation, even where the service provider does not bear responsibility pursuant to Articles 8-10. Paragraph 1 declares that 'service providers shall be responsible for their own information which they keep ready for use, in accordance with general legislation'.[377]

In any case, as in England and as opposed to France, the German safe harbours have so far been put to little use in practice. As shall be shown

376. *Telemediengesetz, 26 February 2007, BGBl. I S. 179.* It is worth noting that the E-Commerce safe harbours are very close to the immunities Germany had proactively adopted earlier with Art. 5 of its 1997 *Teledienstegesetz*. Indeed, that act inspired the horizontal approach adopted by the EU, encompassing both civil and criminal liability. The *Teledienstegesetz* however only included safe harbours for the protection of the providers of host and mere conduit services; no immunity in favour of caching was incorporated. The conditions for the *Teledienstegesetz* hosting immunity were more permissive than in its later incarnation, in that providers of hosting services with actual knowledge of the unlawfulness of stored content were protected from liability unless the prevention of further dissemination was technically possible and could reasonably be expected of them. This reasonability factor harkens back to the rules establishing the scope of a duty of care under general German tort norms. It would thus indeed seem to speak of an attempt at legal clarification more than immunisation. Mere conduit activities were provided with an absolute immunity for the mere provision of access for use and for automatic and temporary copying and storage in the course of the provision of access. See *Gesetz über die Nutzung von Telediensten (Teledienstegesetz – TDG)*, incorporated in the *Gesetz zur Regelung der Rahmenbedingungen für Informations- und Kommunikationsdienste (Informations- und Kommunikationsdienste-Gesetz – IuKDG),* 22 July 1997, BGBl. I S. 1870. See also T Hoeren & S Yankova, 'The Liability of Internet Intermediaries – The German Perspective' (2012) International Review of Intellectual Property and Competition Law (IIC) 501.

377. For more information see, T Hoeren & V Bensinger, *Haftung im Internet – Die Neue Rechtslage* (De Gruyter 2014) 355-361 and 398-402 and A-S Hollanders, *Mittelbare Verantwortlichkeit von Intermediären im Netz* (Nomos 2011) 199 et seq.

below, this is because the German rules on accessory liability for the most part exclude liability for monetary relief of their own accord.[378]

3.3.1 *Störerhaftung* or Disturber Liability

In Germany intermediary contribution to copyright infringements committed by others is dealt with primarily through the doctrine of *Störerhaftung*. This is usually, and somewhat misleadingly, translated into English as 'interferer', 'disturber' and 'accessory' liability or even sometimes as 'breach of a duty of care'.[379] It is however a German idiosyncrasy with no real equivalent in English-speaking legal systems. The doctrine of *Störerhaftung* permits cease and desist orders (*Unterlassungsansspruchen*) to be imposed not only on the immediate wrongdoer (*(Mit-)täter*) and any participants in the wrongdoing (*Teilnehmer*), but also on so-called *Störer*, i.e., 'disturbers', who knowingly and causally contribute to an infringement by another. It is important to emphasise that this is all it can ground. As we shall see below, it is not possible to claim against a defendant for damages unless she was acting with fault.[380] At the same time, culpable breach of an injunction constitutes contempt of court and is punishable with a disciplinary fine.[381]

Störerhaftung is accordingly essentially a form of strict liability limited to injunctive relief. As a result, when applied to internet intermediaries for copyright enforcement the doctrine effectively functions as a tool for the extension of liability to third parties who have not in fact themselves committed an infringement or even participated in its commission, but who are in a prime position to provide relief – in other words, it does precisely what the European legislator was aiming at with the introduction of Article 8(3) of the Copyright Directive.

It should be noted that, although not technically subsidiary in the sense that it is not necessary to exhaust all routes of action against the direct tortfeasor to turn against a disturber, as a general rule, *Störerhaftung* is intended to be available only in cases where that direct infringer is not known or within legal reach or where, although the direct infringer might be known, the nature of the infringement requires action against the disturber in order

378. J B Nordemann, 'Intellectual Property Liability of Consumers, Facilitators and Intermediaries: the Position in Germany' in A Kamperman Sanders & C Heath, *Intellectual Property Liability of Consumers, Facilitators and Intermediaries* (Kluwer Law International 2012) 37.
379. The final translation can lead to confusion between the legal concepts of *Störer* (disturbers) and *Teilnehmer* (participants – see s. 3.3.2) however and is not recommended.
380. A Wandtke, *Urheberrecht* (De Gruyter Recht 2009) 286-290.
381. G Spindler, 'Country Report – Germany' for 'Study on the Liability of Internet Intermediaries' (2006), available at: http://ec.europa.eu/internal_market/e-commerce/directive_en.htm.

to ensure immediate and effective relief.[382] It is worth noting that this will be especially likely in cases of online infringement: in a networked environment, after an initial posting, copies of infringing content will be particularly probable to surface at multiple other sources, giving any action taken against the direct infringer only limited effect.

From a doctrinal point of view, *Störerhaftung*'s origins are somewhat unusual. Although injunctive relief is not explicitly provided for by the tort provisions of the German *Bürgerliches Gesetzbuch* (BGB) (see Book 2 on the Law of Obligations), it has been made available by the German courts by analogy to the law of property.[383] Unusually for Germany's mainly civil law based system therefore, the theory of *Störerhaftung* was primarily developed through extensive case law in the area of unfair competition, as well as for the protection of absolute rights, i.e., rights which are enforceable against everyone, including copyright, trademark and patent law.[384] *Störerhaftung* thus finds its roots outside tort liability in the property defence claims laid out in Articles 862 and 1004 BGB of Book 3 of the BGB, which enable injunctive relief essentially against cases of nuisance.[385] Specifically for copyright, this legislative framework is completed by Article 97(1) of the German copyright act (*Gesetz über Urheberrecht und verwandte Schutzrechte* – UrhG).[386] According to this:

> Any person who infringes copyright or any other right protected under this Act may be required by the injured party to eliminate the infringement or, where there is a risk of repeated infringement, may be required by the injured party to cease and desist. Entitlement to prohibit

382. A Bayer, 'Liability 2.0 – Does the Internet Environment Require New Standards for Secondary Liability? An Overview of the Current Legal Situation in Germany' in M J Adelmann et al., *Patents and Technological Progress in a Globalized World* (Springer 2009) 365. See J B Nordemann, 'Intellectual Property Liability of Consumers, Facilitators and Intermediaries: the Position in Germany' in A Kamperman Sanders & C Heath, *Intellectual Property Liability of Consumers, Facilitators and Intermediaries* (Kluwer Law International 2012) 37, where he states that the '*Störer* can be held liable even if the infringer or intentional contributor to the infringement cannot be prosecuted. The breach of duty of care is thus not a subsidiary liability'.
383. T Hoeren et al., *Handbuch Multimedia Recht* (41st ed., C.H. Beck 2015) Rn. 19; G Bauer et al., *Harbauer Rechtsschutzversicherung – Kommentar zu den Allgemeinen Bedingungen für die Rechtsschutzversicherung* (8th ed., C.H. Beck 2010) Rn 66; F J Säcker & R Rixecker (eds.), *Münchener Kommentar Zum Bürgerlichen Gesetzbuch* (6th ed., C.H. Beck 2013) Rn 583; A Walter, 'Zivilrechtliche Störerhaftung' (2012) JA 658.
384. BGH, *Internetversteigerung I*, 11 March 2004, I ZR 304/01; J Bornkamm, 'E-Commerce Directive vs. IP Rights Enforcement – Legal Balance Achieved?' (2007) GRUR Int 642; T Hoeren, 'German Law on Internet Liability of Intermediaries', LIDC Congress, Oxford 2011.
385. CJEU, Opinion of Advocate General Jääskinen, case C-324/09, *L'Oréal v. eBay International*, 9 December 2010, para. 56.
386. T Hoeren & V Bensinger, *Haftung im Internet – Die Neue Rechtslage* (De Gruyter 2014) 381-382.

> the infringer from future infringement shall also exist where the risk of infringement exists for the first time.[387]

The reference here to the 'infringer' – in German, '*Verletzer*' – should be given a broad interpretation, extending beyond the *Täter* and *Teilnehmer* to include any potential *Störer*. Significantly, the provision expands the reach of injunctive relief in copyright law beyond its usual applicability, as, whereas the regular rules require actual knowledge of the infringement, this is not necessary under Article 97(1) UrhG, so that even a mere unknowing *Störer* may be subjected to *Haftung* regardless.[388] In *Cybersky* the German *Bundesgerichtshof* (BGH) linked *Störerhaftung* to Article 97(1) UrhG, stating that:

> Der vorbeugende Unterlassungsanspruch [aus § 97 Absatz 1 UrhG] kann sich nicht nur gegen den möglichen Täter, sondern auch gegen denjenigen richten, der als potenzieller Teilnehmer oder Störer eine Erstbegehungsgefahr für eine Verletzungshandlung begründet hat.[389]

3.3.1.1 *The Conditions of* Störerhaftung

But what are the conditions for a finding of *Störerhaftung*? Although the first relevant decisions of the BGH date back to the mid-1950s, the development of the doctrine has not been consistent and, as a result, its requirements and scope remain ambiguous.[390] *Automobil-Onlinebörse* gives a concise definition of the current condition of the concept:

> Als Störer kann bei der Verletzung absoluter Rechte auf Unterlassung in Anspruch genommen werden, wer – ohne Täter oder Teilnehmer zu sein – in irgendeiner Weise willentlich und adäquat kausal zur Verletzung des geschützten Rechts beiträgt. Da die Störerhaftung nicht über Gebühr auf

---

387. Translation taken from the official English text provided by the *Bundesministerium der Justiz und für Verbraucherschutz*, available at: http://www.gesetze-im-internet.de/englisch_urhg/englisch_urhg.html.
388. J Wimmers, 'Who Interferes? Liability for Third Party Content on the Internet in Germany' (2007) Intellectual Property Today 32. However, it is worth noting that under Art. 100, where the injuring party acts neither intentionally nor negligently, he may, in order to avert injunctive relief under Art. 97, pay pecuniary compensation instead to the injured party, if the fulfilment of the claims would cause disproportionate harm and the injured party can be expected to accept that. The compensation shall total that amount which would constitute equitable remuneration were the right to be contractually granted. Payment of such compensation shall be equivalent to granting the injuring party permission to exploit the right to the customary extent.
389. BGH, *Cybersky*, 15 January 2009, I ZR 57/07.
390. A Bayer, 'Liability 2.0 – Does the Internet Environment Require New Standards for Secondary Liability? An Overview of the Current Legal Situation in Germany' in M J Adelmann et al., *Patents and Technological Progress in a Globalized World* (Springer 2009) 365.

> Dritte erstreckt werden darf, die nicht selbst die rechtswidrige Beeinträchtigung vorgenommen haben, setzt sie die Verletzung von Prüfpflichten voraus. Deren Umfang bestimmt sich danach, ob und inwieweit dem als Störer in Anspruch Genommenen nach den Umständen eine Prüfung zuzumuten ist.[391]

As this indicates therefore, for claims against a disturber to be acknowledged two main conditions must be met: a) a deliberate and adequately causal contribution to a legal violation; and b) the breach of a reasonable duty to review (the so-called *Prüfpflicht*).[392] Below, after a brief examination of the first, simpler criterion, the analysis shall focus in detail on the second.

(a) Deliberate and Adequately Causal Contribution to a Legal Violation

In order to qualify for *Störerhaftung*, the disturber must have, as a first condition, in any way, deliberately, adequately and causally contributed to the creation or maintenance of a legal wrong, including through taking advantage of infringements committed by others. In this context, 'deliberately' refers not to an intention to contribute to an infringement, but rather an intention to perform the action which creates or maintains the infringement.[393] Good faith on behalf of the *Störer* is not relevant.[394] The disturber

391. BGH, *Automobil-Onlinebörse*, 22 June 2011, I ZR 159/10. For an older definition moving along very similar lines see, BGH, *Constanze II*, 6 July 1954, I ZR 38/532: '*Störer i. S. entsprechender Anwendung des § BGB § 1004 BGB ist auch derjenige, der die unzulässige Wettbewerbshandlung eines aus eigenem Antrieb und selbstverantwortlich handelnden Dritten durch die sachlichen und persönlichen Mittel seines Betriebes unterstützt, obwohl er die rechtliche Möglichkeit hat, den Dritten an der Störungshandlung zu hindern -- dies selbst dann, wenn er sich im guten Glauben befindet.*'
392. A Bayer, 'Liability 2.0 – Does the Internet Environment Require New Standards for Secondary Liability? An Overview of the Current Legal Situation in Germany' in M J Adelmann *et al.*, *Patents and Technological Progress in a Globalized World* (Springer 2009) 365. A third condition of the legal and factual possibility of preventing infringement is sometimes also identified, see e.g. M Leistner, 'Common Principles of Secondary Liability?' in A Ohly (ed.), *Common Principles of European Intellectual Property Law* (Mohr Siebeck 2012) 128 and I Garrote Fernandez-Diez, 'Comparative Analysis on National Approaches to the Liability of Internet Intermediaries for Infringement of Copyright and Related Rights' WIPO study, 35, available at: www.wipo.int/copyright/en/internet_intermediaries. However, here we shall treat this possibility as part of the first condition of an adequate causal contribution. Similarly, a clear, easily recognisable infringement is sometimes treated as an additional condition, while here this shall be analysed under the reasonable duty to review, see T Hoeren & V Bensinger, *Haftung im Internet – Die Neue Rechtslage* (De Gruyter 2014) 363-366.
393. J Becher, 'Copyright and User-Generated Content: Legal Challenges for Community-Based Businesses in Germany and the USA' (Master's Thesis, Bucerius Law School/ WHU Otto Beisheim School of Management 2010).
394. BGH, *Constanze II*, 6 July 1954, I ZR 38/532.

must have had either the legal or the factual possibility of exerting influence on the infringing conduct of the direct infringer to prevent the infringement.

When is this the case? In the 1960s the German courts concluded that such an adequate causal connection existed between the manufacture and supply of blank tapes and tape recorders and the commission of copyright infringements by buyers.[395] Similarly, causal contribution was found between the making available of photocopying machines in a copy-shop and the production of infringing copies by the shop's customers.[396] The decisive question was whether, after objective consideration, the infringing use lay outside of all probability and whether the owner of the machine could therefore be reasonably held liable. The existence of a wilful behaviour which endangers the copyright of the claimant or of significant cause for concern for such a danger is sufficient – significantly therefore, preventive injunctive action against an intermediary which has not yet contributed to a specific unlawful activity by a third person should be considered possible.[397]

(b) Breach of a Reasonable Duty to Review

Liability as a *Störer* may not be extended unduly to innocent third parties. In *Architektenwettbewerb,*[398] for example, the BGH held that, in order that an alleged disturber be held liable, the disturbing circumstances must be readily apparent. However, if that was not the case because the disturber ignored a *Prüfungspflicht* (i.e., a duty to review), liability will be imposed regardless. What does this mean?

It should be noted that the notion of *Prüfungspflichten* is a relatively recent addition to the doctrine of *Störerhaftung*. In the classic leading cases, the disturber was simply understood as somebody who participated organisationally or technically in an infringement committed by another. Under this laxer approach, reasonableness was injected into the process indirectly through the limitation of the legal consequences of the *Störer's* behaviour by the principles of good faith. *Störerhaftung* thus gave rise merely to a duty to take all reasonable measures to exclude or seriously reduce the endangerment of the plaintiff's rights.[399] So, for example, in the 1960s a general prohibition on the manufacture and retail of blank tapes,[400] as well as a prohibition on allowing customers to use the photocopiers in the copy-shop was found to be unreasonable by the BGH, as was the suggestion of a requirement of ID verification prior to each purchase.[401] Privacy concerns

395. BGH, *Personalausweise,* 29 May 1964, Ib ZR 4/63.
396. BGH, *Kopierladen,* 9 June 1983, I ZR 70/81.
397. BGH, *Kleidersack*, 30 January 2003, I ZR 142/00 (this matter was still undecided in BGH, *Paperboy*, 17 July 2003, I ZR 259/00).
398. BGH, *Architektenwettbewerb,* 10 October 1997, I ZR 129/96.
399. BGH, *Kopierladen,* 9 June 1983, I ZR 70/81.
400. BGH, *Magnettonband II*, 8 January 1965 - Ib ZR 10/63.
401. BGH, *Personalausweise,* 29 May 1964, Ib ZR 4/63.

also came into play: in *Kopierladen,* a 1983 decision concerning photocopying by customers on the defendant's premises, the BGH found that an obligation to inspect the copied material would unbearably impair the third party's right to confidentiality, which is founded in the constitutionally protected rights of personal freedom.[402] This would moreover harm the defendant's business activities in a disproportionate manner. However, it was not required that the infringement of third party rights be impeded with certainty; it was instead sufficient that the measures in question contributed to a limitation of the risk of infringement.[403] Thus, as in the British *Amstrad* case, the very simple requirement of adding a warning to any advertisement of such devices to the effect that lawful copying of copyright-protected works would require prior right-holder permission was deemed suitable. The same obligation to prominently display warning signs was imposed on the owner of the copy-shop.

From these beginnings, a shift took place in the late 1990s. Beginning with the BGH's 1999 decision in *Möbelklassiker,* the disturber's liability was treated as arising from the violation of the duty to review possible infringements. This has been described as a 'remarkable turnabout' in the *Störerhaftung* case law and arguably constitutes a considerable restriction on the scope of the doctrine's application.[404] Interestingly, the introduction of the duty to review as a control mechanism for *Störerhaftung* was likely a response to criticism levelled against the BGH due to its 'almost limitless' overexpansion of disturber liability, particularly in the area of unfair competition law.[405]

What kind of duty to review applies? The duty to review must be reasonable. This requirement significantly restricts the reach of *Störerhaftung* and has been described as offering a type of 'safe harbour' protection in itself.[406] In *Paperboy,*[407] the BGH held that if the risk of unlawful conduct is not qualitatively altered by the alleged disturber's behaviour, no room for *Störerhaftung* exists – thus, the setting of hyperlinks to copyright-protected articles which have been placed online by the right-holder does not give rise to liability for injunctive relief, as the hyperlink merely increases the accessibility of the article, while the decision as to whether the work should remain available to the public or not remains with the initial publisher. On this basis, it was found that hyperlinking is no different to referencing in

---

402. BGH, *Kopierladen*, 9 June 1983, I ZR 70/81.
403. BGH, *Magnettonband II*, 8 January 1965 - Ib ZR 10/63.
404. G Spindler & M Leistner, 'Secondary Copyright Infringement – New Perspectives from Germany and Europe' (2006) 37(7) International Review of Intellectual Property and Competition Law (IIC) 788.
405. J Wimmers, 'Who Interferes? Liability for Third Party Content on the Internet in Germany' (August 2007) Intellectual Property Today 32.
406. J Wimmers, 'Who Interferes? Liability for Third Party Content on the Internet in Germany' (August 2007) Intellectual Property Today 32.
407. BGH, *Paperboy*, 17 July 2003, I ZR 259/00.

traditional printed matter. In *Schöner Wetten*,[408] it was established that the scope of the duty to review should be determined according to the overall context within which the alleged disturber was acting, the purpose of her behaviour, her knowledge of circumstances that suggest unlawful activity and the possibilities available to reasonably recognise the unlawfulness of the act. In that specific case it was found that the defendant had not violated a duty of care simply because it could not have excluded the possibility that by placing the hyperlink it was assisting an act punishable in Germany. At the same time, it must be acknowledged that both *Paperboy* and *Schöner Wetten* have been heavily influenced by the laxer liability standards applicable to German press law.[409]

A duty to review is considered to be unreasonable if it would unduly impair the business of the alleged disturber.[410] On this basis, in its *Internetversteigerung* trademark trilogy,[411] the BGH established that an online auction platform does not have to examine each and every listing for trademark infringement prior to allowing its publication on its website, as such an obligation would jeopardise the site's entire business model. At the same time, the reasonability criterion does not mean that legitimate business models enjoy absolute protection: the BGH has upon occasion demanded that service providers amend their business plan to counter infringing third party conduct.[412]

What does the above mean for intermediaries? Significantly, in *Internetversteigerung I,* a trademark case involving an online marketplace, the Court made clear that, after gaining knowledge through a concrete notification, the operator does have a duty both to take down or block access to the specific infringing content to which its attention was drawn and to prevent further similar violations.[413] It clarified that, while a general monitoring obligation would make the provider's business model impossible, specific monitoring obligations in response to notifications were acceptable, to the extent that they was technically feasible. Thus, a *Prüfungspflicht* is essentially an 'inquiry notice', i.e., a duty to check (inquire into) whether

408. BGH, *Schöner Wetten,* 1 April 2004, I ZR 317/01.
409. T Hoeren, 'Liability for Online Services in Germany' (2009) 10(5) German Law Journal 561.
410. T Hoeren & V Bensinger, *Haftung im Internet – Die Neue Rechtslage* (De Gruyter 2014) 366.
411. BGH, *Internetversteigerung I,* 11 March 2004, I ZR 304/01; BGH, *Internetversteigerung II,* 19 April 2007, I ZR 35/04; BGH, *Internetversteigerung III,* 30 April 2008, I ZR 73/05.
412. J B Nordemann, 'Liability for Copyright Infringements on the Internet: Host Providers (Content Providers) – The German Approach' (2011) 2(1) Journal of Intellectual Property, Information Technology and Electronic Commerce Law (JIPITEC) 37.
413. BGH, *Internetversteigerung I (Rolex),* 11 March 2004, I ZR 304/01. *Internetversteigerung II* confirmed the applicability of its previous findings under the new (E-Commerce Directive-inspired) *Telemediengesetz.*

infringements have occurred.[414] This obligation does not actualise spontaneously, but is triggered only by a clear ('*klar*') notice of an existing infringement. The decision was important, as it established that the *Prüfungspflicht* operates continuously from the moment of receipt of notification, so that the intermediary may operate under obligations to monitor and forestall future predictable infringements.[415] This may include making use of filter software or, if necessary, conducting manual follow-up checks.

Indeed, the duty to review is not limited only to identical copies or copies offered by the same person, but extends to all easily recognisable future unlawful acts of an essentially similar nature.[416] This is the so-called *Kerntheorie,* according to which in order to trigger *Störerhaftung* the infringements must be similar in their core (*Kern*).[417] Thus, while the relevance of notice-and-take-down regimes is confined in Germany to cases where there has not previously been any similar infringement on the same platform, once the operator has been alerted to an infringement, as long as its business operations are not unreasonably impaired, it is expected to proceed with blocking obvious re-occurrences without waiting for right-holder notification.[418] Essentially therefore, the doctrine amounts to the same – if not slightly broader – result as the French judge-made 'notice-and-stay-down' regime.

Which circumstances will indicate a clear infringement of the same type as the initial offence such as to trigger an obligation to remove or block without the need for new notification? Nordemann suggests that infringements will be of the same type if:

(a) the same work is infringed through the communication to the public of the same copy or another just as obviously infringing copy;
(b) other works of the same kind are infringed, provided the infringements originate from the same perpetrator and do not require a new legal assessment. This is the case of 'repeat offenders'; and
(c) other works of different types are infringed by a different infringer, provided the service is particularly susceptible to infringements and the provider is aware of this. This will be the case for example, where the provider advertises the infringing capabilities of the

414. A Dietz, 'Germany' in L Bently, P Geller & M Nimmer, *International Copyright Law and Practice* (Matthew Bender/LexisNexis 2013) § 8[1][c][i].
415. A Dietz, 'Germany' in L Bently, P Geller & M Nimmer, *International Copyright Law and Practice* (Matthew Bender/LexisNexis 2013) § 8[1][c][i].
416. J Bornkamm, 'E-Commerce Directive vs. IP Rights Enforcement – Legal Balance Achieved?' (2007) GRUR Int 642.
417. M Leistner, 'Störerhaftung und mittelbare Schutzrechtsverletzung' (2010) GRUR-Beil 1.
418. A Bayer, 'Liability 2.0 – Does the Internet Environment Require New Standards for Secondary Liability? An Overview of the Current Legal Situation in Germany' in M J Adelmann *et al., Patents and Technological Progress in a Globalized World* (Springer 2009) 365.

service or where otherwise neutral services happen to be predominately used for infringing purposes.

Unclear infringements would include e.g., tricky cases of exceptions or limitations, where expert legal advice would be necessary to clarify the situation. It remains uncertain whether a duty to review arises where the provider is made aware of unclear infringements.[419]

The emphasis on 'clear' indications of infringement is reminiscent of the French preoccupation with 'manifest' unlawfulness. In *Blog-Eintrag,*[420] the BGH accepted that it will not always be possible to immediately determine whether an infringement has taken place. It stated that a host provider is only required to take action if the notice sent to the intermediary was concrete and enabled the latter to identify the infringement without excessive difficulty, i.e., without an in-depth legal and factual review. It is not immediately clear how this strict interpretation of notification is compatible with a subsequent duty to remove similar infringements. Interestingly, in that case, the court seemed to accept a certain degree of subsidiarity:

> As a rule, the affected person's objection is first to be communicated to the person responsible for the blog for comment. If a comment is not provided within a reasonable deadline in the circumstances, it is to be assumed that the objection is justified and the contested entry is to be deleted. If the person responsible for the blog denies, with substantiation, that the objection is justified, and if as a result there are legitimate doubts, the provider is as a matter of principle required to notify such to the party affected and if appropriate request evidence that shows the alleged infringement of the rights. If the person affected fails to comment or fails to submit any evidence required, there is no occasion for any further investigation.[421]

In any case, the scope of the duty to investigate should be determined according to whether and to what extent the alleged disturber can reasonably be expected to carry out an investigation in the light of the circumstances of the individual case, taking into account his function and duties, as well as the

419. J B Nordemann, 'Liability for Copyright Infringements on the Internet: Host Providers (Content Providers) – The German Approach' (2011) 2(1) Journal of Intellectual Property, Information Technology and Electronic Commerce Law (JIPITEC) 37; J B Nordemann, 'Intellectual Property Liability of Consumers, Facilitators and Intermediaries: the Position in Germany' in A Kamperman Sanders & C Heath, *Intellectual Property Liability of Consumers, Facilitators and Intermediaries* (Kluwer Law International 2012) 37.
420. BGH, *Blog-Eintrag,* 25 October 2011, I ZR 93/10.
421. Translation from case comment, 'Federal Supreme Court, 25 October 2011 - Case No. VI ZR 93/10: GERMANY – "Blog Entry"*' (2012) 8 International Review of Intellectual Property and Competition Law (IIC) 982. See also: BGH, *Stiftparfüm,* 17 August 2011, I ZR 57/09.

individual responsibility of the direct infringer.[422] In other words, the extent of the *Prüfungspflicht* will depend on the circumstances.[423]

The comparative importance of the opposing protected interests is also relevant here: in *Jugendgefährdende Medien bei eBay,* the BGH considered that the scope of the *Prüfungspflicht* will depend on the importance of the protected right and the possibilities open to the intermediary to acquire knowledge.[424] On this basis, it concluded that protection measures deemed sufficient for protection against trademark infringements will not necessarily suffice to protect minors against unsuitable material (in that case computer games glorifying violence and Nazi-type propaganda).[425] Similarly, in *Schöner Wetten* the author of the editorial article containing the hyperlink was protected by his freedom of expression under Article 5(1) of the *Grundgesetz* (GG): obliging an intermediary which lacks the necessary professional knowledge to evaluate content for legal violations risks forcing them into blocking content that might be fully legal, thus engendering de facto censorship and an impairment of the communication means they offer and opening themselves up to legal action on the part of the alleged direct infringer.[426]

In this regard, it should be noted that the disturber is also subject to a secondary burden of proof, in that, despite its position as defendant, it has to present to the court the measures it has taken to protect against unlawful activity, indicate any potential sources of ineffectiveness of these measures and explain and why it cannot be expected to take further action. A defendant who has taken all reasonable measures to impede infringements cannot be held liable for infringements for which it does not bear fault. This will be the case for infringements that the prior examination process (e.g., automatic filtering), which it was ordered to implement, could not identify.[427]

In the final analysis, the duty to review emerges as an exceptionally flexible criterion, influenced by a host of factors. The tasks that can be demanded of a disturber are likewise variable, ranging from attempts to

---

422. BGH, *Blog-Eintrag,* 25 October 2011, I ZR 93/10.
423. BGH, *Cybersky,* 15 January 2009, I ZR 57/07.
424. See also, BGH, *Blog-Eintrag,* 25 October, I ZR 93/10.
425. BGH, *Jugendgefährdende Medien bei eBay,* 12 July 2007, I ZR 18/04. See: A Kur, 'Secondary Liability for Trademark Infringement on the Internet: the Situation in Germany and throughout the EU' (2014) 37(4) Columbia Journal of Law & the Arts 525.
426. A Bayer, 'Liability 2.0 – Does the Internet Environment Require New Standards for Secondary Liability? An Overview of the Current Legal Situation in Germany' in M J Adelmann *et al., Patents and Technological Progress in a Globalized World* (Springer 2009) 365. For a more comprehensive analysis of the relevance of fundamental rights to the establishment of duties of care, see P Breyer, 'Verkehrssicherungspflichten von Internetdiensten im Lichte der Grundrechte' (2009) MMR 14.
427. BGH, *Internetversteigerung I,* 11 March 2004, I ZR 304/01. As an example of an infringement for which the disturber would not have fault, the court suggested the case of a Rolex watch sold on an online auctioning site at a price appropriate for an original and without any indication that it is an imitation.

detect unlawful conduct in advance to more passive behavioural standards.[428] Moreover, the unreasonableness threshold rises and falls with the behaviour of the operator: the more the operator provokes infringement by third parties, the more strident the requirements of the duty to review will be.[429] As is typical in cases of complicated conflicts of interests, the effect is that the exact scope of the duty to review can only be decided on a case-by-case basis after comprehensive weighing of the relevant constellation of circumstances in the specific situation, with a view to finding an appropriate balance between the interests of the parties involved.[430] Nordemann puts forth a number of factors that will be relevant in this regard, namely the intensity of the risk, the commercial advantage of the hosting provider from the infringements, the weight of the interests of the copyright holder, the expense of limiting the risk and the lack of possibilities to neutralise the source of the infringement in a different way with equal effectiveness.[431]

While this approach has undisputable advantages, *Störerhaftung's* duty to review has also been criticised as overly broad. Despite the numerous instructions coming down from the BGH, the regional courts of Germany remain confused about the exact scope and requirements of *Störerhaftung,* especially in the area of internet service providers. Conflicting rulings have been handed down by the German courts, while it remains unclear what precautions an internet service provider must take in order to avoid being labelled a *Störer* before the courts. A general, unambiguous standard for interferer liability is currently absent.[432] Nevertheless, despite its disadvantages, this adjustability is arguably appropriate, as the only way to avoid falling into the 'typology' approach that, as we saw above, has obscured the essence of the intermediary liability question in France.

3.3.1.2 Störerhaftung *and Intermediary Liability in Copyright*

The seminal *Internetversteigerung* cases that decided so much with regard to *Störerhaftung's* applicability to the internet all concerned trademarks. Do the same conclusions hold true with regard to copyright? In more recent years,

---

428. A Bayer, 'Liability 2.0 – Does the Internet Environment Require New Standards for Secondary Liability? An Overview of the Current Legal Situation in Germany' in M J Adelmann et al., *Patents and Technological Progress in a Globalized World* (Springer 2009) 365.
429. J B Nordemann, 'Liability for Copyright Infringements on the Internet: Host Providers (Content Providers) – The German Approach' (2011) 2(1) Journal of Intellectual Property, Information Technology and Electronic Commerce Law (JIPITEC) 37.
430. BGH, *Schöner Wetten,* 1 April 2004, I ZR 317/01; T Hoeren, 'German Law on Internet Liability of Intermediaries', LIDC Congress, Oxford 2011.
431. J B Nordemann, 'Liability for Copyright Infringements on the Internet: Host Providers (Content Providers) – The German Approach' (2011) 2(1) Journal of Intellectual Property, Information Technology and Electronic Commerce Law (JIPITEC) 37.
432. J Wimmers, 'Who Interferes? Liability for Third Party Content on the Internet in Germany', (August 2007) Intellectual Property Today 32.

the BGH has addressed this question in the complicated *Rapidshare* saga. This concerned a Swiss-based online file-hosting service that came under attack for the storage of copyright-infringing files uploaded onto the cloud by users. The site undertook prompt take-downs upon receiving notices, but refused to accept that it had a duty to prevent future infringements.

Previously the regional courts had had some difficulty with the question. In 2010, in *Rapidshare I*,[433] the Düsseldorf *Oberlandesgericht* (OLG) found that the preventive measures Rapidshare had taken to avoid infringement were reasonable and adequate. According to the court, there was no obligation to take proactive manual action to supervise the material exchanged by end-users or to install automatic filters against unlawful content. The threat of over-blocking posed by word-based filters was specifically cited to justify this, while IP-address blocking was rejected, since IP addresses are often shared by many different people. As the court declared, notice-and-take-down measures are sufficient and no duty to examine content to prevent similar infringements is necessary. Later the same year, in *Atari v. Rapidshare (Alone in the Dark)*,[434] the same court confirmed that imposing a duty on Rapidshare to automatically filter the content posted by its users would be 'arbitrary', since keywords were not compelling evidence that a file included infringing material. Similarly, manual checks of content were found to be too work-intensive to be feasible. The court emphasised that, although it was undisputed that copyright infringements were committed by Rapidshare's users, the legal uses to which Rapidshare was put were numerous and common: its business model did not depend on infringement.

Yet a couple of years later, in *Rapidshare II*,[435] on very similar facts, the Hamburg OLG reached the exact opposite conclusion. This court held that deleting links after being notified by the copyright holders was not enough and that Rapidshare was under a duty to carry out active monitoring of any content appropriately notified as unlawful, so as to identify and remove any future hyperlinks in its system leading to infringing files. For this purpose, Rapidshare was also obliged to keep up with current developments through regular web searches for infringing links. The court emphasised as particularly relevant in this regard the fact that Rapidshare's business plan had previously incorporated a system of incentives offering financial rewards to users who uploaded popular files.[436] Although the court acknowledged that Rapidshare had since changed this practice, it nonetheless found that users were still likely to associate the service with illegal content.

When the case came before the BGH, the federal court, predictably in view of the *Internetversteigerung* jurisprudence, sided with the Hamburg judge. On 12 July 2012 (clearly a fateful date in the intermediary liability

433. OLG Düsseldorf, *Rapidshare I*, 27 April 2010, I-20 U 166/09.
434. OLG Düsseldorf, *Rapidshare III*, 21 December 2010, I-20 U 59/10.
435. OLG Hamburg, *Rapidshare II*, 14 March 2012, 5 U 87/09.
436. For a similar case, see OLG Hamburg, *Sharehoster II*, 30 September 2009, 5 U 111/08.

world), the BGH went in the exact opposite direction being opted for on the very same day by its French counterpart. So, in *Rapidshare (Alone in the Dark)*,[437] the BGH confirmed the neutrality and usefulness of the Rapidshare service, but nevertheless found Rapidshare to be a *Störer.* As such, Rapidshare did not have a duty to perform proactive monitoring of the files uploaded by its users, but could only be liable if it ignored a reasonable *Prüfungspflicht.* Such a duty could only arise once Rapidshare was made aware of a clear infringement through notification. Nevertheless, in such cases, the provider could not simply rest at deleting existing infringing files, but had to go further and perform searches for future infringements of the notified content, as well as take all reasonable measures to make sure users could not proceed with such infringements in the first place, as long as these did not threaten Rapidshare's business model. This could include automatic word filters supplemented by subsequent manual controls. Contrary to what the Düsseldorf court had ruled, these measures could not be excluded simply because they might not be entirely effective. The filtering moreover should aim to delete all files, regardless of the identity of the uploader. In addition, according to the BGH, Rapidshare might also be obligated, by means of regular search facilities, to review a 'small number' of link collections[438] manually to see if they contain references to infringing material.

Subsequently, in a second case the next year, *Rapidshare III (GEMA v. Rapidshare,* also known as *The Reader)*,[439] the BGH went one step further. Here the Court again agreed that Rapidshare's business model was not *a priori* designed to facilitate infringement and that the provided hosting services could also be used for lawful purposes, thus again validating Rapidshare's business model as deserving of protection against disruption.[440] Nevertheless, Rapidshare was found to have increased through its activities the risk of the illegal use of its services. As a result it had lost its neutrality. The different outcome in comparison to *Alone in the Dark* was explained by dint of the different factual findings of the appeal courts. For example, in this case, it had been found that Rapidshare advertised the fact that certain files on its platform had been downloaded 100.000 times, a circumstance that suggested 'highly attractive and hence as a rule illegal' content. Rapidshare's services could also be used anonymously, increasing its appeal for illegal

437. BGH, *Rapidshare I,* 12 July 2012, I ZR 18/11.

438. 'Link collections' means 'collections of search results after searching for specific content through search tools', see J Wang, 'Development of Hosting ISPs' Secondary Liability for Primary Copyright Infringement in China – As Compared to the US and German Routes' (2015) International Review of Intellectual Property and Competition Law (IIC) 275. An example is given: 'if a person searches keywords of "alone in dark, Rapidshare" in Google, the results are links from which a person can download "alone in dark" residing on Rapidshare.'

439. BGH, *Rapidshare III,* 15 August 2013, I ZR 80/12.

440. T Hoeren, 'BGH: Störerhaftung von RapidShare – Alone in the Dark', case comment (2013) MMR 185.

use, while points were awarded to users depending on their number of downloads, a further indication that Rapidshare encouraged unlawfulness. The BGH stated that, if the business model of a file-hosting service significantly facilitates copyright infringement, the provider can reasonably be expected to extensively and regularly monitor its service for preventive purposes – indeed, the more hazardous the service, the more extensive the monitoring obligations. While Rapidshare was not obliged to examine each and every file uploaded to its server by its users, it had a duty to do everything that could be technically and commercially expected of it to prevent further infringements with respect to the works on its servers. The court was adamant that the high number of infringing works available on Rapidshare's servers could not serve as an excuse to reduce its monitoring obligations, which applied to every work for which a notification of a clear infringement has been received: '[c]opyright protection cannot be diluted by virtue of the fact that there are a large number of infringements within a business model that per se is permissible'.

As a result, Rapidshare was obliged to take preventive measures in addition to expeditious removal. This was understood to constitute 'a duty of care to be expected of [the website] according to reasonable judgment and set down in national legal regulations in order to discover and prevent specific types of illegal activity'.[441] In particular, according to the BGH, Rapidshare should have implemented a word filter to retrieve and delete all infringing files already in its system; this automated monitoring should additionally have been supplemented with a subsequent manual reassessment for the avoidance of over-blocking. Again, the BGH dismissed the possibility that these measures might not be entirely effective, as it stated that they would be sufficient to at least reduce infringements. In addition, the BGH found that Rapidshare is under general '*Marktbeobachtungspflicht*', i.e., market monitoring duty to search, by use of general search engines 'such as Google, Facebook or Twitter' through suitably formulated search questions, 'and possibly also through the assistance of so-called web-crawlers', for further illegal links to its service with regard to all 4815 relevant works. The fact that the BGH referred to Facebook and Twitter as 'general search engines' should be alarming enough on its own, but its complete disregard for proportionality and user rights, as well as its lip-service to the need to protect the intermediary's business model is additional cause for concern.[442] The ruling is clearly in no way compatible with underlying EU law.

441. Translation borrowed from Case comment, 'The Federal Supreme Court (Bundesgerichtshof): "Rapidshare III"' (2014) International Review of Intellectual Property and Competition Law (IIC) 716.

442. For a general analysis of the liability of such 'Sharehoster' service providers, as they are known in Germany, see T Hoeren & V Bensinger, *Haftung im Internet – Die Neue Rechtslage* (De Gruyter 2014) 353-390.

The lower courts have continued along the path carved by the BGH. So, for example, in 2012, the *Hamburg Landgericht* (Hamburg district court) in *GEMA v. YouTube* concluded that the popular video-sharing platform had infringed its take-down duties by only removing allegedly infringing videos seven months after receipt of a notification. This conclusion poses no problems in view of the E-Commerce Directive. Not stopping here however, the court also found that YouTube was obliged to undertake automated filtering of its platform, so as to uncover any future infringement of content whose previous infringement had already been brought to its attention.[443] Thus, YouTube was obliged to use its Content ID software itself, instead of expecting the right-holder to do so, as is its usual practice. In addition to this, YouTube was also under an obligation to install a word-based filter designed to examine the title of the video and the artist concerned, as the Content ID system would only block identical audio recordings. The court did make reference to proportionality, but considered that that requirement was satisfied by the fact that YouTube was not obliged to conduct searches before receiving a notification. The court bypassed the question of compatibility with CJEU case law, noting that the word filter ordered only captured the name of the uploaded video, which was already in the public domain. It also suggested that fundamental rights were not relevant to the discussion, as YouTube did not handle end-users' personal data (a controversial idea, as personal data is a broader concept than that of sensitive private information), while any risk to freedom of expression would be eliminated by the appropriate application of the measures ordered. On 1 July 2015, the Hamburg Court of Appeal confirmed the ruling.[444]

Notably, the above cases all concerned host providers of one kind or another. Curiously, *Störerhaftung* has had a far less happy fate in cases of blocking requests against mere conduits with regard to websites responsible for infringement. For example, in *g-stream.in* the OLG Hamburg refused to grant a website blocking order against an access provider, arguing that such an injunction was not provided for in German law, while Article 8(3) of the Copyright Directive could not be directly applied.[445] The court also denied that such an interpretation of *Störerhaftung* brought German law out of line with Article 8(3) of the Copyright Directive, as this says nothing about blocking injunctions per se, but leaves considerable room for interpretation

443. LG Hamburg, 20 April 2012, 310 O 461/10.

444. OLG Hamburg, 1 July 2015, 5 U 87/12. For another case on YouTube as a *Störer* see: OLG München, 17 November 2011, 29 U 3496/11 and, more recently, OLG Hamburg, 1 July 2015, 5 U 87/12.

445. OLG Hamburg, 22 December 2010, 5 U 36/09. For a similar decision see OLG Frankfurt, 22 January 2008, 6 W 10/08, with commentary by G Spindler (2008) MMR 166.

to the Member States.[446] In view of the already expansive interpretation of *Störerhaftung* embraced by the German courts, this seems a strange hill to die on.

The OLG Köln in *Hinweisbeschluss* went in a slightly different direction: while rejecting a similar request, it did concede that in principle *Störerhaftung* against access providers should be possible, as long as these resist reasonable precautions.[447] Thus, *Störerhaftung* must be interpreted and applied in a way that complies with the European directives, while an interpretation of German law that exempts access providers from injunctive orders should no longer be possible. As a result, the requirements for labelling the access provider a *Störer* were found to be fulfilled in the case there examined. At the same time, it was not shown that the provider had reasonable measures at its disposal to prevent infringement. In line with the principle of proportionality, the question of reasonableness should be assessed in view of both the applicant's rights to the protection of his intellectual property, the intermediary's freedom to conduct a business and its users' freedom of expression. The only measures that the provider could take would be URL, IP or DNS-blocking. In view of the danger of over-blocking, the ease with which these blocking measures may be circumvented, the fact that the webpages in question did not contain illegal content themselves, but simply links to such content, and the fact that the intermediary operated a legitimate and socially significant business, the order was not granted. However, an appeal to the BGH was permitted, as that court has never addressed the question of access providers' *Störerhaftung* for third party copyright infringements.

Finally, it is also relevant to note the numerous *Usenet* decisions emanating from the German courts. The question has not yet made it to the BGH and the lower courts have issued a number of rulings with conflicting outcomes. So, in different cases, Usenet service providers have been found to act as mere conduits,[448] caching providers[449] or even hosts.[450] Again, the difficulty in application of *Störerhaftung* has revolved around the lack of

446. See also: G Spindler, '"Die Tür ist auf" – Europarechtliche Zulässigkeit von Auskunftsansprüchen gegenüber Providern Urteilsanmerkung zu EuGH "Promusicae/ Telefónica"' (2008) GRUR 574.

447. OLG Köln, 18 July 2014, 6 U 192/11. See also: T Raab, 'OLG Köln: Keine Pflicht von Access-Providern zur Sperrung rechtswidriger Angebote' (2014) MMR-Aktuell 361783. See also: J B Nordemann, 'Internet Copyright Infringement: Remedies against Internet Intermediaries – the European Perspective on Host and Access Providers' (2012) 59(4) Journal of the Copyright Society of the USA 773.

448. OLG Hamburg, 14 January 2009, 5 U 113/07; OLG Hamburg, 28 January 2009, 5 U 255/07.

449. OLG Düsseldorf, 15 January 2008, I-20 U 95/07; LG München, 19 April 2007, 7 O 3950/07.

450. Hamburg LG, 19 February 2007, 308 O 32/07.

reasonable and effective control measures.[451] The most recent decision on the service regards it as an access provider that is subject to *Störerhaftung.*[452]

In view of the ease with which German courts have been willing to apply filtering to host service providers, their reluctance to apply the far less invasive blocking measures against access providers, as well as their confusion with regard to the application of any injunctive relief against the (arguably guiltier) Usenet providers is remarkable. Again, there appears to be some confusion: Hoeren and Yankova state that filtering and blocking measures would be a violation of the user's secrecy of telecommunication that thus contrary to the German constitution[453] – but this would only be true of the first of these. The question of effectiveness is a much better objection to blocking measures, but as the CJEU's *Telekabel* decision has shown, (depending on the objective) not an impenetrable one.

On 26 November 2015, the BGH partially overcame the German courts hesitation towards website blocking injunctions in two decisions issued against two German access providers, Deutsche Telekom and O2 Deutschland.[454] At the time of writing the full decision had not yet been handled down, but the court's press release offers helpful insights.[455] According to this, the court, in conformity with EU case law, relied primarily on the concept of a fair balance to reach its decision. For this purpose, it took into account the right-holders' copyright, the intermediary's freedom to conduct a business and end-users' right to information. The court reasoned that it should not be necessary that a targeted website contain nothing but infringing content in order that a blocking order be considered reasonable, as long as the lawful content is negligible. This approach echoes the US's 'substantial non-infringing uses' doctrine. In a clear evocation of *Telekabel,* the court also confirmed that the availability of circumvention technology should not affect the reasonableness of blocking orders, as long as the blocks prevent or at least make more difficult access to the infringing content. At the same time, in one important caveat, the BGH insisted on the subsidiarity of the blocking orders. According to the court, internet access providers can only be held liable as *Störer* if the right-holder has first made reasonable efforts to take action against the primary infringers, such as the website operators, or those

451. T Hoeren & S Yankova, 'The Liability of Internet Intermediaries – The German Perspective' (2012) International Review of Intellectual Property and Competition Law (IIC) 501.
452. OLG Hamburg, 9 January 2014, 5 U 52/10.
453. T Hoeren & S Yankova, 'The Liability of Internet Intermediaries – The German Perspective' (2012) International Review of Intellectual Property and Competition Law (IIC) 501.
454. BGH, *GEMA v. Deutsche Telekom*, 26 November 2015, I ZR 3/14 and *Universal Music v. O2 Deutschland*, 26 November 2015, I ZR 174/14.
455. Bundesgerichtshof, 'Bundesgerichtshof zur Haftung von Access-Providern für Urheberrechtsverletzungen Dritter', press release Nr. 194/2015, available at: http://juris.bundesgerichtshof.de/cgi-bin/rechtsprechung/document.py?Gericht=bgh&Art=pm&Datum=2015&Sort=3&nr=72928&pos=14&anz=209.

who have contributed to the infringement by the provision of services, such as the host service providers. The BGH moreover set a high standard for such efforts, by suggesting that they could include hiring a private investigator or involving criminal prosecution authorities to determine the identity and location of the primary infringer. This interesting twist confirms that the BGH indeed views hosts as more culpable than mere conduits.

3.3.1.3 Compatibility with the E-Commerce Directive

From the above it is clear that *Störerhaftung* can, in many ways, be seen as the German (pre-)implementation of Article 11 of the Enforcement Directive. At the same time, *Störerhaftung*'s compatibility with the safe harbour provisions of the E-Commerce Directive has been heavily disputed.

The BGH has brushed aside such concerns. In *Internetversteigerung,* the BGH considered its interpretation regarding the inapplicability of the safe harbours to injunctive relief to be an *acte clair* that required no reference to the CJEU. The Court observed that Article 14(1) of the Directive on the immunity of host service providers demands actual knowledge only as regards claims for damages, but otherwise allows constructive knowledge to exclude the safe harbour. If claims for cease and desist orders were covered by the safe harbour, the Court expounded, this would have the unacceptable consequence of imposing more stringent conditions ('actual knowledge') on these than on claims for damages ('awareness of facts or circumstances from which illegal activity or information is apparent').[456] This result being unacceptable, the BGH concluded that the safe harbours do not apply to claims for injunctive relief against host providers who have been notified of infringing activity on their websites.

This argument is not very strong. The court might have done better to examine the Explanatory Memorandum to the Directive, which makes clear that claims for damages are to be contrasted in the context of Article 14(1) not with injunctive orders, but with criminal liability.[457] The safe harbours certainly do not extend to injunctive relief, but, as has been explained in Chapter 2, the legal basis for that is to be found in the final paragraph of each of the liability privileges of Articles 12-14, which contain explicit exceptions permitting national courts or administrative authorities, in accordance with the Member State's legal system, to require service providers to terminate or prevent infringements. Recital 45 of the Directive further confirms the permissibility of injunctive relief and, in particular, orders by courts or administrative authorities requiring the termination or prevention of any

456. BGH, *Internetversteigerung I,* 11 March 2004, I ZR 304/01. See for an analysis in support of this argument, J Bornkamm, 'E-Commerce Directive vs. IP Rights Enforcement – Legal Balance Achieved?' (2007) GRUR Int 642.

457. Commission Proposal for a European Parliament and Council Directive on certain legal aspects of electronic commerce in the internal market, 18 November 1998, COM (1998) 586 final.

infringement, including the removal of illegal information or the disabling of access to it. Article 8 of the Copyright Directive and Article 11 of the Enforcement Directive, both of which confirm IPR owners' right to apply for injunctions against intermediaries whose services are used by third parties to infringe, strengthen the case in favour of compatibility.

In any case, while the permissibility of injunctive relief and specific monitoring obligations under the E-Commerce Directive cannot be doubted, the compatibility of *Störerhaftung's* extension to clear future repetitions of a notified infringement with the general monitoring obligation of Article 15 of the E-Commerce Directive is another matter.[458] Bornkamm argues that this 'continuous' *Störerhaftung* does not impose *ex ante* monitoring, but only an *ex post* obligation to react. He then claims that Article 15(1) is limited to *ex ante* obligations, but that *ex post* injunctive relief relating to further infringements once an infringement has been shown is permissible.[459] On this basis, he concludes that 'the directive does not rule out injunctive relief as to further infringements once an infringement has been shown'. Leistner agrees, suggesting that, since the doctrine does not require the prevention of '*any* future comparable infringement at *any* cost', its specificity is assured.[460] In *Rapidshare III,* the BGH again confidently stated that its *Störerhaftung* principles are compatible with the standards laid down by the CJEU in *L'Oréal v. eBay*. According to that ruling, the 'appeal court rightly assumed that the defendant can be subjected not to a general but rather an incident-related monitoring obligation to trace an infringement already made and prevent further infringements'. Yet the final part of this statement is by no means self-evidently true.

Indeed, the same obstacles encountered by the French notice-and-stay-down regime arise here as well. Specifically, Justice Bornkamm's interpretation of Article 15 seems wrong-headed: the provision makes no reference at all to *ex ante* versus *ex post* monitoring. There is therefore nothing to suggest that timing influences the legality of general obligations to monitor or general obligations actively to seek facts or circumstances indicating illegal activity. Admittedly, as discussed in Chapter 2, the interpretation of the provision's phrasing is open for debate. The CJEU has however offered some additional clarity, by establishing unequivocally in its *SABAM* judgments that the filtering of all electronic communications that applies indiscriminately to all users as a preventive measure, at the expense of the intermediary and for an unlimited period of time should be understood as encompassed by the provision. A 'continuous' application of *Störerhaftung*

458. J B Nordemann, 'Liability for Copyright Infringements on the Internet: Host Providers (Content Providers) – The German Approach' (2011) 2(1) Journal of Intellectual Property, Information Technology and Electronic Commerce Law (JIPITEC) 37.

459. J Bornkamm, 'E-Commerce Directive vs. IP Rights Enforcement – Legal Balance Achieved?' (2007) GRUR Int 642.

460. M Leistner, 'Common Principles of Secondary Liability?' in A Ohly (ed.), *Common Principles of European Intellectual Property Law* (Mohr Siebeck 2012) 128.

does not seem compatible with this finding: although certainly the rights for the protection of which the *Störerhaftung*-imposed monitoring is undertaken are specific, the measures that must be adopted for their protection require precisely this type of filtering, which scrutinises the entirety of the hosted content as posted by all users with no end in sight.

Technical limitations confirm this conclusion. In *Internetversteigerung I,* the BGH explained that the provider:

> cannot reasonably be expected to check every offer placed directly on the internet in an automated process for a possible infringement of third-party property rights. If a service provider acquires notice of a trade mark infringement, it must not only immediately block the specific sale but must also take technically feasible and reasonable measures to prevent further such infringements.[461]

However, it is entirely unclear how further infringements are supposed to be prevented without checking every offer for a possible infringement. The dichotomy suggested here is therefore a false one. To draw a real-life analogy, it matters little if airport security services give airplane travellers routine pat-downs in search of any kind of weapon or only semi-automatic pistols – the pat-down is in either case occurring. And, while it would certainly be convenient if it were possible to limit pat-downs only to persons carrying the weapon in question, that idea ignores that fact that identifying those individuals is the precise the objective of the pat-down in the first place. Moreover, even if one were to take a very permissive approach to the differentiation between 'general' and 'specific' and allow that descriptor to depend on the specificity of the infringements the monitoring is intended to uncover, it is not hard to see how the 'specific' duties as imagined by the BGH may easily accumulate and cross the line into generality.[462] This is made especially obvious in *GEMA v. Rapidshare,* which involved an exceptionally large number of protected works and where the provider was, alarmingly, ordered to supervise not only its own platform, but (however selectively) the entire internet – this particular slope thus appears to be a very slippery one. In copyright this problem is particularly acute, as the limitation to copies similar in their 'core' offers limited guarantees: the same posting might be illegal when done by one person at one point in time and legal when done by another or at a different time, the work might in the meantime have fallen into the public domain, it might have been released under an open-content license or it might simply have been posted by the right-holder

461. Translation taken from Case comment, 'Federal Supreme Court (Bundesgerichtshof): GERMANY' (2005) International Review of Intellectual Property and Competition Law (IIC) 573.

462. A Kur, 'Secondary Liability for Trademark Infringement on the Internet: the Situation in Germany and throughout the EU' (2014) 37(4) Columbia Journal of Law & the Arts 525.

herself. Automatic filters or busy customer service teams would have little way of knowing any of this.

Along similar lines, Leistner's logic can also be questioned: his conclusion seems more relevant to the issue of proportionality. Certainly, there is room for differentiations with regard to the invasiveness of general monitoring measures: requiring that every infringement without exception be in fact uncovered might represent a more unreasonable interference than simply demanding that economically viable filtering occur while accepting the limits of this measure's effectiveness. But this ignores the fact that both Article 15 of the E-Commerce Directive and the CJEU have declared that all obligations for general monitoring are prohibited regardless of their proportionality – or, perhaps more accurately, that all such obligations are by definition disproportionate regardless of their invasiveness or unreasonableness.

Indeed, in this regard there seems to be a widespread misunderstanding among German jurists. For example, Nordemann also suggests that, 'hosting providers are not obliged to use [audio and audiovisual filters] filters on all content uploaded by any user, as this would result in a general monitoring duty', but they 'may be obliged to install are audio-visual filters only for certain works upon knowledge that such works were made publicly available on the site'. This again transplants the generality of the monitoring to the works the measure is intended to protect, rather than the content being filtered. He also suggests that keyword filters do not breach the principle that providers must not be obliged to generally monitor their content:

> In *Netlog,* the CJEU held that all filtering duties that apply indiscriminately to all users as a preventive measure at the expense of the host provider and for an unlimited period of time breach Article 15 of the EU E-Commerce Directive. This does not mean that word filters may not be imposed on hosting providers. Word filters by their nature only search for certain film titles, game titles, audio book titles, music titles, band names etc. Also, they only filter the keywords belonging to the filed stores but not the file itself.[463]

There appears to be a disconnect in the reasoning here, as first one set of conditions as required by the CJEU are acknowledged, but then these are swept aside in favour of a different criterion never mentioned by the Luxembourg court. Hoeren and Yankova have a better grasp of the situation: 'An injunction to prevent future similar infringements refers neither to a specific field nor to a specific time period and can in no way represent a

463. J B Nordemann, 'Internet Copyright Infringement: Remedies against Internet Intermediaries – the European Perspective on Host and Access Providers' (2012) 59(4) Journal of the Copyright Society of the USA 773.

monitoring obligation in a specific case. This proactive duty establishes rather a monitoring obligation of a general nature'.[464]

In any case, the exact location of the divide between specificity and generality aside, it is also important to note that not all 'specific monitoring' will be permitted under EU law – even if a measure is not general in the sense of Article 15 of the E-Commerce Directive, according to the CJEU, it will still be obliged to strike a 'fair balance' between all competing fundamental rights it impacts, a matter not considered at all by the BGH. In this regard, the compatibility of the German notion of 'reasonableness' with the CJEU's 'diligent economic operator' could, for example, bear analysis. After all, although in *Rapidshare III,* the BGH considered that measures should not be taken that threaten the host provider's business model, this is exactly what it subsequently proceeded to do. Ultimately, after an attempt, in the face of legal pressure, to discourage the use of its service for the distribution of files to large numbers of anonymous users and instead focus on personal subscription-only cloud-based file storage, Rapidshare's popularity fell sharply and, at the end of March 2015, the provider ceased to operate.[465] This would have been an acceptable legal result if Rapidshare's business model had been declared illegal, but it had been explicitly recognised as deserving of legal protection by the BGH. Similarly, the familiar question of effectiveness is also worth considering. As Hoeren notes, the ease with which the *Rapidshare III* court concluded that popular content must be illegal fails to convince:[466] if the internet has made one thing clear then that should be that the most professionally produced content cannot compete in popularity with home videos of pet cats. Hoeren also pertinently questions the effectiveness of word filters for the exclusion of files with titles too close to the titles of protected content, at least where these are based on generic phrases such as 'alone in the dark'.[467]

As a result of the above discrepancies the German courts have been accused of 'misconceiving the main goals which national and European legislators have pursued when drafting the Telemedia Act and the E-Commerce Directive'.[468] A referral on these matters to the Court of Justice

464. T Hoeren & S Yankova, 'The Liability of Internet Intermediaries – The German Perspective' (2012 International Review of Intellectual Property and Competition Law (IIC) 501.
465. See, entry on 'Rapidshare' on Wikipedia.
466. T Hoeren, 'Konkretisierung der Störerhaftung für Urheberrechtsverletzungen bei File-Hosting', case comment (2013) NJW 3245.
467. T Hoeren, 'BGH: Störerhaftung von RapidShare – Alone in the Dark', case comment (2013) MMR 185.
468. T Hoeren, 'German Law on Internet Liability of Intermediaries', LIDC Congress, Oxford 2011; J Wimmers, 'Who Interferes? Liability for Third Party Content on the Internet in Germany' (August 2007) Intellectual Property Today 32.

would be particularly welcome.[469] Interestingly, Bornkamm in his defence of *Störerhaftung* makes an appeal for a further substantive European harmonisation that would give greater concrete information on how a fair balance may be struck.[470] The CJEU has since moved in exactly this direction, but, unfortunately for the German courts, its edicts seem to be in conflict with their own conclusions.

3.3.1.4 **Störerhaftung** ***as Injunctive Relief for 'Neutral' Intermediaries***

One BGH decision does seem to hit the right note. In 2009, in *Cybersky* the BGH took an extremely strict approach to the designers and distributers of software that enabled users to share television signals using P2PTV (Peer-To-Peer Television) technology.[471] In view of the active part that the defendant played in inducing copyright violations, mere warning notices (as had been accepted as sufficient in the older *Möbelklassiker* judgment) were not, in this case, deemed sufficient. Instead, the court ordered a complete prohibition of the distribution of the application, as long as it continued to allow the transmission or reception of the decrypted signal of the applicant broadcasting organisation. Interestingly, the ban rested not so much on the software's capabilities for infringing use per se (indeed, no actual infringement had been proven), but on the promotion of those capabilities by the company in an online advertising campaign. In this way, the ruling explicitly avoided condemning P2P as such, describing the technology instead as 'legally unobjectionable', and limited itself only to companies whose business model depended on the promotion of the violation of the rights of others: '*der Schutz der Berufsfreiheit kann für sie nicht in Anspruch genommen werden*'.

The solution is an intriguing one. On its basis, Spindler and Leistner have argued that the courts' approach towards more 'neutral' providers, whose technology has a significant potential for legal use and is not exclusively designed for infringing activities is much more generous than that towards intermediaries who actively induce copyright infringements on the part of their users: instead of the positive obligation to prevent illegal

---

469. In pending case C-484/14, *McFadden,* the Munich district court has asked the CJEU to clarify whether Art. 12 precludes the issue of injunctive orders by national courts requiring the access provider to refrain in future from enabling third parties to make a particular copyright-protected work available for electronic retrieval from online exchange platforms via a specific internet connection. While concerning access providers, rather than hosts, whose treatment by the German courts has been much harsher and more problematic in view of EU law, this request is a step in the right direction.

470. J Bornkamm, 'E-Commerce Directive vs. IP Rights Enforcement – Legal Balance Achieved?' (2007) GRUR Int 642.

471. BGH, *Cybersky,* 15 January 2009, I ZR 57/07.

activity on their systems that encumbers the second, the first can rely much more confidently on the classic measures of warning notices and preventive action.[472] The two authors accordingly conclude that recent German case law shows a preoccupation in the area of *Störerhaftung* with a differentiation between the 'active' inducement of infringement and 'neutral' technology providers.[473] Nordemann echoes this view, connecting *Störerhaftung* with indications of bad faith on the part of the disturber:

> the unreasonableness threshold rises more the more hosting providers, through their behaviour, provoke rights infringements by third parties, for example by advertising using illegally hosted content or setting up categories susceptible to infringements. One must also take into account whether the hosting provider receives a commission for the infringing acts or at least indirectly profits through increased advertising revenue due to the illegal acts. An example would be if the income of advertising financed hosting providers such as link referrers, file hosts and link encrypters rises with the number of times the hosted content is illegally accessed.[474]

If this interpretation is accepted, it would indicate that, just as the English and French courts – not to mention the CJEU itself – the German judges too are intent on making a distinction between worthy and unworthy intermediaries, innocent bystanders and those which have made the infringement their own – *Störerhaftung* does not apply to all intermediaries, but only those that aren't neutral. It would thus appear that the insistence on injecting a moral, mental element into the question of third party liability crosses European borders.

Incidentally, it is also arguable that a desire to treat differently neutral and non-neutral intermediaries can explain the BGH's differentiated approach towards hosts and mere conduits, as the first will almost inevitably by their nature be more involved in the infringing content than the second. Such an inclination is also discernible in the *Rapidshare* case law analysed above – although the BGH eventually brushes it off to impose the same measures in both *Rapidshare* cases. If *Störerhaftung* really is a purely causal liability that only applies injunctive relief and thus need not care about the safe harbour provisions, this outcome is entirely appropriate. If however it is agreed that the neutrality or lack thereof of a service should make a

472. G Spindler & M Leistner, 'Secondary Copyright Infringement – New Perspectives from Germany and Europe' (2006) 37(7) International Review of Intellectual Property and Competition Law (IIC) 788.
473. G Spindler & M Leistner, 'Secondary Copyright Infringement – New Perspectives from Germany and Europe' (2006) 37(7) International Review of Intellectual Property and Competition Law (IIC) 788.
474. J B Nordemann, 'Liability for Copyright Infringements on the Internet: Host Providers (Content Providers) – The German Approach' (2011) 2(1) Journal of Intellectual Property, Information Technology and Electronic Commerce Law (JIPITEC) 37.

difference and the courts wish to impose consequences on intermediaries for the 'active' inducement of third party copyright infringement, it might make more sense to bite the bullet and impose liability in a more straightforward manner as a participant in the commission of a wrong.

Beyond *Störerhaftung* what other options are there in the German legal system for the third party copyright liability of internet intermediaries? From the above, it is clear that a *Störer* is somebody who causally contributes to the unlawful behaviour of another without however desiring the infringement as such. The central question therefore becomes: how close to the main perpetrator must the disturber be to attract liability? The wider the circle of possible prohibited action is drawn, the more a disturber begins to look like a primary wrongdoer – i.e., a *Täter* or *Teilnehmer.*[475]

3.3.2 The General Rules of Tort Law

Intriguingly, the doctrine of *Störerhaftung* is currently being argued in Germany as dogmatically unnecessary and replaceable.[476] It has come under particularly intense attack in the area of unfair competition. The criticism seems to be provoked precisely by *Störerhaftung's* intended purpose of extending liability to encompass persons not directly involved in the commission of the infringement. This is seen as particularly inappropriate for unfair competition law, in which unlawfulness is supposed to emanate from the unfair competition practice itself (*Verhaltungunrecht*). Overextending the reach of the law to persons whose conduct does not of itself constitute a breach of the standard business conduct is thus considered by many as inappropriate. By contrast, this argument is weaker in the field of copyright: IPRs are *erga omnes* absolute rights, any infringement of which is by definition unlawful. In this area therefore, unlawfulness resides not in the type of behaviour, but in the achievement of the illegal result (*Erfolgsunrecht*). As a result, any infringement of an absolute right constitutes in and of itself an illegal act, irrespective of the behaviour that led to it, making *Störerhaftung's* objectionable characteristics less pertinent. While some suggest that *Störerhaftung* should nevertheless be viewed as generally inapplicable in all areas of law, the strongest case against it is thus still limited to the realm of unfair business practices. And indeed, in the case law of the BGH, while application of *Störerhaftung* has been severely restricted

475. H Schack, 'Täter und Störer: Zur Erweiterung und Begrenzung der Verantwortlichkeit durch Verkehrspflichten im Wettbewerbs- und Immaterialgüterrecht' in 'Festschrift für Dieter Reuter zum 70. Geburtstag am 16. Oktober 2010' (2010) De Gruyter 1167.

476. T Hoeren & S Yankova, 'The Liability of Internet Intermediaries – The German Perspective' (2012) International Review of Intellectual Property and Competition Law (IIC) 501; M Leistner, 'Störerhaftung und mittelbare Schutzrechtsverletzung' (2010) GRUR-Beil 1; H Köhler, '"Täter" und "Störer" im Wettbewerbs- und Markenrecht Zur BGH-Entscheidung "Jugendgefährdende Medien bei eBay"' (2008) GRUR 1;

in recent years with regard to unfair competition, the court continues to employ the doctrine in intellectual property matters, albeit circumscribed by the principle of reasonable review duties.[477]

Regardless, the discussion itself indicates that, as in England and France, in Germany too, as a result of the perceived inadequacies of *Störerhaftung,* a slow push towards the doctrinal reintegration of accessory liability in copyright into the underlying rules of general tort law can be discerned.[478] This is more openly talked about in the literature, but hints may be found in the case law as well. The idea is to transform the *Störer* into a '*mittelbarer Verletzer',* a true 'indirect infringer' by relying on the general rules on tortfeasance and participation.[479] The possibilities for such a solution shall be examined below.

It should be noted that the relationship between *Störerhaftung* and general tort law is currently unclear.[480] A bright line division between the two is lacking, not least because in both areas the relevant duties of care have been developed gradually by the courts, leading to flexible, adaptive, but badly demarcated doctrines.[481]

3.3.2.1 Täterhaftung*: Liability as a Joint Tortfeasor*

As in other jurisdictions, in Germany too, the theories not only of accessory liability (if that is what *Störerhaftung* can be called), but also of direct liability have to be considered when examining intermediary liability for online copyright infringement – an intermediary may be considered to have participated in a third party infringement in such a way as to label itself a primary tortfeasor and thus attract liability of this type. Direct liability in Germany can accrue both to a tortfeasor and to a participant in an

477. T Hoeren, 'German Law on Internet Liability of Intermediaries', LIDC Congress, Oxford 2011; G Spindler & M Leistner, 'Secondary Copyright Infringement – New Perspectives from Germany and Europe' (2006) 37(7) International Review of Intellectual Property and Competition Law (IIC) 788; H Schack, 'Täter und Störer: Zur Erweiterung und Begrenzung der Verantwortlichkeit durch Verkehrspflichten im Wettbewerbs- und Immaterialgüterrecht' in 'Festschrift für Dieter Reuter zum 70. Geburtstag am 16. Oktober 2010' (2010) De Gruyter, 1167.
478. G Spindler & M Leistner, 'Secondary Copyright Infringement – New Perspectives from Germany and Europe' (2006) 37(7) International Review of Intellectual Property and Competition Law (IIC) 788.
479. Hamburg LG, 3 September 2010, 308 O 27/09, see comment by P Christiansen (2010) MMR 833.
480. H Schack, 'Täter und Störer: Zur Erweiterung und Begrenzung der Verantwortlichkeit durch Verkehrspflichten im Wettbewerbs- und Immaterialgüterrecht' in 'Festschrift für Dieter Reuter zum 70. Geburtstag am 16. Oktober 2010' (2010) De Gruyter 1167.
481. H Schack, 'Täter und Störer: Zur Erweiterung und Begrenzung der Verantwortlichkeit durch Verkehrspflichten im Wettbewerbs- und Immaterialgüterrecht' in 'Festschrift für Dieter Reuter zum 70. Geburtstag am 16. Oktober 2010' (2010) De Gruyter 1167.

infringement.[482] In true civil law manner, the font of the relevant tort rules is found in the civil code, *das BGB.*

The key provision here is Article 823(1) BGB. According to this, any person who, intentionally or negligently, unlawfully injures the life, body, health, freedom, property or any other legal right of another person or commits a breach of a statute that is intended to protect another person is liable to compensate the other party for the damage incurred. Paragraph 2 follows up by clarifying that the same duty to compensate is held by a person who commits a breach of a statute that is intended to protect another person. In this case, if, according to the contents of the specific provision, a statutory breach may also be committed without fault, liability for monetary relief only exists in the case of fault.[483] Either way, the basic constituent elements of a tort are four: the violation of a right (*Tatbestand*), unlawful behaviour (*Rechtswidrigkeit*), causal connection (*Kausalität*) and culpability (*Verschulden*). The most important condition here is the last one, indicating the big difference between *Täterhaftung* and the fault-free *Störerhaftung*.

Somewhat redundantly,[484] the element of *unlawfulness* (*Rechtswidrigkeit*) is automatically satisfied whenever a legal right is violated intentionally. If the protected right is violated unintentionally, unlawfulness will only accrue if the defendant has failed to satisfy the standard of care demanded by society. In other words, an act or omission is only unlawful in the event that a defendant either acts intentionally or violates a duty of care (*Sorgfaltspflicht* or *Verkehrspflicht*). Such a duty of care will arise to anybody who through his activity or property creates a source of potential danger which is likely to affect the interests and rights of others. This will include a duty to prevent the misuse of one's property by third persons in violation of another's rights. As with *Störerhaftung*, here too the rule of reason (*Zumutbarkeit*) prevails: the measures that a person can be expected to take to prevent a violation of the legal rights of others must be legally and physically feasible. The usual balancing act will require that the advantages of maintaining a source of danger must be weighed against potential damages to the rights of others.[485] So, similarly to *Störerhaftung*, measures which endanger the business model of the company and blanket manual checks are deemed unreasonable, while the examination of certain offers and the use of filters to identify similar content is permissible.[486] In contrast to the

482. T Hoeren & S Yankova, 'The Liability of Internet Intermediaries – The German Perspective' (2012) International Review of Intellectual Property and Competition Law (IIC) 501.
483. Article 823(2) BGB.
484. C von Bar, *The Common European Law of Torts – Vol. II* (Clarendon Press 2000) 235-245. For more on this, please see below, s. 4.3.1.
485. Koelman, K, 'Liability for On-Line Intermediaries', Imprimatur/Institute for Information Law, Amsterdam, 1997.
486. G Spindler & K Anton in G Spindler & F Schuster, *Recht der Electronischen Medien* (2nd ed., C.H. Beck 2011).

Prüfpflichten of *Störerhaftung* however, a breach of this duty of care leads not to the imposition of an injunctive order, but to liability as a *Täter*, i.e., main perpetrator, which can encompass both monetary and injunctive relief.

A statutory tort as required by Article 823(2) is provided by Article 97 of the German copyright act (UrhG).[487] Article 97(2) obliges anybody who infringes a copyright or related right intentionally or as the result of negligence to pay compensation for damages suffered. Calculation of the appropriate height of such compensation may take into account any profit made by the infringing party as a result of the infringement, as well as reasonable royalties that would have been payable had the infringing party sought permission to use the infringed right. Entitlement to damages may also be assessed on the basis of the amount the infringer would have had to pay in equitable remuneration if the infringer had requested authorisation to use the right infringed. Authors, including authors of scientific editions, photographers and performers may also recover monetary compensation for injury through breach of the statutory rights granted under the act, even if no pecuniary loss occurred. This last provision is an exception to the general rule under German law according to which only actual, not punitive, damages can be compensated. Its scope is limited to those right-holders who enjoy moral rights protection under the UrhG. Thus liability for such immaterial damage will be limited to the severe and substantial infringement of a moral right.[488]

Accordingly, whoever uses an IPR has an obligation to check whether proper permission has been granted. Failure to fulfil this obligation, to the extent that it is technically, legally and financially feasible, will constitute a breach of a duty of care, making the person in question fully liable for any injury incurred to the right-holder.[489] Article 97 UrhG is generally interpreted as encompassing typical preparatory acts, such as the importation or offering for sale of infringing goods. As a result, the person who, in any way willingly engages in behaviour that results in copyright infringement – for example, by making available online an unlawful copy of a copyright-protected work – can be held responsible as a primary wrongdoer for the infringement. All forms of participation are covered by this broad definition, from complicity and indirect delinquency to inducement and contributory infringement.[490]

487. For a brief analysis see, T Hoeren & V Bensinger, *Haftung im Internet – Die Neue Rechtslage* (De Gruyter 2014) 379-382. See also, A Waldenberger, 'Zur Zivilrechtlichen Verantwortlichkeit für Urheberrechtsverletzungen im Internet' (1997) ZUM 176.

488. A Klett et al., *Intellectual Property Law in Germany – Protection, Enforcement and Dispute Resolution* (C.H. Beck/LexisNexis 2008) 71.

489. K Koelman, 'Liability for On-Line Intermediaries', Imprimatur/Institute for Information Law, Amsterdam, 1997.

490. G Spindler & M Leistner, 'Secondary Copyright Infringement – New Perspectives from Germany and Europe' (2006) 37(7) International Review of Intellectual Property and Competition Law (IIC) 788.

The BGH has recently made a timid attempt to find an alternative basis for intermediary liability to *Störerhaftung* in the general principles of tort law. This is based on the familiar concept of the 'adoption' of content. So, in *marions-kochbuch.de*[491] the Court found that the operator of a website on which third party users can make content (in the particular case, recipes) publicly, if it examines the posted information itself for completeness and accuracy, must be understood as having adopted it as its own. As a result, it will be liable under the general provisions as a content provider. In that particular case, the determining factors of such a '*Zu-Eigen-Machen*' ('one's-own-making') included the fact that: (a) the content was editorially checked and approved by the website; (b) the photos were tagged with the platform's logo; (c) the contributing users were required to grant extensive use rights to the site, which the court interpreted as an economic appropriation of the content; and (d) the content in question constituted the core value of the website.[492] Remarkably, whether or not internet users could perceive that the content originated with third parties was deemed irrelevant.

It has been suggested that the case instituted a general principle. According to this, where the structure and contents of a given website create in the mind of a reasonably informed internet user the impression that the platform operator intends to adopt the UGC as its own, the operator should be held directly liable as *Täter* for any infringement.[493] If this interpretation were to be accepted, it would lead German jurisprudence on intermediary liability to converge with the French solution of negligence-based liability: where the intermediary can reasonably be considered to be itself at the origin of the infringing material, it may be held liable as a direct infringer either under the copyright provisions or, in the default, under the basic tort principles for a dereliction of a duty of care. This approach fits in nicely with the exception to the mere conduit and hosting safe harbours carved out by their German implementation for providers who intentionally work together with a recipient of their service to commit illegal acts,[494] as well as the exception already given in the E-Commerce Directive regarding hosting providers with authority and control.[495]

Yet, the doctrine of '*Zu-Eigen-Machen*' has not had much further success before the German courts.[496] Although the turn away from

491. BGH, *marions-kochbuch.de*, 12 November 2009, I ZR 166/07.
492. J Becher, 'Copyright and User-Generated Content: Legal Challenges for Community-Based Businesses in Germany and the USA' (Master's Thesis, Bucerius Law School/ WHU Otto Beisheim School of Management 2010).
493. T Hoeren & V Bensinger, *Haftung im Internet – Die Neue Rechtslage* (De Gruyter 2014) 357.
494. See Arts 8 and 9 TMG.
495. Article 14(2) of the E-Commerce Directive.
496. The same approach was taken by Hamburg LG the next year against YouTube. Again, YouTube was found to have 'made the third-party content its own' on the basis of the prominent use of its logo in comparison to the name of the uploading user and its

Störerhaftung has been applauded by commentators, in itself *'Zu-Eigen-Machen'* has been criticised as inappropriate: Hoeren and Yankova suggest that the BGH based the ruling directly on Article 7(1) of the TMG, without sufficient grounding in the general rules of direct trademark liability, thus incorrectly assuming that the inapplicability of the safe harbour provisions provides a basis for liability in and of itself, something obviously far from the European legislators' intention.[497] In 2011, in *Sevenload,* the Hamburg OLG declined to apply *'Zu-Eigen-Machen'*, as the content in question was not subjected to prior examination for accuracy, even though a structure had been provided by the intermediary enabling online publication.[498] This perspective would seem to depend the German doctrine of adoption on editorial control along the lines discussed above for France.

As with the very similar French application of the rules of CPI directly onto intermediaries, the German 'adoption' approach of *marions-kochbuch.de* yet again reveal the blurriness of the line separating direct from indirect liability. It also raises familiar questions regarding the balancing of opposing interests and the need for case-specific evaluations in the context of a rule of reason: presumptions of consent might be appropriate, but only to the extent that they remain reasonable. The right-holder cannot be expected to take extraordinary measures to prove lack of consent to inappropriate reproduction.[499]

Regardless, it should be noted that Germany has not had the same difficulty with other types of hyperlinking as France has: in *Paperboy,* the BGH held that hyperlinks (including deep links) to a website containing a copyright work made available to the public by the authorised user does not infringe the reproduction right or the right to make the work available to the public.[500] In this way, *'Linkfreiheit'* was confirmed.[501] In *Schöner Wetten,* it

---

editorial input in proposing content to users, as well as the placement of ads on user-provided material, see Hamburg LG, 3 September 2010, 308 O 27/09. The LG Hamburg has now changed this interpretation and views YouTube as a host service provider, see Hamburg LG, 20 April 2012, 310 O 461/10.

497. T Hoeren & S Yankova, 'The Liability of Internet Intermediaries – The German Perspective' (2012) International Review of Intellectual Property and Competition Law (IIC) 501.

498. OLG Hamburg, 29 September 2010, 5 U 9/09, see (2010) MMR-Aktuell 311084.

499. T Pihlajarinne, 'Setting the Limits for the Implied License in Copyright and Linking Discourse – The European Perspective' (2012) International Review of Intellectual Property and Competition Law (IIC) 700.

500. In 2005 however, the Munich court of appeal did impose *Störerhaftung* against a third party for linking to the website of a producer of new DVD-copying software. The freedom of the press was not found to be relevant in that case, as copyright was a permissible limitation to that right. See München OLG, 28 July 2005, 29 U 2887/05.

501. T Hoeren & V Bensinger, *Haftung im Internet – Die Neue Rechtslage* (De Gruyter 2014) 419.

further found that, in light of freedom of expression and of the freedom of the press, as protected by Article 5(1) of the *Grundgesetz*, a press enterprise is not obliged under particular circumstances to refrain from placing hyperlinks simply because it could not, following a reasonable examination, exclude the possibility that it was thereby assisting in a wrongful act. In that case of course, the company was not protected by the safe harbours, as it was not acting as an intermediary.[502]

Finally, other provisions of the German copyright act that can be used as sources of direct liability might also be listed: under Article 96 of the UrhG, illegally produced copies may not be distributed or used for the purposes of communication to the public. This provision could be directly applied to intermediaries handling infringing material. Additionally, according to Article 53, copies made under the private copying exception may not be distributed or communicated to the public – this again could create problems for intermediaries where users upload copies of protected works that they have obtained in this way.

3.3.2.2 Mittäter and Teilnehmer*: Participants, Instigators and Accessories*

Another potential basis for intermediary liability can be found in Article 830(1) of the BGB. This establishes that joint tortfeasors (in German, *Mittäter*) are to be held responsible for the loss they caused to the plaintiff. Article 830(1)II BGB applies the same rule of joint and several liability to cases where it cannot be established which of the multiple persons involved (known as *Teilnehmer* or *Beteiligte*) caused the damage. Joint tortfeasors in German law are persons who commit a wrong jointly, '*durch eine gemeinschaftlich begangene unerlaubte Handlung*'. The BGH confirms: '*Mittäterschaft erfordert eine gemeinschaftliche Begehung, also ein bewusstes und gewolltes Zusammenwirken*'.[503] This will be the case where the parties commit a breach of a joint duty or act in pursuance of a common design. The concept is therefore very close to the English understanding of joint tortfeasance.

As opposed to English law however, German joint tortfeasance does not stop here: under Article 830(2), instigators (*Anstifter*) or accessories (*Gehilfen*) (together: *Teilnehmer* or participants) are subject to the same liability scheme as joint tortfeasors. The definitions of 'instigator' and 'accessory' can be sourced from the criminal law.[504] Instigators are thus understood as being

502. Cf. CJEU, case C-291/13, *Papasavvas*, 11 September 2014.
503. BGH, *Automobil-Onlinebörse*, 22 June 2011, I ZR 159/10.
504. See Arts 25(2), 26 and 27 of the *Stefgesetzbuch (StGB)*, i.e., the German Criminal Code. This was confirmed in BGH, *Kinderhochstühle im Internet*, 22 July 2010, I ZR 139/08 and BGH, *Automobil-Onlinebörse*, 22 June 2011, I ZR 159/10.

persons who incite the decision to infringe, i.e., who 'intentionally induce someone else to intentional wrongful conduct'. Intentional assistance to wrongful conduct will brand one an accessory.[505]

The conduct of each of the *Mittäter* and *Teilnehmer* must be such as to meet all the conditions for the establishment of liability, with the exception of causation. The plaintiff is thus obliged to show only injury, wrongful and faulty conduct on the part of the principal and a causal connection between the two.[506] Accordingly, the very participation of the joint tortfeasor, instigator or accessory in the commission of the wrong serves as a substitute for causation.[507] The logic behind this solution rests on the idea that that joint tortfeasors, instigators and accessories will have all willed the damage. It is therefore fair to relieve the plaintiff from the difficulties that would accompany attempts to establish what will often be limited to what in Germany is called '*psychisch vermittlete Kausalität*' – 'psychological causation'. As a result, how significant the contribution of each such party was in causal terms becomes irrelevant: even mental participation in the form of planning the tortious act or facilitation will suffice.[508] At the same time, since the provision constitutes an exception to the principle according to which the plaintiff must prove a causal connection between the behaviour of the defendant and the damage occasioned, it has to be interpreted strictly.[509]

According to the jurisprudence of the BGH, joint tortfeasors must have knowingly and wilfully cooperated to bring about the inflicted loss. A necessary element of joint tortfeasance is therefore a shared intention between the co-authors (*gemeinschaftlicher Engschluss*). At least contingent intent (*bedingtem Vorsatz*) is necessary for this purpose, i.e., the participant must have seriously considered the risk of infringement and approvingly accepted it.[510] Knowledge of the objective circumstances that form the main offence and awareness of their unlawfulness are required.[511] In this way, the laxer causation requirement is replaced by a stricter standard for fault. This is in congruence with the widely accepted principle according to which the rules of causation are relaxed in cases of intentional harm. So, under German

505. J von Staudinger et al., *Kommentar zum Bürgelichen Gesetzbuch,*(15th ed., De Gruyter 2008) § 830; H Köhler & J Bornkamm, *Gesetz gegen den Unlauteren Wettbewerb* (30th ed., C.H. Beck 2012) Rn. 2.15.
506. W van Gerven et al., *Tort Law* (Hart Publishing 2000) 276.
507. W V H Rogers, 'Comparative Report on Multiple Tortfeasors' in W V H Rogers (ed.), *Unification of Tort Law: Multiple Tortfeasors* (Kluwer Law International 2004) 273.
508. B Markesinis, *The German Law of Torts* (3rd ed., Clarendon Press 1994) 906.
509. W van Gerven et al., *Tort Law* (Hart Publishing 2000) 445.
510. J Becher, 'Copyright and User-Generated Content: Legal Challenges for Community-Based Businesses in Germany and the USA' (Master's Thesis, Bucerius Law School/ WHU Otto Beisheim School of Management 2010).
511. BGH, *Halzband,* 11 March 2009, I ZR 114/06.

law, it is generally accepted that, when a defendant acted with intention, she is liable for all consequences – the principles of adequate causation do not apply to limit the reach of liability.[512]

Under Article 840 BGB, if more than one person is responsible for damage arising from a tort, they are jointly and severally liable (*Gesamtschuldner*) towards the victim. Article 840 BGB refers to the general regime of joint and several liability set out in Article 421 et seq BGB. This allows the plaintiff to pursue any of the multiple *Mittäter* for up to the full amount of damages due. Until the entire compensation has been paid, all defendants remain under an obligation to pay. As between the *Mittäter* themselves, Article 426 I BGB envisions equal contributions, unless otherwise provided.

Finally, it should be noted that where several persons have caused damage, the only case where it is correct to combine their spheres of responsibility and therefore make each responsible for the contribution to the harm made by the others is when the conditions of Article 830(1) BGB are met. If the defendants did not share any common purpose and the injurious result was brought about by the coincidental concurrence of separate tortious behaviours, they are considered *Nebentäter*, i.e., several concurrent tortfeasors. Their wrongful behaviours are in this case seen as constituting separate torts. The concurrence of these torts and the fact that they may coincide closely in time and space is not considered as justifying an apportionment which burdens each debtor with the contributions of the others. The issue is therefore not approached as one of multiple tortfeasors of a single tort, but of multiple causes of a single damage. Unlike *Mittäter*, *Nebentäter* do not receive express special treatment by the BGB. The plaintiff must therefore establish all conditions for liability, including causation, for all involved tortfeasors. If that is done, Article 840 BGB applies exactly as it would for *Mittäter* and the *Nebentäter* are held liable jointly and severally – like *Mittäter*, *Nebentäter* are also *Gesamtschuldner*.[513] The German legal system accordingly reproduces the same distinction between joint tortfeasors and several concurrent tortfeasors that was encountered above with regard to England.

The notion of *Nebentäter* is relevant in intermediary liability with regard to negligent participation in an infringement. As the scope of Article 830 BGH is limited to intentional wrongs, in cases of mere negligence (*Fahrlässigkeit*), the plaintiff is not spared the need to prove causation for all tortfeasors. Instead, such cases are dealt with in the same way as cases where there is a plurality of established causes (in German known as *Nebentäterschaft*) and are termed '*fahrlässige Nebentäterschaft*'.

512. W van Gerven et al., *Tort Law* (Hart Publishing 2000) 429.
513. W van Gerven et al., *Tort Law* (Hart Publishing 2000) 436.

3.3.2.3 Towards a Negligence-Based Accessory Liability

Could the rules on joint tortfeasors and accessories be applied to hold intermediaries liable for the copyright infringements committed by third parties using their services? The knowledge of the objective circumstances that form the main offence and awareness of their unlawfulness necessary to prove contingent intent are not usually met in such circumstances.[514] It should be mentioned however that in its early case law the old *Reichsgericht* took a broader view, under which a combination of a series of negligent actions was sufficient to trigger liability as a joint tortfeasor under Article 830(1) BGB, even in the absence of shared intent on the part of the co-authors.[515] Using this as a springboard, in a significant step, the German lower courts have attempted to extend negligence liability as a participant to cases of gross and insistent breach of the obligation to examine a notification of alleged infringements: thus, a defendant may also be held liable, if she consistently violates duties of care over a longer period of time.[516]

For example, such gross and insistent breaches of the obligation to examine have been accepted where service providers ignored specific notices of unlawful activities and failed to prevent further infringement.[517] So, in 2013, an online hosting provider which had received several notices of concrete infringements that it had, through the supply of storage facilities, made possible, but which had continuously and obstinately refused to react, was found by the OLG Hamburg to have pushed past the limits of mere *Störerhaftung* and branded itself a *Gehilfe* – an accessory. In this way, it had opened itself up to not only injunctive orders, but liability for monetary relief as well.[518] The persistent refusal to intervene by the provider in this case was key, as it indicated *Gehilfenvorsatz*, i.e., intent to act as an accessory to an infringement and thus opened up the possibility of liability *stricto sensu*.

---

514. See for example, BGH, *Internetversteigerung I,* 11 March 2004, I ZR 304/01, where the court stated that '*eine Tätigkeit als Teilnehmerin an der Markenverletzung der Anbieter scheidet aus, weil die hier allein in Betracht zu ziehende Gehilfenstellung zumindest einen bedingten Vorsatz voraussetzt, der das Bewusstsein der Rechtswidrigkeit einschließen muss*'. See also more recently OLG Hamburg, 1 July 2015, 5 U 87/12 and LG München, 30 June 2015, 33 O. 9639/14.
515. W van Gerven et al., *Tort Law* (Hart Publishing 2000) 431.
516. BGH, *Internetversteigerung I,* 11 March 2004, I ZR 304/01; J B Nordemann, 'Liability for Copyright Infringements on the Internet: Host Providers (Content Providers) – The German Approach' (2011) 2(1) Journal of Intellectual Property, Information Technology and Electronic Commerce Law (JIPITEC) 37.
517. OLG München, 11 January 2006, 21 O 2793/05.
518. OLG Hamburg, 13 May 2013, 5 W 41/13. Another example is offered by OLG München, 11 January 2006, 21 O 2793/05. See also O Löffel, 'Host-Provider Kann als Gehilfe Haften' (2013) GRUR-Prax 298 and A Dietz, 'Germany' in L Bently, P Geller & M Nimmer, *International Copyright Law and Practice* (Matthew Bender/LexisNexis 2013) § 8[1][c][i].

Other German courts have found online intermediaries liable where, regardless of the operator's knowledge, an infringement had to be expected[519] or where the operator had knowledge of repeated infringements in the past or persistently violated the inspection duties that this knowledge imposed.[520] This kind of conduct is considered to constitute *infringement by forbearance.*[521] The lines between this approach and *Störerhaftung* have not been discussed. As usual, the differentiation between the two can only be assessed on the basis of a case-by-case assessment. In any case, it is worth noting that, so far, this approach has not been confirmed by the BGH.[522]

The pursuit of infringement by forbearance by the lower German courts shows the way towards the possible development of a German tort-based accessory liability. This could be founded on the infringement of duties of care similar to those of *Störerhaftung,* but accompanied by contingent intent. A general duty of care to prevent all third party infringement of course cannot exist – however, where the intermediary ignores concrete indications of possible copyright infringement a relevant obligation could be established. The result would be what has been called *Täterhaftung wegen Verletzung der zumutbaren Prüftungspflichten als Verkehrssicherungspflichten* that results in an *objective Beihilfehandlung*[523] – a direct liability based on the violation of reasonable duties of care that amounts to facilitation. Commentators have argued in favour of such a construct, noting the similarity between the conditions for liability under the general provisions for the violation of duties of care (*Haftung wegen Verkehrspflichtverletzung*) and the conditions for *Störerhaftung.* Promisingly, in *Jugendgefährdende Medien bei eBay,* the BGH appeared to be moving in precisely this direction. Here, eBay was held liable for the violation of an independent, tort-based duty of care to prevent acts of unfair competition by its users.[524] In that case, the court found that the platform, having gained concrete knowledge of a specific violation by means of a notice, had to remove the disputed content and prevent similar violations from occurring in the future. If it did not, it would face liability as a *Täter.* Similarly, in *Halzband,*[525] an eBay account-holder was held liable for the tortious violation of a duty of care to prevent infringement by controlling access to his eBay account and protecting the confidentiality of his account information.[526]

519. OLG Köln, 26 September 2008, 6 U 111/08, MMR 2009, 197.
520. OLG Hamburg, 4 February 2008, 2-81/07, WRP 2008, 1569.
521. T Hoeren & S Yankova, 'The Liability of Internet Intermediaries – The German Perspective' (2012) International Review of Intellectual Property and Competition Law (IIC) 501.
522. F Hafenbrädl et al., ALAI Cantagena 2013, National Report for Germany.
523. A Wandtke, *Urheberrecht* (De Gruyter 2009) 288-289.
524. BGH, *Jugendgefährdende Medien bei eBay,* 12 July 2007, I ZR 18/04.
525. BGH, *Halzband,* 11 March 2009, I ZR 114/06.
526. *Halzband* also shows the broad range of people which might, under German law, be designated *Störer.*

What makes the prospect of a move in this direction particularly interesting is that the fact that the main difference between *Störerhaftung* and such a tort-based construct would be limited to the legal consequences: the first allows for monetary relief, while the second is limited to injunctions.[527] Commentators object to this differentiation as legally unaccountable. On this basis, it has been argued that *Störerhaftung* should be reintegrated into the codified tort law by being developed into a concept of tortious liability for the wilful facilitation of third party infringements.[528] As Gräbig explains, if that were to happen and *Störerhaftung* were to be replaced by an actual negligence-based *Täterhaftung,* the liability of current *Störer* would be transformed into a *Nebentäterschaft.*[529]

It is interesting to note that precisely such a tort-based approach to accessory liability exists within German patent law. This has been developed from the general tort rules of 823 et seq BGB by the Tenth Civil Senate of the *BGH*. According to Leistner, three conditions must be met for a finding of such an accessory liability for breach of a duty of care in patent law: a) the indirect infringer must have willingly[530] made an adequate causal contribution to the direct act of infringement; b) the prevention of the infringement must have been legally and practically possible; and c) negligence on the part of the indirect infringer in the form of a violation of a duty of care to prevent the infringement must be established.[531] Thus, a so-called *Doppelvorsatz* – double fault – is required: the facilitation of an third party's fault through, at

527. M Leistner, 'Common Principles of Secondary Liability?' in A Ohly (ed.), *Common Principles of European Intellectual Property Law* (Mohr Siebeck 2012) 128.

528. M Leistner, 'Common Principles of Secondary Liability?' in A Ohly (ed.), *Common Principles of European Intellectual Property Law* (Mohr Siebeck 2012) 128; G Spindler & M Leistner, 'Secondary Copyright Infringement – New Perspectives from Germany and Europe' (2006) 37(7) International Review of Intellectual Property and Competition Law (IIC) 788; M Leistner, 'Störerhaftung und mittelbare Schutzrechtsverletzung' (2010) GRUR-Beil 1; M Leistner, 'Von "Grundig-Reporter(n) zu Paperboy(s)": Entwicklungsperspektiven der Verantiwortlichkeit im Urheberrecht' (2006) GRUR 801; M Leistner & F Stang, 'Die Neuerung der Wettbewerbsrechtlichen Verkehrspflichten – Ein Siegeszug der Prüfpflichten?' (2008) WRP 533; J Gräbig, 'Akluelle Entwicklungen bei Haftung für[nbsp] mittelbare Rechtsverletzungen: Vom Störer zum Täter – ein neues einheitliches Haftungskonzept?' (2011) MMR 504; H Köhler, '"Täter" und "Störer" im Wettbewerbs-und Markenrecht: Zur BGH-Entscheidung "Jugendgefährdende Medien bei eBay"' (2008) GRUR 1; G Spindler & F Schuster (eds), *Recht der Electronischen Medien* (2nd ed., C.H.Beck 2011) § 1004 Rn. 10. But see also: H Ahrens, '21 Thesen zur Störerhaftung im UWG und im Recht des Geistiges Eigentums' (2007) WRP 1281.

529. J Gräbig, 'Akluelle Entwicklungen bei Haftung für[nbsp] mittelbare Rechtsverletzungen: Vom Störer zum Täter – ein neues einheitliches Haftungskonzept?' (2011) MMR 504;

530. This willingness does not impose a requirement of intention with regard to the infringing result, but merely with regard to the adequate and causal contribution to what in the even proved to be infringing.

531. M Leistner, 'Common Principles of Secondary Liability?' in A Ohly (ed.), *Common Principles of European Intellectual Property Law* (Mohr Siebeck 2012) 128. Section 10 of the German Patent Act (*Patentgesetz*) also establishes a statutory tort of indirect

least, negligence. Contingent intent (*dolus eventualis*) or actual knowledge on the part of the accessory are both sufficient.[532] Under this model, while the facilitation of infringement itself is not alone sufficient to establish liability, if it occurs through the breach of a legal duty, liability will follow. To determine whether a legal duty exists, all involved interests must be weighed against each another.[533] As a result, breach of duty and reasonableness become the guiding lights, indicating the border between accessory infringements and permitted neutral acts.[534] As soon as a breach of a duty of care has occurred, the behaviour of the accessory must be considered negligent and thus capable of triggering sanctions. The doctrine allows for all the legal consequences that accompany direct patent infringement, including both damages and injunctive relief – and all on the basis of the mere violation of a duty of care.

Leistner observes that, although in view of the conditions it relies on it could be supposed that the reach of doctrine would be wide, its relevance in practice has in fact been limited. He attributes this to several factors, including the need to respect the limitations placed on the exclusive rights of the patent-holder; the codification of the supply or offer of supply essential means by Article 10 of the *Patentgesetz*; the doctrine's limited practical relevance in the realm of patents, where larger commercial or technological infringements are more typical; and its sweeping legal consequences, which might serve to inhibit courts.

In any case, as its requirements reveal, accessory liability for breach of a duty of care in patent law functions almost identically to *Störerhaftung*. The main difference is that it allows for monetary compensation alongside injunctive relief. German commentators have noticed the similarity and calls for the reformulation of *Störerhaftung* into a facet of a single tortious liability for the infringement of a duty of care have been made. Notably, such a *Haftung wegen Verkehrspflichtverletzung* would be remarkably similar to the French *droit commun* construction under Article 1382 and 1383 of the C.civ.. It is worth mentioning that doubts have been expressed concerning the possible arbitrariness of a fault-based approach, but most commentators recognise the need for the flexibility this system allows.[535] Encouragingly,

---

parent infringement for the knowing or obvious supply or offer of supply for use to unauthorised persons of an essential element of the invention.

532. S Boos, 'Carrier's Liability for Patent Infringement under German Law' (2010) International Review of Intellectual Property and Competition Law (IIC) 428.
533. BGH, *Füllstoff,* 10 September 2009, Xa ZR 18/08.
534. S Boos, 'Carrier's Liability for Patent Infringement under German Law' (2010) International Review of Intellectual Property and Competition Law (IIC) 428.
535. S Boos, 'Carrier's Liability for Patent Infringement under German Law' (2010) International Review of Intellectual Property and Competition Law (IIC) 428; See also: M Leistner & F Stang, 'Die Neuerung der Wettbewerbsrechtlichen Verkehrspflichten – Ein Siegeszug der Prüfpflichten?' (2008) WRP 533.

recent jurisprudence of the BGH in the area of unfair competition has seen the emergence of precisely such a heading.[536]

Sadly, the expansion of this approach to copyright law seems unlikely in the near future. For the time being, the First Civil Senate of the *BGH*, which is in charge of matters related to copyright and trademarks, seems settled on separating itself from the tort-based analysis of the Tenth Civil Senate in patent matters and approaching questions of indirect liability through the *Störerhaftung* lens. Indeed, in *Jugendgefährdende Medien bei eBay,* the First Civil Senate explicitly stated that these new concepts of tortious contributory liability should be limited to the specific areas of competition law and personal account monitoring.[537]

3.3.3 Information Claims

Finally, as in the UK and France, Germany too allows for information claims against intermediaries. Article 101 UrhG is dedicated to the 'right to information' ('*Anspruch aus Ankunft*'). This was introduced on 1 September 2008 and has since been used extensively by right-holders. According to paragraph 2, in cases of manifest infringement or where the right-holder has brought a court action against the primary infringer, such a right shall exist against any person who, among other possibilities, was providing services used in infringing activities on a commercial scale. This clearly also encompasses internet intermediaries of various kinds. In such cases, the fundamental right to secrecy of communications of Article 10 of the *Grundgesetz* is limited. Under paragraph 3, the information that must be supplied would include the name and address of the users of the services.

Where the information can be provided only by using traffic data ('*Verkehrsdaten*') – e.g., in cases of dynamic IP addresses which are not consistently allocated to the same customer, but change with each internet session – a prior judicial order on the admissibility of the use of that data is first required, to be obtained according to a special procedure. Traffic data is defined as 'data that is collected, processed or used in the provision of a telecommunications service'.[538] The costs of the judicial order should be borne by the applicant, although he is then allowed to claim these from the direct infringer.

---

536. G Spindler & C Volkmann in G Spindler & F Schuster (eds), *Recht der Electronischen Medien* (3rd ed., C.H.Beck 2015) § 1004 Rn. 11-12; H Köhler & J Bornkamm, *Gesetz gegen den unlauteren Wettbewerb* (30th ed., C.H.Beck 2012) Rn 2.15-2.15b and 2.2-2.2d.
537. See also: BGH, *Sommer unseres Lebens,* 12 May 2010, I ZR 121/08 and M Leistner, 'Common Principles of Secondary Liability?' in A Ohly (ed.), *Common Principles of European Intellectual Property Law* (Mohr Siebeck 2012) 127.
538. Article 3, item 30 of the Telecommunications Act (*Telekommunikationsgesetz*).

The *BVerfG* has confirmed that only billing data and not data retained under the Data Retention Directive[539] may be used in response to an information claim.[540] Additionally, according to the dominant line of case law, information claims against ISPs are limited to infringements that occur on a commercial scale. What qualifies as 'commercial scale' however is a matter of some disagreement.[541]

As is usual, the right to information is always precluded where its assertion is disproportionate in the individual case.[542]

3.4 CONCLUSION: THREE VIEWS ON ACCESSORY LIABILITY

The elaborate country-by-country analysis engaged in above reveals three very different national European approaches to accessory copyright liability.

As the chapter makes clear, all three selected national systems have, as a first resort, experimented with intra-copyright solutions to intermediary accessory liability. This is most evident in England, where the courts' first instinct has been the resolution of cases of intermediary liability for third party copyright infringements through the CDPA-based doctrine of authorisation – yet, the original intention behind this concept was its limitation to those who 'grant or purport to grant to a third person the right to do' the restricted act. As a result, authorisation must often be stretched beyond its natural meaning if it is to be applied to cases of intermediary liability. French law has been less subtle yet. Lacking a special regime for accessory liability in copyright along the lines of the cascading system applicable in France to press crimes, the French courts have attempted instead to use the CPI provisions on primary copyright infringement so as to extract liability from intermediaries for infringements committed by others. For this purpose, they have attempted to interpret the notion of the 'provision of means to infringe' as indicative of a direct copyright infringement or even, depending on the

539. Directive 2006/24/EC of the European Parliament and of the Council of 15 March 2006 on the retention of data generated or processed in connection with the provision of publicly available electronic communications services or of public communications networks and amending Directive 2002/58/EC [2006] OJ L 105/54. It should be noted that that directive has now in any case been annulled by the CJEU in Case C-293/12, *Digital Rights Ireland and Seitlinger and Others*, 8 April 2014.

540. BVerfG, 2 March 2010, 1 BvR 256/08.

541. For more information see: A Wandtke, *Urheberrecht* (De Gruyter Recht 2009) 302-305; J B Nordemann, 'Internet Copyright Infringement: Remedies against Internet Intermediaries – the European Perspective on Host and Access Providers' (2012) 59(4) Journal of the Copyright Society of the USA 773; J B Nordemann, 'Intellectual Property Liability of Consumers, Facilitators and Intermediaries: the Position in Germany' in A Kamperman Sanders & C Heath, *Intellectual Property Liability of Consumers, Facilitators and Intermediaries* (Kluwer Law International 2012) 37.

542. Article 101(4) UrhG.

circumstances, suggest that intermediaries may 'occupy' foreign infringements, thus turning them into their own. This approach confuses primary and accessory liability by misidentifying the source of any potential liability of an intermediary for the infringements of third parties. It thus emphasises the need for stricter EU-level guidance on the differentiation between the two concepts. Finally, Germany, while also having experimented with a notion of 'adoption' of third party infringements reminiscent of the French intra-copyright approach, relies primarily on its distinctive *Störerhaftung* regime. This imposes liability on persons who causally contribute to an infringement in violation of a duty to review (*Prüfungspflicht*) incumbent upon them. While not, strictly speaking, limited to copyright (it notably also applies to unfair competition) and in fact finding its roots in property law, *Störerhaftung* has been most enthusiastically applied to this area, which remains it prime stronghold. However, the doctrine focuses only on injunctive relief, denying any monetary compensation to the plaintiff, while in addition, like authorisation and the French primary liability approach, *Störerhaftung* too has been overstretched by overenthusiastic courts at a loss for more appropriate ways to extract liability from providers they instinctively deem blameworthy.

In view of the lack of satisfactory accessory liability theories internal to copyright, all three selected systems have turned for an alternative way of tackling the legal questions raised by internet intermediation to their national tort law rules. The solutions thus supplied vary considerably. On the basis of the comparative analysis undertaken above, two basic national takes on accessory copyright liability can be identified. We can name these as follows: the 'single fault' or 'residual liability' model, favoured primarily by England, the 'multiple faults' or 'concurrent liability' model, favoured primarily by France. A brief summary of each is at this point appropriate:

(a) Residual Liability or Single Fault: the English System of Joint Tortfeasance

In view of the unsatisfactory applicability of authorisation to intermediary accessory copyright liability, the English courts are falling back onto the, doctrinally more convincing, principles of joint tortfeasance. The basic rule here is that the accessory should be held liable for any infringement committed jointly with another. This approach to accessory liability sees the accessory as participating in the wrongdoing of the main tortfeasor and therefore as liable, not for its acts of participation per se, but for that wrongdoing. In such cases therefore, we can talk of a 'residual liability' approach to accessory liability that identifies a 'single fault' for which both parties are equally liable. Recognised modes of participation in English law include the procurement or inducement of an infringement, as well as common design. Participation through facilitation is more controversial, having traditionally encountered strong resistance in English law. However, the UK Supreme Court's decision in *Sea Shepherd* seems to have brought this final barrier down, by clarifying that joint tortfeasance for facilitation is possible, as long as intent – i.e., 'common design' – is shown. While mere facilitation therefore remains incapable of resulting in joint tortfeasance, facilitation accompanied by intent is incorporated into the joint tortfeasance sub-category of common design.

(b) Concurrent Liability or Multiple Faults: the French System of Negligence Liability for the Acts of Others

In France, the approach is entirely different. French law recognises no hierarchy between the joint tortfeasors: one is not prime and the other accessory, only seen as participating in the tort of the other.[543] Instead, the indivisible damage caused by both is understood as resulting from *plusieurs faits générateurs.* Each involved party is thus considered to have committed its own *faute,* all of which are at the origin of the indivisible injury.[544] As opposed to the English 'residual liability' approach, this approach holds the accessory as liable for a separate, self-standing standard of conduct that prohibits acts of facilitation of the wrongdoing of another. In other words, the solution is essentially one of joint and several liability. In contrast to the English 'residual liability' approach, this interpretation of accessory liability can accordingly be identified as one of 'concurrent liability', that recognises the existence of 'multiple faults'. In order for an intermediary to be held liable under this scheme, it must satisfy the requirements of the Basic Rule of Articles 1382 and 1383 *C. civ.* – in other words, violate the traditional standard of the '*bon père de famille*'. Specifically for intermediary liability, this has been reworked into the standard of the '*prestataire diligent et avisé*'. Some debate has surrounded the development of the *diligences appropriées* that indicate when this standard has been violated. Generally speaking, it should be understood as resting on the identification of the duties that are considered reasonable, i.e., on a '*responsabilité de raison*'.

Where does Germany fit within this scheme? The theory of German tort law offers great range, encompassing tools that could enable the application of both the residual and the concurrent approaches to accessory liability. So, while Article 830 of the BGB incorporates a notion of joint tortfeasance, explicitly covering not only co-authors, but also instigators and facilitators, a negligence-based 'infringement by forbearance' is also conceivable. Yet, the second of these possibilities currently remains largely theoretical, while the first requires intent. Unhappy with the limits on accessory liability this

543. Quoted in C von Bar, *The Common European Law of Torts, Vol. I* (Clarendon Press 1998) para. 55.

544. P le Tourneau, *Droit de la responsabilité et des contrats – Régimes d'indemnisation* (9th ed., Dalloz 2013) 1738; C von Bar, E Clive, H Schulte-Nölke et al. (eds), *Principles, Definitions and Model Rules of European Private Law: Draft Common Frame of Reference (DCFR)*, prepared by the Study Group on a European Civil Code and the Research Group on EC private law (Acquis Group), Outline Edition (Sellier 2009) 3447.

imposes, but unwilling to put their negligence law into action, German courts continue to rely primarily on *Störerhaftung*. To the consternation of commentators, this remains very badly integrated into general tort law.

On the basis of these differing theoretical approaches to accessory liability, it is easy to conclude that the three national systems of intermediary liability for third party copyright infringements are fundamentally incompatible. Nevertheless, amid all the confusion of disparate doctrines evolving in parallel, points of convergence are not hard to identify.

In this regard, it is first worth noting that the differences between the two main approaches of residual and concurrent liability are not, upon close examination, as dissimilar as they might at first sight appear. Indeed, the main divergences can be identified between the two approaches are only two: the positioning of the liability within the overall scheme of tort law and the applicable culpability standard. The first issue being a question of doctrine, from a practical perspective it is only the second that has great relevance: while under the 'residual liability' approach, intent is required before an accessory can be shown to have implicated itself sufficiently into the wrong in question, the 'concurrent liability' model allows for a negligence-based liability, as demonstrated through the violation of duties of care. Moreover, notably, both England and France are showing signs of experimentation with the other's point of view: while in France the intra-copyright '*fonction active*' approach wanders close to the logic that supports joint tortfeasance, in England, calls for the integration of accessory liability within the tort of negligence are not unheard-of. Indeed, the English courts themselves have been known to establish liability for 'authorisation' on the back of what amounts to a failure to abide by identified duties of care, thus striving, through the tools available to them, to impose what in essence constitutes a liability for negligence on intermediaries.

Other signs of conversion between the three systems can also be discerned. Most prominently, all three selected jurisdictions appear to be attempting a division of intermediaries into two basic categories: 'innocent' providers that are not involved in the third party infringement and 'guilty' ones that are. This desire for a differentiation reveals a preoccupation with the intermediary's state of mind: in accessory liability, where the material act of infringement is committed by a third party, while the intermediary's culpability is indicated by its mental connection to the infringement, the strict liability rule applicable in copyright to primary liability reaches its limits. In France, if it weren't for the inconvenient jurisprudence of the *Cour de cassation,* this would be easily dealt with, as the fundamental delictual principle of extra-contractual liability for civil offences applies directly, placing fault at centre stage. In this way, 'direct' infringement by means of the CPI norms could be reserved for intentional accessories, while negligent intermediaries could be dealt with only through the rules of the C.civ.. England has had the opposite problem: the mental participation link in both authorisation and joint tortfeasance is much more strictly delineated in

English law, leading judges to an impasse, as they struggle to reconcile their instinctive conviction of the blameworthiness of certain service providers with the rigid standards of their national law. The CDPA's provisions on the knowledge-based notion of secondary liability would offer a potential solution, however they are not at the moment worded so as to allow for their application to the online environment. Finally, Germany seems, in this regard too, to have placed itself on the intersection between the two systems: although the fault-free theories of disturber liability have dominated the discussion in recent decades, the adoption of infringing content can establish direct intermediary liability for unlawful content, while, alternatively, dereliction of duties of care, whether in the context of *Störerhaftung* or *Täterhaftung,* can also substantiate liability. At the end of the day, although their courts might disagree about (or be completely unclear on) where the normative basis for such requirements might lie, all three jurisdictions seem to be, at the very least, leaning towards including some kind of mental element as a requirement for liability for monetary compensation. Promisingly, this tendency towards a culpability-based bifurcation clearly mirrors the similar inclination of the EU legislator, already noted in Chapter 2, to distinguish between 'neutral' and 'non-neutral' intermediaries.[545]

In addition to the above, common areas of uncertainty with regard to the interpretation of the relevant EU provisions can also be discerned in the national case law. The most obvious of these relates to the proper interpretation of the European provisions on the scope of obligations that can be imposed on intermediaries for the enforcement of copyright. Most conspicuously, in all three examined European countries, domestic courts have been toying with the idea of demanding, not only the take-down by intermediaries of notified infringing material, but also of targeted monitoring intended to prevent future infringement: in France, due diligence considerations ballooned into a notice-and-stay-down regime that had to be curtailed by Supreme Court intervention. In Germany, the notoriously vague *Störerhaftung* has led courts to stray in the same direction. And even England has experimented, to a much more limited degree, with similar ideas, by inserting them into its authorisation doctrine. These expansive interpretations clearly push the boundaries of European fundamental rights law. They thus require EU guidance, if they are to be cut back down to size.

Finally, the EU requirements for injunctive relief have also inspired comparable musings across national borders. Through the doctrine of

545. See s. 2.2.1. Nor are European jurisdictions alone is this desire. It is worth noting, for example, that a similar division is encountered in US law through the introduction of the 'inducement' rule an inducement rule with its 2005 Supreme Court *Grokster* case. See *MGM Studios, Inc. v. Grokster, Ltd.*, 545 U.S. 913 (2005). For further analysis of the evolution of US law in this regard see AYen '*Sony,* Tort Doctrines, and the Puzzle of Peer-to-Peer' (2005) 55 Case Western Law Review, 815 and A Yen 'Third Party Copyright after Grokster' (2007) 16(3) Information & Communications Technology Law 233.

Störerhaftung, the German courts have had the greatest ease with implementing Article 8(3) of the Copyright Directive into national law: liability for damages is rarely acknowledged by the German courts, while all parties involved in a wrongdoing can be subjected to an injunction, without any need to establish participation in the commission of the tort. England and France have, on the other hand, both had to resort to the introduction of special provisions to their intellectual property acts to achieve the same effect. At the same time, perhaps precisely due to this need to start from scratch, in comparison with their German counterparts, the courts of these two countries have had the greater success with injecting the necessary proportionality into their respective regimes. Tellingly, in recent years, the national courts' concern, in both countries, for the proper representation of end-users' interests in such processes has been increasing, as has their attention to the proper confinement of relevant orders through appropriate time limits, due regard for the question of effectiveness and a refusal to allow plaintiffs to add new websites to existing blocking orders. The German courts seem to be having greater difficulty in this regard, with German analyses of proportionality taken to extremes that both deny the application of *Störerhaftung* to access providers and impose an exceptionally strict interpretation of the doctrine onto hosts. Even here however, recent BGH rulings would seem to suggest that, under the guidance of CJEU case law, discrepancies may be beginning to iron themselves out.

The re-occurrence of similar patterns across European borders is unsurprising in view of the negative, round-about nature of the E-Commerce special liability regime and the terse demands of 8(3) of the Copyright Directive: the current EU framework on intermediary liability and the CJEU case law that accompanies it have set the tone for the discussion of intermediary liability in Europe, but have failed to provide real answers. Instead, national courts have been left struggling to fit the EU's hints as to the correct solution ('control', 'knowledge', 'neutrality', 'duties of care', 'general monitoring', 'fair balance', 'proportionality') into their heterogeneous home-grown regimes. This problem is exacerbated by the lack of well-founded, systematic national theories on the issue: in all three examined states, accessory liability remains a difficult, under-analysed area of private law, only recently brought to real prominence by the emergence of widespread internet intermediation. Absent well-structured existing solutions, judges and legal practitioners are left to rely on their personal intuitive sense of justice in the application of very general norms to a very specific problem. The result is doctrinal tension, legal uncertainty and conflicting, only sluggishly maturing, interpretations by courts even within individual Member States. Not only does this approach not make for good harmonisation, but it also undermines coherence on the national level. Ultimately, the first steps towards the European harmonisation of intermediary liability have perhaps, counter-intuitively and counter-productively, contributed towards the very confusion that now necessitates further intervention. In this situation, a definitive answer to AG Jääskinen suggestion as to the nature of the safe harbours is impossible: are they exceptions or clarifications? Without a sounder understanding of the substantive rules it is impossible to say.

How can proper structure be returned to the process? The next chapter shall delve into the underlying tort law norms that have determined the national responses to accessory liability, in order to reveal the right way forward towards a well-founded and well-rounded substantive European regime for intermediary accessory copyright liability.

Chapter 4

Back to the Basics: The Elements of a European Accessory Liability

In the previous chapter a country-by-country analysis of the accessory copyright liability regimes applicable to internet intermediaries in the three EU jurisdictions of England, France and Germany was undertaken. Each national system was traced back to the underlying general tort rules that guide it: intermediary liability for third party copyright was thus revealed as a sub-category of the broader concept of accessory tortious liability.

As the analysis indicated, each national system approaches this connection a different manner: England prefers a model of 'residual liability' or 'single fault', wherein accessory liability is seen as a form of 'joint tortfeasance' and accessories are treated as primary tortfeasors. France prefers a 'concurrent liability' or 'multiple faults' approach, under which accessories are held liable not for participating in the infringement as such, but for violating the general standard of conduct that requires all legal subjects to avoid causing others harm. Here, accessory liability essentially amounts to negligence liability for the acts of another. Germany adopts a system both in-between the other two and divergent from both: theoretically the provisions of the German BGB on extra-contractual liability equip the German legal system with general tort rules that would allow it both to treat intentional accessories as joint tortfeasors (along the English example) and to apply a general duty of care to avoid causing another harm (along the French example). At same time, a distinct preference is shown by the German legislator for the first option. In order to overcome the exclusion of accessory liability in negligence that this implies, the German courts have mainly dealt with accessory copyright liability by developing the distinctive *Störerhaftung* regime, which focuses only on injunctive relief.

While the different general tort rules on accessory liability explain the differences between the national approaches to the liability of intermediaries in third party copyright, what explains the differences between those general rules? As Norrgård observes, true harmonisation can only be achieved through a thorough understanding of the national legal traditions in which divergences are grounded.[1] The construction of a European intermediary accessory liability regime for copyright therefore requires the comparative academic analysis of the reasons that push the different countries toward their different solutions: why does France opt for a negligence-based solution and what gave rise to the English notion of joint tortfeasance? What dissuaded each of these countries from applying the system used in the other? Why has Germany eschewed both in favour of a special nuisance-inspired regime? This chapter shall seek to answer these questions by positioning the national rules on accessory liability within the national tort structures that dictate their configuration. Through the resultant deconstruction, the roots of the national divergences can be uncovered, thus enabling the identification of the areas in which harmonisation is necessary.

The ultimate objective shall be the construction of a common European route to the regulation of accessory liability: a bridge over the gaps that separate the Member States. This shall eventually be crossed in the next chapter in the pursuit of the creation of an intermediary liability for accessory copyright infringement. In this way, the emergent European regime for intermediary accessory copyright liability shall be grounded on a strong theoretical framework: as they say, there is nothing more practical than good theory.

Of course, the lack of a common European tort law mindset will inevitably raise obstacles to this exercise. At the same time, the harmonisation of all of European tort law is clearly beyond the scope of this book. To address this problem, the output of two major recent academic projects focused on building a unified European system of tort law shall be heavily relied on to supply the necessary harmonisation 'glue':

(a) The PETL [2] developed by the EGTL (formerly also called the 'Tilburg Group').[3]

1. M Norrgård, 'The European Principles of IP Enforcement: Harmonisation through Communication?' in A Ohly, *Common Principles of European Intellectual Property Law* (Mohr Siebeck 2012) 203.
2. Available at: www.egtl.org. See also, European Group on Tort Law, *Principles of European Tort Law – Text and Commentary* (Springer 2005).
3. For more information see the website of the EGTL at: www.egtl.org.

(b) Book VI on 'Non-contractual liability arising out of damage caused to another' of the DCFR[4] compiled by the Study Group on a European Civil Code and the Research Group on Existing EC Private Law (Acquis Group).[5]

Although neither of these projects is currently formally enacted as an official European tort code,[6] they both nevertheless have all the characteristics in a substantive sense of a restatement of the common core of the national tort laws of Europe, as well as of the existing *acquis communaitaire* in that area, such that they can serve as normative models of what a truly European tort law *would be*. As a result, they constitute prima facie authoritative sources on that topic.[7] The EGTL explains:

> we propose to address the fundamental questions underlying every tort law system […] we shall aim at identifying these principles, thus searching for a common law of Europe, without the necessity yet to lay these principles down in formal legal texts, such as a European civil code.[8]

The Introduction to the DCFR expresses a similar sentiment:

> The CFR project is not an attempt to create a single law of the whole of Europe. Rather, the purpose of the CFR as a legislator's guide or toolbox

4. C von Bar et al. (eds), *Principles, Definitions and Model Rules of European Private Law: Draft Common Frame of Reference (DCFR)*, prepared by the Study Group on a European Civil Code and the Research Group on EC private law (Acquis Group), Outline Edition (Sellier 2009).
5. For more information the website of the Study Group at: www.sgecc.net.
6. It should be noted that, as opposed to the PETL, which is an entirely academic undertaking (see B A Koch, 'The "European Group on Tort Law" and its "Principles of European Tort Law"' (2005) 53 American Journal of Comparative Law 189), the initiative behind the DCFR came from the European Commission, which commissioned the project with a view to implementing its 2003 Action Plan on European contract law. On this see, Communication from the Commission to the Council and the European Parliament on European Contract Law, COM(2001) 398 final, Brussels, 11 July 2001; Communication from the Commission to the European Parliament and the Council, 'A More Coherent European Contract Law – An Action Plan', COM(2003) 68 final, Brussels, 12 February 2003; Communication from the Commission to the European Parliament and the Council, 'European Contract Law and the Revision of the Acquis – The Way Forward', COM(2004) 651 final, Brussels, 11 October 2004). It should be noted that these initiates have focused on the development of European contract law and consider tort law only incidentally. The European Parliament has extrapolated from these plans to envision a true European Civil Code and call for greater political input in its creation, see European Parliament, 'Resolution of 23 March 2006 on European Contract Law and the Revision of the *Acquis*: The Way Forward', (2005/2022(INI)), Brussels 23 March 2006, [2006] OJ C 292 E, 109.
7. M W Hesselink, 'The Common Frame of Reference as a Source of European Private Law' (2009) 83(4) Tulane Law Review 919.
8. See European Group on Tort Law, 'Principles of European Tort Law – A Harmonization Project', available at: http://civil.udg.edu/php//index.php?id=126.

is to enable the meaning of European legislation to be clear to people from diverse legal backgrounds.[9]

In this book, it is precisely as such 'toolboxes' for better law-making that both the DCFR and the PETL shall be employed: important reference points that can aid mutual understanding between the diverse legal systems of the EU and guide a holistic development of European tort legislation, in this case specifically in the sub-section of a European intermediary accessory copyright liability.[10] In other words, the prototypical codifications of the PETL and the DCFR shall be here used as the backbone of the unification exercise, sourcing European definitions for the constituent elements of intermediary accessory copyright liability and positioning those notions within a common European structure.

Of course, it should be noted that both the DCFR and the PETL have been criticised in terms of their quality[11] and effectiveness,[12] as well as pie-in-the-sky projects that deny the essential plurality of the divergent European tort systems[13] and are, moreover, deprived of sufficient democratic legitimacy.[14] In this regard, their lack of formal recognition, if anything, is an advantage: the approach taken in both projects is one of soft, not hard

9. C von Bar et al. (eds), *Principles, Definitions and Model Rules of European Private Law: Draft Common Frame of Reference (DCFR)*, prepared by the Study Group on a European Civil Code and the Research Group on EC private law (Acquis Group), Outline Edition (Sellier 2009) 16.
10. See House of Lords, European Union Committee, 'European Contract Law: The Draft Common Frame of Reference – Report with Evidence', 12th Report of Session 2008-2009, HL Paper 95 (The Stationary Office Limited, London 2009), 5 as quoted in M W Hesselink, 'A Toolbox for European Judges' (2011) 17(4) European Law Journal 441.
11. N Jansen, 'The Authority of an Academic "Draft Common Frame of Reference"' in H-W Micklitz & F Cafaggi (eds), *European Private Law after the Common Frame of Reference* (Edward Elgar 2010) 147. For a response see, M W Hesselink, 'The Common Frame of Reference as a Source of European Private Law' (2009) 83(4) Tulane Law Review 919.
12. E.g., J M Smits, 'European Private Law: A Plea for a Spontaneous Legal Order' in D M Curtin & J M Smits, European Integration and Law (Intersentia 2006) 55.
13. See for example, P Legrand, 'The Impossibility of Legal Transplants' (1997) 4 *Maastricht Journal of European and Comparative Law* 111; P Legrand, 'Antivonbar' (2005) 1 Journal of Comparative Law 13 or (from a far less reactionary perspective) J M Smits, 'Plurality of Sources in European Private Law, or: How to Live with Legal Diversity?' in R Brownsword, H-W Micklitz, L Niglia & S Weatherill (eds.), *The Foundations of European Private Law* (Hart Publishing 2011) 323.
14. See also, Y Laquette, 'Quelques remarques a propos du projet de code civil europeen de M. von Bar' (2002) Dalloz 2202. See also, P Giliker, 'The Draft Common Frame of Reference and European Contract Law: Moving from the "Academic" to the "Political"' in J Devenney & M B Kenny, *The Transformation of European Private Law: Harmonisation, Consolidation, Codification or Chaos?* (Cambridge University Press 2013) 23. For a discussion of this issue see, J M Smits, 'Democracy and (European) Private Law: A Functional Approach' (2009) 5 European Journal of Legal Studies 26.

harmonisation[15] that aims at a convergence, not *ratione imperii,* but *imperio rationis.*[16] In this way, they allow for what Zimmermann calls an 'organically progressive' process of Europeanisation to be pursued.[17] Accordingly, while in this book the DCFR and the PETL shall be used as sources of inspiration in the search for European answers, they shall not be treated as binding, but shall instead be integrated directly into the flexible 'better law' comparative exercise applied.[18] Additionally, the provisions of the two model codes shall be further fleshed out by reference to the accompanying analyses by their respective drafters.[19] Certain key academic works on European tort law, in particular those of Von Bar,[20] Van Dam,[21] Van Gerven, Lever and Larouche[22] and Markesinis and Lawson[23] shall supplementarily be relied on.

Ultimately, the direct appeal to European tort law shall serve to imbue the analysis with much-needed coherence: if a European harmonisation of intermediary accessory liability is to be attempted, it is suggested that that should be done in a systematic manner that would allow for its seamless integration into a future hypothetical European tort code. Notably, this approach runs counter to the usual tactic of EU legislators, which has instead rested on the assumption that it is possible to divide tort law into a core of general rules and a 'special part' that deals with diverse narrowly defined subject matter and harmonise only the latter.[24] It is suggested, however, that

---

15. G Wagner, 'The Project of Harmonizing European Tort Law' (2005) 42 Common Market Law Review 1269.
16. M W Hesselink, 'The Common Frame of Reference as a Source of European Private Law' (2009) 83(4) Tulane Law Review 919; S Weatherill, 'Can There Be a Common Interpretation of European Private Law?' (2002) 31(1) Georgia Journal of International and Comparative Law 139; M Infantino, 'Making European Tort Law: the Game and its Players' (2010) 18(1) Cardozo Journal of International & Comparative Law 45.
17. R Zimmermann, 'The Civil Law in European Codes' in D Carey Miller & R Zimmermann (eds.), *The Civilian Tradition and Scots Law* (Duncker & Humblot, Berlin 1997) 293, as quoted in J M Smits, 'Rethinking Methods in European Private Law' in M Adams & J Bomhoff (eds), *Practice and Theory in Comparative Law*, (Cambridge University Press 2012) 170.
18. See the methodology applied in this book above in Ch. 1, s. 1.6.1.
19. For the PETL see, European Group on Tort Law, *Principles of European Tort Law – Text and Commentary* (Springer 2005), as well as the various other publications of the EGTL on the unification of tort law (full list available at: http://civil.udg.edu/php//index.php?id=133). For the DCFR, see C von Bar et al. (eds), *Principles, Definitions and Model Rules of European Private Law: Draft Common Frame of Reference (DCFR)*, prepared by the Study Group on a European Civil Code and the Research Group on EC private law (Acquis Group), Outline Edition (Sellier 2009).
20. C von Bar, *The Common European Law of Torts – Vol. II* (Clarendon Press 2000).
21. C van Dam, *European Tort Law* (2nd ed., Oxford University Press 2013).
22. W van Gerven et al., *Tort Law* (Hart Publishing 2000).
23. F H Lawson & B Markesinis, *Tortious Liability for Unintentional Harm in the Common Law and the Civil Law* (Cambridge University Press 1982).
24. M Infantino, 'Making European Tort Law: The Game and Its Players' (2010) 18 Cardozo Journal of International & Comparative Law 45; C van Dam, *European Tort Law* (2nd ed., Oxford University Press 2013) para. 610-5.

such selective harmonisation is not conducive to sound legal theory. It instead results in what has been termed by Koziol a 'double shattering of the law': on the one hand national legal systems are infiltrated with foreign provisions and, on the other, no internal consistency is ensured between the EU directives and regulations that comprise existing EU tort legislation.[25] A solution integrated into a strong theory of European tort law would overcome these problems and return coherence to the process of harmonisation.

Arguably, such a systematic approach is particularly appropriate in the area of intermediary accessory copyright liability, which, as shown above, suffers from a troubling under-theorisation even at the national level. A re-grounding of accessory liability in tort law theory is thus necessary at the very least in the three national jurisdictions examined in this book. While this might more efficiently be achieved simultaneously across the board of EU Member States through a single smooth move, the comparative analysis that a European perspective would bring to the area can also serve as a source of inspiration for the improvement of the individual national doctrines. Thus, by re-contextualising accessory copyright liability within general European tort law, a clearer picture of the confines within which it must operate and the options that exist therein can emerge, all on the basis of a strong theoretical foundation.

How do the general national rules of tort law relate to their corresponding regimes on intermediary accessory copyright liability? Before beginning the analysis, it is first necessary to examine the fundaments of European liability in tort.

4.1 A EUROPEAN FAULT LIABILITY

Roughly speaking, tortious liability can be divided into three main areas: fault liability, vicarious liability and strict liability.[26] The area of tort law that interests us here is that of fault liability: as stated in Chapter 1, accessory liability is defined as fault liability for the acts of others.[27] Fault liability

25. H Koziol, 'Comparative Conclusions' in H Koziol, *Basic Questions of Tort Law from a Comparative Perspective* (Jan Sramek Verlag 2015) 690.
26. See European Group on Tort Law, *Principles of European Tort Law – Text and Commentary* (Springer 2005) 70, referring to Art. 1:101(1) PETL that lists three main 'grounds of accountability': conduct constituting fault, an abnormally dangerous activity and the conduct of an auxiliary. See also W van Gerven, J Lever & P Larouche, *Tort Law* (Hart Publishing 2000) Chs 3, 5 and 6.
27. See s. 1.4.1. The other two main headings of tort liability – vicarious liability and strict liability – may of course occasionally be applied to determine questions of third party copyright liability. Vicarious liability concerns liability for the conduct of another that is founded on the defendant's relationship to that other (see W van Gerven, J Lever & P Larouche, *Tort Law* (Hart Publishing 2000) 467. See also P Giliker, 'Vicarious Liability or Liability for the Acts of Others in Tort: A Comparative Perspective' (2011) 2(1) Journal of European Tort Law 31). Common relationships that substantiate vicarious liability in

(sometimes also called 'Aquilian liability' after the Roman *Lex Aquilia*, which provided compensation to the owners of property injured by another person's fault) is the simplest and most classical form of tort liability. By and large, it holds a sovereign position among the possible attributive causes of liability, with the other two alternatives seen as exceptions to its rule: for much of tort law's history, the commonly held view was that 'all fault entails liability, but also that there is no liability without fault'.[28] Despite the recent rise of strict liability in certain areas of tort law, fault is still considered the 'cornerstone', 'core' and 'principal rule' of tort,[29] the 'fundamental and in a certain sense socially and ethically pre-eminent principle of responsibility' – as Van Dam puts it, the '*prima donna* of tort'.[30]

4.1.1 Defining Fault Liability

What is fault liability? The heading takes its name from its most prominent condition: fault, the criterion of imputation that is necessary to make a person accountable for the consequences of their own conduct. The condition of fault is what separates fault liability from strict or vicarious liability, which employ the creation of a source of danger and the relationship of the defendant with the tortfeasor respectively as criteria of imputation. Traditionally, fault in Europe was understood in a purely subjective way as conduct for which one can be personally blamed. This interpretation is however now visibly on the retreat: during the twentieth century, in response to the rise in the use of machinery and the uptake of insurance, the equation of fault with blameworthiness lost ground in modern Western tort systems.

European tort law are those between employer and employee, principle and agent or parent and child (see C van Dam, *European Tort Law* (Oxford University Press 2007) para. 105-4. See also Arts 6:101-6:102 PETL and Arts VI.-3:104-3:201 DCFR). Strict liability is liability that is not based on conduct at all, whether of the defendant or a third party for which the defendant is responsible, instead resulting solely from the existence of a damage and a free-standing obligation to compensate the victim (W van Gerven, J Lever & P Larouche, *Tort Law* (Hart Publishing 2000) 537). Examples of areas in which strict liability is generally considered justified include liability for defective products, traffic accidents and environmental liability (see also Arts 5:101-5:102 PETL and Arts VI.-3:202-3:207 DCFR). As a general rule, a user of the services provided by an internet intermediary cannot accurately be described as connected to the intermediary in a relationship that might give rise to vicarious liability. Vicarious liability is therefore irrelevant to the issue of intermediary liability. Likewise, strict liability is inappropriate: no current rule exists in an EU member state or at the EU level that imposes strict liability on intermediaries for the copyright infringements of their users.

28. See B Markesinis and Deakin as quoted in W van Gerven, J Lever & P Larouche, *Tort Law* (Hart Publishing 2000) 280, note 5.
29. European Group on Tort Law, *Principles of European Tort Law – Text and Commentary* (Springer 2005) 64; P Widmer, 'Comparative Report on Fault as a Basis of Liability and Criterion of Imputation (Attribution)' in P Widmer (ed.), *Unification of Tort Law: Fault* (Kluwer Law International 2005) 332.
30. C van Dam, *European Tort Law* (2nd ed., Oxford University Press 2013) para. 801.

Fault liability has instead embarked on a process of *objectivisation,* wherein the individual's conduct is measured against that which society expects of her.[31] As a result, fault is now seen as encompassing any conduct unacceptable in society, regardless of the personal culpability that can be lain at the tortfeasor's door.

It is worth noting that the term 'fault liability' is somewhat controversial among European tort scholars. Von Bar, for example, prefers to call the concept 'liability for misconduct', arguing that 'fault' is incompatible with an objective appreciation of conduct. Under this labelling scheme, strict liability is designated 'liability without misconduct'.[32] Similarly, Van Gerven, Level and Larouche talk of 'liability for one's own conduct', which they contrast to 'liability for the conduct of others' and 'liability without conduct'.[33] The argument here is that 'fault' is too risky a term, as there is no general European agreement on its definition.[34] However, this objection need not concern the present analysis: this book shall stick to the term 'fault', as that is the one used in the PETL.[35] This allows it to sidestep controversy, by simply relying on the interpretation of that term as given in that project. The term also accords as well as of the binary notion of 'intent and negligence' referenced in the DCFR, which clearly is intended to amount to what might, indeed, collectively be termed 'fault'.[36]

31. W van Gerven et al., *Tort Law* (Hart Publishing 2000) 279.
32. C von Bar, *The Common European Law of Torts – Vol. II* (Clarendon Press 2000) paras 179 and 231.
33. W van Gerven, et al., *Tort Law* (Hart Publishing 2000) Chs 3, 5 and 6.
34. C von Bar, *The Common European Law of Torts – Vol. II* (Clarendon Press 2000) paras 226-227 and 231. Von Bar himself seems to interpret 'fault' as a blameworthiness or culpability. In this is was no doubt influenced by the German term '*Verschulden'*. Although often translated as 'fault', this usually receives a much more limited interpretation that sees it merely as a defective will: blameworthiness or culpability. Koziol agrees, suggesting that 'according to the basic principles fault is assessed according to a subjective yardstick': H Koziol, *Basic Questions of Tort Law from a Germanic Perspective* (Jan Sramek Verlag, Vienna 2012) 176; see also H Koziol, 'Austria: Wrongfulness under Austrian Law' in H Koziol (ed.) *Unification of Tort Law: Wrongfulness* (Kluwer Law International 1998) 11.
35. Under this approach fault will be viewed as synonymous to wrongfulness, i.e., as a combination of unlawfulness and culpability following the French unitary example. German tort scholars' propensity for precision is admirable, but not well-calculated to ease the way of EU tort harmonisation. For this a more flexible framework that can be more easily compatible with all local peculiarities is preferable.
36. The DCFR avoids the issue altogether, by opting for a unitary approach that concentrates simply on the general notion of 'non-contractual liability'. A condition for this is identified in what is broadly termed 'accountability'. This is then divided into 'intentional and negligence' and 'accountability without intention or negligence', a term that refers to vicarious and strict liability. From a technical perspective, this is probably the clearest and most accurate division of the relevant concepts, but suffers from a pronounced chunkiness of terminology. Given that this book does not aim at the harmonisation of all of European tort law, but only a corner of it that is not significantly impacted by this terminological debate, less accuracy in the name of a more natural wording can be tolerated.

4.1.2 The Conditions of Fault Liability

What are the conditions of fault liability? The basic building blocks differ from country to country. Of the three jurisdictions examined here, France keeps things the simplest – only three conditions are demanded by Articles 1382 and 1383 of the French C.civ.:

(a) *faute*;
(b) *causation;* and
(c) *dommage.*[37]

The English law of negligence adds one more requirement to the mix:

(a) duty of care;
(b) breach of that duty of care;
(c) causation; and
(d) damage.[38]

Finally, Germany's Articles 823 and 826 BGB go all out, demanding that no less than five basic conditions be met:

(a) the violation of a codified normative rule (*Tatbestandswidrigkeit*);
(b) unlawfulness (*Rechtswidrigkeit*);
(c) blameworthiness (*Verschulden*);
(d) causation (*Kausalität*); and
(e) damage (*Schaden*).[39]

How do these systems differ from each other? As is apparent, causation and the existence of a legally relevant damage are common to all three. The divergence lies instead in the number of factors into which each breaks down the central requirement of fault liability: the notion of a fault. France has a unitary notion of fault (*faute*), English law splits fault into duty of care and breach and German law prefers a three-pronged approach. The disparity can be explained by the extent to which each legal system is happy to let fault self-define: while France is content to let *faute* be *faute*, England and Germany feel the need to control against its overexpansion. To this end, in England a fault is defined as a breach of duty, requisitioning the additional identification of a specific duty of care as a formal requirement limiting the permissible breadth of such breaches. Germany deconstructs fault further into three constitutive elements, those of unlawfulness, blameworthiness and

37. P le Tourneau, *Droit de la responsabilité et des contracts – Régimes d'indemnisation* (9th ed., Dalloz 2013) 1301; C van Dam, *European Tort Law* (2nd ed., Oxford University Press 2013) para. 301-2.
38. N McBride & R Bagshaw, *Tort Law* (4th ed., Pearson 2012) 92 et seq; W van Gerven, et al., *Tort Law* (Hart Publishing 2000) 44-45; W V H Rogers, *Winfield & Jolowicz on Tort* (18th ed., Sweet & Maxwell 2010) 150.
39. C van Dam, *European Tort Law* (2nd ed., Oxford University Press 2013) para. 402-1.

the violation of a codified normative rule, all of which must be established before a fault can be found.

Although at first glance this might give the impression that a finding of liability will be easier under French fault liability than in the English law of negligence and that both of these systems will set up a less demanding standard than Germany, practice does not confirm this hypothesis.[40] Instead, in all three systems, the basic requirement for fault liability is, properly understood, only one: the existence of a fault. The difference between them lies merely in how explicit each system chooses to be about the component elements of this notion and in particular the mechanisms which restrain it.

The roots of the discrepancy can be found in the difference between the underlying theories grounding the three systems, those of casuistry and conceptualism. While casuistic systems favour an exhaustive, but necessarily incomplete list of possible faults, conceptualist ones meet the vagueness of reality head-on. So, France opts for the conceptualist route that begins with the very vague general rules of Article 1382 and 1383 and leaves it to the courts to set the limits. English and German tort law follow a casuistic approach instead, which prefers limiting the scope of fault liability *ex ante,* by identifying conditions that must be met before it can be considered. The International Encyclopaedia of Comparative Law breaks these distinctions down further by distinguishing between the 'single-rule approach' followed by France, the 'restricted pluralism' of Germany and the 'unrestricted pluralism' of England. This ensconces German law comfortably between the other two systems[41] – thus incidentally also supplying the first indication of its attitude to accessory liability. Nevertheless, despite these formal classifications, as Van Dam points out, in the final analysis, both Article 823 of the German BGB and the English tort of negligence essentially operate as general liability rules in the French fashion. Although the systems set out from opposite extremes, therefore, they meet in the middle.[42] Ultimately, the French concept of a *faute* is therefore comparable to the combined effect of the English duty of care and breach of duty, which in turn is strikingly similar to the German tripartite approach. As a result, the disparity is largely theoretical, looming in lawyers' minds far more menacingly than it does in the reality of court practice.[43]

Where do these divisions leave European tort law? The DCFR and the PETL lead the search for composite solutions. Both of these begin by articulating a general precept not to harm others along the civil law tradition of '*neminem laedere*'. So, according to the 'Basic Norm' of Article 1:101(1) of the PETL:

40. C van Dam, *European Tort Law* (2nd ed., Oxford University Press 2013) para. 605-1.
41. See C van Dam, *European Tort Law* (2nd ed., Oxford University Press 2013) para. 605-2, note 33.
42. C van Dam, *European Tort Law* (2nd ed., Oxford University Press 2013) para. 605-2.
43. C van Dam, *European Tort Law* (2nd ed., Oxford University Press 2013) para. 605-2.

> A person to whom damage to another is legally attributed is liable to compensate that damage.

On this basis, it is then explained that, among other possibilities, damage may be legally attributed to a person whose conduct constituting fault has caused it (Article 1:101(2)(a)).

The DCFR takes a very similar approach. The 'Basic Rule' enshrined in Article 1:101(1) of Book VI contains a summary of the basic elements of non-contractual liability:

> A person who suffers legally relevant damage has a right to reparation from a person who caused the damage intentionally or negligently.

It therefore seems that both proposals favour vagueness over exactness. From a comparison of these provisions it becomes clear that the basic building blocks of a European fault liability are the French three:

(a) fault (i.e., intent or negligence);
(b) causation; and
(c) legally relevant damage.

A unitary conception of fault is accordingly adopted. This approach makes sense. Precision is admirable, but it does not make for a very good starting point for a cross-border legal harmonisation. For this purpose, a simple solution is instead to be preferred that employs concepts which can be understood in all relevant systems. Refinement can come later. At any rate, this basic three-fold approach provides a good skeletal representation of all three national systems: whether fault is further sub-divided into more refined conditions is another matter.

How can this three-factor skeleton framework be applied to intermediary accessory copyright liability? In cases of copyright infringement the element of damage can be taken as given and requires no further analysis. Thus, in the following, the basic structure of European tort liability can be reduced to the second two: fault and causation. These will be analysed in turn below. A third element of defences will also be considered: once we know the conditions that will generally lead to liability, what circumstances can negate such liability must also be examined.

4.2 FAULT

If fault liability is first and foremost defined by the existence of a fault, what is a fault? If fault is measured against an objective standard, from where does that standard arise? Generally speaking, the standard of care expected of members of a society may be set in the law in one of two ways: either as a specific or as a general rule of appropriate conduct. In the first case, the standard of care appropriate to a given situation is explicitly foreseen by the law, either through statutory means or, at least in the common law, in the form of a nominate tort.[44] This is, for example, the case with direct liability in copyright law, which, through statutory provisions, prohibits the reproduction, communication to the public or other infringement of the right-holder's recognised exclusive rights. Direct liability for copyright infringement is therefore fault liability resulting from the violation of a specific rule of appropriate conduct.

Abiding exclusively by such specific duties is not however sufficient. In the continental legal systems, any loopholes overlooked by the legislator are filled in by means of what Von Bar calls an 'autonomous *Normgenerator*':[45] the general standard of care. Both French and German tort systems are constructed precisely around such a general standard of care, although, as we shall see below, the French general standard of care of is somewhat more general than the German general standard of care. The common law originally lacked such an all-encompassing theory of extra-contractual liability, consisting instead exclusively of a series of individual 'torts', each of which follows its own rules, in accordance with its particular nature. Nevertheless, nowadays the same purpose is increasingly served by the ever-expanding tort of negligence: the king of the English torts.[46]

Given that, as seen in Chapter 3, copyright laws by and large omit to codify accessory liability and those provisions that are included in the various copyright codes tend to be insufficient or maladapted to modern technological conditions, no specific standard of care exists for that area: clearly, accessory copyright liability must therefore rest on the general standard of care. Investigating the meaning of this standard therefore becomes paramount for the purposes of this book. What does the general standard of care require of its subjects? By its very generality, the standard inconveniently precludes a simple definition of the conduct it would allow and disallow. Instead, what must be taken is a step-by-step approach to the determination of permissible behaviour that breaks the general standard of care down into its constituent elements and dissects each in turn.[47] A good starting point is found in the identification of the two fundamental bases of fault liability: intent and negligence.[48]

So, according to the drafters of the PETL, fault is any 'deviation from or violation of "the required standard of conduct", whether wilfully (through the *intentional violation* of such a standard) or by omitting to act with the necessary care and circumspection that can be "reasonably" be expected of

44. C von Bar, *The Common European Law of Torts – Vol. II* (Clarendon Press 2000) paras 220-223.
45. C von Bar, *The Common European Law of Torts – Vol. II* (Clarendon Press 2000) para. 224.
46. W van Gerven et al., *Tort Law* (Hart Publishing 2000) 304.
47. European Group on Tort Law, *Principles of European Tort Law – Text and Commentary* (Springer 2005) 70.
48. C van Dam, *European Tort Law* (2nd ed., Oxford University Press 2013) para. 800.

the defendant (through the *negligent violation* of the standard)'.[49] This would indicate that the most straightforward definition of fault consists simply of its break down into its two main alternative forms. And indeed, Article 4:101 of the PETL follows exactly that approach:

> A person is liable on the basis of fault for intentional or negligent violation of the required standard of conduct

This also accords with the approach of the DCFR, which bypasses the fault conjunction entirely and speaks simply of causing damage intentionally or negligently. The investigation of the concept of fault shall therefore begin with the investigation of each of its two possible variations: intent and negligence.

It is worth noting that tort law's differentiation between intent and negligence echoes the more refined classifications of criminal law. As opposed to civil law, criminal law distinguishes between the objective element of the crime, the *actus reus*, and the subjective element, the *mens rea.* Both are necessary conditions of criminal liability: '*nulla poena sine culpa'*. Given its importance for criminal liability, criminal law expends considerable energy into identifying intricate series of nuanced degrees of criminal blameworthiness, these differing of course slightly from jurisdiction to jurisdiction. Blomsma, in his thesis on general principles of European criminal law, identifies three distinct types of European criminal *mens rea: dolus, culpa* and a third category he refers to as recklessness. *Dolus* may be further sub-divided into *dolus directus,* the most serious kind of fault that refers to the deliberate causation of a result, *dolus indirectus,* covering cases where the actor deliberately acts in a manner she knows will almost certainly bring about a result, and *dolus eventualis* or quasi-intent, the conscious acceptance of a substantial risk. *Culpa,* in its turn, is primarily distinguishable into *culpa lata,* i.e., gross negligence that consists of a serious and unethical failure to abide by the proper standard of care,[50] *culpa levis,* a failure to abide by the proper standard of care by any measure and *culpa levissima,* i.e., a very slight negligence arising from the failure to exercise the most exact care. Other categories of culpability can also be discerned: so, for example, recklessness and its civil law brother of *dolus eventualis* form an independent in-between category that fits into neither intent nor negligence.[51] The difference between these and *culpa lata* resides in whether or not the defendant accepted the possibility of the injurious result or considered it

49. European Group on Tort Law, *Principles of European Tort Law – Text and Commentary* (Springer 2005) 69-70.
50. C von Bar, *The Common European Law of Torts – Vol. II* (Clarendon Press 2000) para. 243.
51. J Blomsma, *Mens Rea and Defences in European Criminal Law* (Intersentia 2013) 509-526.

unlikely and relied on the idea that it would not occur.[52] Detailed country-by-country study can also reveal other local peculiarities, such as, e.g., the concept of *luxuria,* a distinct, aggravated form of *culpa* that is recognised in Germany (*'Leichtfertigkeit'*) and the Netherlands (*'roekeloosheid'*).

As in criminal law, gradations of fault can also be identified in private law, although these are less structured and attract less attention.[53] Even the basic distinction between intent and negligence is less significant in tort law than in criminal law: although in some cases the establishment of intent is necessary for a finding of liability (particularly in English law, where intent and negligence are applied to individual torts rather than forming two varieties of a single concept of fault), in most situations, degree is not relevant to a finding of extra-contractual liability: the lowest bar of negligence will generally suffice.[54] This is the logical consequence of the move in private law described above away from the concept of personal responsibility that still dominates criminal law towards a more objectivised standard. This is also the reason why fault liability is often also referred to as 'negligence liability': although intent is certainly a most acceptable basis for most faults, mere negligence usually suffices.[55] As a result, intent is often downplayed in modern tortious liability, while a more complicated gradation of types of fault along the criminal law paradigm becomes entirely redundant.[56] At the same time, even in tort law, the level of fault retains relevance in peripheral ways, including in the assessment of causation or in the choice of the appropriate remedies.[57] The distinction between intent and negligence therefore remains important, especially for accessory liability,

---

52. C von Bar, *The Common European Law of Torts – Vol. II* (Clarendon Press 2000) para. 238.
53. European Group on Tort Law, *Principles of European Tort Law – Text and Commentary* (Springer 2005) 66.
54. W van Gerven, J Lever & P Larouche, *Tort Law* (Hart Publishing 2000) 332.
55. It should be noted that even in the English common law, 'the tort of negligence' may perfectly well be committed intentionally. There is no good reason after all why the intentional violation of the requisite standard of care should be less culpable than its negligent violation. One can equally commit the tort of negligence through deliberate, as well as inadvertent behaviour. That the tortfeasor intended the damage is not a defence against claims in negligence. A differentiation must accordingly be made between negligence as a standard of conduct (a 'tort' in common law parlance) and negligence as a state of mind, i.e., essentially carelessness. See N McBride & R Bagshaw, *Tort Law* (4th ed., Pearson 2012) 93-94 and W V H Rogers, *Winfield & Jolowicz On Tort* (18th ed., Sweet & Maxwell 2010) 90-91.
56. C von Bar et al. (eds), *Principles, Definitions and Model Rules of European Private Law: Draft Common Frame of Reference (DCFR)*, prepared by the Study Group on a European Civil Code and the Research Group on EC private law (Acquis Group), Outline Edition (Sellier 2009) 3266.
57. C von Bar, *The Common European Law of Torts – Vol. II* (Clarendon Press 2000) para. 235 and P Widmer, 'Comparative Report on Fault as a Basis of Liability and Criterion of Imputation (Attribution)' in P Widmer (ed.), *Unification of Tort Law: Fault* (Kluwer Law International 2005) 353-354.

which, as we shall see below, operating as it does on the very edges of fault, often relies on the added element of extra culpability for an additional nudge towards or away from liability.

Below, the analysis shall be split into two parts: after a brief inspection of intent, this section will focus more *intently* on negligence.

4.2.1 Intention

Of the two dominant forms of fault, intent is the simplest and easiest to regulate in theory, if not always to substantiate in practice. Currently, there is no uniform definition of intent in European private law. Von Bar notes that the concepts of '*faute intentionelle*', '*Vorsatz*' and 'intention' in the English sense of the word do not always coincide: in particular, in the English context, the term 'intention' may often refer simply to conscious controlled conduct ('intention *simpliciter*'), while 'malicious intent' is instead usually used to signify the blameworthiness indicated by the French and German terms.[58] What about the model European tort law codifications? The PETL contain no unified definition of intention. The DCFR on the other hand gets straight to the point. Under Article VI.-3:101 of the DCFR:

> A person causes legally relevant damage intentionally when that person causes such damage either: (a) meaning to cause damage of the type caused; or (b) by conduct which that person means to do, knowing that such damage, or damage of that type, will or will almost certainly be caused.

This definition indicates that intention can be separated into two primary variants. A person will be seen as acting intentionally, when the behaviour causing the damage was deliberate and they either: (a) meant to cause the damage; or (b) knew the damage would almost certainly result from their behaviour. In other words, the defendant must have aimed at causing the loss as an end in itself or, alternatively, as a means of achieving another purpose: she must have either wanted the damage or known it would happen and not changed course.[59] Thus, clear parallels can be drawn between the DCFR approach to intent and the classic criminal law distinction mentioned above between *dolus directus* and *dolus indirectus.* In the following, we shall label these two possible types of intent 'direct intent' or 'intent *stricto sensu'* and 'indirect intent' or 'oblique intent'.[60]

Both types of DCFR intent rest on two basic elements: the wanting of the damage and the knowing of the damage – as the German lawyers put it,

58. C von Bar, *The Common European Law of Torts – Vol. II* (Clarendon Press 2000) para. 240.
59. N McBride & R Bagshaw, *Tort Law* (4th ed., Pearson 2012) 679.
60. P S Davies, Accessory Liability (Hart Publishing 2015) 41.

'der Wissen und Willen'.[61] It is important that the defendant be conscious of causing the damage, whether or not he realised that it would be legally relevant. If he was not aware of the harmful consequences of his behaviour, even if he knew that the behaviour violated a statutory rule of conduct, he cannot be understood to have acted with intent. So, when a person makes a mistake in the calculation of the damaging effect of their actions, they may be found to have acted with negligence, but cannot be held liable for intent. Similarly, if the defendant was not in control of his actions, either because he did not know what he was doing or because he was unable to act differently, he cannot be said to have intended the resulting damage. Intent will also usually be absent in cases of error of law or fact. At the same time, if that error could have been avoided through abiding by an appropriate standard of care, negligence may still be established.[62]

The damage the defendant wanted or knew would occur must at least be of the same type as that which eventually took place. It is not necessary, however, that the defendant should have anticipated the exact chain of events that resulted in the damage. So, if the damage would have occurred regardless of the defendant's behaviour, he cannot be said to have intended to cause it, even if he approved of the damage and hoped it would come about. Indeed, the defendant's hopes regarding the outcome of his actions are entirely irrelevant to the assessment of intent, as long as the defendant understands the real possibilities: if he desperately hoped that the damage would be avoided, but recognised that that hope was futile and the damage would almost certainly arise, he must be said to have had intention to cause it. If, conversely, he was relying on what he believed were low odds of the damage materialising, negligence will probably be a better descriptor.[63]

It should be noted that establishing intent becomes more troublesome where the defendant's behaviour consisted of an omission. In principle, the same rule applies to omissions as to positive actions: a person can be said to have intentionally caused a legally relevant damage through her omission if she meant to cause the damage in that way (i.e., remained inactive precisely in order to allow the damage to occur) or if she meant to omit the action that would have prevented the damage, knowing that the damage would almost certainly come about as a result. If she neither meant for the damage to happen nor knew it almost certainly would, she may be found negligent, but cannot be said to have had intent.

---

61. C von Bar, *The Common European Law of Torts – Vol. II* (Clarendon Press 2000) para. 237.
62. C von Bar, *The Common European Law of Torts – Vol. II* (Clarendon Press 2000) para. 237.
63. C von Bar et al. (eds), *Principles, Definitions and Model Rules of European Private Law: Draft Common Frame of Reference (DCFR)*, prepared by the Study Group on a European Civil Code and the Research Group on EC private law (Acquis Group), Outline Edition (Sellier 2009) 3263-3273.

What about recklessness or *dolus eventualis*? In the Annex of the DCFR[64] definitions of both recklessness and the adjacent notion of gross negligence are provided: a person is reckless if he 'knows of an obvious and serious risk of proceeding in a certain way but nonetheless voluntarily proceeds without caring whether or not the risk materialises'. He is grossly negligent if he 'is guilty of a profound failure to take such care as is self-evidently required in the circumstances'.[65] In some legal systems (notably Germany), *dolus eventualis* is considered to be a type of intent.[66] Indeed, even gross negligence will sometimes be treated as intent for practical reasons.[67] The DCFR however takes care to avoid using either term when referring to intent in non-contractual liability. Instead, although they do note the similarities between the second sub-paragraph of their definition of intent and the concept of *dolus eventualis* as that exists in some Member States, the DCFR drafters make clear that intent is supposed to establish a stricter standard that excludes both recklessness and gross negligence. Both unreasonable want of care and conscious carelessness are therefore relegated to the area of negligence. In the following, we shall be abiding by this approach, as more in keeping with the natural meaning of the word 'intention': both *dolus eventualis* and gross negligence sit more comfortably within negligence, whose focus on objective standard violation and stricter causation requirements allow for better guarantees against the creation of 'thought torts'.

As can be gathered from the above, in general, the European standard of intent in tort is a remarkably high one. This demanding test is reinforced by the practical difficulties of divining the workings of another person's mind that make proving intent an inherently challenging exercise. So, while intent may occasionally be substantiated where the defendant admits to it or her mindset is made clear through discovery devices (such as requests for the production of documents or depositions), proving intent through circumstantial evidence is far harder. This is appropriate: an accusation of intent is a serious one and should be substantiated with serious evidence.

At the same time, although intent might be difficult to prove, once it is established, liability follows with relative ease. This is because, as shall be

64. See Art. I.-1:108 of the DCFR's Book 1 on General Principles: '(1) The definitions in the Annex apply for all the purposes of these rules unless the context otherwise requires. (2) Where a word is defined, other grammatical forms of the word have a corresponding meaning.'
65. C von Bar et al. (eds), *Principles, Definitions and Model Rules of European Private Law: Draft Common Frame of Reference (DCFR)*, prepared by the Study Group on a European Civil Code and the Research Group on EC private law (Acquis Group), Outline Edition (Sellier 2009) 4785 and 4791.
66. C van Dam, *European Tort Law* (Oxford University Press 2007) para. 802-2.
67. C von Bar, *The Common European Law of Torts – Vol. II* (Clarendon Press 2000) paras 237 and 242.

shown below,[68] the threshold of causation is affected by the degree of fault: where the defendant wanted the victim to suffer the damage or knew that that was going to be the inevitable result of her conduct, the law is less inclined to worry about whether she in fact 'caused' it.[69] So, according to the English courts, '[i]ntention to injure the plaintiff disposes of any question of remoteness'.[70] The German BGH agrees: '*vorsätzlich herbeigeführte Tatfolgen sind immer "adäquat"*'.[71] As a result, if a person intentionally causes harm to another, she will be liable for all direct consequences of her actions, regardless of how distant.[72] In this way, the range of legally relevant causation expands and contracts depending on the intensity of the tortfeasor's culpability. Given that the need for a causative link is one of the strongest obstacles against the establishment of accessory liability, a finding of intention can thus significantly ease the process of substantiating it.

The equivalency between intention and causation can be explained by dint of the close connection between the concepts of fault and causation: as we shall see below, in the context of tort law, causation is not only a mechanical link that binds the resultant damage to the tortfeasor's behaviour ('factual causation'), but a conceptual bridge between the two ('legal causation').[73] Fault and causation are therefore mutually referential, interdependent concepts. This means that what is established by the first need not be re-visited by the second: damage will always be foreseeable to the tortfeasor who intended to cause it – deliberately bringing about of a certain result is always causatively sufficient. This realisation gives a first indication of the source of the difference between the French 'multiple faults' approach to accessory liability and the English and German joint tortfeasance/*Mittäterschaft* solution: if a person intends somebody else's infringement, they have caused it and therefore, barring a defence, they are liable.

While the objectivisation of fault liability has diminished the relevance of intention in tort, its survival indicates that a subjective core does remain within the objectivised notion of fault: a person will always be unreasonable – and therefore at fault – if they intend to inflict damage on another. As Von Bar notes therefore, although modern European tort systems agree that, as a general rule, it is not the defendant's blameworthiness that attracts the liability, but instead the deviation from the prescribed standard of care,

---

68. See s. 4.4.
69. R Bagshaw, 'Causing the Behaviour of Others and Other Causal Mixtures' in R Goldberg (ed), *Perspectives on Causation* (Hart Publishing 2011) 361.
70. *Quinn v. Leathem* [1901] AC 495, 537 (Lord Lindley). See also G Williams, *Joint Torts and Contributory Negligence* (Stevens & Sons 1951) 201.
71. BGH, 27 January 1981, VI ZR 204/79, BGHZ 79, 259-264.
72. C van Dam, *European Tort Law* (Oxford University Press 2007) paras 803 and 1101.
73. P Widmer, 'Comparative Report on Fault as a Basis of Liability and Criterion of Imputation (Attribution)' in P Widmer (ed.), *Unification of Tort Law: Fault* (Kluwer Law International 2005) 337-338.

blameworthiness nonetheless remains a relevant notion in tort law.[74] At the same time, both the practical difficulties in proving intention and the, sometimes alarming, simplicity with which it leads to liability once it has been found, have pushed intent to the side-lines of modern tort law. The bulk of fault analyses have instead concentrated on its tamer – if more complicated – sister-fault of negligence. It is to this that we will now turn. As we shall see below, negligence is the opposite of intention, in that the standard for finding it is lower, but more intricate, and the causation requirements considerably more demanding.

4.2.2 Negligence

If intention still retains a strong attachment to fault's historical roots in culpability, negligence embraces with a vengeance its modern preoccupation with objectivity, which depends the existence of tortious behaviour on the expectations of the society within which it occurs. But what is negligence? As it does with intention, the DCFR also provides a definition of that notion. According to Article VI.-3:102 DCFR:

> A person causes legally relevant damage negligently when that person causes the damage by conduct which […] does not otherwise amount to such care as could be expected from a reasonably careful person in the circumstances of the case.

The PETL move along similar lines. According to Article 4:102(1) PETL:

> The required standard of conduct is that of the reasonable person in the circumstances.

Notably, both these definitions centre around the legal fiction of the 'reasonable person'. It is with this therefore that the analysis will begin.

4.2.2.1 The Reasonable Person

The 'reasonable person' is a classic concept in European tort law that is encountered across the continent and has deep roots in European legal history. It essentially constitutes the modern reincarnation of the Roman *bonus pater familias,* i.e., the prudent (*prudens*) and industrious (*diligens, studiosus*) head of the family, who does not rashly leap into action, but circumspectly considers the consequences of his conduct for the interests of others.[75]

---

74. C von Bar, *The Common European Law of Torts – Vol. II* (Clarendon Press 2000) para. 235.
75. A Berger, *Encyclopedic Dictionary of Roman Law – Volume 43* (The American Philosophical Society 1953) 377.

The EGTL notes that the model for the PETL provision was the German notion of *Fahrlässigkeit,* as defined in Article 276(1) of the BGB. According to this, 'a person acts negligently if he fails to exercise reasonable care'.[76] The point of reference here, known as the *objektivierter Fahrlässigkeits-maßstab,* the 'objective negligence standard', is that of a *sorgfältiger Mensch von durchschnittlicher Umsicht und Tüchtigkeit,* i.e., a careful person of average prudence and capability. The 'reasonable person' threshold is also fundamental to the French and English tort systems.[77] So, the objective test of the *bon père de famille* or *homme raisonnable et avisé,* which is used to interpret and apply Article 1382 of the French C.civ., was already encountered above in Chapter 3,[78] while this venerable hypothetical individual also makes frequent appearances in English negligence jurisprudence,[79] often under the various guises of the 'reasonable man placed in the same situation as the defendant', 'the man of ordinary prudence and intelligence', the 'man using ordinary care and skill', the 'man on the Clapham omnibus'[80] and, more recently, 'the traveller on the London Underground'.[81]

What purpose does this multifaceted persona serve? The basic idea is to allow negligence to be assessed through the comparison of the behaviour of the defendant with that of a hypothetical model citizen. Naturally, an actual reasonable person's assessment of the defendant's conduct is not literally required. The reasonable person instead is nothing more than a legal device and conceptualising tool:

> it would misconceived for a party to seek to lead evidence from actual passengers on the Clapham omnibus as to how they would have acted in a given situation or what they would have foreseen, in order to establish how the reasonable man would have acted or what he would have

76. European Group on Tort Law, *Principles of European Tort Law – Text and Commentary* (Springer 2005) 65-66.
77. See C van Dam, *European Tort Law* (Oxford University Press 2007) paras 804 and 811-2; P Widmer, 'Comparative Report on Fault as a Basis of Liability and Criterion of Imputation(Attribution)' in P Widmer (ed.), Unification of Tort Law: Fault (Kluwer Law International 2005) 331 et seq.
78. See s. 3.2.3.2.
79. The UK Supreme Court is clear on the connection between these notions: 'The Clapham omnibus has many passengers. The most venerable is the reasonable man, who was born during the reign of Victoria but remains in vigorous health. Amongst the other passengers are the right-thinking member of society, familiar from the law of defamation, the officious bystander, the reasonable parent, the reasonable landlord, and the fair-minded and informed observer, all of whom have had season tickets for many years. […] They belong to an intellectual tradition of defining a legal standard by reference to a hypothetical person, which stretches back to the creation by Roman jurists of the figure of the *bonus paterfamilias*[...] In recent times, some additional passengers from the European Union have boarded the Clapham omnibus.' See *Healthcare at Home Limited v. The Common Services Agency* [2014] UKSC 49 (30 July 2014).
80. *McQuire v. Western Morning News Co Ltd* [1903] 2 K.B. 100.
81. *McFarlane v. Tayside Health Board* [1999] 3 WLR 1301.

> foreseen. […] The behaviour of the reasonable man is not established by the evidence of witnesses, but by the application of a legal standard by the court.[82]

Essentially therefore, the reasonable person constitutes the personification of proper conduct, the anthropomorphised yardstick of lawful behaviour, the symbolic representation of the composite judgment of the community within which the defendant operates as to response expected of legal subjects in situations that pose a threat of harm to others: ultimately, the touchstone of care. Through its application judges are provided with a mental metric to be used for the assessment of the defendant's behaviour outside of those cases for which a customised standard of care is detailed in the law (as is the case in e.g., road traffic regulations or, indeed, direct copyright infringement).[83] As Van Dam explains, in negligence law 'the factual "is" conduct of the actual defendant is compared with the normative 'should' conduct of an average careful person in the same situation and, where there is a difference because the defendant's conduct did not meet this standard of care, negligence can be established'.[84] The reasonable person stands in for the 'should' aspect of the equation. Through this lens, the pertinent question in determining whether a person has acted negligently becomes the following: 'what would a reasonable person have done?'

It should be noted that the use of an external reference point for the assessment of negligence is no accident: its establishment makes clear that the European concept of negligence is, as mentioned above, truly an objective or 'objectivated', i.e., one that it hinges on an abstract representation of the conduct everybody must match. Negligence is thus intended to be independent of the personal idiosyncrasies of the defendant.[85] This is appropriate for a method of determining fault in a legal sense, as opposed to one dependant on morality. As American jurist Oliver Wendall Holmes famously quipped:

> The standards of the law are standards of general application. The law takes no account of the infinite varieties of temperament, intellect, and education which make the internal character of a given act so different in different men. […] If, for instance, a man is born hasty and is always having accidents and hurting himself or his neighbours, no doubt his congenital defects will be allowed for in the courts of Heaven, but his slips are no less troublesome to his neighbours than if they sprang from guilty neglect. His neighbours accordingly require him, at his proper

82. *Healthcare at Home Limited v. The Common Services Agency* [2014] UKSC 49 (30 July 2014).
83. Article VI.-3:102(a) of the DCFR.
84. C van Dam, *European Tort Law* (Oxford University Press 2007) para. 805-1.
85. *Glasgow Corp v. Muir* [1943] AC 448.

> peril, to come up to their standard, and the courts which they establish decline to take his personal equation into account.[86]

For society to function, liability for negligence cannot be adjusted to the judgment of each individual or else we would end up with a standard is 'as variable as the length of the foot' of each of its members.[87] A sacrifice of personal idiosyncrasies to a generally applicable single standard is instead necessary. At the same time, the standard is intended to be a human one – it does not require conduct that would be impossible to carry out. Winfield & Jolowicz give us a poetic description:

> He has not the courage of Achilles, the wisdom of Ulysses or the strength of Hercules, nor has he the prophetic vision of a clairvoyant. He will not anticipate folly in all its forms but he never puts out of consideration the teachings of experience shows such negligence and so will guard against negligence of others when experience shows such negligence to be common. He is a reasonable man but not a perfect citizen, nor a 'paragon of circumspection'.[88]

Tort law therefore presumes or requires that everybody possess ordinary capacity to avoid harming their neighbours. Having said that, it should be noted that any limitations under which the individual defendant was operating must also be considered. According to Article I.-1:104 of the DCFR:

> Reasonableness is to be objectively ascertained, having regard to the nature and purpose of what is being done, to the circumstances of the case and to any relevant usages and practices.

In other words, the reasonableness standard takes account on the concrete circumstances in which the defendant found herself. There 'is not absolute or intrinsic negligence; it is always relative to some circumstances of time, place or person'.[89] The standard is that of '*l'homme raisonnable placé dans les même circonstances de temps, de lieu et d'action*'.[90] Thus, most jurisdictions agree that, in certain circumstances, subjective elements may take over: a 'blind man is not required to see at his peril'.[91] Such

86. O Wendell Holmes, *The Common Law – Dover Edition* (Dover Publications 1991) 108.
87. *Vaughan v. Menlove* [1837] 132 ER 490.
88. W V H Rogers, *Winfield & Jolowicz on Tort* (18th ed., Sweet & Maxwell 2010) 92-93. French scholars move along similar lines, explaining that the *bon père de famille* '*c'est celui qui n'est ni extrêmement vigilant, ni anormalement negligent, ni un héros, ni un lâche, ni un pur égoïste, ni un exceptionnel altruiste, mais entre les deux, un homme ordinaire*' see M Fabre-Magnan, *Droit des obligations* (2nd ed., PUF 2010) 89-90.
89. *Degg v. Midland Railway Co* (1857) 1 H&N 773.
90. W van Gerven et al., *Tort Law* (Hart Publishing 2000) 310.
91. O Wendell Holmes, *The Common Law – Dover Edition* (Dover Publications 1991) 108.

exceptions however usually require some sort of clear and manifest incapacity to live up to the regular standard, such as is the case with children or people acting in emergency situations. As long as the defendant in such cases cannot be blamed for getting into an unmanageable situation, he will not be held liable for the damage that arose from his behaviour once he was immerged in it. This concession is intended to forestall the transformation of a fault-based liability standard into one of strict liability on the mere basis of the personal abilities of the defendant.[92] In this way, despite the recent turn to objectivity, a hint of blameworthiness or culpability is ultimately retained not only in intention, but as an element of negligence as well, albeit a peripheral one that emerges only when necessary for a specific purpose.[93]

In any case, the malleability of the 'reasonable person' standard indicates how it can be adjusted for the purposes of not only of primary, but also accessory liability: the concept of the 'reasonable person' shifts gear depending on the exact demands society has of a person in the defendant's position. Accordingly, where a person acts in such a way as to participate in the tort of another, whether or not he should be held liable will depend on how that participation measures up to the, by definition, irreproachable conduct that in which perfect paragon of lawfulness would have engaged in the same situation: would the reasonable person have acted in a similar way?

4.2.2.2 The Factors of Negligence

How is that question to be answered? What *would* a reasonable person who finds herself in the circumstances of the defendant do? It is obviously not possible to give an unequivocal and clear-cut description of the comportment of the reasonable person in all situations. The best that can be offered is the identification of appropriate factors. The PETL and DCFR provide exactly that.

So, according to Article 4:102 PETL, the behaviour of the reasonable person will depend, among other considerations, on:

- the nature and value of the protected interest involved;
- the dangerousness of the activity;
- the expertise to be expected of a person carrying it out;
- the foreseeability of the damage;
- the relationship of proximity or special reliance between those involved; and

92. *Mansfield v. Weetabix* [1998] 1 WLR 1263; C van Dam, *European Tort Law* (Oxford University Press 2007) para. 804-1 and European Group on Tort Law, *Principles of European Tort Law – Text and Commentary* (Springer 2005) 79.
93. C Von Bar, *The Common European Law of Torts – Vol. II* (Clarendon Press 2000) paras 226-243.

– the availability and the costs of precautionary or alternative methods.[94]

Article 4:102(2) introduces some subjective elements to the equation: the standard may be adjusted for the age, mental or physical disability of the person or any extraordinary circumstances that might prevent them from conforming. Finally, according to Article 4:102(3), statutory duties or interdictions also have to be taken into consideration in determining proper conduct.

Although the PETL did go to pains to enumerate as precisely and completely as possible all the relevant factors to be taken into account when defining proper conduct,[95] it should be noted that this list is not intended to be exhaustive nor will the enumerated factors be relevant in all cases: the importance of a given factor will depend not only on the legal system in operation, but more importantly on the specifics on display in the case at hand. The 'reasonable person' standard is intended to be a flexible one that can be calibrated at the court's discretion: by its very nature, negligence is *ius in causa positum* – law found in the facts of the case.[96]

The drafters of the DCFR were much more reticent. They refused to draw a list of negligence indicators, emphasising instead that the variety of factors which may become relevant in an individual case is beyond conclusive enumeration. Yet tellingly, their supporting analysis rests on very similar catchwords as those used by the EGTL. So, they explain, the person who turns a blind eye to the foreseeable consequences of their actions can only be saved by sheer luck from harming others. Likewise, the type and extent of the damage should be taken into consideration, as well as the relationship between the parties, whether the parties are children or adults or whether the danger was known or arose for the first time.[97] Finally, in view of the objective nature of the standard, they caution that a person cannot escape liability by claiming to be a slow learner or especially forgetful. This indicates that what is necessary for the determination of negligence is an appropriately pliable formulation of a list of criteria that can allow room for all relevant circumstances in a given case to be taken into account. Naturally, '[a]ny attempt to provide an exhaustive list of every factor which might

94. This list compares well with similar lists of criteria as identified in e.g.,: G Viney, 'France: Le 'Wrongfulness' en Droit Français' in H Koziol (ed.) *Unification of Tort Law: Wrongfulness* (Kluwer Law International 1998) 57.
95. European Group on Tort Law, *Principles of European Tort Law – Text and Commentary* (Springer 2005) 76; D Nolan & J Davies, 'Torts and Equitable Wrongs' in A Burrows, *English Private Law* (Oxford University Press 2013), 17 and 59.
96. C van Dam, *European Tort Law* (Oxford University Press 2007) para. 805-1.
97. C von Bar et al. (eds), *Principles, Definitions and Model Rules of European Private Law: Draft Common Frame of Reference (DCFR)*, prepared by the Study Group on a European Civil Code and the Research Group on EC private law (Acquis Group), Outline Edition (Sellier 2009).

conceivably weigh in the scale is to pursue a will-o'-the-wisp'.[98] However, criteria can be identified that are broadly defined and adjustable, in such a way as to enable them to operate in catch-all manner in response to the circumstances of each case. In this way an appropriately sized hole can be provided by the legal framework for any peg thrown up by individual cases, while both flexibility and structure can be achieved. The judge is not left floundering for lack of guidance, but is also permitted to adjust to the specificities at hand.

Van Dam, in his *magnum opus* detailing the evolving condition of European tort law, has undertaken precisely this task of formula-finding. He has approached the issue by means of the systematisation of the six PETL factors. To this end, he first separates the notion of negligence into two basic elements: an 'outer', 'visible' element of negligent conduct and an 'inner', 'invisible' one of the negligent person. He picks out four of the six PETL factors as relevant to the first of these. These, he organises into two categories. On the one hand he lists, as measures of the expected risks:

(1) the seriousness of the anticipated harm (corresponding to the 'nature and value of the protected interest involved' in the PETL); and
(2) the probability of that harm taking place (the PETL's 'dangerousness of the activity').

On the other hand, as measures of the due care that the wrongdoer owes the victim, he suggests:

(1) the character and benefit of the conduct (the notion of 'relationship of proximity or special reliance between those involved' that are mentioned by the PETL can be subsumed here); and
(2) the burden of precautionary measures (i.e., 'the availability and costs of precautionary or alternative methods' in the PETL).[99]

In a second analytical step, the two leftover PETL factors (the expertise to be expected of a person carrying it on and the foreseeability of the damage) are then translated in the Van Dam approach into the complementary 'inner negligence' standard, that assesses the person of the tortfeasor. Here, whether the defendant possessed the reasonable person's knowledge and abilities is analysed.[100] In the final analysis, the negligence test is thus divided into two parts: the defendant must not only prove that her conduct was that of a reasonable person, but, moreover, that she had the knowledge

98. S Todd, 'Negligence: the Duty of Care' in S Todd (ed.), *The Law of Torts in New Zealand* (3rd ed., Brookers, Wellington 2001) 151–152.
99. C van Dam, *European Tort Law* (2nd ed., Oxford University Press 2013) para. 805-2, see note 38.
100. C van Dam, *European Tort Law* (2nd ed., Oxford University Press 2013) para. 805-2, see note 38.

and abilities that such a person would possess.[101] As with the question of negligent conduct, in the case of the negligent person, the standard is an objective one: the question is not whether the tortfeasor *personally* knew the danger and could have avoided it, but whether she was under an *obligation* to know of and to avoid it.[102]

As is clear, Van Dam's factors, although renamed, are not greatly dissimilar to those listed by Article 4:102 PETL. What the Van Dam approach adds however is an organisation of the identified criteria into antipodal groups that showcase the conditions' relationship to each other and their relevance to the overall process of assessing of the defendant's behaviour. This structure illuminates tort law's preoccupation with accommodating the conflicting interests of the claimant and defendant: the standard of care lies at the intersection of due care with the expected risks, between freedom and protection, the objective assessment of harmful behaviour and the personal attributes of the particular wrongdoer.[103] As with the law of fundamental rights explored in Chapter 2 therefore, the search for a balance is revealed to lie at the heart of tort law as well. In the words of Van Dam: 'the negligent character of the defendant's conduct has to be established by balancing the expected risk, on one hand, and the precautions, on the other: 'As the danger increases, so must the precautions increase'.[104] The two opposing sides represent the two facets of liberty: the freedom to develop one's personality and participate in the economic, artistic and social life is typically countered by the freedom to enjoy one's health and property without external disturbance.[105] The EGTL names these the 'activity interest' and the 'integrity interest'. Tort law is intended to provide the framework for the balancing act necessary to reconcile these opposing forces, by requiring that the risks created in the pursuit of one's own activity interest be tempered

---

101. C van Dam, *European Tort Law* (2nd ed., Oxford University Press 2013) para. 805-1.
102. The distinction between the negligence conduct and negligence person is strongly reminiscent of the German distinction between *äußere und innere Fahrlässigkeit,* i.e., outer and inner negligence. 'Outer' negligence in German law refers to conduct which diverges from the conduct required by the situation. 'Inner' negligence by contrast refers to the tortfeasor's lack of concentration, the laziness that stopped him from seeking out pertinent information or in general any internal mechanism that result in the 'outer' manifestation. German law retains the distinction as it retains the boundary between unlawfulness and fault: *äußere Fahrlässigkeit* is part of unlawfulness and *innere Fahrlässigkeit* is part of fault. See below, s. 4.3.1. See also, C von Bar, *The Common European Law of Torts – Vol. II* (Clarendon Press 2000) paras 228-229 and C van Dam, *European Tort Law* (2nd ed., Oxford University Press 2013) para. 804-2; H Koziol, *Basic Questions of Tort Law from a Germanic Perspective* (Jan Sramek Verlag 2012) 190-191.
103. C van Dam, *European Tort Law* (Oxford University Press 2007) paras 609-1 and 805-1.
104. C van Dam, *European Tort Law* (2nd ed., Oxford University Press 2013) para. 805-2, quoting *Lloyds Bank Ltd v. Railway Executive* [1952] 1 All ER 1248.
105. European Group on Tort Law, *Principles of European Tort Law – Text and Commentary* (Springer 2005) 76.

by the appropriate care for the integrity interests of others.[106] The reasonable person test is, therefore, in the end, revealed as another kind of balancing act. This time however, the exercise provides an answer, not to the question of how the State should interact with private persons, but of what behaviour can be expected of one private person with respect to the rights of others. The answer is: whatever the reasonable person would do.

In the analysis below we will follow the Van Dam approach, as it covers all the criteria identified in the PETL, but organises them into a coherent framework. In this way, it clarifies the relationship between the constituent elements of the standard of care. As Van Dam himself observes, although it cannot be said that every court in Europe applies it as such, this systematic scheme provides an accurate description of the way in which the courts usually approach negligence. It therefore works as a good formula to help structure thought around these abstract, elusive concepts.[107]

4.2.2.3 Outer Negligence: Risk and Care

The first question to be answered in any investigation of negligence is the one that concerns the defendant's conduct: did the defendant behave as a reasonable person would have done in the same circumstances? The answer depends on the careful examination of the counterbalancing factors of risk and care. The higher the risk taken by the defendant, the higher the requisite accompanying care. Here, we shall begin by considering the concept of risk.

(a) Risk

As mentioned above, the level of the risk encountered in a given situation is determined by two main factors: the seriousness of the harm occasioned and the probability of that harm coming about. The graver the expected damage and the more likely it is that it will occur, the bigger the risk. Each of these elements deserves individual analysis.

- *The seriousness of the harm*

With regard to the seriousness of the harm, the first thing that should be noted is the hierarchy of values recognised by most legal systems. The PETL explicitly acknowledge this in their Article 2:102. According to that, '[t]he scope of protection of an interest depends on its nature; the higher its value, the precision of its definition and its obviousness, the more extensive is its protection'. The higher the value therefore, the higher the risk when that value is threatened – and, naturally, the higher the standard of care to which that the defendant has to adhere to prevent damage. Life, bodily or mental integrity, human dignity and liberty are placed on the highest pedestal of

106. C van Dam, *European Tort Law* (2nd ed., Oxford University Press 2013) para. 711-2.
107. C van Dam, *European Tort Law* (Oxford University Press 2007) para. 805-2.

protection. Pure economic interests or contractual relationships are granted far more circumscribed protection. Interestingly for the purposes of this book, paragraph 2 explicitly grants extensive protection to property rights, including those of intangible property. Finally, if the damage suffered by the claimant is not legally relevant, no duty to avoid it will of course be incumbent upon the defendant: where there is no harm, there is no need for care.

It should be noted that the defendant's negligent conduct does not exist in isolation, but must be examined with reference to the overall context within which it occurs. For example, in the English case of *Paris v. Stepney Borogh Council,* the employer of man who was blind in one eye was found liable for damage caused in the course of the man's work to his only seeing eye. In that case, the employer was deemed to be under a duty of care to provide protective goggles to his employee, regardless of whether there could be said to be a general duty of care incumbent upon him to do the same for two-eyed workers. 'Blindness', declared the court, 'is so great a calamity that even the loss of one of two good eyes is not comparable'. Thus, the more serious the damage which will happen if an accident occurs, the more thorough the precautions which an employer must undertake to avoid it.[108]

- *The probability of harm*

According to Lord Dunedin, '[p]eople must guard against reasonable probabilities, but they are not bound to guard against fantastic possibilities'. In addition to the seriousness of the damage, the element of probability or dangerousness is therefore also relevant to the balancing of negligence. This should be understood in a general sense, as encompassing any activity which the abilities of the tortfeasor are incapable of controlling. As common sense dictates, the question of dangerousness intersects with the question of the abilities of the defendant: where somebody undertakes an activity they are not equipped to carry out, the probably of harm increases. Crucially, the danger of harm occurring has to be measured *ex ante,* with reference to the moment right before it takes place. Liability is also due only if the danger exceeded the socially accepted level; risky activities, such as driving or playing sports, do not in themselves give rise to an obligation to compensate all loss that they occasion, as long as their execution was not negligent in comparison with the generally accepted standards. At the same time, it should be understood that dangerousness can often be underestimated in daily life. The use of empirical data can be helpful in this regard. In addition, it is the probability of the harmful event occurring that is relevant, not the probability of the ultimate damage resulting from that event: probability should be assessed in a generalised way – it is not necessary to consider how probable is was that the victim of an accident would break his vertebrae, only

108. *Paris v. Stepney Borough Council* 1950] UKHL 3 [1951] AC 367 (13 December 1950).

that the accident would happen. It should be noted that a low probability of harm does not equate a complete absence of liability. Instead, the seriousness of the danger should be considered in parallel: a highly probable, but insignificant harm may be less worrisome than an improbable serious harm.[109]

(b) Care

Where it is established that the defendant's behaviour made probable a serious harm and thus caused a risk, that risk has to be considered against the appropriate care that a reasonable person would undertake to avoid it. Like risk, care too comprises two elements: so, whether the danger was justified in view of the 'character and benefit of the conduct' that caused it must first be considered. If it was not, whether the defendant took all available precautionary measures should also be examined.

- *The nature and benefit of the conduct*

The character and benefit of the defendant's conduct can operate as a justification for her behaviour, by reversing or nullifying the collective effect on society of the damage occasioned. So, it is possible to envision situations where it may not be desirable to ask the defendant to desist from her activity even where the conduct harms others, as long as the behaviour results in great benefit to the defendant herself, to third parties or to the public interest. So, Article 2:102(6) of the PETL explains that '[i]n determining the scope of protection, the interests of the actor, especially in liberty of action and in exercising his rights, as well as public interests also have to be taken into consideration'. As the EGTL elaborates, 'the higher appears the value of the 'activity interest', the more one should be sparing in restricting its exercise in favour or the 'integrity interest' of third persons', unless those interests enjoy the nearly absolute priority of personality rights.[110] Thus, claimants may be expected to tolerate a certain degree of harm in the face of more highly valued interests of others.[111] As England's Jackson LJ puts it, it is 'the function of the law of tort to deter negligent conduct and to compensate those who are the victims of such conduct. It is not the function of the law to eliminate every iota of risk or to stamp out socially desirable activities'.[112] The idea is to discourage excessive risk aversion and the creation of a so-called compensation culture that imposes too high a price on generally desirable activities.[113]

---

109. C van Dam, *European Tort Law* (Oxford University Press 2007) para. 806-2.
110. European Group on Tort Law, *Principles of European Tort Law – Text and Commentary* (Springer 2005) 76-77.
111. C van Dam, *European Tort Law* (2nd ed., Oxford University Press 2013) para. 809-1.
112. *The Scout Association v. Barnes* [2010] EWCA Civ 1476 (21 December 2010).
113. For a recent codification of this idea, see s. 1 of the UK's Compensation Act 2006, which explicitly permits courts, when considering a claim in negligence or breach of statutory

The individual circumstances of the case will be relevant in evaluating the nature of the conduct. In particular, the relationship between the tortfeasor and the victim must be taken into account when assessing the nature and value of the conduct of the former. The closer the proximity between the parties, the more they can be expected to pay attention to each other's interests and, therefore, the higher the standard of care that will be imposed on the defendant. So, for example, if a person is or presents themselves as an expert in a specific field, they must assume the corresponding responsibility towards any persons who rely on their knowledge.

- *The burden of precautionary measures*

As mentioned above, tort liability is based on a balancing act that takes equal consideration of the claimant's rights as of the defendant's freedom to act.[114] This balancing act informs us of the obligations incumbent upon us as members of society. Thus, it can be said that the reasonable person is the one that correctly balances her own rights against the freedom of others. Precautionary measures are part of that balancing. How each available precautionary measure compares to the damage which its omission would cause to the claimant will determine whether the defendant was reasonable or not. The English courts explain:

> if all the trains in this country were restricted to a speed of five miles an hour, there would be fewer accidents, but our national life would be intolerably slowed down. The purpose to be served if sufficiently important, justifies the assumption of abnormal risk.[115]

Obviously, if it were possible to take a precautionary measure which enabled fast travel, while also eliminating the possibility of accidents, it would be wholly unreasonable to fail to do so. However, in its absence, the only precautionary measure that remains is omitting fast travel, which in most cases is a completely unreasonable demand. Accordingly, where his interests can be pursued and his goals attained by alternative methods that don't carry the same penalty for the claimant, the defendant who knows or should know of the dangers that his behaviour poses for others should choose the less dangerous avenue. This is an application of the general principle of proportionality and of good faith ('*schonende Rechtsausübung*').

A more interesting question concerns the costs of such safer alternative methods: what expense and inconvenience must the defendant accept while

duty, in determining whether the defendant should have taken particular steps to meet a standard of care (whether by taking precautions against a risk or otherwise), to have regard to whether a requirement to take those steps might: (a)prevent a desirable activity from being undertaken at all, to a particular extent or in a particular way; or (b)discourage persons from undertaking functions in connection with a desirable activity.

114. C van Dam, *European Tort Law* (2nd ed., Oxford University Press 2013) para. 711-2.
115. *Daborn v. Bath Tramways Motor Co. Ltd* [1946] 2 All ER 333.

remaining observant of the requisite standard of care? Some guidelines can be constructed: for example, the cost of one-off precautionary measures will generally be found to be proportionate to a persistent danger. By contrast, continuous precautionary measures are imposed far more cautiously, as they generally require greater time, money and effort in their maintenance that will less easily outweigh the gravity and probability of the expected damage.[116] In cases where the complete elimination of the danger would be too costly or impossible, a duty might still burden the defendant to take measures to reduce the risk or to warn others.[117]

It should be noted that the question of precautionary measures necessarily features heavily in the area of accessory liability. After all, in accessory liability – at least where the defendant is accused of negligence rather than intent – it is not the accessory themselves who is committing the tort. Instead, they are simply found to have fallen short of the required standard of care, by either creating circumstances that make it more likely for another to commit the tort or failing to prevent them from committing it. In either case, whether precautionary measures could in fact have offset the liability is relevant. The issue will receive further attention below, in the examination of the tricky question of omissions.[118]

4.2.2.4 Inner Negligence: Knowledge and Abilities

If it is established that a person's conduct was negligent, the question remains whether their *personal capacities* measured up to those of the reasonable person. As with the negligent conduct, so too with the negligent person is the standard an objective one: the question is not whether the tortfeasor *personally* knew the danger and could have avoided it, but whether she was under an obligation to know and avoid.

As was shown above, the personal capacities of the tortfeasor consist of two elements: knowledge and abilities. The defendant will thus meet the standard of negligence if she knew the risk or ought to have known it and if she could have avoided the risk or ought to have been able to avoid it. In other words, the person who caused damage to another while both knowing the danger their behaviour posed and having the ability to avoid it will be liable for that damage. The same will be true if that person did not know or could not have stopped the harm, but should have been able to know of it or should have been able to stop it. Only if it would not have been possible to become aware of the risk or to avoid it once it has been discovered, then the defendant cannot be held liable. As Van Dam notes, as opposed to the first four indicators of negligent conduct, which are only *factors* suggesting

116. C van Dam, *European Tort Law* (Oxford University Press 2007) para. 807.
117. C van Dam, *European Tort Law* (Oxford University Press 2007) para. 807-3.
118. See s. 4.3.3.2.

possible aberration from proper conduct, knowledge and ability are *conditions* of liability.[119]

(a) Knowledge

Of what must the defendant have knowledge? The knowledge required of the reasonable person must be related to the risk at hand, i.e., the first factor of negligent conduct analysed above. The necessary knowledge may also comprise any common safety rule regarding the avoidance of the risk that indicates its existence. It will however not refer to the exact sequence of events that precede the damage: the defendant need not have been in a position to predict the exact details of the way in which the damage would unfold in order to be held liable. If the risk is unclear, then the reasonable person may be required to engage in further research to refine their knowledge regarding whether or not preventive measures are necessary. The obvious upper limit of knowledge is always the state of the art: if nobody at the time could possibly have known of the risk, then the defendant cannot be held responsible for neglecting to predict it. The state of the art is determined by the time at which the defendant's suspect behaviour occurred: 'the court must not look at the 1947 accident with 1954 spectacles'.[120]

The reliance on the state of the art indicates the flip side of the knowledge question, that of foreseeability. As the knowledge of the defendant is objectively assessed, it can also be described in terms of how predictable it was: the pertinent level of knowledge is the knowledge that the reasonable person would have had – in other words, the knowledge the defendant ought to have had. The question therefore can be rephrased as 'how foreseeable was the risk?' As shall be seen below,[121] foreseeability is often also applied as an element of causation, the idea being that if the defendant could not have foreseen the damage, she may not be said to have caused it.

Foreseeability is affected by a variety of different factors. The relationship of proximity or special reliance between those involved, mentioned by Article 4:102(1) of the PETL, is particularly relevant. So, the closer the relationship between the defendant and the claimant, the more the former can be expected to pay attention to the interests of the latter. The obviousness of the interest, mentioned in Article 2:102(1) of the PETL, is also pertinent: the more recognisable an interest is to the defendant, the higher the defendant's obligation to take care to safeguard it.[122] In this way, an element of subjectivity does enter the area: the objective assessment of the knowledge

119. C van Dam, *European Tort Law* (Oxford University Press 2007) para. 805-2.
120. *Roe v. Minister of Health* [1954] 2 QB 66.
121. See s. 4.4.1.
122. European Group on Tort Law, *Principles of European Tort Law – Text and Commentary* (Springer 2005) 78.

the defendant should have had depends, among other factors, on the person of the defendant.

(b) Abilities

The second characteristic of a negligent person is his lack of ability to avoid the damage. Just as knowledge is related to risk, ability or skill is related to care: the abilities of the reasonable person must correspond to the precautionary measures that are necessary to avoid the harm. This includes safety measures taken in advance in order to forestall the creation of an unavoidable harm. As with knowledge, personal capacity is not, in principle, relevant: a junior doctor cannot rely on his lack of experience to provide sub-par care.[123] If a task is beyond the defendant's capabilities, they may be expected to turn for help to more experienced persons. If they nevertheless proceed, knowing that they do not have the capacity to carry it out safely, liability will result for any resultant harm. This is what the Germans name '*Übernahmeverschulden*', i.e., fault for the undertaking of a dangerous or otherwise unmanageable activity.

As with knowledge, the state of the art marks the limit to the reasonable person's required skill: if nobody could have avoided the damage, the defendant cannot be held liable for its occurrence. As a result, all of the above considerations are controlled by what is feasible in view of the information and technical possibilities available: *impossibilium nulla obligatio est.*

4.3 THE LIMITS OF FAULT

Clearly, not all harmful conduct can result in liability. A limit must somehow be set. Different jurisdictions incorporate this need for boundaries into their tort systems in different ways.[124] Although limitations to fault liability can also be introduced by means of the remaining conditions of fault liability (e.g., damage),[125] they may also be internal to the concept of fault itself. As noted above, the number of conditions for a finding of fault varies from legal system to legal system: France supports a unitary approach to fault, under which the condition for a finding of fault is fault and fault alone. This obviously leaves room for only a single internal fault-limiting device, i.e., the interpretation of fault itself. The English tort of negligence breaks fault down into two elements, duty of care and breach of duty and uses the first to put the brakes on the second. Germany, ever the most analytic national European

123. *Wilsher v. Essex Area Health Authority* [1987] QB 730.
124. For a detailed comparative analysis see, J Spier, *The Limits of Liability – Keeping the Floodgates Shut* (Kluwer Law International 1995).
125. This is the usual approach in France, see C van Dam, *European Tort Law (2nd ed., Oxford University Press 2013)* para. 701-2.

legal system, opts for three conditions of fault: *Tatbestandswidrigkeit* or the violation of a codified normative rule; *Rechtswidrigkeit* or unlawfulness; and *Verschulden* of blameworthiness.[126] The above being said, it is important to understand that the requirements for a finding of fault do not differ in real terms between the three jurisdictions: what changes is simply the formal divisions to which the single fundamental condition on which they depend is subjected: fault.[127] Unitary, dual or three-pronged, fault is still fault. In all three cases, ultimately what is necessary is that the defendant must be, in the words of the DCFR, 'accountable for the causation of the damage'[128] – as the PETL puts it, the damage must be 'legally attributable' to him.[129]

Whatever form they take, the limits of fault are of particular relevance to accessory copyright liability. Accessory liability by definition operates on the very fringes of fault liability: an overexpansion of fault will therefore immediately result in excessive accessory liability, while too strict of a definition will exculpate accessories who arguably deserve to be held liable. As a result, the question of the appropriate limits of fault liability lies at the heart of the European divisions on the topic of the appropriate approaches to accessory liability that were described in Chapter 3.[130] The concept therefore deserves closer attention.

4.3.1 Germany: Unlawfulness

As mentioned above, the German notion of fault comprises three sub-notions: *Tatbestandswidrigkeit, Rechtswidrigkeit* and *Verschulden.* This means that, in order that a person be found to be at fault under German law, he must have violated a codified rule, his conduct must have been unlawful and he must have acted with intention or negligence.[131] The main liability-limiting tool among this conceptual trio is the middle one of unlawfulness; at the same time, unlawfulness cannot be examined without consideration of the two surrounding concepts of *Tatbestandswidrigkeit* and *Verschulden.* Some explanation is therefore here necessary. In the following, we will examine each of these notions in turn.

Tatbestandswidrigkeit is a peculiarly Germanic notion. It originates in the German legislator's attempt to combine a casuistic approach to wrong-doing (similar to the common law's collection of multiple nominate torts)

126. C van Dam, *European Tort Law* (2nd ed., Oxford University Press 2013) para. 605-1; W van Gerven et al, *Tort Law* (Hart Publishing 2000) 300-302.
127. C van Dam, *European Tort Law* (2nd ed., Oxford University Press 2013) para. 605-1.
128. See Art. 1:101(1) DCFR. See also C van Dam, *European Tort Law* (2nd ed., Oxford University Press 2013) paras 701-1 and 701-2: 'It all boils down to the fact that negligent conduct must be legally wrong or that the damage needs to be legally relevant. These are usually two sides of the same coin.'
129. See Art. 1:101(1) PETL.
130. See Ch. 3, s. 3.4.
131. C van Dam, *European Tort Law (2nd ed., Oxford University Press 2013)* para. 802-2.

with the civil law's preference for codification. The German BGB adopts a general duty of care along the Napoleonic example – albeit one broken down into three different provisions: the three general rules of Articles 823(1), 823(2), and 826 of the BGB. At the same time however it is not as comfortable as the C.civ. with the vagueness that accompanies such broadly stated norms. In a bid to curtail legal uncertainty and ensure improved unity in judicial application, these three basic provisions accordingly require the violation of a codified normative rule or *Tatbestand*.[132] This violation what is termed *Tatbestandswidrigkeit*.[133] According to this approach, a person's conduct will only be able to give rise to liability under German tort law under three basic possibilities (*Grundtatbestände)*:[134]

(a) the conduct violated a right (in particular, the life, body, health, freedom, property or another right of another person) (Article 823(1) BGB);
(b) the conduct violated a statutory rule (*Schutzgesetz)* (Article 823(2) BGB); or
(c) the conduct violated a rule pertaining to proper social conduct, i.e., was *contra bonos mores* (Article 826 BGB).

Accordingly, under German law, unreasonable behaviour alone is not enough to substantiate fault: the unreasonableness must be found to be in violation of a codified normative rule.[135] Thus, the German provisions on fault are stated much more reticently than the *grands principes* of Articles 1382 and 1383 of the French C.civ.. At the same time, the provisions of Articles 823 and 826 BGB are wide enough that the limitation imposed by *Tatbestandswidrigkeit* is easily overcome. The main focus of the discussion on the limitations to fault in the German context lies instead on the second condition of fault, that of *Rechtswidrigkeit*. The exact meaning of *Rechtswidrigkeit* is a controversial matter. Among those that recognise it, the answer differs from jurisdiction to jurisdiction, while even within single system opinions clash. In the area of fault liability, the only common denominator seems to be the idea that unlawfulness subsists if the defendant's behaviour was legally incorrect.[136]

---

132. C van Dam, *European Tort Law* (2nd ed., Oxford University Press 2013) para. 604-2.
133. C van Dam, *European Tort Law* (2nd ed., Oxford University Press 2013) para. 402-1.
134. In addition to these three general provisions, the BGB also incorporates three specific provisions (*Einzeltatbestände*): Art. 824 on financial and economic trustworthiness; Art. 825 on infringements of sexual integrity; and Art. 839 on the breach of an official duty, see C van Dam, *European Tort Law* (2nd ed., Oxford University Press 2013) para. 402-1.
135. C van Dam, *European Tort Law* (2nd ed., Oxford University Press 2013) para. 402-1.
136. It is not coincidental that Weir describes the European Group of Tort Law's book on wrongfulness as the least satisfactory of the comparative volumes produced by the estimable group (see T Weir, 'Unification of Tort Law: Wrongfulness.(Review)' (1999) 58(3) Cambridge Law Journal 643): each chapter seems to be talking about something entirely different and, although in his conclusion Koziol suggests that 'wrongfulness'

There are two main schools of thought in this regard: the Result Theory (*Erfolgsunrechtlehre*) and the Conduct Theory (*Verhaltensunrechtlehre*).[137] In Germany, the first system is generally considered to be the prevalent one, although the issue continues to be debated. Other European countries, such as Austria, prefer the Conduct Theory. According to the Result Theory, unlawfulness derives from the causation of a negative result. Clearly, this approach leads to a considerable overlap between unlawfulness and *Tatbestand*: under this interpretation, unlawfulness exists as soon as the *Tatbestand* is established, as long as a ground of justification is not found. Unlawfulness is therefore the violation of a legal norm in the absence of a legally recognised excuse. Consequently, an infringement by means of a positive act of e.g., one of the legal interests enumerated in Article 823(1) BGB, will always automatically result in unlawfulness. On the other hand, according to the Conduct Theory, it is the defendant's behaviour that must be qualified as unlawful. The idea here is that it is possible to infringe somebody else's protected interests without necessarily acting unlawfully. Legal rules can only be violated by the persons who are subject to them, which means that only that behaviour and not the damaging result should be qualified as unlawful. So, under this system, the infringement of one of the legal interests enumerated in Article 823(1) BGB will not be unlawful unless done with intent or negligence.

As a result, where the Conduct Theory is accepted, a different overlap occurs, this time between unlawfulness and the third German condition for fault, *Verschulden*. Although often translated as 'fault' itself, *Verschulden* is best understood as concerning the state of mind of the person who acted in an unlawful manner.[138] A better rendition in English might be blameworthiness, culpability or imputability. As with the *Tatbestand,* its exact contours depend on whether the Result or Conduct Theory is accepted. If the Conduct Theory applies, *Verschulden* is limited exclusively to the subjective element

---

plays an important role in the tort norms of every country, (see H Koziol (ed.) *Unification of Tort Law: Wrongfulness* (Kluwer Law International 1998) 129), this hardly seems surprising: in its broadest meaning, 'wrongful' simply means 'actionable under private law'. See W V H Rogers, 'England: Wrongfulness under English Tort Law' in H Koziol (ed.) *Unification of Tort Law: Wrongfulness* (Kluwer Law International 1998) 39. 'Wrong' is the civil law equivalent of 'crime' and in effect equally vague.

137. W van Gerven et al., *Tort Law* (Hart Publishing 2000) 302-305; K Zweigert & H Kötz, *An Introduction to Comparative Law* (3rd ed., Clarendon Press 1998) 599-600; C von Bar et al. (eds), *Principles, Definitions and Model Rules of European Private Law: Draft Common Frame of Reference (DCFR)*, prepared by the Study Group on a European Civil Code and the Research Group on EC private law (Acquis Group), Outline Edition (Sellier 2009) 2986-2988; H Koziol, *Basic Questions of Tort Law from a Germanic Perspective* (Jan Sramek Verlag 2012) 171-174; H Koziol, 'Austria: Wrongfulness under Austrian Law' in H Koziol (ed.) *Unification of Tort Law: Wrongfulness* (Kluwer Law International 1998) 13-18.

138. W van Gerven et al., *Tort Law* (Hart Publishing 2000) 302.

of the imputability of the conduct to a defendant. As a result, its impact becomes very limited, concerning only questions such as whether the defendant was aware that the conduct was unlawful or whether she was able to properly appreciate the circumstances which made the situation dangerous.[139] Thus, under the Result Theory, *Verschulden* expands to include parts of the objective element of fault as well. In this way, German tradition retains a distinction between the objective and subjective elements of fault, the first being supplied by *Tatbestand* and *Rechtwidrigkeit* and the second by *Verschulden,* with the dividing line between the two moving back and forth depending on the prevalent doctrine.[140]

Is this three-way break down of fault useful to a European tort law? The concept of unlawfulness is entirely alien not only to the common law, but a number of European civil law countries as well.[141] Within France in particular, although the introduction of a notion of *illicéité* has been occasionally discussed, it has been routinely rejected in favour of the unitary notion of *faute*.[142] Indeed, French jurists have concluded that unlawfulness is '*inutile*', '*illusoire*' and '*dangereuse*'.[143] These concerns are by no means to be dismissed as mere Gallic pride. Speaking from within the German tradition itself, Von Bar is equally condemnatory, describing wrongfulness as 'nothing more than a pleonasm [that] only irritates those who are not brought up under German law'. And indeed: if a right is recognised, it adds nothing to say that its violation is wrongful. Given that Article 823(1) BGB anyway recognises the liability of any 'person who, intentionally or negligently, unlawfully injures the life, body, health, freedom, property or another right of another person', the reference to unlawfulness simply foreshadows the detailed list of absolute rights that follows immediately after it. Moreover, the casuistic attempt to enumerate all duties whose infringement is wrongful beyond those listed in statute is, by its nature, doomed to failure, as it is both 'too ambitious from a theoretical point of view and too restrictive in practical

139. W van Gerven et al., *Tort Law* (Hart Publishing 2000) 303-304.

140. Van Gerven et al., suggest that the combination of the objective element of unlawfulness and the subjective element of culpability amounts to wrongfulness (in German, *Widerrechtlichkeit*) – i.e., essentially as a synonym for what in this book is called fault (see W van Gerven, J Lever & P Larouche, *Tort Law* (Hart Publishing 2000) 300-301).

141. Including French, Czech, Belgian, Maltese, Luxemburgian, Slovakian, Slovenian, Spanish law, as well as the law of Nordic countries, see C von Bar et al. (eds), *Principles, Definitions and Model Rules of European Private Law: Draft Common Frame of Reference (DCFR)*, prepared by the Study Group on a European Civil Code and the Research Group on EC private law (Acquis Group), Outline Edition (Sellier 2009) 2986. See also, C Von Bar, *The Common European Law of Torts – Vol. II* (Clarendon Press 2000) paras 213-219.

142. Although see W van Gerven et al., *Tort Law* (Hart Publishing 2000) 301, who notes that upon closer inspection *faute* can be separated into two elements: (i) an objective element of unlawfulness and (b) a subjective element of culpability or imputability.

143. C Von Bar, *The Common European Law of Torts – Vol. II* (Clarendon Press 2000) para. 218. The same could be said of the English preoccupation with nominate 'torts'.

terms'.[144] It could of course simply be said that wrongfulness should be assumed, as long as a ground of justification is not proven – but again, this would be simply stating the obvious purpose of legally recognised defences.

The debate on the precise contours of the notion that unlawfulness has engendered even within the single jurisdiction of Germany is further indication of the difficulties that the concept poses. Zweigert and Kötz criticise the *Erfolgsunrechtlehre v. Verhaltensunrechtlehre* discussion, noting that it lacks real practical significance: 'given that a person who causes harm despite observing all the requisite precautions is not liable, it is normally quite immaterial whether his non-liability is attributed to want of *unlawfulness* or want of *culpability*'.[145] Widmer also admits that the distinction 'is more one of philosophical and dogmatical perspectives than of effective practical importance'.[146] More fundamentally, the very differentiation between unlawfulness and culpability is not always respected by the courts, even in countries which do recognise the difference in their legal theory. This is the case for example in the Netherlands.[147]

As a result, unlawfulness does not make an impressive candidate for incorporation in a harmonised European tort law – including therefore a harmonised European system for accessory liability. And indeed, precisely in view of the theoretical difficulties that accompany it, as well as its relative lack of popularity across the EU, unlawfulness has not been incorporated as such into either the PETL or the DCFR.[148] More significantly for the purposes of this book, unlawfulness as a condition of fault also causes significant problems for accessory liability,[149] as declaring the unlawfulness of a violation of a legal norm not through a direct positive act, but through an omission or by means of the conduct of a third party is far less straightforward.[150] As Von Bar observes, it 'is impossible to operate with an 'accessory' law of delict which basically can only produce three types of

144. C Von Bar, *The Common European Law of Torts – Vol. II* (Clarendon Press 2000) para. 214.
145. K Zweigert & H Kötz, *An Introduction to Comparative Law* (3rd ed., Clarendon Press 1998) 599-600.
146. P Widmer, 'Switzerland: The Concept of Unlawfulness – Function and Relevance under Swiss Law' in H Koziol (ed.) *Unification of Tort Law: Wrongfulness* (Kluwer Law International 1998) 115.
147. J Spier, 'The Netherlands: Wrongfulness in the Dutch Context' in H Koziol (ed.) *Unification of Tort Law: Wrongfulness* (Kluwer Law International 1998) 87.
148. C von Bar et al. (eds), *Principles, Definitions and Model Rules of European Private Law: Draft Common Frame of Reference (DCFR)*, prepared by the Study Group on a European Civil Code and the Research Group on EC private law (Acquis Group), Outline Edition (Sellier 2009) 2986.
149. C von Bar, *The Common European Law of Torts – Vol. II* (Clarendon Press 2000) paras 212-214.
150. C von Bar, *The Common European Law of Torts – Vol. II* (Clarendon Press 2000) para. 214, footnote 216; W van Gerven et al., *Tort Law* (Hart Publishing 2000) 286-287; C van Dam, *European Tort Law* (2nd ed., Oxford University Press 2013) para. 402-2.

'unlawful' omission: breach of a statutory duty, breach of a contractual duty, and omission in cases of conduct creating potential danger'.[151] The result would be a dramatic overexpansion, as all cases of violation of a right protected by Article 823 BGB could be attributed to another's omission to prevent it.[152] To overcome this issue the German jurisprudence has turned to the notion of *Verkehrspflichten* or duties of care as a control device. So, now, shall we. The primary proponent of duties of care in the EU is England. The analysis is therefore best situated in an examination of that jurisidiction's law.

4.3.2 England: Duty of Care

As mentioned above, in English law the basic conditions for the establishment of the tort of negligence are four: (a) a duty of care; (b) a breach of that duty; (c) a damage; and (d) causation. The tort of negligence thus hinges first and foremost on the notion of a duty of care:

> The cardinal principle of liability is that the party complained of should owe to the party complaining a duty to take care and that the party complaining should be able to prove that he has suffered damage in consequence of a breach of that duty.[153]

The existence of a notion of duty of care is not in itself atypical among the European tort systems. What is however striking in the approach of English law is the emphasis placed on it. This can be attributed to the nature of English tort law as a collection of separate heads of liability: the notion of 'duty' is not confined to the tort of negligence, but is an elemental part of every English tort, as each is specialised to cater to a particular duty. However, as opposed to most torts (defamation, trespass, assault, etc.), where the concept of duty can only refer to an obligation to not commit that particular tort, in the tort of negligence the contours of the duty of care are much less obviously defined. As Rogers points out, in English law there is no general liability for carelessly or unreasonably causing harm to others: '[i]t is not for every careless act that a man may be held responsible in law, nor even for every careless act that causes damage'. Unreasonable carelessness will only be legally relevant when it is in violation of a duty to not be careless in that specific way. Where there is no such duty, the defendant is allowed to act unreasonably.[154] To put it another way, unreasonableness that is legally

151. C von Bar, *The Common European Law of Torts – Vol. II* (Clarendon Press 2000) para. 214, footnote 216.
152. C van Dam, *European Tort Law* (2nd ed., Oxford University Press 2013) para. 402-2.
153. *Donoghue v. Stevenson* [1932] UKHL 100 (26 May 1932).
154. D Howarth, 'Many Duties of Care – Or A Duty of Care? Notes from the Underground' (2006) 26(3) Oxford Journal of Legal Studies 449.

irrelevant does not give rise to duty: we are all free to obstinately refuse to put our dirty socks in the laundry basket without any legal repercussions.

When then does a duty of care arise under English law? Over the course of the development of the tort of negligence a variety of different models have been proposed for determining when such a duty is owed.[155] A huge revolution in the modern English law of negligence occurred in the first half of the twentieth century when Lord Atkin declared his famous 'neighbour principle':

> The rule that you are to love your neighbour becomes in law you must not injure your neighbour; and the lawyer's question 'Who is my neighbour?' receives a restricted reply. You must take reasonable care to avoid acts or omissions which you can reasonably foresee would be likely to injure your neighbour. Who, then, in law, is my neighbour? The answer seems to be persons who are so closely and directly affected by my act that I ought reasonably to have them in contemplation as being affected when I am directing my mind to the acts or omissions which are called in question.[156]

This formulation gives negligence a particularly wide reach, transforming it into the most general and most important of the English torts. English lawyers have been trying to claw it back from the precipice of a civil-law-like *clausula generalis* ever since.

In 1978, the *Anns*[157] formula attempted a stronger hold on the concept by declaring that a duty of care will exist if the relationship between the claimant and the defendant was of sufficient proximity or neighbourhood, such that it was reasonable foreseeable that the defendant's conduct would result in the claimant suffering harm and as long as no policy considerations exist that would negate or limit the scope of the duty of care. This again was accused of being overly permissive.

The currently best-accepted standard however is the so-called *Caparo* or *threefold* test. According to this, the defendant will be found to have owed a duty of care where: (a) it was reasonably *foreseeable* that the defendant's actions or inaction would cause the claimant damage; (b) the relationship between the claimant and the defendant was sufficiently *proximate*; and (c) the imposition of a duty of care would be '*fair, just and reasonable*'.[158] Of these three conditions the most important is the last one. When sufficient 'fairness, justness and reasonableness' will be found to exist will depend on the individual circumstances at hand: in some cases, mere foreseeability of

155. N McBride & R Bagshaw, *Tort Law* (4th ed., Pearson 2012) 104.
156. *Donoghue v. Stevenson* [1932] UKHL 100 (26 May 1932).
157. *Anns v. Merton LBC* [1977] 2 All ER 118.
158. *Caparo Industries plc v. Dickman* [1990] 1 All ER 568; W van Gerven et al., *Tort Law* (Hart Publishing 2000) 53; N McBride & R Bagshaw, *Tort Law* (4th ed., Pearson 2012) 107.

the harm will be sufficient to label the imposition of a duty of care 'fair, just and reasonable', while in others something more, e.g., a kind of special relationship binding the defendant to the claimant or a special obligation of some sort, will be required. As Lord Oliver observed:

> But although the cases in which the courts have imposed or withheld liability are capable of an approximate categorisation, one looks in vain for some common denominator by which the existence of the essential relationship can be tested. Indeed it is difficult to resist a conclusion that what have been treated as three separate requirements are, at least in most cases, in fact merely facets of the same thing, for in some cases the degree of foreseeability is such that it is from that alone that the requisite proximity can be deduced, whilst in others the absence of that essential relationship can most rationally be attributed simply to the court's view that it would not be fair and reasonable to hold the defendant responsible. 'Proximity' is, no doubt, a convenient expression so long as it is realised that it is no more than a label which embraces not a definable concept but merely a description of circumstances from which, pragmatically, the courts conclude that a duty of care exists.[159]

From this, McBride and Bagshaw conclude that more important than any test of duty of care are the factors that determine when it has been satisfied. For this purpose, they suggest such elements as the reasonable foreseeability of the harm, the seriousness of the harm, the lawmakers' intention, whether the defendant's behaviour was an act or an omission, the reasonableness of the defendant's behaviour, the contributing responsibility of the claimant or a third party, the public interest, the novelty of the claim and 'fairness', i.e., the proportionality of the fault to the harm.[160]

As a result, duty of care in English law remains as hard to pin down as any other area of negligence. A simple rule for establishing duty of care is impossible to state. If one must be put forth, perhaps the best that can realistically be offered is simply the same one applied to the accompanying condition of breach of duty: the vague reasonable person standard. The defendant will owe a duty to do what the reasonable person would. All other tests are arguably nothing more than an interpretation of that rule.

At its simplest therefore, the English duty of care refers merely to a restriction on acceptable conduct limiting it to that which the reasonably careful person in similar circumstances would display.[161] But if duty is the obligation to behave as a reasonable person in similar circumstances would and breach of duty is the failure to behave in such a way, it can reasonably be questioned whether they are not in fact two sides of the same coin. If that

---

159. *Caparo Industries plc v. Dickman* [1990] 1 All ER 568.
160. N McBride & R Bagshaw, *Tort Law* (4th ed., Pearson 2012) 108-119.
161. P Winfield, 'Duty in Tortious Negligence' (1934) 34 Columbia Law Review 41.

is the case, whether both deserve to be independent conditions of the tort of negligence is worth considering.

As a result, like unlawfulness in German law, duty of care in English law has also received its fair share of criticism. A number of 'duty sceptics' have thus suggested abandoning the notion altogether in favour of a fault-based approach. Buckland, for example, famously called duty of care 'the fifth wheel of the coach'.[162] Winfield suggested that duty of care is but a superfluous historical accident, which should be retained in English law simply in order to avoid upsetting the tradition of centuries.[163] Markesinis has complained precisely that the 'blunderbuss weapon' of duty can more satisfactorily be replaced by the reasonable person test:[164] instead of complicating fault by attempting to explain it by reference to a different, but equally indeterminate notion, it would be far more elegant to simply state that the standard of care has not been breached, as the defendant did not exhibit legally relevant lack of reasonableness. Setting the standard of care is of course the hard part – but no harder than deciding whether or not there is a duty. In addition, the language of standard of care would have the advantage of allowing for greater flexibility, by not removing the option of liability off the table categorically: instead of contriving categories of duties of care, judges should instead be invited to examine each case on its merits. This is of course exactly how the French deal with cases of 'no duty': they are not cornered by their system into recognising obligations incumbent on legal subjects where they do not wish such obligations to exist, but attempt to identify what is expected of the defendant by means of an indeterminate number of socially constructed rules.

Nevertheless, the idea of abandoning duty of care remains a highly controversial position in English law. McBride and Bagshaw argue that an excessive reliance on fault would imply that for a claimant to win her case, the only thing that would be necessary would be a showing of carelessness on the part of the defendant and a resulting damage to the claimant. On this basis they warn that:

> a system of law which was genuinely based on a 'fault principle' that losses should fall on those who were at fault for causing them would destabilise society – both because people would be paralysed from doing anything by the fear that if their conduct was judged to have fallen below the standard of a 'reasonable man' they might be fixed with a huge bill for damages, and because the normal business of the courts would collapse under the weight of the claims for compensation with which they would be flooded.[165]

---

162. W Buckland, '*The Duty to Take Care*' (1935) 51 Law Quarterly Review 637.
163. P Winfield, 'Duty in Tortious Negligence' (1934) 34 Columbia Law Review 41.
164. B Markesinis, 'Negligence, Nuisance and Affirmative Duties of Action' (1989) Law Quarterly Review 104.
165. N McBride & R Bagshaw, *Tort Law* (4th ed., Pearson 2012) 120.

Viney is flatly dismissive of this 'floodgates' argument: '*cet argument me parait dangereux car il manque totalement de rigueur. Il n'a guère d'impact actuellement sur la jurisprudence française*'.[166] And indeed, the suggestion assumes that the standard of care will be either be a closely guarded secret of the courts inaccessible to the (wo)man on the street or entirely determined by the notions of 'carelessness' and 'reasonableness' in common parlance. But why this would be the case for those legal terms, when it is not for the concept of 'duty', which also has a different meaning in everyday life than it does in the law? Instead, it must be accepted that the difference between English and German tort law, on the one hand, and French tort law, on the other, is that, rather than treating the notion of duty of care as an independent condition for liability, French law folds duty into breach, so that they become one and the same: the famous French *faute*.

So, do duty of care and unlawfulness have no usefulness at all? More a propos to our purposes, do they have no effect on the law of intermediary accessory liability for copyright? To determine this, their application must be examined in practice.

4.3.3 The Limits of Fault and Intermediary Accessory Liability in Copyright

Can the stricter view taken by the English and German rules on the conditions for a finding of fault explain the reluctance experienced in these two jurisdictions for the application of a negligence-based solution to intermediary accessory liability in copyright? In other words: is intermediary accessory liability in copyright pushed out of English and German negligence liability by unlawfulness and the duty of care? Those jurisdictions' concern with the overexpansion of fault would suggest as much.[167]

How does that exclusion operate in practice? The main 'no fault' enclaves relevant to intermediary accessory copyright liability that have been carved out in English and German law by the formal limitations of unlawfulness and duty of care are two: pure economic loss and omissions.[168] Both are relevant to the analysis of accessory copyright liability. The first relates to the extent of the protection afforded to copyright as an interest and the second to the extent of the protection afforded against failures to act, including therefore the failures to act to prevent copyright infringements by others.

166. G Viney, 'France: Le 'Wrongfulness' en Droit Français' in H Koziol (ed.) *Unification of Tort Law: Wrongfulness* (Kluwer Law International 1998) 57. For an analysis of how and why this has been achieved see, J-S Borghetti, 'The Culture of Tort Law in France' (2012) 3 Journal of European Tort Law 158.
167. *CBS Songs v. Amstrad* [1988] UKHL 15 (12 May 1988).
168. B Markesinis, 'Negligence, Nuisance and Affirmative Duties of Action' (1989) Law Quarterly Review 104; N McBride & R Bagshaw, *Tort Law* (4th ed., Pearson 2012) 106.

4.3.3.1 Copyright and Pure Economic Loss

Arguments could be made that copyright infringement constitutes pure economic loss, i.e., damage unconnected to personal injury or property damage. For example, Riordan declares that the common law's refusal to recognise a general duty not to facilitate an end-user's infringements is rooted in precisely its dismissal of the idea of negligence for pure economic loss beyond the established principles.[169] Weir likewise explains Lord Templeman's rejection of a negligence-based solution in *Amstrad* by pointing out the mere economic nature of the harm suffered by the plaintiffs.[170] While there is no reason to challenge the limited protection of pure economic loss in negligence, can it really be said that copyright constitutes such loss?

Upon first inspection, the idea does seem to hold some water. Pure economic loss is loss which does not arise from personal injury or damage to property.[171] In most European systems, this type of damage is placed on the lower levels of the totem pole of protected interests. It is indicative that Article 2:102(4) PETL shares the general European reluctance to allow tort claims for pure economic loss:

> Protection of pure economic interests or contractual relationships may be more limited in scope. In such cases, due regard must be had especially to the proximity between the actor and the endangered person, or to the fact that the actor is aware of the fact that he will cause damage even though his interests are necessarily valued lower than those of the victim.[172]

The denigration of pure economic loss is particularly evident in the common law, where no duty of care to prevent such loss encumbers the defendant unless a compelling reason so demands.[173] As a result, pure economic loss (setting aside the case of certain specially designated

169. J Riordan, *The Liability of Internet Intermediaries* (PhD thesis, University of Oxford 2013, forthcoming Oxford University Press 2016) 148.
170. T Weir, 'Liability for Knowingly Facilitating Mass Breaches of Copyright' (1988) 47(3) The Cambridge Law Journal 348.
171. M Bussani & V V Palmer, 'The Notion of Pure Economic Loss and Its Setting' in M Bussani & V V Palmer (eds), *Pure Economic Loss in Europe* (Cambridge University Press 2003) 5; M Lunney & K Oliphant, *Tort Law – Text and Materials* (3rd ed., Oxford University Press 2007) 376.
172. It is also worth observing that, on the European level, the Directive on Liability for Defective Products makes a similar distinction when it limits its protection to death, personal injury and damage to property. See Council Directive of 25 July 1985 on the approximation of the laws, regulations and administrative provisions of the Member States concerning liability for defective products (85/374/EEC) [1985] OJ L210/29.
173. N McBride & R Bagshaw, *Tort Law* (4th ed., Pearson 2012) 172-206. See, for example, *Hedley Byrne & Co Ltd v. Heller & Partners Ltd* [1964] AC 465; *Leigh and Sillivan Ltd v. The Aliakmon Shipping Co. Ltd* (*The Aliakmon*) [1986] AC 785; *Caparo Industries plc v. Dickman* [1990] 2 AC 605.

economic torts) is generally only recoverable if inflicted intentionally. Similarly, Article 823 of the German BGB does not list *reiner Vermögensschaden* among the *Rechtsgüter* it protects, meaning that the infliction of pure economic loss cannot be unlawful under that provision. Instead, the only means available for a finding of fault for pure economic loss is Article 826 of the BGB. This prohibits the causation of damage of any kind (therefore including pure economic loss) on another person in an immoral manner ('*gegen die guten Sitten*' or, in Latin, '*contra bonos mores*') only when done intentionally. So in Germany, as in English law, the causation of pure economic loss only constitutes a fault if accompanied by intent. Pure economic loss in negligence is the exception, recognised only under certain very circumscribed conditions.

By contrast, French law draws no bright line between pure economic loss and graver forms of damage. Instead, equal protection is extended in theory to all types of loss, with interferences to property and interferences with legitimate economic interests both being viewed as reprehensible *atteintes au patrimonie.* 'At a conceptual level there are no limits' to the recovery of pure economic loss in France.[174] Can this permissive attitude explain the relative ease the French enjoy in finding internet intermediaries liable in negligence for third party copyright infringements? It should be noted that, although France does indeed lack the formal control mechanisms that allow England and Germany to lock pure economic loss out of fault in an overt fashion, significant barriers against the recovery of pure economic loss can be found in the French system as well, although located in the additional conditions for fault liability of causation and damage. Thus, in France, before it may be compensated, the damage must be found to be *direct et personnel, licite, légitime, présent et certain.* Additional safeguards are incorporated into the concept of *faute* itself: in cases of pure economic loss the existence of a *faute* in France is not assessed with reference to the standard of *le bon père de famille,* but according to the stricter principles of *loyauté,* honnête, et bonne foi.[175]

Adding to these observations, it is also worth noting that, while the legal theory in England and Germany is certainly more hostile towards the idea of pure economic loss than that of France, the judiciaries in both countries have found ways to permit a laxer standard in practice.[176] Ultimately, the conclusion must be that, while the divisions between the various European national approaches are real, they are not as black and white as might at first glance appear and are, moreover, mainly vested in the shape of the different legal frameworks rather than in practical effect. The question is one of

---

174. C van Dam, *European Tort Law* (2nd ed., Oxford University Press 2013) para. 710-2.
175. W van Gerven et al., *Tort Law* (Hart Publishing 2000) 205-208; C van Dam, *European Tort Law* (2nd ed., Oxford University Press 2013) paras 710-1 to 710-5.
176. C van Dam, *European Tort Law* (2nd ed., Oxford University Press 2013) para. 710-1.

degree: pure economic loss enjoys lesser protection in all three systems, but to a greater extent in England and Germany than in France.

Can the national differences in approach towards pure economic loss explain the national differences in approach towards intermediary accessory copyright liability? Even if the first were considerably starker, a more fundamental obstacle to this theory exists. As, simply put, in no European jurisdiction can copyright be described as a form of pure economic loss. Instead, in all EU Member States, copyright is very clearly a form of the more serious concept of property damage.[177] As Article 2:102(3) PETL explicitly recognises as much:

> Extensive protection is granted to property rights, including those in intangible property.

This makes sense. It should be recalled that copyright also comprises moral rights,[178] while even the author's economic rights represent something weightier than the mere monetary value of the work: the connection of the author to the fruit of his creative labour.[179] Certainly, different European legal systems do justify copyright by reference to different schools of thought: so, while the French tradition of *droits d'auteur* takes a distinctly natural law-inspired position, the common law is more inclined towards a pragmatic conception,[180] which might conceivably indicate a lesser interest in a far-reaching protection extending to accessory liability. Nevertheless, neither legal system is inclined to deny the nature of intellectual property as, precisely, property.[181]

In any case, the property nature of copyright has recently found added confirmation at the highest level in European human rights law: according to the ECtHR the term 'possessions' used in Article 1 of the First Protocol 1 to the ECHR on the right to property is intended to cover 'assets, including claims, in respect of which the applicant can argue that he has at least a

177. Indeed, Murphy and Witting define pure economic loss negatively as 'a loss which is not a physical damage or injury to intellectual property rights or reputation. […] The concern is with loss not immediately bound up in one of the primary interests of person, property (including intellectual property), or reputation'; see J Murphy & C Witting, *Street on Torts* (13th ed., Oxford University Press 2012) 93.

178. L Bently & B Sherman, *Intellectual Property Law* (3rd ed., Oxford University Press 2009) 241; P Goldstein & P B Hugenholtz, *International Copyright: Principles, Law, and Practice* (Oxford University Press 2012) 357; S Ricketson & J Ginsburg, *International Copyright and Neighbouring Rights: The Berne Convention and Beyond* (Oxford University Press 2006) 585; E Adeney, *The Moral Rights of Authors and Performers: An International and Comparative Analysis* (6th ed., Oxford University Press 2006). See also, C van Dam, *European Tort Law* (2nd ed., Oxford University Press 2013) para. 701-1.

179. A Mossoff, 'Is Copyright Property?' (2005) 42(1) San Diego Law Review 29.

180. P Goldstein & P B Hugenholtz, *International Copyright: Principles, Law, and Practice* (Oxford University Press 2012) 6-7.

181. L Bently & B Sherman, *Intellectual Property Law* (3rd ed., Oxford University Press 2009) 1-3.

'legitimate expectation' of obtaining effective enjoyment of a property right'.[182] This indicates that the ECHR protects not only tangible property, but intangible property as well, which some legal orders might classify as pure economic interests.[183] Subsequent case law makes clear that, although Article 1 of Protocol 1 does not expressly mention intellectual property, its protection extends to copyright: so, in *Anheuser-Busch Inc v. Portugal,* the Court stated that, 'intellectual property as such undeniably attracts the protection of Art. 1 of Protocol No.1'.[184] That case was relevant to trademark protection, but the same conclusion was repeated with regard to copyright in *Balan v. Moldova.*[185] The Charter goes one step further and explicitly incorporates IPRs into its Article 17 on the right to property. There, it decrees that 'intellectual property shall be protected'. On this basis, as already mentioned in Chapter 2, the case law of the CJEU has acknowledged that the protection of the fundamental right to property includes IPRs.[186]

In the final conclusion, it becomes clear that any economic loss resulting from intellectual property infringement must be viewed as consequential upon the accompanying property loss and therefore cannot be seen as 'pure'. As a result of its property status, copyright, while not quite as imposing an interest as the personal rights of life, bodily or mental integrity, human dignity and liberty (to which Article 2:102(2) PETL, for example, grants 'the most extensive' protection) finds itself on a middle tier of protected interests: its protection is not absolute, but it is compelling.[187]

182. ECtHR, *Prince Hans-Adam II of Liechtenstein v. Germany,* application. no. 42527/9812, 12 July 2001.
183. C van Dam, *European Tort Law* (2nd ed., Oxford University Press 2013) para. 709-2.
184. *Anheuser-Busch Inc. v. Portugal* [GC] (Appl. No. 73049/01) 11 January 2011.
185. *Balan v. Moldova* (Appl. No. 19247/03) 29 January 2008.
186. It should be noted of course that property rights can be said to be among the weakest in the human rights arsenal; for example, the ECHR allows interference with the right to property 'in the public interest and subject to the conditions provided for by law and by the general principles of international law'. States can accordingly 'enforce such laws as it deems necessary to control the use of property in accordance with the general interest or to secure the payment of taxes or other contributions or penalties.' It should also be considered that copyright is only an artificial, not a natural property right, potentially further weakening its defenses. See, E Barendt, *Freedom of Speech* (2nd ed., Oxford University Press 2007) 253-254. Nevertheless, these considerations should not affect copyright's standing within the tort law framework as a property right, but simply indicate that it might be more vulnerable than other more consequential rights within a human rights setting.
187. The protection of property, aside from being mandated by ECHR and the EU Charter, is in line with the status of the right in the tort law of the Member States. For example, English law recognises, in addition to a series of property-related torts such as private nuisance and trespass to goods, that the tort of negligence may also apply to for the protection of property, including economic loss consequential on physical damage (see *Spartan Steel & Co Ltd v. Martin* [1973] 1 QB 27). Thus, it is assumed that a tortfeasor owes a duty of care towards persons whose property may foreseeably be damaged by her negligence conduct. Likewise, Germany includes '*das Eigentum*' and similar rights among the protected *Rechtsgüter* of Art. 823(1) BGB, while in France there is likewise

While the mere infliction of copyright infringement will therefore not in itself be enough to establish negligence, as might be the case where personal rights are involved,[188] it is likewise not the case that damage to copyright may be freely inflicted. This is as true of England and Germany, as it is of France. Once that is accepted, it becomes clear that different jurisdictional approaches to pure economic loss are irrelevant to the national approaches to accessory copyright liability.

4.3.3.2 Accessory Liability and Omissions

A far more promising explanation of the German and English caution as concerns the idea of a negligence-based accessory liability is provided by the second area on which the formal limitations to fault recognised by these two jurisdictions concentrate, that of omissions. What happens where the only way in which the defendant can prevent the creation of harm for the claimant is, not simply to avoid conduct that would result in the imposition of harm, but to undertake *positive action* to intervene between the potential victim and the oncoming damage? The question of omissions is central to accessory liability: liability for others has in fact been said to be the very 'prototype' of liability for omissions,[189] while at the same time, as McIvor observes, the troublesome history of liability for omissions lies at the heart of the misunderstandings surrounding accessory liability law.[190] Clarifying negligence by omission therefore represents an important step in elucidating the European law of third party liability. To this end, below under which circumstances such a positive duty of care may be imposed on the tortfeasor will be examined in each of the selected national jurisdictions.

The first thing that must be observed in this regard is that most national legislators shy away from requesting persons to do what they do not wish to: when a positive act is prohibited, many other options remain available to legal subjects, but when it is demanded, freedom of choice evaporates. This explains why no modern European legal order imposes a general duty to save another from damage by taking action, rather than omitting it: there is no duty to be a good Samaritan. At the same time, all examined systems

no question that interference with a property right is a forbidden '*dommage*' in the sense of Arts 1382 and 1383. See W van Gerven et al., *Tort Law* (Hart Publishing 2000) 203-204.

188. See Art. 823(1) BGB.
189. C von Bar, *The Common European Law of Torts – Vol. II* (Clarendon Press 2000) para. 203.
190. C McIvor, *Third Party Liability in Tort* (Hart Publishing 2006) 9; M Lunney & K Oliphant, *Tort Law – Text and Materials* (3rd ed., Oxford University Press 2007) 481.

recognise significant exceptions to this basic rule.[191] So, in *Blyth v. Birmingham Waterworks,* Alderson B confirmed that negligence may arise through either commission or omission:

> Negligence is the omission to do something which a reasonable man, guided upon those considerations which ordinarily regulate the conduct of human affairs, would do, or doing something which a prudent and reasonable man would not do.[192]

Accordingly, liability may be imposed for the violation of a positive obligation to refrain from a negligent omission just as much as it might from the violation of a negative obligation to refrain from negligent action. Indeed, it is the only way it may be: as Von Bar notes, just 'as there is no liability without a duty, so there can be no liability for an omission in the absence of an obligation to act'.[193] The liability for breaching such an affirmative obligation to act is termed *nonfeasance*, as opposed to liability for breaching a negative obligation of refrain from acting, i.e., *misfeasance*. An affirmative duty arises when a reasonable person could be expected to engage in an activity.[194] But when might that be?

This question is a particularly vexatious one that has been the epicentre of considerable doctrinal disagreement across and within European jurisdictions. In their attempt to deal with the problem, the first instinct of most European legal systems seems to have been to try to squeeze answers out of the factual realities. Thus, English law distinguishes between omissions that are part of a chain of negligent affirmative conduct and 'pure omissions' that stand alone. It then enables liability only for the first. This is similar to the French distinction between '*omissions dans l'action*' and '*omissions pure et simple*'.[195] The idea behind the division is that, if a defendant has played a causative part in the train of events that led to the ultimate harm, liability is appropriate in a way that it is not for mere bystanders that fail to intervene. But this solution seems to beg the question: although it gives us a clearer idea of when omissions may be negligent, it still doesn't tell us much about what differentiates an omission from positive action.

Indeed, a big source of the confusion surrounding the idea of a negligent failure to act lies precisely in the difficulty of drawing a clear-cut line

---

191. H Koziol, *Basic Questions of Tort Law from a Germanic Perspective* (Jan Sramek Verlag 2012) 188. For further explanations of the law's unwillingness to impose a general obligation for positive action, see N McBride & R Bagshaw, *Tort Law* (4th ed., Pearson 2012) 213-217.
192. *Blyth v. Birmingham Waterworks* [1856] EWHC Exch J65.
193. C von Bar, *The Common European Law of Torts – Vol. II* (Clarendon Press 2000) para. 288.
194. C van Dam, *European Tort Law* (2nd ed., Oxford University Press 2013) para. 808-1.
195. P le Tourneau, *Droit de la responsabilité et des contracts – Régimes d'indemnisation* (9th ed., Dalloz 2013) 7201-7233; C van Dam, *European Tort Law* (2nd ed., Oxford University Press 2013) para. 808-1.

between acts and omissions. What may at first sight appear to be a case of nonfeasance might upon closer inspection prove to constitute misfeasance. Should, for example, a driver who fails to brake and, as a result, hits a pedestrian be considered to be liable for misfeasance or for nonfeasance? Has she omitted to press the brake and slow down the car or has she engaged in a positive act by getting behind the wheel and knocking somebody down? Applying natural laws to solve this conundrum leads to legally unsatisfactory results. To give another traffic-related example, is there a real difference between the driver moving downhill that has enough momentum to carry the car into the pedestrian unassisted and the driver moving uphill who has to apply his foot to the brake to achieve the same result? The only fair answer can be no: both drivers are simply adjusting their behaviour to the differing physical realities of their situations in order to achieve the precise same result. The first driver is not avoiding pressing down on the accelerator to circumvent the act the second driver is pursuing, but because the incline of the road means that that is not necessary. The more pertinent question is indeed a different one: why did each of the two drivers engage in this behaviour?

With this in mind, a simpler approach treats the classification of conduct as either an act or omission as no more than mere *l'art pour l'art.*[196] For instance, Hart and Honoré suggest that the proof is in the pudding: 'if there is a legal duty to do an act, and the subject has not done it, the legally relevant description will be in terms of an omission to perform the act in question'.[197] In this way, whether an act or omission occurred will depend entirely only on the content of the duty of care. Von Bar agrees. He suggests that the distinction between act and omission is a reflection of the distinction between the rule and the exception. As a rule, only the person who caused damage is liable for it. Uninvolved third parties cannot be dragged into problems they did not create. Harm caused by another can only be attributed to a third party exceptionally, if there is a good reason to do so.[198] In conclusion therefore, the answer can ever only be found in the law:

> It is not the rights and objects of legal protection which generate the duties whose violation constitutes misconduct, but rather the laws, the principle of *neminem laedere*, and the general duty of care.[199]

At this point, it is worth considering in greater detail the individual solutions adopted in the three selected Member States.

---

196. C von Bar, *The Common European Law of Torts – Vol. II* (Clarendon Press 2000) para. 194.
197. H L A Hart & T Honoré, *Causation in the Law* (2nd ed., Clarendon Press 1985) 138-139.
198. C von Bar, *The Common European Law of Torts – Vol. II* (Clarendon Press 2000) para. 194.
199. C Von Bar, *The Common European Law of Torts – Vol. II* (Clarendon Press 2000) para. 214.

- *England*

Despite the increasing importance it gives to the tort of negligence, English law has been exceedingly resistant to the imposition of positive duties of care.[200] Lord Hoffman is usually cited as delivering the English position on the topic and the main arguments supporting it:

> There are sound reasons why omissions require different treatment from positive conduct. It is one thing for the law to say that a person who undertakes some activity shall take reasonable care not to cause damage to others. It is another thing for the law to require that a person who is doing nothing in particular shall take steps to prevent another from suffering harm from the acts of third parties […] or natural causes. One can put the matter in political, moral or economic terms. In political terms it is less of an invasion of an individual's freedom for the law to require him to consider the safety of others in his actions than to impose upon him a duty to rescue or protect. A moral version of this point may be called the 'why pick on me?' argument. A duty to prevent harm to others or to render assistance to a person in danger or distress may apply to a large and indeterminate class of people who happen to be able to do something. Why should one be held liable rather than another? In economic terms, the efficient allocation of resources usually requires an activity should bear its own costs. If it benefits from being able to impose some of its costs on other people (what economists call 'externalities',) the market is distorted because the activity appears cheaper than it really is. So liability to pay compensation for loss caused by negligent conduct acts as a deterrent against increasing the cost of the activity to the community and reduces externalities. But there is no similar justification for requiring a person who is not doing anything to spend money on behalf of someone else. Except in special cases (such as marine salvage) English law does not reward someone who voluntarily confers a benefit on another. So there must be some special reason why he should have to put his hand in his pocket.[201]

As a result, it is considered rare for English law to find that one person owes another a positive duty of care to undertake a specific action, as

---

200. B Markesinis, 'Negligence, Nuisance and Affirmative Duties of Action' (1989) Law Quarterly Review 104.
201. *Stovin v. Wise* [1996] UKHL 15 (24 July 1996). J Logie has also put forth a good summary of these arguments in his article entitled 'Affirmative Action in the Law of Tort: The Case of a Duty to Warn' ([1989] CLJ 115), as has J Kortmann in *Altruism in Private Law: Liability for Nonfeasance and Negatorium Gestio* (Oxford University Press 2005).

opposed to a negative duty to avoid one. Nevertheless, although this is sometimes not readily apparent in the scholarship, this is not to say that English law does not accept any affirmative duties of care under any circumstances; rather that the mere causative link between the omission of the tortfeasor and the harm to the claimant are not of themselves enough to ground a positive duty of care: 'something more', as it is usually put, will always be necessary. In the words of Lord Nicholls, 'compulsory altruism needs more justification than an obligation not to create dangers to others when acting for one's own purposes'.[202] When will such a more convincing justification be said to exist?

As much as English law has done its best to keep the answer narrowly defined, it is impossible to fully catalogue all the possible cases of duty. What can be said is that that special 'something more' is usually agreed to be present where:

(a) the defendant created the risk of harm, including through interference to prevent help;
(b) the defendant has assumed responsibility for the plaintiff's welfare;
(c) the defendant is in a special position of control over the source of the damage;
(d) the defendant has a special relationship with the third party that caused the damage.[203]

This list is not exhaustive and it should be noted that different analyses will compose different categories. The catalogued circumstances, moreover, are only intended to be loosely defined and, indeed, often overlap. It is, therefore, a combination of factors, not one decisive criterion that will, in the end, determine liability, in this area too, as in the rest of tort law. In any case, what is clear is that, despite the English starting point of no liability for omissions, significant exceptions puncture the rule, accumulated in the case law on an incremental and ad hoc basis. Indeed, in recent years it could be argued that a tipping point has been reached, so that the exceptions appear to be submerging the 'no duty for omissions' rule. Although therefore there are still those that insist that in England omissions may not incur liability, strong

202. *Stovin v. Wise* [1996] UKHL 15 (24 July 1996), Lord Nicholls (dissenting).
203. N McBride & R Bagshaw, *Tort Law* (4th ed., Pearson 2012) 207-243; W V H Rogers, *Winfield & Jolowicz on Tort* (18th ed., Sweet & Maxwell 2010) 194-218; J Kortmann, *Altruism in Private Law: Liability for Nonfeasance and Negatorium Gestio* (Oxford University Press 2005) and E Quill, 'Affirmative Duties of Care in the Common Law' (2011) 2 Journal of European Tort Law 151; M Lunney & K Oliphant, *Tort Law – Text and Materials* (3rd ed., Oxford University Press 2007) 466. Honoré encompasses these duties of care into his broader theory of 'distinct duties', see T Honoré, 'Are Omissions Less Culpable?' in P Cane & J Stapleton (eds), *The Law of Obligations: Essays for Patrick Atiyah* (Clarendon Press 1991) 31.

voices are calling for a re-formulation of the law and an abandonment of the 'no duty' approach in favour of one that applies the usual reasonable person test, in omissions just as much as in commissions – a breach-based one.[204]

The English oscillation between duty and breach is reflected in the leading case of *Smith v. Littlewoods.*[205] This examined a failure on the part of the defendant Littlewoods to prevent hooligans from breaking into their disused cinema and starting a fire, which then spread to and destroyed the plaintiffs' property. The ruling featured substantial opinions by four judges, but it is that of Lord Goff that has attracted the most attention in the literature. Lord Goff relied on the concept of absence of a duty of care to declare that Littlewoods could not be held liable. Yet, as numerous commentators have pointed out, Lord Goff's opinion probably does not represent the law: instead is it the opinion of Lord Mackay that was the leading one, endorsed by the majority of the court. Lord Mackay based his analysis not on the concept of duty of care, but on that of breach of duty, i.e., on the violation of the standard of care. This indeed brings us back, not to the artificial closed list of cases where duty is acknowledged or rejected, but to the familiar figure of the reasonable person. The central issue in English negligence law is therefore, not remoteness or break of the chain of causation, but fault.[206] Indeed, it is worth noting that Lord Goff accepted that liability may arise where 'persons trespass upon the defender's property and the defender either knows or has the means of knowing that they are doing so and that in so doing they constitute a danger to neighbouring property'. This concession might serve to undermine his main thesis: after all, liability will fail if the defendant neither knew nor could have known that the risk existed under a standard of care approach as well.

204. See for example, B Markesinis, 'Negligence, Nuisance and Affirmative Duties of Action' (1989) Law Quarterly Review 104; B Markesinis et al., *Tortious Liability for Unintentional Harm in the Common Law and the Civil Law* (Cambridge University Press 1982); E Quill, 'Affirmative Duties of Care in the Common Law' (2011) 2 Journal of European Tort Law 151; J Kortmann, 'Liability for Nonfeasance: A Comparative Study' (2001) Oxford U Comparative L Forum 1, available at: ouclf.iuscomp.org and T Honoré, 'Law, Morals and Rescue' in J Ratcliffe (ed.), *The Good Samaritan and the Law* (Anchor Books 1966) 241. Markesinis is especially acerbic in his condemnation of the duty approach, attributing it to an 'extreme individualism' (F H Lawson & B Markesinis, *Tortious Liability for Unintentional Harm in the Common Law and the Civil Law* (Cambridge University Press 1982) 73) and an 'irrational conviction that because the law and morals do not always coincide there is some value in their being different' that gave rise to it. He accordingly wryly suggests that even if the common law is to be understood as still subscribing to the idea that there is no duty to rescue, the reasonable person would probably disagree (B Markesinis, 'Negligence, Nuisance and Affirmative Duties of Action' (1989) Law Quarterly Review 104).
205. *Smith v. Littlewoods* [1987] AC 241.
206. D Howarth, 'My Brother's Keeper? Liability for Acts of Third Parties' (1994) 14(1) Legal Studies 88.

Howarth summarises the ultimate effect:

> In contrast, therefore, to Lord Goff's attempt to freeze the law so that it cannot easily recognise any more social democratic mutual obligations, Lord Mackay is giving the law room to develop. To locate the important decision in these cases firmly in the question of fault or breach means that the courts are in a position, if they wish, to strike a new balance between the specific utility of preventing harm and the general utility of leaving people alone to make their own decisions. It must be stressed that Lord Mackay's approach does not require the courts to shift the balance - it is more than possible for the court to decide in any particular case that liability would amount to imposing too much of a burden on the defendant. But Lord Mackay's approach does give the courts an opportunity to come to a conclusion on a question that Lord Goff considers in nearly all circumstances to be unaskable.[207]

In this regard, it is worth noting a comment made by Lord Woolf, in 2000, in *Kent v. Griffiths.*[208] Here, the judge noted of duty of care:

> in this area of the law there is a danger that statements made in judgments will be applied more widely and more rigidly than was in fact intended. The statements are intended to assist in the difficult task of determining whether a duty of care exists. They are tools not rules. There are cases in which even the three requirements identified by Lord Bridge [in *Caparo*] may not by themselves provide an answer. Other tools may be needed to provide assistance.

In the final conclusion, while the legal certainty that the duty of care approach brings with it is certainly often helpful, the introduction of greater flexibility to the English law of negligence might be welcome. It is, in any case, worth pointing out that these discussions are primarily relevant only as regards doctrine. When it comes to practical outcome, the differences between the two approaches will rarely differ: after all, in *Littlewoods,* both Lords Goff and Mackay reached the same conclusion of a lack of liability for the defendant. As we shall now see, the same would most likely also have been the outcome had the case been tried in France or Germany.[209]

- *France*

As with all things *faute,* compared to England, France takes a much more relaxed approach to the question of omissions. The unitary French notion of fault accommodates omissions effortlessly: just as with cases of negligent

207. D Howarth, 'My Brother's Keeper? Liability for Acts of Third Parties' (1994) 14(1) Legal Studies 88.
208. *Kent v. Griffiths & Ors* [2000] EWCA Civ 3017 (3 February 2000).
209. B Markesinis, 'Negligence, Nuisance and Affirmative Duties of Action' (1989) Law Quarterly Review 104.

action, omissions are governed by Articles 1382 and 1383 *C. civ.* and, by extension, the doctrine of the reasonable person.[210] As a result, French law takes omissions in its stride and the question has not raised great debate in the literature.[211] No objections to liability for failure to act arise on the sole basis of principle.

Nevertheless, even in the flexible French system the substantive question of when a reasonable person would omit preventive action to avoid damage to another cannot be escaped. Satisfying the reasonable person standard through an omission will always be seen as harder.[212] So, the *Cour de cassation* in its landmark 1929 *Branly* case[213] ruled that a historian who omitted to mention the contributions of the plaintiff scientist to the development of wireless telegraphy in an article accounting the history of that technology was liable for failing to live up to the standard of objectivity expected of a prudent professional in his field. This confirms that liability for nonfeasance may be imposed if the omission violated an affirmative duty created not only by a legislative or regulatory prescription, but also by a customary rule of proper social conduct.[214] While the case clearly concerned an *abstention dans l'action,* it has nevertheless had a significant effect on the development of *abstentions pures et simples* as well, with French theorists showing less inclination to acknowledge a difference between the two following the ruling.[215] Indeed, the subsequent case law has interpreted the ruling as constituting an abandonment of any distinction between nonfeasance and misfeasance and a recognition of the courts' prerogative to impose legal duties, both affirmative and negative, wherever they deem them to be appropriate. This development was precipitated in the 1940s by the introduction of affirmative duties of care into the French criminal code, something which inevitably – given the unitary approach France takes to civil and criminal faults that regards the commission of any criminal offence which causes harm to others as substantiating a simultaneous *faute* within the meaning of Articles 1382 and 1383 of the C.civ. as well – affected the interpretation of French tort law as well.[216]

---

210. P le Tourneau, *Droit de la responsabilité et des contracts – Régimes d'indemnisation* (9th ed., Dalloz 2013) 7202; W van Gerven, J Lever & P Larouche, *Tort Law* (Hart Publishing 2000) 281; G Viney, *Traité de Droit Civil - Vol. IV* (Libr. Générale de Droit et de Jurisprudence 1982) nr 456.
211. C van Dam, *European Tort Law* (2nd ed., Oxford University Press 2013) para. 808-3.
212. P le Tourneau, *Droit de la responsabilité et des contracts – Régimes d'indemnisation* (9th ed., Dalloz 2013) 7202-7209.
213. *Branly v. Turpain,* Cour de Cassation, 27 February 1951, Jur. 329.
214. Juristische Blätter 9. (Hart Publishing 2000) 281.
215. W van Gerven et al., *Tort Law* (Hart Publishing 2000) 283; J Kortmann, 'Liability for Nonfeasance: A Comparative Study' (2001) Oxford U Comparative L Forum 1, available at: ouclf.iuscomp.org.
216. J Kortmann, 'Liability for Nonfeasance: A Comparative Study' (2001) Oxford U Comparative L Forum 1, available at: ouclf.iuscomp.org.

In any case, even in France, once again, the basic precept that affirmative duties require a special link of some kind can be discerned. Indeed, it is in this theory where we find the source of the *diligences appropriées* summoned for the regulation of intermediary liability in copyright that was noted above in Chapter 3.[217] In France, such duties are referred to generally as *obligations de sécurité,* i.e., obligations to safeguard another's interests. Following the flexible French approach, these come in many shades, including *obligations de prudence, de surveillance, de vigilance, d'information, de conseil,* the violation of all of which may be considered to be *abstentions* which – if causative of harm – may lead to liability.[218] Naturally, such obligations are generally understood to be limited to *obligations de moyens,* which impose only a duty to take measures, not extending to *obligations de résultat.*[219]

When will an *obligation de sécurité* be found to exist? As in English law, in French law as well, the recognition of affirmative *obligations* will depend on a holistic appreciation of each individual case. At the same time, French law takes a more fluid approach to the matter, being far less restricted by rigid categories of recognised duties or plausible circumstances. France is also perhaps more eager to recognise that such duties exist – but that is perhaps due simply to a greater willingness as a point of policy among French law-makers to recognise broader liability possibilities, as evidenced, for example, by the country's comprehensive rules of strict liability devised to deal with questions that in other jurisdictions would amount to cases of omission.[220] At the same time, French courts also seem to take the defendant's personal characteristics and subjective experience of the situation into account, especially in cases of *omissions sans action.* So, if the defendant was a child or was physically or mentally unable to provide the required assistance, the courts are disinclined to find liability. On the other hand, if the omission was malicious and the harm was intended, liability is more likely to arise.[221]

- *Germany*

The German treatment of omissions presents a middle way between the English and French solutions. Much like France, Germany too sees no reason in principle for a different treatment for omissions as opposed to actions. For

217. See s. 3.2.3.2.
218. P le Tourneau, *Droit de la responsabilité et des contracts – Régimes d'indemnisation* (9th ed., Dalloz 2013) 7203-7205.
219. W van Gerven et al., *Tort Law* (Hart Publishing 2000) 281-285.
220. C van Dam, *European Tort Law* (2nd ed., Oxford University Press 2013) para. 808-3; W van Gerven et al., *Tort Law* (Hart Publishing 2000) 298.
221. J Kortmann, 'Liability for Nonfeasance: A Comparative Study' (2001) Oxford U Comparative L Forum 1, available at: ouclf.iuscomp.org; P le Tourneau, *Droit de la responsabilité et des contracts – Régimes d'indemnisation* (9th ed., Dalloz 2013) 7208.

example, Article 823 of the German BGB does not distinguish between the two, but refers only to the infringement of rights. Larenz writes:

> the omission to act in a way that would have prevented a result repugnant to the legal order is equivalent to a positive action to produce this result, as long as the person alleged to be liable was under an obligation to avoid this result and to act in consequence.[222]

Again therefore, the same theme encountered above takes shape: while a positive act that breaches the right of another is presumed to be unlawful and only a justification can rebut this presumption, a failure to act will require the violation of a *Pflicht zum Handeln,* i.e., an obligation to act, before unlawfulness can be established. It is law that determines the existence of an omission, not fact.

As a result, as in the previous two legal systems therefore, the crucial question which arises is when such an obligation to act can be said exist. As mentioned above, the Result Theory is very limited in this regard offering no guidance that would not lead to an over-expansive rule. Less comfortable with this open-endedness than the French courts, the German courts have sought to overcome the gap through judicial inventiveness.[223] So, the German *Reichsgericht* decided early on that the general provision of Article 823(1) must also apply to cases in which the infringement of a right was the consequence of the defendant's omission.[224] On this basis, it established in 1903 that local authorities had an obligation ('*Pflicht zur Anwendung von Sorgfalt*') to make sure that the snow-covered public steps on which the plaintiff has slipped and injured himself were gritted and safe to walk on. At the same time however, it was recognised that *Tatbestand*, *Rechtswidrigkeit* and *Verschulden* alone cannot apply unmodified to cases of omissions or perfectly innocent activities, such as the production of knives or the sale of motor vehicles, would result in liability if a third party used the product to cause harm. A solution was found in the development of the doctrine of *Verkehrssicherungspflichten* or (more shortly) *Verkehrspflichten* as an additional liability-limiting device applicable only in cases of omissions. These are legal duties that that require that somebody who, within the scope of her responsibility, established a source of potential danger or allows such a danger to persist must protect others against its realisation[225] – in other words, they represent the German answer to the English affirmative duties of care, scaled back to apply only to omissions. What the concept of *Verkehrspflichten* therefore essentially attempts to do is delineate where and when a person is obliged to take positive action to protect others against a

222. K Larenz, *Lehrbuch des Schuldrechts – Vol. I* (C. H. Beck, Munich 1987) 457, as quoted in W van Gerven et al., *Tort Law* (Hart Publishing 2000) 286.
223. W van Gerven et al., *Tort Law* (Hart Publishing 2000) 286-289.
224. RG 23 February 1903, RGZ 54, 53.
225. For a detailed analysis of *Verkehrspflichten* see C von Bar, *Verkehrspflichten: Richterliche Gefahrsteuerungsgebote im deutschen Deliktsrecht* (Heymanns 1980).

risk.[226] Over the decades, the German courts have recognised an ever increasing variety of *Verkehrspflichten*. What standard of duty each *Verkehrspflicht* imposes will depend on the circumstances of each individual case. In general, the courts will be more reluctant to recognise an obligation to act where the defendant was merely negligent, while intentional omissions will be more likely to result in liability.[227] At the same time, the German courts have become more and more willing to resort to findings of *Verkehrspflichten* even under the most ordinary circumstances. So, illustratively, in a 1981 case, the OLG Hamburg found a supermarket liable for having failed to pick up a dangerous lettuce leaf lying on the floor of its establishment that had caused a customer to slip and fall.[228] As in England, precedent and the pre-establishment of recognised duties remains important: as a result, despite essentially arising from the same basic idea, less flexibility therefore infuses the German and English systems than that enjoyed by France.

4.3.4 A European Rule for Omissions

In the final analysis, illustrating the differences between the three systems, Kortmann suggests:

> [in] the parable of the Good Samaritan, […] the priest and the Levite would have had nothing to fear from English law. In Germany they would have been liable [if a *Verkehrspflicht* or a *Schutzgesetz* could be found to have been violated] and arguably under par. 826 *BGB* if it could have been proved that they 'passed by on the other side' with the intent to harm. Under French law they would also have incurred criminal liability, while the victim would have had a claim for damages in negligence.[229]

As with liability for pure economic loss, real divisions accordingly separate the different European legal systems on omissions. As opposed to liability for pure economic loss however, those differences in omissions do in fact do a lot to explain the divergent approaches of the three systems to intermediary accessory copyright liability. France, whether due to its theory or as a matter of policy, is simply much more willing than either England or Germany to overcome the barrier set by nonfeasance and impose liability on

226. W van Gerven et al., *Tort Law* (Hart Publishing 2000) 287.
227. C van Dam, *European Tort Law* (2nd ed., Oxford University Press 2013) para. 808-3; J Kortmann, *Altruism in Private Law: Liability for Nonfeasance and Negatorium Gestio* (Oxford University Press 2005) 38-44.
228. OLG Hamm, 26 October 1981, 13 U 153/81; W van Gerven et al., *Tort Law* (Hart Publishing 2000) 289.
229. J Kortmann, 'Liability for Nonfeasance: A Comparative Study' (2001) Oxford U Comparative L Forum 1, available at: ouclf.iuscomp.org. See also: Lord Diplock in *Home Office v. Dorset Yacht Co Ltd* [1970] UKHL 2 (6 May 1970).

negligent omitters, with only minor adjustments to account for the particularities of failures to act.[230] It thus has no problems locating accessory liability within negligence liability on the basis of Articles 1382 and 1383 *C. civ*. England and Germany, on the other hand, first have to account for the formal limitations that their systems rely on to keep negligence liability in check, which require the existence of an *a priori* rule stating that a duty encumbers intermediaries to this effect. As a result, a negligence-based solution is mostly foreclosed, leaving the two countries instead to craft complicated 'joint tortfeasance' or 'interferer liability' solutions.

At the same time, these divergences should not be overstated: the main thrust of the identified differences lies primarily not in effect, but in rigidity of structure. In all three jurisdictions the ultimate rule is that a duty should not be imposed where it would be excessively cumbersome to do so.[231] The main practical difference lies in their willingness to acknowledge such cumbersomeness: as was seen in Chapter 3, at least in the area of intermediary accessory copyright liability, the French courts are the most willing. The English courts are the least, although they too are happy to stretch the notion of intent to fit circumstances they deem worthy of liability. The German courts have given up on the idea altogether, taking refuge in *Störerhaftung* and injunctions instead.

It should be noted that this background is not always properly understood. McBride for example suggests that the English recognition of duties of care of care as a separate condition for fault indicates a view of negligence that rests on the idea of obligations as organisers of communal living which is at odds with the French focus on fault as a prerequisite for compensation. According to this view, under the first 'wrong-based' approach, people are obligated to act reasonably, whereas under to the second 'fault-based' approach, they are merely obligated to pay compensation after acting unreasonably.[232] On this understanding, McBride rejects the idea of a common European tort law as necessitating a sacrifice of the English 'idealistic' view, in favour of the French 'cynical' approach.

But this portrayal of harmonisation is misleading. For one thing, even if the divisions between the different systems were to truly run that deep, it is unclear why the French system should be assumed to be the one that would set the tone of a European tort law, as opposed to any of the other twenty-seven national systems. Indeed, as we saw above, German law achieves more or less the same effect as duty of care through the notion of unlawfulness and even goes as far as to, in cases of omissions, reconfigure that notion precisely into a duty of care along the English lines. More importantly, upon close inspection, it is clear that French law too is no real

230. C van Dam, *European Tort Law* (2nd ed., Oxford University Press 2013) para. 808-3.
231. W van Gerven et al., *Tort Law* (Hart Publishing 2000) 300.
232. N McBride, 'Duties of Care – Do They Really Exist?' (2004) 24(3) Oxford Journal of Legal Studies 417.

outlier.[233] As Le Tourneau explains, '*il y a faute à violer une règle de conduit*'.[234] Such a '*règle de conduit*' can result from statutory provisions, but also from the '*règles coutumières*'. It is thus clear that '*règle de conduit*' is simply the French equivalent of duty of care:[235] while the concept of duty of care might not be explicitly mentioned in the wording of Articles 1382 and 1383 *C. civ.*, it is no less missing from French tort law than it is from the entirely unwritten English tort of negligence.[236] Instead, it should be accepted that all three systems are based on an 'idealistic' notion of wrongfulness that is dependent on the obligations incumbent on members of a society, although each may go about achieving this effect in different ways. While English and German law treat the notion of duty of care as an independent condition for liability, French law folds duty into breach, so that the two become one and the same: the famous French *faute*. From this perspective, it becomes clear that a bid for the European harmonisation of the area is by no means a bid for 'cynicism'. This should not be surprising: if there is one thing of which the proponents of a single European tort law certainly cannot be accused, that is of not being idealistic enough.

It thus becomes clear that the divergent national approaches towards omissions are not representative of a fundamental incompatibility, but may be overcome where there is sufficient political will. If nowhere else, at least in intermediary accessory liability for copyright, the difficulties experienced by the British courts in applying the general accessory liability rules, as well as the German turn to the property law-based *Störerhaftung* indicate that that will does exist.[237] In any case, naturally, a copyright-focused duty to take positive action against infringements could of course be explicitly introduced as such in each national system that requires it in a self-standing manner, whether as part of a harmonisation project or as an independent attempt to rationalise the national handling of this difficult area. At the same time, it is nevertheless worth examining how such a duty might fit within a broader European rule on liability for failure to act. Again, the model European codifications lead the way. From among these, the PETL provides the best solution.

233. D Howarth, 'Many Duties of Care – Or A Duty of Care? Notes from the Underground' (2006) 26(3) Oxford Journal of Legal Studies 449.

234. P le Tourneau, *Droit de la responsabilité et des contracts – Régimes d'indemnisation* (9th ed., Dalloz 2013) 7201-7233.

235. Indeed, just as the English duties of care can be classified as affirmative and negative duties, the French too speak of 'agissements fautifs' and 'abstentions fautives': P le Tourneau, *Droit de la responsabilité et des contracts – Régimes d'indemnisation* (9th ed., Dalloz 2013) 7201-7233.

236. On the other hand, cases of omission are often covered by one of the many French strict liability rules, see C van Dam, *European Tort Law* (2nd ed., Oxford University Press 2013) para. 808-3. The French predilection for strict liability represents a far greater source of incompatibility between European tort systems. This issue does not however impact the question of intermediary accessory copyright liability.

237. See Ch. 3, s. 3.1 and 3.3. above.

So, to begin with, the EGTL confirms the general conclusion that people do not, for the most part, have to concern themselves with promoting the interests of others: '[a]s a general rule, one need not care about the security and the well-being of other people, with or towards whom one has no special relationship or supervisory function'. [238] Von Bar agrees:

> [a]n event occurring without the doing of another does not ordinarily concern the third party. It can only be attributed to him if there is a special closeness between him and the victim, or if he bears a particular responsibility for the relevant source of danger. Although it goes without saying that nobody may harm another, this does not mean that every individual has a duty to save everybody else from all possible dangers.[239]

An omission is wrongful only if there is a norm which imposes a duty to act. After all, any contrary conclusion would lead to an insufferable limitation on the range of permissible conduct, such that everybody would constantly have to worry about even the most far-fetched consequences of their actions. The starting point should consequently always be a lack of duty. This is not of itself objectionable: '[t]he world is full of harm for which the law furnishes no remedy'.[240]

Operating on this basis and taking clear inspiration from the English duties of care and the German *Verkehrspflichten,* the PETL then introduces the notion of 'duties to protect' as intra-fault clarifying devices applicable in cases of omissions. In this way, the duty of care is both folded into a unitary conception of fault along the French example and overtly recognised, as in England and Germany, where greater clarity is needed.[241] Article 4:103 PETL provides four such possibilities:

> A duty to act positively to protect others from damage may exist if law so provides, or if the actor creates or controls a dangerous situation, or when there is a special relationship between parties or when the

238. European Group on Tort Law, *Principles of European Tort Law – Text and Commentary* (Springer 2005) 86.
239. C von Bar, *The Common European Law of Torts – Vol. II* (Clarendon Press 2000) para. 194.
240. N McBride & R Bagshaw, *Tort Law* (4th ed., Pearson 2012) 119.
241. This makes sense, as the English notion of breach of duty corresponds more smoothly with the conduct-oriented approach to unlawfulness, while also offering a better way of dealing with omissions than both unlawfulness and the harmonising 'legally relevant damage' approach, see European Group on Tort Law, *Principles of European Tort Law – Text and Commentary* (Springer 2005) 26-27 and C Von Bar, *The Common European Law of Torts – Vol. II* (Clarendon Press 2000) para. 214. Koziol notes that, as French law applies a unitary notion that does not distinguish fault from wrongfulness, it should be assumed that it also focuses on the behaviour rather than the result, see H Koziol (ed.) *Unification of Tort Law: Wrongfulness* (Kluwer Law International 1998) 129.

> seriousness of the harm on the one side and the ease of avoiding the damage on the other side point towards such a duty.

It is suggested that, of these four possibilities, the second on the creation and control of a source of danger and the fourth on the ease of addressing the danger will be the most relevant to intermediary accessory copyright liability. The first exception for legal provisions could also of course be relevant, if a European harmonising provision were to declare that such a duty must be imposed.[242]

4.4 CAUSATION

Fault and its limits are only part of the liability equation. Once it is established that a person has acted negligently, the next question that arises is whether a link can be established that binds that negligent behaviour with the subsequent damaging outcome. Causation refers to exactly that connection between the triggering conduct of the tortfeasor and the injury suffered by the victim. It is, in other words, as Van Gerven et al. point out, the element of tort that answers the following:

> under the circumstances of the case and assuming all other conditions for liability are met, ought *this* defendant to be held liable for *this* damage?[243]

Thus, causation is the missing piece of the liability puzzle, the essential link that binds the other two indispensable pillars of tort liability together.[244] Consequently, it does not stand alone, but is positioned between and therefore influenced by fault and damage. Von Bar explains:

> In tort law […] causation is no more than the connection deemed necessary […] between, on one hand, a defendant's misconduct, that of a person for whom the defendant is responsible, or the existence of a source of danger, and on the other, compensable damage. There is no generalized answer as to the qualities of that link. It can generally be said that the causation test combines elements of the categories which it associates: breach of duty and damage.[245]

As a result, fault and damage are needed to prove causation and vice versa. This means that, as Von Bar puts it, whether liability will result depends on a closed-system normative evaluation. Damage, fault and

242. For more on this, see Ch. 5, s. 5.4.3.4.
243. W van Gerven et al., *Tort Law* (Hart Publishing 2000) 395.
244. See for example Art. VI.-1:101 of the DCFR.
245. C von Bar, *The Common European Law of Torts – Vol. II* (Clarendon Press 2000) para. 440.

attributive cause are communicating vessels; although they are formally divided for the purposes of legal study, an appreciation of their fundamental interconnectedness is necessary for their successful application in practice. Pertinently to our purposes, as noted above,[246] the requirements of causation and negligence are particularly closely intertwined.

So, among other things, the concept of *probability* is central to both these notions: while in the negligence test, the critical question is how likely it was at the time the harmful conduct was undertaken that harm *would* be caused by the defendant's conduct, in the causation test the focus is on how likely it is that the damage *was in fact* caused by the defendant's conduct. The related concept of *foreseeability* also features heavily in both areas. Causation is additionally closely connected to such negligence elements as the scope of the defendant's duty or of the rule in question, the kind of loss sustained by the plaintiff, any contributory negligence on the part of the plaintiff and indeed the very level of fault of the defendant: the more at fault somebody is, the easier it is to substantiate a causal connection between their behaviour and the harm.[247] This means that, importantly, what is governed by the vehicle of causation in one country can be located in fault in another. As we shall see below, this is precisely the case for accessory liability in Europe.

As a result of these blurred lines, causation is a particularly flexible – and correspondingly volatile – concept. It is telling that, although referenced heavily, causation is not defined in the law of any of the three examined jurisdictions: even civil law jurisdictions omit a description from their codes. The rules of causation in all three countries have instead been primarily developed by the courts. This has probably been wise given the difficulty of formulating a generally applicable causation test: there can be no 'one-size-fits-all' rule of causation – the standard must be adjusted depending on the kind of damage incurred and the grounds on which liability is claimed.[248] For the same reason, causation is particularly susceptible to differently weighted interpretations depending on the modalities of the other two elemental particles of liability – attributive cause and the legally relevant damage – within the legal system in question.[249] This explains why the same issue might be differently categorised in different jurisdictions: what might be considered a matter for causation in one country, will often fall under the

---

246. See s. 4.2.1.
247. C van Dam, *European Tort Law* (2nd ed., Oxford University Press 2013) para. 1102.
248. C von Bar et al. (eds), *Principles, Definitions and Model Rules of European Private Law: Draft Common Frame of Reference (DCFR)*, prepared by the Study Group on a European Civil Code and the Research Group on EC private law (Acquis Group), Outline Edition (Sellier 2009) 3424.
249. C von Bar et al. (eds), *Principles, Definitions and Model Rules of European Private Law: Draft Common Frame of Reference (DCFR)*, prepared by the Study Group on a European Civil Code and the Research Group on EC private law (Acquis Group), Outline Edition (Sellier 2009) 3423.

rubric of breach of duty in another or damage in a third.[250] At the same time, although different theories of causation prevail in different Member States, the end results of their application are often strikingly similar.[251] As with fault therefore, while different countries might prefer to follow different routes, their final destination is usually the same.

The malleability of causation naturally makes it a particularly receptive concept to policy considerations. Indeed, Van Dam goes as far as to suggest that courts often decide the outcome that they wish to reach and subsequently morph their rulings on causation around that.[252] As noted in Chapter 3, in intermediary accessory copyright liability at least, that does not seem a far-fetched conclusion. There are however limits: although causation is never alone sufficient to establish liability, liability cannot be found without it. While policy considerations do play an important part in formulating standards of causation therefore, liability is never imposed merely for political or moral reasons: it is not enough that somebody be simply best-placed, well-insured or affluent enough to handle liability, some causal link that traces the harm back to the sphere of control of the defendant is necessary.[253] Entirely innocent bystanders cannot be touched. This immediately reveals causation's relevance to accessory liability: causation helps distinguish the involved from the uninvolved, the neutral onlooker from the true participant. If somebody did not at least contribute to the causation of the harm, they cannot be held liable for it.[254] Accessory liability is perched right on the edge of that divide: cases of a necessary, but insufficient fault-based cause of the harm.[255]

It should be noted that the causative link should always bind the fault of the defendant – and not the defendant's activity – to the plaintiff's loss.

---

250. C van Dam, *European Tort Law* (2nd ed., Oxford University Press 2013) para. 437; P Widmer, 'Comparative Report on Fault as a Basis of Liability and Criterion of Imputation (Attribution)' in P Widmer (ed.), *Unification of Tort Law: Fault* (Kluwer Law International 2005) 337; W van Gerven et al., *Tort Law* (Hart Publishing 2000) 455; K Zweigert & H Kötz. *An Introduction to Comparative Law* (3rd ed., Clarendon Press 1998) 673.
251. European Group on Tort Law, *Principles of European Tort Law – Text and Commentary* (Springer 2005) 43.
252. C van Dam, *European Tort Law* (2nd ed., Oxford University Press 2013) para. 1111.
253. C von Bar et al. (eds), *Principles, Definitions and Model Rules of European Private Law: Draft Common Frame of Reference (DCFR)*, prepared by the Study Group on a European Civil Code and the Research Group on EC private law (Acquis Group), Outline Edition (Sellier 2009) 3422.
254. This observation explains why Art. 8(3) of the Copyright Directive imposes injunctions on neutral intermediaries whose services are used to commit infringements, but does not go as far as to suggest liability in the strict sense, i.e., for damages. Such an imposition would amount, not to a statutory rule on fault liability, but a strict liability that would require very strong policy justifications.
255. J Riordan, *The Liability of Internet Intermediaries* (PhD thesis, University of Oxford 2013, forthcoming Oxford University Press 2016) 37.

This is what is referred to in Germany as the '*Rechtmäßiges Alternativverhalten*' or 'lawful alternative'. If the defendant can prove that the same damage would have occurred even if they had taken due care, then they cannot be held liable. So, if a puck is shot over the fence surrounding a hockey rink and hits a member of the audience, as long as the trajectory of the puck took it higher than the requisite height of a hockey rink fence by law, the owners of the rink cannot be held liable for the harm suffered by the fan, even if the fence in question was too short according to the appropriate standard:[256] where the defendant was powerless to stop the damage, they cannot be held liable for that damage.

4.4.1 Causation in the National Systems

The most prevalent method of assessing causation and that which provides the starting point of legal analysis in all three systems under study is the so-called theory of *conditio sine qua non*. Known in English-speaking world as the 'but-for' test and in France and Germany as the 'theory of equivalence of conditions' (*théorie de l'équivalence des conditions/Äquivalenztheorie*), this requires that, in order that the defendant's behaviour to be considered as a cause of the plaintiff's injury, it must be demonstrated that the injury would not have occurred *but for* that behaviour.[257] The crucial question here is therefore 'would the harm have occurred without the conduct?' Depending on the jurisdiction, different levels of certainty are necessary in answering this question. Under English law, the focus lies on probabilities, with causation being substantiated when the chances that the alleged tortfeasor's

256. R Van Den Bergh & L Visscher, 'The Principles of European Tort Law: The Right Path to Harmonization?' (2006) 4 European Review of Private Law 511.

257. In Germany this process is labelled *Hinwegdenken:* the defendant's behaviour must be 'thought away' to reveal whether the damaging event would have occurred without its influence, see F H Lawson & B Markesinis, *Tortious Liability for Unintentional Harm in the Common Law and the Civil Law* (Cambridge University Press 1982) 109. It should be noted that *conditio sine qua non* can apply to omission just as well as it does to commission. Instead however of applying a method of elimination to examine what would have happened if the alleged tortfeasor's conduct is omitted, what is necessary in omissions is the substitution of the defendant's inactivity by the positive act which they were under a duty to perform. If the harmful result would not have occurred without the omission, causation can be established, see F H Lawson & B Markesinis, *Tortious Liability for Unintentional Harm in the Common Law and the Civil Law* (Cambridge University Press 1982) 109; C von Bar et al. (eds), *Principles, Definitions and Model Rules of European Private Law: Draft Common Frame of Reference (DCFR)*, prepared by the Study Group on a European Civil Code and the Research Group on EC private law (Acquis Group), Outline Edition (Sellier 2009) 3423.

conduct led to the plaintiff's injury are higher than 50%.[258] By contrast, in Germany, full proof and effective certainty is necessary.[259]

The main merit of the *conditio sine qua non* test lies in its ability to deftly exclude all *causally irrelevant* occurrences from the consideration of causation. On the other hand, the rule has also been heavily criticised for being incapable of distinguishing between real causes and mere circumstances.[260] As a result of this shortcoming, under the 'but-for' test, the scope of causation can be extended *ad infinitum*,[261] a clearly unworkable solution. As Williams observes '[w]hat is the use of defining cause so widely that it goes back to the primeval slime?'[262] At the same time, while further normative fine-tuning through more discerning standards is clearly necessary, *conditio sine qua non* nonetheless offers a good rudimentary starting point for the appraisal of causation.

In view of its limited powers of discernment, once *conditio sine qua non* has been established, an additional mechanism for its limitation must thus be introduced.[263] To this end, English lawyers distinguish between what is called 'cause-in-fact' on the one hand and 'legal cause' on the other. 'Cause-in-fact' employs the 'but-for' test. 'Legal cause' then investigates whether the alleged tortfeasor *ought to* be held liable for the harm, thus focusing less on 'scientific' questions regarding the actual occurrences than issues of policy.[264] German legal theory takes a similar path, by distinguishing between *Kausalität im naturlichen Sinne* and *Kausalität im rechtlichen Sinne*.[265] As in English law, *conditio sine qua non* forms the centrepiece of the first, while multiple complementary theories of legal causation have been

258. C van Dam, *European Tort Law* (2nd ed., Oxford University Press 2013) para. 1104.
259. See Art. 286 of the Code of Civil Procedure (Zivilprozessordnun – ZPO). See also, C van Dam, *European Tort Law* (2nd ed., Oxford University Press 2013) para. 1103-1.
260. C von Bar, *The Common European Law of Torts – Vol. II* (Clarendon Press 2000) paras 440-442.
261. W van Gerven et al., *Tort Law* (Hart Publishing 2000) 397.
262. G Williams, 'Causation in the Law (1961) Cambridge Law Journal 62. For a detailed analysis of the drawbacks of *conditio sine qua non* see C von Bar, *The Common European Law of Torts – Vol. II* (Clarendon Press 2000) paras 415-439.
263. C van Dam, *European Tort Law* (2nd ed., Oxford University Press 2013) para. 1102.
264. W van Gerven et al., *Tort Law* (Hart Publishing 2000) 408.
265. On a similar note, German legal theory also distinguishes between *Haftungsbegründende Kausalität,* i.e., causation that establishes liability, and *Haftungsausfüllende Kausalität,* i.e., causation as a determinant of the scope of liability. The first refers to the causal link that binds the conduct of the alleged tortfeasor to the infringement of the plaintiff's right. It is essential in establishing unlawfulness, since it links the conduct of the defendant to the unlawful result. The second represents the causal link between the infringement of a right and the items of damage alleged by the plaintiff. While some authors argue that the equivalence theory provides sufficient basis for the establishment of *Haftungsbegründende Kausalität, Haftungsausfüllende Kausalität* requires something more. The distinction between *Haftungsbegründende* and *Haftungsausfüllende Kausalität* is primarily relevant in the context of Art. 823(1) BGB and has consequences with regard to matters of standards of proof. See: W van Gerven, J Lever & P Larouche, *Tort*

put forward to correct its misfires in the second. French authors, ever the pragmatists of tort law, take a more 'unitary' approach that ignores fussy distinctions between 'science' and 'policy'.[266] Indeed, it should be noted that the division does not enjoy universal recognition even within the other two jurisdictions: Hart and Honoré, for example, have taken issue with its use in English law, arguing for a 'common sense' approach to causation that eliminates references to policy entirely.[267] Malone has also argued that policy constitutes as important a consideration in the first stage of the inquiry as it is in the second. There is probably some truth in both these statements: findings of causation cannot be said to be either a pure inquiry into fact or only a matter of policy. Instead, they straddle the fence between the two, attempting to identify results that satisfy both the courts' perception of what is just and fair and the integrity of legal reasoning.[268]

Given that the different legal systems employ different legal theories of causation, once again a brief country-by-country run-down is at this point useful. For this purpose the selected jurisdictions shall be examined in order of the interest they take in the matter: the intricate German theories of causation provide the best starting point, followed by the middle ground approach represented by England. The empirical French system shall be studied last.[269]

4.4.1.1 Germany

Three are the main theories of causation put forth in Germany as a suitable adjustments of the *Äquivalenztheorie*. The first of these is the so-called *Adequänztheorie* or adequate cause theory, which made its debut in German tort law at the turn of the nineteenth century. According to this, a cause will be deemed legally relevant, if it was 'adequate' for the creation of the damage suffered by the plaintiff, i.e., generally apt to cause the harm or at least to significantly increase the chance that it would happen. It is therefore essentially based on probabilities.[270] There are many different options available with regard to determining adequacy, but in general it can be said that the defendant will only be liable for harmful consequences that were reasonably to be expected or foreseeable or at least not very unlikely for an objective and optimal observer.[271]

Law (Hart Publishing 2000) 396 et seq; C van Dam, *European Tort Law* (2nd ed., Oxford University Press 2013) para. 1103.

266. F H Lawson & B Markesinis, *Tortious Liability for Unintentional Harm in the Common Law and the Civil Law* (Cambridge University Press 1982) 107.
267. H L A Hart & T Honoré, *Causation in the Law* (Clarendon Press 1985). See also N McBride & R Bagshaw, *Tort Law* (4th ed., Pearson 2012) 275.
268. N McBride & R Bagshaw, *Tort Law* (4th ed., Pearson 2012) 327.
269. W van Gerven et al., *Tort Law* (Hart Publishing 2000) 395.
270. W van Gerven et al., *Tort Law* (Hart Publishing 2000) 397.
271. C van Dam, *European Tort Law* (2nd ed., Oxford University Press 2013) para. 1103-1.

Other causation limiting theories have also been suggested by German scholars: an alternative popular approach is the so-called *Schutzzweck der Norm* or 'scope of the rule' theory. Under this, damage is only recoverable if it is within the 'scope of protection' of the rule allegedly violated. The general concept here is that compensation will not be owed if the damage sustained was not protected by the law applied. The scope of the rule theory allows for quite unlikely consequences to be attributed to the defendant.[272] It also explicitly takes the focus away from the actual circumstances of each case towards the analysis of the legal norm applied; as a result, Honoré correctly labels this a 'legal policy' theory.[273] More recently, German causation scholars have developed the additional concept of the *Risikobereich* or 'sphere of risk'. Although not yet as fully developed as its predecessors, this approach suggests that everybody has to accept a certain amount of risk; if a certain harm comes therefore within the claimant's *Risikobereich,* it cannot be imputed to the defendant. The best-known incarnation of this theory is the so-called *allgemeines Lebensrisiko* or 'general risk associated with living', which everybody has to bear.[274]

There is no general consensus among German lawyers as to which of these theories is preferable. Case law does not seem to subscribe to one particular school of thought, but tends to employ them all in parallel, depending on the requirements of the case at hand. At the end of the day, policy will always play a decisive role, particularly in borderline cases.[275]

4.4.1.2 England

The main tool for the establishment of legal causation under English law is what usually labelled the 'remoteness of damage'. The basic rule here is that of 'reasonable foreseeability', according to which damage is too remote to be attributed to the defendant if it is of such a kind that a reasonable person could not have foreseen it. This test bears an obvious resemblance to the German adequacy theory. It was first developed in the 1961 case of *The Wagon Mount*[276] and replaced the previously prevailing *Re Polemis*[277] criterion, which (more reminiscent of the laxer French approach to be analysed below) held the defendant liable for all 'direct consequences' of his action. The foreseeability principle was later elaborated upon in *Hughes v. Lord Advocate,* where Lord Guest clarified that:

272. C van Dam, *European Tort Law* (2nd ed., Oxford University Press 2013) para. 1103-2.
273. W van Gerven et al., *Tort Law* (Hart Publishing 2000) 398.
274. W van Gerven et al., *Tort Law* (Hart Publishing 2000) 398.
275. W van Gerven et al., *Tort Law* (Hart Publishing 2000) 398; C van Dam, *European Tort Law* (2nd ed., Oxford University Press 2013) para. 1103-2.
276. *Overseas Tankship (UK) Ltd v. Morts Dock and Engineering Co Ltd ('Wagon Mound (No. 1)')* [1961] UKPC 1.
277. *Re Polemis & Furness, Withy & Co Ltd* [1921] 3 KB 560.

> it is sufficient if the accident which occurred is of a type which should have been foreseeable by a reasonable careful person ... ; the precise concatenation of circumstances need not be envisaged.[278]

This 'reasonable foreseeability' standard is intended to avoid imposing an erratic rule that is impossible for anybody to abide by, by ensuring that everyone should only have to avoid harm that they can predict. As opposed to the intricate German theories set out above therefore, the general objective here is the construction of a 'common sense' standard:[279] '[c]ausation is to be understood as the man in the street, and not as either the scientist or the metaphysician would understand it'.[280] In practice of course, this has not been an easy result to achieve, leading a number of authors to denounce the test as inapplicable fiction.[281] As a result, as in German law, in English law too policy considerations end up playing a vital role in the determination of legal causation.

4.4.1.3 France

In France, the question of causation has traditionally been overlooked in favour of the all-consuming notion of *faute*. Consequently, although in recent years more attention has been paid to the topic, the French approach to causation remains a practical one that eschews over-theorisation.[282] Accordingly, as opposed to what is the case in England and Germany, for the most part, French law is satisfied with the theory of *équivalence des conditions*. As a result, the French system has a much more permissive approach to findings of a causal link.

Of course, even in French law some limitations to causation do exist. At a theoretical level, French tort law has been considerably influenced by German writings on causation. Especial consideration has been given by French authors to the adequacy theory (in French, *théorie de la causalité adequate*). Ultimately however, the general conclusion in the French literature is that, although *conditio sine qua non* certainly has its faults,

---

278. *Hughes v. Lord Advocate* [1963] AC 837.
279. C van Dam, *European Tort Law* (2nd ed., Oxford University Press 2013) para. 1104.
280. See Lord Wright in *Yorkshire Dale Steamship Co. Ltd v. Minister of War Transport* [1942] AC 691.
281. F H Lawson & B Markesinis, *Tortious Liability for Unintentional Harm in the Common Law and the Civil Law* (Cambridge University Press 1982) 120; W van Gerven et al., *Tort Law* (Hart Publishing 2000) 412 and 453 et seq; C van Dam, *European Tort Law* (2nd ed., Oxford University Press 2013) para. 1104.
282. See F H Lawson & B Markesinis, *Tortious Liability for Unintentional Harm in the Common Law and the Civil Law* (Cambridge University Press 1982) 106. Van Dam agrees: 'French legal writers have not expressed a strong inclination to develop profound theories and thoughts about causation; they have only developed some small-scale theories, none of which has gained a firm foothold in the doctrine, and their voices are not being heard in the case law.' See: C van Dam, *European Tort Law* (2nd ed., Oxford University Press 2013) para. 1105.

adequacy is too vague and less logical.[283] Likewise, the scope of the law theory, known in France as *relativité aquilienne,* has not found wide recognition and is rarely applied in practice.[284] Van Gerven et al. point towards the development of an 'explanatory theory' in French causation writings. According to this, in order to be deemed to be the cause of an injury, the alleged tortfeasor's actions must offer a convincing *explanation* of the course of events, so that the harm can be said to have 'followed a continuous path that can be traced back from the injury to the [...] fault of the defendant'.[285] Van Dam also mentions the emergent theory of 'efficient causation', wherein the court weighs the respective importance of various factors in determining the legal cause of the damage.[286] Both of these however remain underdeveloped, while any other theories are only partial, dedicated to particular problems, but not conducive to the formulation of a single, overarching general doctrine.[287] In the end, *équivalence des conditions* still wins the day in France, particularly in cases of fault liability.[288]

Thus, the only real limitation to causation consistently applied by the French courts is the requirement that the causal connection be *certain et directe*.[289] The probability of damage is also taken into consideration, with causation being denied if the damage was not a *consequence normale* of the defendant's conduct. This makes for a simple and easy rule. At the same time, as Lawson and Markesinis observe, the distinction between direct and indirect liability is, in effect, 'anything the judge feels inclined to make of it'.[290] In French law therefore the policy considerations behind causation are made even more obvious than in the more circumspect English and German systems. There is a lot to sympathise with in the French approach. Starck, Roland and Boyer have stated that:

> causation is one of the most obscure issues in the law of torts. Masses of cases shed no further light on the subject-matter, dominated as they

283. W van Gerven et al., *Tort Law* (Hart Publishing 2000) 419.
284. C van Dam, *European Tort Law* (2nd ed., Oxford University Press 2013) para. 1105.
285. N Dejean de la Bâtie, quoted in W van Gerven et al., *Tort Law* (Hart Publishing 2000) 418.
286. C van Dam, *European Tort Law* (2nd ed., Oxford University Press 2013) para. 1105.
287. See for example the theories of *perte d'une chance* or *cause étrangère*, W van Gerven et al., *Tort Law* (Hart Publishing 2000) 419-420.
288. By contrast, some French authors suggest that strict liability should be compensated for through the application of more exacting causation regimes, such as adequacy or the explanatory theory, see Le Tourneau & Cadiet, mentioned in W van Gerven, J Lever & P Larouche, *Tort Law* (Hart Publishing 2000) 420.
289. This rule stems from Art. 1151 of the *Code civil* on contract law. See C van Dam, *European Tort Law* (2nd ed., Oxford University Press 2013) para. 1105.
290. F H Lawson & B Markesinis, *Tortious Liability for Unintentional Harm in the Common Law and the Civil Law* (Cambridge University Press 1982) 120.

are by the individuals' circumstances of the case and the intuition of the court.[291]

They are probably not wrong.

4.4.2 Causation and Intermediary Accessory Liability in Copyright

As with fault and its limitations, the examination of the national systems for causation makes clear how and why France has such ease with applying the regular rules on negligence to solve problems of accessory liability in a way that England and Germany cannot: the laxer French system simply grants causation a broader reach, capable of embracing accessories excluded from liability by the more exacting 'legal causation' rules of the other two systems. Accordingly, as shown above, in France, the only real limitation over and beyond the simple test of *sine qua non*, is the requirement of directness. Of course, directness too can have obvious consequences for third party victims: 'indirect liability' is not for nothing an alternative term for accessory liability. So, for example, a concert organiser's claim for compensation from the person who was liable for an accident that resulted in a singer cancelling a concert has been rejected by the *Cour de cassation* as being insufficiently direct.[292] But the breathing space directness allows to causation is nevertheless considerable. As a result, France does not need special rules dedicated to causation in accessory liability over and beyond those related to the *fautes concurrentes* of several concurrent tortfeasors.[293] *Conditio sine qua non* is permissive enough to allow liability for accessories, including in cases of mere facilitation. Any over-expansive results of this set-up are delegated to the normative realm of *faute.*

By contrast, the English and German systems' 'legal causation' theories will usually pre-emptively exclude a negligence-based accessory liability: clearly the provision of the means to commit a tort will not in and of itself constitute an 'adequate' cause for its commission nor will it easily be seen as either falling within the scope of the applicable law or giving rise to a risk that the primary tort will be committed.[294] Similarly, without further reason to suspect that such means will be used for tortious purposes, it cannot be said that it is 'reasonably foreseeable' that any assistance provided by an accessory will result in wrongdoing. In such cases, the primary party's wrongdoing is usually considered instead to constitute a *novus actus interveniens* – an unforeseeable intervening event that, as it is said, 'breaks'

291. B Starck et al., *Obligations I – Responsabilité délictuelle* (5th ed., Litec 1996) 438, quoted in W van Gerven, J Lever & P Larouche, *Tort Law* (Hart Publishing 2000) 418.
292. See C van Dam, *European Tort Law* (2nd ed., Oxford University Press 2013) para. 1105.
293. See above Ch. 3, s. 3.2.3. See also W van Gerven et al., *Tort Law* (Hart Publishing 2000) 432.
294. F H Lawson & B Markesinis, *Tortious Liability for Unintentional Harm in the Common Law and the Civil Law* (Cambridge University Press 1982) 129.

the 'chain of causation', i.e., occurs after the defendant's negligent act and operates to precipitate or worsen the claimant's injury, thereby severing the defendant's causative link to the damage.[295] The third party in such circumstances is as a result viewed as the sole cause of the harm and the accessory is released from liability. Indeed, the causation standard for accessory liability is usually interpreted as even stricter than that for primary liability. So, for example, in *Dorset Yacht,* Lord Reid observed on the topic of causation and third party liability:

> [W]here human action forms one of the links between the original wrongdoing of the defendant and the loss suffered by the plaintiff, that action must at least have been something very likely to happen if it is not to be regarded as *novus actus interveniens* breaking the chain of causation. I do not think that a mere foreseeable possibility is or should be sufficient, for then the intervening human action can more properly be regarded as a new cause than as a consequence of the original wrongdoing.[296]

This conclusion echoes the dubiousness English and German law both show towards liability for omissions, by requiring a duty of care or *Verkehrssicherungspflicht* before liability can be found, compounding the unlikeliness of a finding of fault liability and expanding it beyond mere omissions into all third party cases.

What does this mean for intermediary liability? As a result of their stricter causation theories, both the English and German systems essentially lock themselves out of a negligence-based accessory liability. In order to re-enable the possibility, special rules must be established that supersede the regular avenues of causation. This is achieved in England through the rules of joint tortfeasance and in Germany by means of Article 830 BGB's *Mittäterschaft*. So, as with the rule of no liability for omissions, an exception to the rule of *novus actus interveniens* will apply if special circumstances occur that bring causation back to the table. But from where does the causal power of these circumstances derive? How do they achieve the necessary causal leap?

The answer is found in intent: although an aspect of fault, in all three legal systems, as already hinted at above,[297] intent is a decisive factor in determining whether the defendant's conduct was causative of damage.[298] This makes sense: after all, if an accessory intends that the action of another

295. P S Davies, *Accessory Liability* (Hart Publishing 2015) 33-36; C von Bar, *The Common European Law of Torts – Vol. II* (Clarendon Press 2000) para. 464. For examples of relevant court rulings see: *Home Office v. Dorset Yacht Co* [1970] AC 1004 and *Smith v. Littlewoods* [1987] AC 241.
296. *The Home Office v. The Dorset Yacht Company Ltd* [1970] AC 1004 at 1030.
297. See s. 4.2.1.
298. C von Bar, *The Common European Law of Torts – Vol. II* (Clarendon Press 2000) para. 457.

cause injury, it becomes harder to argue that that other broke the chain of causation connecting the accessory to the damage.[299] In this way, the third party's behaviour is recast as a link in the causative chain, forged by the accessory's plans of inflicting that harm either as a means to an end or an end in itself. Thus, according to the English courts, '[i]ntention to injure the plaintiff disposes of any question of remoteness'.[300] The German BGH agrees: '*vorsätzlich herbeigeführte Tatfolgen sind immer "adäquat*"'.[301] If a person intentionally causes harm to another, she will be liable for all direct consequences of her actions, regardless of how distant.[302] The obstacle of *novus actus interveniens* is thus surmountable where the accessory used the other party as a tool to achieve their tortious ends or at least knew about the others harmful plans and persisted in contributing towards them. It should be noted that this conclusion holds true for both direct and indirect intent.

The relevance of intent to causation can be explained by dint of the equivocation between causation and fault that was mentioned above:[303] in no European system is the determination of legally relevant causation seen exclusively as a mere mechanical link that binds the resultant damage to the tortfeasor's behaviour. Causation is instead also affected by normative considerations that form a supplementary conceptual bridge.[304] As a result, fault and causation are mutually referential, interdependent concepts, so that what is established by the first, need not be re-visited by the second. Von Bar explains this well:

> Often, not only is the causal analysis directly dependent on the terms of the duty, but also the exact content of the duty is only observable as a result of the causal analysis. [...] The general rule set out above, under which 'the intervention of intentional or reckless–conduct of–a third party resulting in–injury or damage breaks the chain of causation and renders the–injury or damage too remote', is thus applicable only where the defendant was [not] under a duty [either] to protect against a third party's action [or] to influence the behaviour of the third party whose gross fault caused the damage.[305]

---

299. R Bagshaw, 'Causing the Behaviour of Others and Other Causal Mixtures' in Richard Goldberg (ed), *Perspectives on Causation* (Hart Publishing 2011) 361.
300. *Quinn v. Leathem* [1901] AC 495, 537 (Lord Lindley). See also G Williams, *Joint Torts and Contributory Negligence* (Stevens & Sons 1951) 201.
301. BGH, 27 January 1981, VI ZR 204/79, BGHZ 79, 259-264.
302. C van Dam, *European Tort Law* (Oxford University Press 2007) paras 803 and 1101.
303. See s. 4.4. See also F H Lawson & B Markesinis, *Tortious Liability for Unintentional Harm in the Common Law and the Civil Law* (Cambridge University Press 1982) 184.
304. P Widmer, 'Comparative Report on Fault as a Basis of Liability and Criterion of Imputation (Attribution)' in P Widmer (ed.), *Unification of Tort Law: Fault* (Kluwer Law International 2005) 337-338.
305. C von Bar, *The Common European Law of Torts – Vol. II* (Clarendon Press 2000) paras 463-464.

In this way, the range of legally relevant causation expands and contracts depending on the intensity of the tortfeasor's culpability.[306] As a result, where the tortfeasor acted with intent, only cause-as-fact needs to be found.[307] The *conditio sine qua non* or 'but-for' test is usually sufficient for this purpose: if the harm would not have occurred *but for* the behaviour of the defendant, the defendant can be said to have caused the harm and will be liable. If, conversely, the defendant intended the damage, but failed to bring it about, only for it to take place anyway as a result of a different cause, the defendant will not be liable: *novus actus* arguments accordingly remain relevant, but must be grounded in a different source, such as a natural event, the behaviour of the claimant or the behaviour of an independent outside party. So, for example, if A intended to set B's house of fire, but failed in that attempt due to rainy weather, A will not be liable if the next day C independently successfully sets fire to the same house. Accessory liability accordingly provides an excellent example of the different partitioning between the different elements of fault liability in the different legal systems: what is dealt with as a question of causation in England and Germany is delegated to fault in France. At the same time, the causative potency of English joint tortfeasance and German *Mittäterschaft* derives from precisely where it resides in France as well: the defendant's fault.

And indeed, intent is at the heart of both the English doctrine of joint tortfeasance and the German provisions of Article 830 BGB. This has been made most obvious in Germany. As noted in Chapter 3, the BGH limits the scope of application of Article 830 BGB to intent or by requiring that the participants knowingly and intentionally combined to bring about the damage.[308] And, although rarely explicitly identified as such, intent, as mentioned in Chapter 3, is also clearly what is hiding behind the English 'participation links' of authorisation, procurement and common design.[309] If this was never explicitly stated before, Lord Sumption's interpretation of *Amstrad* in *Sea Shepherd* is clear:

> Intent in the law of tort is commonly relevant as a control mechanism limiting the ambit of a person's obligation to safeguard the rights of others, where this would constrict his freedom to engage in activities

---

306. The generous consequences of intent can also be explained in terms of an expanding scope of protection that allows all damage flowing from intentional behaviour to be recoverable. So, according to Art. 826 of the BGB, a person who, in a manner contrary to public policy (*'gegen die guten Sitten'* or, in Latin, *contra bonos mores)*, intentionally inflicts damage on another person is liable to the other person to make compensation for the damage. This will encompass even the relatively less protected mere economic loss. So, a finding of intent not only loosens the requirements of causation, but also expands the boundaries of the character of the loss.
307. C McIvor, *Third Party Liability in Tort* (Hart Publishing 2006) 19.
308. C van Dam, *European Tort Law* (Oxford University Press 2007) para. 1108-1; W van Gerven, et al., *Tort Law* (Hart Publishing 2000) 430-431.
309. See s. 3.1.3.

> which are otherwise lawful. The economic torts are a classic illustration of this. The cases on joint torts have had to grapple with the same problem, and intent performs the same role. What the authorities, taken as a whole, demonstrate is that the additional element which is required to establish liability, over and above mere knowledge that an otherwise lawful act will assist the tort, is a shared intention that it should do so. The required limitation on the scope of liability is achieved by the combination of active co-operation and commonality of intention. It is encapsulated in Scrutton LJ's distinction between concerted action to a common end and independent action to a similar end, and between either of these things and mere knowledge of the consequences of one's acts.[310]

It should be noted that this interpretation is perhaps mildly contentious. Davies explicitly disagrees with it, arguing instead for a knowledge-based standard.[311] However, that is not the generally accepted approach and, although Lord Sumption was here dissenting with the opinion of the majority, it is clear that, as was explained already in Chapter 3, any disagreement between the judges was not on this matter.

Some discussion surrounds the exact nature of the resultant link in joint tortfeasance. Cooper suggests that intent acts an alternative to causation.[312] According to this interpretation, in view of the lack of a true causal link binding the accessory to the wrong, a different kind of nexus must be forged: a nexus of complicity. He explains:

> This is not, however, to say that causation is entirely irrelevant to secondary liability. The acts of secondary participation must in some way contribute to the primary wrong, and this may be described as a requirement of causation in the broadest sense of the word.[313]

The German interpretation is similar: German scholars interpret *Mittäterschaft* as resting on a notion of '*psychisch vermittelte* Kausalität', i.e., psychological causation.[314] Von Bar analyses this nuanced concept:

---

310. *Sea Shepherd UK v. Fish & Fish Ltd* [2015] UKSC 10 (4 March 2015) at 44.
311. P S Davies, *Accessory Liability* (Hart Publishing 2015) 40-54 and 203-210.
312. D Cooper, *Secondary Liability for Civil Wrongs* (unpublished PhD thesis, University of Cambridge 1995) 4-6.
313. D Cooper, *Secondary Liability for Civil Wrongs* (unpublished PhD thesis, University of Cambridge 1995) 4.
314. W van Gerven et al., *Tort Law* (Hart Publishing 2000) 430; C von Bar, *The Common European Law of Torts – Vol. II* (Clarendon Press 2000) paras 416-417; C van Dam, *European Tort Law* (2nd ed., Oxford University Press 2013) para. 1108-1; C von Bar et al. (eds), *Principles, Definitions and Model Rules of European Private Law: Draft Common Frame of Reference (DCFR)*, prepared by the Study Group on a European Civil Code and the Research Group on EC private law (Acquis Group), Outline Edition (Sellier 2009) 3425 and 3445.

> In 'psychological causation' the German-language jurisdictions provide for a further tort construct which, although related to the concept of factual causation, cannot be demonstrated by scientific experiment. It covers cases in which both the defendant and a third party (possibly including the victim) contributed to the injury, which resulted from the third party acting in a manner wrongfully suggested by the defendant. The problem here is that, given the lack of knowledge of the detailed workings of the human brain, laws of nature regarding its functioning cannot be formulated. Rather, the law is concerned with a legal evaluation of whether one person's conduct is a reaction to another's misconduct.[315]

Davies diverges slightly from this interpretation and sees the rules of joint tortfeasance not as an alternative to, but as a specific type of causal connection.[316] This seems to better reflect the language used by the British courts,[317] while also explaining why the *novus actus* principle is only ever invoked as regards acts of assistance, but not cases of inducement or procurement. Accordingly, Davies views the 'culpability' link essentially as an interpretation of the 'but-for' test. Under this approach, the recognised 'participation links' are those identified by theory as contributing to the primary wrong in a factually causative manner.[318]

Although therefore the theory of joint tortfeasance is disguised as a matter of causation, it is perhaps better read as an attempt to bypass causation so as enable the establishment of an alternative connection binding the damage to the conduct of the accessory that is justified by general considerations of justice: a person who participates in the tort of another should not be exonerated from liability simply because 'but-for' causation is hard to establish. Instead, the accessory is held liable for the damage, regardless of whether the claimant can show proper causation linking her

315. C von Bar, *The Common European Law of Torts – Vol. II* (Clarendon Press 2000) para. 417.
316. P S Davies, *Accessory Liability* (Hart Publishing 2015) 31-32.
317. Davies gives a number of examples from a variety of areas of law. Indicatively, in *Attorney-General's Reference (No. 1 of 1975)*, Lord Widgery CJ stated that you 'cannot procure an offence unless there is a causal link between what you do and the commission of the offence' (see Attorney-General's Reference No 1 Of 1975 [1975] EWCA Crim 1). In *OBG Ltd v. Allan,* Lord Hoffmann observed that 'the real question which has to be asked [is]: did the defendant's acts of encouragement, threat, persuasion and so forth have a sufficient causal connection with the breach by the contracting party to attract accessory liability?' (see Douglas & Ors v. Hello! Ltd & Ors [2007] UKHL 21 (2 May 2008)). In *Brown v. Bennett*, Morritt LJ stated that 'if there is no causative effect and therefore no assistance given by the person … on whom is sought to establish the liability as [an accessory], for my part I cannot see that the requirements of conscience require any remedy at all' (see *Brown & Anor v. Bennett & Ors* [1998] EWCA Civ 1881).
318. P S Davies, *Accessory Liability* (Hart Publishing 2015) 39-40.

behaviour to it – it is enough that the plaintiff prove merely damage, fault on the part of the main tortfeasor and the cognitive participation of the accessory.[319] Participation accordingly essentially implements failure to abide by a standard of care – fault in the form of a participation in the tort of another – as *ersatz* causation.[320]

Of course, the differences in the interpretation of the culpability connection do not have any practical effect on ultimate outcomes. Yet Davies' suggestion does further illuminate the close connection of the English approach to the French one in real terms, if not in structural theory. Indeed, it is worth noting that in France as well, some authors do argue in favour of depending the choice of causation theory on the type of liability. So, Le Tourneau & Cadiet suggest that the equivalence theory is only suitable for fault liability, while strict liability should be compensated for through the application of more exacting causation regimes, such as adequacy. Starck, Roland and Boyer move ever closer to their fellow Europeans' systems and suggest that *équivalence des conditions* should be limited to intentional fault liability, while the explanatory or adequacy theories should instead be applied to all other cases, including cases of non-intentional fault.[321]

Movement towards approximation is evidenced from the other side of the causation fence as well. So, as was shown in Chapter 3, in both England and Germany, what should happen if the accessory's conduct is due, not to intent, but to negligence has become a biting issue. In such cases there would be no intent and therefore no 'participation link' establishing 'psychological causation'. Joint tortfeasance would thus be off the table and causation would have to be otherwise established. While this sets up a small roadblock, significantly, in neither of the two jurisdictions should the possibility of liability be understood to be entirely closed off. In Germany, although as a general rule it is true that, as mentioned in Chapter 3,[322] mere *Fahrlässigkeit* does not suffice for the application of Article 830 BGB, some wiggle room can be found in the older jurisprudence that accommodates gross negligence established by a combination of a series of negligent courses of conduct. This 'persistent negligence' approach has been revived in recent writings, especially with regard to copyright.[323]

English scholars seem more reluctant than their German counterparts to embrace this interpretation, but the same option cannot be excluded under English law either. The best example is again provided by *Smith v.*

---

319. C von Bar, *The Common European Law of Torts – Vol. II* (Clarendon Press 2000) para. 55.
320. U Magnus, 'Multiple Tortfeasors under German Law' in W V H Rogers, *Unification of Tort Law: Multiple Tortfeasors* (Kluwer Law International 2004) 88.
321. B Starck et al., *Obligations I – Responsabilité délictuelle* (5th ed, Litec 1996) 160-166, mentioned in W van Gerven et al., *Tort Law* (Hart Publishing 2000) 420.
322. See s. 3.3.2.3.
323. W van Gerven et al., *Tort Law* (Hart Publishing 2000) 430-431.

Littlewoods.[324] As part of his flexible fault-based analysis, Lord Mackay made the connection between breach of duty and causation clear:

> It is plain from the authorities that the fact that the damage, upon which a claim is founded, was caused by a human agent quite independent of the person against whom a claim in negligence is made does not, of itself, preclude success of the claim, since breach of duty on the part of the person against whom the claim is made may also have played a part in causing the damage.

This indicates that the general rule that persons must not cause harm by their negligence may continue to apply in cases of accessory liability as well: not all third party interventions break the chain of causation.[325] Naturally, liability under negligence will be harder to substantiate than under joint tortfeasance[326] – but that much should be obvious and is the case in France and Germany as well. The ultimate effect is one of combining causation with either intent or negligence in all three jurisdictions. In all three systems, moreover, where one person's negligence, e.g., due to an omission to take precautions, combines with another's intentional action inflicting harm, given that they will have both contributed through independent acts to the creation of a single indivisible injury, the accessory and main party must be understood to be a several concurrent tortfeasors.[327]

4.4.3 A European Rule for Causation

What would a European compromise on causation look like? Causation is enshrined as one of the 'indispensable pillars' of liability in the DCFR alongside legally relevant damage and accountability in the Basic Rule of VI.-1:101. Article VI. – 4:101 attempts a definition:

> A person causes legally relevant damage to another if the damage is to be regarded as a consequence of that person's conduct or the source of danger for which that person is responsible.

---

324. *Smith v. Littlewoods* [1987] AC 241.
325. T Weir, 'Liability for Knowingly Facilitating Mass Breaches of Copyright'(1988) 47(3) The Cambridge Law Journal 348; W V H Rogers, 'Multiple Tortfeasors under English Law' in W V H Rogers, *Unification of Tort Law: Multiple Tortfeasors* (Kluwer Law International 2004) 66; W V H Rogers, 'Comparative Report on Multiple Tortfeasors' in W V H Rogers, *Unification of Tort Law: Multiple Tortfeasors* (Kluwer Law International 2004) 277.
326. P S Davies, *Accessory Liability* (Hart Publishing 2015) 56-57.
327. C von Bar et al. (eds), *Principles, Definitions and Model Rules of European Private Law: Draft Common Frame of Reference (DCFR)*, prepared by the Study Group on a European Civil Code and the Research Group on EC private law (Acquis Group), Outline Edition (Sellier 2009) 3446.

In the formulation of this provision, the authors of the DCFR were careful to avoid a simple reduction to *conditio sine qua non*:[328] a conduct or a source of danger will be considered to be the cause of a legally relevant damage, if the damage is to be regarded as a consequence of that conduct or source of danger. The DCFR intentionally eschews the distinction between factual and normative causation. Accordingly, there is no bifurcation between a 'scientific' test that requires supplementation by further 'legal' value judgments, while no particular specific normative 'causation limiting' theory is adopted. Instead, the drafters note that the factors that must be taken into consideration in deciding whether a particular legally relevant damage is to be considered to be a consequence of the defendant's conduct or a source of danger do not lend themselves to an exhaustive listing or weighting in relation to each other – in each individual case, a separate calibration is necessary. At the same time, probability, foreseeability, the type of damage and the type of the attributive cause, the protective scope of the norm and general policy considerations are all identified as relevant factors in this calibration process.[329]

The PETL are much braver. Chapter 3 of the PETL expressly espouses the principle of *conditio sine qua non.* Article 3:101 PETL, headed by that exact term, declares that:

> An activity or conduct (hereafter: activity) is a cause of the victim's damage if, in the absence of the activity, the damage would not have occurred.

The drafters point out that the test is intended to provide the lowest common denominator of causation: '[i]f this test is not met, that is the end of the story.' This indicates that the purpose of the rule is mere law-in-fact. Beyond this, the drafters suggest a very practical approach, observing that, in most cases, the answer to the question of causation will be obvious, as the 'normal' consequences of an activity (e.g., damage to a car after a collision) can be easily agreed upon by reasonable people. To assist with this assessment, Article 3:201 PETL, provides a non-exhaustive list of factors very similar to those mentioned by the drafters of the DCFR:

a) the foreseeability of the damage at the time of the activity to a reasonable person, taking into account in particular the closeness in time or space between the damaging activity and its consequence,

328. C von Bar et al. (eds), *Principles, Definitions and Model Rules of European Private Law: Draft Common Frame of Reference (DCFR)*, prepared by the Study Group on a European Civil Code and the Research Group on EC private law (Acquis Group), Outline Edition (Sellier 2009), 3425.

329. C von Bar et al. (eds), *Principles, Definitions and Model Rules of European Private Law: Draft Common Frame of Reference (DCFR)*, prepared by the Study Group on a European Civil Code and the Research Group on EC private law (Acquis Group), Outline Edition (Sellier 2009), 3426.

or the magnitude of the damage in relation to the normal consequences of such an activity;
b) the nature and the value of the protected interest (Article 2:102);
c) the basis of liability (Article 1:101);
d) the extent of the ordinary risks of life; and
e) the protective purpose of the rule that has been violated.

What do these rules mean for accessory liability? The two projects' different starting points indicate divergent approaches. So, on the basis of its more cautious general rule on causation, the DCFR follows the 'joint tortfeasance' lead of England and Germany,[330] while, as indicated by its permissive 'but-for' solution to causation, the PETL prefers France's 'multiple faults' approach.

Article VI.–4:102 of the DCFR – located in Chapter 4 on 'Causation' – is dubbed 'collaboration' in its title:

> A person who participates with, instigates or materially assists another in causing legally relevant damage is to be regarded as causing that damage.

As the drafters clarify, the provision presupposes intent: the participation, instigation or material assistance offered by the collaborator must be conscious and wilful if it is to establish liability.[331] The liability of the primary party must also be based on fault: collaboration is not conceivable where the primary party acted without intention or negligence. In cases of instigation or assistance in particular, the bar is set higher yet, as all parties – including the instigator or facilitator – must have acted intentionally; mere negligence on the part of the secondary party will not suffice. The drafters justify the provision by reference to the idea of psychological causation.[332]

Although the DCFR does not itself provide any definitions, the accompanying commentary fills this gap. According to this, 'participants' are described as those persons who either play a part in carrying out an overall plan or persons who, although not participating in the actual act of wrongdoing themselves, maintain command or co-command over the course of events from the background. Unless extraordinary circumstances can be

---

330. G Wagner, 'The Law of Torts in the DCFR' in G Wagner (ed.), *The Common Frame of Reference - A View from Law and Economics* (Sellier European Law Publishing 2009) 254.
331. C von Bar et al. (eds), *Principles, Definitions and Model Rules of European Private Law: Draft Common Frame of Reference (DCFR)*, prepared by the Study Group on a European Civil Code and the Research Group on EC private law (Acquis Group), Outline Edition (Sellier 2009) 3445.
332. C van Dam, *European Tort Law* (2nd ed., Oxford University Press 2013) para. 1108-1; C von Bar et al. (eds), *Principles, Definitions and Model Rules of European Private Law: Draft Common Frame of Reference (DCFR)*, prepared by the Study Group on a European Civil Code and the Research Group on EC private law (Acquis Group), Outline Edition (Sellier 2009) 3445.

proven, harmful behaviour of the direct wrongdoer that goes beyond the original common plan will also be attributed to them as a consequence of their participation in the act. Instigators are defined as those persons who provided the active party with at least an additional motivating reason. It is not necessary that the instigator be the first to give the primary wrongdoer the idea and the fact that the main party might have wished to carry out the act without the instigator's intervention is irrelevant. Finally, accessories or aiders are described as persons supporting the primary tortfeasor in carrying out the act, but who have no influence over whether or not it actually comes to fruition. The requirement here is that the accessory know the general outline of the primary wrong and wished to assist in it. [333]

Article VI.–4:102 of the DCFR should be read in conjunction with Article VI.–6:105. This establishes a rule of joint and several liability (here named 'solidary liability') for several persons who are liable for the same damage. As a result, the 'collaborators' of Article VI.–4:102 will be liable as against the victim alongside the principle wrongdoer for the whole of the damage done. Again, this is reminiscent of English joint tortfeasance and the German *Mittäterschaft.* Paragraph 2 acknowledges that, as between themselves, such solidary debtors are liable severally and in equal parts, unless different shares are more appropriate, having regard to all circumstances of the case and in particular to fault or to the extent to which a source of danger contributed to the occurrence or extent of the damage. Book VI of the DCFR does not contain a provision on the allocation of liability between solidarily liable parties. This is instead covered by Article III.-4:106. According to this, the default rule is equal apportionment, but this is subject to the reasonableness test. Particular consideration should thus be taken of the degree of fault of each defendant.[334] According to the drafters of the DCFR, Article VI.–6:105's rule on solidary liability also applies in cases of concurrent tortfeasors.[335] Whether based on intent or negligence therefore, the ultimate result as regards responsibility towards the claimant should be the same.

In the PETL, the topic of multiple tortfeasors is dealt with in Title V. Thus, instead of being situated in causation, as it is in the DCFR, in imitation

333. C von Bar et al. (eds), *Principles, Definitions and Model Rules of European Private Law: Draft Common Frame of Reference (DCFR)*, prepared by the Study Group on a European Civil Code and the Research Group on EC private law (Acquis Group), Outline Edition (Sellier 2009) 3446-3447.
334. C von Bar et al. (eds), *Principles, Definitions and Model Rules of European Private Law: Draft Common Frame of Reference (DCFR)*, prepared by the Study Group on a European Civil Code and the Research Group on EC private law (Acquis Group), Outline Edition (Sellier 2009) 3600.
335. C von Bar et al. (eds), *Principles, Definitions and Model Rules of European Private Law: Draft Common Frame of Reference (DCFR)*, prepared by the Study Group on a European Civil Code and the Research Group on EC private law (Acquis Group), Outline Edition (Sellier 2009) 3446.

of the French system, the issue is located directly in the rules on apportionment. According to Article 9:101(1)(a), where the whole or a distinct part of the damage suffered by the victim is attributable to two or more persons, liability is solidary. As in the DCFR, the term 'solidary liability' is used to designate joint and several liability.[336] Among other possibilities, this will be the case where:

> a person knowingly participates in or instigates or encourages wrongdoing by others which causes damage to the victim.

As with the DCFR, this cannot happen unless the accessory was aware of the purpose of the person inflicting the damage: the participation, instigation or encouragement must be 'knowing'. On the other hand, contrary to the DCFR, Article 9:101(1)(a) of the PETL makes no mention of facilitation, thereby favouring a more restrictive approach to joint tortfeasance – although of course it is certainly conceivable that a specific act of facilitation might always qualify as 'participating in' the wrongdoing.

As opposed to Article VI.–4:102 of the DCFR, in the PETL participation is therefore not seen as a form of causation. The matter dealt with is instead much more mundane: simply to bind the tortfeasors to each other through solidary liability, so that accessories are held liable alongside the main tortfeasor for the whole of the damage that that person caused. As in the DCFR, the exact same regime is established in subparagraph (b) for cases where 'one person's independent behaviour or activity causes damage to the victim and the same damage is also attributable to another person', i.e., several concurrent tortfeasors or *Nebentäter*,[337] at least as long as there is 'no reasonable basis for attributing only part of the [damage] to each of the [multiple tortfeasors]' (see (Article 9:101(3)).

The PETL goes into much further detail than the DCFR concerning the exact parameters of this arrangement. Article 9:101 deals with the 'external' aspect concerning the situation between the tortfeasors and the victim. Here, it is made clear that each of the multiple tortfeasors will be individually liable to the victim for the whole of the damage suffered, provided no more than the full amount is recovered (Article 9:101(2)). Article 9:102 moves on to the 'internal' issue of contributions among the tortfeasors. According to this, a tortfeasor who has paid more than his share, without prejudice to any contractual arrangements to the contrary, may recover a contribution from any of the other joint tortfeasors (Article 9:102(1)). The obligation to make such a contribution is several, meaning that the person subject to it is liable only for his apportioned share of responsibility for the damage. The amount

336. European Group on Tort Law, *Principles of European Tort Law – Text and Commentary* (Springer 2005) 138. The term is also encountered in the US and Australia, see for example: K L Aubert, 'So Long Solidary Liability: Is Parting Such Sweet Sorrow?' [1997] 42(4) Loyola Law Review 745.

337. European Group on Tort Law, *Principles of European Tort Law – Text and Commentary* (Springer 2005) 143.

of the contribution owed by each joint tortfeasor shall be what is considered just in the light of the relative responsibility for the damage of the persons liable, having regard to their respective degrees of fault and to any other matters which are relevant to establish or reduce their liability. If it is not possible to determine the relative responsibility of joint tortfeasors, they are to be treated as equally responsible (Article 9:102(2)). Where it is not possible to enforce a judgment for contribution against one person liable, his share should be re-allocated among the other persons liable, in proportion to their responsibility (Article 9:102(4)). So, while as against the victim, the tortfeasors' liability for compensation is not apportioned, as among themselves, the tortfeasors main claim apportionment according to their relative responsibility. The objective here is that the victim should not suffer because more than one person was responsible for the damage, by having to pursue each individually.[338]

Ultimately, the two harmonisation projects illustrate the significant overlap between the two basic national approaches of 'multiple faults' and 'single fault'. They both accept a rule of solidary (joint and several) liability for both joint and several tortfeasors and several concurrent tortfeasors. The only question is how to get there. Like French law, the PETL jumps straight to the solidarity result, from the easy springboard of a lax causation rule and a permissive notion of fault. At the same time, it does take a cue from English and German law and first gives a nod in its apportionment rules to the idea that there is something special about the type of accessories identified in those jurisdictions as joint tortfeasors that needs to be overtly acknowledged. The DCFR's starting point is different. Its causation rule is far more cautious. However, like England and Germany, it quickly overcomes this difficulty by noting in the very next provision that 'collaborators' should be understood as having caused the damage. At the same time, it also adopts a broader definition of such collaborators than what is usually accepted in those countries, re-positioning its solution closer to the French one. Interestingly, English and German law are showing indications of wanting to move in that direction as well. Either way, both systems offer good indications of the ways in which the differences between the national European approaches to causation can be bridged, as well as demonstrating that those differences aren't in fact as great as might at first be imagined.

4.5 DEFENCES

A final word must be said on the last element of fault liability: defences. Obviously, if the conditions of fault liability as described in the preceding sections are not established, the defendant will not be found to be liable and

338. C von Bar, *The Common European Law of Torts – Vol. I* (Clarendon Press 1998) para. 318.

the claim will fail. However, it is also possible for the defendant to invoke a defence that protects her from liability that would otherwise attach. This provides an additional manner of inserting safeguards into the law against an over-expansive liability.[339] Below, we shall be examining such defences to the extent that they are relevant to intermediary liability.

4.5.1 Defences in the National Systems

Before we begin, a clarification regarding the use of the term 'defences' in this context is necessary. Considerable differences exist between national European approaches to defences against negligence. Von Bar and Van Dam make a distinction between a broader category of 'defences', which would include any argument made by the defendant with the aim of proving non-liability (including 'excuses' for conduct recognised as faulty), and a narrower category of 'grounds of justification', i.e., counter-indications of fault. Goudkamp expresses a similar distinction by using the terms 'absent element defences', which he defines as 'denials by the defendant of one or more of the elements of the tort in which the claimant sues',[340] and 'public policy defences', which 'exempt the defendant from liability even though he committed a tort'. The difference between the two is the difference between arguing 'I did no wrong' and 'I may have done wrong, but I should not be held liable anyway'.[341] The latter are therefore, to use a different terminology, pleas in 'confession and avoidance', as opposed to denials of wrongdoing.[342] As noted by McBride and Bagshaw, such defences require high levels of justification: tort law is primarily dedicated to the remedying of wrongs and only exceptional reasons should allow for a deviation from this rule.[343]

How do the national systems approach defences? German tort law understands 'grounds of justification' ('*Rechtfertigungsgründe*') in the first of the above meanings, i.e., as a neutraliser of unlawfulness, which (as noted above)[344] is a precondition of German fault; from this perspective, if grounds for justification apply, the defendant's conduct will not be unlawful and there thus can, by definition, be no fault, since fault requires 'unlawful' conduct. Naturally, this phenomenon will be even more evident where a legal system has no notion of 'unlawfulness', meaning that 'grounds of justification' will

339. European Group on Tort Law, *Principles of European Tort Law – Text and Commentary* (Springer 2005) 121-122.
340. J Goudkamp, *Tort Law Defences* (Hart Publishing 2013) 2.
341. N McBride & R Bagshaw, *Tort Law* (4th ed., Pearson 2012) 717.
342. J Goudkamp, *Tort Law Defences* (Hart Publishing 2013) 2.
343. N McBride & R Bagshaw, *Tort Law* (4th ed., Pearson 2012) 717.
344. See s. 4.3.1.

become even more entwined with the existence of a fault.[345] So, in France, 'grounds of justification' ('*faits justificatifs*') are seen as incompatible with the very notion of *faute:* if there is a justification, then there is no fault.[346] '*Faits justificatifs*' are accordingly merely classified in France as a type of *force majeure,* itself a subcategory of *cause étrangère,* an unforeseeable and unavoidable external cause of the damage. On the other end of the spectrum, English law sees defences in a broader way, as circumstances that may either justify or excuse conduct. It thus includes concepts such as the contributory negligence of the claimant and time limits for actions within the ambit of the term.[347] The cumulative result of these national approaches is a complete confusion with regard to the classification and consequences of European 'defences'. Even Von Bar, usually the harmonisation optimist, admits that the diversity in this area 'can pose a considerable obstacle for a common European law of delict', such that it may only be overcome if European lawyers 'show their willingness to reconsider everything they have learnt'.[348] He accordingly suggests that harmonisers discard their old, incompatible ideas and focus instead on developing new approaches, guided exclusively by the factor of effectiveness.[349]

4.5.2 A European Rule for Defences

This solution makes particular sense for a European intermediary liability: one that pulls free from the confines of the traditional notions of the German *Rechtfertigungsgründe,* the French *causes étrangères* or the English concept of defences and is instead developed independently as an organic response to the demands of the specific field. What defences are appropriate for a European regime of intermediary accessory liability in copyright?

To answer this it is first necessary to identify the defences used in tort law generally. Regardless of their classification, what kind of circumstances can serve as defences? To find a European answer to this question, we shall once again be taking cues from the academic tort unification projects of the PETL and the DCFR.

The PETL distinguish between defences based on justification and those that are not. On the non-justificatory front, only 'contributory negligence or activity' is listed (Article 8:101 PETL). Defences based on justification are

345. C von Bar, *The Common European Law of Torts – Vol. II* (Clarendon Press 2000) paras 486-487.
346. C van Dam, *European Tort Law* (2nd ed., Oxford University Press 2013) para. 809-2.
347. C von Bar, *The Common European Law of Torts – Vol. II* (Clarendon Press 2000) para. 486.
348. C von Bar, *The Common European Law of Torts – Vol. II* (Clarendon Press 2000) para. 488.
349. C von Bar, *The Common European Law of Torts – Vol. II* (Clarendon Press 2000) para. 490.

dealt with in Article 7:101 of the PETL. According to this, liability can be excluded if and to the extent that the actor acted legitimately:

a) in defence of his own protected interest against an unlawful attack (self-defence);
b) under necessity;
c) because the help of the authorities could not be obtained in time (self-help);
d) with the consent of the victim, or where the latter has assumed the risk of being harmed; or
e) by virtue of lawful authority, such as a licence.

The ultimate result will depend on the importance of these justifications as weighed against the conditions of liability. In extraordinary cases, liability may instead simply be reduced.

In its Chapter 5 on the topic, the DCFR distinguishes between three types of defences: 'Consent or Conduct of the Injured Person' (Articles VI.-5:101-5:103), 'Interests of Accountable Persons or Third Parties' (Articles VI.-5:201-5:203) and 'Inability to Control' (Articles VI.-5:301-5:302). The first includes consent and contributory fault; the second authority conferred by law, self-defence, benevolent interventions and necessity, as well as the protection of the public interest; and the third mental incompetence and events beyond control.

Both projects clearly move along very similar lines. They are also both clearly influenced by the civilian perspective, concentrating heavily as they do on the more circumscribed 'grounds for justification'.[350] This arguably makes sense given their breadth: where a variety of different torts are handled in a single document, establishing bright lines beyond which liability in all cases cannot pass offers a sensible way of providing more concrete guidance on the appropriate standard of care for each case. The same approach can be just as useful in accessory as in primary liability. Indeed, Davies, declares that the 'most significant defence to accessory liability is that of justification'.[351] Again however, this is in reference to accessory liability in its totality, ranging across not only all of tort law, but also equity, contract and criminal law.

By contrast, given that this book is concentrated on the formulation of a standard of care in a very specific area of liability, it is suggested that the examination of grounds of justification within a heading of defences is counter-indicated. For the sake of greater coherence (and in the absence of any European concept of unlawfulness), denials of fault should instead be best integrated into the examination of fault itself: after all, they essentially

350. C van Dam, *European Tort Law* (2nd ed., Oxford University Press 2013) para. 809-2.
351. P S Davies, *Accessory Liability* (Hart Publishing 2015) 222.

constitute another way of saying that the defendant has not acted negligently, while it makes little sense to elaborate a standard of care for a specific area of law only to subsequently undermine it with extraneous justifications. For the purposes of this book therefore, 'defences' shall be understood to include only defences in the form of excuses: Goudkamp's 'public policy defences', which shield defendants from liability where a wrong has nevertheless been committed.

This is however not to say that the above-listed justifications should be entirely disregarded: instead, their relevance shall simply be transported back into the determination of the standard of care appropriate for intermediary accessory liability in copyright. Having said that, the majority of the justifications mentioned by the PETL and the DCFR do not seem particularly relevant to intermediary accessory liability for copyright infringement. The obvious exception is presented by the interests of accountable persons and third parties. Article VI.-5:203 DCFR in particular stands out. This declares that:

> [a] person has a defence if legally relevant damage is caused in necessary protection of values fundamental to a democratic society, in particular where damage is caused by dissemination of information in the media.

The provision constitutes a clear reference to the importance of fundamental rights, particularly in the context of the modern information society.[352] The fact that this idea is singled out in the DCFR as a justification indicates the particular importance such counterbalancing indications should receive. Accordingly, they must play a heightened role in the elaboration of the standard of care suitable for intermediary liability. Happily, this justification fits in very nicely with concept of the character and benefit of the defendant's conduct that acts as a factor in fault.[353] It can therefore be incorporated into the dedicated balancing exercise of intermediary accessory copyright liability and shall receive especial emphasis there.[354]

Are any other defences relevant to accessory liability? Not much is left, although contributory negligence and limitations[355] should always certainly be considered. Finally, statutory defences[356] will of course also be a possibility in any field of law. Indeed, that is exactly what, at the end of the day, the E-Commerce Directive's safe harbours really are.

---

352. On the relevance of human rights to defenses against accessory liability, see P S Davies, *Accessory Liability* (Hart Publishing 2015) 230-234. He notes that freedom of expression is particularly important in the context of IPRs.
353. Indeed, it is exactly there that Van Dam also positions the issue, see C van Dam, *European Tort Law* (2nd ed., Oxford University Press 2013) para. 809-1.
354. See below, Ch. 5, para. 5.4.
355. P S Davies, *Accessory Liability* (Hart Publishing 2015) 251-253.
356. W V H Rogers, *Winfield & Jolowicz on Tort* (18th ed., Sweet & Maxwell 2010) 1131.

4.6 NEGLIGENCE BALANCING AND THE 'FAIR BALANCE'

In the sections above, the individual elements of a tort have each been examined in turn. What can we conclude from this analysis regarding the central theme of tort law? This is clearly one: balancing. Van Gerven et al. put this well:

> Tort law is therefore about the (re-)distribution of losses and in consequence allocation of risks. Reduced to its bare essentials, it strikes a balance between the respective interests of the victim and the injurer, taking into account broader social interests as well.[357]

Van Dam is even more succinct: '[t]ort law is about balancing the freedom of conduct against the protection of rights and interests'.[358] Every individual's integrity interests stand – by their very nature – in opposition to the potential activity interests of all others.[359] As a result, each time the legal system recognises one person's right to live free from the interferences of others, everybody else's freedom of action is circumscribed. Tort law is the battlefield upon which this conflict between private autonomy and social solidary is resolved for the purpose of application to private interactions.[360]

As a result of the central role it plays, the seed of balancing sprouts up continuously across the landscape of tort: balancing is how legally relevant interests are identified, how duties of care are decided upon, how legal causation is determined and how appropriate defences are settled upon. But the main tool with which tort law's balancing act is achieved is of course the famous 'reasonable person'.[361] As Prosser and Keeton state: 'So far as there is one central idea [to tort law], it would seem that it is that liability must be based upon conduct which is socially unreasonable. The common thread woven into all torts is the idea of unreasonable interference with the interests

357. W van Gerven et al., *Tort Law* (Hart Publishing 2000) 13.
358. C van Dam, *European Tort Law* (2nd ed., Oxford University Press 2013) para. 711-2.
359. P Widmer, 'Required Standard of Conduct' in P Widmer (ed.), *Unification of Tort Law: Fault* (Kluwer Law International 2005) 76.
360. C van Dam, *European Tort Law* (2nd ed., Oxford University Press 2013) para. 711-2; H Koziol, *Basic Questions of Tort Law from a Germanic Perspective* (Jan Sramek Verlag 2012) 188; M W Hesselink, 'Common Frame of Reference & Social Justice', available in NARCIS (National Academic Research and Collaborations Information System).
361. Vam Dam states: 'It is generally accepted that the negligent character of the defendant's conduct has to be established by balancing the expected risk, on one hand, and the precautions, on the other: 'As the danger increases, so must the precautions increase. 'This balancing of care and risk reflects the general task of tort law to balance freedom and protection.' See: C van Dam, *European Tort Law* (2nd ed., Oxford University Press 2013) para. 805-2.

of others.'[362] All other balancing exercises can thus be viewed as interpretations of tort law's one quintessential quest: the identification of the reasonable person as the ultimate measure of lawful (i.e., non-tortious) behaviour. After all, the reasonable person would not cause legally relevant damage either intentionally or negligently or, if he did, it would be with good legal reason – absent any of the necessary conditions of fault liability or given a recognised defence, the defendant must be accepted as reasonable; given all the necessary conditions of fault liability and absent a recognised defence, the reasonable person by definition is no longer so. In the final analysis, legal reasoning in tort law consists of the search for socially reasonable behaviour and that search is called balancing.

4.6.1 Negligence Balancing: A Rights-Based or Utility-Based Approach?

The realisation of the central role that balancing plays within the tort law framework raises one big question: if tort law is about balancing, what exactly does the balancing process entail? How should tort-based balancing be approached? Above, in the exposition of the European notion of negligence, Van Dam's formula organising the pertinent factors that determine negligence was heavily relied upon. What is the history of this approach? According to Van Dam himself, his proposed model was partially inspired by what has become known as the 'Learned Hand test' or the 'calculus of negligence'.[363] This has often been described as the main balancing tool of modern tort law.[364] According to this, in order to assess whether the defendant took a sufficient amount of care, a comparison must be made between the costs of the precautionary measures necessary to eliminate the damage and the benefit of achieving that result.

The rule was first formulated by US judge Learned Hand (from whom it takes its name) in 1947 in *US v. Carroll Towing,* a case involving an improperly secured barge that had drifted away from a pier and caused damage to several other boats. Justice Hand proposed an algebraic formula to determine whether the standard of care had been met:

> Since there are occasions when every vessel will break from her moorings, and since, if she does, she becomes a menace to those about her; the owner's duty, as in other similar situations, to provide against resulting injuries is a function of three variables: (1) The probability that

362. W Page Keeton et al., *Prosser and Keeton on Torts* (5th ed. West Group, St Paul, MN 1984) 6.
363. C van Dam, *European Tort Law* (2nd ed., Oxford University Press 2013) para. 805-2.
364. McBride and Bagshaw for example equate 'balancing' with the Hand formula and differentiate this from other formulae of legal reasoning (See, N McBride & R Bagshaw, *Tort Law* (4th ed., Pearson 2012) 252-256).

she will break away; (2) the gravity of the resulting injury, if she does; (3) the burden of adequate precautions. Possibly it serves to bring this notion into relief to state it in algebraic terms: if the probability be called P; the injury, L; and the burden, B; liability depends upon whether B is less than L multiplied by P: i.e., whether $B < PL$.

If the harm could have been avoided for less than what it cost ($B < PL$), then the individual *should* have taken precautions to avoid it, rather than allowing the harm to occur. If these precautions were not taken, then there has been a breach of duty and liability must be imposed on the defendant to pay for the harm. If the harm could not be avoided for less than what it cost ($B > PL$), then no liability should be imposed. A catchier rendition of the test formulates it as $C > GL$: **C**ost is greater than **G**ravity of **L**oss.[365] At a later stage, this simple equation was amended to add consideration for the benefit of the conduct as well.[366]

Is this an appropriate summary of European tort law? Although the Learned Hand test has indubitably exercised greater influence on the common law and especially on American tort law, comparative scholars note that the same factors are also used and balanced in the same way in civil law jurisdictions.[367] So, aside from Van Dam, Van Den Bergh and Visscher have also observed the correspondence between the elements of the Learned Hand rule and the formulation of Article 4:102(1) PETL.[368] The cost of precautions, they agree, is rendered as the 'availability and costs of precautionary or alternative methods', the probability of incurring a damage is referred to as the 'dangerousness of the activity' and the losses are 'the value of the protected interests involved'. Foreseeability, they concede, is also relevant, as it is not possible to take precautionary measures against risks one cannot foresee.

But the Hand formula is not without its critics. Detractors have observed that the costs of care and the expected loss should not be expressed in absolute numbers, when it is the marginal values that are what is relevant: the pertinent question is whether the cost of any additional measures would be higher or lower than the benefit they would yield in reduced losses. An efficient level of care should therefore be determined in an incremental, not an absolute, manner. Brown has accordingly suggested rejecting the literal interpretation of the Hand formula in favour of two alternative tests of care, which he terms the 'Incremental Standard' and the 'Limited Information Incremental Standard', both of which require more complicated

365. N McBride & R Bagshaw, *Tort Law* (4th ed., Pearson 2012) 252-256.
366. C van Dam, *European Tort Law* (2nd ed., Oxford University Press 2013) para. 805-2.
367. See also, H Kerkmeester & L Visscher, 'Learned Hand in Europe: A Study in the Comparative Law and Economics of Negligence' (2003) 6 German Working Papers in Law and Economics.
368. R Van Den Bergh & L Visscher, 'The Principles of European Tort Law: The Right Path to Harmonization?' (2006) 4 European Review of Private Law 511.

calculations.[369] Grady has further expressed doubts as to whether the Hand formula truly promotes the minimisation of social costs. Instead of comparing the defendant's actual precautions with the level of precaution demanded by due care, he suggests that what should be examined is the costs and benefits of a particular untaken precaution, as proposed by the plaintiff, that functions as a condition of the harm.[370]

Yet the problems with the Hand formula go deeper than simple tweaks of the equation representing it. McBride and Bagshaw, for example, point out that the Hand rule reaches its limits in what they call 'high risk-high cost' situations, i.e., where guarding against a great risk would also have highly negative repercussions. What to do in such cases is a tricky question.[371] They quote Lord Denning, who in *Miller v. Jackson,* a case involving a choice between closing down a cricket ground and exposing the neighbours to a high likelihood that a ball could fly into their house, resorted to the concept of the public interest:

> There is a contest here between the interest of the public at large; and the interest of a private individual. The public interest lies in protecting the environment by preserving our playing fields in the face of mounting development, and by enabling our youth to enjoy all the benefits of outdoor games, such as cricket and football. The private interest lies in securing the privacy of his home and garden without intrusion or interference by anyone. […] As between their conflicting interests, I am of opinion that the public interest should prevail over the private interest. The cricket club should not be driven out. In my opinion the right exercise of discretion is to refuse an injunction.

The fact that what was requested in this case was not damages, but an injunction, a discretionary remedy in English law, was significant in leading him to form this view. At the same time, his two fellow judges on the Court of Appeal disputed his assessment:

> The risk of injury to person and property is so great that on each occasion when a ball comes over the fence and causes damage to the Plaintiffs, the Defendants are guilty of negligence.[372]

It therefore appears that reasonable people can disagree on how a reasonable person would behave. Courts may be similarly divided on 'low cost-low risk' cases.[373]

---

369. J P Brown, 'Towards an Economic Theory of Liability' (1973) Journal of Legal Studies 323.
370. M F Grady, 'A New Positive Economic Theory of Negligence' (1983) 92(5) The Yale Law Journal 799; M F Grady, 'Untaken Precautions' (1989) 18 Journal of Legal Studies 139.
371. N McBride & R Bagshaw, *Tort Law* (4th ed., Pearson 2012) 255-256.
372. *Miller v. Jackson,* [1977] QB 966.
373. N McBride & R Bagshaw, *Tort Law* (4th ed., Pearson 2012) 254.

More fatally however, critics of the Learned Hand test have also objected to its very objective: the attempt to transmogrify complex legal problems into mathematic equations. Indicatively, Wright has observed that, although the Hand formula persists as an academic myth, in actual fact even the US courts overwhelmingly do not apply it to determine negligence. Those that do fail to derive useful conclusions from it, but instead primarily use it as window-dressing for decisions reached by different methods.[374] The Hand Formula, he therefore asserts, is based on speculation, generalisations, selection bias and superficial descriptions of sophisticated analyses.[375] One problem here is the lack of reliable statistical information on which to undertake the aggregate cost-benefit analysis. Indeed, in most cases, such data is impossible to collect, as (as Hand himself acknowledged) the factors comprising the test are – just as is the case with fundamental rights balancing – incommensurable and thus not susceptible to quantitative determination.[376] Accurate values can therefore not be assigned to them and comparison is impossible. Without such data, the Hand formula is reduced to a mere thought experiment.[377]

Finally, disagreements concerning the nature and aims of tort law as a category of law also beleaguer the test. The basic schism that divides tort law theoreticians is between corrective justice and distributive justice. Corrective justice focuses on fixing wrongs. Distributive justice on the other hand is concerned with optimising the distribution of goods in society.[378] Although distributive justice sits well alongside the teleology of the Hand approach, corrective justice theoreticians observe that the legal tradition of Western tort law relies more strongly on an individualistic morality that focuses not on social policy, but on interpersonal equality.[379] The idea here is not to maximise benefit for society as a whole, but to create the 'conditions that allow each person to realise his or her humanity as a self-legislating free rational being'.[380] Thus, Wright suggests that, not utilitarianism, but a Kantian-Aristotelian theory of legal responsibility best explains the traditional structures of European tort law. It is worth noting in this regard that an earlier version of the DCFR made an explicit reference to this underlying understanding:

---

374. R W Wright, 'Hand, Posner, and the Myth of the "Hand Formula"' (2003) 4(1) Theoretical Inquiries in Law 144.
375. R W Wright, 'Hand, Posner, and the Myth of the "Hand Formula"' (2003) 4(1) Theoretical Inquiries in Law 144.
376. *Conway v. O'Brien,* 111 F.2d 611 (2d Cir. 1940).
377. G Brüggermeier, *Modernising Civil Liability Law in Europe, China, Brazil and Russia: Texts and Commentaries* (Cambridge University Press 2011) 75.
378. C van Dam, *European Tort Law* (Oxford University Press 2007) para. 609-1.
379. J Fleming, *The Law of Torts* (7th ed., The Law Book Company, Sydney 1987) 108-109, as quoted in R W Wright, 'The Standards of Care in Negligence Law' in D Owens, *The Philosophical Foundations of Tort Law* (Oxford University Press 1997) 252.
380. R W Wright, 'The Standards of Care in Negligence Law' in D Owens, *The Philosophical Foundations of Tort Law* (Oxford University Press 1997) 252.

> The DCFR is particularly concerned to promote what Aristotle termed 'corrective' justice. This notion is fundamental to […] non-contractual liability for damage. The DCFR is less concerned with issues of 'distributive justice', but sometimes distributive or 'welfarist' concerns may be reflected in the DCFR.[381]

And indeed, while legal economist Richard Posner has claimed that tort law 'is best explained as if the judge who created the law through decisions operating as precedents in later cases were trying to promote efficient resource allocation',[382] a brief overview shows that a number of features of modern tort law are entirely incompatible with such a utilitarian explanation: tort law is in fact remarkably unconcerned with efficiency or resource allocation. For example, the use of an objective rather than a subjective standard for assessing fault makes no sense under a utilitarian approach, which, instead of imposing a minimum threshold, would logically insist on each individual being required to undertake only that care which does not exceed the benefits of the risk at all times. Likewise, the utilitarian approach fails to explain why there is not always liability for failure to act in a way that would maximise social benefit or why, as a general rule, the law does not forbid persons from acting against their own interests, even when those interests coincide with social utility. Furthermore, a genuine application of the cost-benefit analysis would allow – or even oblige – us to use others as means to our own ends, as long as the ultimate result would be a net social positive.[383]

Theoretically, it could of course be argued that the utilitarian approach can be salvaged by moving past a money-based understanding of costs and benefits.[384] But this assertion too is dubious. The trouble is the way in which this perspective clings to the idea of quantifying unquantifiable concepts. While it therefore would be correct to suggest that tort law strives for optimal outcomes, that optimisation is to be judged through the lens of justice and not social utility. Thus, even such a non-mercantile understanding of the Hand formula still cannot rid itself of the need for a comparison of ultimate outcomes against the standard of social utility. It therefore fails to account for the possibility of a highly principled or even of a self-destructive society that does not prioritise social benefit, in this way subverting the aggregate-cost-benefit explanation. More pertinently, it does nothing to prove that we do not currently live in a world that is, at least to some extent, either or both of those things.

---

381. As quoted by M W Hesselink, 'Common Frame of Reference & Social Justice', available in NARCIS (National Academic Research and Collaborations Information System).
382. W Landes & R Posner, *The Economic Structure of Tort Law* (Harvard University Press 1987) 1, as quoted in R Stevens, *Torts and Rights* (Oxford University Press 2007) 93.
383. R Stevens, *Torts and Rights* (Oxford University Press 2007) 93-94 and 99.
384. D Dobbs, *The Law of Torts* (West Publishing, St. Paul 2000) 339-340.

Regardless, at this point, it should be noted that this book is not interested in engaging in the philosophical debates behind the preference for one approach or the other. Instead, the analysis here is limited to a merely descriptive observation: the justice-based solution would appear to be the one most accepted by European legal theorists and which best explains modern European negligence liability. In this regard, it is also worth mentioning that the distinction between corrective and distributive justice is often considered to follow territorial lines. So, corrective justice is more strongly associated with English tort law, while France are said to lean more towards distributive justice. Germany, typically, steers a middle course.[385] However, these differences should not be over-estimated, at least within the area of fault liability. All the objections raised above to the calculus of negligence hold true equally in the common law, as in the civil law: both are rights-based. And, although it is true that France is more prone to the unleashing of strict liabilities, this does not affect the workings of French fault liability, but merely the number of areas subject to it.

Unsurprisingly given this background, a justice-based approach is also the preference of the DCFR and the PETL. That is, for example, what the long list of counterbalancing factors forming the negligence standard of Article 4:102 of the PETL suggest. The refusal of the drafters of the DCFR to enumerate any criteria at all, as well as their circumspect take on causation points even more emphatically in the same direction. These multiple factors can be aggregated into a more easily digestible representation in the form of the reasonable person, but that person cannot be located through math. A more precise rule does not at the moment exist and it is doubtful if it even could.[386] Accordingly, as in fundamental rights, the appropriate approach to tort law balancing is a case-by-case consideration of the facts at hand. The Interim Edition of the DCFR explains this best:

> Abstract principles tend to contradict one another. They always have to be weighed up against one another more exactly because only then are optimal outcomes assured. […] It is characteristic for such fundamental aims that they conflict with each other. […] Therefore the aims can never be pursued in a pure and rigid way. The underlying values of a private law system can only be discerned and described by explaining how such fundamental aims are balanced in the individual model rules.[387]

Ultimately, the trouble with the Hand formula is accordingly simply diagnosed: law is not math. As Van Dam acknowledges, the factors of

385. C van Dam, *European Tort Law* (Oxford University Press 2007) paras 609-2 and 609-3.
386. See Pearson J expressing the same idea in *Hazell* v. *British Transport Commission* [1958] 1 WLR 169, 171.
387. C von Bar et al. (eds), *Principles, Definitions and Model Rules of European Private Law: Draft Common Frame of Reference (DCFR)*, Interim Edition (Sellier 2008) 4-7.

negligence 'can be used as a formula but, this is not a matter of simply carrying out a calculation and reaching a conclusion'.[388] Instead, tort law privileges rights over efficiency.[389] A better explanation of European tort law is one that is justice-based. Tort rights, like fundamental rights, are not absolute, but they are also not toothless. They are instead flexible legal concepts that take their cue from social perceptions of justice. As opposed to the blunt, tone-deaf approach of the legal economist, therefore, they allow for more refined decision-making: adjudication instead of calculation. So, while the current reality of European negligence law seems to be a balancing one, this balancing is not geared towards maximum social utility, but at a more sophisticated, if somewhat nebulous, search for justice. As a result, while 'balancing' in tort law is often identified with the Hand approach and more generally with legal teleology, here it shall be used to refer more flexibly to the complex processes of weighing up conflicting interests through legal reasoning.

It is worth noting that, remarkably, balancing seems to be equally accepted as an appropriate basic framework for the analysis and evaluation of private law rules by European privatists from both the right and left of the political spectrum – although different persons might have different ideas about the outcomes it promotes.[390] Indeed, while in the US it can be said to be losing popularity,[391] in Europe, after a post-war dip, balancing is now again on the rise. Balancing sceptics might argue that this represents a de-rationalisation and politicisation of legal methodology. Alternatively, it could also be seen as the 'belated attainment of legal maturity' by the field[392] – indeed, the potential to bridge ideologically driven conflict has been identified as one of the advantages of proportionality balancing as a legal tool.[393] In any case, on a more pragmatic plane, what it certainly suggests is the beginning of a merging of European private law theory with the

388. C van Dam, *European Tort Law* (2nd ed., Oxford University Press 2013) para. 805-2.
389. R Stevens, *Torts and Rights* (Oxford University Press 2007) 93-97. R W Wright, 'Justice and Reasonable Care in Negligence Law' (2002) 47 American Journal of Jurisprudence 143.
390. C von Bar et al. (eds), *Principles, Definitions and Model Rules of European Private Law: Draft Common Frame of Reference (DCFR)*, prepared by the Study Group on a European Civil Code and the Research Group on EC private law (Acquis Group), Outline Edition (Sellier 2009) 10.
391. J Bomhoff, *Balancing Constitutional Rights: the Origins and Meanings of Postwar Legal Discourse* (Cambridge University Press 2013) 1-71; A Stone-Sweet & J Matthews, 'Proportionality Balancing and Global Constitutionalism' (2008) 47(1) Columbia Journal of Transnational Law 72.
392. D Kennedy, 'A Transnational Geneology of Proportionality in Private Law' in R Brownsword, H-W Micklitz, L Niglia & S Weatherill, *The Foundations of European Private Law* (Hart Publishing 2011) 185.
393. D M Beatty, *The Ultimate Rule of Law* (Oxford University Press 2004) 159.

overarching debate on European constitutional law, including the law of fundamental rights.[394] This is the aspect that shall now be explored.

4.6.2 A Return to 'Fair Balance'

The use of balancing as the central deliberative mechanism of tort is strongly reminiscent of the law of fundamental rights. As established in Chapter 2, fundamental rights also employ balancing as a conflict resolution mechanism. Notably, as was also mentioned in Chapter 2, controversy surrounds the notion of balancing in that area as well. Indeed, interestingly, the debate on the utilitarian or justice-based interpretation of tort law balancing outlined above is closely paralleled in the law of fundamental rights. So, Tsakyrakis, for example, echoing some of the fears surrounding the Hand formula, complains that fundamental rights balancing 'constitutes a misguided quest for precision and objectivity in the resolution of human rights dispute' that attempts to invest 'judicial judgements with the precision of the natural sciences'. He thus argues that 'this view leads to a complete erosion of the notion of human rights [that] overlooks the idea that human rights are not merely quantities of freedom but protect some basic status of people as moral agents' and suggests that courts 'should focus, instead, on the real moral issues underlying such disputes'.[395] In essence, this boils down to one accusation:[396] that of incommensurability, i.e., the absence of a common metric that permits comparison between incomparable values that also beleaguers the Hand formula. As Habermas puts it, 'the court's judgement is then *itself* a value judgement […] But this judgement is no longer related to the alternatives of a right or wrong decision'.[397] The accusation is that balancing takes us out of the realm of the just and unjust to one of the adequate and the inadequate and, therefore, out of the realm of law and into

394. D Kennedy, 'A Transnational Geneology of Proportionality in Private Law' in R Brownsword, H-W Micklitz, L Niglia & S Weatherill, *The Foundations of European Private Law* (Hart Publishing 2011) 185.
395. S Tsakyrakis, 'Proportionality: An Assault on Human Rights?' (2009) 7(3) International Journal of Constitutional Law 468.
396. Balancing has also been attacked for watering down human rights by depriving them of their normative power (see, for example, S Tsakyrakis, 'Proportionality: An Assault on Human Rights?' (2009) 7(3) International Journal of Constitutional Law 468, where he states that 'The balancing approach […] is committed to a view whereby everything, even those aspects of our life most closely associated with our status as free and equal, is, in principle, up for grabs.') As Smet points out however, in the context of clashes between human rights, as opposed to conflicts between human right and the public interest, there is no risk that human rights will lose their Dworkian 'trump' status: either way a human right will emerge triumphant, see S Smet, *Resolving Conflicts between Human Rights: A Legal Theoretical Analysis in the Context of the ECHR,* (unpublished PhD thesis, Ghent University 2014) 135.
397. J Habermas, 'Reply to Symposium Participants, Benjamin N. Cardozo School of Law' (1996) 17 Cardozo Law Review 1477.

that of unlimited judicial discretion.[398] Thus, through balancing, it is suggested, all legal debates are reduced to debates on policy.[399]

There is certainly some justification to this criticism. In particular, Alexy's famous 'Law of Balancing', although not without its advantages, has invited criticism by, like the Hand formula, expressing itself in mathematical terms. Thus, according to Alexy, the concept of fundamental rights balancing can be rendered as follows:

$$Wij = \frac{Ii}{Ij}$$

I stands for the intensity of interference with a principle and W for its abstract weight. So, if Pi is the first principle being weighed and Pj the second, Ii refers to the intensity of the interference with the first principle and Ij to the intensity of the interference with the second.[400] Ultimately, Wij is intended to express how the two principles relate to each other in terms of the concrete circumstances of a given case. In order to enable the application of the test, a scale with three basic settings is established for measuring the intensity of a given interference: 'light', 'moderate' and 'serious'. Light *(l)* is assigned a value of 2^0 or 1, moderate *(m)* a value of 2^1 or 2 and serious *(s)* of 2^2 or 4. The result reveals which principle should prevail. Three outcomes are possible: the result may be higher than 1, lower than 1 or equal to 1. In the first case, the concrete weight of the Pi will be found to be higher than that of Pj and it should take precedence. In the second case, the converse will

398. Again Alexy, in R Alexy, 'Constitutional Rights, Balancing and Rationality' (2003) 16(2) Ratio Juris 131.

399. S Greer, '"Balancing" and the European Court of Human Rights: A Contribution to the Habermas-Alexy Debate' (2004) 63(2) The Cambridge Law Journal 412.

400. Alexy has further elaborated on this formula through his second Law of Balancing (dubbed the 'Epistemic Law of Balancing'), as well as by recognises that the abstract weight of a principle may also play a role in balancing. His ultimate Weight Formula is as follows:

$$Wi,j = \frac{Ii \times Wi \times Ri}{Ij \times Wj \times Rj}$$

I stands for the intensity of interference with a principle, W for its abstract weight and R for the reliability of the underlying premises, i.e., the chance that the effects on the principle will materialise. So, if Pi is the first principle being weighed and Pj the second, the Wi,j expresses how the two principles relate to each other in terms of the concrete circumstances of a given case. See, R Alexy, *A Theory of Constitutional Rights* (Oxford University Press 2002); R Alexy, 'Balancing, Constitutional Review, and Representation' (2005) 3(4) International Journal of Constitutional Law 572; R Alexy, 'On Balancing and Subsumption. A Structural Comparison', (2003) 16(4) Ratio Juris 433; S Greer, '"Balancing" and the European Court of Human Rights: A Contribution to the Habermas-Alexy Debate' (2004) 63(2) The Cambridge Law Journal 412; S Smet, *Resolving Conflicts between Human Rights: A Legal Theoretical Analysis in the Context of the ECHR,* (unpublished PhD thesis, Ghent 2014).

be true and Pj will prevail. If the result is equal to 1, there is what Alexy terms a 'stalemate'.[401]

Intriguingly, Alexy's balancing test does manage to address the challenge of incommensurability. The use of the triadic scale on the basis of a common point of view of the importance of each principle enables a rational discourse around competing principles. Accordingly, it is admirable in the way it infuses rationality into a process that otherwise runs the risk of deflating into complete arbitrariness. At the same time, it must be acknowledged that, again, law is not math, and Alexy's balancing formula suffers from the same weakness that the Hand formula does: judicial rulings require reasoning, not calculation. As indicated in Chapter 2, both of the highest courts of Europe have embraced balancing, but they have done so within a context of judicial deliberation. This is especially apparent in the case law of the ECtHR, which, slowly but, hopefully, surely, appears to be pulling together a factor-infused structure for fair balance.[402] While the relevant factors as yet appear to be too mutable to offer great predictive value, the promise of this line of case law is great. Apart from anything else, what it indicates is the same conclusion as that at which tort law balancing hints: the value of the investigation of societal values as guidelines for judicial reasoning through rational, deliberative analysis.

Promisingly, legal theorists are one step ahead in this regard. So, for example, inspired by both Alexy and recent ECtHR case law, Smet has suggested a structured, but factor-based model for balancing. This is intended to apply a principle of balancing for the resolution of conflicts between non-absolute human rights. The criteria it employs are seven: a value criterion, an impact criterion, a core-periphery criterion, an additional rights criterion, a general interest criterion, a purpose criterion and a responsibility criterion.[403] Interestingly, these show considerable overlap with the criteria of the tort-based balancing exercise identified above:[404]

(1) The value criterion is intended to take account of the abstract value of the Convention rights in conflict. Relative rights will generally be considered to be of equal value and therefore worthy of equal respect. They will accordingly cancel each other out, rendering the value criterion irrelevant in most cases of conflict between relative rights. It should be noted that scholars have suggested the

---

401. R Alexy, *A Theory of Constitutional Rights* (Oxford University Press 2002); R Alexy, 'Balancing, Constitutional Review, and Representation' (2005) 3(4) International Journal of Constitutional Law 572; R Alexy, 'On Balancing and Subsumption. A Structural Comparison', (2003) 16(4) Ratio Juris 433; Greer, explaining Alexy: S Greer, '"Balancing" and the European Court of Human Rights: A Contribution to the Habermas-Alexy Debate' (2004) 63(2) The Cambridge Law Journal 412.

402. See s. 2.3.

403. S Smet, *Resolving Conflicts between Human Rights: A Legal Theoretical Analysis in the Context of the ECHR,* (unpublished PhD thesis, Ghent University 2014) 192-193.

404. See s. 4.2.2.

recognition of a hierarchy of Convention rights. Ducoulombier, for example, proposes a ranking that, interestingly for our purposes, would place the freedom of expression of Article 10 in second place among the relative Convention rights, closely followed by privacy in Article 8 and only then the property rights of Protocol 1.[405] However, both the ECtHR and the CJEU have made their position on the equal value of relative rights clear and that is the approach that shall be followed here.

(2) The impact criterion examines two relevant factors: the damage suffered by each of the conflicting Convention rights and the danger that such damage will actually occur. It therefore bears close resemblance to the tort analyses of the risk element in the determination of the standard of care. Under the impact criterion, preference should be given to the right that would suffer the greatest damage if the other were to prevail.

(3) The core-periphery criterion assesses whether damage is done to a central or to a peripheral aspect of the rights in conflict. The core-periphery distinction should be understood as existing on a continuum, in the sense that an interference with a right can hit closer to or further from that right's central or secondary aspects. Smet describes it as a circle with a centre and circumference. In assessing where given aspects of a right place in the circle, the case law of the ECtHR should be used to provide guidance. It should be noted that even the 'core' of a non-absolute right is not inviolable: measures that touch it may nonetheless be justified in appropriate circumstances. If it is difficult or impossible to locate the position of an aspect of a right in the circle or, if it has been located but is equal to the competing aspect of the conflicting right, the core-periphery criterion will be placed out of action.

(4) The additional rights criterion evaluates the potential relevance of other rights, held by one of the parties to the conflict or by third parties. It is thus intended to allow for a more rounded appreciation of the interests at stake. Smet warns that the assessment of the criterion should not be reduced to a game of numbers: more rights should not necessarily outweigh fewer rights. The convergence of numerous rights is relevant, but not conclusive. The additional rights criterion has clear parallels with tort law's consideration of the benefit of the conduct, as well as of the burden of the precautionary measures.

---

405. P Ducoulombier, *Les Conflits de Droits Fondamentaux devant la Cour Européenne des Droits de l'Homme*, (PhD thesis, University of Strasbourg, 2008, published by Bruylant2011) 521-525.

(5) The general interest criterion likewise examines whether either or both of the competing rights affects positively or negatively the general interest. In this way, it assesses what the global social value of avoiding an interference with a person's right is. Like the additional right criterion, the general interest criterion mirrors the notions of the benefit of the conduct and the burden of the precautionary measures in tort.

(6) The purpose criterion is reminiscent of the tort doctrine of the *Schutzzweck der Norm*. It is intended to account for the fact that certain rights support other rights, in the sense that one of the purposes of one set of rights may to ensure adequate protection of a different set. Like the value criterion, the purpose criterion has a rather limited area of applicability, as it is incompatible with the inherent equal value of all relative Convention rights. Smet limits its relevance to exceptional cases, such as those that involve the best interests of a child.

(7) Finally, the responsibility criterion allows for the assessment of the relevance of the flip side of rights: duties. Care is needed here, as under the Convention system obligations cannot be directly imposed on private individuals. It does find relevance however in the area of freedom of expression, which under Article 10 ECHR 'carries with it duties and responsibilities'.[406] As with its sibling-criteria, the responsibility criterion has obvious parallels in tort law and in particular in the notion of duties of care.

As Smet explains, under his 'structured balancing model', the identified factors are intended to be handled, not through the more traditional deductive approach of chained arguments, but as 'nets' that are mutually, rather than sequentially, supportive. Nets of arguments, he suggests, instead of presenting an ultimate argument that is susceptible to subjectivity[407] and 'only as strong as its weakest link',[408] result in a group of coherent reasons that mutually reinforce each other to create a holistic case in favour of a certain outcome. In this way, they allow for the making of a rational comparative judgment on the strength of the case in favour of each of the opposing rights. Smet calls this process 'balancing as reasoning', explaining that, rather than applying a mechanical balancing exercise, it takes a practical approach to judicial deliberation that allows for a clear picture to emerge indicating

406. S Smet, *Resolving Conflicts between Human Rights: A Legal Theoretical Analysis in the Context of the ECHR*, (unpublished PhD thesis, Ghent University 2014) 193-256.
407. S Smet, *Resolving Conflicts between Human Rights: A Legal Theoretical Analysis in the Context of the ECHR*, (unpublished PhD thesis, Ghent University 2014) 174.
408. S Smet, *Resolving Conflicts between Human Rights: A Legal Theoretical Analysis in the Context of the ECHR*, (unpublished PhD thesis, Ghent University 2014) 146.

which right should take priority in a given case.[409] As a result, he suggests, the structured balancing test forces judges into deliberative reasoning, which mitigates the danger of an excessive reliance on intuition, insufficiently coherent judicial reasoning, preferential framing and subjectivity.[410] Ultimately, a framework is set out that is capable of guiding deliberation. From this perspective, balancing, far from irrational as its opponents claim, is revealed an 'indispensable form of rational practical discourse'.[411]

Curiously, on the basis of his structured balancing test, Smet argues that a wide margin of appreciation need not be automatically granted to national authorities in cases of balancing. The default position should instead be one that allows for a 'certain' margin of appreciation to be determined with reference to a number of 'traditional' factors, including the type of aim pursued by the rights-restricting measure, the nature and importance of the Convention rights at stake, the recognition that national authorities are better placed to handle the issue and the absence or presence of a European consensus on the matter.[412] Yet, clearly, absent a broad margin of appreciation, at least in the area of adjudication on cases of interpersonal relationships, the gap between fundamental rights and tort law would narrow: depending on the extent to which the margin of appreciation is limited, the human rights court is no longer telling the State within what margin it must operate to avoid breaching a fundamental right, but what its law must in fact say.

4.6.3 Bridging the Gap to Fundamental Rights

The parallel development of balancing in both the areas of human/fundamental rights and tort law can be attributed to the nature of both sets of rights: as with (most) human rights, tort rights too are non-absolute[413] – even the highest ranking interests[414] may be restricted under the appropriate circumstances. As a result, in both areas, a resolution mechanism for cases of conflicting rights is necessary. In both areas moreover, the mathematical formulation of such a mechanism has been rejected: the algebraic representation of the scales of justice through the Hand formula, just as with Alexy's Laws of Balancing, is accepted by most modern tort scholars as having only symbolic value. The ultimate conclusion, therefore, in both tort law and

409. S Smet, *Resolving Conflicts between Human Rights: A Legal Theoretical Analysis in the Context of the ECHR,* (unpublished PhD thesis, Ghent University 2014) 118.
410. S Smet, *Resolving Conflicts between Human Rights: A Legal Theoretical Analysis in the Context of the ECHR,* (unpublished PhD thesis, Ghent University 2014) 181.
411. R Alexy, 'Constitutional Rights, Balancing and Rationality' (2003) 16(2) Ratio Juris 131.
412. S Smet, *Resolving Conflicts between Human Rights: A Legal Theoretical Analysis in the Context of the ECHR,* (unpublished PhD thesis, Ghent University 2014) 236-256.
413. See Ch. 2, s. 2.3.
414. E.g., Art. 2:102 PETL's rights to life, bodily integrity, human dignity and liberty.

human rights must be one of multi-factorial normative reasoning. And, although in both fields concerns have been expressed as to whether this approach might function only a vehicle for judicial discretion,[415] ultimately, in both, this deontological deliberation emerges as, not only one acceptable, but as the essentially unavoidable mechanism for deciding which restrictions are appropriate for a justice-based social ordering within a democracy.

Against this backdrop, it should come as no surprise that balancing takes a strikingly similar form in both areas of law. Tony Weir explains tort-based legal reasoning as follows:

> In fact a tort claim is really more of a boxing match than a hurdle race; […] success depends on the number of points you make overall. The plaintiff gets extra points if the harm he has suffered is of serious nature – especially personal injury – or if he is particularly deserving or especially reliant on the defendant; so too if the defendant's conduct was very reprehensible, or if the contribution his conduct made to the harm was very obvious and direct, or if he was very close to the plaintiff so that he should have been especially concerned for his well-being and interest.[416]

This approach is strongly reminiscent of the 'nets of arguments' method adopted by Smet to describe structured balancing in the Convention context. Liability in tort law, like interferences with human rights, is not based on a one-sided determination of a violation of the claimant's interests, but on the search for an equilibrium between those interests and any opposing them, so that all relevant interests can be at least 'more or less' protected.[417]

The similarity between tort law balancing and human rights balancing is a reflection of the inevitable interconnectedness and complementarity of the two fields of law. At its most basic, this relationship requires that tort law be interpreted in conformity with the law of human rights. In their formulation of European rules for tort law, both the PETL and the DCFR have emphasised this aspect. So, the EGTL makes clear that the PETL are to be read and interpreted in the spirit of human rights law.[418] In the same spirit, the Study Group on a European Civil Code recognises the protection of human rights as one of the 'overriding principles' of the DCFR.[419] This idea

415. M Moran, 'The Reasonable Person: A Conceptual Biography in Comparative Perspective' (2010) 14(4) Lewis & Clark Law Review 1233.
416. T Weir, *A Casebook on Tort*, (10th ed., Sweet & Maxwell 2004), 5, as quoted in C van Dam, *European Tort Law* (2nd ed., Oxford University Press 2013) 711-2.
417. C van Dam, *European Tort Law* (2nd ed., Oxford University Press 2013) para. 711-2.
418. European Group on Tort Law, *Principles of European Tort Law – Text and Commentary* (Springer 2005) 17.
419. C von Bar et al. (eds), *Principles, Definitions and Model Rules of European Private Law: Draft Common Frame of Reference (DCFR)*, prepared by the Study Group on a European Civil Code and the Research Group on EC private law (Acquis Group), Outline Edition (Sellier 2009) 14.

is furthermore explicitly enshrined in the requirement that its provisions on non-contractual liability be interpreted and applied in a manner compatible with the constitutional law of Article VI.-7:101. More generally, Article I.-1:102(2) reads as follows:

> [These rules] are to be read in the light of any applicable instruments guaranteeing human rights and fundamental freedoms and any applicable constitutional laws.

This requirement derives from the State's duty to respect human rights. And indeed, the construction of tort law constitutes one of the ways with which the State interacts with private individuals. In that interaction, the State has a duty to abide by the demands of the human rights that bind it.[420] Van Dam explains:

> the State must provide effective remedies for the violation of a Convention right, regardless of whether this violation was due to governmental, corporate, or an individual's conduct. Such remedies are often provided by the national tort law system. Hence, by having a proper tort law system in place, a State can discharge its duty to provide for an effective remedy. In this way, the victim of a human rights violation can obtain damages to remedy the harm.[421]

In this regard, it is important to note the distinction between the State's so-called 'negative' and 'positive' obligations: 'negative obligations' are the obligations of the State to abstain from interference with the human rights of private individuals. 'Positive obligations' are the obligations of the State to take active steps to ensure that human rights are effectively secured within their territory.[422] In the formulation of its tort law therefore – including in the execution of the various balancing exercises entailed therein and in particular in the definition of the behaviour of the reasonable person – the State must both make sure that it does not infringe human rights and that (assuming a sufficiently effective alternative does not exist elsewhere) it provides a sufficient level of protection for them.[423] As a result, the State's duty to protect moves beyond a mere obligation to refrain from interfering with human rights and impacts the governance of relationships between private individuals. In this way, it becomes relevant to the regulation of the conduct

---

420. C Von Bar, *The Common European Law of Torts – Vol. II* (Clarendon Press 2000) paras 556-557.
421. C van Dam, *European Tort Law* (2nd ed., Oxford University Press 2013) para. 711-4.
422. D J Harris, M O'Boyle, E P Bates, & C Warbrick, *Harris, O'Boyle & Warbrick – Law of the European Convention on Human Rights* (2nd ed., Oxford University Press 2009) 18.
423. On this see ECHR, *Osman v. The United Kingdom,* application no. 23452/94, 28 October 1998 and *Z v. The United Kingdom,* application no. 29392/95, 10 May 2001. See also M Lunney & K Oliphant, *Tort Law – Text and Materials* (5th ed., Oxford University Press 2013) 151; C McIvor, *Third Party Liability in Tort* (Hart Publishing 2006) 150-155. For a detailed analysis see J Wright, *Tort Law and Human Rights* (Hart Publishing 2001).

of non-State actors as well. As Von Bar explains, '[b]y defining the rules of liability governing the 'horizontal' relationships between individuals, the State also fulfils its 'vertical' protective duty'.[424] Likewise, the Study Group on a European Civil Code declares that:

> The non-contractual liability of the DCFR has the function primarily (albeit not exclusively) of providing 'horizontal' protection of human rights – that is to say, a protection not vis-à-vis the state, but in relation to fellow citizens and others subject to private law.[425]

From this perspective tort law can be said to constitute the horizontal application of human rights law. Again Van Dam's succinct maxim bears repeating: 'tort rights are human rights'.[426]

As a result, private and public law balancing are – at least from the point of view of the law-maker –essentially complementary:[427] to avoid liability a private individual must act as a reasonable person would. How a reasonable person must act is determined by tort law. Tort law is adopted and applied by the State. And the State must abide by the requirements of the law of human rights. Ultimately, the State cannot designate behaviour 'reasonable', therefore, where a fair balance of human rights does not permit it to do so. In formulating the standard of the reasonable person, judges and legislators must fairly balance opposing interests.

Digging deeper into this relationship, Mullender identifies a point of intersection between tort and human rights law in the concern of both with the investigation of generally justifiable norms. On this basis, he notes that the classical human rights notion of a 'fair balance' between the general interests of the community and the protection of the individual's human rights correlates with tort law's cardinal concern with notions of 'fairness', 'reasonableness' and 'the ordinary notions of what is fit and proper': both in human rights law and in tort law we find a commitment to the concepts of general justifiability. From this springboard, he suggests that human rights

424. C Von Bar, *The Common European Law of Torts – Vol. II* (Clarendon Press 2000) paras 556-557. See also C van Dam, *European Tort Law* (2nd ed., Oxford University Press 2013) para. 711-4.

425. C von Bar et al. (eds), *Principles, Definitions and Model Rules of European Private Law: Draft Common Frame of Reference (DCFR)*, prepared by the Study Group on a European Civil Code and the Research Group on EC private law (Acquis Group), Outline Edition (Sellier 2009) 64.

426. C van Dam, *European Tort Law* (2nd ed., Oxford University Press 2013) para. 711-4 and 201 to 202-2. See also, C von Bar, *The Common European Law of Torts – Vol. II* (Clarendon Press 2000) 553-564.

427. D M Beatty, *The Ultimate Rule of Law* (Oxford University Press 2004) 165; D Kennedy, 'A Transnational Geneology of Proportionality in Private Law' in R Brownsword, H-W Micklitz, L Niglia & S Weatherill, *The Foundations of European Private Law* (Hart Publishing 2011) 185.

can provide a metric for the development of tort in a way that honours its traditional reverence for such justifiability, by providing a source of inspiration as regards what is considered be a just society.[428] As a result, human rights law can be used to guide the proper formulation of such open-ended tort concepts as the notion of a duty of care, what that famous 'reasonable person' thinks or when liability for omissions should be imposed. It can also, of course, indicate whether private parties may be placed under an obligation to prevent third parties from causing harm, i.e., when and where accessory liability is appropriate. Thus, given that one of the guiding principles in the ECHR case law is the search for a European standard, the usefulness of human rights traditions for a European tort law is great.

The above being said, it should of course at the same time be emphasised that the kinship between the two bodies of law does not mean that a complete tort law system can be derived from the human rights framework. As noted in Chapter 2, the law of human rights is too abstract for definitive solutions suitable for the finicky area of private interpersonal relationships. By contrast, the law of tort is dedicated to exactly this purpose – indeed, it has had centuries of development behind it shaping it for the optimum regulation of human extra-contractual interactions. The much more developed state of tort law balancing in comparison to the only nascent discussion on the identification of criteria capable of guiding balancing in the area of human rights further demonstrates this reality. If the notion of balancing is going to be used, it cannot simply be mindlessly repeated as a mantra, but must achieve concrete solutions[429] and tort law balancing offers more refined guiding formulae with which to reach this purpose. On this basis, it is clear that it is the rules of traditional tortious deliberation that should primarily be relied upon to guide the complicated questions of extra-contractual liability – instead of attempting to directly apply human rights to the proper field of application of tort law, as the CJEU has been

---

428. R Mullender, 'Tort, Human Rights, and Common Law Culture', (2003) 23(2) Oxford Journal of Legal Studies, 301. See also, for example, *Smith v. Sussex Police* [2008] EWCA Civ 39 (05 February 2008), where Rimer LJ stated that 'where a common law duty covers the same ground as a Convention right, it should, so far as practicable, develop in harmony with it.' See also: W Berka, 'Human Rights and Tort Law' in H Koziol, E Karner, A Fenyves & E Steiner, *Tort Law in the Jurisprudence of the European Court of Human Rights* (De Gruyter, Berlin 2011) 237; M Arden, *Human Rights and European Law: Building New Legal Orders* (Oxford University Press 2015) 223-241; C van Dam, 'Tort Law and Human Rights: Brothers in Arms – On the Role of Tort Law in the Area of Business and Human Rights' (2011) 2 Journal of European Tort Law 221; C van Dam, European Tort Law (2nd ed., Oxford University Press 2013) para. 711-4; J Wright, *Tort Law and Human Rights* (Hart Publishing 2001) 1-15; see N McBride & R Bagshaw, *Tort Law* (4th ed., Pearson 2012) 85.
429. L Bently & R Burrell, 'Copyright and the Information Society in Europe: A Matter of Timing as Well as Content' (1997) 34 Common Law Review 1197.

doing in its intermediary liability case law, what should be attempted is the interpretation of tort law in a manner mindful of fundament rights.[430]

What does this mean for copyright and intermediary liability? Geiger suggests that the CJEU's turn to fundamental rights is an attempt to check the recent tendency to overprotection in this area, in order to provide a more balanced framework for IP law, guarantee a certain flexibility in IP law and thereby recover its legitimacy in the eyes of the public.[431] Derclaye points out that there is only a conflict between human rights and copyright where the legislature has eroded the natural limits of the latter so that its internal resolution mechanisms cannot deliver sufficient safeguards for the former: if legislators did not cross lines in their adopted solutions, judges would not have to resort to human rights legislation to restore the proper balance. This underlines the importance of incorporating a fair balance of interests directly into the statutory provisions.[432] In other words, as tort law has not been administering correct weighing, but is overstepping its bounds to apply solutions out of congruence with the broader framework that it is obliged to respect, fundamental rights have been brought back into play by courts concerned with proportionate outcomes. To remedy this distortion, a direct answer should be introduced directly within copyright framework – but that answer cannot be correct if it does not account for the human rights obligations of the legislator that crafts it.

4.7 CONCLUSION

From the above analysis and under the guidance of the PETL and the DCFR, a formula for a truly European intermediary accessory copyright liability standard can begin to take rough shape. What would such a standard look like? As is now clear, its main constitutive elements must comprise a fault, supplemented by a causal link to the copyright infringement. In addition, liability may be deemed to subside, assuming an adequate defence exists that justifies the intermediary's actions.

430. W Berka, 'Human Rights and Tort Law' in H Koziol, E Karner, A Fenyves & E Steiner, *Tort Law in the Jurisprudence of the European Court of Human Rights* (De Gruyter 2011) 237.

431. C Geiger, '"Constitutionalising" Intellectual Property Law? The Influence of Fundamental Rights on Intellectual Property in the European Union' (2006) International Review of Intellectual Property and Competition Law (IIC) 371; C Geiger, 'Fundamental Rights as Common Principles of European (and International) Intellectual Property Law' in A Ohly, *Common Principles of European Intellectual Property Law* (Mohr Siebeck 2012) 223.

432. E Derclaye, 'Intellectual Property Rights and Human Rights: Coinciding and Cooperating' in P Torremans, *Intellectual Property and Human Rights* (Kluwer Law International 2008) 133.

What does this mean? In all three selected jurisdictions, an intermediary's fault may consist of either intent or negligence. Intent is the easy form of fault. It will be found where the intermediary can be said to have meant to cause copyright infringement or knew that its behaviour could result in such infringement and meant to engage in that behaviour. Where intent exists, the importance of a causative link between the intermediary's behaviour and the damage is lessened.

Negligence is more complicated, depending as it does on the adjustable notion of reasonableness. As already mentioned, reasonableness is found at the intersection between risk and care: where there is a risk of a sufficiently grave and probable harm, the defendant is obliged to take the requisite precautionary measures. The higher the risk, the more likely that a duty of care will burden the tortfeasor. Factors that indicate the existence of risk will include the seriousness of the anticipated harm and the probability of that harm taking place. The height of the necessary care, on the other hand, is measured by the character and benefit of the conduct and the burden of precautionary measures. The knowledge and abilities of the tortfeasor are also at this point relevant: the intermediary will only be unreasonable, and thus eligible for liability, if it knew the risk or ought to have known it and if it could have avoided the risk or ought to have been able to avoid it.

Particular attention is necessary where the prescribed precautionary measures are affirmative. In such cases, in order to avoid the damage, the intermediary will be asked, not to omit its negligent activities, i.e., the provision of its services to primary infringers, but to take positive measures of care obstructing the infringements committed by its users. Liability for the omission of such measures of care is sensitive, as it necessarily entails a graver restriction on the defendant's freedom of action. It is thus generally acknowledged as requiring a stricter standard of reasonableness. As a result, an intermediary will only be held liable for the omission of a measure of care, if it can be found that it was burdened by an affirmative duty obliging it to take it. According to the PETL, this will be the case in four types of situations: the law so provides; the intermediary created or controls the danger; a special relationship exists between the intermediary and the right-holder; or the harm threatened against the right-holder is serious and the ease of its avoidance for the intermediary is great. Depending on the strictness of the adopted standard, the range of intermediary accessory copyright liability can be calibrated up or down: the easier it is to recognise a duty to take affirmative action against third party copyright infringements within a given system, the broader the possibilities for fault to be substantiated. Restricting the availability of duties of care means limiting the possibilities for intermediary accessory copyright liability.

In causation, the baseline is provided by the fundamental rule of *conditio sine qua non*: if the copyright infringement would not have occurred *but for* the intermediary, then the latter is a contender for liability. Further considerations in establishing a causative link between the intermediary's act or omission and the copyright infringement may, depending on the legal system, include the following: the foreseeability of the damage; the nature and the value of the protected interest; the basis of liability; the extent of the ordinary risks of life; and the protective purpose of the rule that has been violated. Again, room exists for calibration: a simple 'but-for' test means a wider-reaching rule on liability, while restrictions through additional law-based factors limit the available options. Interestingly, causation and fault are mutually referential concepts, such that the first can also be established on the back of the second. This will usually be the case where the fault is particularly egregious: thus, intending that another commit an infringement will do away with the need to establish negligence through the refusal to implement measures of care, by signifying the direct involvement of the intermediary in the third party's infringement. Ultimately, as the analysis above revealed, the underlying legal system's choice to focus on either of the interdependent concepts of fault or causation will explain the structure of its intermediary accessory liability system: so, France's negligence-based interpretation of intermediary liability emphasises fault, while England and Germany concentrate on causation. In both cases however, the material question is always the same: that of duty. What ought the defendant to have done? What were the obligations incumbent upon him? The realisation of the cross-border central relevance of these matters opens up the way for an integrated, single European solution.

As a final consideration, a broad disagreement as to the meaning of the element of defences exists between the individual Member States. This centres primarily on whether the term should encompass excuses of faulty conduct or only justifications excluding fault. Any future European rule in the area will probably be best advised to adopt an independent definition of its own making. It was suggested that, at least in narrowly defined areas such as intermediary accessory copyright liability, a better solution to the adoption of defences is their avoidance, to the extent possible, by means of a properly constructed regime on fault.

In any case, in all cases, the interpretation of these concepts should be undertaken with due reverence for the edicts of fundamental rights. This will be especially so with regard to any precautionary affirmative action that the intermediary embarks on in order to deflect liability: in seeking to protect one fundamental right, the State cannot introduce legislation that harms another. Fundamental rights will thus mark the outer limits of liability: intermediaries may not be required to take measures that impinge to a disproportionate degree upon the substance of other fundamental rights competing with copyright. In this way, fundamental rights essentially present the intermediary with the ultimate defence against liability for third party copyright infringement.

Naturally, the above-listed concepts are all exceedingly vague. This is especially true of fault's central requirement of 'reasonableness' and its supportive notional paraphernalia in the form of 'risk', 'care', 'knowledge' and 'skills', but is also noticeable as concerns terms such as 'intent', 'recklessness' or 'causation'. Even the concept of 'defences' requires the pre-designation of exceptions or excuses in broad-brush terms. Tort harmonisation projects have thus come under fire for relying excessively on highly abstract notions, put forth without the additional interpretative underpinnings derived from the supportive context of a surrounding jurisprudence, as is the case in the individual national legal systems. As Hesselink explains however, this is a choice both calculated and justified: what the drafters of the ambitious harmonisation projects aiming at covering all of tort law are constructing is structure. Naturally, fully harmonised rules can only be introduced where a clear, common core can be identified in the tort *acquis* – where no obvious best solution or general consensus is at hand however, more open-ended constructions that provide as much normative guidance as may be gleaned from the national sources are better than ill-conceived stand-ins.[433] Indeed, this is the way of national law as well: the more the case law that exists on a topic, the more legal certainty accumulates – the law is generally built as it's applied, especially in such a situation-specific area as tort law. Does this mean that a European tort law-based approach can offer no better solutions to intermediary accessory copyright liability than the existing regime, criticised in Chapter 2 for its incompleteness and vagueness? Structure is an advantage in itself that should not be underestimated. More importantly, the generality necessary for projects set on the harmonisation of all of European tort law need not carry into more targeted schemes focused on the specific area of European intermediary accessory copyright liability. As Van Dam emphasises, formulae can give legal thinkers the tools with which to tackle legal conundrums in a structured manner – at the same time, they cannot fill in the blanks the structure leaves:[434]

> There is no escape from the truth that, whatever formula be used, the outcome in a grey area has to be determined by judicial judgment. Formulae can help to organise thinking but they cannot provide answers.[435]

Those answers shall be sought in the next chapter.

433. M W Hesselink, 'The Common Frame of Reference as a Source of European Private Law' (2009) 83 Tulane Law Review 919.
434. C van Dam, *European Tort Law* (2nd ed., Oxford University Press 2013) para. 805-2.
435. Cooke P in *South Pacific Manufacturing Co. Ltd v. New Zealand Security Consultants & Investigations Ltd* [1992] 2 NZLR 282, as quoted by C van Dam, *European Tort Law* (2nd ed., Oxford University Press 2013) para. 805-2.

Chapter 5

Shaping European Intermediary Accessory Copyright Liability: What Would a Reasonable Intermediary Do?

Building on the set-up of the preceding chapters, Chapter 5 shall now proceed to formulate a plausible model European regime for substantive intermediary accessory copyright liability. For this purpose, it shall seek to align the diverse national and thematic analyses explored in the previous chapters with a view to identifying common threads that could support a harmonised solution.

Chapter 4 brought to the forefront the two key elements of a hypothetical harmonised European intermediary accessory copyright liability: those of fault and causation. A supplementary element of defences was mostly side-lined. What shall now be attempted will be to interpret these broad notions with a view to understanding what they mean specifically in the area of intermediary liability for copyright infringement. In other words, the sub-species of intermediary accessory copyright liability shall be mapped over the genus of general accessory liability to discover, through a combination of deductive and inductive reasoning, a compelling heuristic legal product. This shall help to organise in a coherent manner the criteria that have been identified by European national courts as relevant to intermediary liability, but which have been applied so far in a haphazard fashion. Through the logical organisation of the resultant interpretations, a proposed framework for a future European intermediary accessory liability in copyright shall be put forth.

In this way, a solution that represents not only a cogent policy response to the questions surrounding intermediary liability, but also a well-grounded harmonised legal construction shall be sought: a European answer to a European question. The objective shall be to craft, by learning from, incorporating and simultaneously improving on the national regimes and existing EU law, a truly sensitive and comprehensive system that allows for fine distinctions and delivers clear definitions.

It should be noted that this regime shall be intended to replace the current piecemeal, dual-level one. Although that provided the first step towards the creation of a European intermediary accessory liability in copyright, it has too many gaps and leaves too many unanswered questions to continue to provide a strong solution in the area.[1] At the same time, current law shall be employed as a valuable source of inspiration and an indication of the European legislator's thinking on the topic: the objective should not be to do away with existing interpretations, but to build a sounder, more complete structure around them that can more successfully support them.

Significantly, the envisioned liability regime shall be broadly gauged. Accordingly, it shall encompass both liability in the strict sense of the word, i.e., for monetary compensation, and liability only for injunctive relief. This choice has been made in view of the complementarity of the two notions as they have been developed to date within the current EU legal framework:[2] in intermediary liability more than most fields of law, it seems that the type of remedy influences the extent of the liability. Limiting the analysis to only one of these areas would therefore exclude instrumental context supplied by the other for the purpose of defining the parameters of the first.

Below, the analysis will begin with a choice of a basic accessory liability scheme in section 5.1. This shall be further elaborated upon by means of individual analyses of its constituent elements in sections 5.2-5.4. The resultant theoretical framework will be applied in section 5.5 in a benchmarking exercise examining a set of selected copyright enforcement measures capable of implementation by internet intermediaries. Section 5.6 shall consider the matter of remedies and section 5.7 that of defences. An overview of the ultimate proposed framework shall undertake in section 5.8.

5.1 THE BASIC FRAMEWORK: THE UNREASONABLE INTERMEDIARY

As established in Chapter 4, fault liability or liability for personal misconduct is the main paradigm of European tort law: the pre-eminent basis of European extra-contractual accountability. It is accordingly around this that the framework proposed here for intermediary accessory copyright liability

1. See Ch. 2, which substantiates this statement.
2. See Ch. 2, s. 2.2.1.

will be constructed. After all, accessory liability is a type of fault liability.[3] It therefore follows that a European accessory liability framework – including a framework for intermediary accessory liability in copyright – should follow the basic structure of European fault liability. Accordingly, the central question intermediary accessory liability for copyright poses is this: when is an intermediary committing a fault with regard to the copyright infringements of third parties? As fault consists of a misconduct, i.e., a deviation from the required standard of conduct, two possible answers present themselves: when it violates a specific standard of conduct, as set up by statute or precedent, or when it violates the general standard of conduct.[4]

Specific standards of conduct are what are established by the various national European copyright statutes that require that people refrain from infringing the exclusive rights of copyright holders. The general standard of conduct is what fills any remaining gaps, by imposing a supplementary general duty of care, covering all unreasonable conduct not foreseen as such by the statutory provisions. Intermediary copyright liability – and accessory liability in general – can, as we saw in Chapter 3,[5] be viewed through either of these two legal lenses: it can be interpreted as an alternative method of infringing the right-holder's exclusive rights or it can be understood as the violation of a different, self-standing obligation to avoid acts of participation in an infringement of those rights by another.

The first model of accessory liability is what in Chapter 3 was named the 'residual liability' or the 'single fault' approach. This is the logic primarily applied in England, where those who have 'authorised' or 'procured' an infringement or who have acted in 'common design' to infringe with the person committing the primary act of infringement are considered to be 'joint tortfeasors' that have 'made the primary infringer's tort their own'. The second system is what in Chapter 3 was labelled the 'concurrent liability' or 'multiple faults' approach. In such cases, the accessory will be seen as having committed, not the same tort as the primary tortfeasor, but a different, although obviously connected, one: the accessory is not a joint tortfeasor, but a several concurrent tortfeasor alongside the primary infringer. The independent standard of conduct she has violated is derived from the general standard of conduct: while only the primary infringer is seen as having violated the specific standard of care set in the copyright law, the intermediary is considered to have breached the basic tort principle of '*neminem laedere*', which requires everybody to refrain from injuring each other. This is currently the system in operation in France. Germany, as it is

3. See above, Ch. 1, s. 1.4.1. See also C McIvor, *Third Party Liability in Tort* (Hart Publishing 2006) 1. See also, D Cooper, *Secondary Liability for Civil Wrongs* (unpublished PhD thesis, University of Cambridge 1995) 3; P S Davies, *Accessory Liability* (Hart Publishing 2015) 58.
4. C von Bar, *The Common European Law of Torts – Vol. II* (Clarendon Press 2000) para. 224.
5. See above, s. 3.4.

wont, adopts a system both in-between and separate: although the provisions of the German BGB on extra-contractual liability equip the German legal system with general tort rules that would allow it both to treat intentional accessories as joint tortfeasors in the English manner (see Article 830 BGB) and to apply a general duty of care in line with the French habit (see Article 823(1) BGB), the German courts have mainly dealt with accessory copyright liability by developing the completely independent scheme of *Störerhaftung*, the so-called interferer liability. This finds its roots in property law and focuses on injunctive relief, rather than the monetary compensation of the plaintiff.[6]

On the basis of the analysis undertaken in Chapter 4 and in line with the objective of constructing a truly European harmonised framework for intermediary accessory copyright liability, the following chapters will outline a proposal for an interfused regime that borrows equally from all three of these national prototypes. The starting point shall be found in the second of the two basic systems of accessory liability: the 'concurrent multiple faults' approach that imposes a self-standing standard of care founded on the general duty of care. The choice is an obvious one made in the interests of expediency: while France, which does not employ a notion of 'accessory liability' as such, is lacking the legal theoretical equipment that would enable the application of the 'single fault' approach, all three of the selected European legal systems recognise a general standard of care of some kind. This approach therefore represents the lowest common denominator between diverse national systems. It is indicative that the PETL and the DCFR adopt this solution as their central premise, both beginning with the proposition of a 'Basic Norm' or 'Basic Rule',[7] which they subsequently infuse with elements from across the board of tort systems. In any case, given the confusion that the 'single fault' approach has generated even in the English system where it is most ardently espoused, a return to the very fundaments of general extra-contractual liability in order to investigate accessory liability does not seem ill-advised.[8] Accordingly, the reference point for this chapter's proposed European model regime for intermediary accessory copyright liability will be the concept of a general standard of care requiring all members of a community to refrain from injuring others: the 'autonomous *Normgenerator*', familiar from so many continental civil codes, as well as the common law's 'tort of negligence'.[9]

As a result of this approach, intermediary liability will be understood in the following, not as a participation in the infringement of another, but as the

6. On all of this see above, s. 3.4.
7. See PETL, Art. 1:101 and DCFR, Art. 1:101.
8. On this s especially, s. 3.1.3.3.
9. While nominally the tort of negligence should be understood as only one among a plurality of individual torts, over the past century it has developed into the preeminent English tort, expanding almost – although not entirely – to civil law breadth. See above s. 4.1.

violation of a prohibition against accessorial behaviour with regard to infringements committed by others. At the same time, it is important to emphasise that whether the resultant European model rule is ultimately incorporated into the individual national systems as a specific application of a general standard of care or as an independent *sui generis* rule embedded in statutory provisions will be immaterial to the substance of the standard. This book does not seek to harmonise all of tort law or even all of accessory liability, but only intermediary accessory copyright liability. Accordingly, as with all instances of harmonisation, how the harmonised rule is incorporated into national law should be a matter for the national legislator and may thus vary considerably from EU Member State to EU Member State.[10] The essential part is that intermediaries should be understood as operating under a legal limit to the behaviours in which they may engage with regard to the copyright infringements of others that is consistent across the board of EU Member States.

The suggested solution obviously fits in comfortably with both French and German law: the former already applies its basic provisions of Articles 1382 and 1383 *C.civ.* to deal with intermediary liability; the latter, although it has so far for the most part refrained from using it in intermediary accessory copyright liability, is, in its Article 823(1) BGB, in possession of a similar structure capable of serving the same purpose. English lawyers are perhaps the least likely to react enthusiastically to the suggestion of such a negligence-inspired approach. The use of negligence as an alternative to joint tortfeasance was scoffed at long ago by Lord Templeman in *Amstrad*[11] and English tort lawyers remain dubious ever since. Even Davies, although otherwise enthusiastic about the restatement of English accessory liability, rejects the idea:

> Imposing duties of care more readily may place an 'impossible burden' upon defendants. Accessory liability and negligence are conceptually distinct, and it is important that the elements of one do not twist the requirements of the other. Although negligence has already expanded such that it encompasses a huge area of tort law, it should not cover accessory liability.[12]

This position should be re-considered. While the warnings against the overexpansion of accessory liability are well-advised and should be heeded, there is no reason why an 'impossible burden' should result more readily

10. This was already made clear in the Introduction, see s. 1.4. Even if total unification is to be pursued, that unification need not involve all of tort law. Each Member State would therefore still be free to decide the position of the unified rule within its own legal system.
11. *CBS Songs v. Amstrad* [1988] UKHL 15 (12 May 1988).
12. P S Davies, Accessory Liability (Hart Publishing 2015) 7.

under a negligence-based system than under the current English model:[13] given that that is not what has in fact resulted in France, there is no reason why it should be feared in England.[14] Moreover, not only will such an approach free English law of the confines it has constructed around itself through the exclusion of mere facilitation as a participation link in joint tortfeasance (against which modern jurisprudence, in copyright particularly, is already chafing), but, more importantly, it will move the focus of accessory liability from the area of causation, where joint tortfeasance currently situates it, to that of duty, where it more naturally belongs.[15] What is after all the prohibition against the three recognised English participation links if not a duty to abstain from engaging in a given set of behaviours? From this angle, a breach of duty approach is by no means incompatible with English law.

Any residual discomfort the common law lawyer might feel with this set-up should be mitigated by the further elaboration of the proposed standard: if the fear is that a fundamental prohibition of accessory activity is too vague for the common law, it will be subsequently sharpened with more precise specifications. Accordingly, a detailed framework will be built around the basic rule, clarifying precisely what constitutes a prohibited accessory activity for internet intermediaries in the field of copyright law. This will be infused with devices borrowed by all three informing systems, the most pertinent solutions being picked from each. After all, while a broadly conceived notion of fault allows more room for the identification of common ground, it must always somehow be subsequently contained. The more explicit English and German approach to this containment – especially in the area of omissions – offers greater promise of legal certainty. It is moreover especially appropriate to a narrowly defined area, where it runs fewer risks of closing off potentially useful avenues that have not yet been identified or put to use by lawyers. Ultimately, the end result will, in this way, end up as reminiscent of English and German law, as it is of French.

5.1.1 The Building Blocks of Accessory Liability

As established in Chapter 4, the existence of a fault, i.e., a deviation from a standard of conduct, is determined by means of a comparison to the faulty tortfeasor's hypothetical opposite: the legal construct of the 'reasonable person of ordinary prudence' in her various guises (the *bonus pater*, the *personne normalement soigneuse et prudent*, *sorgfältiger Mensch,* etc.). By

13. Indeed, the carefully-set confines of authorisation and joint tortfeasance seem to have done little to hold English courts intent to extracting liability from internet intermediaries back, see above Ch. 3, ss 3.1.2 and 3.1.3.
14. See Viney, expressing the same sentiment in G Viney, 'France: Le "Wrongfulness" en Droit Français' in H Koziol (ed.) *Unification of Tort Law: Wrongfulness* (Kluwer Law International 1998) 57.
15. C McIvor, *Third Party Liability in Tort* (Hart Publishing 2006) 18-20 and 61.

this standard, fault can be redefined as a failure to behave as the reasonable person would: if you are not reasonable, then your conduct constitutes a misconduct,[16] you are at fault and you will be held liable for any resultant damage.

As should be clear, when the law refers to the 'reasonable person', it is obviously not suggesting that statistics be compiled to determine how prudent people behave in each and every circumstance.[17] References to the opinion of 'travellers on the London Underground' are not meant to imply that metro users are more circumspect than the rest of society or that the views of cyclists, motorists or equestrians are not valued.[18] One does not become more diligent simply by riding the Clapham omnibus, let alone by 'taking the magazines at home, and in the evening pushing the lawn mower in […] shirt sleeves'.[19] The various incarnations of the reasonable person are instead simply personifications of the duties of care by which a diligent member of the group to which the defendant belongs would abide.[20] The 'reasonable person' test is intended to be an adjustable one that can be adapted – not, as a general rule, to the person of the tortfeasor, but to the category which she represents. Thus, a doctor will be measured against the standard of diligent doctors and an architect in accordance with what can be expected of architects.[21] The test can be made stricter when dealing with an expert than with a layperson and vice versa. In the area of intermediary accessory liability for online copyright infringement, the point of reference will obviously become that of the reasonable intermediary: the '*bonus medius interretialis*'. In the words of the CJEU, 'the diligent economic operator'. The relevant question for a finding of liability under this approach will therefore be the following: 'what would a reasonable intermediary do?'

---

16. C von Bar, *The Common European Law of Torts – Vol. II* (Clarendon Press 2000) para. 179.
17. See the analysis of the UK Supreme Court in *Healthcare at Home Limited v. The Common Services Agency* [2014] UKSC 49, which explains: 'It follows from the nature of the reasonable man, as a means of describing a standard applied by the court, that it would be misconceived for a party to seek to lead evidence from actual passengers on the Clapham omnibus as to how they would have acted in a given situation or what they would have foreseen, in order to establish how the reasonable man would have acted or what he would have foreseen. Even if the party offered to prove that his witnesses were reasonable men, the evidence would be beside the point. The behaviour of the reasonable man is not established by the evidence of witnesses, but by the application of a legal standard by the court.'
18. For that matter, although the traditional test refers to the 'reasonable man', women aren't excluded either, as is brought home by the tongue-in-cheek exposition by Sir Alan Herbert, in A P Herbert, *Uncommon Law: Being 66 Misleading Cases Revised and Collected in One Volume* (Methuen 1969) 5.
19. *Hall v. Brooklands Auto Racing Club*, [1933] 1 K.B. 205, [1930. H. 3471.].
20. C von Bar, *The Common European Law of Torts – Vol. II* (Clarendon Press 2000) para. 224.
21. C van Dam, *European Tort Law* (2nd ed., Oxford University Press 2013) paras 804-2 and 812-1.

This chapter shall examine precisely this question: what *would* a reasonable intermediary do in the face of user copyright infringement – and therefore what is the normative 'should' standard by which an intermediary that wishes to dutifully follow in the law-abiding footsteps of this hypothetical paragon must abide?[22] In other words, what is the required standard of conduct, incumbent on intermediaries with regard to the copyright infringements of others conducted using their services?

To answer that question, the basic building blocks of intermediary liability must first be identified. As has already been established, fault liability will require a finding of a fault and a finding of causation. In keeping with the terminology usually employed in accessory liability to refer to each of them,[23] these conditions can be renamed. Intermediary accessory copyright liability can therefore be said to consist of two fundamental elements:

(a) an outer, visible *conduct element*, that examines whether the defendant behaved as a reasonable intermediary would have done in the same circumstances; and
(b) an inner, invisible *mental element*, that examines whether the defendant demonstrated the mindset required of a reasonable intermediary in the same circumstances.

The conduct element constitutes the first requirement of intermediary liability. It serves the purpose of separating the chaff of random bystanders from the grain of the involved intermediaries, i.e., the intermediaries whose liability seems at first blush plausible. As a result, this initial element will be established without reference to the intermediary's state of mind. Once however the conduct element has been substantiated, the liability standard will bifurcate along the lines of the intermediary's mental participation. As established in Chapter 4, a fault may consist of either intent or negligence.[24] In the accessory liability paradigm as well, the first branch of the mental

22. European Group on Tort Law, *Principles of European Tort Law – Text and Commentary* (Springer 2005) 76.
23. See *Sea Shepherd UK v. Fish & Fish Ltd* [2015] UKSC 10 (4 March 2015), which also makes this distinction, specifically in the field of accessory liability, as well as P S Davies, *Accessory Liability* (Hart Publishing 2015) 21-54 and 188-209; P S Davies, 'Accessory Liability for Assisting Torts' (2011) 70(2) Cambridge Law Journal 353; P S Davies, 'Aid, Abet, Counsel or Procure?' in S Pitel, J Neyers, E Chamberlain (eds), *Tort Law: Challenging Orthodoxy* (Hart Publishing 2013) 413.
24. See Ch. 4, s. 4.2. See also, Art. 4:101 of the PETL, Arts VI.-3:101 and VI.-3102 of the DCFR, as well as Art. 828 para. 1 German BGB and Arts 1382 and 1383 French C.civ. See also C van Dam, *European Tort Law* (2nd ed., Oxford University Press 2013) para. 801; C von Bar, *The Common European Law of Torts – Vol. I* (Clarendon Press 2000) para. 11; C von Bar, *The Common European Law of Torts – Vol. II* (Clarendon Press 2000) para. 229; H Koziol, 'Comparative Conclusions' in H Koziol, *Basic Questions of Tort Law from a Comparative Perspective* (Jan Sramek Verlag 2015) 704; J Lahe, 'The Importance of Distinguishing between Forms of Fault in the Law of Delict' (2009) XVI Juridica International 94.

element will govern intermediaries acting with intent and the second intermediaries acting with knowledge. An intermediary will therefore be considered to display a relevant mental element with regard to the copyright infringement of a third party if it either *intended* that the third party commit the infringement in question or if its participation in the third party's copyright infringement was *negligent*. On this basis, two kinds of unreasonable intermediaries – that is to say two kinds of intermediaries at fault with regard to a third party copyright infringement – can be distinguished: the intentional intermediary and the negligent intermediary.

This distinction will be important, as, while a combination of unreasonable conduct and intent can automatically lead to liability as an intentional intermediary, a mental element of knowledge will be insufficient to label an intermediary immediately negligent. For that, an additional third ingredient of liability will be necessary:

(c) the violation of a duty of care. Why should this element be required? The reason is simple: in fault, before liability can materialise, there needs to be a sense that the individual intermediary personally *deserves* liability. Where this cannot be supplied by the intermediary's mental element, as is the case where there is intention to cause infringement, it must be demonstrated through the violation of a reasonable obligation incumbent upon the intermediary: a duty of care.

With this structure in place, the influences of the individual national regimes on the final harmonised European product become a bit easier to trace. The first liability branch of intent takes clear inspiration from the English and German 'joint tortfeasance' approach. Accordingly, where the requisite conduct element is displayed, if the intermediary can also be found to have been acting with intent, liability should automatically follow: no further link connecting the intermediary to the infringement should be necessary beyond its 'psychological causation'. The second, more lenient branch is negligence-inspired: if the conduct element is established, but no intent may be found, as long as the intermediary was nonetheless acting with knowledge of the third party infringement, it will be held liable only if it has been found to also have violated a duty of care, just as is currently the case in France. In this way, although in both cases a 'multiple faults' approach may be said to have been taken to the extent that the accessory intermediary will be understood as having committed a tort different to that of the direct infringer emanating from tort law's 'Basic Norm', as concerns the basic conditions of liability, as well as its inspiration and rationale, the system proposed shall shift between the paradigms of residual and concurrent liability, depending on the gravity of the mental element. In addition of course, in their individual interpretation, the conduct element, mental element and the recognised duties of care will further be infused with analysis inspired from all three national approaches.

5.1.2 Fault Liability and Legal Persons

Before we proceed, it should be noted that, significantly for the purposes of intermediary liability, the concepts of both intent and negligence apply equally to legal as to natural persons. Legal persons should therefore be understood as being capable of behaving both with intent and with negligence. This is perhaps counter-intuitive: a legal person is a legal fiction and therefore cannot physically do wrong, let along exhibit a 'guilty mind' with regard to that wrong.[25] Nevertheless, all European national legal systems seem to be in agreement that a legal person can be held liable, whether that liability is understood to be for its own wrongdoing or for the wrongdoing of natural persons acting on its behalf.[26] The PETL are silent on the matter, but Article VI.-1:103 DCFR, is quite clear: the rules of fault liability 'apply to both legal and natural persons, unless stated otherwise'. According to its drafters, the 'intention of the legal person is found by establishing the state of mind of the natural persons acting as its governing organ'.[27]

What does this mean for intermediary liability? If the intermediary does not have legal personhood, it should be taken to coincide with the natural person(s) who run(s) it and it is to their personal liability that the term 'intermediary liability' should then be understood to refer. If the intermediary is a legal person, not much will in practice be different: the legal person's fault shall be established by reference to the conduct and state of mind of the private individuals in charge. It should be noted that in such cases the intermediary's representatives may additionally be liable in parallel for having violated their own duties.[28] In such cases, logically, the regular rules on solidary (i.e., 'joint and several') liability as between several concurrent tortfeasors apply.

---

25. C von Bar, *The Common European Law of Torts – Vol. II* (Clarendon Press 2000) paras 188-193.
26. C von Bar, *The Common European Law of Torts – Vol. II* (Clarendon Press 2000) para. 188.
27. C von Bar et al. (eds), *Principles, Definitions and Model Rules of European Private Law: Draft Common Frame of Reference (DCFR)*, prepared by the Study Group on a European Civil Code and the Research Group on EC private law (Acquis Group), Outline Edition (Sellier 2009) 3263.
28. E.g., the representative was given false information by his staff preventing him from having the knowledge necessary to make him negligent, see C von Bar, *The Common European Law of Torts – Vol. II* (Clarendon Press 2000) para. 193.

5.2 THE CONDUCT ELEMENT

The first thing that must be established before an intermediary may be found liable as an accessory in the copyright infringement of another is the conduct element: what must an intermediary do before the question of its accessory copyright liability may be raised at all? This question shall be examined below.

Before beginning with that analysis, it is important to first note that, as the comparative examination of the three selected jurisdictions undertaken in Chapters 3 and 4 reveals, regardless of the system followed, accessory liability must, in all cases, be grounded in an actual harm suffered. If a primary infringement has not been committed, then a third party may not be held liable for having participated in that wrongdoing. While, as shall be seen below, some discussion surrounds the question of whether or not the intermediary's behaviour must be associated with a specific infringement or whether the existence of widespread infringement can suffice,[29] what is clear is that there may be no liability in tort for *attempting* to collaborate with another to tortious ends, as long as those ends do not actually materialise.[30] This conclusion should hold strong with regard to intermediary liability for copyright infringement as well: merely offering somebody the means through which they could, but in the event choose not to, commit copyright infringement or disseminating an instigating message encouraging members of the public to infringe copyright, which however nobody in fact takes up, should not result in liability. Intermediary liability for third party copyright infringement may not be inchoate.[31] Any conduct the intermediary exhibits must be linked to a definite injurious result.

5.2.1 'A Psychological Causation'

Can any act on the part of the intermediary connecting it to the final infringement suffice to establish a conduct element for accessory liability? The common law's attempt to break down joint tortfeasance into distinct 'participation links' offers a useful starting point for this discussion.

As detailed in Chapter 3, 'authorising', 'procuring' and agreeing on a 'common design' to infringe copyright will all constitute recognised participation links in English tort law. However, as was already argued above,[32] the problem here is that it is not the intermediary's conduct per se that justifies liability for these actions, but the implied accompanying culpable mindset of the defendant: the three recognised English participation links hinge not so much on the description of the behaviour of the collaborator, but on the

29. See ss 5.3.1.3 and 5.3.2.2.
30. P S Davies, *Accessory Liability* (Hart Publishing 2015) 9.
31. See Ch. 1, s. 1.4.1.
32. See Ch. 3, s. 3.1.3.

mental identification of the collaborator with the primary tortfeasor. And indeed, arguably, an 'authorisation', 'procurement' or 'common design' cannot exist unless the intermediary intended the infringement, while attempting to apply them otherwise distorts the terms' natural meaning. German law moves along similar lines: under the rule of Article 830 of the BGB, those who knowingly and intentionally combine to bring about a copyright infringement,[33] as well as the instigators of such infringement should be treated as *Mittäter,* i.e., joint tortfeasors. German law bases the liability of such *Mittäter* precisely on the existence of a '*psychisch vermittelte Kausalität*',[34] a psychological causation that connects the accessory to the act of the primary infringer. Accordingly, like English joint tortfeasance, to make up for the attenuated causality, German *Mittäterschaft* also requires a finding of an intention to bring about an infringement before *Mittäterschaft* can result.[35] French law, in keeping with its construction around a general duty of care which allows for a very broad conception of fault, does not contain a specific rule on accessory liability.[36] It likewise scarcely acknowledges the relevance of the degree of blameworthiness exhibited by the defendant.[37] However, it does reveal a matching tendency in practice to condemn with greater ease – albeit through the vehicle of negligence liability – those whose actions display a similarly culpable mindset.[38]

All three systems can thus be said to be in agreement as to the liability of defendants whose behaviour indicates some element of intentional involvement in the infringement, if not on the tools to be used to construct their liability. The DCFR and the PETL follow suit: Article VI.-4:102 of the DCFR agrees that a person who 'participates with [or] instigates […] another in causing legally relevant damage' should be understood to have caused that damage, while Article 9:101 of the PETL establishes a rule of solidary liability for persons who 'knowingly participate in or instigate or

33. According to Van Gerven, 'bewußt*es und gewolltes Zusammenwirken zur Herbeiführung des Verletzungserfolges*', see W van Gerven, J Lever & P Larouche, *Tort Law* (Hart Publishing 2000) 430-432.
34. H Koziol, *Basic Questions of Tort Law from a Germanic Perspective* (Jan Sramek Verlag 2012) 139-140; F Bydlinski, 'Haftung bei alternativer Kausalität' (1959) Juristische Blätter 9; F Bydlinski, *Mittäterschaft im Schadensrecht*, [1959-1960] 158 Archiv für die civilistische Praxis (AcP) 410. See also: L Haertlein, *Executionsintervention und Haftung* (Mohr Siebeck 2008) 443. Cf. M Goldmann in H Harte-Bavendamm & F Henning-Bodewig, *Gesetz gegen den Unlauteren Wettbewerb (UWG)* (3rd ed., C. H. Beck 2013) Rn 93-96; I Puppe in U Kindhäuser, U Neumann & H-U Paeffgen, Strafgesetzbuch (4th ed., Nomos 2013) Rn 125-126; H-J Musielak, 'Kausalität und Schadenszurechnung im Zivilrecht' (2013) Juristische Arbeitsblätter 241.
35. W van Gerven et al., *Tort Law* (Hart Publishing 2000) 430-432; H Koziol, *Basic Questions of Tort Law from a Germanic Perspective* (Jan Sramek Verlag 2012) 140.
36. W van Gerven et al., *Tort Law* (Hart Publishing 2000) 432.
37. C van Dam, *European Tort Law* (2nd ed., Oxford University Press 2013) para. 802-1.
38. See Ch. 3, ss 3.2.3 and 3.2.4.

encourage wrongdoing by others'. As with the English and German definitions of joint tortfeasance, here too a concept of intent seems to be inherent to the definition of the conduct identified as wrongful: instigating or encouraging cannot occur without intent. 'Participating' sounds potentially more benign, yet the definition given by the DCFR makes clear that intent is by no means incompatible with the notion: '"[p]articipants" in the sense of the Article are those persons who either play a role in carrying out an overall plan […] or persons who indeed do not participate in the actual act of wrongdoing themselves, and yet stay 'in the background' maintaining command or co-command over the course of events'.[39]

It is the argument of this book that intention should be examined as such, not subsumed in the analysis of the conduct element: it is illogical to depend the definition of the conduct element of intermediary liability on the mindset of the intermediary. Instead, in this proposal, the question of intent will be examined separately, as part of the analysis of the mental element undertaken below.[40]

5.2.2 'Mere' Facilitation

In any case, a much more divisive area of intermediary conduct is that of facilitation or assistance.[41] But here too the confusion is slowly clearing up. According to well-established English precedent, the 'mere' facilitation of a tort is not itself tortious. As was noted in Chapter 3 (section 3.1.3.3) however, 'mere facilitation' should be understood as facilitation that is not accompanied by intention.[42] So, according to the UK's Supreme Court in *Sea Shepherd*:

> [T]here is no tortious liability for aiding and abetting or facilitating the commission of a tort, even knowingly. There may, however, be such a liability if that is done pursuant to a common design.[43]

Accordingly, facilitation should be accepted as fully capable of substantiating accessory liability under English law, as long as it is accompanied

39. C von Bar et al. (eds), *Principles, Definitions and Model Rules of European Private Law: Draft Common Frame of Reference (DCFR)*, prepared by the Study Group on a European Civil Code and the Research Group on EC private law (Acquis Group), Outline Edition (Sellier 2009) 3446.
40. See s. 5.3.
41. Facilitation and assistance should be understood to be synonymous for the purposes of this book, see also P S Davies, *Accessory Liability* (Hart Publishing 2015) 23-24.
42. See also, R Bagshaw, 'Downloading Torts: And English Introduction to On-Line Torts' in H Snijders & S Weatherill, *E-Commerce Law: National and Transnational Topics and Perspectives* (Kluwer Law International 2003) 59.
43. *Sea Shepherd UK v. Fish & Fish Ltd* [2015] UKSC 10 (4 March 2015) at 12 endorsing Hamblen J's summary of the situation in *Fish & Fish Ltd v. Sea Shepherd UK & Anor* [2012] EWHC 1717 (Admlty) (25 June 2012).

by the requisite mental element. As the analysis in this section is focused only on the conduct element, 'mere facilitation', i.e., facilitation unaccompanied by intent, is all that interests it. 'Mere facilitation' must therefore be concluded to be a permitted conduct element under English law.

In Germany, the situation is more nuanced. Article 830(2) of the BGB extends joint tortfeasance to '*Gehilfen*' or 'accessories'.[44] '*Gehilfen*' are therefore considered '*Mittäter'*, joint tortfeasors. However, as analysed above (section 3.3.2.2), this is generally only understood to encompass those accomplices who acted intentionally. Moreover, the provision is not usually applied to internet intermediaries: '*neutrale Beihilfe'*, i.e., neutral acts of assistance that occur in the form of normal commercial activities, will qualify only exceptionally, usually if the accessory was under a duty, particularly as a result of its professional position, to defend the rights of the plaintiff. Opinions differ as to when such exceptions might arise: one position holds that an agreement to commit a wrong must have been reached between the accessory and primary tortfeasor. Another requires that the facilitation must have at least increased the risk of infringement, thus forming a self-standing source of unlawfulness. Finally, a third view sees accessories as liable only as a result of a cocktail comprised of a risk of damage, occupation-specific duties and the foreseeability of the wrongdoing.[45] In any case, as we already know, facilitators are by no means let entirely off the hook even where *Mittäterschaft* cannot be established: the doctrine of *Störerhaftung* covers the gap, enabling courts to issue injunctions against intermediaries that adequately contribute to the causation of an infringement, as long as they can be said to have violated a reasonable duty of review. Accordingly, as in English law, in German law too, 'mere facilitation' should be understood as an accepted conduct element, with regard at least to some kind of liability, if only for injunctive relief.

Finally, as should be expected, the French approach of 'negligence liability for the acts of others' achieves the same result, albeit much more smoothly: although French courts may in practice be more enthusiastic about imposing liability on intentional accessories, French intermediary liability law makes no formal distinction in theory between facilitation and actions that reveal a blameworthy mental attitude. This is an obvious logical consequence of the 'concurrent faults' set-up espoused by France,[46] as well as its main advantage: instead of relying on 'participation links' that bind the accessory to the primary tortfeasor, French law casually subjects the intermediary's behaviour to the same expansive notion of *faute* that it would apply to wrongdoing in any other area. It therefore does not preclude

44. According to the English translation of the Bundesministerium der Justiz, see: http://www.gesetze-im-internet.de/teilliste_translations.html.
45. J Säcker & R Rixecker, *Münchener Kommentar Zum Bürgerlichen Gesetzbuch* (6th Ed., Verlag C. H. Beck 2013) § 830 at 17-26.
46. See above, Ch. 3, s. 3.4.

accessory liability for any kind of participation: all that is necessary is that the intermediary violate the required standard of care vis-à-vis the right-holder's copyright.

In conclusion, all three Member States seem amenable to the idea that facilitation should be included as a possible conduct element of accessory liability. The differences between the three are firmly lodged in the realm of theory and legal *mentalité* rather than outcome: while France gives facilitation the green light with casual nonchalance, England and Germany are far more circumspect, carefully emphasising its coupling with the mental element.

On the European level, the PETL do not mention facilitation as such, but do, as noted above, extend liability across the far-reaching concept of 'participation', a notion that would presumably incorporate the provision of any kind of help or support to the commission of the tort.[47] The DCFR goes one step further, making explicit mention of those who 'materially assist another in causing legally relevant damage' among its potential 'collaborators'. Such 'accessories or aiders' are defined by the drafters of the DCFR as those who 'know of the general outline of the primary act', 'wish to assist' and 'support the person acting directly in carrying out the act, but have no influence over whether it actually comes about or not'.[48] Both models therefore seem to encourage a roomy conduct element that comfortably accommodates assistance within its reach.

5.2.3 Causal Participation

In view of the above, this book will remain neutral regarding the shape of the conduct element in accessory tort liability in general, whether on the individual national level or the European one. With regard to the conduct element specifically in European intermediary accessory copyright liability however, in order to limit the impact of a subjective assessment that relies on the characterisation of the conduct, it is suggested that a broad concept be favoured. Thus, it is suggested that the conduct element should encompass any involvement in the creation of a risk of copyright infringement by another. Davies puts forth the term 'causal participation' to convey this notion.[49] This he defines as incorporating all possible 'modes of participation which have a substantial causal impact upon the primary wrong and the infringement of the victim's rights'. In this way, the element of causation – an awkward and controversial part of accessory liability – can be neatly

47. See PETL, Art. 9:101(1)(a).
48. C von Bar et al. (eds), *Principles, Definitions and Model Rules of European Private Law: Draft Common Frame of Reference (DCFR)*, prepared by the Study Group on a European Civil Code and the Research Group on EC private law (Acquis Group), Outline Edition (Sellier 2009) 3447.
49. P S Davies, *Accessory Liability* (Hart Publishing 2015) 39.

folded into the conduct element.[50] This suggestion shall also be the one adopted here. It should be noted that the appropriate test for causation, in this regard, shall be a very simple 'but-for' one.[51] As a result, the conduct element of 'causal participation' can be understood as extending from an active collaboration with the primary infringer to the inducement of the infringement all the way to the simple offer of material support. The baseline is set at – and includes – facilitation.

If the conduct element must be limited in some way, Davies suggests that that should not be by reference to, not the form of the participation, but to its impact. 'Causal participation' as a conduct element of accessory liability should therefore extend only to cases where the participation contributes in more than a minimal way to the primary wrong. Otherwise, accessory liability should be excluded.[52] This seems sensible: as the general maxim would have it, '*de minimis non curat lex*'. In any case, a contribution that is 'minimal' is unlikely to be truly 'causal'.

There is some precedent for this idea: in the area of criminal law, Williams moves along similar lines when he suggests that as 'matter of common sense a person who gives a very minor assistance ought not to be held liable as an accessory'.[53] Cooper pushes the concept into private law, noting that, '[a]lthough there need not be (and cannot be) a true causal relationship between an inducement and a primary wrong, there is nonetheless a limited requirement of minimal effect, which might in a broader sense be described as a causal connection'.[54] The notion has now received high-level endorsement in the UK by *Sea Shepherd,* where Lord Sumption explained that 'assistance which is said to further [a] common design must be material, but that means no more than that it must be more than *de minimis*'.[55] Finally, from a more European point of view, the DCFR also supports the *de minimis* rule: according to Article VI. – 6:102, 'trivial damage is to be disregarded'. As its drafters observe, the 'idea is that trivial damage must be accepted in highly civilised society as a socially acceptable interference not warranting reparation; and actions for damages should be prevented if they do not primarily involve making good a loss, but rather involve harming the other party through the burden of having to bear the

50. P S Davies, *Accessory Liability* (Hart Publishing 2015) 31-40.
51. See above, Ch. 4, s. 4.4.1.
52. P S Davies, *Accessory Liability* (Hart Publishing 2015) 37 and 40.
53. G Williams, *Criminal Law: The General Part* (Stevens & Sons 1953) 294.
54. D Cooper, *Secondary Liability for Civil Wrongs* (unpublished PhD thesis, University of Cambridge 1995) 9. See also, P Sales, 'The Tort of Conspiracy and Civil Secondary Liability' (1990) 49(3) Cambridge Law Journal 491 at note 62. For case law consider: *Baden v. Societe Générale pour Favoriser le Developpement du Commerce et de l'Industrie en France SA*, [1993] 1 W.L.R. 509; *Fish & Fish Ltd v. Sea Shepherd UK & Ors* [2013] EWCA Civ 544.
55. *Sea Shepherd UK v. Fish & Fish Ltd* [2015] UKSC 10 (4 March 2015) at 49 and 85.

costs of legal proceedings'.[56] Although the wording here is focused on damage rather than participation, this can be explained by the fact that the provision does not focus on accessory liability. The same idea can, nevertheless, be applied to identical effect in that area, if the concept of damage is understood as 'damage attributable to the defendant'.

The conduct element of a European intermediary accessory copyright liability should therefore be accepted as embracing any material causal participation in the infringement. This should include the material causal facilitation of the infringement. For intermediary accessory copyright liability this conclusion is significant: as mentioned in Chapter 1 (see section 1.4.2), internet intermediaries are defined as legal or natural persons who 'bring together or facilitate transactions between third parties on the Internet'.[57] Clearly therefore, where an intermediary's networks or websites are used to conduct a copyright infringement, at a minimum facilitation will always be substantiated: that is simply what intermediaries do. Doing less would simply mean doing nothing – remaining entirely uninvolved. Moreover, it is unlikely that the relevant facilitation will be *de minimis:* as Lord Kerr observes, the *de minimis* rule is concerned with extremes.[58] Providing the means by which a copyright infringement occurred may therefore not easily be allowed to qualify as sufficiently inconsequential. As a result, if material causal facilitation is recognised as the base level conduct element, the conduct element of accessory copyright liability will always be satisfied by internet intermediaries whose services are used by others to infringe. On the basis of this reasoning, in the following, we will be operating on the assumption that the mere offer of online intermediary services will by definition always satisfy the conduct element of intermediary accessory liability, as soon as an infringement is made by another using the intermediary's services.

Obviously, this approach does not offer great scope for meaningful distinctions between different kinds of intermediary conduct. This, it is suggested, is how it should be: a more discriminating conduct standard runs the risk of becoming entirely inscrutable, as it attempts to draw lines where no obvious divisions can be found, as well as quickly outdated, as technology outpaces the adaptability of law, leading to linguistic quagmires precisely

56. C von Bar et al. (eds), *Principles, Definitions and Model Rules of European Private Law: Draft Common Frame of Reference (DCFR)*, prepared by the Study Group on a European Civil Code and the Research Group on EC private law (Acquis Group), Outline Edition (Sellier 2009) 3575.
57. K Perset, 'The Economic and Social Role of Internet Intermediaries', OECD Study, STI/ICCP(2009)9/FINAL, March 2010, 9; R MacKinnon, E Hickok, A Bar & H Lim, 'Fostering Freedom Online: the Role of Internet Intermediaries' (UNESCO/Internet Society 2014) 19; 'Manila Principles on Intermediary Liability – Background Paper', 30 May 2015, 6, available at: www.manilaprinciples.org.
58. *Sea Shepherd UK v. Fish & Fish Ltd* [2015] UKSC 10 (4 March 2015) at 85.

such as those that plague English intermediary liability at the moment.[59] Instead of fastidiously attempting to categorise behaviours based on empty distinctions, embracing any type of causal participation as conditionally capable of substantiating accessory liability should be preferred. We cannot search for answers to intermediary liability in the conduct element, as it is not their conduct that distinguishes the reasonable intermediaries from the unreasonable ones. The difference is to be found elsewhere.

It is worth pointing out that, for those that would favour a wider international approximation of intermediary liability,[60] this approach also accords well with the US doctrine of contributory liability,[61] the fault-based branch[62] of the US's 'secondary liability' regime that rests on a finding of participation by the accessory in the infringement.[63] Such participation can, under US doctrine, include any inducement, cause or material contribution to the infringing conduct of another in the form of either (a) 'personal conduct that encourages or assists the infringement' or (b) the 'provision of machinery or goods that facilitate the infringement'.[64] Accordingly, US accessory copyright liability also relies on an expansive understanding of the notion of a 'participation', encompassing the same wide variety of actions that would lead to liability under the paradigm outlined above.[65]

---

59. See in particular s. 3.1.2 on the doctrine of authorisation.
60. See e.g., B Martinet Farano, 'Internet Intermediaries' Liability for Copyright and Trademark Infringement: Reconciling the EU and US Approaches' (2012) TTLF Working Paper No 14.
61. M B Nimmer & D Nimmer, *Nimmer on Copyright: A Treatise on the Law of Literary, Musical and Artistic Property, and the Protection of Ideas – Volume 3* (Matthew Bender/LexisNexis 2013) § 12.04[A].
62. A Yen, '*Sony*, Tort Doctrines, and the Puzzle of Peer-to-Peer' (2005) 55(4) Case Western Reserve Law Review 815 at 852.
63. M B Nimmer & D Nimmer, *Nimmer on Copyright: A Treatise on the Law of Literary, Musical and Artistic Property, and the Protection of Ideas – Volume 3* (Matthew Bender/LexisNexis 2013) § 12.04[A][3][a].
64. C A Grossman, 'The Evolutionary Drift of Vicarious Liability and Contributory Infringement: from Interstitial Gap Filler to Arbiter of the Content Wars' (2005) 58(2) SMU Law Review 357, quoting *Matthew Bender & Co. v. West Pub'g Co.*, 158 F.3d 693, 706 (2d Cir. 1998).
65. Martinet Farano for examples explains that in 'the United States, the doctrine of contributory liability has thus been extensively used by right holders in their claims against online service providers (for third party infringing content) on the ground that they arguably (i) *furnished the means*, *induced*, *facilitated* or *incentivized* infringement (ii) *while being aware* of such infringement', see B Martinet Farano, 'Internet Intermediaries' Liability for Copyright and Trademark Infringement: Reconciling the EU and US Approaches' (2012) TTLF Working Paper No 14, 49-50. Ginsburg confirms that 'intent to facilitate infringement by enabling end-user copying supposedly forms the keystone of contributory liability', see J Ginsburg, 'Separating the Sony Sheep from the Grokster Goats: Reckoning the Future Business Plans of Copyright-Dependent Technology Entrepreneurs' (2008) 50(2) Arizona Law Review 577. For relevant case law see: *Elektra Entm't Group, Inc. v. Barker*, No. 05-CV-7340 (KMK), 2008 WL 857527 (S.D.N.Y. Mar. 31, 2008); *Sega Enters. Ltd v. Maphia*, 948 F. Supp 923 (N.D. Cal. 1996); *In re Aimster*

In any case, obviously, since the conduct element is only one factor to consider, the facilitation of or other material causal participation in a copyright infringement cannot be made illegal on that basis alone. This is appropriate, as otherwise the result would be the immediate banning of the provision of all intermediary services. In *L'Oréal v. eBay,* the CJEU confirms:

> the mere fact that the operator of an online marketplace stores offers for sale on its server, sets the terms of its service, is remunerated for that service and provides general information to its customers cannot have the effect of denying it the exemptions from liability provided for by Directive 2000/31[66]

Accordingly, under the current safe harbour-based regime, mere facilitation is barred from substantiating intermediary liability on its own, at least for mere conduit, caching and hosting intermediaries. Similarly, according to *Google France*:

> It must be pointed out that the mere facts that the referencing service is subject to payment, that Google sets the payment terms or that it provides general information to its clients cannot have the effect of depriving Google of the exemptions from liability provided for in Directive 2000/31.[67]

These results should also be maintained in any potential future substantive regime that moves beyond the safe harbours: the heart of the analysis of intermediary liability lies not in the assessment of the services offered by the intermediary, but in the accompanying mental element. Accordingly, when found to have facilitated copyright infringement, the intermediary may only be held liable as long as that additional condition accrues. It is therefore to the mental element that the analysis will now turn.

Copyright Litigation, 334 F.3d 643 (7th Cir. 2003) ('The swappers, who are ignorant or more commonly disdainful of copyright and in any event discount the likelihood of being sued or prosecuted for copyright infringement, are the direct infringers. But firms that facilitate their infringement, even if they are not themselves infringers because they are not making copies of the music that is shared, may be liable to the copyright owners as contributory infringers') and *Metro Goldwyn Mayer Studios Inc. v. Grokster* 545 U.S. 913 (2005) where it was held that: 'this evidence of unlawful objective is given added significance by MGM's showing that neither company attempted to develop filtering tools or other mechanisms to diminish the infringing activity using their software. While the Ninth Circuit treated the defendants' failure to develop such tools as irrelevant because they lacked an independent duty to monitor their users' activity, we think this evidence underscores Grokster's and Stream Cast intentional facilitation of their users' infringement'.

66. CJEU, C-324/09, *L'Oréal v. eBay International*, 12 July 2011, para. 115.
67. Joined Cases C-236/08 and C-237/08 *Google France v. Louis Vuitton et al,* 23 March 2010, para. 116.

Before moving on, first a diagram illustrating the framework for intermediary accessory copyright liability as it has been developed in this chapter to this point can help establish clarity. What we know so far about European intermediary accessory copyright liability is represented in Figure 5.1.

Figure 5.1 Basic Intermediary Accessory Copyright Liability Flowchart

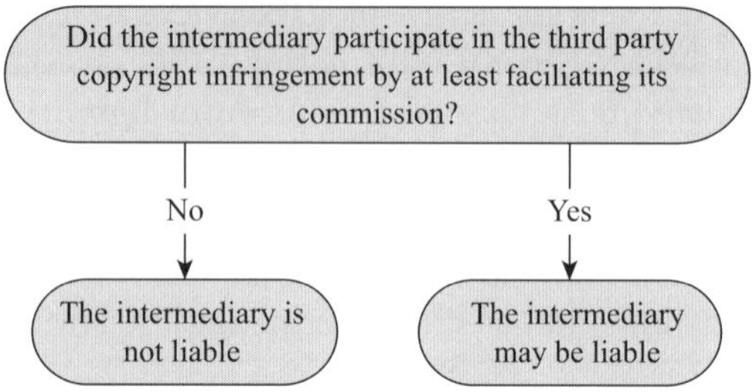

5.3 THE MENTAL ELEMENT

As established in Chapter 4,[68] the differentiation between degrees of mental involvement in the commission of a tort has strong roots in European tort law.[69] The idea finds explicit recognition in Article 2:102(5) of the PETL, which assigns greater weight to intentionally committed torts over merely negligence-based ones. So, according to this:

> The scope of protection may also be affected by the nature of liability, so that an interest may receive more extensive protection against intentional harm than in other cases.

For the most part of course, the notion of degrees of culpability is downplayed in the modern European national tort laws. This makes sense: with the transition towards the modern objective standard of fault, the liability outcome will always be the same regardless of the tortfeasor's blameworthiness.[70] In the area of accessory liability, however, the significance of culpability persists.[71] As was shown in Chapter 3, intention plays a central part in the notion of joint tortfeasance in both English and German theory, while even in France the traditional unitary approach of the *Cour de*

68. See s. 4.2.1.
69. F H Lawson & B Markesinis, *Tortious Liability for Unintentional Harm in the Common Law and the Civil Law* (Cambridge University Press 1982) 181.
70. W van Gerven et al., *Tort Law* (Hart Publishing 2000) 279; C von Bar, *The Common European Law of Torts – Vol. II* (Clarendon Press 2000) para. 226.
71. P S Davies, Accessory Liability (Hart Publishing 2015) 40-54 and 203-209; S K Högberg, 'The Search for Intent-Based Doctrine of Secondary Liability in Copyright Law' (2006) 106(4) Columbia Law Review 909.

cassation that insists on extending copyright's strict liability approach to internet intermediaries has found fierce opposition in the legal scholarship.[72] The desire for differentiation is noticeable on the EU level as well: as Chapter 2 demonstrated, the relevant EU framework also favours a distinction between 'neutral' and 'non-neutral' intermediaries. It is therefore clear that, in order that accessory liability be recognised, the conduct element must be complemented by an appropriate mental element. As Yen observes, it 'is one thing to distribute technology that could be used to infringe in the hope that others will use it legitimately. It is something else to distribute the same technology in the hope that others will use it to infringe'.[73]

Two main types of mental element are relevant to intermediary accessory copyright liability: intent and knowledge. These shall be examined in turn below.

5.3.1 Intention

As noted in Chapter 4, intention is the fast track route to accessory tort liability: where a person who causally participated in somebody else's a tort intended that commission, the standard of care expected of him must be seen as automatically violated. This equivalence is appropriate. Once a strong mental link that binds the defendant's conduct to the damage is established, there need be no further investigation of that conduct and attempt to measure it against an expected standard of reasonability: a reasonable person never intends to cause harm to another and a person who causes harm intentionally, even if indirectly through another, is immediately unreasonable. As opposed to the law of negligence therefore, which centres on the investigation of the notion of duty and only secondarily considers mental participation, in intent the focus is entirely on the mental element of the standard of care. An intentional intermediary is always an unreasonable intermediary. This shall be the rule adopted in this book as well.

It should be noted that it is clear that this conclusion has the backing not only of general tort law, but also of the selected national systems applicable

72. See Ch. 3, ss 3.1.3, 3.3.2 and 3.2.3.1. Indeed, it's worth noting that strict liability is currently being contested by some copyright scholars in the area of primary liability as well, in favour of a return to a fault-based, see e.g., S Hetcher, 'The Kids are Alright: Applying a Fault Liability Standard to Amateur Digital Remix' (2010) 62(5) Florida Law Review 1275; S Hetcher, 'The Fault Liability Standard in Copyright' in S Balganesh (ed.), *Intellectual Property and the Common Law* (Cambridge University Press 2013) 431; S Hetcher, 'The Immorality of Strict Liability in Copyright' (2013) 17(1) Marquette Intellectual Property Law Review 1; D S Ciolino & E A Donelon, 'Questioning Strict Liability in Copyright' (2002) 54(2) Rutgers Law Review 351.
73. A Yen, 'Third Party Copyright after Grokster' (2007) 16(3) Information & Communications Technology Law 233.

specifically to intermediary accessory copyright liability. So, English law rests on an element of 'common design' to craft its joint tortfeasance doctrine, which hold intentional accessories liable alongside the primary party. The German BGB imposes the same requirement of intention – borrowed from German criminal law – for the deployment of its Article 830 on *Mittäterschaft:* intentional participation, encouragement and facilitation result – by means of the connector of 'psychological causation' – in immediate liability. Although that provision finds limited application in the copyright practice of the German courts, it is clear that the German BGH was heading in a very similar direction with the construction of the '*Zu-Eigen-Machen*' doctrine adopted in *marions-kochbuch.de.*[74] Finally, while French tort theory does not recognise a principle of joint tortfeasance per se, the French courts essentially expressed the same idea when applying the direct copyright liability onto intermediaries for 'taking over' third party content.[75]

What about the European law-maker? An indication of the direction in which the EU is leaning can be found in *L'Oréal v. eBay*. Here the CJEU declared that where:

> the operator has provided assistance which entails, in particular, optimising the presentation of the offers for sale in question or promoting those offers, it must be considered not to have taken a neutral position between the customer-seller concerned and potential buyers but to have played an active role of such a kind as to give it knowledge of, or control over, the data relating to those offers for sale. It cannot then rely, in the case of those data, on the exemption from liability referred to in Article 14(1) of Directive 2000/31.[76]

So, according to the CJEU, where the intermediary's involvement was such as to indicate *non-neutrality,* immunity is denied. Again, as noted in Chapter 2, the description of such non-neutrality rests heavily on indications of mental participation: the active promotion of an unlawful outcome, which cannot but be intentional.[77] From this starting point, the explicit recognition of intent as the great line crossing through European intermediary liability is not a great leap.

---

74. See s. 3.3.2. above BGH, *marions-kochbuch.de*, 12 November 2009, I ZR 166/07.
75. See s. 3.2.3.1. above and *Tiscali Media c. Dargaud Lombard, Lucky Comics,* Cour d'appel de Paris, 7 June 2006.
76. CJEU, C-324/09, *L'Oréal v. eBay International*, 12 July 2011 at 115-116. It is recalled that the paragraph is an interpretation of Recital 42 of the E-Commerce Directive.
77. See s. 2.2.1. See also Ginsburg, who explains that the various safe harbour provisions adopted across the world 'share a goal of insulating the innovator whose technology happens, but was not intended, to enable its adopters to make unlawful copies or communications of protected works'. See: J Ginsburg, 'Separating the Sony Sheep from the Grokster Goats: Reckoning the Future Business Plans of Copyright-Dependent Technology Entrepreneurs' (2008) 50(2) Arizona Law Review 577.

5.3.1.1 Defining Intention in Intermediary Liability

When can an intermediary be said to have intended the copyright infringement of another? In accordance with the DCFR definition of intention analysed in Chapter 4 (section 4.2.1), in order to be found to have had intent, the intermediary must have either *meant* to cause the infringement committed by the third party ('direct intent') or have known that its behaviour could result in the commission of the copyright infringement by the third party and *meant* to engage in that behaviour ('indirect intent' or 'oblique intent').

As noted in Chapter 4, the DCFR definition of intent is quite strict. This is contrary to the general trend in European tort systems, which has been towards the 'watering down' of the standard of intention. Thus, Van Dam observes that in England, France and Germany a tendency to include recklessness or *dolus eventualis* in the concept of intent is discernible.[78] As was explained above, recklessness should be understood as the conscious acceptance of a substantial risk. The difference between recklessness and indirect intent centres around probability: if the damage is 'well-nigh certain',[79] there is indirect intent, whereas if it is merely highly probable, there is recklessness. The distinction represents a decision that should be made in a European regime of intermediary liability: should recklessness be included in the notion of intent with regard to intermediary accessory copyright liability? In other words, should an intermediary be understood to be acting with intent if the risk of infringement is not certain, but merely 'obvious and serious' and it 'nonetheless voluntarily proceeds without caring'[80] if the infringement materialises?

Depending on the decision, the line between intent and negligence will be placed at a slightly different position on the scale of intermediary accessory liability. As shall be shown below, this will have consequences with regard to the relevance of the investigation of the applicable duties of care, as well as, potentially, the choice of appropriate remedies. If recklessness is accepted as a form of intent, then an intermediary whose aim is not the infringement itself (whether for its own sake or, e.g., as a means of making profit), but simply the offering of technology which predictably makes infringement easier and therefore more probable, will run a much higher risk of being seen as intentionally infringing copyright and will accordingly be held liable without further ado. Under such a paradigm therefore, merely intending to provide services that in the event facilitated copyright infringement will, far too often, alone be sufficient to create liability. This, however, could have a detrimental effect on a vast array of

78. C van Dam, *European Tort Law* (2nd ed., Oxford University Press 2013) para. 803.
79. C von Bar et al. (eds), *Principles, Definitions and Model Rules of European Private Law: Draft Common Frame of Reference (DCFR)*, prepared by the Study Group on a European Civil Code and the Research Group on EC private law (Acquis Group), Outline Edition (Sellier 2009) 3266.
80. See DCFR, 'Annex – Definitions'.

internet intermediaries, and in particular modern interactive host service providers, which aim at offering services that allow their users to exchange legitimate information, but which must be aware of the fact that, in that process, they are also enabling the exchange of infringing content, despite not wilfully seeking to do so.[81] Such providers presumably know that their conduct results in a serious risk of infringement, however that infringement is not their primary objective, but collateral damage occurring on the side-lines of their business model.

One of the central positions of this book is the idea that mental culpability is important when it comes to intermediary liability. In view of this, it is suggested that the strict definition of intent of the DCFR that excludes recklessness from its scope be retained in intermediary liability.[82] That is not of course to say that reckless intermediaries should be allowed run wild. Rather, instances of recklessness should instead be examined under the rubric of negligence, which imposes more exacting requirements before a misconduct can be found.

5.3.1.2 Proving the Intermediary's Intent

While the theory surrounding the notion of intent is straightforward, proving it in practice remains remarkably difficult. As Howarth notes, '[n]egligence may sometimes speak for itself. Intentional harm does not'.[83] In view of the evidentiary difficulties surrounding the investigation of another person's state of mind, two main methods of proving intent emerge: (a) the intermediary may admit to intending the infringement; or (b) absent such a confession, intent may nonetheless be convincingly inferred from the circumstances.[84]

The first of these is far less likely than the second – it is not however impossible. Davies[85] highlights an indicative section from the autobiography of Amstrad's founder and chairman Alan Sugar, with regard to the warnings the company placed on its recording machines against copying, which

81. Think, for example, of the currently very popular content sharing platforms, reddit.com or Pinterest.com.

82. See also *Grimme Maschinenfabrik GmbH & Co KG v. Scott (t/a Scotts Potato Machinery)* [2010] EWCA Civ 1110 (15 October 2010), talking about indirect patent infringement: 'So far as concerns intention, the cases have shown the need to distinguish between something which has been "targeted" or "aimed at", in the sense of a specific subjective intention, and recklessness or merely a foreseeable consequence. It is established that nothing other than a specific subjective intention is sufficient for liability'.

83. D Howarth, 'My Brother's Keeper? Liability for Acts of Third Parties' (1994) 14(1) Legal Studies 88.

84. P Cane, '*Mens Rea* in Tort Law' (2000) 20(4) Oxford Journal of Legal Studies 533; A N Dixon, 'Liability of Users and Third Parties for Copyright Infringements on the Internet: Overview of International Developments' in A Strowel (ed.), *Peer-to-Peer File Sharing and Secondary Liability in Copyright Law* (Edward Elgar Publishing 2009) 38.

85. P S Davies, *Accessory Liability* (Hart Publishing 2015) 220.

proved so instrumental in their release from liability before the House of Lords:

> This was a cheeky tactic. People would read it and think to themselves, 'hey, that's a good idea! I can use this machine to copy my mate's Abba cassette'. That was the effect the warning had, yet there was I, keeping within the law, whiter than white, telling people that the product should not be used for that purpose. Is that called reverse psychology?[86]

This admission sheds an entirely different light on the *Amstrad* case.[87] Amstrad's liability for the copyright infringements committed by the users of their machines was rejected by the House of Lords in 1988 on the premise that it amounted to 'mere facilitation'. According to the Court, Amstrad could not be said to have procured or induced the infringement – it had no intent: 'a defendant who procures a breach of copyright […] intends and procures and shares a common design that infringement shall take place. [But] Amstrad are not concerned to procure and cannot procure unlawful copying'. Sugar's admission casts doubt on that conclusion: the use of the word 'tactic' suggests that Amstrad did, at least in a generalised manner, intend that their machines be used for infringing purposes – indeed, they intended the very warning against copying to incite their customers towards such infringement! While they did not therefore have control over how their customers used their machines, they had attempted to subtly manipulate them into infringing activity. It is their customers' fault that they responded to the invitation – but it was Amstrad's for issuing it. Arguably, if this could have been proven at the time, both parties should have been held liable.

Of course, it is no coincidence that the publication of Sugar's admission was decades too late to impact Amstrad's liability: intermediaries with nefarious plans are unlikely to voluntarily share these with right-holders, while it can by no means be assumed without further evidence that every intermediary which cautions others against infringement is secretly hoping to inspire it. Nevertheless, it is not to be excluded that sloppy providers may betray themselves in other ways. In this regard, evidence-gathering can prove fruitful, particularly in the era of digital communications. An excellent example is provided by the US *Grokster* case,[88] where incriminating emails presented a key piece of evidence against the defendant file-sharing client. As the Supreme Court noted:

> An internal e-mail from a company executive stated: 'We have put this network in place so that when Napster pulls the plug on their free service ... or if the Court orders them shut down prior to that ... we will be positioned to capture the flood of their 32 million users that will be actively looking for an alternative'.

86. A Sugar, *What You See Is What You Get: My Autobiography* (Macmillan 2010) 230.
87. *CBS Songs v. Amstrad* [1988] UKHL 15 (12 May 1988).
88. *Metro Goldwyn Mayer Studios Inc. v. Grokster* 545 U.S. 913 (2005).

Inconveniently, while such give-aways might have been likely in the early days of the internet, when inexperienced intermediaries did not take sufficient safeguards against liability, smart company executives are by now most likely exceptionally careful to avoid committing this kind of incriminating evidence to writing.

What about the second method of proving intent through extrapolation from the surrounding circumstances? This offers a far more promising avenue. As Dixon suggests, 'courts can determine intention on the basis of oral and behavioural evidence that encourages infringement, even including inactivity or indifference of such a nature that a certain desired result may be inferred'.[89] Again, discovery can uncover mines of incriminating information: in the UK's *Newzbin (No. 1)* case, for example, attention focused heavily on the damning evidence collected at cross-examination. According to Kitchin J, this showed that the site 'actively encouraged its editors to make reports on films, has rewarded them for so doing and has instructed and guided them to include URLs in their reports and well knows of the common practice of using NFOs too'.[90] On this basis, the judge concluded that it was 'the defendant's intention to make available through Newzbin all films posted on Usenet, so inevitably including the copyright films in the claimants' repertoire both now and in the future'. This time, the court was thus not content to take any warnings issued by Newzbin against infringement at face value:

> I should also draw attention to the user terms and conditions which include the following restriction which mirrors that which applies to editors:
>
> 'You may only use the Site for lawful purposes. In particular you may not use the Site to transmit defamatory, offensive or abusive material or material of an obscene or menacing character, or which promotes hatred, violence or illegal conduct, or in breach of copyright or any other intellectual property rights, or in breach of the Computer Misuse Act 1990 or other relevant legislation or the rights of another User.'
>
> I have no doubt that this is another superficial attempt to conceal the purpose and intention of the defendant to make available binary content of interest to its users, including infringing copies of films. As will be seen, the defendant has done nothing to enforce this restriction. To the contrary, it has encouraged its editors to report and has assisted its users to gain access to such infringing copies.

---

89. A N Dixon, 'Liability of Users and Third Parties for Copyright Infringements on the Internet: Overview of International Developments' in A Strowel (ed.), *Peer-to-Peer File Sharing and Secondary Liability in Copyright Law* (Edward Elgar Publishing 2009) 38.
90. *Twentieth Century Fox Film Corporation & Anor v. Newzbin Ltd* [2010] EWHC 608 (Ch).

Warnings with no enforcement are therefore deemed to amount to empty words that cannot disguise an obvious intention to incite infringement. A similar judicial attitude was also evident in *Dramatico,*[91] where Justice Arnold declared that infringement 'is not merely an inevitable consequence of the provision of torrent files by [TPB]. It is the operators of [TPB]'s objective and intention'. He deduced this from a collection of circumstances including:

i) The website's name – The Pirate Bay – and associated pirate ship logo, which clearly reference the popular terminology applied to online copyright infringement, that of piracy.
ii) A statement published on the site, according to which it was founded by a 'Swedish anti-copyright organisation'.
iii) The site's 'about page', which, among other things, intransigently declared that 'any complaints from copyright and/or lobby organisations will be ridiculed and published at the site' and that '0 torrents have been removed and 0 torrents will ever be removed'
iv) A quote by one of the investors in the site, who was recorded as stating that 'the purpose of the site was pirate copying'.
v) Numerous proceedings in other European jurisdictions, where injunctions and other orders against the operators of TPB had been ignored and orders against TPB's hosting service providers had been circumvented by moving TPB to new providers. This made it clear that the operators of TPB were well-aware that the website was engaged in copyright infringement.

5.3.1.3 General versus Specific Intent

Yet one big stumbling block remains: even if the House of Lords had been aware of Sugar's scheming in *Amstrad*, it would still have been difficult to link any intent this might have demonstrated on the company's part to particular instances of infringement,[92] a requirement central to the traditional conception of joint tortfeasance in the tort laws of Europe: as Lord Templeman expounded, '[g]enerally speaking, inducement, incitement or persuasion to infringe must be by a defendant to an individual infringer and must identifiably procure a particular infringement in order to make the defendant liable as a joint infringer'.[93] This approach reflects the general wisdom of tort law, which does not as a rule attach liability to the creation

91. *Dramatico Entertainment Ltd & Ors v. British Sky Broadcasting Ltd & Ors* [2012] EWHC 268 (Ch) (20 February 2012).
92. P S Davies, Accessory Liability (Hart Publishing 2015) 220-221; A Yen, 'Third Party Copyright after Grokster' (2007) 16(3) Information & Communications Technology Law 233.
93. *CBS Songs v. Amstrad* [1988] UKHL 15 (12 May 1988).

of a repetitive risk through the distribution of products: account must be taken of the specific circumstances of each case. After all, many companies will be 'well-nigh certain' that their products have the potential to cause injury to others in a general way: car manufacturers, for example, must be aware that eventually somebody will be hurt in a car accident, just as breweries and distilleries know that intoxicated people can be dangerous. There are nevertheless legitimate reasons for the making and selling of items such as automobiles, alcohol, knives or guns.[94] Arguably, a distinction must therefore be made between a vague intent regarding the potential of numerous unspecified infringements and intent targeted at a particular infringement:[95] there is difference between selling many cars, one of which was subsequently used as a getaway vehicle in a bank robbery, and making a sales pitch to a potential buyer on the basis of the excellent suitability of a specific vehicle in getaway situations.

Yet, as *Newzbin (No. 1)* and *Dramatico* demonstrate, in copyright the English courts at least seem to be overcoming these qualms.[96] And indeed, it could potentially be argued that the intent in many such cases is sufficiently expansive: if an intermediary intended numerous infringements, then it also intended each infringement within that group, even if it did not plan it individually. After all, a group of infringements is nothing more than a collection of individual infringements – does an individual case need to be made for each? Surely, if it were common knowledge that most car dealerships rely to a significant degree on bank robberies, it would be time to rethink the law governing the liability of car dealers for bank robberies as well. On this reasoning, there is a strong case to be made that such cases are ones of 'oblique intent' that relies on so-called Nelsonian knowledge – i.e., a wilful blindness that allows a provider to remain 'content agnostic', while promoting infringement under the table.[97] Indicatively, it was precisely along these lines of thought that, in its *Grokster* ruling, the US Supreme Court famously re-routed American secondary liability law by introducing the intent-focused doctrine of inducement.[98] According to this, 'one who

---

94. A Yen, 'Third Party Copyright after Grokster' (2007) 16(3) Information & Communications Technology Law, 233; A Yen, '*Sony,* Tort Doctrines, and the Puzzle of Peer-to-Peer' (2005) 55(4) Case Western Reserve Law Review 815.
95. A Yen, '*Sony,* Tort Doctrines, and the Puzzle of Peer-to-Peer' (2005) 55(4) Case Western Reserve Law Review 815.
96. P S Davies, 'Accessory Liability: Protecting Intellectual Property Rights' (2011) 4 Intellectual Property Quarterly 390.
97. P S Davies, *Accessory Liability* (Hart Publishing 2015) 43; J Riordan, *The Liability of Internet Intermediaries* (PhD thesis, University of Oxford 2013, forthcoming Oxford University Press 2016) 74. As concerns inducement of breach of contract see: *Douglas & Ors v. Hello! Ltd & Ors* [2007] UKHL 21 (02 May 2007): 'If the defendant deliberately turned a blind-eye and proceeded regardless he may be treated as having intended the consequence he brought about.'
98. A Yen, 'Third Party Copyright after Grokster' (2007) 16(3) Information & Communications Technology Law 233; T Wu, 'The Copyright Paradox' (2005) 27 Supreme Court

distributes a device with the object of promoting its use to infringe copyright, as shown by clear expression or other affirmative steps taken to foster infringement, is liable for the resulting acts of infringement by third parties'.[99] What does this mean for internet intermediaries? Ginsburg makes a tentative suggestion: 'Speculation is hazardous, but one might predict that where a device or service facilitates infringement on a massive scale, its distributor will likely be found to have intended that result'.[100] As Wu suggests, the inducement doctrine was tailor-made to 'pistol-whip the bad guys' – to punish those companies with a bad attitude.[101]

Should the EU follow suit? Is this approach sensible or sweeping? Should an intermediary that has been found to have intended mass infringements generally, but no specific infringement individually be held liable on the basis of that intention or is it necessary to connect the intent to a specific infringement? In the first case, intent would allow liability where intermediaries have general substantial certainty of wide-spread infringement. As in the *Grokster* case, this could be extrapolated from the intermediary's behaviour. So, for example, if an intermediary creates categories of downloadable content available on its website that include suggestive keywords such as 'recent Hollywood blockbusters', this would be a clear indication of its intention that its users infringe copyright. The same could be said where the intermediary advertises its infringing capabilities to its users.[102]

In view of the immediate and severe consequences it would entail, such a broad inducement rule would certainly have to be carefully controlled so as to avoid an excessive expansion that nullifies the relevance of the mental element and imposes liability on anybody that in any way demonstrates a causal participation in another's copyright infringement. Back in the US, Justice Souter explains:

> mere knowledge of infringing potential or of actual infringing uses would not be enough here to subject a distributor to liability. Nor would

---

Review 229; J Ginsburg & S Ricketson, 'Inducers and Authorisers: A Comparison of the US Supreme Court's Grokster Decision and the Australian Federal Court's Kazaa Ruling' (2006) 11 Media & Arts Law Review 1; P K Yu, 'Digital Copyright and Confuzzling Rhetoric' (2011) 13 Vanderbilt Journal of Entertainment and Technology Law 881; S K Högberg, 'The Search for Intent-Based Doctrine of Secondary Liability in Copyright Law' (2006) 106(4) Columbia Law Review 909; D L Zimmerman, 'Daddy, Are We There Yet? Lost in Grokster-land (The Unintended Consequences of Legislating Technology: The Digital Millennium Copyright Act)' (2005) 9(1-2) New York University Journal of Legislation and Public Policy 75.

99. *Metro Goldwyn Mayer Studios Inc. v. Grokster* 545 U.S. 913 (2005) at 19-20.
100. J Ginsburg, 'Separating the Sony Sheep from the Grokster Goats: Reckoning the Future Business Plans of Copyright-Dependent Technology Entrepreneurs' (2008) 50(2) Arizona Law Review 577.
101. T Wu, 'When Code Isn't Law' (2003) 89 Virginia Law Review 679.
102. This was the case for example the Norwegian case of *Tono et. al v. Frank Allan Bruvik d/b/a Napster*, Hr-2005-00133-A, Rt-2005-41 (Supreme Court of Norway, 27 January 2005 – Docket No. 2004/822), otherwise known as the 'Norwegian Napster' case.

> ordinary acts incident to product distribution, such as offering customers technical support or product updates, support liability in themselves. The inducement rule, instead, premises liability on purposeful, culpable expression and conduct, and thus does nothing to compromise legitimate commerce or discourage innovation having a lawful promise.[103]

Alternatively of course, intent could only be allowed to substantiate liability where it is attached to a specific infringement committed by a specific third party. For example, in the US case of *A & M Records v. Abdallah,*[104] the defendant sold time-loaded cassettes designed to run for a specific time so as to enable better counterfeit copies of specific protected works by specific individuals who he knew full-well intended to commit precisely such infringements.[105] In the online realm, a corresponding example can be imagined of the intermediary that offers support services to specific users in troubleshooting problems with downloading specific infringing files. Clearly, such instances will be harder to prove – but that's probably simply because they rarely occur. Absent a strong concrete attachment to a specific infringement, it might be fair to conclude that the intermediary did not in fact intend the infringement – at worst, like Alan Sugar, it gleefully anticipated the boost that it could only hope – but not ensure – that the possibility of infringement would give to its own business. As Wu warns, a broad inducement test runs the risk of allowing courts to see what they want to and apply a stricter liability test for those intermediaries they simply don't like, without however really being able to prove in what way they are different from the 'innocent' ones.[106]

In view of these cautionary considerations, in the model for European intermediary accessory copyright liability proposed in this book, the more conservative approach that requires a specifically targeted intention shall be espoused. At the same time, the strict results of this solution shall be mitigated through the rules on negligent accessory liability. So, as we shall see below, one final option for proving intent aside from the two discussed above shall be introduced: a substantiation of intention on particularly egregious cases of persistent negligence. This however, cannot be properly explained before the analysis of negligence itself is first undertaken.[107]

In conclusion, while intention offers a clear and strong ethical basis for liability, it is pragmatically often difficult to prove. This leaves it by and large on the fringes of fault. At the same time, if it can be shown, provided the conduct element has already been established, the result will be automatic, full liability. At this point, we can expand on our initial simplistic flowchart.

---

103. *Metro Goldwyn Mayer Studios Inc. v. Grokster* 545 U.S. 913 (2005).
104. *A & M Records v. Abdallah*, 948 F.Supp. 1449.
105. A Yen, 'Third-party Copyright Liability after Grokster' (2007) 16(3) Information & Communications Technology Law 233.
106. T Wu, 'The Copyright Paradox' (2005) 27 Supreme Court Review 229.
107. See s. 5.5.7.2.

As shown in Figure 5.2., one branch of the intermediary liability decision tree is already complete.

Figure 5.2 Intermediary Accessory Copyright Liability Flowchart: Intent

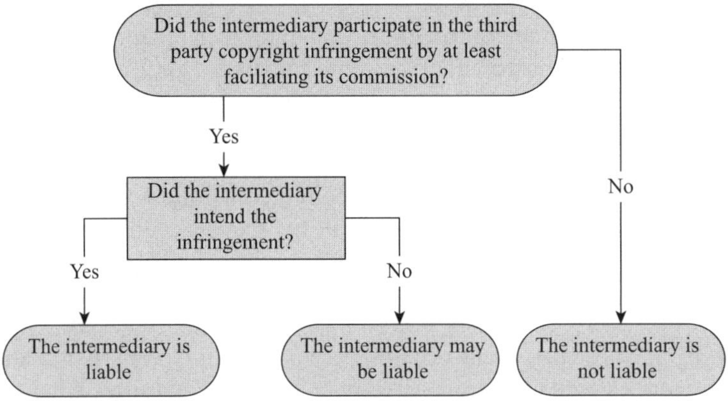

5.3.2 Knowledge

Although intention is a sufficient, it should not be understood as a necessary mental element for a finding of intermediary accessory copyright liability.[108] Merely not intending to cause another to commit copyright infringement cannot alone be enough to let an intermediary off the hook of accessory liability: if the conduct element is established and no intent may be found, in order to be free of all liability, the intermediary must still be shown to not have been negligent with regard to the occurrence of the infringement.

It should be noted that, while this suggestion is par for the course in French accessory liability law,[109] it goes against established precedent in English law, while German jurisprudence might also have to make some adjustments to accommodate it. In particular, accessory liability in England definitively presupposes intent of some kind. As has been suggested earlier however, this restriction is inappropriate and results in unhappy courts manipulating doctrine to achieve desired outcomes.[110] German law faces a similar problem, although *Störerhaftung* has done much to suppress the problems it creates. While traditionally therefore under German doctrine intent is seen as a requirement for the activation of Article 830 BGB, a slight tendency is discernible among the lower German courts towards the introduction of a notion of joint tortfeasance by forbearance.[111] In any case, in the face of modern efficient and extensive intermediation, arguably the law

108. P S Davies, *Accessory Liability* (Hart Publishing 2015) 42.
109. See Ch. 3, s. 3.2.3.2.
110. See Ch. 3, s. 3.1.3.
111. See Ch. 3, s. 3.3.2.3.

in both countries should open itself up to the possibility of an accessory liability based in negligence.

The mental element of negligence liability can be found in knowledge: it is not possible, after all, to take care to avoid a risk one does not know is there. Under this book's proposed model, knowledge therefore shall be the second mental element an intermediary can exhibit that can establish liability for the copyright infringements of others. Of course, knowledge and intent are closely connected concepts – for one thing, intent pre-supposes knowledge.[112] Knowledge however represents a lower standard on the mental element bar.[113]

It should be emphasised that knowledge constitutes only the base level of negligent intermediary accessory liability: more serious mental involvement in the infringement of another, although not necessary to establish negligence liability, will by no means exclude it. So, for example, as noted above (section 5.3.1) recklessness on the part of the intermediary with regard to the copyright infringement of another will certainly establish a sufficient mental element to enable discussion of negligence liability. After all, like intent, recklessness also assumes knowledge.

Where exactly should the knowledge threshold be placed? Two choices must be made in this regard.

5.3.2.1 Actual versus Constructive Knowledge

The first choice that must be made by the European legislator related to the standard of knowledge for intermediary negligence liability for third party copyright infringements is that between actual and constructive knowledge: must the intermediary have actual knowledge so as to be found to be negligent with regard to another's copyright infringement or is constructive knowledge sufficient? Actual knowledge is subjective knowledge. Constructive knowledge is objective knowledge.[114]

As established in Chapter 4, the test applied in general European negligence liability to determine whether a defendant had the necessary level of knowledge is an objective one. According to this, the pertinent question is not whether the defendant *in fact* knew the risk of infringement (as would be the case under a subjective test), but whether it *ought* to have known of it. Yet, the hosting safe harbour of Article 14 of the E-Commerce Directive sets a slightly different threshold. According to that provision, in order to benefit from immunity, a host service provider must not have 'actual knowledge of illegal activity or information and, as regards claims for damages, [must not be]

112. *Douglas & Ors v. Hello! Ltd & Ors* [2007] UKHL 21 (2 May 2007).
113. P S Davies, *Accessory Liability* (Hart Publishing 2015) 42.
114. S K Högberg, 'The Search for Intent-Based Doctrine of Secondary Liability in Copyright Law' (2006) 106(4) Columbia Law Review 909.

aware of facts or circumstances from which the illegal activity or information is apparent'.

As noted in Chapter 2, considerable discussion has surrounded the interpretation of this sentence.[115] Van Dam suggests that the hosting test is a subjective one that deviates from the normal standards of tort law for the benefit of host service providers.[116] However, as was shown above, this does not seem to be entirely correct: although the standard set in Article 14 is not explicitly identified as an objective one and the words 'ought to' are not used, the reference to 'facts or circumstances from which the illegal activity or information is apparent' would seem instead to depend the knowledge standard not on what the intermediary personally – *subjectively* – did or did not know, but on what could have *objectively* been deduced by a reasonable person in the same position. It is therefore probably more accurate to speak of an adjustment of the objective test to meet the needs of intermediary liability: a hybrid subjective/objective standard, wherein the objectivity is assured through the word 'apparent', while some subjectivity is allowed through by reference to the intermediary's individual 'awareness'.[117]

This conclusion is strengthened by the juxtaposition of this standard of 'constructive knowledge' with the alternative criterion offered in Article 14 of 'actual knowledge'. The first is confined to 'claims for damages', while the second applies unconstrained to both criminal and civil law. Criminal law concerns itself with punishing those who act badly. By contrast, civil law is about establishing proper standards of behaviour. An objectivated test that does not seek to lay blame, but merely to compensate for harm caused by unfortunate, if human, lapses in attention, is therefore more appropriate to the realm of civil law. It accordingly seems most likely that this was also the distinction the E-Commerce Directive sought to make when differentiating the standard of knowledge applicable in a criminal context to that reserved for private law. Final confirmation of this interpretation can be found in the CJEU's elucidation of the word 'apparent' in *L'Oréal* by means of reference to a hypothetical 'diligent economic operator', clearly intended to function as the reasonable person of the intermediary liability world: only if the intermediary was 'aware of facts or circumstances on the basis of which a diligent economic operator should have identified' the infringement, will it be obliged to face up to its responsibilities and accept the obvious.[118]

As was explained in Chapter 2,[119] this hybrid standard is the product of the overall structure surrounding the safe harbours: any proactive investigation of infringements made using an intermediary's services will generally

115. See above, Ch. 2, s. 2.2.4.1.
116. C van Dam, *European Tort Law* (2nd ed., Oxford University Press 2013) para. 811-2.
117. B Martinet Farano, 'Internet Intermediaries' Liability for Copyright and Trademark Infringement: Reconciling the EU and US Approaches' (2012) TTLF Working Paper No 14, 83.
118. CJEU, C-324/09, *L'Oréal v. eBay International*, 12 July 2011 at 120.
119. See s. 2.2.4.1.

involve some kind of general monitoring, the imposition of which by law is foreclosed by Article 15 of the E-Commerce Directive. As the law cannot demand that intermediaries undertake such monitoring, it is clear that the reasonable intermediary cannot be defined by its willingness to do so. The subjective elements of Article 14's knowledge standard are therefore a necessary nod to Article 15. Any knowledge or awareness must be brought to the host service provider by others or by circumstance – it cannot be obliged to hunt it out.

Should this seemingly offbeat standard be limited to the exclusive ambit of Article 14 of the E-Commerce Directive? This does not seem appropriate. Again as explained in Chapter 2, while Article 15 of the E-Commerce Directive applies only to safe harbour activities, the prohibition of general monitoring has subsequently been extended by the CJEU beyond that limited purview to all intermediary activities through the Charter-based mechanism of a 'fair balance'. In this way, Article 15 is revealed as an elaboration of more expansive principles drawn directly from the law of fundamental rights.[120] Accordingly, general obligations to monitor end-user activities on their services and networks should not be understood as capable of being legally imposed on internet intermediaries, even where the conditions of the safe harbour provisions are not met. In turn, this means that the hybrid standard of care of Article 14 of the E-Commerce Directive deserves more general application.

On the basis of this analysis, in the model suggested by this book, the hybrid standard shall be retained for application to a full, substantive European intermediary liability regime. For this purpose, that standard can therefore be rephrased into a classic reasonable person question: 'would a reasonable intermediary aware of the same facts and circumstances as the defendant have known about the risk?' From the *ex ante* perspective of an intermediary wishing to avoid a negligent mindset, this then becomes: 'what ought I to conclude from the facts or circumstances at my disposal? Is an infringement apparent to me on their basis?'

5.3.2.2 General versus Specific Knowledge

How can that question be answered? The second important choice that must be made by the legislator related to the standard of knowledge is that between general and specific knowledge. What precisely must the accessory intermediary know? Must it have specific knowledge of a particular act of infringement or will general knowledge of a widespread disregard for copyright do?[121] The choice between a general or specific standard of knowledge has become particularly acute since the advent of modern

120. See s. 2.3.
121. S K Högberg, 'The Search for Intent-Based Doctrine of Secondary Liability in Copyright Law' (2006) 106(4) Columbia Law Review 909.

information-sharing technologies, particularly in the area of peer-to-peer exchanges.[122] While an intermediary might know full-well that its product or services are used for significant amounts of infringing activities, it is less likely to be aware of particular instances of infringement – indeed, following the early cases pursued against first generation file-sharing providers such as Napster, the emergence of higher-bandwidth computers has allowed the relevant technology to evolve towards decentralised, distributed frameworks, which allow providers to facilitate infringement, while avoiding specific knowledge.[123] Once again, a choice must be made and, while historically European courts seem to have opted for the stricter 'specific' approach, a definite relaxing of the standard towards the general is discernible.[124]

It should be noted that, although the notions are connected and often used interchangeably, the distinction between specific and general knowledge has a different focus from the distinction between actual and constructive knowledge. While the latter refers to the type of knowledge, the former concerns the object or content of that knowledge: is the provider aware of a particular primary wrong or it is just party to the 'common knowledge' that infringement is rampant on its site? It follows that knowledge of a specific infringement may be actual or construed: the intermediary may have been made aware of it in an explicit way or it may simply have surmised the risk of infringement from the circumstances. General knowledge is a bit trickier in this regard: it has been argued that actual knowledge cannot take the form of general knowledge.[125] Although probably rarer however, technically there doesn't seem to be a reason why knowledge of rampant infringement shouldn't be able to be both actual (where for example it is measured by experts and communicated to the intermediary) or simply construed from rumours, anecdotes and common sense.

Specific knowledge

The most damning kind of knowledge will naturally be specific knowledge. Specific knowledge will arise where the intermediary knows or has reason to know of a particular instance of infringement by a particular infringer. This will most commonly be the case where the intermediary has received

122. S K Högberg, 'The Search for Intent-Based Doctrine of Secondary Liability in Copyright Law' (2006) 106(4) Columbia Law Review 909; M Bartholomew & P F McArdle, 'Causing Infringement' (2011) 64(3) Vanderbilt Law Review 675.
123. R Dickinson & A Watt, 'How Litigation Changed Peer-to-Peer File-Sharing' (2010) 197 Copyright World 19; D W Opderbeck, 'Peer-to-Peer Networks, Technological Evolution, and Intellectual Property Reverse Private Attorney General Litigation' (2005) 20(4) Berkeley Technology Law Journal 1685; R Giblin, *Code Wars – 10 Years of P2P Software Litigation* (Edward Elgar 2011) 148-153.
124. The difference between the stricter *Amstrad* standard and the approach taken in *Newzbin* and *Dramatico* (see Ch. 3, ss 3.1.2 and 3.1.3) is indicative.
125. Commission Staff Working Paper, 'Online Services, Including E-Commerce, in the Single Market', SEC(2011) 1641 final, 11 January 2012, 34.

notification of a copyright infringement by the right-holder: indeed, furnishing intermediaries with specific knowledge that forces them to take action is the very purpose of notice-and-take-down schemes.[126] Other ways in which an intermediary might acquire specific knowledge might include the flagging of an infringement by filtering software or manual supervision of the platform by human employees.

Specific knowledge should always be interpreted in a strict manner. The knowledge-imparting circumstances must thus be brought to the intermediary's attention in targeted ways: the knowledge must be specific not just with regard to the infringement and the identity of primary infringer, but as concerns the intermediary as well – it cannot simply be knowledge conveyed to the world at large. So, for example, publication in a newspaper of a court ruling establishing that a particular file-sharing website is widely used for copyright infringement cannot be construed as 'specific knowledge' of that website's illegal nature on the part of every internet access provider in the country, thereby establishing an obligation on the part of such providers to block the site or face liability.[127] Moreover, notices of illegality imparted to the intermediary must be held to a high standard.[128]

At the moment, as noted in Chapter 2, EU law offers very little guidance in this regard, leaving the requirements of specific knowledge up to interpretation by the national authorities under the guidance of general principles of law.[129] However, in *L'Oréal,* the CJEU did provide some input, by noting that any notification from a third party of illegal content must be 'sufficiently precise' and 'adequately substantiated' if they are to preclude safe harbour protection.[130] Outside of the EU regime, it is worth noting that the Manila Principles on Intermediary Liability,[131] proposed in March 2015 by a forum of civil societies from around the world, supply more detail in their Principle III: 'Requests for restrictions of content must be clear, be unambiguous, and follow due process'. According to Principle III.b. in particular, a content restriction request pertaining to unlawful content must, at a minimum, contain the following:

126. R MacKinnon et al., 'Fostering Freedom Online: the Role of Internet Intermediaries' (UNESCO/Internet Society 2014) 41-42.
127. 'Manila Principles on Intermediary Liability – Background Paper', 30 May 2015, 28, available at: www.manilaprinciples.org.
128. J Lahe & K Turk, 'The Web Host's Privilege of Limited Liability: Its Application to Operators of Commentary Rooms' (2012) 2 European Review of Private Law 447.
129. See above, Ch. 2, ss 2.2.4.1, 2.2.5 and 2.3. Other national systems are more illuminating. See e.g., s. 512(c)(3)(A)-(B) of the Digital Millennium Copyright Act (DMCA), 17 U.S.C. For other national examples see N Zingales, 'Internet Intermediary Liability: Identifying Best Practices for Africa' (2013) Association for Progressive Communications (APC).
130. CJEU, C-324/09, *L'Oréal v. eBay International*, 12 July 2011 at 122.
131. Available at: www.manilaprinciples.org.

(1) The legal basis for the assertion that the content is unlawful. This should include a detailed description of the content alleged to be illegal and make specific reference to the law allegedly violated, as well as the country where it applies.
(2) The internet identifier and description of the allegedly unlawful content (such as a specific URL). Intermediaries cannot be required to search for the content themselves, as that would involve general monitoring.
(3) The consideration provided to limitations, exceptions and defences available to the content provider. This requirement is particularly relevant to copyright, where limitations and exceptions play an important role.[132]
(4) Contact details of the issuing party or their agent, unless this is prohibited by law.
(5) Evidence sufficient to document legal standing to issue the request.
(6) A declaration of good faith that the information provided is accurate. These final three requirements help limit the incidence of bogus notices. They are again also particularly relevant to copyright, as they indicate that no permission to engage in the protected acts has been given by the right-holder, something that would eliminate the possibility of infringement.[133]

Of the three Member States examined in this book, the most detailed provisions on notice-and-take-down are found in the law of France.[134] Like the Manila Principles, this also imposes significant conditions on valid notices, including that they provide the date of the notification; specific identifying details of the notifying natural or legal person and of its recipient; a description of the alleged illegal information and its precise location; the reason why the content should be removed, including the legal basis for its removal; and a copy of the letter sent to the content provider or publisher requesting the termination of the illegal activity (see Article 6-I-5 LCEN). Given the general dissatisfaction with the current rudimentary E-Commerce notice-and-take-down regime, it would not be inappropriate if a substantive European regime for intermediary accessory copyright liability provided a sounder definition of specific knowledge along these lines.[135]

Can specific knowledge be assumed by the nature of the content – in other words, may content be considered to be 'manifestly' infringing? The Manila Principles maintain that intermediaries should not be required to substantively evaluate the legality of third-party content themselves (Manila

132. For an exhaustive list of the limitations and exceptions possible in the EU see Art. 5 of the Copyright Directive.
133. Electronic Frontier Foundation, 'Manila Principles on Intermediary Liability – Background Paper', 30 May 2015, 28, available at: www.manilaprinciples.org.
134. See Ch. 3 above, s. 3.2.
135. See Ch. 2 above, s. 2.2.4.4.

Principles, Principle III.a.). Again, French jurisprudence tends to agree.[136] As has been noted before, at least in the area of copyright this makes a lot of sense, as the infringing nature of particular content will often not be readily apparent without a clear understanding of the applicable law and access to all relevant information. It should be noted that this requirement does not go against the establishment of a threshold of constructive knowledge, as constructive knowledge is knowledge that emerges from the circumstances generally and not necessarily from the defendant's own research.

Finally, some consideration must also be had for the tricky question of knowledge of the future. Can specific knowledge be said to be had of an infringement that has not yet been committed? It has been argued that such a requirement would be unreasonable: a person cannot possibly know future facts. While generally of sound logic, this does perhaps represent an excessively formalist definition of knowledge: clearly, many future events are readily predictable. As Davies observes, 'I can know that there will be daylight tomorrow'.[137] AG Jääskinen in *L'Oréal* also accepted that the repetition of the same infringement by the same actor should be taken to constitute, not two separate events, but a single 'ongoing activity' that 'covers past, present and future'.[138] At the same time, a cautious interpretation should be favoured in this regard. Perhaps it could be said that actual knowledge of a specific existing infringement constitutes a 'fact or circumstance' that enables constructive knowledge of very similar future infringements, but only in so far as the CJEU has allowed this in *L'Oréal*: the same infringement of the same work by the same primary infringer at the same location should be necessary. Anything more and proactive investigations will be required of the intermediary for the uncovering of the future infringement, to the potential detriment of users' fundamental rights.

General knowledge

What about general knowledge? Should that be considered to constitute a sufficient mental element to ground accessory copyright liability?[139] The question is a difficult one. Davies explains:

> Attempts by defendants to deny the huge number of infringements of copyright committed by the various users of the site ring very hollow

136. See Ch. 3 above, s. 3.2.
137. P S Davies, *Accessory Liability* (Hart Publishing 2015) 43.
138. CJEU, Opinion of Advocate General Jääskinen, case C-324/09, *L'Oréal v. eBay International*, 9 December 2010. See *also* Ch. 2, s. 2.2.4.1.
139. In the US in *Tiffany. v. eBay*, 600 F.3d 93, 107 (2d Cir. 2010), it was held that 'a service provider must have more than a general knowledge or reason to know that its service is being used to sell counterfeit goods ... [s]ome contemporary knowledge of which particular listings are infringing or will infringe in the future is necessary.').

> indeed, and it is unrealistic to expect prosecutors to prove every specific infringement committed. Indeed, a principal reason for prosecuting website owners rather than end-users is that it is a more efficient and effective way of protecting copyright. […] However, although there may be a shift to 'general knowledge' in this context, the knowledge requirement must remain a very high threshold to cross. This is because the accessories are not those who *actually* infringe the rights of the copyright holders, and extending liability from the primary infringers to accessories should only occur if the accessories are culpable and blameworthy; this can only be established by a strict mental element.[140]

So, while a high knowledge threshold is appropriate in view of the parasitic nature of accessory liability, at the same time it obviously impedes attempts to hold intermediaries accountable for their users' actions.[141]

Once again, a return to the basics can be illuminating. As established in Chapter 4, as a rule, in European tort law the knowledge requirement must be applied in a generalised manner.[142] It is therefore not necessary for the defendant to have foreseen or been aware of the precise sequence of events that resulted in the injury, as long as it was clear that certain conduct was highly likely to cause it. Instead, knowledge must be related to risk, so that what is relevant is whether or not a particular conduct can foreseeably cause harm of a general type, e.g., to bodily integrity or property.[143] Of course, such generalised knowledge won't necessary include a mere hunch that another may potentially commit a wrong: in the words of the infallible Hercule Poirot, 'knowledge is one thing; suspicion is another'.[144] This will be all the more so, when the suspicion refers to anonymous parties of unascertainable numbers infringing unidentified works. At the same time, it is entirely possible for general knowledge to exist that is more than mere suspicion. Van Dam gives an example from the German BGH involving a pregnant woman who was injured in a car accident:

> When she delivered the baby three months later, it was found that the child suffered from brain damage. The BGH decided that it was not required that the driver knew or could have known that he would injure a pregnant woman or her child. 'It suffices to render the person liable who inflicted the injury if he should have realised the possibility of a

140. P S Davies, 'Accessory Liability: Protecting Intellectual Property Rights' (2011) 4 Intellectual Property Quarterly 390.

141. See also, P S Davies, *Accessory Liability* (Hart Publishing 2015) 44-49.

142. See s. 4.2.2.3.

143. C van Dam, European Tort Law (2nd ed., Oxford University Press 2013) para. 810-2.

144. A Christie, *Death in the Clouds* (Hercule Poirot Series Book 12) (Kindle edition, Harper Collins 2010); Longmore J expressed the same sentiment in *Credit Lyonnais Bank Nederland NV (now Generale Bank Nederland NV) v. Export Credits Guarantee Department*, [1996] C.L.C. 11. See, P S Davies, *Accessory Liability* (h 2015) 44-49.

damaging result in general; it need not be foreseeable what form the damage would take in detail and what damage might occur.'[145]

Accordingly, in the same way that a supermarket does not need to know the identity of the person who will slip on a cabbage leaf and break her knee for the risk that somebody might do so to be foreseeable,[146] an internet intermediary does not need to know the exact copyright-protected work that will be infringed or the identity of the primary infringer to be said to have sufficient knowledge to predict that a copyright infringement is highly likely.[147] General knowledge should, accordingly, be an acceptable standard.

In this regard, it is important to emphasise that knowledge is not intent: its results are not as immediate or detrimental – as shall be shown below, other safety valves against inappropriately wide knowledge-based accessory liability are built into the system, in particular in the form of the pairing of different kinds of knowledge with different appropriate duties of care. What this means is that the standard of care can subsequently be further calibrated to the type of knowledge, so that different obligations attach to general knowledge than those generated by specific knowledge.[148] Once this is understood, it becomes far less crucial to carefully control against an overexpansion of the definition of knowledge in the same way that is necessary in intent. As a result, a divergence at this point from the general tort framework is at this point not required, while, at the same time, the inclusion of general knowledge into the proposed liability framework can go a long way to compensating for any excessive difficulties in the establishment of liability caused by the exclusion of general intent.

Finally, as with specific knowledge, in the area of general knowledge too, some consideration must be had for the concept of knowledge of the future. Is it possible for an intermediary to be said to have general knowledge of impending infringement? One way of establishing future-oriented general knowledge might be through statistical research that reveals high percentages of infringing content on the intermediary's website or network. Simester, talking about complicity as a requirement for criminal liability, suggests that a computer manufacturer who knows that, statistically speaking, 30% of its customers will use the product to copy files illegally cannot be said to have sufficient knowledge to ground liability: there is insufficient evidence to

145. C van Dam, *European Tort Law* (2nd ed., Oxford University Press 2013) para. 810-2, referring to BGH 11 January 1972, BGHZ 58, 48, 56 = NJW 1972, 1126 = JZ 1972, 363.

146. See e.g., BGH 28 January 1976, BGHZ 66, 51 = NJW 1976, 712 = JZ 1976, 776 = VersR 1976, 589.

147. A N Dixon, 'Liability of Users and Third Parties for Copyright Infringements on the Internet: Overview of International Developments' in A Strowel (ed.), *Peer-to-Peer File Sharing and Secondary Liability in Copyright Law* (Edward Elgar Publishing 2009) 38.

148. M Bartholomew & P F McArdle, 'Causing Infringement' (2011) 64(3) Vanderbilt Law Review 675.

make the commission of an infringement by a given customer foreseeable.[149] Davies, returning the discussion to tort, agrees that vagaries must not be allowed to suffice, but wonders whether that conclusion should hold if the infringing percentage is raised to 60%, 75% or 90%.[150] At this point it is worth again considering more traditional types of manufacturers: although obviously a knife producer cannot be held accountable for every murder committed with its knives, fatal stabbings are thankfully relatively rare events. The situation might therefore be different for a manufacturer who has good reason to know that its knives are highly likely to be used for murderous purposes.[151] So if, hypothetically, a knife seller were to operate in a location where a significant percentage of knives sold are used to commit crimes, it might not be unreasonable to suggest that the shopkeeper and the supplier who kept him in stock could foresee with reasonable certainty that a given sale would result in criminal activity and should therefore bear some responsibility. For the sake of legal certainty, it might be convenient in such cases if a legal limit were to be set by law. Returning to the area of intermediary accessory copyright liability, it could, thus, hypothetically be pre-established by the legislator that, if the infringing content on an online platform is, for example, over 50%, general knowledge must be assumed. Stricter or more lenient thresholds could also be envisioned.

How would an intermediary know if it has crossed such a general knowledge threshold? Is the resultant conclusion that all intermediaries must undertake regular statistical research of the content available on their services to investigate the prevalence of copyright infringement? That seems a bit excessive, as well as of doubtful legality in view of Article 15 of the E-Commerce Directive and the 'fair balancing' of fundamental rights. It will moreover be mostly unnecessary: if infringement on a website is indeed of such formidable proportions, less exact indications will be hard to avoid. So, if an intermediary regularly receives high numbers of notices of infringement, it may be said that it, at least, ought to have known that its platform posed a high risk for copyright infringement, if nowhere else than with regard to infringements of a similar kind as those notified. General knowledge of the risk of infringement may also be established if the intermediary was aware of the existence of a safety rule that required it to take certain precautionary measures in order to avoid infringement: if an intermediary knows that measures are necessary to avoid infringement, then presumably it will also know that there is a risk that infringement might otherwise occur.

149. A Simester, 'The Mental Element in Complicity' (2006) 122 Law Quarterly Review 578, at note 54.

150. P S Davies, 'Accessory Liability: Protecting Intellectual Property Rights' (2011) 4 Intellectual Property Quarterly 390; P S Davies, 'Accessory Liability for Assisting Torts' (2011) 70(2) Cambridge Law Journal 353.

151. P S Davies, 'Accessory Liability for Assisting Torts' (2011) 70(2) Cambridge Law Journal 353.

5.3.2.3 Knowledge Floors and Knowledge Ceilings

What are the highest and lowers levels of knowledge that may be expected of an intermediary? It should be clear that the scientific state of the art provides the floor for the assessment of an intermediary's knowledge:[152] if acquiring the knowledge of the infringement would have been simply impossible for anybody in the same position as the intermediary, liability cannot be imposed. As a result, the possibilities enabled by current technology, such as automated monitoring and filtering tools, are particularly significant:[153] where it would be technically impossible to implement a system that allows the intermediary to acquire knowledge of the risk of infringement, it will not be possible to suggest that the intermediary had or ought to have had sufficient knowledge to ground negligence. At the other end of the spectrum, a definite ceiling to such fact-finding missions is set by the legality of the measures used to collect knowledge: if it would be illegal for the intermediary to implement a certain knowledge-creating measure or for the State to demand that an intermediary implement it, then it cannot be said that the intermediary 'ought to' have had the knowledge it could only have received by using it. The legality of a selection of knowledge-giving measures will be examined in detail below in the section on duties of care.[154]

Aside from these general rules that bind all intermediaries, the ceiling and floor of the requisite knowledge may not be fixed, but will depend on the circumstances of each case. So, for example, the size of an intermediary might play a role in this regard: a higher standard of knowledge could conceivably be expected of a world-class behemoth such as Google than of an SME or a single-author blog. Conversely of course, it might also be that, in a material case, the opposite effect is encountered, so that a big intermediary which has larger quantities of content passing through its networks might have a harder time acquiring certain knowledge. The social role of the intermediary could also be relevant in this regard. Consequently, when determining the level of knowledge that may be required of a reasonable intermediary, an examination the professional ethics expected in the sector is pertinent. If an intermediary does not have knowledge that similar operators agree is expected, that should be taken as a reliable indication that something is amiss[155] – the diligent economic operator once again raises its head.

---

152. C van Dam, *European Tort Law* (2nd ed., Oxford University Press 2013) para. 810-4.
153. C van Dam, *European Tort Law* (2nd ed., Oxford University Press 2013) para. 810-4.
154. See s. 5.5.
155. Codes of conduct adopted by groups of similar intermediaries could theoretically offer a good point of reference in this regard. Unfortunately, those that exist however for the most part don't consider copyright. So, for example, according to the code of practice of the UK's internet services providers' association (ISPA UK), 'Members shall provide ISPA with a point of contact to receive notices from the IWF' (the Internet Watch Foundation, responsible for removing criminal information from the internet). Violation

To summarise the above analysis, it is suggested that knowledge should constitute the mental element of a European negligence-based framework for intermediary accessory copyright liability. For this purpose, the standard set in the E-Commerce Directive's hosting safe harbour should be copied. This establishes a hybrid objective/subjective threshold that consists of awareness of facts and circumstances that would make infringement apparent to a diligent economic operator. In addition, a broad reach that encompasses both general and specific knowledge as acceptable possibilities is proposed, under the understanding that further refinement should be picked up further down in the duty-determination process.

The investigation of the concept of knowledge allows another section to be added to the liability flowchart. Although it is not yet complete, as can be seen in Figure 5.3, the European regime for the accessory copyright liability of the negligent intermediary is slowly beginning to take clear shape.

Figure 5.3 Intermediary Accessory Copyright Liability Flowchart: Knowledge

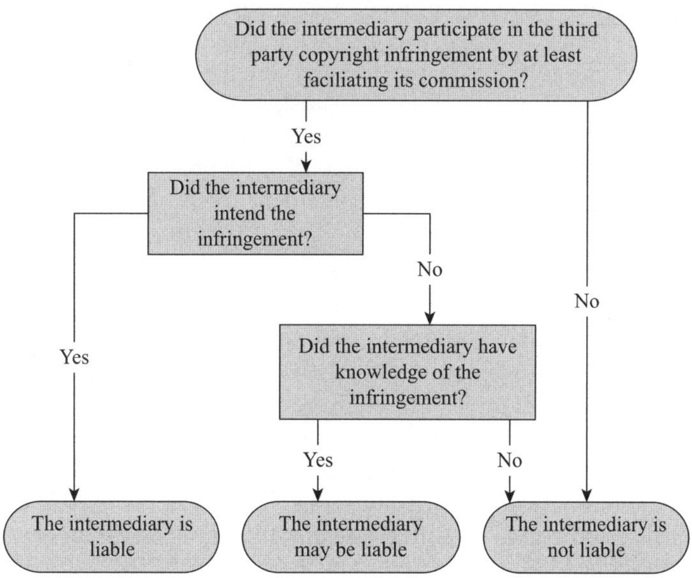

5.4 'SOMETHING MORE': DUTIES OF CARE

If an intermediary causally and knowingly participated in the copyright infringement of a third party – that is to say, if the conduct element of intermediary accessory liability is supplemented by a mental element of

of this obligation should therefore be equated with wilful blindness. ISPA UK, 'Code of Practice', adopted 25 January 1999, available at: www.ispa.org.uk.

knowledge of the risk of infringement – does liability automatically ensue? Is knowing causal participation alone sufficient to substantiate liability? For that to be the case, it would have to be identified as a violation of the standard of conduct in its own right, i.e., as negligent behaviour in which the reasonable intermediary would refuse to engage.[156]

A comparative overview of the national intermediary liability regimes for accessory copyright infringement, as well as of existing European provisions, would suggest that that is not the case. In England and Germany, joint tortfeasance requires intent or, at a very minimum, gross negligence.[157] This indeed is the precise roadblock both countries have encountered in trying to adapt their existing law to the context of the internet.[158] France in theory applies a more permissive negligence approach, but sets high standards for the finding of a *faute* in intermediary accessory liability, which first require the violation of *obligations de sécurité,* i.e., duties to safeguard another's interests.[159] In intermediary liability specifically, these obligations translate into a set of *diligences appropriées,* as identified by the case law and parsed down by the legislature.[160] Even Germany's *Störerhaftung* approach, despite being limited only to injunctive relief, is predicated on the violation of a 'duty to review'.[161] Finally, none of the safe harbours enshrined in the E-Commerce Directive allow for liability on the basis of mere knowing causal assistance. Instead, Article 14's hosting safe harbour – arguably the strictest of the three – requires a failure to take-down or disable an infringement upon acquitting knowledge of it before liability can come into question. This approach has the endorsement of the CJEU. In *L'Oréal v. eBay,* that court declared of an online marketplace that:

> the mere fact that the operator of an online marketplace stores offers for sale on its server, sets the terms of its service, is remunerated for that service and provides general information to its customers cannot have

156. See e.g., Art. 4:101 PETL or Art. 3:102 DCFR.
157. W van Gerven et al., *Tort Law* (Hart Publishing 2000) 430. For England see also *Sea Shepherd UK v. Fish & Fish Ltd* [2015] UKSC 10 and *CBS Songs v. Amstrad* [1988] UKHL 15 (12 May 1988). For Germany see also Art. 830 BGB, as interpreted in view of the definitions borrowed from German criminal law.
158. See above Ch. 3, ss 3.12, 3.1.3 and 3.3.2.
159. P le Tourneau, *Droit de la responsabilité et des contracts – Régimes d'indemnisation* (9th ed., Dalloz 2013) 7203-7205.
160. A Lepage, *Libertés et droits fondamentaux à l'épreuve de l'internet* (Litec 2003) 287; C Féral-Schuhl, *Cyberdroit – Le Droit à l'Épreuve de l'Internet* (6th ed., Dalloz 2010) 743-901.
161. A Bayer, 'Liability 2.0 – Does the Internet Environment Require New Standards for Secondary Liability? An Overview of the Current Legal Situation in Germany' in MJ Adelmann et al., *Patents and Technological Progress in a Globalized World* (Springer 2009) 365; M Leistner, 'Common Principles of Secondary Liability?' in A Ohly (ed.), *Common Principles of European Intellectual Property Law* (Mohr Siebeck 2012) 128.

the effect of denying it the exemptions from liability provided for by Directive 2000/31.[162]

The comparative conclusion is clear: knowledge is not intent. Absent the strong mental participation that intent demonstrates, in view of the immediate and severe consequences that the opposite approach would have, accessory liability must be carefully controlled so as to avoid an over-expansion that nullifies the relevance of the mental element and imposes liability on anybody who in any way demonstrates a causal participation in another's copyright infringement. As a result, liability on the basis of a coupling of the conduct standard with a mental element of knowledge should be excluded as an option.[163] An intermediary may not be held liable for simply unintentionally, if knowingly, facilitating or otherwise causally participating in a copyright infringement committed by somebody else.[164]

Are there any other options? Yen provides a hint: '[s]omething more is required, namely a finding that the defendant's behavior was unreasonable with respect to the plaintiff. Fault significantly limits third party copyright liability because many individuals who might limit or stop infringing behavior are not unreasonable for having failed to do so'.[165] And indeed, knowledge as a mental element brings us into the realm of negligence.[166] In negligence, the reasonable intermediary – the diligent economic operator – steps into the limelight: while infringing intention is always unreasonable, in negligence, reasonability is much harder to pin-point. How should it be attempted? Negligence, as has been repeatedly emphasised, is found at the intersection between risk and care: if a defendant creates a risk of a sufficiently grave and probable harm, she will be obliged to take corresponding measures of care.[167] Only if she does not, will liability result. This indicates the next step in the liability flowchart: that of affirmative duties of

162. CJEU, C-324/09, *L'Oréal v. eBay International*, 12 July 2011 at 115.

163. Davies disagrees, see P S Davies, *Accessory Liability* (Hart Publishing 2015) 52-54 and 213-222; P S Davies, 'Accessory Liability for Assisting Torts' (2011) 70(2) Cambridge Law Journal 353; P S Davies, 'Accessory Liability: Protecting Intellectual Property Rights' (2011) 4 Intellectual Property Quarterly 390. However Davies also recommends a stricter knowledge standard of actual knowledge, thus controlling accessory liability in a different way. That might make sense for accessory liability generally, but in European intermediary accessory liability for copyright, existing provisions, by setting a knowledge standard of constructive knowledge and encouraging the expeditious removal or disabling of injurious information, push in a different direction.

164. G Williams, *Joints Torts and Contributory Negligence* (Stevens & Sons Ltd 1951), 14-15.

165. A Yen, 'Third Party Copyright after Grokster' (2007) 16(3) Information & Communications Technology Law 233.

166. C van Dam, *European Tort Law* (2nd ed., Oxford University Press 2013) paras 801 and 805-1.

167. See above, Ch. 4, s. 4.2.2.

care. Since liability by misfeasance for the provision of the means or opportunity to commit the infringement must be excluded, whether liability for nonfeasance on the basis of the violation of an obligation to act exists should instead be examined.[168]

This possibility should come as no surprise. Indeed, as already noted in Chapter 4, the essence of accessory negligence liability lies in omission.[169] In the area of intermediary accessory copyright liability, this will mean the omission of affirmative duties to attempt to prevent, discontinue or limit third party copyright infringement.[170] An intermediary should consequently be said to have behaved negligently (and therefore unreasonably) with regard to the copyright infringement of another when it took a risk of, at a minimum, causally participating in another's copyright infringement, knew that it was taking such a risk, and did not take all reasonable affirmative counterbalancing measures of care incumbent upon it to avoid or terminate the infringement. If the intermediary did diligently take all the precautionary measures that due care dictates it should to counteract the risk it knows it has created, it will nullify that risk and with it its own liability. In other words, the knowing risky behaviour of an intermediary places it under a duty to expend all appropriate efforts to avoid facilitating infringement.[171] Only dereliction of that duty will result in liability.

The E-Commerce Directive sanctions this scheme, at least in the area of host service providers: according to Recital 48, Member States are entirely free to require host service providers 'to apply duties of care, which can reasonably be expected from them and which are specified by national law, in order to detect and prevent certain types of illegal activities', even where they are protected by the safe harbour of Article 14. Even beyond this provision, all three safe harbours designate conditions for their enjoyment – arguably, these indicate the duties of care that the European legislator thinks are reasonable to impose on intermediaries offering the services in question. A substantive regime on intermediary liability would therefore best account for this in the identification of the measures of care incumbent on the providers of mere conduit, caching and hosting activities. Greater flexibility could surround the identification of the duties incumbent on other providers.

168. C van Dam, *European Tort Law* (2nd ed., Oxford University Press 2013) para. 808-1.
169. C von Bar, *The Common European Law of Torts – Vol. II* (Clarendon Press 2000) para. 203; C McIvor, *Third Party Liability in Tort* (Hart Publishing 2006) 9; M Lunney & K Oliphant, *Tort Law – Text and Materials* (3rd ed., Oxford University Press 2007) 481.
170. A N Dixon, 'Liability of Users and Third Parties for Copyright Infringements on the Internet: Overview of International Developments' in A Strowel (ed.), *Peer-to-Peer File Sharing and Secondary Liability in Copyright Law* (Edward Elgar Publishing 2009) 38-39.
171. See Art. 4:103 of the PETL.

On this basis, the European intermediary accessory copyright liability flowchart gains another step. This is shown in Figure 5.4.

Figure 5.4 Intermediary Accessory Copyright Liability Flowchart: Duties of Care

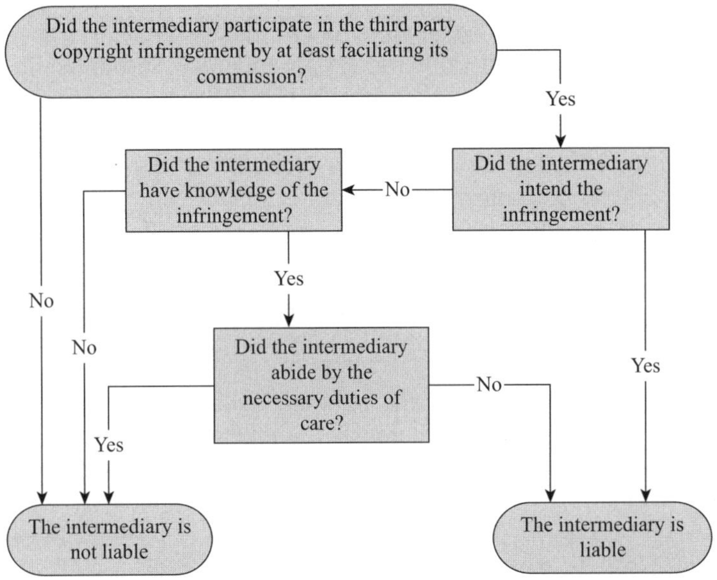

What duties of care are incumbent on intermediaries who know that their services are used by third parties in a copyright infringement? In other words, what is the requisite standard of care that is expected of an internet intermediary that fulfils both the conduct and mental element of negligence liability with regard to the copyright infringements of others? Much that has been written about the precautionary measures available to intermediaries in the service of copyright enforcement, yet a general system that can be applied to specific measures to provide concrete answers regarding whether or not they can be expected of internet intermediaries in the enforcement of copyright has not yet been explicitly formulated in EU law. In its absence, answers must be searched for in the surrounding framework.[172] Two main sources of law comprise this framework: the rules of European tort law and the law of fundamental rights. Both of these steer in the same direction, by emphasising the centrality of balancing to a justice-based solution.

---

172. C Angelopoulos, 'Sketching the Outline of a Ghost: the Fair Balance between Copyright and Fundamental Rights in Intermediary Third Party Liability' (2015) 17(6) Info – The Journal of Policy, Regulation and Strategy for Telecommunications, Information and Media 72.

5.4.1 Balancing the Duties of Care

As we saw in Chapter 4, the determination of the duties incumbent under the rules of tort law on persons for the avoidance of liability depends on a process of justice-based legal reasoning. This is usually described in the language of balancing:[173]

> In this world, absolute rights are rare. Even the probably highest-ranking rights such as the right to life, to bodily integrity, and to health may be infringed by someone without him being liable for the consequences. This is because these rights have to be balanced against society's pivotal freedom to act. Tort law systems usually provide for this balancing act through the requirement of negligent conduct which means that the freedom to act must be used in a careful way, sufficiently taking into consideration other persons' rights and interests.[174]

Thus, when deciding whether tort liability will exist or not, the claimant's interests must be assessed in the context of the interests of the defendant. The general interest, as well as the interests of third parties must also be taken into account.[175] The resultant balancing act represents the behavioural boundaries that continuously impinge upon each individual in all aspects of our communal existence, informing us of the obligations incumbent upon us, as well as of the freedoms we enjoy as members of a society. Seen from this angle, it can therefore be said that the reasonable person is the person that correctly executes this balancing act within the context of her own behaviour. By the same logic, the reasonable intermediary, from a copyright perspective, will be the one that strikes, in its treatment of infringements, the right balance between its interests and the interests of all other involved parties.

How is the outcome of this balancing process to be determined? Significantly, tort law balancing is mirrored in a sister balancing act situated within the law of fundamental rights. As we saw in Chapter 2, the standard according to which conflicts between non-absolute fundamental rights are usually approached by Europe's highest courts is that of proportionality. In the case of conflicting relative fundamental rights, this will boil down to a balancing test. Fundamental rights balancing is particularly important from a copyright perspective, given that, absent a valid European tort law regime, the CJEU has turned, in its search for an appropriate conflict resolution mechanism, to fundamental rights as the only common touchstone between the national legal systems.[176] As a result, the relevant EU-level case law rests

---

173. See above, Ch. 4, s. 4.6.
174. C van Dam, *European Tort Law* (2nd ed., Oxford University Press 2013) para. 711-2.
175. European Group on Tort Law, *Principles of European Tort Law – Text and Commentary* (Springer 2005) 77-78.
176. X Groussot, 'Rock the KaZaA: Another Clash of Fundamental Rights' (2008) 45 Common Market Law Review 1745.

heavily on the notion of a 'fair balance' between copyright and conflicting fundamental rights to assess the duties that rest on intermediaries to prevent infringing conduct on their networks and websites.[177]

This substitution is not inappropriate. As shown in Chapter 4, tort rights and human rights are intrinsically intertwined: tort rights enable the 'horizontal' protection of human rights, while, through the proper formulation of their tort laws, States likewise fulfil their vertical protective duties towards private persons. Although the two systems of law therefore differ drastically as to their field of application and in particular the identification of the relevant 'duty-bearers',[178] in their parallel pursuit of a basic standard of decent human behaviour they constitute two sides of the same coin. This interconnection means that the standard of care that can be imposed on private individuals by State-enacted legal provisions must be delineated by reference to the underlying human rights obligations of that State: the duties imposed upon private parties by the State are reflections of the duties incumbent upon the State towards private parties. In the EU context, the fundamental rights recognised under the Charter serve the precise same purpose: according to Article 51 of the Charter, the fundamental rights protected therein are addressed to the institutions and bodies of the Union, as well as – by extension – to the Member States when they are implementing Union law. Accordingly, they should always be accounted for in both the formulation and application of any EU-level legal provision.

As a consequence of this interconnectivity, while EU copyright law can be seen as a implementation of the European legislator's obligation[179] to protect copyright under Article 17(2) of the Charter ('[i]ntellectual property shall be protected'), the EU law-maker is also under equally pressing obligations to ensure that, in the construction of that law, it does not overstep the mark to the detriment of other competing fundamental rights. European fundamental rights law in this way guides European tort law by indicating what may or may not be required of individuals through the enactment of tort rules, as well as what must or must not. This approach is particularly pertinent to the process of constructing a European regime for intermediary accessory copyright liability, such as that which is proposed in this chapter: by introducing such a regime, the European legislator would be instructing the Member States on what obligations to impose on intermediaries with regard to copyright enforcement. In its formulation, it must therefore avoid the issue of rules that would impose duties on intermediaries that would

177. C Angelopoulos, 'Sketching the Outline of a Ghost: the Fair Balance between Copyright and Fundamental Rights in Intermediary Third Party Liability' (2015) 17(6) Info – The Journal of Policy, Regulation and Strategy for Telecommunications, Information and Media 72.

178. Internet Governance Forum, Dynamic Coalition on Platform Responsibility, draft document on 'Recommendations on Terms of Service and Human Rights', available at http://review.intgovforum.org.

179. With due regard for the principle of subsidiarity, see Art. 51 of the Charter.

violate fundamental rights law: EU tort law must operate within the confines of EU fundamental rights law.

In the final analysis therefore, fair balance guides the reasonable person. Yet crucially, fundamental rights can also not provide the full picture: fundamental rights law can only tell us whether a provision of tort law encroaches upon the very basic standards that it sets. The construction of a full, substantive European intermediary liability regime will obviously require something more intricate. It is at this point that European tort law can step forward to fill in the gaps between the rough outlines set by fundamental rights. Ultimately, balancing operates at the meeting point between private law and public law. Tort law balancing and fundamental rights law balancing each provide a differing perspective that can illuminate separate parts of the same puzzle: a reasonable intermediary must be defined as one that strikes the right balance between its own interests and those of others, but that right balance cannot be determined by the law-maker in a way that would impinge on the fundamental rights of other private parties. The notion of the reasonable person in tort law can therefore be seen as an extension of the notion of fair balance in fundamental rights law: from this perspective, tort rights really are fundamental rights.

5.4.2 Structuring Balancing: The Criteria of Care

Whether occurring within the framework of tort law or of fundamental rights, balancing is a quintessentially open-ended instrument. As a result, merely observing that a fair balance must be struck in the imposition of duties of care on internet intermediaries in the pursuit of copyright enforcement is not sufficient.[180] Although useful as a starting point for the legal analysis, on its own, the notion balancing as a legal principle is much too vague to offer sufficient guarantees of rationality, objectivity, transparency and legal theoretical coherence.[181] If no other tools are provided to help flesh it out, intuition, obscure reasoning and subjectivity will thus inevitably be left to fill the gaps. As Smet correctly argues, to overcome these deficiencies, the balancing exercise must be structured, so that instead of resulting in ad hoc, unpredictable assessments for each individual case it grapples with on the basis of the subjective assessments of the individual employing it, it may be

180. J Griffiths, 'Constitutionalising or Harmonising? The Court of Justice, the Right to Property and European Copyright Law' (2013) 38(1) European Law Review 65; T-E Synodinou, 'Intermediaries' Liability for Online Copyright Infringement in the EU: Evolutions and Confusions' (2015) 31 Computer Law & Security Review 57; O Fischman Afori, 'Proportionality – A New Mega Standard in European Copyright Law' (2014) International Review of Intellectual Property and Competition Law (IIC), 889; S Kulk & F Borgesius, 'Filtering for Copyright Enforcement in Europe after the Sabam Cases' (2012) 34(11) European Intellectual Property Review 791.

181. S Smet, *Resolving Conflicts between Human Rights: A Theoretical Analysis in the Context of the ECHR* (unpublished PhD thesis, Ghent University 2014) 118.

turned into a useful legal device capable of delivering reliable, well-grounded, justice-based conclusions.[182] To this end, the balancing exercise – whatever the level of law at which it is executed – must be infused with objective criteria that can guide its correct deployment.[183]

It therefore becomes clear that, instead of offering a silver bullet for a resolution of conflicts between rights that is simultaneously effortless, tidy and justice-based, in practice, in both the areas of tort law and of fundamental rights, considerable further refinement is necessary before balancing can achieve a proper control of judicial arbitrariness. In this light, the main criticisms against balancing as a useful judicial tool outlined in Chapters 2 and 4 must be conceded. At the same time, it should be understood that balancing is to be approached merely as a metaphor intended to guide juridical thought[184] – or perhaps more precisely, a formula for the investigation of what is ultimately a policy choice.[185] The language of balancing can thus be seen simply as a way of explaining that no obvious solution to a given problem exists: the issue at stake is a complex one, comprised of multiple factors that must all be considered – 'weighed', so to speak.[186] At the same time, as opposed to the simplistic Hand Formula or even Alexy's more intricate Law of Balancing, which limit themselves to mathematical equations, balancing properly understood can be used to welcome multiple, potentially shifting criteria into its fold.[187] At the end of the day, while balancing might be a metaphor, it is not necessarily an empty promise: instead, it can be fleshed out into a toolkit of rational deliberation

182. S Smet, *Resolving Conflicts between Human Rights: A Theoretical Analysis in the Context of the ECHR* (unpublished PhD thesis, Ghent University 2014) 9-10 and 193-257.

183. E Barendt, 'Balancing Freedom of Expression and Privacy: The Jurisprudence of the Strasbourg Court' (2009) 1 Journal of Media Law 49.

184. See also, M Kumm & A D Walen, 'Human Dignity and Proportionality: Deontic Pluralism in Balancing' in G Huscroft, B W Miller & G Webber, *Proportionality and the Rule of Law: Rights, Justification, Reasoning* (Cambridge University Press 2014), where the authors clarify: 'Balancing is not a mechanical exercise. Balancing is a metaphor we use to describe a residual category within rights analysis that registers the importance of the various concerns at stake. But the idea of balancing itself says nothing about what kind of things are relevant or what weight to assign the relevant concerns. When balancing is misunderstood as a technique that somehow allows lawyers and courts to avoid substantive moral reasoning or engagement with policy it is likely to lead to bad results'.

185. See M W Hesselink, 'How Many Systems of Private Law Are There in Europe? On Plural Legal Sources, Multiple Identities and the Unity of Law' in L Niglia (ed.), *Pluralism and European Private Law* (Hart Publishing 2013) 199.

186. A Barak, *The Judge in a Democracy* (Princeton University Press 2009) 165; J Stapleton, 'Duty of Care Factors: A Selection from the Judicial Menus' in P Cane & J Stapleton (eds.), *The Law of Obligations: Essays in Celebration of John Fleming* (Clarendon Press 1995) 59-95.

187. J Stapleton, 'Duty of Care Factors: A Selection from the Judicial Menus' in P Cane & J Stapleton (eds.), *The Law of Obligations: Essays in Celebration of John Fleming* (Clarendon Press 1995) 59-95.

– like any toolkit, however, its usefulness lies not in the box, but in the devices it contains.

What are the tools of balancing? The legal criteria that provide a rational standard for balancing, as they present themselves in both tort law and the law of fundamental rights, were described in Chapter 4. Here we will briefly revisit them before moving on to their application to the issue of intermediary negligence accessory liability.

As was shown in Chapter 4, the central balancing act in European tort law is that between risk and care: a high risk indicates a need for great care, while a lower risk might be counterbalanced with lesser care. Risk consists of *the seriousness of the expected damage* and *the probability that the damage will happen*. But risk is measured by reference only to the right-holder. Risk therefore cannot be allowed to alone determine the height of care due: consideration must also be had for the interests of others. Against the pressure that risk imposes to heighten the care taken, there therefore push other opposing forces: the *character and benefit of the conduct* and the *burden of precautionary measures*. Finally, two elements relating to the person of the defendant must also be considered: the *knowledge* of the defendant regarding the risk of damage and his *ability* to avoid it.[188] Although these latter two also function as hard conditions of liability, not merely factors to be balanced, they are at the same time relevant to the determination of duties of care: both the type of knowledge and extent of ability can influence whether or not a specific measure of care is warranted or not. A certain measure might require specific knowledge, while another might be acceptable only with general knowledge. Ability too must be applied to each assessed measure of care to determine its eligibility and effectiveness.

On this basis, six main criteria of the balancing test that determine the standard of care in negligence emerge: (a) the seriousness of the expected damage; (b) the probability that an accident will happen; (c) the character and the benefit of the conduct; (d) the burden of precautionary measures; (e) the defendant's knowledge; and (f) the defendant's abilities. Where the duties of care in question are duties of affirmative care, an optional seventh can be added to the set, in the form of (g) a 'special reason' justifying an obligation to act. In accordance with Article 4:103 PETL, these shall be: (a) the existence of a specific legal provision requiring it; (b) the creation or control of a dangerous situation; (c) a special relationship between parties; or (d) the seriousness of the harm on the one side and the ease of avoiding the damage on the other side. The reasonable person should be understood as the person who correctly balances all seven of these forces.

Balancing in the law of fundamental rights moves along strikingly similar lines. As shown in Chapter 2, Smet also suggests a list of seven criteria that can be used to apply a structured balancing test to cases of

188. C van Dam, *European Tort Law* (2nd ed., Oxford University Press 2013) para. 805-2.

conflicting relative fundamental rights: the value criterion, the impact criterion, the core-periphery criterion, the additional rights criterion, the general interest criterion, the purpose criterion and the responsibility criterion.[189] When applied to intermediary liability these can be whittled down to only five: the value criterion is not useful in cases of conflicts between relative rights, all of which should be considered as being of equal intrinsic value.[190] Likewise, the purpose criterion is only relevant in exceptional cases, which cannot be said to include matters of intermediary liability for copyright infringement.[191] This leaves five: the impact criterion, the core-periphery criterion, the additional rights criterion, the general interest criterion and the responsibility criterion.

These criteria pose a marked resemblance to the seven factors of negligence: the impact criterion, like tort law's notion of risk, considers the seriousness and probability of the damage. The core/periphery criterion can be seen as a further elaboration of the notion of risk that digs deeper into the seriousness element: how essential were the aspects of the right that were damaged? The criteria of additional rights and the general interest also offer a new dimension to the question of risk, opening it up to the interests of others besides the copyright holder – mainly however, these two criteria should be seen as corresponding to risk's counterbalancing factors, as considered though the lens of the benefit of the conduct and the burden of precautionary measures: the promotion of the rights of third parties or the additional rights of the defendant, as well as the general interest might reveal a possible benefit of the defendant's conduct or at least a strong argument against taking action to counteract the risk through damaging those rights. Finally, the responsibility criterion could be seen as corresponding to the defendant's knowledge and abilities, as well as any 'special reasons' for the imposition of affirmative duties.

In conclusion, the balancing criteria used in tort law and in the law of fundamental rights can essentially be interpreted as corresponding terms in a different legal language. On the basis of this analysis, we can thus identify four main factors dictated by both the law of fundamental rights and by European tort law as appropriate considerations through which a 'fair balance' may be achieved in intermediary liability and which will indicate what can be demanded of the intermediary in the provision of online

---

189. S Smet, *Resolving Conflicts between Human Rights: A Theoretical Analysis in the Context of the ECHR* (unpublished PhD thesis, Ghent University 2014) 192-193.
190. As was shown in Ch. 2 all non-absolute relative rights are of equal value in absolute terms within the fundamental rights framework. See s. 2.3. Although a stronger hierarchy of rights is often adopted within the tort law framework (Art. 2:102 PETL is indicative), the rights involved in the balancing of intermediary liability are all neither top (life, bodily or mental integrity, human dignity and liberty) nor bottom-rung rights (pure economic loss).
191. See above, s. 4.6.2.

services. These are: (1) the *risk* created, (2) the *benefit* of the conduct; the (3) *burden* of the measures of care; and (4) any potential *responsibility* of the intermediary. Each criterion must be examined both through the lens of European tort law and of the law of fundamental rights, the first to determine the contours of reasonable intermediary behaviour by reference to consistent legal theory and social perceptions of justice and the second to make sure that the final standard is a permissible one.

Just as in Van Dam's formula of negligence,[192] these four criteria of a 'fairly-balanced negligence liability' for the copyright infringements of others can be viewed as consisting of two sets of antipodal factors: the risk of the conduct is counterbalanced by the benefit of the conduct and the burden the measures of care must be weighed against the intermediary's responsibility to take them. Accordingly, two different factions of factors can be discerned: those criteria pushing in favour of liability (risk and responsibility), as opposed to those pushing against (the benefit of the conduct and the burden of the measures of care).

Moving one step further, in the specific area of intermediary liability, the following further specifications of the four basic criteria can be identified. The notion of risk can be broken down into: (a) *the seriousness of the damage* (including the core/periphery aspect) and (b) *the probability of damage*. The factor of the benefit of the conduct should be examined in view of: (a) *the interests of the intermediary*; (b) *the interests of the intermediaries' users*; and (c) *the general interest*. The same holds for the third factor of the burden of the measures of care. Finally, responsibility to take measures might arise from: (a) the type of knowledge of the risk that the intermediary has (*foreseeability* of the risk); (b) its skills with regard to the measure in question (*avoidability* of the risk); and (c) the existence of *a special duty* to take affirmative care. The resultant scheme can be represented as in Figure 5.5.

192. See Ch. 4, s. 4.2.2.2.

Figure 5.5 The Criteria of Balancing

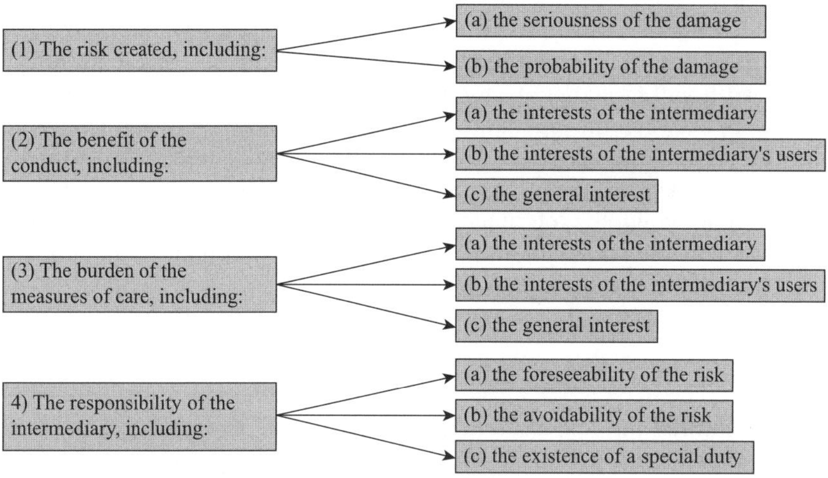

Of course, it should be kept in mind that, as has been noted numerous times above, attempts to provide an exhaustive list of every factor which might conceivably weigh in the scale will inevitably constitute an exercise in futility. In view of this, the criteria identified above are suitably broadly defined and adjustable, so as to enable them to operate in a catch-all manner in response to the circumstances of each case.

How can these criteria help us identify the duties of care incumbent on intermediaries for the enforcement of copyright? The standard of care for accessory intermediary copyright liability will lie at the crossroad between these four opposing forces: the carrefour of care. A reasonable intermediary is the one that navigates its way through this junction successfully. The higher the risk imposed by the intermediary's facilitating behaviour to the right-holder's copyright and the higher the intermediary's responsibility to prevent the damage, the more likely that a duty of care will burden the intermediary and the more exacting those duties might be. At the same time, the benefit the intermediary's conduct confers to its users, itself and society in general must also be considered, as must the harm that any measures of care could case to all these parties.

The optimum combination of all relevant factors indicates the answer to the intermediary's question as to the behaviour expected of it with regard to user copyright infringements: 'How much out of my own way should I go to protect somebody else's rights? How much of a hit to my own interests, the interests of my users and the general interest should I accept to protect the interests of copyright holders?' The answer that the optimally reasonable intermediary would give will signify the care that every intermediary should take or else face liability.

Ultimately, in this way, rather than attempting to apply fundamental rights tools to solve tort law problems *ex post*, through the *ex ante* creation, under the guidance of fundamental rights, of a tort law structure, more reliable solutions can be identified and put into practice. In the end, through a very traditional conception of fundamental rights that limits them to the relationship between the legislator and the private individual and keeps them out of the private interactions, a radical re-conceptualisation of accessory tort liability can be achieved.[193] This confirms the conclusion reached in Chapter 2 according to which the reference to fundamental rights by the CJEU should be approached not as an indication of the constitutionalisation of private law,[194] but of the Europeanisation of tort law.[195]

5.4.3 The Four Criteria of Care

Having identified the four criteria of care, we shall now proceed to analyse each in greater detail within the context of intermediary accessory copyright liability.

5.4.3.1 The Risk of Infringement

The first identified criterion is that of the risk of infringement. How should 'risky intermediary conduct' be determined? When does an intermediary act in a risky manner, such that it invites third party copyright infringement? As already noted, factors that indicate the existence of a risk are the *seriousness of the anticipated harm* and the *probability of that harm taking place*.

(a) The seriousness of the infringement

According to Article 17(2) of the EU's Charter, '[i]ntellectual property shall be protected'. Article 1 of Protocol 1 to the ECHR does not explicitly

193. Indeed, this phenomenon can be perceived in tort law generally, see M Arden, *Human Rights and European Law: Building New Legal Orders* (Oxford University Press 2015) 237, where she notes that the 'introduction of Convention values offered a means of modernizing the common law when it became out of touch with the needs of contemporary society'.

194. J M Smits, 'Private Law and Fundamental Rights: A Sceptical View' in T Barkhuysen & S Lindenbergh (eds.), *Constitutionalisation of Private Law* (Martinus Nijhoff, Leiden 2006) 9.

195. See Ch. 2, s. 2.4. See also: J Pila, 'Intellectual Property as a Case Study in Europeanization: Methodological Themes and Context' in A Ohly and J Pila (eds), *The Europeanization of Intellectual Property Law: Towards A European Legal Methodology* (Oxford University Press 2013) 23; J Griffiths, 'Constitutionalising or Harmonising? The Court of Justice, the Right to Property and European Copyright Law' (2013) 38(1) European Law Review 65; O Fischman Afori, 'Proportionality – A New Mega Standard in European Copyright Law' (2014) International Review of Intellectual Property and Competition Law (IIC) 889.

mention intellectual property, but has been interpreted by the ECHR as including it.[196] Nevertheless, it is 'not a particularly strong fundamental right that dominates all other fundamental rights'.[197] This middle-tier status is reflected in copyright's standing as a tort right as well: so, for example, according to the PETL, intellectual property is certainly not as important as the rights of life, bodily or mental integrity, human dignity and liberty (placed at the top of the hierarchy by Article 2:102(2) PETL), but is also not as insignificant as pure economic loss (at the very bottom of the pile under Article 2:102(4) PETL). Instead, under Article 2:102(3) PETL, it is due 'extensive protection'. It therefore also requires correspondingly serious protective measures.

In this regard, it is relevant to observe that the seriousness of the harm caused by a copyright infringement may not be as extensive as the seriousness of the harm caused by the violation of other more weighty rights. Consequently, it will not always follow that where a measure is taken for the protection of a certain right or interest, the same measure will be appropriate for the protection of copyright as well. This helps put into perspective assertions according to which, if a measure is employed to combat a different type of illegal online behaviour, it should also be enlisted for the enforcement of copyright. Instead, the different magnitude that different interests carry may very well result in different levels of protection.[198] So, in their 2011 Joint Declaration on Freedom of Expression and the Internet, the four rapporteurs on freedom of expression suggested that the '[m]andatory blocking of entire websites, IP addresses, ports, network protocols or types of uses (such as social networking) is an extreme measure – analogous to banning a newspaper or broadcaster – which can only be justified in accordance with international standards, for example where necessary to protect children against sexual abuse'.[199] The same mechanisms may, by

196. ECtHR, *Anheuser-Busch Inc v. Portugal,* application no. 73049/01, 11 January 2007; *Balan v. Moldova,* application no. 19247/03 29 January 2008*; Ashby Donald,* application no. 36769/08, 10 January 2013; *Neij and Sunde Kolmisoppi v. Sweden,* application no. 40397/12, 19 February 2013.

197. P Torremans, 'Article 17(2)' in S Peers, T Hervey, J Kenner & A Ward, *The EU Charter of Fundamental Rights: A Commentary* (Hart Publishing 2014) 504.

198. 'Filtering Away Infringement: Copyright, Injunctions and the Role of ISPs', Panel Session at 'Information Influx' International Conference, Amsterdam, 2-4 July 2014.

199. The United Nations (UN) Special Rapporteur on Freedom of Opinion and Expression, the Organization for Security and Co-Operation in Europe (OSCE) Representative on Freedom of the Media, the Organization of American States (OAS) Special Rapporteur on Freedom of Expression and the African Commission on Human and Peoples' Rights (ACHPR) Special Rapporteur on Freedom of Expression and Access to Information, 'Joint Declaration on Freedom of Expression and the Internet', 1 June 2011, p. 68. Indeed, child sexual abuse will often fall under the heading of torture, one of the few absolute rights protected under the ECHR and the Charter, see S Peers, 'Taking Rights Away – Limitations and Derogations' in S Peers & A Ward, *The EU Charter of Fundamental Rights: Politics, Law and Policy* (Hart Publishing 2004) 142-143, M

contrast, be disproportionate when applied for the protection against lesser harm, such as might result from the online infringement of a copyright. It is worth observing on this note that, in *Delfi,*[200] the ECtHR took a particularly severe view of intermediary liability that come into direct conflict with the previously established case law of the CJEU.[201] This discrepancy can arguably be ascribed to the fact that that case dealt, not with copyright infringement, but with hate speech, i.e., information that does not enjoy the same protection under freedom of expression:[202] a reasonable intermediary will not protect against copyright infringement to a greater or even necessarily equal extent as against other illegal activities of greater consequence.

In any case, this *in abstracto* assessment of the 'extensive' value of copyright as a property right is not enough. Further analysis of the specificities of the situation at hand will additionally be necessary.[203] In particular, the seriousness of the particular infringement will depend on the value of the work infringed: the higher that value, whether commercial or sentimental, the higher the level of care that may be demanded of the intermediary; conversely, the lower the value, the correspondingly lower or non-existent the expected duties of care as well. The number of infringements threatened could also prove important in this regard: an upload of a file by a user onto a BitTorrent client that makes it available to millions of potential downloaders must be assessed differently than a one-on-one exchange between friends conducted via an email service. Finally, it may also be possible that the circumstances of the right-holder should be taken into consideration: just as the loss of an eye by a one-eyed man is more detrimental than the loss of an eye by a fully sighted person,[204] the infringement of the copyright of an impoverished independent artist might carry different weight from the infringement of the rights held by a global multi-national conglomerate.

Finally, it should be considered that, aside from copyright, additional rights may strengthen the seriousness of the damage that the infringement occasions and, with it, the position of the right-holder: for example, extra

Nowak & A Charbord, 'Article 4 – Prohibition of Torture' in S Peers, T Hervey, J Kenner & A Ward, *The EU Charter of Fundamental Rights: A Commentary* (Hart Publishing 2014) 92-93. See also CJEU, C-112/00, *Schmidberger,* 12 June 2003.

200. ECtHR, *Delfi v. Estonia,* application no. 64569/09, Grand Chamber, 16 June 2015, at 15.

201. See above Ch. 2, s. 2.3.3.

202. See Joint dissenting opinion of Judges Sajó and Tsotsoria in ECtHR, *Delfi v. Estonia,* application no. 64569/09, Grand Chamber, 16 June 2015, at 15.

203. It is worth noting that, although the matter is controversial, most experts agree that despite significant efforts, it is difficult, if not impossible, to quantify the net effect of copyright piracy on the economy as a whole, see I Hargreaves, 'Digital Opportunity – A Review of Intellectual Property and Growth', Independent Report, May 2011, 73. This however is not a decisive fact in a justice-based approach.

204. C van Dam, *European Tort Law* (2nd ed., Oxford University Press 2013) para. 806-1; *Paris v. Stepney BC* [1950] UKHL 3 (13 December 1950).

ammunition for the claimant might be found in the protection of privacy, the right to reputation or freedom of expression. This could indicate, for example, that greater enforcement is necessary for the protection of a work that includes sensitive personal data, whether of the right-holder or another party: attempts to halt the online distribution of a person's private diaries may thus require more serious measures of care than cases of merely monetary concern.[205] Freedom of expression might also, under certain circumstances, be interpreted to include an author's right to disclose his work as he desires, thus requiring intermediaries to take action to ensure that right is not hijacked by users posting without the author's consent.[206] Finally, there is an argument that an infringement of the author's moral right to be identified in connection to his work and have that work treated appropriately by others constitutes a violation of human dignity.[207] This could indicate that copyright should be more strongly enforced where the work constitutes an important exercise of such additional rights on the part of the author. So, works of satire or parody or works which represent important contributions to a greater political or societal discussion may, for example, attract more substantial protection than cases of merely monetary concern.[208]

(b) The probability of infringement

The magnitude of the risk threatened to the copyright holder by online intermediary activities is not only dependant on the seriousness of the copyright infringement, but also on the probability that that infringement will occur. Accordingly, intermediaries must adapt their diligence to the dangerousness of their activities. At the same time, intermediaries only need to guard against reasonable possibilities, not far-fetched scenarios.

The nature of the intermediary may be relevant in this regard, as may the market it caters to: if an intermediary specialises as an Italian language social networking service provider, demanding that it safeguard against the infringement of Lithuanian poetry readings through the incorporation of

205. H MacQueen, '"My Tongue Is Mine Ain": Copyright, the Spoken Word and Privacy' (2005) 68(3) The Modern Law Review 349; H MacQueen et al., *Contemporary Intellectual Property – Law and Policy* (2nd ed., Oxford University Press 2011) 243; E Barendt, *Freedom of Speech* (2nd ed., Oxford University Press 2007) 256. For an example of a case in which both breach of confidence and infringement of copyright were alleged on the basis of the publication of private diaries, see *HRH Prince of Wales v. Associated Newspapers Ltd* [2007] 3 W.L.R. 222; [2006] EWHC 522 (Ch); [2006] EWCA Civ 1776 (Civ Div).

206. E Barendt, *Freedom of Speech* (2nd ed., Oxford University Press 2007) 260. Indeed, the traditional conception of copyright would seem to suggest that freedom of expression is only ever relevant in cases of *self-expression,* see e.g., M B Nimmer, 'Does Copyright Abridge the First Amendment Guarantees of Free Speech and Press?' (1970) 17 UCLA Law Review 1180.

207. H MacQueen et al., *Contemporary Intellectual Property – Law and Policy* (2nd ed., Oxford University Press 2011) 243.

208. E Barendt, *Freedom of Speech* (2nd ed., Oxford University Press 2007) 256.

Lithuanian language fingerprints into automated filtering software or the hiring of Lithuanian-speakers as portal moderators will probably be excessive. Similarly, the owner of a cooking blog might be excused for not anticipating the unauthorised reproduction of extracts from a physics textbook in her comment section. By contrast, it is not improbable that protected music videos of the latest pop hit or scenes from the a Hollywood blockbuster will crop up on a platform dedicated to the exchange of home-videos or that copyright-protected original photographs and other imagery might appear on a site intended for the sharing of visual bookmarks. In this regard, the popularity of a platform as a tool for infringement should be taken into consideration: if a website is a hotspot for unauthorised exchanges of copyrighted works, the probability of a given interaction between users including a copyright infringement increases. These considerations harken back to the initial instincts of the national courts that examined the architecture of the platform and the business model of the intermediary in question:[209] although the liability of an intermediary may not be based on these considerations alone, in combination with other elements they are relevant as indicators of the appropriate level of counterbalancing care.

Finally, the contributory negligence of the right-holder might also come into play: if a right-holder makes a work available online on a free access basis, their right to complain against future re-sharing by others may be negated.[210] This is reminiscent of the CJEU's refusal in both *Svensson*[211] and *Bestwater*[212] to recognise the embedding of another person's work already made available to the public on a third party website as a form of communication to the public within the meaning of Article 3(1) of the Copyright Directive, as long as the work was not directed at a new public. Although the language of contributory negligence is not used here, the controversial construct of a 'new public' introduced by the CJEU seemed to serve a similar purpose and effect, at least in those two instances: as the Court stated, if 'there is no new public, the authorisation of copyright holders is not required'. No infringement consequently exists and therefore no accessory liability. Caution should be had however, as 'failure to guard against folly is

209. On this see especially the early French rulings, s. 3.2.1.
210. See Art. 8:101(1) of the PETL, according to which, '[l]iability can be excluded or reduced to such extent as is considered just having regard to the victim's contributory fault and to any other matters which would be relevant to establish or reduce liability of the victim if he were the tortfeasor.' Likewise, according to Art. VI.-5:101(1) of the DCFR, '[w]here the fault of the person suffering the damage contributes to the occurrence or extent of legally relevant damage, reparation is to be reduced according to the degree of such fault.' A *de minimis* rule applies here as well (Art. VI.-5:101(2)(a) and (b).
211. CJEU, C-466/12, *Svensson,* 13 February 2014.
212. CJEU, C-348/13, *Bestwater International,* 21 October 2014.

sometimes folly in itself'.[213] Accordingly, intermediaries should not assume that right-holders will appropriately defend their own interests at all times and may, depending on how risky their behaviour was, be expected to pro-actively undertake some of that burden, at least by issuing a warning beforehand.

5.4.3.2 The Benefit of the Conduct

As mentioned above, the interests of the claimant aren't the only ones under evaluation: according to Article 2:102(6) of the PETL, '[i]n determining the scope of protection, the interests of the actor, especially in liberty of action and in exercising his rights, as well as public interests also have to be taken into consideration'. In the area of intermediary liability, we can also add the interests of the intermediary's users, as per the case law of the CJEU, to this list. Accordingly, the benefits that the provision of intermediary services confers on these three parties must be considered, as counterbalancing considerations to the risk for the right-holder, speaking against the intermediary's obligation to prevent it. Fundamental rights law and in particular the 'fair balance' copyright case law of the CJEU, which indicates the interests that public law demands be taken into consideration, shall be used to guide this analysis.

(a) The interests of the intermediary

The most obvious benefit from the provision of an intermediary service is reaped by the intermediary itself in its free participation in electronic commerce: the provision of an intermediary service in exchange for a fee constitutes the essence of an internet intermediary's business model and it is through its pursuit of that business model, that the intermediary makes profit. This was acknowledged by CJEU in *Scarlet Extended*[214] and *Netlog*[215] by reference to the intermediary's freedom to conduct a business under Article 16 of the EU's Charter[216] as a counterbalancing interest to intellectual property. Article 16 acts to protect 'economic initiative and the ability to participate in a market'. This should be distinguished from the protection of

---

213. *Lang v. London Transport Executive* [1959] 1 WLR 1168, as quoted in C van Dam, *European Tort Law* (2nd ed., Oxford University Press 2013) para. 806-3.

214. CJEU, C-70/10, *Scarlet Extended SA v. Société belge des auteurs, compositeurs et éditeurs SCRL (SABAM)*, 24 November 2011.

215. CJEU, C-360/10, *Belgische Vereniging van Auteurs, Componisten en Uitgevers CVBA (SABAM) v. Netlog NV*, 16 February 2012.

216. The freedom to conduct a business is not protected under the ECHR. For an analysis see M Everson & R Correia Gonçalves, 'Article 16 – Freedom to Conduct a Business' in S Peers, T Hervey, J Kenner & A Ward, *The EU Charter of Fundamental Rights: A Commentary* (Hart Publishing 2014) 437.

'actual profit, seen in financial terms, that is earned in that market'.[217] Instead, the right includes the freedom of any business to freely use, within the limits of its liability for its own acts, the economic, technical and financial resources available to it.[218] The consideration of the intermediary's business model in cases of copyright enforcement has already found application on the national level; for example, it should be recalled that, in the German *Störerhaftung* system, a duty to review is considered to be unreasonable if it would unduly impair the business of the alleged disturber.[219]

Another point to consider should be whether the provision of an information society service might constitute an exercise of the intermediary's freedom to provide information. As may be recalled,[220] this was the question under dispute in *Delfi,*[221] where the applicant intermediary complained that holding it liable for the comments posted by the readers of its internet news portal interfered with its rights under Article 10 of the ECHR. Of course, in *Delfi,* no violation was ultimately found by the ECtHR, potentially suggesting that less gravity is assigned to the right of host providers to store and communicate the expression of others, at least within the human rights framework.

(b) The interests of the intermediary's users

On the flip-side of this exchange are the intermediary's users, who subscribe to its services so as to receive their share of the benefit in the form of capabilities to distribute and/or access content. As the Explanatory Memorandum to the proposal of the E-Commerce Directive declared, '[a]ctivities involved in Information Society services constitute both services within the meaning of Articles 59 and 60 of the Treaty and information within the scope of the principle of freedom of expression laid down in Article 10 of the European Convention on Human Rights'.[222] Recital 9 of the E-Commerce Directive confirms the connection: '[t]he free movement of information society services can in many cases be a specific reflection in Community law of a more general principle, namely freedom of expression'. To the extent therefore that the content accessed or distributed through the use of

217. See CJEU, Opinion of AG Cruz Villalón, case C-426/11, *Alemo-Herron and Others,* 19 February 2013, paras 50-51.
218. CJEU, C-314/12, *UPC Telekabel Wien GmbH v. Constantin Film Verleih GmbH,* 27 March 2014, para. 49.
219. See above, Ch. 3, s. 3.3.1. The BGH *Rapidshare* case law deserves particular consideration in this regard, for the emphasis the Court gave to this criterion, see BGH, *Rapidshare I,* 12 July 2012, I ZR 18/11 and *Rapidshare III,* 15 August 2013, I ZR 80/12.
220. See above, Ch. 2, s. 2.3.3.
221. ECtHR, *Delfi v. Estonia,* application no. 64569/09, 10 October 2013.
222. Commission Proposal for a European Parliament and Council Directive on certain legal aspects of electronic commerce in the internal market, 18 November 1998, COM (1998) 586 final.

intermediary services is lawful, the use of those services will constitute an exercise of the users' freedom 'to receive and impart information and ideas without interference by public authority and regardless of frontiers', as protected by Article 11 of the Charter and Article 10 of the ECHR. As with the intermediary's freedom to conduct a business, *Scarlet Extended* and *Netlog* also recognised the users' freedom of expression as relevant to the intermediary liability debate.

In this regard, it should be noted that the type of service in question might be relevant to the assessment of its benefit to end-users: with the subscription to the services of an internet access provider, for example, a user is immediately positioned to connect with the entire internet. By contrast, joining a social networking service allows access to a much more limited pool of content; a single blog even less. On this basis, it might be said that denying somebody internet connectivity altogether would constitute a greater interference with their freedom of expression than merely blocking their access to a particular website. At the same time, it should be considered that these services are by their nature interdependent: accessing blogs and social networking sites is not possible without internet access, while the possibility of visiting such sites provides incentive to connect to the internet. The interference with a person's freedom of expression will consequently be dependent on the purpose they intended to pursue. As a result, which services will provide the greatest benefit to an individual user will be a matter of circumstance, as well as of perspective. For example, while removing or blocking particular content might constitute a small interference with the freedom to access information of the user attempting to consume it, it might constitute a far graver interference with the freedom of expression of the person attempting to distribute it. A lot will also depend on the importance that the information contained in the disputed material has for the involved parties, as well as, as the ECHR suggested in *Appleby,*[223] the existence of viable alternatives.

(c) The general interest

Finally, the benefit accrued to society as a whole should also be considered. Obviously, the collective enjoyment of freedom of expression and the freedom to conduct a business by the majority of society's members results in a certain societal benefit. In that regard, it is worth recalling the particular importance of the internet in the modern communications landscape, as confirmed by the ECtHR: 'the Internet has now become one of the principal means by which individuals exercise their right to freedom of expression and information, providing as it does essential tools for participation in activities and discussions concerning political issues and issues of general interest.'.[224]

223. ECtHR, *Appleby and others v. the UK*, application no. 44306/98, 6 May 2003.
224. ECtHR, *Ahmet Yildirim v. Turkey*, application no. 3111/10, 18 December 2012.

This is such that 'a right to unhindered Internet access should also be recognised.'[225] Indeed, the uninterrupted provision of internet intermediary services would arguably allow 'the widest possible dissemination of works, ideas and new know-how', an aim which Recital 2 of the Enforcement Directive declares that the protection of intellectual property should not inhibit. Recital 2 of the E-Commerce Directive further indicates the positive economic consequences of the unencumbered development of electronic commerce, suggesting that it 'offers significant employment opportunities in the Community, particularly in small and medium-sized enterprises, and will stimulate economic growth and investment in innovation by European companies, and can also enhance the competitiveness of European industry, provided that everyone has access to the Internet'. Finally, it should be considered that the transmission of information over the internet is particularly beneficial with regard to the free movement of information across European borders and, consequently, the creation of a 'connected digital single market', incidentally one of the ten priorities of the current President of the European Commission Jean-Claude Juncker. According to President Juncker, by 'creating a connected digital single market, we can generate up to EUR 250 billion of additional growth in Europe in the course of the mandate of the next Commission, thereby creating hundreds of thousands of new jobs, notably for younger job-seekers, and a vibrant knowledge-based society'.[226] Recital 1 of the E-Commerce Directive indicates the loftier aspirations behind this idea: 'the development of information society services within the area without internal frontiers is vital to eliminating the barriers which divide the European peoples'. This is connected with the European Union's ultimate objective of 'seeking to forge ever closer links between the States and peoples of Europe, to ensure economic and social progress'.

The contemplation of the general interest requires taking a step back from the circumstances of the specific case and their meaning to the involved parties to observe the bigger picture. In this regard, the difference between a piece of technology and the use to which it was put in a given case should be noted. Even, for example, peer-to-peer technology, so commonly demonised as dedicated to infringement, can be used to lawfully distribute content, whether copies of the user's own work, public domain works or works for the distribution of which permission has been obtained from the right-holder. Indeed, the technology's popularity as a tool for copyright infringement is rooted in its very strength as a mass content distribution tool: peer-to-peer file-sharing is cheap, fast, easy to maintain and, due to its lack of reliance on

225. ECtHR, *Ahmet Yildirim v. Turkey*, application no. 3111/10, 18 December 2012.
226. J-C Juncker, 'A New Start for Europe: My Agenda for Jobs, Growth, Fairness and Democratic Change – Political Guidelines for the next European Commission', opening statement in the European Parliament plenary session, Strasbourg, 15 July 2014.

a single central distribution point, reliable.[227] It should additionally be considered that the societal benefit of a given piece of technology need not be immediately apparent: it may take years or decades before its full advantages come to fruition, while old technologies will often be repurposed for new objectives that could not be anticipated in advance. As a result, any court that ignores the potential for the future productive development of intermediary technology will run the risk of short-changing society in the long run.[228] The US Supreme Court's emphasis in *Sony* on, not only existing, but also possible non-infringing uses is indicative in this regard:

> The sale of copying equipment, like the sale of other articles of commerce, does not constitute contributory infringement if the product is widely used for legitimate, unobjectionable purposes, or, indeed, is merely capable of substantial noninfringing uses.[229]

The evolution in the uses of videocassette recorders, examined in that case, illustrates this point beautifully: far form spelling catastrophic losses for the film industry, as was argued at the time, video recorders eventually opened up a whole new lucrative market in the sale and rental of videotapes.[230] With this in mind, pronouncements on the liability of intermediaries must only be made on a case-by-case basis: content distribution technology will always have potential beneficial applications that will speak against blanket prohibitions.[231] A finding against one provider should not spell liability for all others offering similar capabilities as well. Room for

---

227. A Yen, '*Sony,* Tort Doctrines, and the Puzzle of Peer-to-Peer' (2005) 55(4) Case Western Reserve Law Review 815.
228. A Yen, '*Sony,* Tort Doctrines, and the Puzzle of Peer-to-Peer' (2005) 55(4) Case Western Reserve Law Review 815.
229. Sony Corp. v. Universal City Studios, (1984) 464 U.S. 417. See also, *CBS Songs v. Amstrad* [1988] UKHL 15 (12 May 1988), where Lord Templeman noted that '[a]ll recording machines and many other machines are capable of being used for lawful or unlawful purposes but manufacturers and retailers are not infringers if purchasers decide to break the law'.
230. A Yen, '*Sony,* Tort Doctrines, and the Puzzle of Peer-to-Peer' (2005) 55(4) Case Western Reserve Law Review 815. Unfortunately, nowadays the standard seems to have shrunk to only actual, not potential non-infringing uses, see P Savola, 'Blocking Injunctions and Website Operators' Liability for Copyright Infringement for User-Generated Links' (2014) 5 European Intellectual Property Review 279. On the need for the protection of technology with substantial non-infringing uses see also, P S Davies, 'Accessory Liability for Assisting Torts' (2011) 70(2) Cambridge Law Journal 353; P S Davies, 'Accessory Liability: Protecting Intellectual Property Rights' (2011) 4 Intellectual Property Quarterly 390; A N Dixon, 'Liability of Users and Third Parties for Copyright Infringements on the Internet: Overview of International Developments' in A Strowel (ed.), *Peer-to-peer File Sharing and Secondary Liability in Copyright Law* (Edward Elgar Publishing 2009) 38.
231. A Yen, '*Sony,* Tort Doctrines, and the Puzzle of Peer-to-Peer' (2005) 55(4) Case Western Reserve Law Review 815.

the responsible development of technology should be given, even while unreasonable behaviour is condemned.[232]

5.4.3.3 The Burden of the Measures of Care

The benefit conferred by the provision of intermediary services should be distinguished from the burden imposed by measures seeking to limit or interrupt those services so as to eliminate or minimise copyright infringement. Obviously, the questions of benefit and burden are closely connected: an immediate burden will be imposed on an interested party where the benefit conferred to it by the conduct of intermediary service provision is removed. However, unconnected burdens might also manifest. In the context of the counterbalancing considerations to the questions of risk and the responsibility it implies therefore, the burden of the measures of care deserves a separate analysis. As with the question of the benefit of the conduct, here too regard should be had to the interests of the intermediary itself, those of the users and the general interest.

(a) The interests of the intermediary

As with the question of the benefit of the conduct, with regard to the burden of the precautionary measures on the intermediary, the obvious starting point is offered by the freedom to conduct a business. This requires that economic actors not be exposed to undue or unfair business costs.[233] What does this mean for copyright enforcement? In *Scarlet Extended* and *Netlog,* the CJEU declared the expansive filtering measures envisaged by the referring court to constitute a disproportionate interference with the intermediary's freedom to conduct a business, in view of their complicated, costly and permanent nature.[234] The outcome in the *SABAM* cases should be contrasted to that in the subsequent ruling on *Telekabel,*[235] which instead of filtering injunctions concerned a blocking order. Here, the CJEU acknowledged that the injunction in question constituted an interference with the intermediary's freedom to conduct a business, as it restricted the free use of the resources at its disposal and obliged it to take measures which may represent a significant cost, have a considerable impact on the organisation of its activities or require difficult and complex technical solutions. At the same time however, the blocking injunction was not deemed to infringe the very substance of the freedom to conduct a business, as it did not require 'unbearable sacrifices' on

232. A Yen, '*Sony,* Tort Doctrines, and the Puzzle of Peer-to-Peer' (2005) 55(4) Case Western Reserve Law Review 815.
233. M Everson & R Correia Gonçalves, 'Article 16 – Freedom to Conduct a Business' in S Peers, T Hervey, J Kenner & A Ward, *The EU Charter of Fundamental Rights: A Commentary* (Hart Publishing 2014) 453.
234. See *Scarlet* para. 51 and *Netlog,* para. 49.
235. CJEU, C-314/12, *UPC Telekabel Wien GmbH v. Constantin Film Verleih GmbH,* 27 March 2014.

the part of the intermediary.[236] This result was enabled by the freedom left to the intermediary in the choice of the measures to be adopted, which allowed it to opt for those which were best suited to its resources and abilities and which were compatible with any other obligations and challenges encountered in the exercise of his business activities, thus alleviating the oppressiveness of the burden upon it. The possibility of exoneration before a court, allowing the intermediary to prove that it has taken all reasonable measures to achieve the result ordered, was also central to this outcome.

Special attention should be given to this last condition in view of the ECtHR's ruling in *Delfi*. There, the Grand Chamber noted that Delfi had published a disclaimer warning users against posting unlawful comments, installed an automatic filtering system for the deletion of comments containing the stems of certain vulgar words and put in place a notice-and-take-down system, in addition to undertaking occasional human moderation. The company could thus not be said to have wholly neglected its duty to avoid causing harm to third parties. Nevertheless, the Court observed that these mechanisms had proved insufficient in the event, making liability appropriate. This reasoning is suspect and indeed, the dissenting judges took great issue with it:

> It was decisive for the Court that the filtering mechanism failed. There is no review of the adequacy of the filtering mechanism (was it state-of-the-art; can there be a duty to apply state-of-the-art systems; is there any reason for being held liable with a state-of-the-art filtering system?). The Court itself finds that filtering must have been a simple task and that the system failed. No expert opinion, no cross-examination. We are simply assured that setting up a dedicated team of moderators is not 'private censorship'.[237]

The trap they point out is obvious and important to avoid: the intermediary cannot be allowed to be exonerated only where it has achieved the desired effect and condemned where it has not. Such a rule would be circular and leave no room for justice or proportionality, thereby imposing an excessive burden on the provider that makes it solely responsible for the damage caused to another regardless of the control it enjoys over the situation at the source of the problem. In this regard, it is important to point out that, to the extent that it does not even deem filtering measures – already rejected by the CJEU in *Scarlet* and *Netlog* – sufficient, the findings of the ECtHR in this case are wholly incompatible with EU law.[238]

---

236. CJEU, C-314/12, *UPC Telekabel Wien GmbH v. Constantin Film Verleih GmbH*, 27 March 2014, paras 48-54.
237. Joint dissenting opinion of Judges Sajó and Tsotsoria, ECtHR, *Delfi v. Estonia*, application no. 64569/09 [GC], 16 June 2015, at 36.
238. For more on this see s. 2.3.3. above.

(b) The interests of the intermediary's users

What about the interests of the intermediary's users? Recital 2 of the Enforcement Directive indicates the areas that could potentially expect to take a hit, by declaring that the protection of intellectual property 'should not hamper freedom of expression, the free movement of information, or the protection of personal data, including on the Internet'.

Again, the *Scarlet Extended* and *Netlog* cases provide examples of how an interference with end-users' freedom of expression[239] may result from the imposition of a measure of care for the enforcement of copyright. So, according to *Scarlet,* the broad filtering injunction requested by the plaintiffs:

> could potentially undermine freedom of information since that system might not distinguish adequately between unlawful content and lawful content, with the result that its introduction could lead to the blocking of lawful communications. Indeed, it is not contested that the reply to the question whether a transmission is lawful also depends on the application of statutory exceptions to copyright which vary from one Member State to another. Moreover, in some Member States certain works fall within the public domain or can be posted online free of charge by the authors concerned.[240]

In other words, the danger of over-blocking imposes an excessive burden in this area, particularly troublesome in view of copyright protection's mutable nature both in terms of its complicated systems of exceptions and limitations and its persistent territoriality. Collateral damage thus indicates unreasonable measures.

The CJEU's conclusions in the two *SABAM* cases are once more to be contrasted with that reached in the subsequent case of *Telekabel,* where the discussed blocking measure was deemed far less burdensome, not only to the intermediary (as discussed above), but also to its users. Notably, in *Telekabel,* the Court opted to, in effect, outsource responsibility for the consideration of users' freedom of information to the intermediary itself.[241] This approach

239. For an analysis of the right to freedom of expression and information in the Charter, see L Woods, 'Article 11 – Freedom of Expression and Information' in S Peers, T Hervey, J Kenner & A Ward, *The EU Charter of Fundamental Rights: A Commentary* (Hart Publishing 2014) 311.

240. CJEU, C-70/10, *Scarlet Extended SA v. Société belge des auteurs, compositeurs et éditeurs SCRL (SABAM)*, 24 November 2011, at 52. See also, case C-360/10, *Belgische Vereniging van Auteurs, Componisten en Uitgevers CVBA (SABAM) v. Netlog NV*, 16 February 2012, at 50, which expresses the exact same sentiment, this time with regard to host service providers instead of mere conduits.

241. C Angelopoulos, 'Are Blocking Injunctions against ISPs Allowed in Europe? Copyright Enforcement in the Post-Telekabel EU Legal Landscape' (2014) 10 Journal of Intellectual Property Law & Practice, 812.

was enabled by the flexibility of the order examined, which, as noted in Chapter 2, was intended to allow the intermediary the freedom to choose the specific technological means that it would implement to achieve the desired result. Within this context however, the Court warns that 'the measures adopted by the internet service provider must be strictly targeted, in the sense that they must serve to bring an end to a third party's infringement of copyright or of a related right but without thereby affecting internet users who are using the provider's services in order to lawfully access information'.[242] This makes clear that measures that do not allow for an appropriate consideration of end-users' freedom of information would be 'unjustified in the light of the objective pursued'[243] and thus cannot be expected of the intermediary. The key term here is 'targeted': the distinction between infringing and lawful use emerges as central to the Court's balancing approach. This finding accords with Article 15 of the E-Commerce Directive and its prohibition of general monitoring obligations, as well as Recital 46 of the E-Commerce Directive, according to which 'the removal or disabling of access has to be undertaken in the observance of the principle of freedom of expression'. This is to be expected: as noted above, these provisions should be seen as clarifications of the broader fundamental rights framework.[244] The Manila Principles move along similar lines: according to their Principle IV(a), '[a]ny restriction of content should be limited to the specific content at issue'.[245]

As opposed to freedom of expression and the freedom to conduct a business, the protection of users' privacy and personal data entails, not simply the removal of a benefit, but a positive act of interference into the 'burden' side of the scales. According to Article 8 of the ECHR, 'everyone has the right to respect for his private and family life, his home and his correspondence'. This covers the confidentiality of all private communications, whatever their form or content.[246] It therefore also includes the protection of internet usage.[247] The Charter of the EU is more specific, distinguishing between the protection of 'private and family life, home and

242. CJEU, C-314/12, *UPC Telekabel Wien GmbH v. Constantin Film Verleih GmbH,* 27 March 2014, at 55-56.
243. CJEU, C-314/12, *UPC Telekabel Wien GmbH v. Constantin Film Verleih GmbH,* 27 March 2014, at 56.
244. See Ch. 2, s. 2.3.
245. 'Manila Principles on Intermediary Liability – Best Practices Guidelines for Limiting Intermediary Liability for Content to Promote Freedom of Expression and Innovation - A Global Civil Society Initiative', Version 1.0, 24 March 2015, available at: www.manilaprinciples.org.
246. ECtHR, *Michaud v. France*, application no. 12323/11, 6 December 2012.
247. ECtHR, *Copland v. the United Kingdom*, application no. 62617/00, 3 April 2007. See also: D J Harris, M O'Boyle, E P Bates, & C M Buckley, *Harris, O'Boyle & Warbrick – Law of the European Convention on Human Rights* (3rd ed., Oxford University Press 2014) 530.

communications' in its Article 7[248] and the protection of personal data in its Article 8.[249]

The protection of privacy and personal data will become relevant to the balancing process primarily with regard to such enforcement measures as seek to identify infringers through the surveillance of all users with a view to picking out those from among the crowd that exhibit infringing behaviours.[250] Accordingly, as noted earlier,[251] the protection of privacy and personal data in intermediary liability serves similar ends as the prohibition of general monitoring under Article 15 of the E-Commerce Directive, although obviously extending beyond the limited scope of that provision. The *SABAM* rulings again provide useful examples, by clarifying that IP addresses are protected personal data, as they allow users to be precisely identified.[252] On this basis, the CJEU concluded that enforcement measures that consist of the systematic collection and analysis of the IP addresses from which unlawful content on the network in general is sent will constitute an unacceptable interference with data protection. On the other hand, in *Bonnier Audio,* the CJEU accepted that a disclosure order issued by a court against a specific user would be possible, on the condition that:

> there be clear evidence of an infringement of an intellectual property right, that the information can be regarded as facilitating the investigation into an infringement of copyright or impairment of such a right and that the reasons for the measure outweigh the nuisance or other harm which the measure may entail for the person affected by it or for some other conflicting interest.[253]

This again confirms what Article 15 of the E-Commerce Directive suggests, i.e., that it is the 'general' character of measures that impact

248. J Vested-Hansen, 'Article 7 – Respect for Private and Family Life (Private Life, Home and Communications' in S Peers, T Hervey, J Kenner & A Ward, *The EU Charter of Fundamental Rights: A Commentary* (Hart Publishing 2014) 153.
249. For an analysis see H Kranenborg, 'Article 8 – Protection of Personal Data' in S Peers, T Hervey, J Kenner & A Ward, *The EU Charter of Fundamental Rights: A Commentary* (Hart Publishing 2014) 223.
250. It has been argued that balancing is entirely inappropriate for the right to the protection of personal data, and that instead account must be taken of the substantial requirements listed in Art. 8(2) and Art. 8(3) of the Charter, see G González Fuster & S Gutwirth, 'Opening up Personal Data Protection: A Conceptual Controversy' (2013) 29(5) Computer Law & Security Review: The International Journal of Technology Law and Practice 531. It should be noted though that in the cases discussed the requirements of Art. 8(2) and (3) were satisfied. It could of course be argued that processing for the purposes of filtering out copyright infringements was not 'fair' in the sense of Art. 8(2), but it is unclear how this would differ in substance from saying that a 'fair balance' has not been struck in that processing.
251. See above, Ch. 2, s. 2.3.
252. See *Scarlet* para. 48 and *Netlog* para. 46.
253. CJEU, C-461/10, *Bonnier Audio,* 19 April 2012, at 58.

innocent bystanders in addition to infringers that forces measures below the fair balance threshold.

Although the case law of the CJEU so far has focused only on the rights of the users' of intermediary services, it should additionally be noted that other third parties might also be adversely affected. So, for example, if a mere conduit provider blocks access to a website for all its subscribers, not only the freedom of information of a visitor to the site, but, more importantly, the freedom of expression of its owner will be clearly impacted.

(c) The general interest

Finally, the cumulative negative effect of the imposition of burdens on intermediaries' freedom to conduct a business, on intermediaries' and users' freedom of expression and on users' privacy and data protection should be considered with regard to the general interest. In accordance with the analysis on the benefit of the conduct (section 5.4.2), it must be concluded that the removal of the benefit that these rights and freedoms confer will inevitably result in a burden for society in the form of the diminished participation of individuals in public debate, a more limited dissemination of works, ideas and know-how, the inhibition of the development of electronic commerce and of the digital single market and the furtherance of closer links between the peoples and states of Europe. Troublingly, this effect could moreover extend beyond the mere total damage occasioned collectively to individual users to the creation of a culture of fear regarding the repercussions of the use of internet services, particularly worrisome in the area of freedom of expression. So, for example, a connection exists between the protection of users' privacy and personal data and the overall robustness of freedom of expression within a society, as arguably fear of interference with the former might serve as a deterrent to the exercise of the latter, thereby creating a chilling effect on free speech that incentivises an over-compliance by non-infringers.[254]

5.4.3.4 The Responsibility of the Intermediary

As mentioned above, a responsibility on the part of the intermediary to take measures to enforce copyright on its websites or networks might arise from: (a) the type of knowledge of the risk that the intermediary has (i.e., the *foreseeability* of the risk); (b) the intermediary's skills with regard to the measure in question (i.e., the *avoidability* of the risk); and (c) the existence of a 'special reason' justifying an obligation to act. These three factors will be examined in turn below.

254. A chilling effect occurs when an individual chooses to self-censor due to fear of punishment created by law. For more information see G McCord, *What You Need to Know about Privacy Law* (Libraries Unlimited 2013) 42; K D Kumayama, 'A Right to Pseudonymity' (2009) 51 Arizona Law Review 427.

(a) The foreseeability of the risk

An analysis of the types of knowledge which an intermediary might have with regard to the copyright infringements occurring on its website or networks was undertaken above (section 5.3.2). As mentioned in that section, while an intermediary must be understood as having sufficient knowledge of a risk of infringement, and therefore displaying the mental element of negligence liability, whether its knowledge is general or specific, the distinction between these two types of knowledge is relevant to the balancing of the duties of care incumbent on the intermediary. A differentiated treatment with regard to the next step of identifying the appropriate duties of care therefore results.

What this means is that specific and general knowledge indicate different possibilities with regard to the duties incumbent on an intermediary. This result is the necessary outcome of the factual possibilities on offer: if an intermediary has specific knowledge of a particular infringement, it will be able to take action targeted at the removal or disabling of access to that infringement. If it only has general knowledge however, targeted measures of care will clearly not be possible: the identification of infringing content will present an added hurdle that must first be tackled. As a result, specific knowledge may be seen as creating a responsibility to take specific duties of care, while general knowledge may only create a responsibility to seek out specific knowledge, which then might result in the recognition of further duties. At the same time, duties to take more general measures, such as the placement of warning signs, may also emanate from general knowledge.

(b) The avoidability of the risk

According to Article 3 of the Enforcement Directive, any 'measures, procedures and remedies' of care that the intermediary undertakes to enforce copyright 'shall also be effective'. The defendant must therefore not only have the expected level of knowledge of a diligent economic operator as indicated above (section 5.3.2), but also the skill to take the measures required of him to eliminate the risk. As opposed to what is the case with regard to knowledge, where the generally applicable objective standard is diluted in the area of intermediary liability by an inevitable element of subjectivity imposed by the law of fundamental rights, in accordance with the rules of tort law identified in Chapter 4,[255] the standard for skills should be a fully objective one. So, while technically an intermediary might not have violated a duty of care to undertake a specific measure if it could not possibly have abided by it, that lack of ability might in its own right constitute a violation of a different duty of care to make sure that it is vested

255. See above, s. 4.2.2.3.

with the appropriate abilities.[256] If, on the other hand, the risk could not have been prevented by any intermediary, regardless of skill, no liability will attach.

What this means is that duties of care will arise for the intermediary to take the measures that a company of its kind would be expected to take – the measures that a 'diligent economic operator' would take. Individual inability to take such measures will not relieve the intermediary from this duty or the resultant liability in case of its failure. As with knowledge, the technological state of the art sets the bottom line for ability, while codes of conduct provide guidance. The size of the intermediary might also be relevant in this regard: different technological abilities unlock for bigger, more financially powerful intermediaries than for smaller players.[257] Finally, as again with knowledge, an upper limit is set to the skills that can be expected of the intermediary by the legal possibilities: no duty to take illegal measures may be imposed on an intermediary in the pursuit of copyright enforcement. If the risk is unavoidable, then the intermediary cannot be held liable for omitting to neutralise it.

In this regard, one big question with regard to the avoidability of the risk will concern the effectiveness of the available enforcement measures. In *Telekabel,* the CJEU indicated that the measures taken by the intermediary to avoid or terminate copyright infringement do not have to be incapable of being circumvented. Instead, the 'avoidability' bar is set quite low:

> None the less, the measures which are taken by the addressee of an injunction, such as that at issue in the main proceedings, when implementing that injunction must be sufficiently effective to ensure genuine protection of the fundamental right at issue, that is to say that they must have the effect of preventing unauthorised access to the protected subject-matter or, at least, of making it difficult to achieve and of seriously discouraging internet users who are using the services of the addressee of that injunction from accessing the subject-matter made available to them in breach of that fundamental right.[258]

This approach is to be contrasted with the *SABAM* cases' zero tolerance stance on false positives, that was noted above: while taking down non-infringing material is not acceptable, failing to remove all infringements can be seen as reasonable, as long as it is clear that nothing else could have legally been done. At the same time, *Telekabel* does indicate is that, what can be done, should be done, even if that is of little effect: if only a small part of the risk is avoidable, that small part should be avoided. If nothing else, such

256. A N Dixon, 'Liability of Users and Third Parties for Copyright Infringements on the Internet: Overview of International Developments' in A Strowel (ed.), *Peer-to-Peer File Sharing and Secondary Liability in Copyright Law* (Edward Elgar Publishing 2009) 38.
257. See 'Manila Principles on Intermediary Liability – Background Paper', 30 May 2015, 7, available at: www.manilaprinciples.org.
258. CJEU, C-314/12, *UPC Telekabel Wien GmbH v. Constantin Film Verleih GmbH,* 27 March 2014, at 62.

measures on the part of the intermediary can serve as an indication that it is opposed to piracy (helping to establish is good mental element credentials), as well as be of educational value for the public.[259] As Savola observes:

> the underlying goal of copyright enforcement has implications on how the scale tilts. In particular, ineffective enforcement mechanisms can be more easily accepted if the goal of symbolic, educational or politically motivated enforcement is considered legitimate. On the other hand, if the goal is to decrease the impact of infringement, higher efficiency and economically quantifiable results may be required.[260]

The CJEU's wording would seem to indicate a preference for the first approach. Hustinx, the European Data Protection Supervisor, indicates that the reason lies in the relative weakness of the right under protection:

> While intellectual property is important to society and must be protected, it should not be placed above individuals' fundamental rights to privacy, data protection, and other rights such as presumption of innocence, effective judicial protection and freedom of expression.[261]

In view of the equal normative value of the opposing fundamental rights involved in this debate,[262] this interpretation is clearly not entirely correct. It might instead be more accurate to say that the measures undertaken in the pursuit of copyright enforcement often have greater potential to cause graver damage to the relevant counterbalancing rights than that imposed on the right-holder's copyright by the initial end-user infringements whose elimination they pursue. They must therefore be excluded from the list of measures which the intermediary is legally able to apply, often leaving it with the only alternative of measures of low effectiveness.

(c) A 'special reason' justifying an obligation to act

According to Article 4:103 PETL, a special reason justifying an obligation to act may arise in four different ways: the law so provides, the defendant created or controls the source of the danger of infringement, a special relationship exists between the parties or the harm threatened against the claimant is serious and the ease of its avoidance for the defendant great. The first two of these possibilities is largely inapplicable in cases of intermediary

---

259. C Angelopoulos, 'Are Blocking Injunctions against ISPs Allowed in Europe? Copyright Enforcement in the Post-Telekabel EU Legal Landscape' (2014) 10 Journal of Intellectual Property Law & Practice, 812.
260. P Savola, 'Proportionality of Website Blocking: Internet Connectivity Providers as Copyright Enforcers' (2014) 5(2) Journal of Intellectual Property, Information Technology and Electronic Commerce Law (JIPITEC) 116.
261. 'Opinion of the European Data Protection Supervisor on the Current Negotiations by the European Union of an Anti-Counterfeiting Trade Agreement (ACTA)' (2010/C 147/01), 22 February 2010, OJ C147/1, 19.
262. See above Ch. 2, s. 2.3.

accessory copyright liability: currently, no relevant legal provision in EU law or the law of the selected national jurisdictions imposes a special obligation on internet intermediaries to undertake actions to combat copyright enforcement above and beyond the general provisions applicable to any person – indeed, the E-Commerce Directive's safe harbours go in the exact opposite direction, immunising intermediaries against obligations that would otherwise apply. Similarly, the third option provided by the PETL does not offer great promise of applicability to intermediary accessory copyright liability: in the vast majority of intermediary liability cases, far from being bound together by a relationship of proximity or reliance, intermediaries and right-holders are nothing more than random actors brought together exclusively by the interference of others. The second and forth possibilities however deserve greater attention: an intermediary will always by definition have created and be in control of the source of danger for the copyright infringements that occur on its own platform and are facilitated by its services. Where that danger can be easily mitigated, no excuse for a lack of affirmative action will exist.

The issue of responsibility was particularly apparent in the ECtHR's famous *Delfi* decision. So, while discussing the context in which the comments had been posted, the Court in that case emphasised that Delfi was 'a professionally managed Internet news portal run on a commercial basis which sought to attract a large number of comments on news articles published by it'. The provider has actively called for comments to its news articles, while it also exercised a substantial degree of control over those comments and an economic interest in their posting.[263] As the Court also noted, Delfi had not put instruments in place that could help with identifying the authors of the illegal comments.[264] Finally, the ECtHR attached weight to the consideration that the ability of a potential victim to continuously monitor the internet is more limited than the ability of a large commercial internet news portal to prevent or rapidly remove such comments.[265] In the view of the Court, all of these considerations combined to create an impression of an exceptional duty on Delfi's part to take especial affirmative actions of care.

Although this analysis is worth considering for the insight it gives into the relevant theory, it should be noted that whether the majority applied that theory correctly to the material case can be questioned. As dissenting judges Sajó and Tsotsoria observed, '[c]ontrol *presupposes* knowledge', while such

263. ECtHR, *Delfi v. Estonia,* application no. 64569/09, Grand Chamber, 16 June 2015, para. 144.
264. ECtHR, *Delfi v. Estonia,* application no. 64569/09, Grand Chamber, 16 June 2015, para. 151.
265. ECtHR, *Delfi v. Estonia,* application no. 64569/09, Grand Chamber, 16 June 2015, para. 158.

knowledge does not automatically accrue simply because a comment has been published on a news portal. Instead, in most cases, the publication of comments by end-users occurs without any editorial input on the part of the provider. Whether Delfi had the necessary degree of control over its users' comments to create a special obligation can therefore be questioned. Moreover, given this set-up, any knowledge the intermediary does acquire cannot, even after publication, arise without either its notification – which Delfi allowed through its notice-and-take-down platform, but which the majority in that case deemed insufficient – or active monitoring: '[t]he duty to remove offensive comments without actual knowledge of their existence and immediately after they are published means that the active intermediary has to provide supervision 24/7'.[266] Clearly such general monitoring would be not be easy for the intermediary to implement – nor, for that matter, legal for the EU legislator to demand under the Charter, if not the ECHR. The existence of a special obligation to undertake filtering derived from the ease of its adoption would therefore also appear to be inapplicable to internet intermediaries under EU law.

It should be considered that, as noted above in *Scarlet* and *Netlog,* it was the complicated, expensive and permanent nature of the filtering measures under examination that prohibited their application.[267] This limitation is indeed enshrined in Article 3 of the Enforcement Directive, according to which, measures, procedures and remedies necessary to ensure the enforcement of IPRs 'shall not be unnecessarily complicated or costly, or entail unreasonable time-limits or unwarranted delays'. This confirms that general filtering cannot be deemed sufficiently 'easy' under EU copyright law to warrant the creation of a special obligation to deploy it.

5.5 'FAIRLY BALANCED' MEASURES OF CARE: INDIVIDUAL ANALYSIS

In view of the above it becomes clear that, as Yen observes, balancing is as much an art as it is science:

> Courts must therefore make sensitive, almost philosophical, judgments about the society importance of deterring infringement, compensating victims, and holding the culpable liable, and they must do so likewise for the social costs of exposing reasonable (and therefore potentially

266. Joint dissenting opinion of Judges Sajó and Tsotsoria in ECtHR, *Delfi v. Estonia,* application no. 64569/09, Grand Chamber, 16 June 2015, at 35.
267. CJEU, C-70/10, *Scarlet Extended SA v. Société belge des auteurs, compositeurs et éditeurs SCRL (SABAM)*, 24 November 2011, at 48 and C-360/10, *Belgische Vereniging van Auteurs, Componisten en Uitgevers CVBA (SABAM) v. Netlog NV*, 16 February 2012 at 46.

innocent) defendants to liability and suppressing legitimate, noninfringing behaviour.[268]

This means that context is paramount: both tort law balancing and the notion of a 'fair balance' as this applies in the law of fundamental rights are abstract tests that cannot find real meaning until applied to a specific case: as already established, the behaviour of the reasonable person depends on the circumstances in which she finds herself.[269] The diagnosis of a fair balance – and with it the requirements of reasonableness – will therefore hinge on the nature of each available measure of care and its interaction with the situation at hand.[270] Recital 17 of the Enforcement Directive confirms this need for a case-by-case analysis:

> The measures, procedures and remedies provided for in this Directive should be determined in each case in such a manner as to take due account of the specific characteristics of that case, including the specific features of each intellectual property right and, where appropriate, the intentional or unintentional character of the infringement.

Below we shall consider a list of specific measures that intermediaries may take to prevent or end copyright infringements by third parties. This list includes the main duties of care that have been considered by the courts on both the national and EU level, as identified on the basis of the analyses undertaken in Chapters 2 and 3. The objective shall be to examine whether and under which circumstances these measures may be considered to be fairly balanced within the meaning of this chapter – and thus to be expected of the reasonable intermediary within a substantive European law on intermediary accessory copyright liability. Naturally, this list cannot be exhaustive.[271] However, the consideration of the advantages and disadvantages that each of these measures presents can allow a frame of reference to be created for the more confident assessment of other possible alternatives as well. The measures identified here are:

---

268. A Yen, 'Third Party Copyright after Grokster' (2007) 16(3) Information & Communications Technology Law 233.
269. On the need for case-by-case weighing in the fair balance principle of the law of fundamental rights, see s. 2.3 and in traditional tort law s. 4.2.2.
270. T-E Synodinou, 'Intermediaries' Liability for Online Copyright Infringement in the EU: Evolutions and Confusions' (2015) 31 Computer Law & Security Review 57.
271. Indicatively, Riordan suggests another measure in the form of asset freezing by payment intermediaries, J Riordan, *The Liability of Internet Intermediaries* (PhD thesis, University of Oxford 2013, forthcoming Oxford University Press 2016) 247. Another possibility is the so-called 'three strikes' or 'graduated response' approach – however, since in France this has been essentially downgraded to little more than a notice-and-notice regime and the UK has set the possibility (theoretically enabled by the Digital Economy Act 2010) aside, while Germany never even considered it, it shall not be examined here.

- The suspension of the perpetrator of the infringement.
- Measures for the identification of the perpetrator.
- The monitoring of content, including filtering.
- The blocking and removal of infringing content, including notice-and-take-down.
- Warning systems.
- Notification to the authorities.

Which of these measures would a reasonable intermediary take and when? An individual balancing of the opposing forces at play with regard to each should be engaged in order to consider whether or not they may be said to be reasonable in view of the risk of infringement facilitation. Each will accordingly be examined individually below.

Before that analysis begins, it should be reiterated that the notion of liability considered in this chapter is a broad one, in keeping with the wide definition that the concept finds in the practice of the Member States. It will thus be understood to encompass both liability for damages and for injunctive relief. Accordingly, the measures examined shall be considered with respect to both of these options.

In this regard, it should be noted that most of the CJEU case law so far has concerned either injunctive orders[272] or the reach of the E-Commerce Directive's safe harbours.[273] This is unsurprising, given that those two matters are also the main focus of the EU directives. As a result, no definitive European law currently exists outlining the reasonability of measures as duties of care for the avoidance of liability for monetary compensation. Nevertheless, the existing framework can provide reliable indicators in this respect as well. So, if a measure cannot be ordered against an intermediary by a court, it is unlikely to be permissible as a duty of care either. Similarly, if a measure is required for the enjoyment of a safe harbour provision, it is reasonable to suggest that its absence should function as a condition for liability within a substantive regime as well.[274] For all remaining issues, national solutions, the limitations of practical realities, as well as a systematic interpretation by reference to the surrounding framework can supply the answer. In this way, existing provisions of law can be approached as individual pieces of an incomplete puzzle, whose gaps can be filled

---

272. This is the case for the two *Sabam* cases, *Promusicae* and its follow-up cases, *L'Oréal* and *Telekabel.*
273. This is the case for *L'Oréal* and *Google France.*
274. Indeed, Recital 41 of the E-Commerce Directive reveals its role as a harbinger of fair balance: 'This Directive strikes a balance between the different interests at stake and establishes principles upon which industry agreements and standards can be based.' See also, Commission Staff Working Paper, 'Online Services, Including E-Commerce, in the Single Market', SEC(2011) 1641 final, 11 January 2012, 24, according to which, 'the liability regime strikes a balance between the several interests at stake, in particular between the development of intermediary services, the societal interest that illegal information is taken down quickly, and the protection of fundamental rights'.

through logical extrapolation, by utilising the information provided by the Copyright, Enforcement and E-Commerce Directives, the case law of the CJEU and ECHR and their national equivalents as balancing reference points.[275] The EU-level constitutional debate on the question of intermediary obligations for copyright enforcement might at the moment be patchy, but it is there.

In *L'Oréal v. eBay,* the CJEU gave two particularly helpful indications of measures that respect all relevant fundamental rights, at least when deployed in the form of injunctions: an intermediary can be expected to suspend the perpetrator of the copyright infringement and it can be expected to make it easier for right-holders to identify its infringing users.[276] These two suggestions manage to achieve the desired result of preventing further infringements of the same kind by the same user in respect of the same IPR, while also avoiding disproportionate interferences with the rights and interests of the intermediary and its users – in other words, they attain a fair balance. They therefore should also be the first port of call in any action against intermediaries for copyright infringements committed by their users.

5.5.1 The Suspension of the Perpetrator of the Infringement

The CJEU's first suggestion in *L'Oréal* was to suspend the perpetrator of the infringement. This could include both the uploading and downloading parties, depending on whether national law designates both of these acts as constituting copyright infringement.[277] The measure is simple, sensible, easy to implement and sends a clear message. It follows the suggestion by AG Jääskinen of a 'double requirement of identity', as set out in his Opinion in *L'Oréal*, according to which, where the infringing third party is the same and the right infringed is the same, an injunction may be issued ordering the termination of the client account of the user in question.[278] The suggestion is entirely appropriate, at least as concerns online platforms:[279] such a suspension would satisfy the balance between too lax and too aggressive an enforcement of IPRs, i.e., – as the AG himself put it – between the Scylla of allowing the rampant infringement of copyright and the Charybdis of

275. See for another attempt of the same exercise with regard to filtering: Q van Enis, 'Les mesures de filtrage et de blocage de contenus sur l'internet: un mal (vraiment) necessaire dans une société démocratique? Quelques réflexions autour de la liberté d'expression' (2013) 96 Revue trimestrielle des droits de l'homme 859.
276. CJEU, C-324/09, *L'Oréal v. eBay International*, 12 July 2011, at 141-142.
277. In the interests of achieving a fully harmonised EU regime for primary copyright liability, further EU guidance on this point might be desirable.
278. CJEU, Opinion of AG Jääskinen, C-324/09, *L'Oréal v. eBay,* 9 December 2010, para. 182.
279. R MacKinnon et al., 'Fostering Freedom Online: the Role of Internet Intermediaries' (UNESCO/Internet Society 2014) 136.

infringing the rights of users and intermediaries.[280] Arguably of course, it might be easy to circumvent a suspension simply by setting up a new account – however, nothing in the relevant national or European case law indicates that measures for the enforcement of copyright must be infallible before they may be imposed. Indeed, as seen above, the standard set up by the CJEU in *Telekabel* for injunctions is remarkably porous, requiring merely that the measures imposed 'make difficult' and 'seriously discourage' infringement and certainly not that they be 'capable of leading to a complete cessation of infringement'.[281] As Arnold J stated in *Cartier,* to 'allow such a defence would not only undermine IPRs, it would also be inimical to the rule of law'.[282] While these cases both concerned the imposition of injunctions on intermediaries, the same approach should arguably be equally appropriate to duties of care.

Suspensions could of course be strengthened by extending their reach beyond a user account to the IP address with which this is associated. As the wording of the Court concentrates on the 'perpetrator', thus indicating the actual person committing the infringement, this is a possibility worth considering. This is particularly so, given the judgment's deviation from the more conservative reference simply to the account the infringer happened to hold while executing the infringement that was favoured by AG Jääskinen. Courts and intermediaries should tread carefully however, as attempts to target IP addresses, as opposed to user accounts, although probably more effective at banning actual infringers, can potentially also cause over-blocking, by affecting other members of the perpetrator's household or even entirely uninvolved third parties – that will be the case, for example, where the IP address corresponds to a school or business. Additionally, they may also require general filtering technology that would present much more serious fair balance challenges.[283] In any case, it should be obvious that requiring that the intermediary proactively attempt to hunt out cases of such 'double identity' would necessitate the monitoring of innocent bystanders and thereby clearly also tip the scales into the realm of 'unfair'. Suspension should only be attempted when the knowledge is specific and acquired by the intermediary by notification or chance.

Although the CJEU in *L'Oréal* had online hosting platforms in mind, other possibilities may also be envisioned, especially in the form of the

---

280. CJEU, Opinion of AG Jääskinen, C-324/09, *L'Oréal v. eBay,* 9 December 2010, para. 171. See also M Norrgård, 'The Role Conferred on the National Judge by Directive 2004/48/EC on the Enforcement of Intellectual Property Rights' (2005) 6(4) ERA Forum, 503.

281. See ss 2.3.1. and 5.4.4. See also CJEU, C-314/12, *UPC Telekabel Wien GmbH v. Constantin Film Verleih GmbH,* 27 March 2014, at 61-63.

282. *Cartier International AG & Ors v. British Sky Broadcasting Ltd & Ors* [2014] EWHC 3354 (Ch) (17 October 2014).

283. See below s. 5.5.3. See also B Clark & M Schubert, 'Odysseus between Scylla and Charybdis? The ECJ Rules in *L'Oréal v. eBay*' (2011) 6(12) JIPLP 880.

suspension of a user's account with an internet access provider. As shown in Chapter 3, France famously implements precisely such a process. As part of the French graduated response regime, the HADOPI agency can, as a last resort, in cases of persistent copyright infringement (Article 335-7 CPI) or of gross negligence linked to the breach of end-users' duty to secure their internet connection against infringement (Article 335-7-1 CPI), ask the access provider to suspend a user's internet connection for a limited period of time.[284] This possibility however explicitly requires a court order.[285] This would seem to suggest that an internet access provider cannot be held liable for failing to proactively suspend an infringer absent such an injunction: it may have the freedom to do so, but should not be obliged to. The wording in *L'Oréal* ('if the operator […] does not decide, on its own initiative, to suspend the perpetrator […] it may be ordered, by means of an injunction, to do so') suggests that this would also be the solution favoured by the CJEU. It should therefore be concluded that the proportionality of suspension measures should depend on the importance of the service offered by the intermediary: suspension from a single platform is one thing, the exclusion from the most important modern mode of communication another. The balance of care depends *inter alia* on the burden imposed by the measure in question. As a rule of thumb, it could be suggested that online platforms might be expected to suspend perpetrators or face liability, but internet access providers will not.

5.5.2 Measures for the Identification of the Perpetrator

As a second possibility, the CJEU in *L'Oréal* mentions injunctions against intermediaries ordering measures that make it easier to identify the infringer – at least in cases where the user is operating in the course of trade. Paragraph 2 of Article 15 of the E-Commerce Directive backs this option and expands it, by acknowledging that Member States may establish obligations for information society service providers to communicate to the competent authorities at their request information enabling the identification of recipients of their service with whom they have storage agreements. Recital 40 of the E-Commerce Directive confirms that its provisions 'should not preclude the development and effective operation, by the different interested parties, of technical systems of protection and identification and of technical surveillance instruments made possible by digital technology', within the limits laid down by the EU's data protection and privacy rules. Article 8(d) of the Enforcement Directive allows the judicial authorities to order that information on the origin and distribution networks of goods or services that infringe

284. See above, Ch. 3, s. 3.2.5.
285. Conseil Constitutionnel, Décision n° 2009-580 DC du 10 juin 2009, Journal officiel du 13 juin 2009, page 9675, texte n° 3.

an IPR be supplied by any person who was found to be providing services used on a commercial scale for infringing activities or who was indicated as being involved in a commercial-scale production, manufacture or distribution of goods or provision of services used in infringing activities. An intermediary that satisfies these requirements could therefore be forced to supply any information it has available that could lead to the identification of the primary perpetrators.

Here again caution should be had: whether identification measures should be available in all cases is questionable, as the relevant information may be protected as personal data. As *Promusicae*[286] established, care must accordingly be taken. For example, the CJEU has already ruled in *Scarlet Extended* that IP addresses constitute protected personal data in the sense of Article 8 of the EU Charter in view of the fact that they allow users to be precisely identified.[287] Where the only information available for the identification of the user is contained in private communications, thus threatening the user's Article 7 Charter rights, the balance will shift even more aggressively towards the exclusion of identification measures.

Regardless, both *L'Oréal* and the directives limit themselves to the discussion of injunctive measures. For the identification of the user, judicial guarantees in the form of a court order must be ensured: the intermediary cannot be forced into such a duty of care merely as a requirement for avoiding accessory liability. The Manila Principles confirm: according to Principle V(e), '[a]n intermediary should not disclose personally identifiable information about a user without an order by a judicial authority. An intermediary liability regime must not require an intermediary to disclose any personally identifiable user information without an order by a judicial authority'. Proactive duties of identification should therefore be excluded. Intermediaries can also not be understood to be under an obligation to reveal the identity of users to right-holders or other private petitioners upon their request. Indicatively, under Article 6-II of the French LCEN, host service providers are under an obligation to retain information that enables the identification of the primary offender – but they are only forced to reveal it upon request by the judicial authorities. Similarly, the UK's *Norwich Pharmacal* obligations can only take the form of court orders,[288] while the German UrhG's '*Anspruch aus Ankunft*' also requires a prior judicial order, if the necessary information can only be provided using traffic data.[289]

286. See above, Ch. 2, s. 2.2.7.2. See also CJEU, C-275/06, *Promusicae*, 29 January 2008, para. 58.
287. On this, see F J Zuiderveen Borgesius, *Improving Privacy Protection in the Area of Behavioural Targeting* (Kluwer Law International 2015) 131-132.
288. *Norwich Pharmacal Co. v. Customs and Excise Commissioners* [1973] UKHL 6. See also J Riordan, *The Liability of Internet Intermediaries* (PhD thesis, University of Oxford 2013, forthcoming Oxford University Press 2016) 189-245.
289. UrhG, Art. 101(9).

Aside from these two *L'Oréal*-based possibilities, what other measures against intermediaries for the enforcement of copyright can be envisioned? The CJEU emphasised that its suggestions were non-exhaustive. Two main types of measures have been focused on in the remaining copyright case law of that court to date for the obligations of intermediaries with regard to third party copyright infringement: the installation of filtering mechanisms and the blocking or removal of copyright-protected content. Warning systems and the notification of illegal activity to the authorities offer two additional possibilities, inspired in turn by traditional national case law in the area and the current provisions of EU law.

5.5.3 The Monitoring Content, Including Filtering

Filtering can be defined as the combination of monitoring measures with the objective of blocking access to or removing unwanted content.[290] Essentially, filtering therefore refers to the identification of objectionable content with a view to its subsequent disposal. This result can be achieved through a variety of different methods. The most straightforward approach would be the human supervision of a platform by editorial staff with blocking and removal powers. Adding technological involvement into the mix, another very simple filtering strategy would involve the blocking or removal of content on the basis of the IP address or URL at which it is located, achieved through a human decision to blacklist specifically targeted material. More sophisticated results are possible: on the conduit level, for example, the use of so-called deep packet inspection is possible, i.e., the automatic examination of the data part of network packets for the identification and blocking of material containing certain predefined elements.[291] On the platform level, the usual technique employed for the same effect would entail the application of so-called fingerprinting technology, that relies on the use of unique digital representations of each piece of protected content (a 'fingerprint' of the content) so as to identify it among all the traffic uploaded on a hosting website or flowing through a network by means of comparison with a pre-existing extensive reference database of all fingerprints collected and then remove it.[292]

---

290. For a more detailed definition of filtering, blocking and monitoring see, T McGonagle et al., 'Study of Fundamental Rights Limitations for Online Enforcement through Self-Regulation', Institute for Information Law (IViR), University of Amsterdam, forthcoming.
291. R MacKinnon et al., 'Fostering Freedom Online: the Role of Internet Intermediaries' (UNESCO/Internet Society 2014) 196.
292. An example is offered by YouTube's Audible Magic. This was the technology discussed in the two *Sabam* cases, see *SABAM c/ SA Scarlet (anciennement Tiscali),* Tribunal de Première Instance de Bruxelles, 29 juin 2007, available at: tinyurl.com/avnvj2.

The obvious starting point of the legal analysis of filtering in the EU is to be found in the *SABAM* case law. Both the *Scarlet* and *Netlog* rulings concerned injunctions for the installation of exceptionally broad filtering mechanisms, covering all electronic communications, both incoming and outgoing, of all of the intermediary's customers, *in abstracto* and as a preventive measure, at the cost of the provider and for an unlimited period of time. As such, they were found to be in conflict with Article 15 of the E-Commerce Directive, as well as the principle of a fair balance of the relevant fundamental rights, and were consequently disallowed by the CJEU. However, as noted in Chapter 2, the rulings must technically be read as leaving open the possibility of ordering narrower filtering obligations.[293] And indeed, Recital 47 of the E-Commerce Directive explicitly permits monitoring obligations 'in a specific case'.

That said, it is hard to envision a filtering duty that would not perforce involve general monitoring, particularly given that, in order to be effective, filtering has to be systematic, universal and progressive, bringing it out of proportion with its aims.[294] Filtering, by the very definition of the word, necessarily involves examining each from among a group of communications in order to identify and 'filter out' the objectionable ones. So, while in *L'Oréal* the Court explicitly permitted the imposition of measures seeking to prevent future infringements, achieving this purpose through pre-emptive filtering against illegality from unknown sources must nevertheless be excluded, as it will require de facto general monitoring, i.e., monitoring that extends to all communications, including non-infringing ones, there being no other way to stop infringing activity of whose existence intermediaries cannot otherwise become aware without outside assistance.[295] In *Scarlet Extended,* the fair balance doctrine was also found to exclude such general monitoring – and with it the filtering that relies on such monitoring to identify any infringing data from among the pool of lawful communications that must be screened out – as such monitoring also means a disproportionate interference with users' privacy rights and data protection. Accordingly, the imposition of a duty of care for online intermediaries to carry out prior control by means of the installation of a general filtering system, i.e., a

293. See s. 2.2.7.1. See also S Kulk & F Borgesius, 'Filtering for Copyright Enforcement in Europe after the Sabam Cases' (2012) 34(11) European Intellectual Property Review 791.

294. CJEU, Opinion of AG Cruz Villalón, C-70/10, *Scarlet Extended SA v. Société belge des auteurs, compositeurs et éditeurs SCRL (SABAM)* 14 April 2011, para. 48.

295. T Verbiest et al., 'Study on the Liability of Internet Intermediaries', EU Commission study (MARKT/2006/09/E), 12 November 2007; DLA Piper, 'EU Study on the Legal Analysis of a Single Market for the Information Society – New Rules for a New Age?', November 2009, available at: http://ec.europa.eu/information_society/newsroom/cf/itemdetail.cfm?item_id=7022.

filtering system that relies on a general monitoring system, would appear to be excluded under both the E-Commerce Directive and fair balance theory.

Does this mean that filtering that is 'specific' within the meaning of Recital 47 of the E-Commerce Directive is entirely impossible? Certainly, the term should be interpreted very restrictively, as *L'Oréal* shows. One possibility for such permissible 'specific' filtering measures would involve the application of filtering technology to the content of only a single specific user account or IP address which has previously been determined to be associated with illegal activity, in order to identify and block infringements of IPRs that have been previously violated by that user or using that address.[296] So, for example, in *Newzbin (No. 2),* Arnold J ordered a two-stage system of IP address re-routing and DPI-based URL blocking to avoid the danger of over-blocking, while limiting the number of end-users subjected to invasive 'deep packet inspection' monitoring.[297] This takes a lead from the CJEU's 'suspension' suggestion and would serve the purpose of preventing further infringements of the same kind by the same user in respect of the same copyright. However, it is worth noting that, although filtering out such a user's infringements would certainly be a much more refined approach in comparison to the prohibition of all communications from the user account or IP address, as long as no over-blocking is threatened, a blunt suspension, as detailed above in section 5.5.1, would be much easier to implement, while also remaining proportionate. As a result, the incentives for the implementation of such 'narrow' filtering measures are not great, particularly for host service providers, as opposed to mere conduits. Moreover, even such specific filtering should, by rights, require a court order, as it will very likely involve a significant interference with the user's data protection and freedom of expression. An intermediary should not be held liable for failing to filter a specific user's communications for copyright infringement.

Alternatively, monitoring could also conceivably be labelled 'specific' where it involves only a 'minimal' or 'summary' analysis of the monitored content.[298] For example, in reference to conduit-level filtering, the avoidance of 'deep packet inspection' in favour of so-called shallow packet inspection, that limits itself to the analysis of packet headers and avoids the contents of data packets, could be said to avoid the general monitoring obstacle. This of course depends on the accepted definition of 'general monitoring'. It should be noted that the 'depth' of the inspection will not affect its breadth, so that summary analysis still requires the examination of every data packet, making

296. T-E Synodinou, 'Intermediaries' Liability for Online Copyright Infringement in the EU: Evolutions and Confusions' (2015) 31 Computer Law & Security Review 57.

297. *Twentieth Century Fox Film Corporation & Ors v. British Telecommunications Plc* [2011] EWHC 2714 (Ch) (26 October 2011) at 56.

298. T-E Synodinou, 'Intermediaries' Liability for Online Copyright Infringement in the EU: Evolutions and Confusions' (2015) 31 Computer Law & Security Review 57.

it just as 'general' as deep packet inspection. At the same time, the inspection involved will arguably not be invasive enough to qualify as proper 'monitoring'.

These conclusions find additional confirmation from the ECHR side of the fence. So, for example, according to the 2008 Recommendation on internet filters of the Council of Europe's Committee of Ministers,[299] while filtering resulting from state intervention may certainly be demanded for the protection of copyright,[300] nationwide general blocking or filtering may only be required of intermediaries if the filtering concerns specific and clearly identifiable content, a competent national authority has taken a decision on its illegality and the decision may be reviewed by an independent and impartial tribunal or regulatory body. In addition, the effects of the filtering must be proportionate to the purpose of the restriction. According to the Recommendation, this involves assessment of the filter both prior to and during the implementation, so as to exclude the unreasonable blocking of lawful content.[301]

In conclusion, it would seem that duties to filter, although not in principle forbidden, may, in view of a balanced consideration of all relevant factors, only be ordered by a judge. Even then, the reach of such filtering injunctions should be severely limited. As the Joint Declaration on Freedom of Expression and the Internet of the four freedom of expression rapporteurs observes, 'content filtering systems which are imposed by a government [...] are a form of censorship and are not justifiable as a restriction on freedom of expression'.[302] In any case, what is definite is that a reasonable intermediary cannot be expected to proactively filter as a condition for the avoidance of liability.

---

299. 'Recommendation CM/Rec(2008)6 of the Committee of Ministers to member states on measures to promote the respect for freedom of expression and information with regard to Internet filters', 26 March 2008, available at: tinyurl.com/cna63u.
300. The underlying report to the Recommendation expressly explains that filtering may be utilised for the blocking of access to unlawfully disseminated copyrighted content, see Council of Europe, 'Report by the Group of Specialists on human rights in the information society (MC-S-IS) on the use and impact of technical filtering measures for various types of content in the online environment', CM(2008)37 add, 26 February 2008. See also P B Hugenholtz, 'Copyright and Freedom of Expression in Europe' in R Dreyfuss et al. (ed.), *Expanding the Boundaries of Intellectual Property. Innovation Policy for the Knowledge Society*, (Oxford University Press 2001) 343-363.
301. See also C Angelopoulos, 'Filtering for Copyrighted Content in Europe' (2009) (4) IRIS plus 1.
302. The United Nations (UN) Special Rapporteur on Freedom of Opinion and Expression, the Organization for Security and Co-Operation in Europe (OSCE) Representative on Freedom of the Media, the Organization of American States (OAS) Special Rapporteur on Freedom of Expression and the African Commission on Human and Peoples' Rights (ACHPR) Special Rapporteur on Freedom of Expression and Access to Information, 'Joint Declaration on Freedom of Expression and the Internet', 1 June 2011.

5.5.4 The Blocking and Removal of Infringing Content, Including Notice-and-Take-Down

What about duties to block or remove copyright-infringing content? While blocking involves the disabling of access for the intermediary's users to undesirable content, removal eliminates it entirely: the content is not just inaccessible, it is gone. As opposed to filtering, blocking[303] and removal require the identification of the targeted material through means other than monitoring. One of the most obvious ways in which this can be achieved is through notification of the unlawful material by the right-holder or a third party – indeed that is the precise purpose of notice-and-take-down regimes. Other ways of achieving knowledge of an infringement on the part of an intermediary can also be imagined, in particular the accidental uncovering of infringements by an intermediary that was mentioned by the CJEU in *L'Oréal*.[304] The blocking or removal may take place either at the point which the data is requested or at that at which it is sent and it may involve specifically identified communications, user accounts or entire websites.

If the logic developed above for filtering is to be completed, the blocking and removal of content should be deemed acceptable under EU law. Insightfully, in *Scarlet,* AG Cruz Villalón pointed out that filtering and blocking mechanisms, although closely related to each other with regard to the objectives they pursue, differ essentially as to their nature. They consequently carry very different legal implications.[305] And indeed, while blocking or removing content is also part of filtering, it is not the objectionable part. As long as they are not accompanied by general monitoring, mere duties to suppress specific and clearly identifiable users, websites or content that have been found to engage in or contain illicit information should therefore not pose problems. This conclusion is not at all surprising: as seen in Chapter 2, notice-and-take-down constitutes the cornerstone of the EU's current safe harbour-based intermediary liability regime.

At the same time, it should be noted that both the blocking and the removal of content can have more extensive – and potentially unlawful – repercussions than intended: blocking entire websites, for example, risks collateral damage in the form of disallowing access to perfectly legal content that happens to be hosted at the same address.[306] More significantly yet, a clear distinction between blocking and filtering cannot be made, given that even cases of targeted and therefore 'specific' blocking will often necessitate,

303. In the case of search engines, blocking takes the form of 'de-indexing', see J Riordan, *The Liability of Internet Intermediaries* (PhD thesis, University of Oxford 2013, forthcoming Oxford University Press 2016) 247.
304. See CJEU, C-324/09, *L'Oréal v. eBay International*, 12 July 2011, at 122.
305. CJEU, Opinion of AG Cruz Villalón, case C-70/10, *Scarlet Extended SA v. Société belge des auteurs, compositeurs et éditeurs SCRL (SABAM)* 14 April 2011, para. 46.
306. M Horten, *A Copyright Masquerade* (Zed Books 2013) 27.

if not the processing of the content itself, the examination of identifying data that can help locate the content and differentiate it from other material. This can ring alarm bells. So, for instance, URL-based blocking, which compares the website requested by the user with a pre-determined 'blacklist' or 'whitelist' of URLs of objectionable websites, will result in the indiscriminate processing of all URLs passing through the filter, even if only few of these are subsequently blocked.[307] The same will be the case for IP-based blocking, the only difference being that this uses IP (Internet Protocol) addresses instead. As mentioned above, IP addresses are protected personal data. IP-based blocking also has a higher chance of resulting in unintended 'over-blocking' than targeted URL blocking, as a result of IP-sharing, as a given unique IP address may correspond to multiple URLs of different websites hosted on the same server.[308] User freedom of expression might therefore also be at stake. Great care is accordingly needed in establishing that measures that might at first sight appear to be sufficiently 'specific' are indeed so. In this regard, it should be noted that, while in *Telekabel,* an open-ended blocking order was deemed acceptable by the CJEU, that case involved the imposition of an injunctive order. Duties of care should arguably be more restrictive. An internet access provider cannot be expected to block infringing websites simply on the demand of a copyright holder or face liability.

As opposed to blocking, the removal of content will not require the processing of any data. It is therefore safe from accusations of general monitoring or the unlawful processing of protected personal information. But removal also has its downsides. For one thing, it does not allow for discerning solutions: while blocking can be 'target-specific', meaning that it is able to discriminate between users for whom the content should be available (e.g., those who have paid a fee) and those for whom it should be locked off (e.g., those who have not), once content is removed from a server it will not be available to anybody. Secondly, content removals can logically be executed only by the party who has control over the hosting service where the content is stored.[309] While removal is therefore a good option for platform providers, it is one that is foreclosed to access providers, who are instead limited to blocking.

307. T McGonagle et al., 'Study of Fundamental Rights Limitations for Online Enforcement through Self-Regulation', Institute for Information Law (IViR), University of Amsterdam, forthcoming.

308. Council of Europe, 'Report by the Group of Specialists on human rights in the information society (MC-S-IS) on the use and impact of technical filtering measures for various types of content in the online environment', CM(2008)37 add, 26 February 2008.

309. R MacKinnon et al., 'Fostering Freedom Online: the Role of Internet Intermediaries' (UNESCO/Internet Society 2014) 136; T McGonagle et al., 'Study of Fundamental Rights Limitations for Online Enforcement through Self-Regulation', Institute for Information Law (IViR), University of Amsterdam, forthcoming.

Again a good rule of thumb would be that the removal of specific content by platform providers through targeted measures may be imposed on intermediaries as part of the standard of care. The more erratic and severe blocking of content by access providers on the other hand should require a court order. This division is already indicated in the differing criteria imposed for the enjoyment of immunity by the E-Commerce Directive's safe harbours for mere conduits and for host service providers: while the latter must comply with notice-and-take-down requests or forfeit immunity, the former enjoy protection as long as the content is not theirs in any meaningful way.[310]

5.5.5 Warning Systems

Besides the technology-heavy measures analysed so far, inspiration can also be taken from earlier solutions adopted by national courts in the analogue world. Prominent here is the requirement imposed by numerous national courts requiring intermediaries to pin up warning notices reminding users that copyright infringement is illegal and that their facilities are not available for its commission. As we saw in Chapter 3, in *Amstrad,* the inclusion of a warning in advertisements of a double-spin twin-tape recorder noting that copying may require prior permission by a copyright owner and that the recorder's manufacturer did not have the authority to grant such permission was central in deciding against liability for that manufacturer by the UK's House of Lords.[311] Similarly, in *Kopierladen,* the German BGH, while holding that an obligation that the employees of a copy-shop inspect the material photocopied by its customers would disproportionately impair the customers' right to confidentiality, landed on the prominent display of warning signs instead as a suitable compromise.[312]

As with the suspension of the perpetrator, the posting of warnings is an elegantly simple solution that will be effective in the majority of cases: no significant burdens are associated with its implementation for the intermediary, its users or society at large, while the mere reminder of the illegality of the activity can be enough to deter everybody but committed infringers. The warning also achieves the purpose of dissociating the intermediary with any unlawful copying taking place, thus signalling its disapproval and lack of active encouragement.[313] That is perhaps the most that can be expected of otherwise uninvolved parties. Of course, if the intermediary is found to be

310. Cf Arts 12(1) and 14(1) of the E-Commerce Directive and ss 2.2.1 and 2.2.3 above.
311. *CBS Songs v. Amstrad* [1988] UKHL 15 (12 May 1988).
312. BGH, *Kopierladen*, 9 June 1983, I ZR 70/81.
313. See the Canadian case of *CCH Canadian Ltd v. Law Society of Upper Canada* [2004] 1 SCR 339 in this regard.

encouraging infringement in other ways, so that the warnings are revealed as nothing more than a façade, the protective effect should dissipate.[314]

How would such a notice be posted in the modern online world? One solution would be the inclusion of a warning in the intermediary's terms and conditions, although it is unlikely that this would be noticed by the user. For some intermediaries, e.g., access providers, this might nonetheless be the only possible option. Alternatively, in the case of web 2.0 providers, prominent featuring on the front page of the platform could also be considered, e.g., similar to that recently introduced in the EU for user consent to the use of cookies.[315] A pop-up message sent whenever a user posts new content is another possibility – such messages however should be sent to all users indiscriminately. They cannot involve examining the posted content in order to only issue warnings to users who look as though they might be engaging in suspicious activity, as that would risk problematic general monitoring. For the same reason, the requirement of the French HADOPI system that access providers send warning emails to subscribers who do not abide by their duty of surveillance should be deemed excessive.[316] On the other hand, the obligation introduced by the LCEN, according to which mere conduit providers that enable the downloading of files that they have not themselves provided warn their clients in a clear manner that piracy damages artistic creation (Article 7 LCEN) or inform their subscribers of the existence of voluntary private filtering options (Article 6-I-1 LCEN), is eminently sensible.

5.5.6 Notification to the Authorities

Paragraph 2 of Article 15 of the E-Commerce Directive states that Member States may establish obligations for information society service providers promptly to inform the competent public authorities of alleged illegal activities undertaken or information provided by recipients of their service.

---

314. On this see *Twentieth Century Fox Film Corporation & Anor v. Newzbin Ltd* [2010] EWHC 608 (Ch).

315. Directive 2009/136/EC of the European Parliament and of the Council of 25 November 2009 amending Directive 2002/22/EC on universal service and users' rights relating to electronic communications networks and services, Directive 2002/58/EC concerning the processing of personal data and the protection of privacy in the electronic communications sector and Regulation (EC) No 2006/2004 on cooperation between national authorities responsible for the enforcement of consumer protection laws [2009] OJ L 337/11 (known as the 'EU Cookie Directive').

316. See www.hadopi.fr for more information and s. 3.2.5, above. See also: C Jasserand, 'Régime français de la responsabilité des intermédiaires techniques' (2013) 25(3) Les Cahiers de la propriété intellectuelle 1135. For an overview in English, see N van Eijk, C Jasserand, C Wiersma & T M van Engers, 'Moving towards Balance: A Study into Duties of Care on the Internet' (2010) Institute for Information Law & Leibniz Center for Law, University of Amsterdam.

This shows the way towards one final possible measure. Of course, any obligation of the intermediary to actively search for such infringements will be subject to the limitations mentioned above incumbent on all user monitoring activities. However, if an intermediary spontaneously stumbles over indications of user-perpetrated unlawfulness on its services, passing this on to the relevant authorities should be as obvious as the obligation of an offline business to inform the authorities of third party illegal activity encountered during its course of business. At the same time, the practical constraints are severe: while the notification of the authorities is more likely to be appropriate in cases of specific infringements, there will usually be other more obvious measures of self-help available which the intermediary can apply. After all, there is little point in a host service provider notifying the authorities of a specific infringement identified on its own servers: if it is certain the material is infringing, the provider will anyway be obliged to remove or block it. Notifying the authorities of general widespread illegality, on the other hand, is unlikely to either inform them of something of which they aren't already aware or have any kind of real effect on the enforcement of copyright. So, while certainly a perfectly legal duty of care, the notification of the authorities will, more often than not, also be a perfectly useless one. Arguably, for this reason alone it should, unless other factors necessitate its adoption, be rejected as a waste of time and effort.

It should be noted that another similar measure that might have some success would be the notification, not of the authorities, but of the infringer. This is the alternative to the usual notice-and-take-down regime, called notice-and-notice. Under such a scheme, instead of removing or blocking the content upon knowledge, the intermediary merely has to forward the notification to the end-user. The intermediary may additionally be required to monitor the specific user's activities for a period of time. This enables the dispute to be directly resolved between the complainant and the potential infringer, while deterring primary infringement through end-user education.[317] The French *riposte graduée* essentially follows this logic, although it does rely on the ultimate spectre of internet disconnection to enforce the scheme.[318]

5.5.7 Choosing a Measure of Care

From this analysis, what can be concluded regarding the measures of care incumbent on a given intermediary? The conclusions of the above measure-by-measure analysis can be condensed as follows:

---

317. This system was adopted in Canada in 2012, see ss 41.25, 41.26 and 41.27(3) of the Canadian Copyright Modernization Act. See also 'Manila Principles on Intermediary Liability – Background Paper', 30 May 2015, 14, available at: www.manilaprinciple-s.org.
318. See above, Ch. 3, s. 3.2.5.

(a) If the intermediary is only aware in a general sense of widespread copyright infringement on its website, all that can reasonably be done by it will be to post warning signs on its website or in its terms and conditions. Other than that, it must simply stay on alert for more specific indications to which to react.
(b) If, on the other hand, the intermediary has knowledge of a specific infringement, more stringent measures will be necessary. In particular, in such cases the blocking or removal of infringements might become necessary; care must be had however, as a proper balance of all competing interests might be hard to maintain. The imposition of a duty to remove a single piece of infringing information from a website (e.g., a video on YouTube or a comment on reddit) will often be appropriate. By contrast, the blocking of entire websites by internet access providers should only be required after a court order has been issued. Additionally, any blocking or removal measures should be carefully formulated to avoid potential collateral damage: notice-and-stay-down obligations may not require the removal or blocking of content that has not yet been communicated to the public. This should hold true regardless of how similar it might be to existing infringements.
(c) The same conclusions can be applied to the measure of the suspension of the perpetrator: while certainly possible, only specific knowledge will justify requiring such action as a duty of care. The type of service offered by the intermediary will again be relevant in this regard: while a duty to suspend a user from an online platform may be reasonable, the suspension of a user's internet connection should require a court order.
(d) Notification to the authorities of possibly infringing content is mostly benign and should arguably always be permissible – whether it should be required of an intermediary as a condition for the avoidance of liability is, however, debatable, if only because it is unlikely to be of any real efficacy in the area of copyright. At the same time, the notification of the primary infringer (i.e., notice-and-notice measures) has a strong educational component. Where legislation or codes of conduct set up such schemes therefore, intermediaries should be expected to comply.
(e) Finally, duties to identify infringers, as well as duties to filter will usually be out of bounds. The intermediary may choose to adopt either voluntarily, but may not be held liable if it fails to do so. Identification measures should always require an injunctive order issued by a court. Filtering measures may not be imposed through duties of care. They should also be mostly excluded from injunctive orders as well, unless the content to be filtered is narrowly defined or the monitoring sufficiently non-invasive.

It thus becomes clear that different duties may lead to different types of liability: sometimes for monetary compensation and sometimes for injunctive relief. This approach has deep roots in the current EU framework.[319] It shall be explored further in the section on remedies.[320]

5.5.7.1 Implementing Measures of Care: Skills

Once the appropriate measure of care has been identified, a final important matter to consider will be the intermediary's skills.[321] The question of skills in many ways constitutes the flip-side of the question of duties, as it involves examining whether the defendant was in a position to live up to the responsibilities incumbent upon it.[322] Just as with knowledge, skills must be judged objectively. So, while technically an intermediary might not have violated a duty of care if did not have the ability to abide by it, that lack of ability might in its own right constitute a violation of a duty of care to make sure it is vested with the appropriate skills necessary to abide by its duties.[323]

5.5.7.2 Persistent Breach of Duty: Intent by Forbearance

A final word must be said at this point on the question of persistent negligence. As suggested above (section 5.3.1.3), depending the situation, it may occasionally be possible to employ a failure to abide by duties of care in order to show intention to cause third party copyright infringement. A strong case can thus be made that, where an intermediary flagrantly persists in ignoring its duties of care, it effectively betrays its intent to cause infringement.[324] It should be recalled that under German doctrine, the *Mittäterschaft* of Article 830(1) BGB can traditionally be deduced from the persistent violation of duties of care.[325] With regard to intermediary liability itself moreover, the lower German courts have occasionally experimented with the idea that the persistent violation of *Prüfpflichten* over a longer period of time can push liability beyond *Störerhaftung* into a proper *Mittäterhaftung* for monetary compensation under a paradigm of liability by forbearance.[326] Incidentally, this also accords well with the CJEU's 'just do

---

319. See above, Ch. 2, s. 2.2.1.
320. See below, s. 5.6.
321. See above, Ch. 4, s. 4.2.2.4.
322. C van Dam, *European Tort Law* (2nd ed., Oxford University Press 2013) s. 810-3.
323. A N Dixon, 'Liability of Users and Third Parties for Copyright Infringements on the Internet: Overview of International Developments' in A Strowel (ed.), *Peer-to-Peer File Sharing and Secondary Liability in Copyright Law* (Edward Elgar 2009) 38.
324. A Yen, 'Third Party Copyright after Grokster' (2007) 16(3) Information & Communications Technology Law 233.
325. W van Gerven et al., *Tort Law* (Hart Publishing 2000) 431.
326. J B Nordemann, 'Liability for Copyright Infringements on the Internet: Host Providers (Content Providers) – The German Approach' (2011) 2(1) Journal of Intellectual Property, Information Technology and Electronic Commerce Law (JIPITEC) 37; T

something' approach, as evidenced in *Telekabel*:[327] more than the effectiveness of the measure undertaken, the willingness of intermediaries to at least attempt to safeguard copyright serves to prove lack of intent. So, it should be recalled that TPB trumpeted its unwillingness to consider take-down requests on its website: '0 torrents have been removed and 0 torrents will ever be removed'. On this basis, the English courts found it liable of joint tortfeasance, a heading that requires intent.[328] Arguably, a truly 'neutral' intermediary might instead be inclined to examine each take-down request individually before declaring them inappropriate to remove – and, while it might argue against them before a court, it will not dismiss all requests out of hand nor refuse to comply with court orders. Thus, it is possible to convert knowledge of infringement into intent to facilitate, if the intermediary has received notice that its services are being used to commit an infringement and it nevertheless persistently takes no measures to inhibit such use: inaction indicates approval and an intentional act of facilitation.[329] The same might be said where the intermediary refuses to comply with court orders requiring the adoption of measures against copyright infringement. Under this interpretation, the possibility of finding an intermediary liable as a joint tortfeasor under intent does not seem quite so unlikely anymore.

In view of this detailed analysis, the flowchart of liability can now become a bit more specific. This is shown in Figure 5.6.

Hoeren & S Yankova, 'The Liability of Internet Intermediaries – The German Perspective' (2012) International Review of Intellectual Property and Competition Law (IIC) 501.

327. C Angelopoulos, 'Are Blocking Injunctions against ISPs Allowed in Europe? Copyright Enforcement in the Post-Telekabel EU Legal Landscape' (2014) 10 Journal of Intellectual Property Law & Practice 812.

328. See above, Ch. 3, s. 3.1.3.4.

329. J Ginsburg & Y Gaubiac, 'Contrefaçon, fourniture de moyens et faute: perspectives dans les systèmes de *common law* et civilistes à la suite des *arrêts Grokster et Kazaa*' (2006) 228 Revue Internationale du Droit d'Auteur 3.

Figure 5.6 Intermediary Accessory Copyright Liability Flowchart: Reasonable Measures

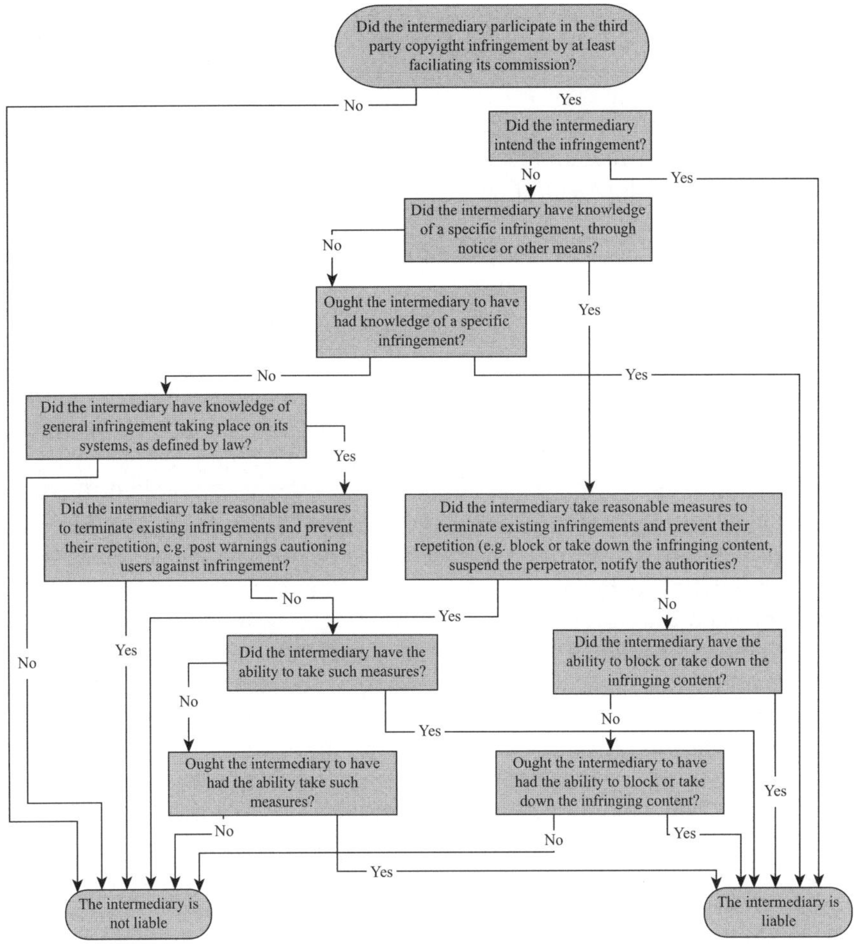

Naturally, this flowchart is just a rough guide intended to service the majority of cases. Practice may deviate from it depending on individual particularities.

5.6 PROPORTIONATE REMEDIES: MATCHING FATE TO FAULT

Although question of remedies for intermediary liability are not within the scope of this book,[330] to the extent that it affects the framework of intermediary liability, one word must be said before this chapter is closed on the divide between solidary and proportionate liability. In this regard, the distinction between intentional and negligent intermediaries is paramount. Arguably, that division should be reflected in the extent of the liability that each type of intermediary attracts. Unfortunately, such a rule would go against the established tort law principles.

5.6.1 THE GENERAL RULE OF SOLIDARY LIABILITY

As noted in Chapter 4, where a single indivisible injury is caused by multiple tortfeasors, both the PETL and the DCFR adopt a rule of solitary liability as against the victim (see Articles 9:101 and 9:102 PETL and Article VI.-6:105 DCFR). Both texts use the term 'solidary liability' as a synonym for what English law calls 'joint and several liability'.[331] This means that each tortfeasor is liable to the victim for the whole of the damage suffered. So, as against the victim, liability is not apportioned between the tortfeasors either equally or according to their degree of fault: it is 'joint'. At the same time, as between the tortfeasors themselves, the liability is 'several', meaning that it can be apportioned according to the relative responsibility of each. So, if one tortfeasor has covered more than her fair share of the damages, she can turn against the rest for compensation. This mitigates somewhat the harsh consequences of joint responsibility for the less blameworthy among the wrongdoers. The rule of solidary liability prevails whether or not the defendants were acting with a common intention to cause the harm. As a result, both Article 9:101 PETL and Article VI.-6:105 DCFR apply equally to both joint tortfeasors and several concurrent tortfeasors.[332] For the same reason, solidary liability is the proffered solution to accessory liability in all three of the national systems examined in this book, despite their theoretical differences.

At first sight this rule seems somewhat counter-intuitive: where a plurality of persons have contributed to the creation of the damage, the

330. See Ch. 1, s. 1.4.4.

331. This is again one of the trickier terminological thickets facing accessory liability, as all available terms come encumbered with national baggage susceptible to causing confusion, see W V H Rogers, 'Comparative Report on Multiple Tortfeasors' in W V H Rogers, *Unification of Tort Law: Multiple Tortfeasors* (Kluwer Law International 2004) 272.

332. European Group on Tort Law, *Principles of European Tort Law – Text and Commentary* (Springer 2005) 138-141.

natural course would seem to be that each should be permitted to invoke the responsibility of the rest in order to diminish their own share of the ultimate liability owed towards the victim.[333] But the logic of solidary liability is based not on the interests of the tortfeasors, but on those of the claimant, which should, under normal circumstances, take precedence. So, under solidary liability, the claimant may start proceedings against the easiest target among the concurrent tortfeasors. If liability were to instead be proportionate, the victim would face the time-consuming and expensive enterprise of identifying and managing separate proceedings against each person involved in the creation of the harm. She would also be burdened with the tricky exercise of determining each tortfeasor's share of responsibility for that harm. Finally, she would be cordoned off from compensation every time one of the multiple tortfeasors proved insolvent, immune, anonymous or absent.[334] To avoid such outcomes, solidary liability is established, in the words of the Spanish Supreme Court, for 'reasons of equity, the interests of society at large and the need to guarantee the protection of victims'.[335]

It should be noted that, in addition to these practical considerations, the idea of proportionate liability has also been attacked as theoretically unsustainable: where indivisible damage is caused, it is argued, it is pointless to talk of partial causation. Each of the defendants has in fact caused the entirety of the damage and it is therefore appropriate that he should be liable to the victim for full compensation.[336] However, as Rogers observes, although this will certainly be the case where each of the multiple causes would have sufficed on its own to bring about the damage (whether through 'alternative' or 'cumulative causation'),[337] it will not obviously be true where each cause was a necessary, but not sufficient condition of harm,[338] as is the case in accessory liability. Indeed, as Lawson and Markesinis argue, the only theory of causation that can provide real support for joint and several liability

333. G Viney & P Jourdain, *Les Conditions de la Responsabilité* (2nd ed., L.G.D.J. 1998) 253.
334. W V H Rogers, 'Comparative Report on Multiple Tortfeasors' in W V H Rogers, *Unification of Tort Law: Multiple Tortfeasors* (Kluwer Law International 2004) 273; C von Bar et al. (eds), *Principles, Definitions and Model Rules of European Private Law: Draft Common Frame of Reference (DCFR)*, prepared by the Study Group on a European Civil Code and the Research Group on EC private law (Acquis Group), Outline Edition (Sellier 2009) 3599-3606.
335. SSTS 7.3.2002, 3 [RJ 2002\4151], as quoted in M Martín-Casals & J Solé, 'Multiple Tortfeasors under Spanish Law' in W V H Rogers, *Unification of Tort Law: Multiple Tortfeasors* (Kluwer Law International 2004) 190.
336. R W Wright, 'The Logic and Fairness of Joint and Several Liability' (1992) 23 Memphis State Law Review 45.
337. See Art. VI.-4:103 DCFR. See also W van Gerven et al., *Tort Law* (Hart Publishing 2000) 441-452.
338. W V H Rogers, 'Comparative Report on Multiple Tortfeasors' in W V H Rogers, *Unification of Tort Law: Multiple Tortfeasors* (Kluwer Law International 2004) 274.

is the theory of the equivalence of conditions – which, among the selected jurisdictions, is popular only in France.[339]

As a result, it must be accepted that the primary arguments in favour of solidary liability in accessory liability are the practical ones driven by compassion towards the victim.

5.6.2 Possible Alternatives

The EGTL notes that the solidary liability rule was accepted by the majority of the Group as representative of the systems in place in the national European jurisdictions, whether of the civil or common law persuasion. As shown in Chapter 4, the DCFR adopts the same approach.[340] To the extent that it exists, EU tort law also seems to embrace the idea of solidary liability: Article 5 of the Product Liability Directive, for example, establishes that where, 'as a result of the provisions of this Directive, two or more persons are liable for the same damage, they shall be liable jointly and severally'.[341] Solidary liability accordingly appears to be of settled legal authority in Europe.

Nevertheless, modern legal developments have raised questions regarding this arrangement, in particular in cases of pollution or disease, where numerous actors might independently have contributed to an eventual damage over a period of years.[342] The US have been the first to react to these challenges. Although steering clear of pure proportionate liability, in the last thirty years, the majority of the US States have moved towards a variegated collection of complex compromise positions.[343] More recently, the trend in favour of proportionate liability has also been picked up in Australia and, to a much more limited degree, Canada.[344]

---

339. F H Lawson & B Markesinis, *Tortious Liability for Unintentional Harm in the Common Law and the Civil Law* (Cambridge University Press 1982) 129.
340. See s. 4.4.3 above.
341. Council Directive 85/374/EEC of 25 July 1985 on the approximation of the laws, regulations and administrative provisions of the Member States concerning liability for defective products [1985] OJ L 210/29.
342. See for example *Barker v. Corus (UK) Plc* [2006] UKHL 20 (3 May 2006), where the UK's House of Lords found that a solvent employer should be liable, not jointly and severally, but only proportionately for mesothelioma contracted by claimants who had worked for a number of different employers, all of whom had negligently exposed them to asbestos. The UK Parliament subsequently introduced a specific provision reversing this outcome in s. 3(2) of the Compensation Act 2006.
343. European Group on Tort Law, *Principles of European Tort Law – Text and Commentary* (Springer 2005) 138-141 and W V H Rogers, 'Comparative Report on Multiple Tortfeasors' in W V H Rogers, *Unification of Tort Law: Multiple Tortfeasors* (Kluwer Law International 2004) 278.
344. K Barker & J Steele, 'Drifting towards Proportionate Liability: Ethics and Pragmatics' (2015) 74(1) The Cambridge Law Journal 49.

Under these influences, in Europe too, in recent years, the dominance of solidary liability is being increasingly challenged.[345] Should proportionate liability be allowed to take over from solidary liability in EU tort law?[346] As a general rule, such a transition would probably have very little to recommend for itself. As mentioned above, the ethical and practical disadvantages of proportionate liability are weighty.[347] At the same time, if proportionality is to be accepted as the essence of tort law, perhaps proportionate liability is also worth considering. Van Gerven, Lever and Larouche note that:

> the balancing of [competing] interests is reflected in the way in which a legal system arranges three basic elements of tort law: sanctioned behaviour on the part of the perpetrator of the harm, protected interests on the part of the injured person and corrective remedies for damage caused by the perpetrator of harm to the injured person[348]

Remedies accordingly must be understood an integral part of the balancing exercise. Perhaps, therefore, a more adjustable rule is appropriate instead of the current immutable one, if not for tort law generally, then at least in the limited area of accessory liability or – more narrowly yet – only for intermediary accessory copyright liability. In this regard, it is worth noting that one of the factors considered by the ECtHR in *Delfi* was precisely the minimal consequences of the outcome of the domestic proceedings for the intermediary: only EUR 320 were imposed as damages, an amount which according to the Court 'can by no means be considered disproportionate'.[349]

A variety of different alternative options can be considered.

5.6.2.1 Proportionate Liability in Negligence

One solution could be to retain a default rule of joint and several liability, but allow proportionate liability in cases where the balance of interests so permits. In particular, in cases of differently culpable several concurrent tortfeasors, as opposed to joint tortfeasance, an upfront apportionment of liability arguably offers a fairer solution.

---

345. See W V H Rogers, *Winfield & Jolowicz on Tort* (18th ed., Sweet & Maxwell 2010) 988-989 and P le Tourneau, *Droit de la responsabilité et des contrats – Régimes d'indemnisation* (9th ed., Dalloz 2013) 1737. See also, J Boré, 'La causalité partielle en noir et blanc ou les deux visages de l'obligation *in solidum*' (1971) JCP I 2369.
346. It is worth noting that law and economics research would favour proportionate liability, see R Van Den Bergh & L Visscher, 'The Principles of European Tort Law: The Right Path to Harmonization?' (2006) 4 European Review of Private Law 511.
347. For an analysis of the disadvantages, see K Barker & J Steele, 'Drifting towards Proportionate Liability: Ethics and Pragmatics' (2015) 74(1) The Cambridge Law Journal 49.
348. W van Gerven et al., *Tort Law* (Hart Publishing 2000) 13.
349. ECtHR, *Delfi v. Estonia*, application no. 64569/09, Grand Chamber, 16 June 2015 at 160-161.

With this in mind, in England, Howarth leans on Lord Mackay's ruling in *Smith v. Littlewoods*[350] to suggest that, if liability in negligence for failure to prevent another from inflicting harm is to be accepted as possible under a fault schematic, proportionate several liability should be introduced to relieve the burden this creates for the negligent defendant.[351] Such cases are particularly noteworthy for the way in which they combine one intentional and therefore more heavily blameworthy tortfeasor with one negligent and therefore less blameworthy accessory. This in itself would perhaps not be problematic, if it weren't for the fact that in the vast majority of such cases the negligent tortfeasor will also be the more accessible and solvent party. In *Smith v. Littlewoods* itself, for example, Littlewoods, a major retail company, had been held liable for its negligence in failing to prevent arson by vandals who broke into a disused cinema the company was intending to convert into a supermarket. It is clear who among the available tortfeasors – Littlewoods or the anonymous and likely impecunious vandals – presents the more appealing target. Disagreeably, that would be the one that is least to blame for the harm occasioned.

Proportionate liability would overcome this problem. Under a proportionate liability scheme, the courts would be in a position to order the defendant to pay only to the extent that that is just and equitable. In practice, a system of proportionate liability should mean that each tortfeasor would only owe the claimant the damages that would, when the current scheme of solidarity functions properly, remain to them after recovering a contribution from each of the other tortfeasors. As Howarth argues, such a system would have the advantage of avoiding saddling the less culpable party with liability appropriate for far more censurable conduct, while at the same time ensuring that the victim can still obtain at least partial compensation. Of course, under such a system, the risk of failing to locate the primary infringer or of finding her insolvent would fall to the plaintiff. But this of course would be the very point: it is not after all always obvious why it should be more just that the damage incurred to the plaintiff should be transferred to an accessory, who, often, will be nothing more than a slightly careless bystander, used by the primary infringer as a tool to inflict damage. Indeed, Davies hypothesises that it is precisely the reluctance to embrace joint and several liability for accessories that has held back the development of accessory tort liability: the small proportion of fault that lies with an accessory to a tort makes the imposition of the full amount of damages on that party, simply because they are more readily accessible, unappetising.[352]

---

350. *Smith v. Littlewoods Organisation Ltd* [1987] UKHL 3 (5 February 1987).
351. D Howarth, 'My Brother's Keeper? Liability for Acts of Third Parties' (1994) 14(1) Legal Studies 88.
352. P S Davies, *Accessory Liability* (Hart Publishing 2015) 216.

A dampening down of a strict solidary liability rule might be particularly pertinent in intermediary accessory liability for copyright infringement. As a general rule, these cases follow precisely the 'least culpable is most reachable' schematic: the internet intermediary, for the most part, will have limited its contribution to only omissions of affirmative action to prevent or remove the intentional infringement of another. At the same time, it will also usually be both wealthier and much easier to locate than the individual primary infringers, who are much more likely to be numerous, penniless, hard to put a name to and safe in far-flung foreign jurisdictions. Arguably, therefore, intermediaries should be shielded from liability in excess of their real fault. Notably, that is exactly what the Manila Principles on Intermediary Liability recommend: according to Principle II(c), '[a]ny liability imposed on an intermediary must be proportionate and directly correlated to the intermediary's wrongful behavior'.[353]

Naturally, such a regime would have to be limited only to those intermediaries whose contributions to the damage took the form of negligence. Intentional participation by an intermediary in the copyright infringements of others should not lead to a lessened share in liability. This in fact follows from the very nature of proportionate liability: it is a system designed to alleviate the burden on the least blameworthy party. Intermediaries acting with intent to cause infringement are not mere bystanders sucked into somebody else's problem – they are, to use the terminology of English law, true joint tortfeasors. Joint tortfeasors are equally responsible for the injury they inflicted with common intent with the primary infringer and therefore should have an equal share of the responsibility for that injury: their proportionate portion of liability amounts to a full compensation. This reveals another one of the advantages of a dual intent/negligence approach: while intentional intermediaries should expect the same penalty as the primary infringer,[354] a negligence rule opens up the possibility for greater granularity.[355]

---

353. 'Manila Principles on Intermediary Liability – Best Practices Guidelines for Limiting Intermediary Liability for Content to Promote Freedom of Expression and Innovation – A Global Civil Society Initiative', Version 1.0, 24 March 2015, available at: www.manilaprinciples.org.
354. So, Cooper explains that 'a secondary party is liable, albeit secondarily, for the same wrong as the primary wrongdoer, and so the liability of each should be joint and equal' see D Cooper, *Secondary Liability for Civil Wrongs* (unpublished PhD thesis, University of Cambridge 1995) 153. Davies, although espousing the classic English joint tortfeasance approach, objects and suggests change, see P S Davies, *Accessory Liability* (Hart Publishing 2015) 255-256. But this bends the nature of joint tortfeasance and requires that it not be joint in reality at all, but an effective negligence-based rule that should be accepted as such.
355. 'Manila Principles on Intermediary Liability – Background Paper', Version 1.0, 30 May 2015, 29, available at: www.manilaprinciples.org.

5.6.2.2 A Principle of Subsidiarity

Of course the acceptance of proportionate liability would be contrary to deep-seated European legal *mentalité*.[356] In view of this obstacle, perhaps an easier way of achieving a very similar effect would instead be through the introduction of a principle of subsidiarity. So, it could be held that a claimant may turn against an intermediary to claim compensation for infringements committed by the intermediary's users, but only after a good faith attempt has been made to start proceedings against those users first. Such a system of hierarchical liability would follow the example of *responsabilité en cascade*, currently applicable in France for certain crimes of the press.[357] As with proportionate liability, a subsidiarity rule would only be appropriate in cases of negligent intermediaries, differently culpable from the intentional direct infringers.

Yet while this approach would have the advantage of avoiding a break with established European doctrine on solidary liability, it could in practice result in a disproportionate burden on right-holders, who would be obliged to start proceedings against nameless, numerous and inaccessible end-users before they could turn against negligent intermediaries.[358] To overcome this problem, subsidiarity could perhaps be limited only to situations where the potential for successfully bringing a claim against the primary tortfeasor is such as to guarantee an effective protection of the right-holder's copyright. Accordingly, a condition could perhaps be imposed according to which, before monetary compensation can be extracted from a negligent intermediary, an injunction against that intermediary requesting any information identifying the intermediary's copyright-infringing users should first be sought – assuming that the communication of such personal data would be proportionate in the circumstances of the case. If this fails to produce fruit, joint and several liability may be applied. Admittedly, this solution would have the disadvantage of incentivising intermediaries towards interference with their users' right to the protection of their personal data. Courts would accordingly have to be barred from ordering injunctions that would lead to such a result: if identifying information may not be legally obtained, the attempt should be abandoned and joint and several liability imposed instead.

---

356. Although it's worth noting that challengers do exist. See, for example, G Wagner, 'The Project of Harmonizing European Tort Law' (2005) 42 Common Market Law Review 1269; G Wagner, 'BGB § 840 Haftung mehrerer' in F J Säcker & R Rixecker (eds.), *Münchener Kommentar Zum Bürgerlichen Gesetzbuch* (6th ed., C. H. Beck 2013) Rn 30-41.

357. See Ch. 3, s. 3.2.2.

358. Indeed, this was the view taken on this suggestion by the ECtHR in Delfi, see *Delfi v. Estonia,* application no. 64569/09, First Section judgment, 10 October 2013 and Grand Chamber judgment, 16 June 2015.

5.6.2.3 The Störerhaftung *Solution*

But perhaps the best option is the one already employed in Germany: *Störerhaftung,* i.e., a limitation of applicable remedies against intermediaries liable under a negligence paradigm to only injunctive relief, leaving monetary compensation to be enforced exclusively against parties (whether intermediaries, end-users or other) acting with intent. After all, if an intermediary is only responsible for a breach of an affirmative duty of care to take precautions against third party infringement, conceivably its liability should be limited only to court orders obliging it to conform to these obligations. In this way, the distinction between true 'joint tortfeasance' (i.e., cases of multiple equally culpable parties all acting with 'common design') and 'accessory liability' (i.e., cases of several concurrent tortfeasors where a negligent party provided an intentional actor with the opportunity to cause harm) can be reflected in the consequences attached.

This approach incorporates the advantages of both the subsidiarity and proportionate liability systems, while deftly avoiding their downsides: crucially, it would achieve the result of a proportionate remedy by providing the claimant with protection, without extracting monetary compensation from a negligent defendant for the intentional wrongdoing of another. The remedy to be imposed would instead be calibrated to the degree of the defendant's blameworthiness. At the same time, as opposed to a proportionate liability solution, this injunction-for-negligence option would not require that the courts undertake the impossible task of attempting to measure shares of liability. Instead, a straightforward binary system would be employed that simply attaches a different type of remedy to two distinct categories of culpability: monetary relief for intent, injunctive relief for negligence. In addition, as opposed to what would be the case with the subsidiarity mechanism, injunctions would need not be limited to the search for data identifying end-users, potentially thus running afoul of privacy and data protection rules. Instead, they could take the form of any of the above-mentioned measures explored as potential duties of care, from blocking infringing content to suspending the perpetrator or installing warning systems: the objective would simply be to force the intermediary to abide by its pre-existing obligations. In that regard, the added guarantee of judicial oversight would be a bonus, offering greater protection for third party rights: courts are, after all, the appropriate venues for the necessary balancing exercise that determines what obligations encumber intermediaries. Arguably, therefore, they should also be the ones to order the applicable measures of care.

Finally, this *Störerhaftung*-inspired approach would not involve conflict with the traditional doctrine of joint and several liability. Indeed, the system enjoys support in the legal theory of at least one national EU jurisdiction, that of Germany, where it in fact springs not only from within private law, but copyright itself.[359] Legal practice in other European countries is also increasingly turning to injunctions as appropriate remedies for intermediary liability: the English courts have been avidly applying section 97A of the CDPA,[360] while France has shown equal enthusiasm for its *action en cessation* procedures.[361] The solution also accords well with existing EU legislation: as has been earlier emphasised, the current EU intermediary liability regime rests on a distinction between 'neutral' and 'non-neutral' intermediaries. While 'neutral' intermediaries, under Article 8(3) of the Copyright Directive, may be liable only for injunctive relief, 'non-neutral' intermediaries open themselves up to the full gamut of applicable liability, at least to the extent that they are denied safe harbour protection.[362] Arguably, this distinction deserves broader application within a substantive European framework for intermediary accessory copyright liability. As a final advantage, this 'injunctions only' approach even has the ECtHR seal of approval: in *Delfi* the Grand Chamber noted that the tangible result of the case for other operators in the post-*Delfi* Estonian legal landscape has been limited to a requirement to take down offending comments, with no need to pay compensation for non-pecuniary damage, a result it seemed to find agreeable.[363]

We can now construct the complete flowchart of intermediary liability. This is given in Figure 5.7.

359. Riordan also supports this suggestion, indicating that the traditional English distinction between tort and equity allows for duties enforceable by injunction where no liability for damages exists, while a strong link can indeed be made with the regular *Norwich Pharmacal* orders commonly used for the protection of intellectual property rights, see J Riordan, *The Liability of Internet Intermediaries* (PhD thesis, University of Oxford 2013, forthcoming Oxford University Press 2016) 248 and 253. As Lord Reid explained: 'a very reasonable principle that if through no fault of his own a person gets mixed up in the tortious acts of others so as to facilitate their wrong-doing he may incur no personal liability but he comes under a duty to assist the person who has been wronged by giving him full information and disclosing the identity of the wrongdoers' see *Norwich Pharmacal* [1974] AC 133 at 175.

360. See Ch. 2, s. 3.1.4.1 and in particular the following recent cases: *Newzbin (No.2)*, *Newzbin (No.3)*, *Dramatico v. Sky (No.2) EMI v. Sky*; *FAPL v. Sky*, *Paramount v. Sky (No. 1)*, *Paramount v. Sky (No. 2) 1967 v. Sky*, *Popcorn Time* and *Cartier v. Sky*.

361. See Ch. 3, s. 3.2.4 and in particular Art. 6-I-8 LCEN and Art. L.336-2 CPI. For examples of application by the courts see the *AAARGH* case, the French Google Suggest cases, *SCPP c. Orange and APC c. Auchan Telecom.*

362. See Ch. 2, s. 2.2.1.

363. ECtHR, *Delfi v. Estonia*, application no. 64569/09, Grand Chamber, 16 June 2015 at 161.

Figure 5.7 Complete European Intermediary Accessory Copyright Liability Flowchart

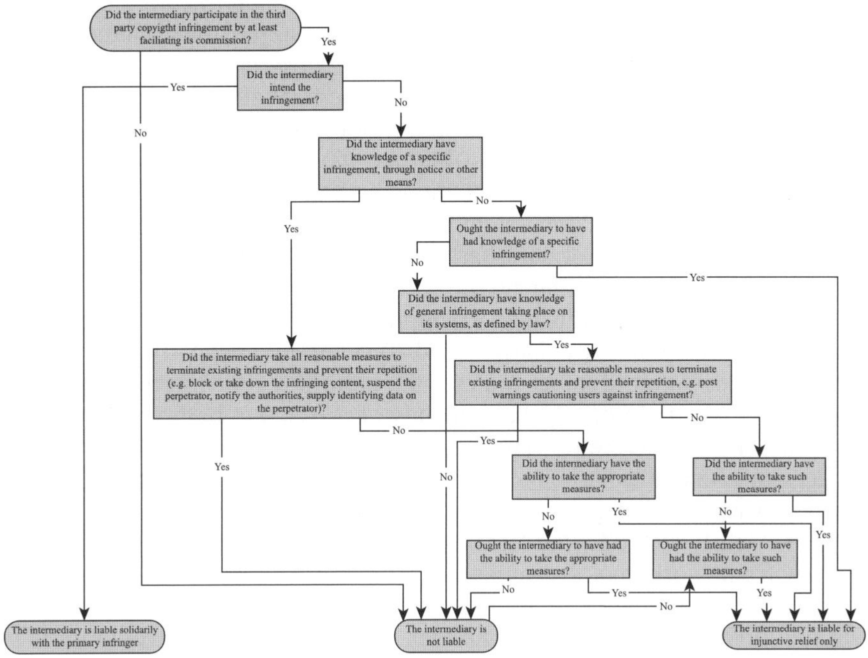

5.7 DEFENCES

Finally, the issue of defences should also be examined. To this end, it should be remembered that the usual excuses of liability, such as time limits on the imposition of liability[364] and contributory negligence, should always be considered. It is not the purpose of this book to delve into such formal conditions. Having said that, in relation to the latter of these two options, it is worth recalling that, as noted in Chapter 2, where a copyright holder has placed material online herself, the CJEU has made clear that primary liability for the re-communication to the public through the placement of hyperlinks cannot ensue.[365] The same protections should be extended to accessory liability as well – but that goes without saying: absent a primary infringement of the right of communication to the public, no accessory liability can be imposed either. With no primary wrong, accessory liability has nothing to which to 'parasitically' attach itself.[366]

---

364. On this see, P S Davies, *Accessory Liability* (Hart Publishing 2015) 251-253.
365. See Ch. 2, s. 2.1.
366. See Ch. 1, s. 1.4.1.

What about defences as grounds of justification? As noted in Chapter 4, the introduction of explicit grounds of justification is not particularly pertinent to an area of law as well-confined as intermediary accessory copyright liability: if properly formulated, the applicable standard itself should be such as to internally account for all appropriate justifications.[367] At the same time, it must be acknowledged that the final outcomes prescribed by the solution suggested in this book might not always be acceptable from a political perspective. It is thus possible that the legislator might decide that fault liability simply does not cut the mustard. In such cases, additional protections for intermediaries might be issued. That is, after all, precisely the point of the current set of safe harbour provisions. However, it should be noted that it is unlikely that retaining those safe harbours would lead to significantly different results than the application of the proposed framework: in the context of a fully harmonised system, the need to plaster over divergences between Member States – the current regime's primary purpose – will be negated. After all, the demands of those safe harbours have been taken into account in the formulation of the proposed framework. Of course, if necessary, the safe harbours as they currently exist – or potential future similar provisions – can always serve clarifying purposes: so, for example, it could be clearly stated by the legislator, as part of the provisions comprising the new framework, that the imposition of liability on host service providers that correctly abide by their notice-and-take-down obligations is excluded or that the most that a reasonable provider of caching services would do is to remove or disable access to information it has stored upon receiving actual knowledge that the information at the initial source of the transmission has been removed from the network or access to it has been disabled. Similarly, it could be declared that the modification of content contained in a transmission by a mere conduit provider will amount to the adoption of said content by the provider, such as to indicate the provider's intention to disseminate it. But such provisions would be – as AG Jääskinen suggested of the current batch of safe harbours in *L'Oréal*[368] – clarifications of the law, not immunities protecting against its application.

Should such clarifications prove insufficient, the alternative of true immunisation might of course also be contemplated.[369] So, provisions could hypothetically be introduced that negate liability entirely for the providers of certain services either on an unconditional basis or provided only very minimal conditions are abided by.[370] Should such a scheme be contemplated,

367. See Ch. 4, s. 4.5.2.

368. CJEU, Opinion of AG Jääskinen, Case C-324/09, *L'Oréal v. eBay*, 9 December 2010, para. 136.

369. This is essentially what is suggested by Principle I(b) of the Manila Principles: 'Intermediaries should be immune from liability for third-party content in circumstances where they have not been involved in modifying that content.'

370. For example, Davies has suggested the adoption of a 'staple article of commerce' defence in the context of intellectual property infringements. This defence finds its

is will nevertheless be best positioned on top of the strong theoretical basis offered by a proper understanding of the demands of the default solution: exceptions to fault should only be introduced after it has become clear what it is that the application of the fault-based regime would require. Failing this, the line between immunities and clarifications will always be uncertain, while the situation of providers that don't qualify for special protection shall remain murky.

Finally, it is worth noting that the exact opposite possibility is also conceivable: a liability regime that moves past defences, past fault liability and lands instead on strict liability for all intermediaries whose services are used to commit an infringement. Again, as with defences, a strong understanding of the default fault position should first be attained. The adoption of exceptional provisions might occasionally be necessary, but they should not detract from the proper construction of the main regime. Regardless, it is worth noting that, while there are those that argue in favour of a *cuius commoda eius* et *incommoda* approach to intermediary accessory copyright liability,[371] it is clear that there is little political appetite in the EU at the moment for a move in that direction.

5.8 CONCLUSION

It is now possible to sketch the contours of the resultant harmonised substantive European system for intermediary accessory copyright liability. The emergent framework rests on two central pillars: the conduct element and the mental element. An optional third pillar of duty becomes relevant depending on the severity of the mental element involved.

1. The conduct element. The conduct element is the first, simplest and broadest condition of intermediary accessory liability. It consists of a causal participation in the copyright infringement of another party. Mere facilitation should suffice. By definition, all internet intermediaries will meet this wide-reaching requirement as soon as their services are used by another to commit a copyright infringement. But the fulfilment of the conduct element

---

origins in patent law (see, for example, s. 60 of the UK's Patents Act 1977) and was famously extended into copyright by the US Supreme Court in the *Sony Betamax* case (464 US 417 (1984)). The intention is to offer protection for technologies with 'significant non-infringing uses'. While the adoption of such a defence makes sense in the context of Davies slightly stricter 'actual knowledge' based regime, in a regime wherein liability for monetary compensation is only contemplated for intentional intermediaries, while negligent intermediaries expose themselves exclusively to injunctive orders, such as that put forth in this book, it is not necessary. P S Davies, *Accessory Liability* (Hart Publishing 2015) 240-247.

371. D Friedman, 'Sinking the Safe Harbour with the Legal Certainty of Strict Liability in Sight' (2014) 9(2) Journal of Intellectual Property Law & Practice 148.

alone cannot lead to liability. Providing technology is not by itself unreasonable: the link is too attenuated to justify a blanket prohibition.[372] At the same time, the expansive reach of the conduct element illuminates the causal connection that links the intermediary to the infringement and gives rise to calls for accessory liability.[373]
2. The mental element. Two possibilities exist here: the intermediary may either have intended the infringement or simply have had knowledge of it. A division must therefore be made:

2A. Intent. The first case is the simplest: if the intermediary intended the infringement, liability will automatically ensue. Indeed, by intending the injury the intermediary has embraced it as its own. Its responsibility for the infringement is therefore not qualitatively different from that of the primary party.[374] Although intent does set a high standard that can be hard to prove, it can be inferred from the circumstances. This will especially be the case where there is a persistent failure to abide by duties of care.

2B. Knowledge. Showing that the intermediary did not intend the infringement is not enough to ward off accessory liability. If the intermediary has no intent, but does have knowledge of the infringement, negligence liability remains an option to consider. The knowledge threshold is a low hybrid objective/subjective one that hovers between actual and constructive knowledge: the intermediary will only be considered to have had knowledge if it was aware of facts or circumstances from which the infringement would have been apparent to a 'diligent economic operator'. Both general and specific knowledge suffice, although they may result in different consequences.

3. Duties of care. As opposed to what is the case for intent, the combination of mere knowledge with the conduct element does not alone suffice to result in liability: as is so often said, 'something more is necessary'. That something more is provided by the violation of an affirmative duty of care incumbent on the intermediary. What duties of care burden the

---

372. A Yen, '*Sony*, Tort Doctrines, and the Puzzle of Peer-to-Peer' (2005) 55(4) Case Western Reserve Law Review 815.
373. J Riordan, *The Liability of Internet Intermediaries* (PhD thesis, University of Oxford 2013, forthcoming Oxford University Press 2016) 38.
374. See Sir Robin Jacob in *Football Dataco Ltd & Ors v. Stan James Plc & Ors* [2013] EWCA Civ 27 (06 February 2013) at 100: 'once a party has procured an act which amounts to infringement by another he has effectively made it his own act. Here the acts of infringement by the punters do not require knowledge. I see no reason why Stan James which causes those acts to happen by providing a link which makes infringement inevitable should have a defence not available to those whose acts it procures. This is not a case of secondary liability but one of primary liability along with another.'

intermediary will depend on the circumstances. Case-by-case balancing is therefore required.

For this purpose, the following balancing criteria were proposed: (1) the *risk* created by the intermediary's behaviour; (2) the *benefit* of that conduct; the (3) *burden* of the measures of care that would be necessary to counteract it; and (4) any potential *responsibility* of the intermediary. These can be further broken as follows. The notion of risk consists of: (a) *the seriousness of the damage*; and (b) *the probability of damage*. The factor of the benefit of the conduct comprises: (a) *the interests of the intermediary*; (b) *the interests of the intermediaries' users;* and (c) *the general interest*. The same holds for the third factor of the burden of the measures of care. Finally, a responsibility to take measures might arise from: (a) the type of knowledge of the risk that the intermediary has (*foreseeability* of the risk); (b) its skills with regard to the measure in question (*avoidability* of the risk); and (c) the existence of *a special duty* to take affirmative care.

On the basis of the balancing exercise – and with the guidance of existing provisions and case law on both the national and the EU level – a number of potential measures of care can be accessed for reasonability. In this chapter, six were examined: the suspension of the perpetrator of the infringement; measures for the identification of the perpetrator; the monitoring of content, including filtering; the blocking and removal of infringing content, including notice-and-take-down; the imposition of warning systems; and notification to the authorities. On the basis of the ensuing analysis, the following was concluded: requiring the blocking or removal of infringements and the suspension of the perpetrator by intermediaries for the enforcement of copyright will often be proportionate, but particular care must be taken in implementation. The type of intermediary will be particularly relevant: the blocking or removal of content can be expected to be undertaken proactively by host service providers, but access providers should require a court order before they must proceed. Requiring notification to the authorities will almost always be proportionate, but often of little use. Obligations to issue general warnings to end-users to avoid copyright infringement will always be proportionate, as long as the intermediary has either general or specific knowledge of infringement. Duties to identify particular primary infringers should always require a court order. Duties to filter content or otherwise generally monitor it, should always be considered out of bounds, both as concerns duties of care and injunctive orders.

If an intermediary finds itself with knowledge of the fact that it has causally participated in a copyright infringement and nevertheless fails to comply with a duty incumbent upon it to take a reasonable measure of care, it will be held liable. As opposed to what is the case in intent-based cases however, in such negligence-based cases, the liability is not comparable to that of the primary infringer. Instead, this time, the term 'accessory liability' is truly justified: the intermediary did not 'make the infringement its own'. It is not using another as a tool to bring about its own malicious ends. It was simply negligent: it failed to take the care a reasonable intermediary would. Arguably, this division between 'true joint tortfeasance' and 'true accessory liability' can have consequences as concerns the remedy imposed. Accordingly, it has been suggested that accessory liability – as opposed to joint tortfeasance – should be proportionate, not solidary. An even better solution – modelled after the German *Störerhaftung* solution and following the lead of the current EU division between 'neutral' and 'non-neutral' intermediaries – would connect accessory liability to only injunctions, relieving negligent intermediaries of the need to pay damages for the infringements of others: a negligent intermediary should, it is suggested, only be forced to abide by its own obligations, not to pay for the misdeeds of others.

The final system that emerges is a two-tiered sliding scale: solidary liability for intentional intermediaries, non-monetary liability for negligent ones. Where an intermediary persistently ignores duties of care, 'intent by forbearance' might be diagnosed, bringing solidary liability back into the game. This is a sleek and elegant construction that remains sensitive to the culpability of the defendants, the social costs and benefits associated with the provision of online intermediary services, as well as the need to ensure due care throughout the supply chain.[375] It also takes due account of all three national systems under examination: the 'true accessory liability' solution of negligence where there is no intent takes its cue from the French regime; the 'true joint tortfeasance' approach established where there is intent draws clear inspiration from the English system; and the non-monetary liability solution for accessories copies the German *Störerhaftung*.

375. A Yen, 'Third Party Copyright after Grokster' (2007) 16(3) Information & Communications Technology Law 233.

Chapter 6

Summary and Conclusion

This book aims at the formulation of a model substantive European framework for the accessory liability of internet intermediaries for copyright infringement. The question is a vexed and multi-dimensional one. While most attempts to address the issue to date have searched for a solution in the analysis of the economic and political stakes, the approach taken here has been one rooted in classic doctrinal legal research: a legal problem deserves, first and foremost, a legal solution. For this purpose the general rules of European tort law have been recruited. The basic idea is that copyright infringement is a tort and it is tort law therefore that is responsible for filling in overlooked gaps in the copyright edifice. Tort law is furthermore fit for the purpose, having been shaped over centuries for the sophisticated case-by-case balancing of social costs and benefits in the regulation of interpersonal interactions. As a result, the reintegration of intermediary accessory copyright liability into the broader tort principles can allow for the doctrinal reconstruction currently necessary in this contentious and overwrought field of law and, ultimately, the emergence of a more stable, effective, cogent and comprehensive analytical structure. Although this structure should certainly be informed by the current piecemeal and incomplete European regime, its purpose should be to replace it. Only once the broader legal landscape surrounding the issue has been properly charted, should routes begin to be plotted to further exceptional policy goals.

How has this objective been pursued? This chapter reprises the course followed throughout the book and summarises its main findings. For this purpose, it shall retrace, in sections 6.1-6.4, the chapter-by-chapter analysis undertaken so far. It shall then move on to an examination of the options for a future actual implementation of the proposed model into law in section 6.5, before finishing off with some closing remarks in section 6.6.

6.1 THE CURRENT EU FRAMEWORK

The analysis above began in Chapter 2 with a detailed appraisal of the current state of European harmonisation for intermediary accessory copyright liability. The objective here was two-fold: to demonstrate the incompleteness of the current harmonised framework, but also to showcase the progress achieved so far: if a European harmonisation of intermediary accessory copyright liability is to be developed, the most efficient way forward would be to build from the groundwork of existing harmonised law up.

The chapter opened with a brief overview of the EU rules on primary copyright liability. These are relevant to accessory liability in two ways: on the one hand, they are often used by the courts as a way to extract liability from intermediaries for the infringements of third parties (a sort of accessory liability by stealth), while on the other hand, they are also necessary to establish the existence of a primary wrong: accessory liability is not inchoate, but parasitic, meaning that it cannot materialise without a wrongdoing by a direct infringer. Where no primary infringement has taken place, no accessory liability can exist. The analysis underlined the importance of crisp rules of primary liability for the sculpting of the proper scope of accessory liability. Without certainty regarding the definition of primary liability, certainty regarding the definition of accessory liability is excluded, while overly expansive rules of primary liability impose on the rightful domain of accessory liability. For this purpose, additional clarification on the details of the current European copyright regime, at least as it pertains to online activities such as hyperlinking, would be beneficial. The adoption of a unified European copyright code might be helpful in this regard.

The analysis subsequently moved on to the current EU framework on intermediary liability. This is scattered across a range of different sources, but its heart is found in the E-Commerce Directive. Here, the EU legislator has set forth a specialised immunity regime for internet intermediaries, shielding them on a conditional basis from all liability they might otherwise encounter, i.e., including for third party copyright infringements, in the provision of three types of services: mere conduit, caching and hosting. Article 15 of the E-Commerce Directive adds an additional element of protection for safe harbour providers in the form of a prohibition against general obligations to monitor the information which such providers transmit or store, as well as general obligations actively to seek out facts or circumstances indicating illegal activity. Specifically for copyright, these provisions are further supplemented by Article 8(3) of the Copyright Directive. This requires Member States to ensure that right-holders can apply for an injunction against intermediaries whose services are used by others to commit an infringement. Assorted peripheral rules helpful with the interpretation of this partial framework can additionally be identified in the Enforcement Directive, as well as relevant EU secondary law on data protection and privacy.

Particularly interesting in this analysis was the emergence of the importance of the concept of neutrality with regard to internet intermediaries. In this regard, a distinction is to be made between the rules of the E-Commerce Directive and those of the Copyright Directive. While the E-Commerce safe harbours provide protection, under certain conditions, to intermediaries that are sufficiently 'neutral', Article 8(3) of the Copyright Directive applies across the board to any intermediary regardless of its neutrality or lack thereof, based solely on optimum placement to bring the infringement to an end. A bifurcation of applicable remedies is thus discernible along the lines of intermediary culpability: injunctions may be issued against any intermediary, but an obligation to pay damages requires non-neutrality – i.e., some sort of active involvement that goes beyond the merely technical and automatic.

In any case, while this patchwork of provisions is of course useful, it is also incomplete: a structured substantive scheme governing EU accessory copyright liability is currently lacking, so that too many unanswered questions slip through the harmonisation gaps. In an attempt to mitigate this problem, the CJEU, in its relevant interpretative case law, has recently reverted to European primary law for clues regarding the appropriate solutions. The relevant rulings rest heavily on the notion of a 'fair balance' between conflicting fundamental rights: according to the CJEU, copyright, as a fundamental right protected under Article 17(2) the EU's Charter of Fundamental Rights, must be weighed against opposing fundamental rights of equal normative value, most notably the right of the intermediary to conduct a business (Article 16 of the Charter) and the rights of its users to the protection of their privacy and personal data (Articles 7 and 8 of the Charter) and their freedom of expression (Article 11 of the Charter). This has elevated the discussion on intermediary liability to hierarchically higher legal planes, while also providing a legal basis for a European regulation of the responsibilities of intermediaries with regard to third party copyright infringements beyond the limited scope of the existing directives. As a result, fundamental rights have been revealed as the driving force behind the harmonisation of European intermediary liability. Accordingly, the existing European provisions can be understood as elaborations on a broader, underlying, unwritten and unified normative framework of intermediary accessory copyright liability, to which any further substantive development must refer.

But the vagueness of the basic rules thus invoked inevitably results in poor guidance as to the appropriate solutions, while the individual cases heard miss the forest for the trees, shedding light only on the specific circumstances that concern them. The CJEU's rulings thus fail to illuminate the boarder picture: where does this 'fair balance' lie? When must an intermediary be held liable for the copyright infringements of others? A harmonised general standard is hinted at, but never detailed. Beyond the safe harbours, the law is all at sea.

To remedy this situation, the doctrine of 'fair balance' was tracked back to its legal theoretical and jurisprudential origins, in order to investigate what it might look like and where it can be located in cases of intermediary accessory copyright liability. It was thus concluded that balancing constitutes the application of the principle of proportionality to cases of clashes between fundamental rights. Where non-absolute rights are involved – as in the case in copyright enforcement against internet intermediaries – this requires an intricate process of rational evaluation taking into account the particular circumstances of each individual case. Balancing thus essentially refers to the constant re-assessment and re-shuffling of basic values and fundamental ideals by a democratic society that is necessary for the resolution of the never-ending flow of legal problems thrown up by evolving social, technological and economic conditions that touch on the basic cornerstones of societal organisation: essentially, to constitutional discourse.

For this purpose, it was noted, the ECtHR is slowly developing an approach that rests on the adoption of sets of factors intended to help courts and legislators navigate the application of fair balance to specific cases. While this factor-infused interpretation is a step in the right direction, the factors identified so far in the case law of the court seem to be changeable depending on the circumstances of the case at hand. In the interests of greater predictability, scholars are therefore calling for more fixed benchmarks, capable of providing better guidance. An even better solution would be the dismounting of European intermediary accessory copyright liability from the lofty realms of fundamental rights and its repositioning within the tort law rules that naturally guide interpersonal legal relationships.

6.2 THE NATIONAL REGIMES

In the absence of a complete EU framework for intermediary accessory copyright liability, the Member States have been forced to rely on their own home-grown solutions. Three of these were meticulously scrutinised in Chapter 3. The jurisdictions chosen for this purpose where those of England, France and Germany, these corresponding to each of the three major tort law traditions of Europe.

All three of these national systems have experimented to a certain extent with intra-copyright solutions to intermediary liability. So, for example, the English courts' first choice of legal device for the resolution of cases of intermediary accessory liability in copyright has been the doctrine of authorisation. Yet, the original intention behind this was its limitation to those who 'grant or purport to grant to a third person the right to do' the restricted act. It must therefore be stretched beyond its natural meaning if it is to be applied to cases of intermediary liability, something for which the English courts have attracted great criticism. France has taken a very different route. Lacking a special liability regime for copyright along the lines of the cascading editorial liability system applicable to press crimes, the French courts have attempted instead to apply the rules of primary copyright infringement directly onto intermediaries, by holding that primary liability encompasses the 'provision of the means' to infringe or even that, depending on the circumstances, intermediaries 'take over' foreign infringements, thus turning them into their own. This will arguably often involve a misapplication of the relevant rules that again emphasises the need for stricter EU-level guidance on primary liability. Finally, Germany relies primarily on its distinctive *Störerhaftung* regime. This imposes liability on persons who causally contribute to an infringement in violation of a duty to review (*Prüfungspflicht*) incumbent upon them. While not limited to copyright (it notably also applies to unfair competition), this is also not a tort-based regime, instead finding its roots in property law. Importantly, *Störerhaftung* focuses only on injunctive relief, denying any monetary compensation to the plaintiff. In addition, like authorisation and the French primary liability rules, *Störerhaftung* too has been overstretched by overenthusiastic courts at a loss for other ways to extract liability from providers they instinctively deem blameworthy.

In the face of the limitations encountered by these options, the courts in all three countries have abandoned the confines of copyright to dig further into their general tort law provisions for better solutions. The analysis revealed two main tort-based approaches to accessory liability. These were labelled 'residual liability' or the 'single fault' model and 'concurrent liability' or the 'multiple faults' model. The prime proponent of the first is England. Here, accessory liability is seen as a form of 'joint tortfeasance' and accessories are therefore treated as equal parties in the commission of the infringement alongside the main infringer. France, by contrast, prefers the second approach. This involves holding accessories liable not for participating in an infringement as such, but for violating, by helping a third party to commit infringement, the general standard of conduct that requires all legal subjects to avoid causing others harm. In other words, while in the residual liability system the accessory is held liable for the same tort as the primary infringer, in the concurrent torts system, the same actions will make her liable for a different, though connected, tortious conduct. The main difference between the residual and concurrent liability models lies in the culpability standard: while residual liability requires that the joint tortfeasor have acted with the intention to cause the infringement, the concurrent liability model is laxer, being satisfied with mere negligence. It should be noted that the multiple faults approach might theoretically have been possible under the English system as well, through the vehicle of the tort of negligence, but for the intense dislike the English courts have always displayed for the idea. A final mixed system is represented by Germany: ever meticulous, the German law-makers have opted to cover all bases, with the provisions of the German BGB on extra-contractual liability equipping the German legal system with general tort rules that would allow it both to treat intentional accessories as *Mittäter,* i.e., joint tortfeasors (along the English example) and to apply a general duty of care to avoid causing another harm (along the French example). Nevertheless, a definite preference for the first solution of *Mittäterschaft* can be discerned, the German Federal Court of Justice having so far refused to apply a negligence-based solution in copyright. At the same time, in the face of *Störerhaftung's* enduring popularity, even this finds little application in practice. In any case, being based on duties of care as well, *Störerhaftung* arguably represents a kind of negligent accessory liability itself, albeit one limited to injunctive relief.

In any case, all three jurisdictions show the clear effects of EU influence. This can certainly be discerned in the rules on liability for damages (e.g., in the rejection of notice-and-stay-down as a basis for liability by the French supreme court), but is most evident in the area of injunctive relief. Given that Article 8(3) of the Copyright Directive, as opposed to the defensive safe harbour provisions, is positively stated, making active demands on national legal systems, this result is unsurprising. Notably, England and France have been obliged to make the most adjustments in this regard, neither having previously contemplated injunctive orders against non-liable parties for the prevention or termination of copyright infringements. Both countries accordingly had to take legislative steps for the introduction of the possibility into their national law. Germany was spared this complication and instead relies on its trusty *Störerhaftung* for the same effect. Regardless, all three systems have adjusted their interpretation of the relevant national rules to the CJEU case law on fair balance. Thus, in recent years, the national courts' concern for the proper representation of end-users' interests in such processes has been increasing, as has their concern with the proper confinement of relevant orders through appropriate time limits, due regard for the question of effectiveness and a refusal to allow plaintiffs to add new listings to existing blocking orders. The German courts seem to be having the most difficulty in this regard, with considerations of proportionality taken to extremes that deny application of *Störerhaftung* to access providers, while imposing an exceptionally strict interpretation of the doctrine onto host service providers. Even here however, recent BGH rulings would seem to suggest that, under the guidance of CJEU case law, discrepancies may slowly be ironing themselves out.

Finally, all three countries have also taken measures for the introduction of additional responsibilities for internet intermediaries in the interests of copyright enforcement, notably in the form of warning obligations, as well as obligations for the disclosure of identifying information of the intermediary's infringing users.

6.3 THE ELEMENTS OF A EUROPEAN ACCESSORY LIABILITY

The descriptive analysis of Chapters 2 and 3 gave way in Chapter 4 to a thematic approach. This focused on the main building blocks of tortious liability relevant to the European harmonisation of intermediary accessory copyright liability. These were identified as fault, causation and, to a lesser extent, defences. Each of these notions was analysed in turn, to discover their common European meaning. Fault was identified as consisting of intent or negligence, the latter being dependant on the mutable notion of the reasonable person. Causation was defined as the link that binds the defendant's behaviour to the damage. Defences were divided into two basic kinds, depending on the jurisdiction: grounds for the justification of the defendant's behaviour and excuses that relieve him from liability that ought otherwise to result. Again, the analysis rested on the comparative examination of English, French and German tort law. Harmonising 'glue' keeping the chapter together was found in existing projects for the unification of European tort law and in particular the PETL, developed by the EGTL, and the DCFR, compiled by the Study Group on a European Civil Code and the Acquis Group. The objective was to ground European intermediary accessory copyright liability in a strong theory of general principles for a truly European tort law.

Through this analysis, the national rules of European intermediary accessory liability in England, France and Germany, as those were laid out in Chapter 3, were associated with the underlying broader tort norms of each respective jurisdiction. In this way, the reasons behind the differences between those diverse rules were identified in the differences between their underlying general tort law frameworks. In particular, two main drivers of divergence in accessory liability were identified: the different limits that the national systems set to the notion of fault and the different approaches they take to causation.

So, the affinity English and German law show for the concept of joint tortfeasance was explained in two ways: (a) their insistence on setting strict limits to liability for omissions – therefore including omissions to prevent the wrongdoing of others – through the construct of 'duties of care' (in England) and '*Verkehrspflichten*' (in Germany); and (b) their restrictive theories of legal causation. Both of these elements carefully control against an overexpansion of fault liability, thus effectively excluding in these two countries the possibility of an accessory liability based in negligence. Instead, the English and German systems are routed into the solution of joint tortfeasance or *Mittäterschaft,* which relies on findings of intention to substantiate accessory liability.

France stands apart in this regard, being shown to take an expansive, unitary approach in both these areas. So: (a) although the French legal system also insists on the substantiation of an obligation to take action before liability for an omission will be found, not only is its theory in this area much more flexible, but the willingness of its courts to make use of this flexibility greater; (b) additionally, by and large, French courts are satisfied with a mere showing of *conditio sine qua non* in order to accept the existence of a causative link binding the defendant's behaviour to the damage. As a result, French liability does not need joint tortfeasance and can rely readily on the basic rules of negligence to support accessory liability.

While these discrepancies might, at first sight, seem to spell despair with regard to the construction of a harmonised European regime in this area, it was shown that great reason for optimism exists. In particular, while the theoretical clashes between the European national systems might be considerable, in practice the results do not greatly differ. Structure, rather than substance is what diverges. On this basis, the PETL and the DCFR were relied upon as examples of the possibilities that exist for harmonised solutions to accessory liability. In particular, the DCFR starts with a cautious causation rule that eschews a simple 'but-for' test. It then sets up a principle of joint tortfeasance based on participation with, instigation of or material assistance in causing the damage. At the same time, it avoids concrete guidelines on omissions, in this way allowing for greater flexibility in the recognition of negligent causation through behaviour that does not meet the standard of the reasonable person. The PETL, on the other hand, shows how a flexible approach to fault can be combined both with the identification of factors indicating the existence of a duty to protect others from damage, as well as guidelines on participation in another's wrongdoing, albeit injected into the rules on apportionment as between multiple tortfeasors.

Finally, the element of defences – i.e., justifications or excuses – was also associated with intermediary liability. As was shown, this is the area that exhibits the least promise of compromise between the three national systems: each refers to something entirely different in its use of the term. At the same time, it was noted that no real need exists for a unitary concept of defences, at least as regards specifically the construction of a European intermediary accessory copyright liability. While the recognition of defences makes sense when creating an entire tort system intended to regulate an endless variety of possible situations, intermediary accessory copyright liability is specific enough that any justifications can be incorporated directly into the rules that comprise the new framework – indeed, that would be a tidier system and the one that should, to the extent possible, be preferred.

The analysis ended on a consideration of the similarities between tort law balancing and the notion of a 'fair balance', as this has been applied to intermediary liability by the CJEU. It was concluded that the substantive overlap between the two is great. The main difference lies in their field of applicability: while fundamental rights balancing is directed towards States, tort law balancing applies to interpersonal legal relationships. As a result, by dismounting the balancing exercise from the inaccessible heights of fundamental rights and positioning it directly on the level of private parties, balancing can be used not only to tell law-makers how to construct their rules on intermediary accessory copyright liability so as not to impinge on fundamental rights, but what in fact those rules should be – i.e., to construct a European substantive rule on intermediary accessory copyright liability. Precisely that was the exercise subsequently undertaken in Chapter 5.

6.4 EUROPEAN INTERMEDIARY ACCESSORY COPYRIGHT LIABILITY

On the basis of the previous analysis, the study finally culminated, in Chapter 5, in the formulation of a proposed framework for a future European intermediary accessory liability in copyright. For this purpose, Chapter 5 attempted to apply the building blocks of liability identified in Chapter 4 to intermediary accessory copyright liability, while relying heavily on the findings of the dissection of the pertinent issues with regard specifically to intermediary accessory copyright liability that was undertaken in Chapters 2 and 3.

The first choice made was for the adoption of a negligence-based solution along the French paradigm: reliance on a 'Basic Norm' that prohibits harming others. As a result of this approach, intermediary liability under the proposed European framework, will be understood, not as a participation in the infringement of others, but as the violation of a prohibition against accessorial behaviour with regard to infringements committed by those others. This decision was motivated by the simplicity of this approach, which is better suited to exercises of harmonisation, as well as by the fact that all examined European systems include the necessary legal theoretical equipment for its application, even if they choose not to make use of it themselves. Additionally, this approach also offers a broader basis for liability, expanding into carelessness as well as intent. It thus enables the examination of all available options within the European accessory liability landscape. At the same time, through the further elaboration of the applicable standard, the proposed solution was infused with elements from English and German law as well, leading to a well-balanced ultimate harmonised outcome.

In keeping with this set-up, the investigation of whether an intermediary is liable for accessory liability in copyright was connected primarily, under the proposed framework, with the examination of its fault, i.e., a comparison of its behaviour with that of the famous 'reasonable person'. To a lesser extent causation was also considered. As a result, the central question guiding the construction of the proposed regime was identified as the following: 'what would a reasonable intermediary do?' The emergent framework rests on two central pillars: a conduct element, examining the extent to which the intermediary caused that damage, and a mental element, examining whether the intermediary demonstrated the mindset of a reasonable intermediary in the same circumstances. An optional third pillar of duties of care becomes relevant depending on the severity of the mental element involved. The conduct element was defined broadly as consisting of any non-minimal causal participation in the copyright infringement of another party. Mere facilitation should accordingly suffice. As all internet intermediaries will meet this requirement as soon as their services are used by another to commit a copyright infringement, liability will depend on how an intermediary fares in the subsequent analysis.

The mental element was subdivided into two types: intent and knowledge. It was concluded that, if an intermediary intended an infringement, its behaviour must be understood as by definition unreasonable. Liability should therefore automatically ensue. As a result, in the final analysis, intentional liability reverts, at least as to its effects, if not its positioning within the system, to the paradigm of 'residual liability' or 'single fault' espoused by English tort law: where an intermediary intends an infringement, that infringement should be seen as its own and its liability should be no different than that of the primary infringer. It has committed the infringement itself – albeit through the vehicle of the primary infringer – and its liability should therefore be assured immediately.

If the intermediary has no intent, but does have knowledge of the infringement, the possibility of negligence liability must be explored. Following the example of Article 14 of the E-Commerce Directive, a hybrid objective/subjective knowledge threshold was opted for: the intermediary will only be considered to have knowledge if it is aware of facts or circumstances from which the infringement would have been apparent to a 'diligent economic operator'. Both general and specific knowledge suffice, although they will result in different consequences. In any event, as opposed to what is the case for intent, the combination of mere knowledge of third party infringement with the conduct element does not alone suffice to render the intermediary's behaviour unreasonable and thereby result in liability: 'something more is necessary'. That something more will be provided by the violation of a duty of care incumbent on the intermediary. What duties of care burden the reasonable intermediary? The answer to this will depend on the circumstances. Case-by-case balancing is accordingly required.

How should that balancing be approached? Four criteria of care were identified for the purpose of guiding the process. These were sourced from the comparative analysis of European tort law principles, as undertaken in Chapter 4, in combination with the factor-infused approach to the doctrine of a fair balance towards which the highest European courts of the CJEU and ECtHR are moving: (1) the *risk* created; (2) the *benefit* of the conduct; the (3) *burden* of the measures of care; and the (4) *responsibility* of the intermediary. In the specific area of intermediary liability, these can be further broken down as follows. The notion of risk can be separated into: (1) *the seriousness of the_damage;* and (1) *the probability of damage*. The factor of the benefit of the conduct should be examined in view of: (1) *the interests of the intermediary*; (2) *the interests of the intermediaries' users;*

and (3) *the general interest*. The same holds for the third factor of the burden of the measures of care. Finally, responsibility to take measures might arise from: (1) the type of knowledge of the risk that the intermediary has (i.e., the *foreseeability* of the risk); (2) its skills with regard to the measure in question (i.e., the *avoidability* of the risk); and (3) the existence of *a special duty* to take affirmative care.

While this reliance on case-by-case balancing makes the accessory liability of internet intermediaries a moving target, the flexibility with which it imbues the resultant framework should be understood as a feature rather than a bug: a strong regime that can face the test of time will provide greater long term legal certainty, as the provision of clear and appropriate factors creates structure, which can help guide effective and targeted deliberative judicial reasoning. At the same time, on this strong theoretical basis, further concretisation to the current situation surrounding intermediary accessory copyright liability becomes easier to achieve. Precisely such concretisation, with a view of revealing the duties of care that encumber reasonable intermediaries with regard to third party copyright infringements, was what was undertaken next. For this purpose, the balancing criteria were applied in a benchmarking exercise that examined the reasonability of six different measures of care:

- the suspension of the perpetrator of the infringement;
- measures for the identification of the perpetrator;
- the monitoring of content, including filtering;
- the blocking and removal of infringing content, including notice-and-take-down;
- warning systems;
- notification to the authorities.

Significantly, the notion of liability considered was a broad one, in keeping with the wide definition that the concept finds in the practice of the Member States. It was thus understood to encompass both liability for damages and for injunctive relief. On the basis of the ensuing analysis, the following was concluded: requiring the blocking or removal of infringements and the suspension of the perpetrator by intermediaries for the enforcement of copyright will often be proportionate, but particular care must be taken in their deployment. The type of intermediary will be particularly relevant: the blocking or removal of content can be expected to be undertaken proactively by host service providers, but access providers should require a court order before they must proceed. Requiring notification to the authorities will most usually be proportionate, but often of little use. Obligations to issue general warnings to end-users to avoid copyright infringement will always be proportionate, as long as the intermediary has either general or specific knowledge of infringement. Duties to identify particular primary infringers should always require a court order. Duties to filter content or otherwise generally monitor it, should invariably be considered out of bounds, even given a court order.

Finally, the question of proportionate liability was examined. The basic idea here is that extracting equal liability from both a primary tortfeasor and an accessory is not always a fair result. Instead, under certain circumstances, the principle of solidary (i.e., joint and several) liability should be exchanged for a proportionate distribution of liability depending on the extent of each party's contribution to the infringement. It was suggested that such a system should be considered where the accessory acted with negligence, but not when there was intent. Under the influence of the current EU framework's distinction between neutral and non-neutral intermediaries with regard to the type of remedy applied and Germany's pragmatic *Störerhaftung* regime, this solution was given a final twist: it was thus proposed that where an intermediary acts with intent, solidary liability should be extracted, but where only negligence can be found, the relief should be limited to the injunctive.

Ultimately, a flowchart of European intermediary accessory copyright liability was put forth. This structures the elemental building blocks of a complete and substantive European answer to this complicated topic. Under the proposed model, where the intermediary intended the third party's infringement of copyright, it should be held liable under a rule of solidarity. Where intention cannot be proven, negligence should be considered. This requires the combination of knowledge with the violation of a duty of care. The type of duty will depend on the type of knowledge. If the intermediary has specific knowledge of a specific infringement, it will be under a duty to take all appropriate measures to remove the infringing content and prevent its repetition, such as (depending on the specific circumstances) blocking or taking it down, suspending the perpetrator, notifying the authorities or supplying identifying data on the perpetrator. If the intermediary had no such specific knowledge, but ought to have had it, then it should be held liable only for injunctive relief. If the intermediary has general knowledge of mass infringements taking place on its systems, it may again be obliged to take all appropriate measures to remove the infringing content and prevent its repetition – however, given the differing circumstances and the limitations these impose, the appropriate measures should this time in all cases be limited to the posting of warning duties or, if requested, the provision of identifying information to the authorities. Again, if the intermediary did not have general knowledge, but ought to have had it, it should be held liable, but only for injunctive relief. What if the intermediary did not take the measures due by it? In that case, whether it had the ability to take those measures and, if not, whether it ought to have made sure that it had the ability to take them becomes relevant. If the answer to either of those questions is in the affirmative, then the intermediary should be held liable only for injunctive relief. If the intermediary has taken all measures appropriate to the knowledge it possessed or if it had no knowledge or, having knowledge, had no ability to take appropriate measures nor an obligation to make sure that it had such ability, then no liability may be sought. A final possibility was also suggested: if the intermediary did not take the appropriate measures that would have been expected of it on a flagrantly persistent basis, arguably intent can be inferred and full liability for damages applied.

Crucially, this system is intended to replace the current fragmented system that combines the EU safe harbours and surrounding vague norms with the national substantive systems. Given that the current EU provisions were considered in its formulation and woven into its structure, it should not result in considerably different outcomes, at least as regards Article 14 and 15 of the E-Commerce Directive, which establish the laxer standard applicable to host services providers. At the same time, once this fundamental substantive framework is in place, the possibility of additional exceptional provisions intended to operate on top on the general rules might be considered. This leaves room for policy considerations to affect the legal regime in more ephemeral and/or targeted ways, as has been the case so far with the safe harbours. Such exceptional provisions could – depending on what is deemed politically or economically desirable and viable – either do what the safe harbours do and introduce further immunities (thus essentially amounting to defences against liability) or impose strict liability. In any case, either option should be understood only as a deviation: strict liability and no liability are exceptions to the generally applicable basic rule of fault. Fault, and the rule of reason it brings with it, must be the default.

6.5 THE WAY FORWARD: IMPLEMENTATION INTO LAW

One final question remains: how could the suggestions of this book be transposed into law – or perhaps more generally, if intermediary accessory liability for copyright infringement were to be harmonised, how would that happen? Five different options present themselves.

Firstly, there is the possibility that a European Civil Code or, less ambitiously, a European Tort Code – based on either the PETL, the DCFR or a third, new text – may truly be adopted in its entirely and used as a basis for the direct regulation of intermediary liability, including for third party copyright infringements. While certainly conceivable, this option seems unlikely to come about in the near future. A certain amount of political will does of course exist.[1] So, for example, the development of the DCFR, intended by its authors to function as a possible model for a political

1. See, for example, European Parliament, 'Resolution of 23 March 2006 on European Contract Law and the Revision of the *Acquis*: The Way Forward', (2005/2022(INI)), Brussels, 23 March 2006, [2006] OJ C 292 E, 109.

Common Frame of Reference,[2] was financed and encouraged by the Commission.[3] However, progress has been exceedingly slow,[4] while the political interest in this area has primarily focused not on tort, but on contract law.[5] The most recent move in the area came in July 2010, when the Commission published a Green Paper for a European contract law, in which it put seven options for the further handling of the DCFR up for discussion.[6] While the prime focus here was again, as the title suggests, on contract, auspiciously, among the possibilities put forth, the paper did include a suggestion for the adoption of a **regulation establishing a European Civil Code**, intended to replace not only national contract laws, but also the rules applicable to other related fields of private law, including tort. Promising as this might sound, no further significant developments on this front have since materialised. In any case, whether a full European Civil Code or even a full European Tort Code is really necessary is questionable, while such an initiative would almost certainly prove controversial in the current political environment. It would also raise sensitive issues of subsidiarity and proportionality: obviously, unifying all of private law simply in order to harmonise the tiny corner of intermediary accessory copyright liability would represent a clear overreaction. At least for the purposes of this one limited area, more circumscribed measures would arguably be much more efficient.

With that in mind, a second option would be to focus exclusively on intermediary accessory copyright liability through the usual route of harmonisation by directive. This is certainly the simplest course of action and therefore arguably the one that should be preferred. Total unification by regulation might also be considered. There is some indication that the EU is contemplating these possibilities. Calls for more detailed regulation of the area have after all been persistent in the relevant consultations and scholarly

2. C von Bar et al. (eds), *Principles, Definitions and Model Rules of European Private Law: Draft Common Frame of Reference (DCFR)*, prepared by the Study Group on a European Civil Code and the Research Group on EC private law (Acquis Group), Outline Edition (Sellier 2009) 8.
3. Green Paper from the Commission of 1 July 2010, 'Policy Options for Progress towards a European Contract Law for Consumers and Businesses', COM(2010) 348 final, Brussels, 1 July 2010.
4. Indicatively, the DCFR arose as an extension of the so-called Principles of European Contract Law, the work on these having begun as early as 1982, see O Lando et al., *Principles of European Contract Law – Part III* (Kluwer Law International 2003) ix.
5. See Communication from the Commission to the Council and the European Parliament on European Contract Law, COM(2001)398 final, 11 July 2001; Commission Communication on 'European Contract Law and the revision of the acquis: the way forward', COM(2004) 651, 11 October 2004; Communication from the Commission to the European Parliament and the Council, 'A More Coherent European Contract Law – An Action Plan', COM(2003) 68, 12 February 2003.
6. Green Paper from the Commission of 1 July 2010, 'Policy Options for Progress towards a European Contract Law for Consumers and Businesses', COM(2010) 348 final, Brussels, 1 July 2010.

output.[7] Encouragingly, as mentioned in Chapter 1, in May 2015, in its Communication on a Digital Single Market Strategy for Europe, the Commission responded by promising to hand down by the end of 2016 legislative proposals for the reform of the EU copyright regime, as well as a comprehensive analysis of the role of intermediaries with regard to illegal content on the internet.[8] The subsequent additional consideration of intermediary liability in a Communication on copyright only in December 2015[9] suggests a possible partitioning of the more general rules of intermediary liability from those dedicated specifically to that area of law. This could foreshadow a move away from the 'horizontal' approach of the E-Commerce Directive's safe harbours towards an – arguably much more sensible – 'vertical' regulation of different areas of law in an independent manner that could add some nuance and granularity to the relevant rules. Even more auspiciously, the Digital Single Market Communication has also made explicit reference to the possible introduction of a 'duty of care' for intermediaries. The concept of 'duty' is of course central to an area of law that forms a sub-species of the so-called law of obligations. Its introduction would essentially be tantamount to the introduction of a concept of fault – after all, presumably any new duty of care would be accompanied by the designation of consequences for its breach. The consideration of this possibility by the Commission therefore strongly suggests a move away from the current negative approach of the safe harbours, towards the adoption of more substantive norms that determine not only when liability cannot result, but when it must.

Would such a move be sensible? Although, as mentioned above, a piecemeal, disjointed development of European tort law does run the risk of a 'double shattering of the law',[10] i.e., of destabilising national structures, while also failing to introduce a solid European one, if such a directive or regulation were to ground itself in a common concept of European tort law based on soft law initiatives such as the PETL and the DCFR, this could be avoided.[11] Such an initiative could also help combat national lawyers natural

7. Commission Staff Working Paper, 'Online Services, Including E-Commerce, in the Single Market', SEC(2011) 1641 final, 11 January 2012, 39-54.
8. Communication from the Commission to the European Parliament, the Council, the European Economic and Social Committee and the Committee of the Regions, 'A Digital Single Market Strategy for Europe' COM(2015)192 final.
9. Communication from the Commission to the European Parliament, the Council, the European Economic and Social Committee and the Committee of the Regions, 'Towards a modern, more European copyright framework', COM(2015) 626 final, 9 December 2015.
10. H Koziol, 'Comparative Conclusions' in H Koziol, *Basic Questions of Tort Law from a Comparative Perspective* (Jan Sramek Verlag 2015) 690.
11. R Van Den Bergh & L Visscher, 'The Principles of European Tort Law: The Right Path to Harmonization?' (2006) 4 European Review of Private Law 511.

'homing' instincts,[12] which might otherwise undermine the uniform implementation and application of the European rules. Indeed, it could be argued that a selective harmonisation of only those areas of tort law that are ripe for the purpose – such as intermediary accessory copyright liability – can be the best ambassador of a common European tort culture, while avoiding the threat to national legal identity that some fear a wholemeal unification of all of tort law might threaten.

Does this exhaust all available options? Instead of relying on 'soft law' instruments such as the PETL and the DCFR to draft a 'hard law' directive or regulation on intermediary accessory copyright liability, it could also be possible, if necessary – as a third alternative – to limit any European instrument on intermediary accessory copyright liability to 'soft law' status itself. Inspiration in this regard can be taken from the aforementioned Green Paper for a European contract law. This makes three such suggestions, all of which could be easily adapted to intermediary accessory liability as well: (a) the adoption of an official legislative 'toolbox' to be used by the EU legislator in the adoption of relevant smaller scale pieces of legislation (e.g., a notice-and-take-down procedure); (b) the adoption of a Commission Recommendation that encourages Member States to replace national law on intermediary accessory copyright liability with a proffered European instrument; and (c) the adoption of a regulation setting up an optional '2nd regime' on intermediary accessory copyright liability in each Member State, while retaining the current national rules in parallel.[13] If all else fails, the Commission also suggests that the mere publication of findings of legal experts can also have some integrating influence.

Failing all else, the possibility always exists that the harmonisation of intermediary accessory copyright liability could also simply proceed precisely as it has done so far: through CJEU case law relying primarily directly on the law of fundamental rights. This is obviously the path of least resistance. It also has the advantage of achieving harmonisation only in those particularly problematic areas where it is most needed (such cases naturally being more likely to make it before the European court), while avoiding pushing the issue too aggressively on a broader front. On the other hand, it is also potentially liable to accusations of a furtive harmonisation not intended by the European legislator,[14] while it would possibly result in little actual guidance for national law-makers and judges: as legal experts from across the EU have been pointing out, there is a limit to how much real

12. M van Eechoud et al., 'The Recasting of Copyright and Related Rights for the Knowledge Economy', final report, Institute for Information Law (IViR), University of Amsterdam, November 2006, 38.
13. See Options 1-4, Green Paper from the Commission of 1 July 2010, 'Policy Options for Progress towards a European Contract Law for Consumers and Businesses', COM(2010) 348 final, Brussels, 1 July 2010.
14. L Bently, 'Harmonisation by Stealth: Copyright and the ECJ', Fordham IP Conference, New York, 2 May 2012.

meaning can be squeezed out of the vague precepts of fundamental rights law. In addition, no coherent unification can possibly come out of case law-based harmonisation in anything approaching the required timeframe:[15] the CJEU cannot hope to keep up with the internet. Finally, and most worryingly yet, this approach would also simply run the risk of resulting in bad law: it is indicative that the ECHR in *Delfi* found no violation of the intermediary's own freedom of expression by the imposition of damages amounting to EUR 320 for a failure to prevent its users' racist speech. Whatever other failings the judges' thought process might have had, this outcome is arguably technically correct: the problem with the outcome of *Delfi* before the Estonian courts was not their interference with Delfi's human rights, so much as a violation of the EU directives and the implementation of bad tort law that fell out of the ECtHR's jurisdiction. The requirements made of Delfi might have been fairly balanced within the Member State's margin of appreciation, but they did not represent the behaviour of the reasonable intermediary. Even if the Charter is seen as more demanding than the ECHR, relying on the same approach within the EU would similarly eventually reach a dead end, where a specific national approach, though undesirable within an EU context, could not be accused of violating fundamental rights. The 'horizontal' governance of relationships between individuals is instead best dealt through the rules of tort law that have been developed for precisely that purpose – and which, at the end of the day, are arguably nothing more than the mirror image of fundamental rights, reflected from the other side of the private/public law divide, albeit with far greater precision.[16]

Finally, it's worth mentioning that, even if no harmonised European accessory intermediary liability framework is adopted in any of the aforementioned ways, it is clear that the national solutions to intermediary accessory copyright liability as they currently exist nevertheless require considerable refurbishment. Accordingly, the suggestions made here, even if not imposed on the Member States by an enterprising EU legislator, could conceivably also be helpful for the improvement of the national systems individually. In that context, inter-European – or even international – dialogue can provide a rich source of best practice. Lord Goff has predicted that 'the next period of our legal history will see the growth of a new influence upon the development of the law […] the growing importance of comparative law'.[17] By looking towards our neighbours for inspiration and lessons, we can better equip ourselves to make decisions as to the appropriate

15. W van Gerven, 'The ECJ Case Law as a Means of Unification of Private Law?' in A Hartkamp, *Towards a European Civil Code* (3rd ed., Kluwer Law International 2004) 101.
16. C von Bar et al. (eds), *Principles, Definitions and Model Rules of European Private Law: Draft Common Frame of Reference (DCFR)*, prepared by the Study Group on a European Civil Code and the Research Group on EC private law (Acquis Group), Outline Edition (Sellier 2009) 64.
17. Quoted in B Markesinis, 'Negligence, Nuisance and Affirmative Duties of Action' (1989) Law Quarterly Review 104.

solutions to apply at home. Indeed, such spontaneous cross-pollination could ultimately end up having a profound harmonising effect in itself. Van Gerven observes that 'convergence of the minds of practitioners, judges, professors and future lawyers is at least as important as convergence of laws. [...] Learning about each other's legal mentalities, and ways of solving concrete legal problems, is therefore of crucial importance'.[18] From this perspective, a 'bottom-up' approach to convergence might, in the end, be as effective as – and encounter less resistance than – a 'top-down' one. Either way, comparative studies with harmonising outlooks, such as that provided in this book, are essential.

6.6 CLOSING REMARKS

What is the ultimate conclusion? The digital environment is characterised by ubiquitous intermediation.[19] Access to the internet requires the set-up of an internet connection by an internet access provider and intermediaries of various kinds are necessary to enable every action undertaken online by a user after that. As a result, everything an individual does on the web will require, in one way or another, the involvement of an internet intermediary. Compounding this escalated prevalence, in comparison to their older, analogue counterparts, internet intermediaries are also equipped with more far-reaching technical powers – their potential uses and misuses are therefore also all the more extensive. Inevitably, intermediaries are also used in the commission of online torts, including the now – owing precisely to modern technical capabilities – quotidian tort of copyright infringement. This raises the obvious question: in a world where intermediaries are necessary to do anything, what is their responsibility when their services are used to do something wrongful?

An obvious answer is missing. With a huge part of modern cultural, commercial and scientific life now situated online, complications arise in the form of the competing, equally compelling interests of the multiple stakeholders involved. At the same time, the obligatory, high-powered and high-stakes intermediation of the information era has thrown settled legal conventions into disarray. Absent set answers, the topic of intermediary liability is therefore forcing us to contemplate the very fundaments of our legal systems: what is required is rational, normative deliberation on our basic values – a legal re-orientation within a re-structured technological landscape.

---

18. W van Gerven, 'The ECJ Case Law as a Means of Unification of Private Law?' in A Hartkamp, *Towards a European Civil Code* (3rd ed., Kluwer Law International 2004) 123.
19. Internet Governance Forum, Dynamic Coalition on Platform Responsibility, draft document on 'Recommendations on Terms of Service and Human Rights', available at http://review.intgovforum.org.

The CJEU has set the ball rolling in precisely this direction by identifying the heart of intermediary liability in the doctrine of a fair balance, as this exists within the law of fundamental rights. This offers an oblique way of introducing new norms by building from the bottom of the legal system's foundational values upwards, under the constitutional guidance of one of Europe's highest courts. But a substantive solution cannot be found in the obscure edicts of primary law alone. A better solution would be one introduced by the legislator as such and based directly on the rules appropriate for the legal regulation of interpersonal relationships, i.e., on tort law. This is the area of law that possesses the necessary conceptual tools that can help properly illuminate the legal stakes and direct judicial attention towards a solution that best serves society's interests.

The benefits of pursuing such a well-grounded, principled solution would be substantial. Most obviously, the result would be a coherent, comprehensive and stable framework to govern the accessory liability of internet intermediaries in copyright, one of the area's trickiest current challenges. But more far-reaching effects could also be envisioned. The essential argument of this book rests on the importance of integrating solutions to specific legal problems within a strong surrounding general theory. As a result, the investigation of intermediary accessory copyright liability, if properly approached, could help indicate the answer to much broader, underlying and so far unresolved questions.

First and foremost, this could include the whole of accessory copyright liability as applicable to any actor. Indeed, while obviously the measures of care identified in this book are tailored specifically to internet intermediaries, the broader structures on which they rest amount to a harmonisation of the theory of accessory copyright liability in its totality. If this solution were to be followed, the last big gap in the harmonised edifice of European copyright law could be closed. Such a move would have positive effects on the rules of European primary copyright liability as well, by allowing them to develop in a more natural fashion, instead of under a distorting pressure to extract liability from actors whose responsibilities are engendered elsewhere.

A further-reaching impact could also be anticipated. Accessory liability generally, not only as applied to internet intermediaries in copyright, remains an underdeveloped and poorly understood area of European tort law. The rectification of this situation in copyright through the adoption of a harmonised European intermediary accessory liability regime could light the way for the correction of this more general problem. This suggestion is not too ambitious: while accessory liability is an overlooked area of tort historically, the rise of the age of intermediation has increased its relevance not only in copyright, but across the tort law board. The liability of internet intermediaries is, therefore, a pressing current topic in assorted other 'cybertorts' as well, including, for example, the online infringement of other IPRs, defamation, privacy, unfair competition or economic torts. While the differing dynamics in each of these fields should result in different outcomes for the inevitable balancing exercise, there is no reason why the general structure of that exercise, if properly conceived, should vary significantly. At the very least, the resolution of intermediary accessory liability in copyright should provide an example of how such problems ought to be approached.

Finally, a bolder outcome yet can also be envisaged: the structured, properly founded harmonisation of intermediary accessory copyright liability could, by providing an example of the harmonisation of a sub-section of tort law, if not open up the road towards the European harmonisation of tort law in its totality, then at least show how that could be achieved. This becomes particularly clear if the harmonisation of intermediary accessory copyright liability is viewed through a methodological lens, as a case study of how European tort harmonisation should be approached. Breaking away from the selective harmonisation approach so far favoured by the EU legislator towards a more structured method that dares to dig into the overarching principles can thus lead the way towards the development of a coherent, truly European concept of tort law. This can guide by example the future harmonisation of other individual tort law areas, leading to the slow emergence of a complete framework. Conversely, if intermediary accessory copyright liability does not follow this path, but takes the easy way that relies on superficial indicators unanchored in theory, the result shall be a contribution to and compounding of the 'double shattering' of European tort law.

Naturally, it is not easy to make the kind of doctrinal adjustments suggested here. They would require comprehensive restructuring, where patching up existing superficial solutions might appear simpler. But the deep-seated problems identified in this book cannot otherwise be properly resolved, while the entrenchment of bad doctrine should be addressed sooner rather than later. A preference for temporary stand-ins might have been advisable in the early years of the internet. But the dust has now settled on information society. Hopefully, this book will contribute to opening a dialogue that can result in the constructive change which that demands.

Bibliography

'Manila Principles on Intermediary Liability – Background Paper', 30 May 2015, available at: www.manilaprinciples.org.

'Manila Principles on Intermediary Liability – Best Practices Guidelines for Limiting Intermediary Liability for Content to Promote Freedom of Expression and Innovation – A Global Civil Society Initiative', Version 1.0, 24 March 2015, available at: www.manilaprinciples.org.

'Opinion of the European Data Protection Supervisor on the Current Negotiations by the European Union of an Anti-Counterfeiting Trade Agreement (ACTA)' (2010/C 147/01), 22 February 2010, OJ C147/1.

'Resolution of 23 March 2006 on European Contract Law and the Revision of the *Acquis*: The Way Forward' (2005/2022(INI) Brussels, 23 March 2006 [2006] OJ C 292 E.

Adams, C W, 'Indirect Infringement from a Tort Law Perspective' (2008) 42(3) University of Richmond Law Review 635.

Adams, M & Bomhoff, J (eds), *Practice and Theory in Comparative Law* (Cambridge University Press 2012).

Adeney, E, *The Moral Rights of Authors and Performers: An International and Comparative Analysis* (6th ed., Oxford University Press 2006).

Agrees, R N, 'Is There Ever a Reason to Know? A Comparison of the Contributory Liability "Knowledge" Standard for Websites Hosting Infringed Trademarked Content versus Infringed Copyrighted Content' (2011) 5(1) Journal of Business Entrepreneurship and the Law 179.

Ahlert, C et al., 'How "Liberty" Disappeared from Cyberspace: The Mystery Shopper Tests Internet Content Self-Regulation', available at: http://pcmlp.socleg.ox.ac.uk/sites/pcmlp.socleg.ox.ac.uk/files/liberty.pdf.

Ahrens, H, '21 Thesen zur Störerhaftung im UWG und im Recht des Geistiges Eigentums' (2007) WRP 1281.

Akturk, A & Malcolm, J, 'Unintended Consequences, European-Style: How the New EU Data Protection Regulation Will be Misused to Censor Speech', Electronic Frontier Foundation, Deeplinks Blog, 20 November 2015.

Alexy, R, 'Balancing, Constitutional Review, and Representation' (2005) 3(4) International Journal of Constitutional Law 572.

Alexy, R, 'Constitutional Rights, Balancing and Rationality' (2003) 16(2) Ratio Juris 131.

Alexy, R, 'On Balancing and Subsumption. A Structural Comparison' (2003) 16(4) Ratio Juris 433.

Alexy, R, *A Theory of Constitutional Rights* (Oxford University Press 2002).

Amadei, X, 'Standards of Liability for Internet for Internet Service Providers: A Comparative Study of France and the United States with a Specific Focus on Copyright, Defamation, and Illicit Content' (2002) 35 Cornell International Law Journal 189.

Angelopoulos, C, 'Sketching the Outline of a Ghost: the Fair Balance between Copyright and Fundamental Rights in Intermediary Third Party Liability' (2015) 17(6) Info – The Journal of Policy, Regulation and Strategy for Telecommunications, Information and Media 72.

Angelopoulos, C, 'Are Blocking Injunctions against ISPs Allowed in Europe? Copyright Enforcement in the Post-Telekabel EU Legal Landscape' (2014) 9(10) Journal of Intellectual Property Law & Practice 812.

Angelopoulos, C, 'Beyond the Safe Harbours: Harmonising Substantive Intermediary Liability for Copyright Infringement in Europe' (2013) 3 Intellectual Property Quarterly 253.

Angelopoulos, C, 'Creative Commons and Related Rights in Sound Recordings: Are the Two Systems Compatible?' in L Guibault & C Angelopoulos (eds), *Open Content Licensing: From Theory to Practice* (Amsterdam University Press 2011).

Angelopoulos, C, 'Filtering for Copyrighted Content in Europe' (2009) (4) IRIS plus 1.

Aplin, T, *Copyright Law in the Digital Society* (Hart Publishing 2005).

Arden, M, *Human Rights and European Law: Building New Legal Orders* (Oxford University Press 2015).

Arezzo, E, 'Hyperlinks and Making Available in the European Union – What Future for the Internet after *Svensson*?' (2014) 45(5) International Review of Intellectual Property and Competition Law (IIC) 524.

Article 19, 'Promoting Free Expression and Access to Information' (2010) Implementation Report.

Atiyah, P S, *Vicarious Liability in the Law of Torts* (Butterworth 1967) 195.

Aubert, K L, 'So Long Solidary Liability: Is Parting Such Sweet Sorrow?' (1997) 42(4) Loyola Law Review 745.

Auvret, V P, 'Application de la loi de 1881 à la communication en ligne: délits de presse' (15 March 2006) JCL Communication, Fasc. 4870.

Azzi, T, 'La responsabilité des nouvelles plates-formes: éditeurs, hébergeurs ou autre voie?' in Colloque de l'IPRI, *Contrefaçon sur internet: les enjeux du droit d'auteur sur le WEB 2.0* (Litec 2009) 59.

Bagshaw, R, 'Causing the Behaviour of Others and Other Causal Mixtures' in R Goldberg (ed), *Perspectives on Causation* (Hart Publishing 2011) 361.

Bagshaw, R, 'Downloading Torts: An English Introduction to On-Line Torts' in H Snijders and S Weatherill (eds), *E-Commerce Law: National and Transnational Topics and Perspectives* (Kluwer Law International 2003) 72.

Balganesh, S, *Intellectual Property and the Common Law* (Cambridge University Press 2013).

Barak, A, 'Constitutional Human Rights and Private Law' in D Friedman & D Barak-Erez (eds), *Human Rights in Private Law* (Hart Publishing 2001) 13.

Barak, A, *Proportionality – Constitutional Rights and their Limitations* (Cambridge University Press 2010) 185.

Barak, A, *The Judge in a Democracy* (Princeton University Press 2009)165.

Barendt, E, 'Balancing Freedom of Expression and Privacy: The Jurisprudence of the Strasbourg Court' (2009) 1 Journal of Media Law 49.

Barendt, E, *Freedom of Speech* (2nd ed., Oxford University Press 2007).

Barker, K & Steele, J, 'Drifting towards Proportionate Liability: Ethics and Pragmatics' (2015) 74(1) The Cambridge Law Journal.

Barkhuysen, T & Lindenbergh, S, *Constitutionalisation of Private Law* (Brill 2005).

Bartholomew, M & McArdle, P F, 'Causing Infringement' (2011) 64(3) Vanderbilt Law Review 675.

Bartholomew, M & Tehranian, J, 'The Secret Life of Legal Doctrine: the Divergent Evolution of Secondary Liability in Trademark and Copyright Law' (2006) 21(4) Berkeley Technology Law Journal 1363.

Basedow, J et al., *The Max Planck Encyclopedia of European Private Law* (Oxford University Press 2012).

Bauer, G et al., *Harbauer Rechtsschutzversicherung – Kommentar zu den Allgemeinen Bedingungen für die Rechtsschutzversicherung* (8th ed., C.H. Beck 2010).

Bayer, A, 'Liability 2.0 – Does the Internet Environment Require New Standards for Secondary Liability? An Overview of the Current Legal Situation in Germany' in M J Adelmann et al. (eds), *Patents and Technological Progress in a Globalized World* (Springer 2009) 365.

Beatty, D M, *The Ultimate Rule of Law* (Oxford University Press 2004).

Becher, J, 'Copyright and User-Generated Content: Legal Challenges for Community-Based Businesses in Germany and the USA' (Master's

Thesis, Bucerius Law School/WHU Otto Beisheim School of Management 2010).
Bechtold, S in T Dreier & P B Hugenholtz (eds), *Concise European Copyright Law* (Kluwer Law International 2006).
Beignier, B et al., *Traité de droit de la presse et les médias* (Litec 2009).
Benabou, V L, 'Quelle(s) responsabilité(s) des intermédiaires techniques sur Internet?' (2006) 61(7-8) Annales Des Télécommunications 865.
Benhamou, Y, 'Compensation of Damages for Infringements of Intellectual Property Rights in France, Under Directive 2004/48/EC and Its Transposition Law – New Notions?' (2009) 40 International Review of Intellectual Property and Competition Law (IIC) 125.
Bently, L & Burrell, R, 'Copyright and the Information Society in Europe: A Matter of Timing as Well as Content' (1997) 34 Common Law Review 1197.
Bently, L et al., 'United Kingdom' in L Bently, P Geller & M Nimmer (eds), *International Copyright Law and Practice* (Matthew Bender/LexisNexis 2013).
Bently, L & Sherman, B, *Intellectual Property Law* (3rd ed., Oxford University Press 2009).
Bently, L et al., *International Copyright Law and Practice* (Matthew Bender/LexisNexis 2013).
Bently, L et al. (eds), *Global Copyright* (Edward Elgar 2010).
Berger, A, *Encyclopedic Dictionary of Roman Law – Volume 43* (The American Philosophical Society 1953).
Berka, W, 'Human Rights and Tort Law' in H Koziol, E Karner, A Fenyves & E Steiner (eds), *Tort Law in the Jurisprudence of the European Court of Human Rights* (De Gruyter, Berlin 2011) 237.
Bermann, G & Picard, E, *Introduction to French Law* (Walters Kluwer 2008).
Bhatia, K L, *Textbook on Legal Language and Legal Writing* (Universal Law Publishing 2010).
Birks, P, 'Civil Wrongs: A New World' in *Butterworth Lectures 1990-91* (Butterworths 1992) 100.
Blomsma, J, *Mens Rea and Defences in European Criminal Law* (Intersentia 2013).
Bomhoff, J, 'Comparing Legal Argument' in M Adams & J Bomhoff (eds), *Practice and Theory in Comparative Law* (Cambridge University Press 2012) 84.
Bomhoff, J, *Balancing Constitutional Rights: the Origins and Meanings of Postwar Legal Discourse* (Cambridge University Press 2013).
Boos, S, 'Carrier's Liability for Patent Infringement under German Law' (2010) International Review of Intellectual Property and Competition Law (IIC) 428.
Boré, J, 'La causalité partielle en noir et blanc ou les deux visages de l'obligation *in solidum*' (1971) JCP I 2369.

Borghetti, J-S, 'The Culture of Tort Law in France' (2012) 3 Journal of European Tort Law 158.
Bornkamm, J, 'E-Commerce Directive vs. IP Rights Enforcement – Legal Balance Achieved?' (2007) GRUR Int 642.
Breyer, P, 'Verkehrssicherungspflichten von Internetdiensten im Lichte der Grundrechte' (2009) MMR 14.
Brown, J P, 'Towards an Economic Theory of Liability' (1973) Journal of Legal Studies 323.
Brownsword, R et al. (eds), *The Foundations of European Private Law* (Hart Publishing 2011).
Brownsword, R et al., *The Foundations of European Private Law* (Hart Publishing 2011).
Brüggermeier, G, *Modernising Civil Liability Law in Europe, China, Brazil and Russia: Texts and Commentaries* (Cambridge University Press 2011).
Buckland, W, 'The Duty to Take Care' (1935) 51 Law Quarterly Review 637.
Büllesback, A et al. (eds), *Concise European IT Law* (Kluwer Law International 2006).
Burrell, R & Weatherall, K, 'Before the High Court – Providing Services to Copyright Infringers: *Roadshow Films Pty Ltd v iiNet Ltd'* (2011) 33 Sydney Law Review 801.
Burrows, A, *English Private Law* (Oxford University Press 2013).
Bussani, M & Palmer, V V (eds), *Pure Economic Loss in Europe* (Cambridge University Press 2003)
Bussani, M & Palmer, V V, 'The Notion of Pure Economic Loss and Its Setting' in M Bussani & V V Palmer (eds), *Pure Economic Loss in Europe* (Cambridge University Press 2003) 5.
Bussani, M & Werro, F, *European Private Law: A Handbook (Vol. I)* (Stämpfli 2009).
Bydlinski, F, 'Haftung bei alternativer Kausalität' (1959) Juristische Blätter 9.
Bydlinski, F, *Mittäterschaft im Schadensrecht*, [1959-1960] 158 Archiv für die civilistische Praxis (AcP) 410.
Cane, P & Stapleton, J (eds), *The Law of Obligations: Essays in Celebration of John Fleming* (Clarendon Press 1995).
Cane, P & Stapleton, J (eds), *The Law of Obligations: Essays for Patrick Atiyah* (Clarendon Press 1991).
Cane, P, '*Mens Rea* in Tort Law' (2000) 20(4) Oxford Journal of Legal Studies 533.
Carty, H, 'Joint Tortfeasance and Assistance Liability' (1999) 10 Legal Studies 489.
Case comment, 'Federal Supreme Court (Bundesgerichtshof): GERMANY' (2005) International Review of Intellectual Property and Competition Law (IIC) 573.

Case comment, 'Federal Supreme Court, 25 October 2011 – Case No. VI ZR 93/10: GERMANY – "Blog Entry"*' (2012) 8 International Review of Intellectual Property and Competition Law (IIC) 982.

Case comment, 'The Federal Supreme Court (Bundesgerichtshof): "Rapidshare III"' (2014) International Review of Intellectual Property and Competition Law (IIC) 716.

Castendyk, O et al., *European Media Law* (Kluwer Law International 2008).

Castets-Renaud, C, 'Le renouveau de la responsabilité délictuelle des intermédiaires de l'internet' (2012) Recueil Dalloz 827.

Christiansen, P, 'Hamburg LG, 3 September 2010, 308 O 27/09' (2010) MMR 833.

Christie, A, *Death in the Clouds* (Hercule Poirot Series Book 12) (Kindle edition, Harper Collins 2010).

Chynoweth, P, 'Legal Research' in A Knight & L Ruddock (eds), *Advanced Research Methods in the Built Environment* (Wiley-Blackwell 2008) 28.

Ciolino, D S & Donelon, E A, 'Questioning Strict Liability in Copyright' (2002) 54(2) Rutgers Law Review 351.

Clark, B & Schubert, M, 'Odysseus between Scylla and Charybdis? The ECJ Rules in *L'Oréal v eBay*' (2011) 6(12) Journal of Intellectual Property Law & Practice 880.

Coffin, F M, 'Judicial Balancing: The Protean Scales of Justice' (1988) 63 New York University Law Review 16.

Collins, H, *The European Civil Code: The Way Forward* (Cambridge University Press 2008)

Colloque de l'IPRI, *Contrefaçon sur internet: les enjeux du droit d'auteur sur le WEB 2.0* (Litec 2009).

Colston, C, *Principles of Intellectual Property Law* (Cavendish Publishing 1999).

Commission Communication to the European Parliament, the Council, the Economic and Social Committee and the Committee of the Regions, 'A Coherent Framework for Building Trust in the Digital Single Market for E-Commerce and Online Services' COM(2011) 942 final/2, 6 February 2012.

Commission Proposal for a Directive of the European Parliament and of the Council on measures and procedures to ensure the enforcement of intellectual property rights, COM(2003) 46 final.

Commission Proposal for a European Parliament and Council Directive on certain legal aspects of electronic commerce in the internal market, 18 November 1998, COM (1998) 586 final.

Commission Staff Working Document, 'A Digital Single Market Strategy for Europe – Analysis and Evidence', SWD(2015) 100 final, 6 May 2015.

Commission Staff Working Paper, 'Analysis of the application of Directive 2004/48/EC of the European Parliament and the Council of 29 April 2004 on the enforcement of intellectual property rights in the Member States', SEC(2010) 1589 final, 22 December 2010.

Commission Staff Working Paper, 'Online Services, Including E-Commerce, in the Single Market', SEC(2011) 1641 final, 11 January 2012.

Communication from the Commission to the Council and the European Parliament on European Contract Law, COM(2001) 398 final, Brussels, 11 July 2001.

Communication from the Commission to the European Parliament and the Council, 'A More Coherent European Contract Law – An Action Plan', COM(2003) 68 final, Brussels, 12 February 2003.

Communication from the Commission to the European Parliament and the Council, 'European Contract Law and the Revision of the Acquis – The Way Forward', COM(2004) 651 final, Brussels, 11 October 2004.

Communication from the Commission to the European Parliament, the Council, the European Economic and Social Committee and the Committee of the Regions, 'A Digital Single Market Strategy for Europe', COM(2015)192 final.

Communication from the Commission to the European Parliament, the Council, the European Economic and Social Committee and the Committee of the Regions, 'Towards a modern, more European copyright framework', COM(2015) 626 final, 9 December 2015.

Cooper, D, *Secondary Liability for Civil Wrongs* (unpublished PhD thesis, University of Cambridge 1995).

Cotter, T F, 'Some Observations on the Law and Economics of Intermediaries' (2005) 1 Michigan State Law Review 2.

Council of Europe, 'Report by the Group of Specialists on human rights in the information society (MC-S-IS) on the use and impact of technical filtering measures for various types of content in the online environment', CM(2008)37 add, 26 February 2008.

Creech, R L, *Law and Language in the European Union: The Paradox of a Babel 'United in Diversity'* (Europa Publishing 2005).

Cryer, R et al., A, *Research Methodologies in EU and International Law* (Hart Publishing 2011).

Curtin, D M & Smits, J M, European Integration and Law (Intersentia 2006).

Dannemann, G et al., 'Language and Terminology' in C Twigg-Flesner (ed.), *The Cambridge Companion to European Union Private Law* (Cambridge University Press 2010) 70.

Davies, P S, 'Accessory Liability for Assisting Torts' (2011) 70(2) Cambridge Law Journal 353.

Davies, P S, 'Accessory Liability: Protecting Intellectual Property Rights' (2011) 4 Intellectual Property Quarterly 390.

Davies, P S, 'Aid, Abet, Counsel or Procure?' in S Pitel, J Neyers, E Chamberlain (eds), *Tort Law: Challenging Orthodoxy* (Hart Publishing 2013) 413.

Davies, P S, *Accessory Liability* (Hart Publishing 2015).

De Greuille, B, Rapport fait au Tribunal, séance du 16 pluviôse an XII (6 février 1803) in Locré, t.XIII.

De Vries, S, 'Balancing Fundamental Rights with Economic Freedoms According to the European Court of Justice' (2013) 9(1) Utrecht Law Review 169.

De Vries, S et al., *The Protection of Fundamental Rights after Lisbon* (Hart Publishing 2013).

Depreeuw, S, *The Variable Scope of the Exclusive Rights in Copyright* (Wolters Kluwer 2014) 487.

Derclaye, E, 'Intellectual Property Rights and Human Rights: Coinciding and Cooperating' in P Torremans (ed), *Intellectual Property and Human Rights* (Kluwer Law International 2008) 133.

Devenney, J & Kenny, M B, *The Transformation of European Private Law: Harmonisation, Consolidation, Codification or Chaos?* (Cambridge University Press 2013).

Dhenne, M, 'Hébergeurs et contrefaçons: de l'usage de la loyauté dans un régime de responsabilité limitée' (2009) 51 RLDI 58.

Dickinson, R & Watt, A, 'How Litigation Changed Peer-to-Peer File-Sharing' (2010) 197 Copyright World 19.

Dickson, J & Eleftheriadis, P, *Philosophical Foundations of European Union Law* (Oxford University Press 2012).

Dietrich, J, 'Accessorial Liability in the Law of Torts' (2011) 31(2) Legal Studies 231.

Dietz, A, 'Germany' in L Bently, P Geller & M Nimmer (eds), *International Copyright Law and Practice* (Matthew Bender/LexisNexis 2013).

Dixon, A N, 'Liability of Users and Third Parties for Copyright Infringements on the Internet: Overview of International Developments' in A Strowel (ed.), *Peer-to-Peer File Sharing and Secondary Liability in Copyright Law* (Edward Elgar Publishing 2009) 38.

DLA Piper, 'EU Study on the Legal Analysis of a Single Market for the Information Society – New Rules for a New Age?', November 2009, available at: http://ec.europa.eu/information_society/newsroom/cf/itemdetail.cfm?item_id=7022.

Dobbs, D, *The Law of Torts* (West Publishing, St. Paul 2000) 339-340.

Dreier, T & Hugenholtz, P B (eds), Concise European Copyright Law (2nd ed., Kluwer Law International, forthcoming).

Dreyfuss, R et al. (ed.), *Expanding the Boundaries of Intellectual Property. Innovation Policy for the Knowledge Society* (Oxford University Press 2001).

Ducoulombier, P, *Les Conflits de Droits Fondamentaux devant la Cour Européenne des Droits de l'Homme* (PhD thesis, University of Strasbourg, 2008, published by Bruylant 2011) 521-525.

Duhen, W, *La responsabilité extra-contractuelle du fournisseur d'accès à Internet* (Presse universitaires d'Aix-Marseille 2013) 64.

Dumitru, C et al., 'Baywatch: Two Approaches to Measure the Effects of Blocking Access to The Pirate Bay' (2014) 4 Telecommunications Policy 383.

Durrande, S et al., *Code de la Propriété Intellectuelle Commenté* (15th ed., Dalloz 2015).
Edwards, L & Waelde, C (eds), *Law and the Internet* (3rd ed, Hart Publishing 2009).
Edwards, L, 'Role and Responsibility of Internet Intermediaries in the Field of Copyright and Related Rights', WIPO Study (2011).
Edwards, L, 'The Fall and Rise of Intermediary Liability Online' in L Edwards and C Waelde (eds), *Law and the Internet* (3rd ed, Hart Publishing 2009) 65.
Edwards, L, 'The Problem of Intermediary Service Provider Liability' in L Edwards (ed), *The New Legal Framework for e-Commerce in Europe* (Hart Publishing 2005) 114-115.
Edwards, L, *The New Legal Framework for e-Commerce in Europe* (Hart Publishing 2005).
Elkin-Koren, N, 'After Twenty Years: Copyright Liability of Online Intermediaries' in S Frankel & D J Gervais (eds), *The Evolution and Equilibrium of Copyright in the Digital Age* (Cambridge University Press 2014).
Elkin-Koren, N, 'Making Technology Visible: Liability of Internet Service Providers for Peer-to-Peer Traffic' (2005) 9(1-2) New York University Journal of Legislation and Public Policy 15.
Ellis, E (ed.), *The Principle of Proportionality in the Law of Europe* (Hart Publishing 1999).
European Commission, 'Initiative on procedures for notifying and acting on illegal online content', last modification: June 2012.
European Commission, 'Summary of the results of the Public Consultation on the future of electronic commerce in the Internal Market and the implementation of the Directive on electronic commerce (2000/31/EC)'.
European Communities, 'Joint Practical Guide of the European Parliament, the Council and the Commission for Persons Involved in the Drafting of Legislation within the Community Institutions' (Office for Official Publications of the European Communities 2003).
European Copyright Society, 'Opinion on the Reference to the CJEU in Case C-466/12 *Svensson*', University of Cambridge Legal Studies Research Paper Series No. 6/2013, 15 February 2013.
European Group on Tort Law, *Principles of European Tort Law – Text and Commentary* (Springer 2005).
European Parliament, 'Resolution of 23 March 2006 on European Contract Law and the Revision of the *Acquis*: The Way Forward', (2005/2022(INI)), Brussels 23 March 2006, [2006] OJ C 292 E, 109.
European Union Ministers, Declaration 'Global Information Networks: Realising the Potential', Bonn, 6-8 July 1997 ('Bonn Declaration').
Eurostat, 'Demography Report – 2015 Edition' (Publications Office of the European Union, Luxembourg 2015).

Everson, M & Correia Gonçalves, R, 'Article 16 – Freedom to Conduct a Business' in S Peers, T Hervey, J Kenner & A Ward (eds), *The EU Charter of Fundamental Rights: A Commentary* (Hart Publishing 2014) 437.

Fabre-Magnan, M, *Droit des obligations* (2nd ed., PUF 2010).

Féral-Schuhl, C, *Cyberdroit – Le Droit à l'Épreuve de l'Internet* (6th ed., Dalloz 2010).

Ficsor, M, *Guide to the Copyright and Related Rights Treaties Administered by WIPO and Glossary of Copyright and Related Rights Terms* (World Intellectual Property Organization 2003).

Fischman Afori, O, 'Proportionality – A New Mega Standard in European Copyright Law' (2014) International Review of Intellectual Property and Competition Law (IIC) 889.

Fleming, J, *The Law of Torts* (8th ed., Law Book Co 1992).

Follesdal, A & Koslowski, P, *Democracy and the European Union* (Spinger 1998).

Frankel, S & Gervais, D J (eds), *The Evolution and Equilibrium of Copyright in the Digital Age* (Cambridge University Press 2014).

Frantz, L B, 'Is The First Amendment Law? A Reply to Professor Mendelson' (1963) 51(4) California Law Review 729.

Friedman, D & Barak-Erez, D (eds), *Human Rights in Private Law* (Hart Publishing 2001).

Friedman, D, 'Sinking the Safe Harbour with the Legal Certainty of Strict Liability in Sight' (2014) 9(2) Journal of Intellectual Property Law & Practice 148.

Gardbaum, S, 'Limiting Constitutional Rights' (2007) 54(4) UCLA Law Review 789.

Garrote Fernandez-Diez, I, 'Comparative Analysis on National Approaches to the Liability of Internet Intermediaries for Infringement of Copyright and Related Rights' WIPO study, available at: www.wipo.int/copyright/en/internet_intermediaries.

Gasser, U & Schulz, W, 'Governance of Online Intermediaries: Observations from a Series of National Case Studies' (18 February 2015) Berkman Center Research Publication No. 2015-5, available at: http://ssrn.com/abstract=2566364.

Geiger, C, '"Constitutionalising" Intellectual Property Law? The Influence of Fundamental Rights on Intellectual Property in the European Union' (2006) International Review of Intellectual Property and Competition Law (IIC) 371.

Geiger, C, 'Fundamental Rights as Common Principles of European (and International) Intellectual Property Law' in A Ohly (ed.), *Common Principles of European Intellectual Property Law* (Mohr Siebeck 2012) 223.

Geiger, C, 'Honourable Attempt but (ultimately) Disproportionately Offensive against Peer-to-peer on the Internet (HADOPI) – A Critical Analysis of the Recent Anti-File-Sharing Legislation in France' (2011) 42(4) International Review of Intellectual Property and Competition Law (IIC) 457.

Geiger, C, *Constructing European Intellectual Property – Achievements and New Perspectives* (Edward Elgar 2013).

Geist, M (ed.), *From 'Radical Extremism' to 'Balanced Copyright': Canadian Copyright and the Digital Agenda* (Irwin Law 2010).

Gendreau, Y, 'Authorisation Revisited' (2001) 48 Journal of the Copyright Society of the U.S.A. 341.

Gerber, D, 'Sculpting the Agenda of Comparative Law: Ernst Rabel and the Façade of Language' in A Riles (ed), *Rethinking the Masters of Comparative Law* (Hart Publishing 2001) 190.

Giblin, R, 'Authorisation in Context – Potential Consequences of the Proposed Amendments to Australian Secondary Liability Law' Australian Digital Alliance, August 2014.

Giblin, R, *Code Wars – 10 Years of P2P Software Litigation* (Edward Elgar 2011) 148-153.

Giliker, P, 'The Draft Common Frame of Reference and European Contract Law: Moving from the "Academic" to the "Political"' in J Devenney & M B Kenny (eds), *The Transformation of European Private Law: Harmonisation, Consolidation, Codification or Chaos?* (Cambridge University Press 2013) 23.

Giliker, P, 'Vicarious Liability or Liability for the Acts of Others in Tort: A Comparative Perspective' (2011) 2(1) Journal of European Tort Law 31.

Ginsburg J, & Gaubiac. Y, 'Contrefaçon, fourniture de moyens et faute: perspectives dans les systèmes de *common law* et civilistes à la suite des *arrêts Grokster et Kazaa*' (2006) 228 Revue Internationale du Droit d'Auteur 3.

Ginsburg J, & Ricketson, S, 'Inducers and Authorisers: A Comparison of the US Supreme Court's Grokster Decision and the Australian Federal Court's Kazaa Ruling' (2006) 11 Media & Arts Law Review 1.

Ginsburg, J, 'A Common Lawyer's Perspective on *Contrefaçon*' in L Bently, J Davis & J Ginsburg (eds), 'Copyright and Piracy: An Interdisciplinary Critique' (Cambridge University Press 2010) 80.

Ginsburg, J, 'Separating the Sony Sheep from the Grokster Goats: Reckoning the Future Business Plans of Copyright-Dependent Technology Entrepreneurs' (2008) 50(2) Arizona Law Review 577.

Glatstein, B H, 'Tertiary Copyright Liability' (2004) 71(4) The University of Chicago Law Review 1605.

Goldberg, R (ed), *Perspectives on Causation* (Hart Publishing 2011).

Goldmann, M in H Harte-Bavendamm & F Henning-Bodewig (eds), *Gesetz gegen den Unlauteren Wettbewerb (UWG)* (3rd ed., C. H. Beck 2013).

Goldstein, P & Hugenholtz, P B, *International Copyright: Principles, Law, and Practice* (3rd ed. University Press 2012).

Gomis, G 'Consécration jurisprudentielle de l'Article L.336-3 du code de la propriété intellectuelle' (2012) 87 Revue Lamy Droit de l'Immatériel 2905.

González Fuster, G & Gutwirth, S, 'Opening up Personal Data Protection: A Conceptual Controversy' (2013) 29(5) Computer Law & Security Review: The International Journal of Technology Law and Practice 531.

González Fuster, G, 'Balancing Intellectual Property against Data Protection: A New Right's Wavering Weight' (2012) 14 IDP: Revista de Internet, Derecho y Política 34.

Goold, P R, 'Is Copyright Infringement a Strict Liability Tort?' (2015) 30(1) Berkeley Technology Law Journal 305.

Goudkamp, J, *Tort Law Defences* (Hart Publishing 2013).

Gräbig, J, 'Akluelle Entwicklungen bei Haftung für[nbsp] mittelbare Rechtsverletzungen: Vom Störer zum Täter – ein neues einheitliches Haftungskonzept?' (2011) MMR 504.

Grady, M F, 'A New Positive Economic Theory of Negligence' (1983) 92(5) The Yale Law Journal 799.

Grady, M F, 'Untaken Precautions' (1989) 18 Journal of Legal Studies 139.

Green Paper from the Commission of 1 July 2010, 'Policy Options for Progress towards a European Contract Law for Consumers and Businesses', COM(2010) 348 final, Brussels, 1 July 2010.

Greer, S, '"Balancing" and the European Court of Human Rights: A Contribution to the Habermas-Alexy Debate' (2004) 63(2) The Cambridge Law Journal 412.

Greer, S, *The Margin of Appreciation: Interpretation and Discretion under the European Convention on Human Rights* (Council of Europe Publishing 2000).

Griffiths, J, 'Constitutionalising or Harmonising? The Court of Justice, the Right to Property and European Copyright Law' (2013) 38(1) European Law Review 65.

Griffiths, J, 'What Is Legal Pluralism?' (1986) 24 Journal of Legal Pluralism and Unofficial Law 1.

Grossman, C A, 'From *Sony* to *Grokster*: the Failure of the Copyright Doctrines of Contributory Infringement and Vicarious Liability to Resolve the War between Content and Destructive Technologies' (2005) 53(1) Buffalo Law Review 141.

Grossman, C A, 'The Evolutionary Drift of Vicarious Liability and Contributory Infringement: from Interstitial Gap Filler to Arbiter of the Content Wars' (2005) 58(2) SMU Law Review 357.

Groussot, X, 'Rock the KaZaA: Another Clash of Fundamental Rights' (2008) 45 Common Market Law Review 1745.

Groussot, X et al., 'The Reach of EU Fundamental Rights on Member State Action after Lisbon' in S de Vries, U Bernitz & S Weatherill (eds), *The Protection of Fundamental Rights after Lisbon* (Hart Publishing 2013) 97.

Guibault, L, & Angelopoulos, C (eds), *Open Content Licensing: From Theory to Practice* (Amsterdam University Press 2011).
Habermas, J, 'Reply to Symposium Participants, Benjamin N. Cardozo School of Law' (1996) 17 Cardozo Law Review 1477.
Habermas, J, *Between Facts and Norms* (Polity Press 1996) 259.
Haertlein, L, *Executionsintervention und Haftung* (Mohr Siebeck 2008).
Hafenbrädl, F et al., ALAI Cantagena 2013, National Report for Germany.
Hagen, G R, '"Modernizing" ISP Copyright Liability' in M Geist (ed.), *From 'Radical Extremism' to 'Balanced Copyright': Canadian Copyright and the Digital Agenda* (Irwin Law 2010) 385.
Harbo, T, 'The Function of the Proportionality Principle in EU Law' (2010) 16(2) European Law Journal 158.
Hardouin, R, 'L'hébergeur et la publicité: la neutralité comme condition d'une coexistence' (2010) 62 Revue Lamy Droit de l'Immatériel 2041.
Hardouin, R, 'La connaissance de l'illicéité par les hébergeurs ou quand etre notifié ne signifie pas nécessairement devoir retirer' (2012) 47 Revue du droit des technologies de l'information 5.
Hardouin, R, 'La jurisprudence, les textes, et la responsabilité des hébergeurs' (2008) 39 RLDI 67.
Hardouin, R, 'Observations sur les nouvelles obligations prétoriennes des hébergeurs' (2007), available at: Juriscom.com.
Hardouin, R, *La responsabilité limitée des prestataires techniques dans la loi pour la confiance dans l'économie numérique* (unpublished PhD thesis, Université de Versailles Saint-Quentin-en-Yvelines 2011).
Hargreaves, I, 'Digital Opportunity – A Review of Intellectual Property and Growth', Independent Report, May 2011.
Harris, D J et al., *Harris, O'Boyle & Warbrick – Law of the European Convention on Human Rights* (3rd ed., Oxford University Press 2014).
Harris, D J et al., *Harris, O'Boyle & Warbrick – Law of the European Convention on Human Rights* (2nd ed. University Press 2009).
Hart, H L A & Honoré, T, *Causation in the Law* (Clarendon Press 1985).
Hartkamp, A S et al. (eds), *Towards a European Civil Code* (4th ed., Ars Aequi Libri 2011).
Hartkamp, A, *Towards a European Civil Code* (3rd ed., Kluwer Law International 2004).
Hays, T, 'The Evolution and Decentralisation of Secondary Liability for Infringements of Copyright-Protected Works: Part 1' (2006) 28(12) European Intellectual Property Review 617.
Helfer, L R, 'New Innovation Frontier – Intellectual Property and the European Court of Human Rights' (2008) 49 *Harvard International Law Journal* 1.
Helman, L, 'Pull Too Hard and the Rope May Break: on the Secondary Liability of Technology Providers for Copyright Infringement' (2010) 19(1) Texas Intellectual Property Law Journal 111.

Herbert, A P, *Uncommon Law: Being 66 Misleading Cases Revised and Collected in One Volume* (Methuen 1969) 5.

Hesselink, M W, 'A European Legal Method? On European Private Law and Scientific Method' (2008) 15(1) European Law Journal 20.

Hesselink, M W, 'A Toolbox for European Judges' (2011) 17(4) European Law Journal 441.

Hesselink, M W, 'Common Frame of Reference & Social Justice', available in NARCIS (National Academic Research and Collaborations Information System).

Hesselink, M W, 'How Many Systems of Private Law Are There in Europe? On Plural Legal Sources, Multiple Identities and the Unity of Law' in L Niglia (ed.), *Pluralism and European Private Law* (Hart Publishing 2013) 199.

Hesselink, M W, 'The Common Frame of Reference as a Source of European Private Law' (2009) 83 Tulane Law Review 919.

Hetcher, S, 'The Fault Liability Standard in Copyright' in S Balganesh (ed.), *Intellectual Property and the Common Law* (Cambridge University Press 2013) 431.

Hetcher, S, 'The Immorality of Strict Liability in Copyright' (2013) 17(1) Marquette Intellectual Property Law Review 1.

Hetcher, S, 'The Kids are Alright: Applying a Fault Liability Standard to Amateur Digital Remix' (2010) 62(5) Florida Law Review 1275.

Hoeren, T & Bensinger, V, *Haftung im Internet – Die Neue Rechtslage* (De Gruyter, Berlin 2014).

Hoeren, T & Yankova, S, 'The Liability of Internet Intermediaries – The German Perspective' (2012) International Review of Intellectual Property and Competition Law (IIC) 501.

Hoeren, T, 'BGH: Störerhaftung von RapidShare – Alone in the Dark', case comment (2013) MMR 185.

Hoeren, T, 'German Law on Internet Liability of Intermediaries', LIDC Congress, Oxford 2011.

Hoeren, T, 'Konkretisierung der Störerhaftung für Urheberrechtsverletzungen bei File-Hosting', case comment (2013) NJW 3245.

Hoeren, T, 'Liability for Online Services in Germany' (2009) 10(5) German Law Journal 561.

Hoeren, T et al., *Handbuch Multimedia Recht* (41st ed., C.H. Beck 2015).

Högberg, S K, 'The Search for Intent-Based Doctrines of Secondary Liability in Copyright Law' (2006) 106(4) Columbia Law Review 909.

Hollanders, A-S, *Mittelbare Verantwortlichkeit von Intermediären im Netz* (Nomos 2011).

Honoré, T, 'Are Omissions Less Culpable?' in P Cane and J Stapleton (eds), *The Law of Obligations: Essays for Patrick Atiyah* (Clarendon Press 1991) 31.

Honoré, T, 'Law, Morals and Rescue' in J Ratcliffe (ed.), *The Good Samaritan and the Law* (Anchor Books 1966) 241.

Hoppner, T, 'Reproduction in Part of Online Articles in the Aftermath of Infopaq (C-5/08): Newspaper Licensing Agency Ltd v Meltwater Holding BV' (2011) 33(5) European Intellectual Property Review 331.

Horsey, K & Rackley, E, *Tort Law* (4th ed., Oxford University Press 2015).

Horten, M, *A Copyright Masquerade* (Zed Books 2013).

Horten, M, *The Copyright Enforcement Enigma – Internet Politics and the 'Telecoms Package'* (Palgrave Macmillan 2012).

Howarth, D, 'Many Duties of Care – Or A Duty of Care? Notes from the Underground' (2006) 26(3) Oxford Journal of Legal Studies 449.

Howarth, D, 'My Brother's Keeper? Liability for Acts of Third Parties' (1994) 14(1) Legal Studies 88.

Hugenholtz, P B (ed.), *Copyright and Electronic Commerce – Legal Aspects of Electronic Copyright Management* (Kluwer Law International 2000).

Hugenholtz, P B, 'Codes of Conduct and Copyright Enforcement in Cyberspace' in I A Stamatoudi (ed.), *Copyright Enforcement and the Internet* (Kluwer Law International 2010) 303.

Hugenholtz, P B, 'Codes of Conduct and Copyright: Pragmatism v. Principle' (2008) 6 International Review of Intellectual Property and Competition Law (IIC) 635.

Hugenholtz, P B, 'Copyright and Freedom of Expression in Europe' in R Dreyfuss et al. (eds), *Expanding the Boundaries of Intellectual Property. Innovation Policy for the Knowledge Society* (Oxford University Press 2001) 343-363.

Husa, J, 'The Method is Dead, Long Live the Methods – European Polynomia and Pluralist Methodology' (2011) 5 Legiprudence 249.

Huscroft, G et al., *Proportionality and the Rule of Law: Rights, Justification, Reasoning* (Cambridge University Press 2014).

Husovec, M & Peguera, M, 'Much Ado about Little – Privately Litigated Internet Disconnection Injunctions' (2015) 46(1) International Review of Intellectual Property and Competition Law (IIC) 10.

Husovec, M, 'Injunctions against Innocent Third Parties: Case of Website Blocking' (2013) 4(2) Journal of Intellectual Property, Information Technology and Electronic Commerce Law (JIPITEC) 116.

Iglezakis, I, 'The Legal Struggle in the EU against Online Piracy' in T-E Synodinou (ed.), *Codification of European Law* (Kluwer Law International 2012) 283.

Infantino, M, 'Making European Tort Law: the Game and Its Players' (2010) 18(1) Cardozo Journal of International & Comparative Law 45.

Intent Governance Forum, Dynamic Coalition on Platform Responsibility, draft document on 'Recommendations on Terms of Service and Human Rights', available at: http://review.intgovforum.org.

International Bureau of WIPO, 'WIPO National Seminar on Digital Technology and the New WIPO Treaties' (WIPO/CNR/SEL/97/1), 22 September 1997.

Jacob, A & Dorfman, A, 'Copyright as Tort' (2011) 12(1) Theoretical Inquiries in Law 59.

Jacobs, F G, 'Recent Developments in the Principle of Proportionality in European Community Law' in E Ellis (ed.), *The Principle of Proportionality in the Law of Europe* (Hart Publishing 1999) 21.

Jans, J, 'Proportionality Revisited' (2000) *Legal Issues of Economic Integration* 239.

Jansen, N, 'The Authority of an Academic "Draft Common Frame of Reference"' in H-W Micklitz & F Cafaggi (eds), *European Private Law after the Common Frame of Reference* (Edward Elgar 2010) 147.

Jasserand, C, 'Régime français de la responsabilité des intermédiaires techniques' (2013) 25(3) Les Cahiers de la propriété intellectuelle 1135.

Johnston, A & Unberath, A, 'European Private Law by Directives: Approach and Challenges' in C Twigg-Flesner (ed.), *The Cambridge Companion to European Union Private Law* (Cambridge University Press 2010) 85.

Juncker, J-C, 'A New Start for Europe: My Agenda for Jobs, Growth, Fairness and Democratic Change – Political Guidelines for the next European Commission', opening statement, European Parliament plenary session, Strasbourg, 15 July 2014.

Kamba, W J, 'Comparative Law: A Theoretical Framework' (1974) 23 International and Comparative Law Quarterly 486.

Kamperman Sanders, A & Heath, C (eds), *Intellectual Property Liability of Consumers, Facilitators and Intermediaries* (Kluwer Law International 2012).

Kamperman Sanders, A, 'Intellectual Property Liability of Consumers, Facilitators and Intermediaries: Comparative Concepts' in A Kamperman Sanders & C Heath (eds), *Intellectual Property Liability of Consumers, Facilitators and Intermediaries* (Kluwer Law International 2012) 14.

Kennedy, D, 'A Transnational Geneology of Proportionality in Private Law' in R Brownsword, H-W Micklitz, L Niglia & S Weatherill, *The Foundations of European Private Law* (Hart Publishing 2011) 185.

Kerkmeester, H & Visscher, L, 'Learned Hand in Europe: A Study in the Comparative Law and Economics of Negligence' (2003) 6 German Working Papers in Law and Economics.

Kinsch, P, 'Human Rights and Fundamental Rights (ChFR and ECHR)' in J Basedow, K J Hopt, R Zimmermann & A Stier, *The Max Planck Encyclopedia of European Private Law* (Oxford University Press 2012) 839.

Kisieliute, I, 'A "Fair Balance" between Intellectual Property Rights and Other Fundamental Rights' (Master's Thesis, Lund University 2012).

Klett, A et al., *Intellectual Property Law in Germany – Protection, Enforcement and Dispute Resolution* (C.H. Beck/LexisNexis 2008) 71.

Knight, A & Ruddock, L (eds), *Advanced Research Methods in the Built Environment* (Wiley-Blackwell 2008).

Koch, B A, 'The "European Group on Tort Law" and Its "Principles of European Tort Law"' (2005) 53 American Journal of Comparative Law 189.

Koelman, K & Hugenholtz, P B, 'Online Service Provider Liability for Copyright Infringement', Workshop on Service Provider Liability, Geneva, 9 and 10 December 1999.

Koelman, K, 'Liability for On-Line Intermediaries', Imprimatur/Institute for Information Law, Amsterdam, 1997.

Koelman, K, 'Online Intermediary Liability' in P B Hugenholtz (ed.), *Copyright and Electronic Commerce – Legal Aspects of Electronic Copyright Management* (Kluwer Law International 2000) 23.

Köhler, C, & Burmeister, K, 'Copyright Liability on the Internet Today in Europe (Germany, France, Italy and the E.U.)' (1999) 21(10) European Intellectual Property Review 485.

Köhler, H & Bornkamm, J, *Gesetz gegen den unlauteren Wettbewerb* (30th ed., C.H.Beck 2012).

Köhler, H '"Täter" und "Störer" im Wettbewerbs- und Markenrecht: Zur BGH-Entscheidung "Jugendgefährdende Medien bei eBay"' (2008) GRUR 1.

Koopmans, T, 'The Birth of European Law at the Cross Roads of Legal Traditions' (1992) 39 The American Journal of Comparative Law 493.

Kortmann, J, 'Liability for Nonfeasance: A Comparative Study' (2001) Oxford U Comparative L Forum 1, available at: ouclf.iuscomp.org.

Kortmann, J, *Altruism in Private Law: Liability for Nonfeasance and Negatorium Gestio* (Oxford University Press 2005).

Koziol, H (ed.) *Unification of Tort Law: Wrongfulness* (Kluwer Law International 1998).

Koziol, H, 'Austria: Wrongfulness under Austrian Law' in H Koziol (ed.) *Unification of Tort Law: Wrongfulness* (Kluwer Law International 1998) 11.

Koziol, H, *Basic Questions of Tort Law from a Comparative Perspective* (Jan Sramek Verlag 2015).

Koziol, H, *Basic Questions of Tort Law from a Germanic Perspective* (Jan Sramek Verlag 2012).

Koziol, H et al., *Tort Law in the Jurisprudence of the European Court of Human Rights* (De Gruyter, Berlin 2011).

Kraakman, R H, 'Gatekeepers: The Anatomy of a Third-Party Enforcement Strategy' (1986) 2(1) Journal of Law, Economics & Organisation 53.

Kranenborg, H, 'Article 8 – Protection of Personal Data' in S Peers, T Hervey, J Kenner & A Ward, *The EU Charter of Fundamental Rights: A Commentary* (Hart Publishing 2014) 223.

Kulk, S & Zuiderveen Borgesius, F J, 'Filtering for Copyright Enforcement in Europe after the Sabam Cases' (2012) 34(11) European Intellectual Property Review 791.

Kumayama, K D, 'A Right to Pseudonymity' (2009) 51 Arizona Law Review 427.

Kumm, M & Walen, A D, 'Human Dignity and Proportionality: Deontic Pluralism in Balancing' in G Huscroft, B W Miller & G Webber, *Proportionality and the Rule of Law: Rights, Justification, Reasoning* (Cambridge University Press 2014).

Kuner, C, 'Data Protection and Rights Protection on the Internet: the Promusicae Judgment of the European Court of Justice' (2008) 30(5) European Intellectual Property Review 199.

Kur, A, 'Secondary Liability for Trademark Infringement on the Internet: the Situation in Germany and throughout the EU' (2014) 37(4) Columbia Journal of Law & the Arts 525.

Laddie, H et al., *The Modern Law of Copyright and Designs* (3rd ed. Butterworths 2000) 1776.

Lahe, J & Turk, K, 'The Web Host's Privilege of Limited Liability: Its Application to Operators of Commentary Rooms' (2012) 2 European Review of Private Law 447.

Lahe, J, 'The Importance of Distinguishing between Forms of Fault in the Law of Delict' (2009) XVI Juridica International 94.

Lando, O, 'Optional or Mandatory Europeanisation of Contract Law' (2000) 59(4) European Review of Private Law 69.

Lando, O et al., *Principles of European Contract Law – Part III* (Kluwer Law International 2003).

Laquette, Y, 'Quelques remarques a propos du projet de code civil europeen de M. von Bar' (2002) Dalloz 2202.

Lawson, E, 'Directors Beware' (2002) 13(2) Entertainment Law Review 44.

Lawson, F H & Markesinis, B, *Tortious Liability for Unintentional Harm in the Common Law and the Civil Law* (Cambridge University Press 1982).

Le Tourneau, P & Cadiet, L, *Droit de la responsabilité et des contrats – Régimes d'indemnisation* (Dalloz-Sirey 2012) 2437-2482.

Le Tourneau, P & Cadiet, L, *Droit de la responsabilité et des contrats* (Dalloz-Sirey 2000) 1152-1155.

Le Tourneau, P, *Droit de la responsabilité et des contracts – Régimes d'indemnisation* (9th ed., Dalloz 2013).

Lefranc, D, 'The Metamorphosis of *Contrefaçon* in French Copyright Law' in L Bently, J Davis & J Ginsburg, 'Copyright and Piracy: An Interdisciplinary Critique' (Cambridge University Press 2010) 55.

Legrand, P, 'The Impossibility of Legal Transplants' (1997) 4 *Maastricht Journal of European and Comparative Law* 111.

Leistner, M & Stang, F, 'Die Neuerung der Wettbewerbsrechtlichen Verkehrspflichten – Ein Siegeszug der Prüfpflichten?' (2008) WRP 533.

Leistner, M, 'Common Principles of Secondary Liability?' in A Ohly, *Common Principles of European Intellectual Property Law* (Mohr Siebeck 2012) 117.

Leistner, M, 'Störerhaftung und mittelbare Schutzrechtsverletzung' (2010) GRUR-Beil 1.
Leistner, M, 'Structural aspects of secondary (provider) liability in Europe' (2014) 9(1) Journal of Intellectual Property Law & Practice 75.
Leistner, M, 'Von "Grundig-Reporter(n) zu Paperboy(s)": Entwicklungsperspektiven der Verantiwortlichkeit im Urheberrehct' (2006) GRUR 801.
Lepage, A, *Libertés et droits fondamentaux à l'épreuve de l'internet* (Litec 2002).
Lescure, P, 'Mission "Acte II de l'exception culturelle" – Contribution aux politiques culturelles à l'ère numérique', May 2013.
Lichtman D & Landes, W, 'Indirect Liability for Copyright Infringement: Napster and Beyond' (2003) 17(2) Journal of Economic Perspectives 113.
Lichtman, D & Landes, W, 'Indirect Liability for Copyright Infringement: An Economic Perspective' (2003) 16(2) Harvard Journal of Law & Technology 395.
Lind, A, & Strand, M, 'A New Proportionality Test for Fundamental Rights? The Joined Cases C-92/09 and C-93/09 Volker und Markus Schecke GbR (C-92/09) and Hartmut Eifert (C-93/09) v. Land Hessen' (2011) 7 European Policy Analysis 1.
Llewelyn, D, 'Intellectual Property Liability of Consumers, Facilitators and Intermediaries: Concepts under Common Law' in A Kamperman Sanders & C Heath (eds), *Intellectual Property Liability of Consumers, Facilitators and Intermediaries* (Kluwer Law International 2012) 26.
Löffel, O, 'Host-Provider Kann als Gehilfe Haften' (2013) GRUR-Prax 298.
Logie, J, 'Affirmative Action in the Law of Tort: The Case of a Duty to Warn' (1989) CLJ 115.
Lomnicka, E, '"Knowingly Concerned"? Participatory Liability to Regulators' (2000) 21 Company Lawyer 120.
Lucas A et al., *Traité de la Propriété Littéraire et Artistique* (4th ed, LexisNexis 2012).
Lucas, A, & Lucas, H-J, *Traité de la Propriété Littéraire et Artistique* (2nd ed., Litec 2001).
Lucas, A et al., 'France' in L Bently, P Geller & M Nimmer, *International Copyright Law and Practice* (Matthew Bender/LexisNexis 2013).
Lunney, M & Oliphant, K, *Tort Law – Text and Materials* (3rd ed., Oxford University Press 2007).
Lunney, M & Oliphant, K, *Tort Law – Text and Materials* (5th ed., Oxford University Press 2013).
MacCormick, N, 'Risking Constitutional Collision in Europe?' (1998) 18(3) Oxford Journal of Legal Studies 517.
MacKinnon, R et al., 'Fostering Freedom Online: the Role of Internet Intermediaries' (UNESCO/Internet Society 2014).
MacQueen, H, '"My Tongue Is Mine Ain": Copyright, the Spoken Word and Privacy' (2005) 68(3) The Modern Law Review 349.

MacQueen, H et al., *Contemporary Intellectual Property – Law and Policy* (2nd ed., Oxford University Press 2011).

Magnus, U, 'Multiple Tortfeasors under German Law' in W V H Rogers, *Unification of Tort Law: Multiple Tortfeasors* (Kluwer Law International 2004) 88.

Manara, C, 'Hébergement des contenu: une decision critiquable!' (2010) Recueil Dalloz 260.

Manara, C, 'Les moteurs de recherche, les sites illicites et leurs utilisateurs' Dalloz actualité, 16 July 2012.

Mann, R J & Belzley, S R, 'The Promise of Internet Intermediary Liability' (2005) 47 William and Mary Law Review 239.

Markesinis, B, 'Negligence, Nuisance and Affirmative Duties of Action' (1989) Law Quarterly Review 104.

Markesinis, B, 'The Not So Dissimilar Tort and Delict' (1977) 93 The Law Quarterly Review 78.

Markesinis, B, *The German Law of Torts* (3rd ed., Clarendon Press 1994) 906.

Martín-Casals, M & Solé, J, 'Multiple Tortfeasors under Spanish Law' in W V H Rogers, *Unification of Tort Law: Multiple Tortfeasors* (Kluwer Law International 2004) 190.

Martinet Farano, B, 'Internet Intermediaries' Liability for Copyright and Trademark Infringement: Reconciling the EU and US Approaches' (2012) TTLF Working Paper No 14.

Matulionytė, R & Nérisson, S, 'The French Route to an ISP Safe Harbour, Compared to German and US Ways' (2011) 42(1) International Review of Intellectual Property and Competition Law (IIC) 55. Max Planck Institute for Intellectual Property and Competition Law, 'Study on the Overall Functioning of the European Trade Mark System' (Munich, 15 February 2011).

McBride, N & Bagshaw, R, *Tort Law* (4th ed., Pearson 2012).

McBride, N, 'Duties of Care – Do They Really Exist?' (2004) 24(3) Oxford Journal of Legal Studies 417.

McCord, G, *What You Need to Know about Privacy Law* (Libraries Unlimited 2013).

McCormick, N, 'Beyond the Sovereign State' (1993) 56 Modern Law Review 1.

McGonagle, T et al., 'Study of Fundamental Rights Limitations for Online Enforcement through Self-Regulation', Institute for Information Law (IviR), University of Amsterdam, forthcoming.

McIvor, C, *Third Party Liability in Tort* (Hart Publishing 2006).

Menell, P S & Nimmer, D, 'Legal Realism in Action: Indirect Copyright Liability's Continuing Tort Framework and Sony's De Facto Demise' (2007) 55(1) UCLA Law Review 143.

Menell, P S, 'Indirect Copyright Liability and Technology Innovation' (2008) 32 Columbia Journal of Law & the Arts 375.

Michaels, R, 'The Functional Method of Comparative Law' in M Reimann & R Zimmermann (eds), *The Oxford Handbook of Comparative Law* (Oxford University Press 2006) 336.

Mimja, P, 'La Definition de l'Éditeur Était dans la Loi …' (March 2009), available at: Juriscom.com.

Monti, M, *A New Strategy for the Single Market – At the Service of Europe's Economy and Society,* Report to the President of the European Commission, José Manuel Barroso, 9 May 2010.

Moran, M, 'The Reasonable Person: A Conceptual Biography in Comparative Perspective' (2010) 14(4) Lewis & Clark Law Review 1233.

Mossoff, A, 'Is Copyright Property?' (2005) 42(1) San Diego Law Review 29.

Mowbray, A, 'A Study of the Principle of Fair Balance in the Jurisprudence of the European Court of Human Rights' (2010) 10 Human Rights Law Review 289.

Mullender, R, 'Tort, Human Rights, and Common Law Culture' (2003) 23(2) Oxford Journal of Legal Studies, 301.

Murphy, J & Witting, C, *Street on Torts* (13th ed., Oxford University Press 2012).

Musielak, H-J, 'Kausalität und Schadenszurechnung im Zivilrecht' (2013) Juristische Arbeitsblätter 241.

Neergaard, U & Nielsen, R, *European Legal Method: In a Multi-level EU Legal Order* (Djøf Publishing 2012).

Neergaard, U & Nielsen, R, *European Legal Method: Paradoxes and Revitalisation* (Djøf Publishing 2011).

Neergaard, U & Nielsen, R, *European Legal Method: Towards a New European Legal Realism?* (Djøf Publishing 2013).

Nérisson, S, 'Intellectual Property Liability of Consumers, Facilitators and Intermediaries: the Position in France' in A Kamperman Sanders & C Heath, *Intellectual Property Liability of Consumers, Facilitators and Intermediaries* (Kluwer Law International 2012) 77.

Nicolaïdis, K, 'European Demoicracy and Its Crisis' (2013) 51(2) Journal of Common Market Studies 351.

Nicolaïdis, K, 'Our European Demoicracy: Is this Constitution a Third Way for Europe?' in K Nikolaides & S Weatherill, *Whose Europe? National Models and the Constitution of the European Union* (Oxford University Press 2003) 137.

Nicolaïdis, K, 'The Idea of European Demoicracy*' in J Dickson & P Eleftheriadis, *Philosophical Foundations of European Union Law* (Oxford University Press 2012) 247.

Nielsen, R, 'Towards an Interactive Comparative Method for Studying the Multi-Layered EU Legal Order' in U Neergaard & R Nielsen, *European Legal Method: In a Multi-level EU Legal Order* (Djøf Publishing 2012) 89.

Niglia, L (ed.), *Pluralism and European Private Law* (Hart Publishing 2013).

Nimmer, M B & Nimmer, D, *Nimmer on Copyright: A Treatise on the Law of Literary, Musical and Artistic Property, and the Protection of Ideas – Volume 3* (Matthew Bender/LexisNexis 2013).

Nimmer, M B, 'Does Copyright Abridge the First Amendment Guarantees of Free Speech and Press?' (1970) 17 UCLA Law Review 1180.

Nolan, D & Davies, J, 'Torts and Equitable Wrongs' in A Burrows, *English Private Law* (Oxford University Press 2013).

Nordemann, J B, 'Intellectual Property Liability of Consumers, Facilitators and Intermediaries: the Position in Germany' in A Kamperman Sanders & C Heath, *Intellectual Property Liability of Consumers, Facilitators and Intermediaries* (Kluwer Law International 2012) 37.

Nordemann, J B, 'Internet Copyright Infringement: Remedies against Internet Intermediaries – the European Perspective on Host and Access Providers' (2012) 59(4) Journal of the Copyright Society of the USA 773.

Nordemann, J B, 'Liability for Copyright Infringements on the Internet: Host Providers (Content Providers) – The German Approach' (2011) 2(1) Journal of Intellectual Property, Information Technology and Electronic Commerce Law (JIPITEC) 37.

Norrgård, M, 'The European Principles of IP Enforcement: Harmonisation through Communication?' in A Ohly, *Common Principles of European Intellectual Property Law* (Mohr Siebeck 2012) 203.

Nowak, M & Charbord, A, 'Article 4 – Prohibition of Torture' in S Peers, T Hervey, J Kenner & A Ward, *The EU Charter of Fundamental Rights: A Commentary* (Hart Publishing 2014).

OECD, 'The Role of Internet Intermediaries in Advancing Public Policy Objectives' (OECD Publishing 2011).

Ohly, A, & Pila. J, (eds), *The Europeanization of Intellectual Property Law: Towards a European Legal Methodology* (Oxford University Press 2013).

Ohly, A, *Common Principles of European Intellectual Property Law* (Mohr Siebeck 2012).

Oliphant, K, 'European Tort Law: A Primer for the Common Lawyer' (2009) 62(1) Current Legal Problems 440.

Olivier, F & Barbry, E, 'Conditions de la responsabilité civile des fournisseurs d'hébergement d'un site sur le réseau Internet' (2000) 13 JCP – La Semaine Juridique Edition Générale 577.

Opderbeck, D W, 'Peer-to-Peer Networks, Technological Evolution, and Intellectual Property Reverse Private Attorney General Litigation' (2005) 20(4) Berkeley Technology Law Journal 1685.

Owens, D, *The Philosophical Foundations of Tort Law* (Oxford University Press 1997).

Page Keeton, W et al., *Prosser and Keeton on Torts* (5th ed. West Group, St Paul, MN 1984).

Peers, S & Prechal, S, 'Article 52 – Scope and Interpretation of Rights and Principles' in S Peers, T Hervey, J Kenner & A Ward, *The EU Charter of Fundamental Rights: A Commentary* (Hart Publishing 2014) 1470.

Peers, S, 'Taking Rights Away – Limitations and Derogations' in S Peers & A Ward, *The EU Charter of Fundamental Rights: Politics, Law and Policy* (Hart Publishing 2004) 142.

Peers, S et al., *The EU Charter of Fundamental Rights: A Commentary* (Hart Publishing 2014).

Peguera, M, 'The DMCA Safe Harbors and their European Counterparts: A Comparative Analysis of some Common Problems' (2009) 32 Columbia Journal of Law & the Arts 481.

Perset, K, 'The Economic and Social Role of Internet Intermediaries', OECD Study, STI/ICCP(2009)9/FINAL, March 2010.

Pessach, G, 'An International-Comparative Perspective on Peer-To-Peer File-Sharing and Third Party Liability in Copyright Law: Framing the Past, Present, and Next Generations' Questions' (2007) 40(1) Vanderbilt Journal of Transnational Law 87.

Picker, R C, 'Copyright as Entry Policy: the Case of Digital Distribution' (2002) 47 (2-3) Antitrust Bulletin 423.

Pihlajarinne, T, 'Setting the Limits for the Implied License in Copyright and Linking Discourse – The European Perspective' (2012) International Review of Intellectual Property and Competition Law (IIC) 700.

Pila, J, 'A Constitutionalized Doctrine of Precedent and the *Marleasing* Principle as Bases for a European Legal Methodology' in J Pila & A Ohly (eds), *The Europeanization of Intellectual Property Law: Towards a European Legal Methodology* (Oxford University Press 2013) 227.

Pila, J, 'Intellectual Property as a Case Study in Europeanization: Methodological Themes and Context' in A Ohly & J Pila, *The Europeanization of Intellectual Property Law: Towards A European Legal Methodology* (Oxford University Press 2013) 23.

Pitel, S et al. (eds), *Tort Law: Challenging Orthodoxy* (Hart Publishing 2013).

Pollack, M A, 'Creeping Competence: The Expanding Agenda of the European Community' (1994) 14(2) Journal of Public Policy 95.

Poort, J & Leenheer, J, 'Filesharing 2©12—Downloading from Illegal Sources in the Nederlands', Report by IviR and CentERdata (16 October 2012), available at: www.ivir.nl.

Puppe, I in U Kindhäuser, U Neumann & H-U Paeffgen, Strafgesetzbuch (4th ed., Nomos 2013).

Quill, E, 'Affirmative Duties of Care in the Common Law' (2011) 2 Journal of European Tort Law 151.

Raab, T, 'OLG Köln: Keine Pflicht von Access-Providern zur Sperrung rechtswidriger Angebote' (2014) MMR-Aktuell 361783.

Ramalho, A, *The Competence of The European Union in Copyright Lawmaking – A Normative Perspective of EU Powers for Copyright*

Harmonization (unpublished PhD thesis, University of Amsterdam 2014).

Ratcliffe, J (ed.), *The Good Samaritan and the Law* (Anchor Books 1966).

Reimann, M & Zimmermann, R (eds), *The Oxford Handbook of Comparative Law* (Oxford University Press 2006).

Report from the Commission to the European Parliament, the Council, the European Economic and Social Committee and the Committee of the Regions on the Application of Directive 2004/48/EC of the European Parliament and the Council of 29 April 2004 on the enforcement of intellectual property rights, COM(2010) 779 final, 22 December 2010.

Ricketson, S & Ginsburg, J, *International Copyright and Neighbouring Rights: The Berne Convention and Beyond* (Oxford University Press 2006).

Riesenhüber, K, *Europäische Methodenlehre: Handbuch für Ausbildung und Praxis* (3rd ed., Walter de Gruyter 2014).

Riester, F, 'Rapport fait au nom de la commission des lois constitutionnelles, de la législation et de l'administration générale de la république sur le projet de loi (n° 1240), adopté par le sénat après déclaration d'urgence, *favorisant la* diffusion *et la* protection *de la* création *sur* internet', 18 February 2009.

Riles, A (ed), *Rethinking the Masters of Comparative Law* (Hart Publishing 2001).

Rimmer, M, 'Canadian Rhapsody: Copyright Law and Research Libraries' (2004) 35(3) Australian Academic & Research Libraries 193.

Riordan, J, *The Liability of Internet Intermediaries* (PhD thesis, University of Oxford 2013, forthcoming Oxford University Press 2016).

Rogers, W V H, 'Comparative Report on Multiple Tortfeasors' in W V H Rogers (ed.), *Unification of Tort Law: Multiple Tortfeasors* (Kluwer Law International 2004) 273.

Rogers, W V H, 'England: Wrongfulness under English Tort Law' in H Koziol (ed.) *Unification of Tort Law: Wrongfulness* (Kluwer Law International 1998) 39.

Rogers, W V H, 'Multiple Tortfeasors under English Law' in W V H Rogers, *Unification of Tort Law: Multiple Tortfeasors* (Kluwer Law International 2004) 66.

Rogers, W V H, *Unification of Tort Law: Multiple Tortfeasors* (Kluwer Law International 2004).

Rogers, W V H, *Winfield & Jolowicz on Tort* (18th ed., Sweet & Maxwell 2010).

Säcker, F J & Rixecker, R (eds), *Münchener Kommentar Zum Bürgerlichen Gesetzbuch* (6th ed., C.H. Beck 2013).

Sales, P, 'The Tort of Conspiracy and Civil Secondary Liability' (1990) 49(3) Cambridge Law Journal 491.

Samuel, G, 'Western Law of Obligations' in M Bussani and F Werro, *European Private Law: A Handbook (Vol. I)* (Stämpfli 2009) 143.

Samuel, G, *An Introduction to Comparative Law and Method* (Hart Publishing 2014).

Saunders, K M & Berger-Walliser, G, 'The Liability of Online Markets for Counterfeit Goods: A Comparative Analysis of Secondary Trademark Infringement in the United States and Europe' (2011) 32(1) Northwestern Journal of International Law & Business 37.

Sauter, W, 'Proportionality in EU Law: A Balancing Act?' TILEC Discussion Paper No. 2013-003, 25 January 2013.

Savola, P, 'Blocking Injunctions and Website Operators' Liability for Copyright Infringement for User-Generated Links' (2014) 5 European Intellectual Property Review 279.

Savola, P, 'Proportionality of Website Blocking: Internet Connectivity Providers as Copyright Enforcers' (2014) 5(2) Journal of Intellectual Property, Information Technology and Electronic Commerce Law (JIPITEC) 116.

Savola, P, *Internet Connectivity Providers as Involuntary Copyright Enforcers – Blocking Websites in Particular* (PhD thesis, University of Helsinki 2015) 9.

Schack, H, 'Täter und Störer: Zur Erweiterung und Begrenzung der Verantwortlichkeit durch Verkehrspflichten im Wettbewerbs- und Immaterialgüterrecht' in 'Festschrift für Dieter Reuter zum 70. Geburtstag am 16. Oktober 2010' (2010) De Gruyter 1167.

Schepel, H, 'The European Brotherhood of Lawyers: the Reinvention of Legal Science in the Making of European Private Law' (2007) 32(1) Law & Social Inquiry 183.

Seng, D, 'Comparative Analysis of the National Approaches to the Liability of Internet Intermediaries', WIPO study, available at: www.wipo.int/copyright/en/internet_intermediaries.

Shillito, M & Meale, D, 'Twentieth Century Fox Film Corp v Newzbin Ltd – Copyright – Online Service Provider Held Liable for Copyright Infringements of Its Users' (2010) 32(8) European Intellectual Property Review 67.

Simester, A, 'The Mental Element in Complicity' (2006) 122 Law Quarterly Review 578.

Sirinelli, P, 'Chronique de Jurisprudence – Droit d\'auteur et réseaux numériques' (2012) 234 Revue Internationale du Droit d'Auteur 412.

Sirinelli, P, 'Chronique de Jurisprudence – Échanges pair à pair non autorisés d'oeuvres protégées (P2P)' (2012) 231 Revue Internationale du Droit d'Auteur 184.

Sirinelli, P, 'Chronique de Jurisprudence – Mise à la disposition illicite d'oeuvres par l'intermédiaire des réseaux numériques' (2011) 228 Revue Internationale du Droit d'Auteur 287.

Sirinelli, P et al., 'Mission to Link Directives 2000/31 and 2001/29 – Report and Proposals', High Council for Literary and Artistic Property, 3 November 2015.

Smet, S, *Resolving Conflicts between Human Rights: A Theoretical Analysis in the Context of the ECHR* (unpublished Phd Thesis, Ghent University 2014).

Smith, E, 'Lord of the Files: International Secondary Liability for Internet Service Providers' (2011) 68(3) Washington and Lee Law Review 1555.

Smits, J M, 'Democracy and (European) Private Law: A Functional Approach' (2009) 5 European Journal of Legal Studies 26.

Smits, J M, 'European Private Law and the Comparative Method' in C Twigg-Flesner (ed.), *The Cambridge Companion to European Union Private Law* (Cambridge University Press 2010) 33.

Smits, J M, 'European Private Law: A Plea for a Spontaneous Legal Order' in D M Curtin & J M Smits, 'European Integration and Law' (Intersentia 2006) 55.

Smits, J M, 'Plurality of Sources in European Private Law, or: How to Live with Legal Diversity?' in R Brownsword, H-W Micklitz, L Niglia & S Weatherill (eds), *The Foundations of European Private Law* (Hart Publishing 2011) 323.

Smits, J M, 'Private Law and Fundamental Rights: A Sceptical View' in T Barkhuysen & S Lindenbergh, *Constitutionalisation of Private Law* (Brill 2005) 9.

Smits, J M, 'Rethinking Methods in European Private Law' in M Adams & J Bomhoff (eds), *Practice and Theory in Comparative Law* (Cambridge University Press 2012) 170.

Smits, J M, 'The Netherlands: Wrongfulness in the Dutch Context' in H Koziol (ed.) *Unification of Tort Law: Wrongfulness* (Kluwer Law International 1998) 87.

Snijders, H & Weatherill, S, *E-Commerce Law: National and Transnational Topics and Perspectives* (Kluwer Law International 2003).

Spier, J, *The Limits of Liability – Keeping the Floodgates Shut* (Kluwer Law International 1995).

Spindler, G & Anton, K in G Spindler & F Schuster, *Recht der Electronischen Medien* (2nd ed., C.H. Beck 2011).

Spindler, G & Leistner, M, 'Secondary Copyright Infringement – New Perspectives from Germany and Europe' (2006) 37(7) International Review of Intellectual Property and Competition Law (IIC) 788.

Spindler, G & Schuster, F (eds), *Recht der Electronischen Medien* (2nd ed., C.H.Beck 2011).

Spindler, G & Volkmann, C in G Spindler & F Schuster (eds), *Recht der Electronischen Medien* (3rd ed., C.H.Beck 2015).

Spindler, G, '"Die Tür ist auf" – Europarechtliche Zulässigkeit von Auskunftsansprüchen gegenüber ProvidernUrteilsanmerkung zu EuGH "Promusicae/Telefónica"' (2008) GRUR 574.

Spry, I, *Equitable Remedies* (9th ed., Sweet & Maxwell 2014).

Stalla-Bourdillon, S, 'Responsabilité civile et strategie de regulation – Essai sur la responsabilité civile des prestataires intermédiaires de service en ligne' (PhD thesis, European University Institute, Florence 2010).

Stalla-Bourdillon, S, 'Sometimes One Is Not Enough! Securing Freedom of Expression, Encouraging Private Regulation, or Subsidizing Internet Intermediaries or All Three at the Same Time: the Dilemma of Internet Intermediaries' Liability' (2012) 7(2) Journal of International Commercial Law and Technology 154.

Stamatoudi, I A & Torremans, P, 'The Information Society Directive' in I A Stamatoudi & P Torremans, *EU Copyright Law* (Edward Elgar 2014).

Stamatoudi, I A & Torremans, P, *EU Copyright Law* (Edward Elgar 2014).

Stamatoudi, I A (ed.), *Copyright Enforcement and the Internet* (Kluwer Law International 2010).

Stapleton, J, 'Duty of Care Factors: A Selection from the Judicial Menus' in P Cane & J Stapleton (eds), *The Law of Obligations: Essays in Celebration of John Fleming* (Clarendon Press 1995) 59.

Starck, B et al., *Obligations I – Responsabilité délictuelle* (5th ed, Litec 1996).

Stevens, R, *Torts and Rights* (Oxford University Press 2007).

Stevens, R, *Wrongs and Rights* (Oxford University Press 2009).

Stone-Sweet, A, & Matthews, J, 'Proportionality Balancing and Global Constitutionalism' (2008) 47(1) Columbia Journal of Transnational Law 72.

Strowel, A (ed.), *Peer-to-Peer File Sharing and Secondary Liability in Copyright Law* (Edward Elgar Publishing 2009).

Sugar, A, *What You See Is What You Get: My Autobiography* (Macmillan 2010).

Synodinou, T-E (ed.), *Codification of European Law* (Kluwer Law International 2012).

Synodinou, T-E, 'Intermediaries' Liability for Online Copyright Infringement in the EU: Evolutions and Confusions' (2015) 31 Computer Law & Security Review 57.

Tambini, D et al., *Codifying Cyberspace* (Routledge 2008).

The United Nations (UN) Special Rapporteur on Freedom of Opinion and Expression, the Organization for Security and Co-Operation in Europe (OSCE) Representative on Freedom of the Media, the Organization of American States (OAS) Special Rapporteur on Freedom of Expression and the African Commission on Human and Peoples' Rights (ACHPR) Special Rapporteur on Freedom of Expression and Access to Information, 'Joint Declaration on Freedom of Expression and the Internet', 1 June 2011.

Thery, J-F & Falque-Pierrotin, I, 'Internet et les réseaux numériques: étude adoptée par l'Assemblée générale du Conseil d'Etat le 2 juillet 1998' (La Documentation française 1998).

Thoumyre, L, 'Etude 464 – La responsabilité pénale et extra-contractuelle des acteurs de l'Internet' (Novembre 2009) Lamy Droit des Médias et de la Communication.

Todd, S, 'Negligence: the Duty of Care' in S Todd (ed.), *The Law of Torts in New Zealand* (3rd ed., Brookers 2001).

Torremans, P, 'Article 17(2)' in S Peers, T Hervey, J Kenner & A Ward, *The EU Charter of Fundamental Rights: A Commentary* (Hart Publishing 2014) 504.

Torremans, P, *Intellectual Property and Human Rights* (Kluwer Law International 2008).

Tsakyrakis, S, 'Proportionality: An Assault on Human Rights?' (2009) 7(3) International Journal of Constitutional Law 468.

Twigg-Flesner, C (ed.), *The Cambridge Companion to European Union Private Law* (Cambridge University Press 2010).

Urban, J & Quilter, L, 'Efficient Process or "Chilling Effects"? Takedown Notices under Section 512 of the Digital Millennium Copyright Act' (2006) 22(4) Santa Clara Computer & High Technology Law Journal 621.

Valcke, P & Dommering, E, 'E-Commerce Directive' in O Castendyk, E Dommering & A Scheuer, *European Media Law* (Kluwer Law International 2008) 1087-1088.

Van Boom, W, 'Comparative notes on Injunction and Wrongful Risk-Taking' (2010) 17(1) Maastricht Journal of European and Comparative Law 10.

Van Dam, C, 'European Tort Law: Features of a Diverse Landscape' in C Twigg-Flesner (ed.), *The Cambridge Companion to European Union Private Law* (Cambridge University Press 2010) 160.

Van Dam, C, 'Tort Law and Human Rights: Brothers in Arms – On the Role of Tort Law in the Area of Business and Human Rights' (2011) 2 Journal of European Tort Law 221.

Van Dam, C, 'Who is Afraid of Diversity? Cultural Diversity, European Co-operation, and European Tort Law' (2009) 20 King's Law Journal 281.

Van Dam, C, *European Tort Law* (Oxford University Press 2007).

Van Dam, C, *European Tort Law* (2nd ed., Oxford University Press 2013).

Van Den Bergh, R & Visscher, L, 'The Principles of European Tort Law: The Right Path to Harmonization?' (2006) 4 European Review of Private Law 511.

Van der Net, C, 'Civil Liability of Internet Providers Following the Directive on Electronic Commerce' in H Snijders & S Weatherill, *E-Commerce Law: National and Transnational Topics and Perspectives* (Kluwer Law International 2003) 49.

Van Dijk, P et al., *Theory and Practice of the European Convention on Human Rights* (4th ed., Kluwer Law International 2006).

Van Eechoud, M et al., *Harmonizing European Copyright Law* (Kluwer Law International 2009).

Van Eechoud, M et al., 'The Recasting of Copyright and Related Rights for the Knowledge Economy', final report, Institute for Information Law (IviR), University of Amsterdam, November 2006.

Van Eecke, P, 'Online Service Providers and Liability: A Plea for a Balanced Approach' (2011) 48 Common Market Law Review 1455.

Van Eijk, N et al., 'Moving towards Balance: A Study into Duties of Care on the Internet' (2010) Institute for Information Law & Leibniz Center for Law, University of Amsterdam.

Van Enis, Q, 'Les mesures de filtrage et de blocage de contenus sur l'internet: un mal (vraiment) necessaire dans une société démocratique? Quelques réflexions utor de la liberté d'expression' (2013) 96 Revue trimestrielle des droits de l'homme 859.

Van Gerven, W, 'The ECJ Case Law as a Means of Unification of Private Law?' in A Hartkamp, *Towards a European Civil Code* (3rd ed., Kluwer Law International 2004) 101.

Van Gerven, W, 'The Effect of Proportionality on the Actions of Member States of the European Community: National Viewpoints from Continental Europe' in E Ellis (ed.), *The Principle of Proportionality in the Law of Europe* (Hart Publishing 1999) 37.

Van Gerven, W et al., *Tort Law* (Hart Publishing 2000).

Van Gestel, R & Micklitz, H-W, 'Why Methods Matter in European Legal Scholarship' (2014) 20(3) European Law Journal 292.

Van Hoboken, J, 'Legal Space for Innovative Ordering: On the Need to Update Selection Intermediary Liability in the EU' (2009) 13 International Journal of Communications Law & Policy 1.

Van Parijs, P, 'Should the European Union Become More Democratic?' in A Follesdal & P Koslowski, *Democracy and the European Union* (Spinger 1998) 287.

Vaver, D, *Copyright Law: Essentials of Canadian Law* (Toronto Irwin Law 1997).

Ventose, E D & Forrester, J J, 'Authorisation and Infringement of Copyright on the Internet' (2010) 14(6) Journal of Internet Law 3.

Verbiest, T et al., 'Study on the Liability of Internet Intermediaries', EU Commission study (MARKT/2006/09/E), 12 November 2007.

Vested-Hansen, J, 'Article 7 – Respect for Private and Family Life (Private Life, Home and Communications' in S Peers, T Hervey, J Kenner & A Ward, *The EU Charter of Fundamental Rights: A Commentary* (Hart Publishing 2014) 153.

Vier, C, 'Counterfeit of a Brand-Name and Infringement of Copyright on the Internet' IRIS 2000-5/18.

Viney, G & Jourdain, P, *Les Conditions de la Responsabilité* (2nd ed., L.G.D.J. 1998).

Viney, G, 'France: Le 'Wrongfulness' en Droit Français' in H Koziol (ed.) *Unification of Tort Law: Wrongfulness* (Kluwer Law International 1998) 57.

Viney, G, 'Tort Liability' in G Bermann & E Picard, *Introduction to French Law* (Walters Kluwer 2008) 238.

Viney, G, *Traité de Droit Civil – Vol. IV* (Libr. Générale de Droit et de Jurisprudence 1982).

Visser, D, 'Europees openbaar maken met ketchup' (2013) 2 AMI: Tijdschriftvoorauteurs-, Media- & Informatierecht 41.

Vivant, M et al., *Lamy – Droit du Numérique: Informatique, Multimedia, Réseaux, Internet* (Wolters Kluwer France 2012).

Vivant, M, 'Conditions de la responsabilité civile des fournisseurs d'hébergement d'un site sur le réseau Internet' (2000) 13 La Semaine Juridique Édition Générale 577.

Vivant, M, 'La responsabilité des intermédiaires de l'internet' (1999) 45-46 JCP – La Semaine Juridique Edition Générale 2021.

Vogenauer, S, 'Eine gemeineuropäische Methodenlehre des Rechts – Plädoyer und Programm' (2005) 13 *Zeitschrift für Europäisches Privatrecht* 234.

Von Bar, C et al. (eds), *Principles, definitions and model rules of European private law: Draft Common Frame of Reference (DCFR),* prepared by the Study Group on a European Civil Code and the Research Group on EC private law (Acquis Group), Outline Edition (Sellier 2009).

Von Bar, C et al. (eds), *Principles, Definitions and Model Rules of European Private Law: Draft Common Frame of Reference (DCFR)*, prepared by the Study Group on a European Civil Code and the Research Group on EC private law (Acquis Group), Interim Edition (Sellier 2008).

Von Bar, C, *The Common European Law of Torts – Vol. I* (Clarendon Press 2000).

Von Bar, C, *The Common European Law of Torts – Vol. II* (Clarendon Press 2000).

Von Bar, C, *Verkehrspflichten: Richterliche Gefahrsteuerungsgebote im deutschen Deliktsrecht* (Heymanns 1980).

Von Staudinger, J et al., *Kommentar zum Bürgelichen Gesetzbuch* (15th ed., De Gruyter 2008).

Wadlow, C, *The Law of Passing-off: Unfair Competition by Misrepresentation* (London, Sweet & Maxwell 2011).

Wagner, G (ed.), *The Common Frame of Reference – A View from Law and Economics* (Sellier European Law Publishing 2009).

Wagner, G, 'BGB § 840 Haftung mehrerer' in F J Säcker & R Rixecker (eds.), *Münchener Kommentar zum BGB* (6th ed., C. H. Beck 2013).

Wagner, G, 'Comparative Tort Law' in M Reimann & R Zimmermann (eds), *The Oxford Handbook of Comparative Law* (Oxford University Press 2006) 1003.

Wagner, G, 'The Law of Torts in the DCFR' in G Wagner (ed.), *The Common Frame of Reference – A View from Law and Economics* (Sellier European Law Publishing 2009) 254.

Wagner, G, 'The Project of Harmonizing European Tort Law' (2005) 42 Common Market Law Review 1269.
Walden, I, 'Directive 2000/31/EC – Directive on Electronic Commerce' in A Büllesback, Y Poullet & C Prins (eds), *Concise European IT Law* (Kluwer Law International 2006) 251.
Waldenberger, A, 'Zur Zivilrechtlichen Verantwortlichkeit für Urheberrechtsverletzungen im Internet' (1997) ZUM 176.
Walter, A, 'Zivilrechtliche Störerhaftung' (2012) JA 658.
Walter, M & Von Lewinski, S, *European Copyright Law: A Commentary* (Oxford University Press 2010).
Wandtke, A, *Urheberrecht* (De Gruyter Recht 2009).
Wang, J, 'Development of Hosting ISPs' Secondary Liability for Primary Copyright Infringement in China – As Compared to the US and German Routes' (2015) International Review of Intellectual Property and Competition Law (IIC) 275.
Weatherill, S, 'Can There Be a Common Interpretation of European Private Law?' (2002) 31(1) Georgia Journal of International and Comparative Law 139.
Weiler, J H H, 'The Transformation of Europe' in J H H Weiler, *The Constitution of Europe: 'Do the New Clothes Have an Emperor?' and Other Essays on European Integration* (Cambridge University Press 1999) 93.
Weiler, J H H, *The Constitution of Europe: 'Do the New Clothes Have an Emperor?' and Other Essays on European Integration* (Cambridge University Press 1999).
Weir, T, 'Liability for Knowingly Facilitating Mass Breaches of Copyright' (1988) 47(3) The Cambridge Law Journal 348.
Weir, T, 'Unification of Tort Law: Wrongfulness (Review)' (1999) 58(3) Cambridge Law Journal 643.
Wendell Holmes, O, *The Common Law – Dover Edition* (Dover Publications 1991).
Widmer, P (ed.), *Unification of Tort Law: Fault* (Kluwer Law International 2005).
Widmer, P, 'Comparative Report on Fault as a Basis of Liability and Criterion of Imputation (Attribution)' in P Widmer (ed.), *Unification of Tort Law: Fault* (Kluwer Law International 2005) 353.
Widmer, P, 'Required Standard of Conduct' in P Widmer (ed.), *Unification of Tort Law: Fault* (Kluwer Law International 2005) 76.
Widmer, P, 'Switzerland: The Concept of Unlawfulness – Function and Relevance under Swiss Law' in H Koziol (ed.) *Unification of Tort Law: Wrongfulness* (Kluwer Law International 1998) 115.
Williams, G, 'Causation in the Law' (1961) Cambridge Law Journal 62.
Williams, G, *Criminal Law: The General Part* (Stevens & Sons 1953).
Williams, G, *Joints Torts and Contributory Negligence* (Stevens & Sons 1951).

Wimmers, J, 'Who Interferes? Liability for Third Party Content on the Internet in Germany' (2007) Intellectual Property Today 32.

Winfield, P, 'Duty in Tortious Negligence' (1934) 34 Columbia Law Review 41.

Wittem Group, *European Copyright Code,* April 2010, available at: copyrightcode.eu.

Woods, L, 'Article 11 – Freedom of Expression and Information' in S Peers, T Hervey, J Kenner & A Ward, *The EU Charter of Fundamental Rights: A Commentary* (Hart Publishing 2014) 311.

Wright, J, *Tort Law and Human Rights* (Hart Publishing, Oxford 2001).

Wright, R W, 'Hand, Posner, and the Myth of the "Hand Formula"' (2003) 4(1) Theoretical Inquiries in Law 144.

Wright, R W, 'Justice and Reasonable Care in Negligence Law' (2002) 47 American Journal of Jurisprudence 143.

Wright, R W, 'The Logic and Fairness of Joint and Several Liability' (1992) 23 Memphis State Law Review 45.

Wright, R W, 'The Standards of Care in Negligence Law' in D Owens, *The Philosophical Foundations of Tort Law* (Oxford University Press 1997) 252.

Wu, T, 'The Copyright Paradox' (2005) 27 Supreme Court Review 229.

Wu, T, 'When Code Isn't Law' (2003) 89 Virginia Law Review 679.

Yen, A, 'Internet Service Provider Liability for Subscriber Copyright Infringement, Enterprise Liability, and the First Amendment' (2000) 88(6) Georgetown Law Journal 1833.

Yen, A, '*Sony,* Tort Doctrines, and the Puzzle of Peer-to-Peer' (2005) 55(4) Case Western Reserve Law Review 815.

Yen, A, 'Third Party Copyright after Grokster' (2007) 16(3) Information & Communications Technology Law 233.

Yu, P K, 'Digital Copyright and Confuzzling Rhetoric' (2011) 13 Vanderbilt Journal of Entertainment and Technology Law 881.

Zimmerman, D L, 'Daddy, Are We There Yet? Lost in Grokster-land (The Unintended Consequences of Legislating Technology: The Digital Millennium Copyright Act)' (2005) 9(1-2) New York University Journal of Legislation and Public Policy 75.

Zimmermann, R, 'Roman Law and the Harmonization of Private Law in Europe' in A S Hartkamp, M W Hesselink, E H Hondius, C Mak & E du Perron (eds), *Towards a European Civil Code* (4th ed., Ars Aequi Libri 2011) 21.

Zimmermann, R, 'The Europeanization of Private Law' in M Reimann & R Zimmermann (eds), *The Oxford Handbook of Comparative Law* (Oxford University Press 2006) 539.

Zimmermann, R, *The Law of Obligations: Roman Foundations of the Civilian Tradition* (Oxford University Press 1996).

Zingales, N, 'Internet Intermediary Liability: Identifying Best Practices for Africa' (2013) Association for Progressive Communications (APC).

Zittrain, J, 'A History of Online Gatekeeping' (2006) 19(2) Harvard Journal of Law & Technology 255.
Zuiderveen Borgesius, F J, *Improving Privacy Protection in the Area of Behavioural Targeting* (Kluwer Law International 2015).
Zweigert, K & Kötz, H, *An Introduction to Comparative Law* (3rd ed., Clarendon Press 1998).

Index

D

O

INFORMATION LAW SERIES

1. Egbert J. Dommering & P. Bernt Hugenholtz, *Protecting Works of Fact: Copyright, Freedom of Expression and Information Law,* 1991 (ISBN 90-654-4567-6).
2. Willem F. Korthals Altes, Egbert J. Dommering, P. Bernt Hugenholtz & Jan J.C. Kabel, *Information Law Towards the 21st Century,* 1992 (ISBN 90-654-4627-3).
3. Jacqueline M.B. Seignette, *Challenges to the Creator Doctrine: Authorship, Copyright Ownership and the Exploitation of Creative Works in the Netherlands, Germany and The United States,* 1994 (ISBN 90-654-4876-4).
4. P. Bernt Hugenholtz, *The Future of Copyright in a Digital Environment, Proceedings of the Royal Academy Colloquium,* 1996 (ISBN 90-411-0267-1).
5. Julius C.S. Pinckaers, *From Privacy Toward a New Intellectual Property Right in Persona,* 1996 (ISBN 90-411-0355-4).
6. Jan J.C. Kabel & Gerard J.H.M. Mom, *Intellectual Property and Information Law: Essays in Honour of Herman Cohen Jehoram,* 1998 (ISBN 90-411-9702-8).
7. Ysolde Gendreau, Axel Nordemann & Rainer Oesch, *Copyright and Photographs: An International Survey,* 1999 (ISBN 90-411-9722-2).
8. P. Bernt Hugenholtz, *Copyright and Electronic Commerce: Legal Aspects of Electronic Copyright Management,* 2000 (ISBN 90-411-9785-0).
9. Lucie M.C.R. Guibault, *Copyright Limitations and Contracts: An Analysis of the Contractual Overridability of Limitations on Copyright,* 2002 (ISBN 90-411-9867-9).
10. Lee A. Bygrave, *Data Protection Law: Approaching its Rationale, Logic and Limits,* 2002 (ISBN 90-411-9870-9).
11. Niva Elkin-Koren & Neil Weinstock Netanel, *The Commodification of Information,* 2002 (ISBN 90-411-9876-8).
12. Mireille M.M. van Eechoud, *Choice of Law in Copyright and Related Rights: Alternatives to the Lex Protectionis,* 2003 (ISBN 90-411-2071-8).
13. Martin Senftleben, *Copyright, Limitations and the Three-Step Test: An Analysis of the Three-Step Test in International and EC Copyright Law,* 2004 (ISBN 90-411-2267-2).
14. Paul L.C. Torremans, *Copyright and Human Rights: Freedom of Expression – Intellectual Property – Privacy,* 2004 (ISBN 90-411-2278-8).
15. Natali Helberger, *Controlling Access to Content: Regulating Conditional Access in Digital Broadcasting,* 2005 (ISBN 90-411-2345-8).
16. Lucie M.C.R. Guibault & P. Bernt Hugenholtz, *The Future of the Public Domain: Identifying the Commons in Information Law,* 2006 (ISBN 978-90-411-2435-7).

17. Irini Katsirea, *Public Broadcasting and European Law: A Comparative Examination of Public Service Obligations in Six Member States,* 2008 (ISBN 978-90-411-2500-2).
18. Paul L.C. Torremans, *Intellectual Property and Human Rights: Enhanced Edition of Copyright and Human Rights,* 2008 (ISBN 978-90-411-2653-5).
19. Mireille van Eechoud, P. Bernt Hugenholtz, Stef van Gompel, Lucie Guibault & Natali Helberger, *Harmonizing European Copyright Law: The Challenges of Better Lawmaking,* 2009 (ISBN 978-90-411-3130-0).
20. Ashwin van Rooijen, *The Software Interface between Copyright and Competition Law: A Legal Analysis of Interoperability in Computer Programs,* 2010 (ISBN 978-90-411-3193-5).
21. Irini A. Stamatoudi, *Copyright Enforcement and the Internet,* 2010 (ISBN 978-90-411-3346-5).
22. Wolfgang Sakulin, *Trademark Protection and Freedom of Expression: An Inquiry into the Conflict between Trademark Rights and Freedom of Expression under European Law,* 2011 (ISBN 978-90-411-3415-8).
23. Stef van Gompel, *Formalities in Copyright Law: An Analysis of their History, Rationales and Possible Future,* 2011 (ISBN 978-90-411-3418-9).
24. Nadezhda Purtova, *Property Rights in Personal Data: A European Perspective,* 2012 (ISBN 978-90-411-3802-6).
25. Brad Sherman & Leanne Wiseman, *Copyright and the Challenge of the New,* 2012 (ISBN 978-90-411-3669-5).
26. Ewa Komorek, *Media Pluralism and European Law*, 2012 (ISBN 978-90-411-3894-1).
27. Joris van Hoboken, *Search Engine Freedom: On the Implications of the Right to Freedom of Expression for the Legal Governance of Web Search Engines,* 2012 (ISBN 978-90-411-4128-6).
28. Natali Helberger, Lucie Guibault, Marco Loos, Chantal Mak, Lodewijk Pessers & Bart van der Sloot, *Digital Consumers and the Law: Towards a Cohesive European Framework*, 2012 (ISBN 978-90-411-4049-4).
29. Tatiana-Eleni Synodinou, *Codification of European Copyright Law: Challenges and Perspectives,* 2012 (ISBN 978-90-411-4145-3).
30. Heather Ann Forrest, *Protection of Geographic Names in International Law and Domain Name System Policy*, 2013 (ISBN 978-90-411-4682-3).
31. Sari Depreeuw, *The Variable Scope of the Exclusive Economic Rights in Copyright*, 2014 (ISBN 978-90-411-4915-2).
32. Vikrant Narayan Vasudeva, *Open Source Software and Intellectual Property Rights*, 2014 (ISBN 978-90-411-5228-2).
33. Frederik J. Zuiderveen Borgesius, *Improving Privacy Protection in the Area of Behavioural Targeting*, 2015 (ISBN 978-90-411-5990-8).

34. Paul L.C. Torremans, *Intellectual Property Law and Human Rights*, Third Edition, 2015 (ISBN 978-90-411-5836-9).
35. Irini A. Stamatoudi, *New Developments in EU and International Copyright Law*, 2016 (ISBN 978-90-411-5991-5).
36. Lodewijk W.P. Pessers, *The Inventiveness Requirement in Patent Law: An Exploration of Its Foundations and Functioning*, 2016 (ISBN 978-90-411-6731-6).
37. Susy Frankel & Daniel Gervais, *The Internet and the Emerging Importance of New Forms of Intellectual Property*, 2016 (ISBN 978-90-411-6789-7).
38. Axel M. Arnbak, *Securing Private Communications: Protecting Private Communications Security in EU Law – Fundamental Rights, Functional Value Chains, and Market Incentives*, 2016 (ISBN 978-90-411-6737-8).
39. Christina Angelopoulos, *European Intermediary Liability in Copyright: A Tort-Based Analysis*, 2017 (ISBN 978-90-411-6835-1).